Cathedral of St. Philip
Music Department

EPISCOPAL EUCHARISTIC LECTIONARY

New Revised Standard Version

St. Mark's Press
Good Shepherd Episcopal Church
8021 West 21st Street
Wichita, KS 67212-4817

PREFACE

In early 1973, Father William R. Bagby, then rector of St. Mark's Episcopal Church, was discussing the financial plight of the parish with Reg Randall, his senior warden. There was a great need to raise more money. It was the sort of conversation in which all kinds of ideas, some good and some not so good, came up. Most were put aside and forgotten. But, Father Bagby made the remark that it would be useful to the Episcopal Church to have available a book containing in a single volume the Sunday eucharistic propers. This was especially true since the adoption of the 3 year cycle of lections made it improbable that these lessons and gospels would be included in the expected revised Book of Common Prayer. Reg Randall, borrowing on his marketing background suggested a mailing that would ask for prepaid orders to cover the cost of printing.

In the weeks following these ideas were picked up and the possibility of publishing such a book came to be considered seriously. The costs of preparing and printing the Lectionary, of mailing brochures announcing its publication, and other related expenses were estimated — and the probable retail price determined from those estimates. The vestry was approached and after much deliberation agreed to support the cost of preparing and mailing flyers to parishes and missions throughout the American Church. Unless the response to those flyers resulted in at least $4500 in orders for the Lectionary, the project could not even make expenses. The orders totaled $5500 — and the *Episcopal Lectionary* became a reality.

There is no longer any question that the *Episcopal Eucharistic Lectionary* has been of service to the Church as well as to Good Shepherd — and for that we are indeed grateful. But the uniqueness of the Lectionary — and the one factor that has made it a possibility in the first place, let alone a successful one — is that it is a project of the laity of this parish. Special thanks are due those involved in the earlier projects: Randy Landis, Mary Ellen Pumphrey, Ed Lester, Carolyn Randall, Betsy Kelly and others. And, deep gratitude is a must for the new team: Maxine Ellis, Jane Thompson, Jean Hite, Marilyn Linn, Diana Hubin, Liz Gomes, Betsy Kelly, Carolyn Randall, Dick Linn, and Reg Randall.

The Lectionary Committee
Wichita, Kansas
January 29, 1991

ACKNOWLEDGEMENTS

The Propers noted in this book are from the Lectionary of the *Book of Common Prayer (1979)* as authorized for use in the Episcopal Church.

"The scripture quotations contained herein are from the New Revised Standard Version of the Bible, copyrighted, 1989 by the Division of Christian Education of the National Council of Churches of Christ in the United States of America, and are used by permission. All rights reserved."

TO ORDER LECTIONARIES
OR TO SUGGEST IMPROVEMENTS

Please contact:

St. Mark's Publishing
Good Shepherd Episcopal Church
8021 West 21st Street
Wichita, KS 67212-4817

Concerning this NRSV Lectionary

The original Lectionary was published in a Revised Standard Version. It has been revised and improved over many reprintings. As of early 1991, over 200,000 Episcopalians have purchased and used it. A New English Bible edition was published several years ago, but the RSV has dominated sales.

In Mid 1990 the United Council of Churches released the New Revised Standard Version (NRSV) of the Bible. The RSV, published in the late 1940's, has been the most widely used and read translations, but it was put out before the discovery of the Dead Sea Scrolls and other recent finds that have enhanced our understanding of the Old and New Testaments. Also, the English Language has undergone significant change in the last 45 years. Thus we made the decision to revamp our most successful publication.

While essentially the same book conceived over a casual kitchen table conversation, significant improvements have been incorporated. First, all of the alternate readings are now printed instead of being cited. Also, the complete text of the Psalms have been added. An important enhancement is the inclusion of the Easter Vigil readings.

The Lectionary is arranged in a three-year cycle, in which year A always begins on the First Sunday of Advent in years evenly divisible by three. (For example, 1977 divided by 3 is 659 with no remainder. Year A, therefore, begins on Advent Sunday of that year.)

The Psalms and Lessons appointed for the Sundays and for other major Holy Days are intended for use at all public services on such days, except when the same congregation attends two or more services. Thus, the same Lessons are to be read at the principal morning service, whether the Liturgy of the Word takes the form given in the Holy Eucharist, or that of the Daily Office.

When the same congregation is present for Morning or Evening Prayer, in addition to the Eucharist, the Lessons at the Office may be selected from one of the other years of the three-year Sunday cycle, or from the Lectionary for the Daily Office. The Psalms at such Offices are normally those appointed in the Office Lectionary; but, when desired, the Psalm cited in the selected Sunday Proper may be used instead.

Opening verses of the Lessons have been edited for liturgical use.

Any Reading may be lengthened at discretion. Suggested lengthenings are shown in parentheses. The texts of the suggested lengthenings are printed in full and placed within brackets for identification.

The symbol □ denotes the page containing collect.

THE FIRST SUNDAY OF ADVENT

The Collect

Almighty God, give us grace to cast away the works of darkness, and put on the armor of light, now in the time of this mortal life in which your Son Jesus Christ came to visit us in great humility; that in the last day, when he shall come again in his glorious majesty to judge both the living and the dead, we may rise to the life immortal; through him who lives and reigns with you and the Holy Spirit, one God, now and for ever. *Amen.*

Almighty God, give us grace that we may cast away the works of darkness, and put upon us the armor of light, now in the time of this mortal life in which thy Son Jesus Christ came to visit us in great humility; that in the last day, when he shall come again in his glorious majesty to judge both the quick and the dead, we may rise to the life immortal; through him who liveth and reigneth with thee and the Holy Ghost, one God, now and for ever. *Amen.*

Year A

The Lesson   Isaiah 2:1-5

The word that Isaiah son of Amoz saw concerning Judah and Jerusalem. In days to come the mountain of the LORD's house shall be established as the highest of the mountains, and shall be raised above the hills; all the nations shall stream to it. Many peoples shall come and say, "Come, let us go up to the mountain of the LORD, to the house of the God of Jacob; that he may teach us his ways and that we may walk in his paths." For out of Zion shall go forth instruction, and the word of the LORD from Jerusalem. He shall judge between the nations, and shall arbitrate for many peoples; they shall beat their swords into plowshares, and their spears into pruning hooks; nation shall not lift up sword against nation, neither shall they learn war any more. O house of Jacob, come, let us walk in the light of the LORD!

The Psalm 122   *Laetatus sum*

1   I was glad when they said to me, *
         "Let us go to the house of the LORD."

2   Now our feet are standing *
         within your gates, O Jerusalem.

3   Jerusalem is built as a city *
         that is at unity with itself;

4   To which the tribes go up,
     the tribes of the LORD, *
         the assembly of Israel,
         to praise the Name of the LORD.

5   For there are the thrones of judgment, *
         the thrones of the house of David.

6   Pray for the peace of Jerusalem: *
         "May they prosper who love you.

7   Peace be within your walls *
          and quietness within your towers.

8   For my brethren and companions' sake, *
          I pray for your prosperity.

9   Because of the house of the LORD our God, *
          I will seek to do you good."

The Epistle   **Romans 13:8-14**
Owe no one anything, except to love one another; for the one who loves another has
fulfilled the law.
The commandments, "You shall not commit adultery; You shall not murder; You
shall not steal; You shall not covet"; and any other commandment, are summed up
in this word, "Love your neighbor as yourself." Love does no wrong to a neighbor;
therefore, love is the fulfilling of the law. Besides this, you know what time it is, how
it is now the moment for you to wake from sleep. For salvation is nearer to us now
than when we became believers; the night is far gone, the day is near. Let us then lay
aside the works of darkness and put on the armor of light; let us live honorably as in
the day, not in reveling and drunkenness, not in debauchery and licentiousness, not
in quarreling and jealousy. Instead, put on the Lord Jesus Christ, and make no
provision for the flesh, to gratify its desires.

The Gospel   **Matthew 24:37-44**
On the Mount of Olives, Jesus said to his disciples privately, "For as the days of
Noah were, so will be the coming of the Son of Man. For as in those days before the
flood they were eating and drinking, marrying and giving in marriage, until the day
Noah entered the ark, and they knew nothing until the flood came and swept them all
away, so too will be the coming of the Son of Man. Then two will be in the field; one
will be taken and one will be left. Two women will be grinding meal together; one will
be taken and one will be left. Keep awake therefore, for you do not know on what day
your Lord is coming. But understand this: if the owner of the house had known in
what part of the night the thief was coming, he would have stayed awake and would
not have let his house be broken into. Therefore you also must be ready, for the Son
of Man is coming at an unexpected hour."

Year B

The Lesson   **Isaiah 64:1-9a**
O that you would tear open the heavens and come down, so that the mountains
would quake at your presence — as when fire kindles brushwood and the fire causes
water to boil — to make your name known to your adversaries, so that the nations
might tremble at your presence! When you did awesome deeds that we did not
expect, you came down, the mountains quaked at your presence. From ages past no
one has heard, no ear has perceived, no eye has seen any God besides you, who works
for those who wait for him. You meet those who gladly do right, those who
remember you in your ways. But you were angry, and we sinned; because you hid

yourself we transgressed. We have all become like one who is unclean, and all our righteous deeds are like a filthy cloth. We all fade like a leaf, and our iniquities, like the wind, take us away. There is no one who calls on your name, or attempts to take hold of you; for you have hidden your face from us, and have delivered us into the hand of our iniquity. Yet, O LORD, you are our Father; we are the clay, and you are our potter; we are all the work of your hand. Do not be exceedingly angry, O LORD, and do not remember iniquity forever.

The Psalm 80 or 80:1-7)   *Qui regis Israel*

1 [Hear, O Shepherd of Israel, leading Joseph like a flock; *
    shine forth, you that are enthroned upon the cherubim.

2 In the presence of Ephraim, Benjamin, and Manasseh. *
    stir up your strength and come to help us.

3 Restore us, O God of hosts; *
    show the light of your countenance, and we shall be saved.

4 O LORD God of hosts, *
    how long will you be angered
    despite the prayers of your people?

5 You have fed them with the bread of tears; *
    you have given them bowls of tears to drink.

6 You have made us the derision of our neighbors, *
    and our enemies laugh us to scorn.

7 Restore us, O God of hosts; *
    show the light of your countenance, and we shall be saved.]

8 You have brought a vine out of Egypt; *
    you cast out the nations and planted it.

9 You prepared the ground for it; *
    it took root and filled the land.

10 The mountains were covered by its shadow *
    and the towering cedar trees by it boughs.

11 You stretched out its tendrils to the Sea *
    and its branches to the River.

12 Why have you broken down its wall, *
    so that all who pass by pluck off its grapes?

13 The wild boar of the forest has ravaged it, *
    and the beasts of the field have grazed upon it.

14 Turn now, O God of hosts, look down from heaven;
    behold and tend this vine; *
    preserve what your right hand has planted.

15   They burn it with fire like rubbish; *
        at the rebuke of your countenance let them perish.

16   Let your hand be upon the man of your right hand, *
        the son of man you have made so strong for yourself.

17   And so will we never turn away from you; *
        give us life, that we may call upon your Name.

18   Restore us, O LORD God of hosts; *
        show the light of your countenance, and we shall be saved.

The Epistle   **1 Corinthians 1:1-9**

Paul, called to be an apostle of Christ Jesus by the will of God, and our brother Sosthenes, to the church of God that is in Corinth, to those who are sanctified in Christ Jesus, called to be saints, together with all those who in every place call on the name of our Lord Jesus Christ, both their Lord and ours: Grace to you and peace from God our Father and the Lord Jesus Christ. I give thanks to my God always for you because of the grace of God that has been given you in Christ Jesus, for in every way you have been enriched in him, in speech and knowledge of every kind — just as the testimony of Christ has been strengthened among you — so that you are not lacking in any spiritual gift as you wait for the revealing of our Lord Jesus Christ. He will also strengthen you to the end, so that you may be blameless on the day of our Lord Jesus Christ. God is faithful; by him you were called into the fellowship of his Son, Jesus Christ our Lord.

The Gospel   **Mark 13:(24-32) 33-37**

[Jesus said, "But in those days, after that suffering, the sun will be darkened, and the moon will not give its light, and the stars will be falling from heaven, and the powers in the heavens will be shaken. Then they will see the son of Man coming in clouds' with great power and glory. Then he will send out the angels, and gather his elect from the four winds, from the ends of the earth to the ends of heaven. From the fig tree learn its lesson: as soon as its branch becomes tender and puts forth its leaves, you know that summer is near. So also, when you see these things taking place, you know that he is near, at the very gates. Truly I tell you, this generation will not pass away until all these things have taken place. Heaven and earth will pass away, but my words will not pass away.] But about that day or hour no one knows, neither the angels in heaven, nor the Son, but only the Father. Beware, keep alert; for you do not know when the time will come. It is like a man going on a journey, when he leaves home and puts his slaves in charge, each with his work, and commands the doorkeeper to be on the watch. Therefore, keep awake — for you do not know when the master of the house will come, in the evening, or at midnight, or at cockcrow, or at dawn, or else he may find you asleep when he comes suddenly. And what I say to you I say to all: Keep awake."

Year C

The Lesson   **Zechariah 14:4-9**

On the day of battle his feet shall stand on the Mount of Olives, which lies before

Jerusalem on the east; and the Mount of Olives shall be split in two from east to west by a very wide valley; so that one half of the Mount shall withdraw northward, and the other half southward. And you shall flee by the valley of the LORD's mountain, for the valley between the mountains shall reach to Azal; and you shall flee as you fled from the earthquake in the days of King Uzziah of Judah. Then the LORD my God will come, and all the holy ones with him. On that day there shall not be either cold or frost. And there shall be continuous day (it is known to the LORD), not day and not night, for at evening time there shall be light. On that day living waters shall flow out from Jerusalem, half of them to the eastern sea and half of them to the western sea; it shall continue in summer as in winter. And the LORD will become king over all the earth; on that day the LORD will be one and his name one.

The Psalm 50 or 50:1-6   *Deus deorum*

1   [The LORD, the God of gods, has spoken; *
        he has called the earth from the rising of the sun to its setting.

2   Out of Zion, perfect in its beauty, *
        God reveals himself in glory.

3   Our God will come and will not keep silence; *
        before him there is a consuming flame,
        and round about him a raging storm.

4   He calls the heavens and the earth from above *
        to witness the judgment of his people.

5   "Gather before me my loyal followers, *
        those who have made a covenant with me
        and sealed it with sacrifice."

6   Let the heavens declare the rightness of his cause; *
        for God himself is judge.]

7   Hear, O my people, and I will speak:
        "O Israel, I will bear witness against you; *
        for I am God, your God.

8   I do not accuse you because of your sacrifices; *
        your offerings are always before me.

9   I will take no bull-calf from your stalls, *
        nor he-goats out of your pens;

10   For all the beasts of the forest are mine, *
        the herds in their thousands upon the hills.

11   I know every bird in the sky, *
        and the creatures of the fields are in my sight.

12   If I were hungry, I would not tell you, *
        for the whole world is mine and all that is in it.

13   Do you think I eat the flesh of bulls, *
        or drink the blood of goats?

14   Offer to God a sacrifice of thanksgiving *
        and make good your vows to the Most High.

15   Call upon me in the day of trouble; *
        I will deliver you, and you shall honor me."

16   But to the wicked God says: *
        "Why do you recite my statutes,
        and take my covenant upon your lips;

17   Since you refuse discipline, *
        and toss my words behind your back?

18   When you see a thief, you make him your friend, *
        and you cast in your lot with adulterers.

19   You have loosed your lips for evil, *
        and harnessed your tongue to a lie.

20   You are always speaking evil of your brother *
        and slandering your own mother's son.

21   These things you have done, and I kept still, *
        and you thought that I am like you."

22   "I have made my accusation; *
        I have put my case in order before your eyes.

23   Consider this well, you who forget God, *
        lest I rend you and there be none to deliver you.

24   Whoever offers me the sacrifice of thanksgiving honors me; *
        but to those who keep in my way will I show the salvation of God."

The Epistle   **1 Thessalonians 3:9-13**

How can we thank God enough for you in return for all the joy that we feel before our God because of you? Night and day we pray most earnestly that we may see you face to face and restore whatever is lacking in your faith. Now may our God and Father himself and our Lord Jesus direct our way to you. And may the Lord make you increase and abound in love for one another and for all, just as we abound in love for you. And may he so strengthen your hearts in holiness that you may be blameless before our God and Father at the coming of our Lord Jesus with all his saints.

The Gospel   **Luke 21:25-31**

Jesus said, "There will be signs in the sun, the moon, and the stars, and on the earth distress among nations confused by the roaring of the sea and the waves. People will faint from fear and foreboding of what is coming upon the world, for the powers of the heavens will be shaken. Then they will see 'the Son of Man coming in a cloud' with power and great glory. Now when these things begin to take place, stand up and raise your heads, because your redemption is drawing near." Then he told them a parable: "Look at the fig tree and all the trees; as soon as they sprout leaves you can see for yourselves and know that summer is already near. So also, when you see these things taking place, you know that the kingdom of God is near."

THE SECOND SUNDAY OF ADVENT

The Collect
Merciful God, who sent your messengers the prophets to preach repentance and prepare the way for our salvation: Give us grace to heed their warnings and forsake our sins, that we may greet with joy the coming of Jesus Christ our Redeemer; who lives and reigns with you and the Holy Spirit, one God, now and for ever. *Amen.*

Merciful God, who didst send thy messengers the prophets to preach repentance and prepare the way for our salvation: Give us grace to heed their warnings and forsake our sins, that we may greet with joy the coming of Jesus Christ our Redeemer; who liveth and reigneth with thee and the Holy Spirit, one God, now and for ever. *Amen.*

Year A

The Lesson   **Isaiah 11:1-10**
A shoot shall come out from the stump of Jesse, and a branch shall grow out of his roots. The spirit of the LORD shall rest on him, the spirit of wisdom and understanding, the spirit of counsel and might, the spirit of knowledge and the fear of the LORD. His delight shall be in the fear of the LORD. He shall not judge by what his eyes see, or decide by what his ears hear; but with righteousness he shall judge the poor, and decide with equity for the meek of the earth; he shall strike the earth with the rod of his mouth, and with the breath of his lips he shall kill the wicked. Righteousness shall be the belt around his waist, and faithfulness the belt around his loins. The wolf shall live with the lamb, the leopard shall lie down with the kid, the calf and the lion and the fatling together, and a little child shall lead them. The cow and the bear shall graze, their young shall lie down together; and the lion shall eat straw like the ox. The nursing child shall play over the hole of the asp, and the weaned child shall put its hand on the adder's den. They will not hurt or destroy on all my holy mountain; for the earth will be full of the knowledge of the LORD as the waters cover the sea. On that day the root of Jesse shall stand as a signal to the peoples; the nations shall inquire of him, and his dwelling shall be glorious.

The Psalm 72 or 72:1-8   *Deus, judicium*
1   [Give the King your justice, O God, *
            and your righteousness to a King's Son;

2   That he may rule your people righteously *
            and the poor with justice;

3   That the mountains may bring prosperity to the people, *
    and the little hills bring righteousness.

4   He shall defend the needy among the people; *
    he shall rescue the poor and crush the oppressor.

5   He shall live as long as the sun and moon endure, *
    from one generation to another.

6   He shall come down like rain upon the mown field, *
    like showers that water the earth.

7   In his time shall the righteous flourish; *
    there shall be abundance of peace till the moon shall be no more.

8   He shall rule from sea to sea, *
    and from the River to the ends of the earth.]

9   His foes shall bow down before him, *
    and his enemies lick the dust.

10 The kings of Tarshish and of the isles shall pay tribute, *
    and the kings of Arabia and Saba offer gifts.

11 All kings shall bow down before him, *
    and all the nations do him service.

12 For he shall deliver the poor who cries out in distress, *
    and the oppressed who has no helper.

13 He shall have pity on the lowly and poor; *
    he shall preserve the lives of the needy.

14 He shall redeem their lives from oppression and violence, *
    and dear shall their blood be in his sight.

15 Long may he live!
and may there be given to him gold from Arabia; *
    may prayer be made for him always,
    and may they bless him all the day long.

16 May there be abundance of grain on the earth,
growing thick even on the hilltops; *
    may its fruit flourish like Lebanon,
    and its grain like grass upon the earth.

17 May his Name remain for ever
and be established as long as the sun endures; *
    may all the nations bless themselves in him and call him blessed.

18 Blessed be the Lord GOD, the God of Israel, *
    who alone does wondrous deeds!

¹⁹ And blessed be his glorious Name for ever! *
   and may all the earth be filled with his glory.
   Amen. Amen.

The Epistle   **Romans 15:4-13**

Whatever was written in former days was written for our instruction, so that by steadfastness and by the encouragement of the scriptures we might have hope. May the God of steadfastness and encouragement grant you to live in harmony with one another, in accordance with Christ Jesus, so that together you may with one voice glorify the God and Father of our Lord Jesus Christ. Welcome one another, therefore, just as Christ has welcomed you, for the glory of God. For I tell you that Christ has become a servant of the circumcised on behalf of the truth of God in order that he might confirm the promises given to the patriarchs, and in order that the Gentiles might glorify God for his mercy. As it is written, "Therefore I will confess you among the Gentiles, and sing praises to your name"; and again he says, "Rejoice, O Gentiles, with his people"; and again, "Praise the Lord, all you Gentiles, and let all the peoples praise him"; and again Isaiah says, "The root of Jesse shall come, the one who rises to rule the Gentiles; in him the Gentiles shall hope." May the God of hope fill you with all joy and peace in believing, so that you may abound in hope by the power of the Holy Spirit.

The Gospel   **Matthew 3:1-12**

In those days John the Baptist appeared in the wilderness of Judea, proclaiming, "Repent, for the kingdom of heaven has come near." This is the one of whom the prophet Isaiah spoke when he said, "The voice of one crying out in the wilderness: 'Prepare the way of the Lord, make his paths straight.'" Now John wore clothing of camel's hair with a leather belt around his waist, and his food was locusts and wild honey. Then the people of Jerusalem and all Judea were going out to him, and all the region along the Jordan, and they were baptized by him in the river Jordan, confessing their sins. But when he saw many Pharisees and Sadducees coming for baptism, he said to them, "You brood of vipers! Who warned you to flee from the wrath to come? Bear fruit worthy of repentance. Do not presume to say to yourselves, 'We have Abraham as our ancestor'; for I tell you, God is able from these stones to raise up children to Abraham. Even now the ax is lying at the root of the trees; every tree therefore that does not bear good fruit is cut down and thrown into the fire. I baptize you with water for repentance, but one who is more powerful than I is coming after me; I am not worthy to carry his sandals. He will baptize you with the Holy Spirit and fire. His winnowing fork is in his hand, and he will clear his threshing floor and will gather his wheat into the granary; but the chaff he will burn with unquenchable fire."

Year B

The Lesson   **Isaiah 40:1-11**

Comfort, O comfort my people, says your God. Speak tenderly to Jerusalem, and cry to her that she has served her term, that her penalty is paid, that she has received from the LORD's hand double for all her sins. A voice cries out: "In the wilderness prepare the way of the LORD, make straight in the desert a highway for our God. Every valley shall be lifted up, and every mountain and hill be made low; the uneven ground shall become level, and the rough places a plain. Then the glory of the LORD shall be revealed, and all people shall see it together, for the mouth of the LORD has spoken." A voice says, "Cry out!" And I said, "What shall I cry?" All people are grass, their constancy is like the flower of the field. The grass withers, the flower fades, when the breath of the LORD blows upon it; surely the people are grass. The grass withers, the flower fades; but the word of our God will stand forever. Get you up to a high mountain, O Zion, herald of good tidings; lift up your voice with strength, O Jerusalem, herald of good tidings, lift it up, do not fear; say to the cities of Judah, "Here is your God!" See, the Lord GOD comes with might, and his arm rules for him; his reward is with him, and his recompense before him. He will feed his flock like a shepherd; he will gather the lambs in his arms, and carry them in his bosom, and gently lead the mother sheep.

The Psalm 85 or 85:7-13   *Benedixisti, Domine*

1   You have been gracious to your land, O LORD, *
      you have restored the good fortune of Jacob.

2   You have forgiven the iniquity of your people *
      and blotted out all their sins.

3   You have withdrawn all your fury *
      and turned yourself from your wrathful indignation.

4   Restore us then, O God our Savior; *
      let your anger depart from us.

5   Will you be displeased with us for ever? *
      will you prolong your anger from age to age?

6   Will you not give us life again, *
      that your people may rejoice in you?

7   [Show us your mercy, O LORD, *
      and grant us your salvation.

8   I will listen to what the LORD God is saying, *
      for he is speaking peace to his faithful people
      and to those who turn their hearts to him.

9   Truly, his salvation is very near to those who fear him, *
      that his glory may dwell in our land.

10   Mercy and truth have met together; *
      righteousness and peace have kissed each other.

11   Truth shall spring up from the earth, *
      and righteousness shall look down from heaven.

12   The LORD will indeed grant prosperity, *
      and our land will yield its increase.

13 Righteousness shall go before him, *
    and peace shall be a pathway for his feet.]

The Epistle
2 Peter 3:8-15a, 18

Do not ignore this one fact, beloved, that with the Lord one day is like a thousand years, and a thousand years are like one day. The Lord is not slow about his promise, as some think of slowness, but is patient with you, not wanting any to perish, but all to come to repentance. But the day of the Lord will come like a thief, and then the heavens will pass away with a loud noise, and the elements will be dissolved with fire, and the earth and everything that is done on it will be disclosed. Since all these things are to be dissolved in this way, what sort of persons ought you to be in leading lives of holiness and godliness, waiting for and hastening the coming of the day of God, because of which the heavens will be set ablaze and dissolved, and the elements will melt with fire? But, in accordance with his promise, we wait for new heavens and a new earth, where righteousness is at home. Therefore, beloved, while you are waiting for these things, strive to be found by him at peace, without spot or blemish; and regard the patience of our Lord as salvation. But grow in the grace and knowledge of our Lord and Savior Jesus Christ. To him be the glory both now and to the day of eternity. Amen.

The Gospel
Mark 1:1-8

The beginning of the good news of Jesus Christ, the Son of God. As it is written in the prophet Isaiah, "See, I am sending my messenger ahead of you, who will prepare your way; the voice of one crying out in the wilderness: 'Prepare the way of the Lord, make his paths straight'", John the baptizer appeared in the wilderness, proclaiming a baptism of repentance for the forgiveness of sins. And people from the whole Judean countryside and all the people of Jerusalem were going out to him, and were baptized by him in the river Jordan, confessing their sins. Now John was clothed with camel's hair, with a leather belt around his waist, and he ate locusts and wild honey. He proclaimed, "The one who is more powerful than I is coming after me; I am not worthy to stoop downand untie the thong of his sandals. I have baptized you with water; but he will baptize you with the Holy Spirit."

Year C

The Lesson
Baruch 5:1-9

Take off the garment of your sorrow and affliction, O Jerusalem, and put on forever the beauty of the glory from God. Put on the robe of the righteousness that comes from God; put on your head the diadem of the glory of the Everlasting; for God will show your splendor everywhere under heaven. For God will give you evermore the name, "Righteous Peace, Godly Glory." Arise, O Jerusalem, stand upon the height; look toward the east, and see your children gathered from west and east at the word of the Holy One, rejoicing that God has remembered them. For they went out from you on foot, led away by their enemies; but God will bring them back to you, carried in glory, as on a royal throne. For God has ordered that every high mountain and the everlasting hills be made low and the valleys filled up, to make level ground, so that Israel may walk safely in the glory of God. The woods and every fragrant tree have shaded Israel at God's command. For God will lead Israel with joy, in the light of his glory, with the mercy and righteousness that come from him.

The Psalm 126 *In convertendo*

1 When the LORD restored the fortunes of Zion, *
    then were we like those who dream.

2 Then was our mouth filled with laughter, *
    and our tongue with shouts of joy.

3 Then they said among the nations, *
    "The LORD has done great things for them."

4 The LORD has done great things for us, *
    and we are glad indeed.

5 Restore our fortunes, O LORD, *
    like the watercourses of the Negev.

6 Those who sowed with tears *
    will reap with songs of joy.

7 Those who go out weeping, carrying the seed, *
    will come again with joy, shouldering their sheaves.

The Epistle
                                                    Philippians 1:1-11
Paul and Timothy, servants of Christ Jesus, to all the saints in Christ Jesus who are in Philippi, with the bishops and deacons. Grace to you and peace from God our Father and the Lord Jesus Christ. I thank my God every time I remember you, constantly praying with joy in every one of my prayers for all of you, because of your sharing in the gospel from the first day until now. I am confident of this, that the one who began a good work among you will bring it to completion by the day of Jesus Christ. It is right for me to think this way about all of you, because you hold me in your heart, for all of you share in God's grace with me, both in my imprisonment and in the defense and confirmation of the gospel. For God is my witness, how I long for all of you with the compassion of Christ Jesus. And this is my prayer, that your love may overflow more and more with knowledge and full insight to help you to determine what is best, so that in the day of Christ you may be pure and blameless, having produced the harvest of righteousness that comes through Jesus Christ for the glory and praise of God.

The Gospel
                                                        Luke 3:1-6
In the fifteenth year of the reign of Emperor Tiberius, when Pontius Pilate was governor of Judea, and Herod was ruler of Galilee, and his brother Philip ruler of the region of Ituraea and Trachonitis, and Lysanias ruler of Abilene, during the high priesthood of Annas and Caiaphas, the word of God came to John son of Zechariah in the wilderness. He went into all the region around the Jordan, proclaiming a baptism of repentance for the forgiveness of sins, as it is written in the book of the words of the prophet Isaiah, "The voice of one crying out in the wilderness: 'Prepare the way of the Lord, make his paths straight. Every valley shall be filled, and every

mountain and hill shall be made low, and the crooked shall be made straight, and the rough ways made smooth; and all flesh shall see the salvation of God.'"

THIRD SUNDAY OF ADVENT

The Collect

Stir up your power, O Lord, and with great might come among us; and, because we are sorely hindered by our sins, let your bountiful grace and mercy speedily help and deliver us; through Jesus Christ our Lord, to whom, with you and the Holy Spirit, be honor and glory, now and for ever. *Amen.*

Stir up thy power, O Lord, and with great might come among us; and, because we are sorely hindered by our sins, let thy bountiful grace and mercy speedily help and deliver us; through Jesus Christ our Lord, to whom, with thee and the Holy Ghost, be honor and glory, world without end. *Amen.*

Year A

The Lesson   Isaiah 35:1-10

The wilderness and the dry land shall be glad, the desert shall rejoice and blossom; like the crocus it shall blossom abundantly, and rejoice with joy and singing. The glory of Lebanon shall be given to it, the majesty of Carmel and Sharon. They shall see the glory of the LORD, the majesty of our God. Strengthen the weak hands, and make firm the feeble knees. Say to those who are of a fearful heart, "Be strong, do not fear! Here is your God. He will come with vengeance, with terrible recompense. He will come and save you." Then the eyes of the blind shall be opened, and the ears of the deaf unstopped; then the lame shall leap like a deer, and the tongue of the speechless sing for joy. For waters shall break forth in the wilderness, and streams in the desert; the burning sand shall become a pool, and the thirsty ground springs of water; the haunt of jackals shall become a swamp, the grass shall become reeds and rushes. A highway shall be there, and it shall be called the Holy Way; the unclean shall not travel on it, but it shall be for God's people; no traveler, not even fools, shall go astray. No lion shall be there, nor shall any ravenous beast come up on it; they shall not be found there, but the redeemed shall walk there. And the ransomed of the LORD shall return, and come to Zion with singing; everlasting joy shall be upon their heads; they shall obtain joy and gladness, and sorrow and sighing shall flee away.

The Psalm 146 or 146:4-9   *Lauda, anima mea*

1   Hallelujah!
     Praise the LORD, O my soul! *
        I will praise the LORD as long as I live;
        I will sing praises to my God while I have my being.

2   Put not your trust in rulers, nor in any child of earth, *
        for there is no help in them.

3   When they breathe their last, they return to earth, *
        and in that day their thoughts perish.

4   [Happy are they who have the God of Jacob for their help! *
       whose hope is in the LORD their God;

5   Who made heaven and earth, the seas, and all that is in them; *
       who keeps his promise for ever;

6   Who gives justice to those who are oppressed, *
       and food to those who hunger.

7   The LORD sets the prisoners free;
    the LORD opens the eyes of the blind; *
       the LORD lifts up those who are bowed down;

8   The LORD loves the righteous;
    the LORD cares for the stranger; *
       he sustains the orphan and widow,
       but frustrates the way of the wicked.

9   The LORD shall reign for ever, *
       your God, O Zion, throughout all generations.
       Hallelujah!]

The Epistle   **James 5:7-10**
Be patient, therefore, beloved, until the coming of the Lord. The farmer waits for the
precious crop from the earth, being patient with it until it receives the early and the
late rains. You also must be patient. Strengthen your hearts, for the coming of the
Lord is near. Beloved, do not grumble against one another, so that you may not be
judged. See, the Judge is standing at the doors! As an example of suffering and
patience, beloved, take the prophets who spoke in the name of the Lord.

The Gospel   **Matthew 11:2-11**
When John heard in prison what the Messiah was doing, he sent word by his
disciples and said to him, "Are you the one who is to come, or are we to wait for
another?" Jesus answered them, "Go and tell John what you hear and see: the blind
receive their sight, the lamewalk, the lepers are cleansed, the deaf hear, the dead are
raised, and the poor have good news brought to them. And blessed is anyone who
takes no offense at me." As they went away, Jesus began to speak to the crowds about
John: "What did you go out into the wilderness to look at? A reed shaken by the
wind? What then did you go out to see? Someone dressed in soft robes? Look, those
who wear soft robes are in royal palaces. What then did you go out to see? A prophet?
Yes, I tell you, and more than a prophet. This is the one about whom it is written,
'See, I am sending my messenger ahead of you, who will prepare your way before
you.' Truly I tell you, among those born of women no one has arisen greater than
John the Baptist; yet the least in the kingdom of heaven is greater than he."

Year B

The Lesson   **Isaiah 65:17-25**
Thus says the Lord God, I am about to create new heavens and a new earth; the
former things shall not be remembered or come to mind. But be glad and rejoice

forever in what I am creating; for I am about to create Jerusalem as a joy, and its people as a delight. I will rejoice in Jerusalem, and delight in my people; no more shall the sound of weeping be heard in it, or the cry of distress. No more shall there be in it an infant that lives but a few days, or an old person who does not live out a lifetime; for one who dies at a hundred years will be considered a youth, and one who falls short of a hundred will be considered accursed. They shall build houses and inhabit them; they shall plant vineyards and eat their fruit. They shall not build and another inhabit; they shall not plant and another eat; for like the days of a tree shall the days of my people be, and my chosen shall long enjoy the work of their hands. They shall not labor in vain, or bear children for calamity; for they shall be offspring blessed by the LORD — and their descendants as well. Before they call I will answer, while they are yet speaking I will hear. The wolf and the lamb shall feed together, the lion shall eat straw like the ox; but the serpent — its food shall be dust! They shall not hurt or destroy on all my holy mountain, says the LORD.

The Psalm 126   *In convertendo*

1   When the LORD restored the fortunes of Zion, *
         then were we like those who dream.

2   Then was our mouth filled with laughter, *
         and our tongue with shouts of joy.

3   Then they said among the nations, *
         "The LORD has done great things for them."

4   The LORD has done great things for us, *
         and we are glad indeed.

5   Restore our fortunes, O LORD, *
         like the watercourses of the Negev.

6   Those who sowed with tears *
         will reap with songs of joy.

7   Those who go out weeping, carrying the seed, *
         will come again with joy, shouldering their sheaves.

or Canticle 3
The Song of Mary   *Magnificat*
Luke 1:46-55
My soul doth magnify the Lord, *
   and my spirit hath rejoiced in God my Savior.
For he hath regarded *
   the lowliness of his handmaiden.
For behold from henceforth *
   all generations shall call me blessed.
For he that is mighty hath magnified me, *
   and holy is his Name.
And his mercy is on them that fear him *
   throughout all generations.

He hath showed strength with his arm; *
   he hath scattered the proud in the imagination of their hearts.
He hath put down the mighty from their seat, *
   and hath exalted the humble and meek.
He hath filled the hungry with good things, *
   and the rich he hath sent empty away.
He remembering his mercy hath holpen his servant Israel, *
   as he promised to our forefathers,
   Abraham and his seed for ever.
Glory to the Father, and to the Son, and to the Holy Spirit: *
   as it was in the beginning, is now, and will be for ever. Amen.

or Canticle 15
The Song of Mary   *Magnificat*
Luke 1:46-55
My soul proclaims the greatness of the Lord,
my spirit rejoices in God my Savior; *
   for he has looked with favor on his lowly servant.
From this day all generations will call me blessed: *
   the Almighty has done great things for me,
   and holy is his Name.
He has mercy on those who fear him *
   in every generation.
He has shown the strength of his arm, *
   he has scattered the proud in their conceit.
He has cast down the mighty from their thrones, *
   and has lifted up the lowly.
He has filled the hungry with good things, *
   and the rich he has sent away empty.
He has come to the help of his servant Israel, *
   for he has remembered his promise of mercy,
The promise he made to our fathers, *
   to Abraham and his children for ever.
Glory to the Father, and to the Son, and to the Holy Spirit: *
   as it was in the beginning, is now, and will be for ever. Amen.

The Epistle   **1 Thessalonians 5:(12-15) 16-28**
[We appeal to you, brothers and sisters, to respect those who labor among you, and
have charge of you in the Lord and admonish you; esteem them very highly in love
because of their work. Be at peace among yourselves. And we urge you, beloved to
admonish the idlers, encourage the faint hearted, help the weak, be patient with all of
them. See that none of you repays evil for evil, but always seek to do good to one
another and to all.] Rejoice always, pray without ceasing, give thanks in all
circumstances; for this is the will of God in Christ Jesus for you. Do not quench the
Spirit. Do not despise the words of prophets, but test everything; hold fast to what is
good; abstain from every form of evil. May the God of peace himself sanctify you
entirely; and may your spirit and soul and body be kept sound and blameless at the

coming of our Lord Jesus Christ. The one who calls you is faithful, and he will do this. Beloved, pray for us. Greet all the brothers and sisters with a holy kiss. I solemnly command you by the Lord that this letter be read to all of them. The grace of our Lord Jesus Christ be with you.

The Gospel
John 1:6-8,19-28

There was a man sent from God, whose name was John. He came as a witness to testify to the light, so that all might believe through him. He himself was not the light, but he came to testify to the light. This is the testimony given by John when the Jews sent priests and Levites from Jerusalem to ask him, "Who are you?" He confessed and did not deny it, but confessed, "I am not the Messiah." And they asked him, "What then? Are you Elijah?" He said, "I am not." "Are you the prophet?" He answered, "No." Then they said to him, "Who are you? Let us have an answer for those who sent us. What do you say about yourself?" He said, "I am the voice of one crying out in the wilderness, 'Make straight the way of the Lord,'" as the prophet Isaiah said. Now they had been sent from the Pharisees. They asked him, "Why then are you baptizing if you are neither the Messiah, nor Elijah, nor the prophet?" John answered them, "I baptize with water. Among you stands one whom you do not know, the one who is coming after me; I am not worthy to untie the thong of his sandal." This took place in Bethany across the Jordan where John was baptizing.

or John 3:23-30

John also was baptizing at Aenon near Salim because water was abundant there; and people kept coming and were being baptized — John, of course, had not yet been thrown into prison. Now a discussion about purification arose between John's disciples and a Jew. They came to John and said to him, "Rabbi, the one who was with you across the Jordan, to whom you testified, here he is baptizing, and all are going to him." John answered, "No one can receive anything except what has been given from heaven. You yourselves are my witnesses that I said, 'I am not the Messiah, but I have been sent ahead of him.' He who has the bride is the bridegroom. The friend of the bridegroom, who stands and hears him, rejoices greatly at the bridegroom's voice. For this reason my joy has been fulfilled. He must increase, but I must decrease."

Year C

The Lesson
Zephaniah 3:14-20

Sing aloud, O daughter Zion; shout, O Israel! Rejoice and exult with all your heart, O daughter Jerusalem! The LORD has taken away the judgments against you, he has turned away your enemies. The king of Israel, the LORD, is in your midst; you shall fear disaster no more. On that day it shall be said to Jerusalem: Do not fear, O Zion; do not let your hands grow weak. The LORD, your God, is in your midst, a warrior who gives victory; he will rejoice over you with gladness, he will renew you in his love; he will exult over you with loud singing as on a day of festival. I will remove disaster from you, so that you will not bear reproach for it. I will deal with all your oppressors at that time. And I will save the lame and gather the outcast, and I will change their shame into praise and renown in all the earth. At that time I will bring you home, at the time when I gather you; for I will make you renowned and praised among all the peoples of the earth, when I restore your fortunes before your eyes, says the LORD.

The Psalm 85 or 85:7-13   *Benedixisti, Domine*

1   You have been gracious to your land, O LORD, *
        you have restored the good fortune of Jacob.

2   You have forgiven the iniquity of your people *
        and blotted out all their sins.

3   You have withdrawn all your fury *
        and turned yourself from your wrathful indignation.

4   Restore us then, O God our Savior; *
        let your anger depart from us.

5   Will you be displeased with us for ever? *
        will you prolong your anger from age to age?

6   Will you not give us life again, *
        that your people may rejoice in you?

7   [Show us your mercy, O LORD, *
        and grant us your salvation.

8   I will listen to what the LORD God is saying, *
        for he is speaking peace to his faithful people
        and to those who turn their hearts to him.

9   Truly, his salvation is very near to those who fear him, *
        that his glory may dwell in our land.

10   Mercy and truth have met together; *
        righteousness and peace have kissed each other.

11   Truth shall spring up from the earth, *
        and righteousness shall look down from heaven.

12   The LORD will indeed grant prosperity, *
        and our land will yield its increase.

13   Righteousness shall go before him, *
        and peace shall be a pathway for his feet.]

or Canticle 9
The First Song of Isaiah   *Ecce, Deus*
Isaiah 12:2-6
Surely, it is God who saves me; *
    I will trust in him and not be afraid.
For the Lord is my stronghold and my sure defense, *
    and he will be my Savior.

Therefore you shall draw water with rejoicing *
  and the springs of salvation.
And on that day you shall say, *
  Give thanks to the Lord and call upon his Name;
Make his deeds known among the peoples; *
  see that they remember that his Name is exalted.
Sing the praises of the Lord, for he has done great things, *
  and this is known in all the world.
Cry aloud, inhabitants of Zion, ring out your joy, *
  for the great one in the midst of you is the Holy One of Israel.
Glory to the Father, and to the Son, and to the Holy Spirit: *
  as it was in the beginning, is now, and will be for ever. Amen.

The Epistle   Philippians 4:4-7 (8-9)

Rejoice in the Lord always; again I will say, Rejoice. Let your gentleness be known to everyone. The Lord is near. Do not worry about anything, but in everything by prayer and supplication with thanksgiving let your requests be made known to God. And the peace of God, which surpasses all understanding, will guard your hearts and your minds in Christ Jesus. [Finally, beloved, whatever is true, whatever is honorable, whatever is just, whatever is pure, whatever is pleasing, whatever is commendable, if there is any excellence and if there is anything worthy of praise, think about these things. Keep on doing the things that you have learned and received and heard and seen in me, and the God of peace will be with you.]

The Gospel   Luke 3:7-18

John the baptizer said to the crowds that came out to be baptized by him, "You brood of vipers! Who warned you to flee from the wrath to come? Bear fruits worthy of repentance. Do not begin to say to yourselves, 'We have Abraham as our ancestor'; for I tell you, God is able from these stones to raise up children to Abraham. Even now the ax is lying at the root of the trees; every tree therefore that does not bear good fruit is cut down and thrown into the fire." And the crowds asked him, "What then should we do?" In reply he said to them, "Whoever has two coats must share with anyone who has none; and whoever has food must do likewise." Even tax collectors came to be baptized, and they asked him, "Teacher, what should we do?" He said to them, "Collect no more than the amount prescribed for you." Soldiers also asked him, "And we, what should we do?" He said to them, "Do not extort money from anyone by threats or false accusation, and be satisfied with your wages." As the people were filled with expectation, and all were questioning in their hearts concerning John, whether he might be the Messiah, John answered all of them by saying, "I baptize you with water; but one who is more powerful than I is coming; I am not worthy to untie the thong of his sandals. He will baptize you with the Holy Spirit and fire. His winnowing fork is in his hand, to clear his threshing floor and to gather the wheat into his granary; but the chaff he will burn with unquenchable fire." So, with many other exhortations, he proclaimed the good news to the people.

FOURTH SUNDAY OF ADVENT

The Collect

Purify our conscience, Almighty God, by your daily visitation, that your Son Jesus Christ, at his coming, may find in us a mansion prepared for himself; who lives and reigns with you, in the unity of the Holy Spirit, one God, now and for ever. *Amen.*

We beseech thee, Almighty God, to purify our consciences by thy daily visitation, that when thy Son our Lord cometh he may find in us a mansion prepared for himself; through the same Jesus Christ our Lord, who liveth and reigneth with thee, in the unity of the Holy Spirit, one God, now and for ever. *Amen.*

Year A

The Lesson   Isaiah 7:10-17

Again the LORD spoke to Ahaz, saying, Ask a sign of the LORD your God; let it be deep as Sheol or high as heaven. But Ahaz said, "I will not ask, and I will not put the LORD to the test." Then Isaiah said: "Hear then, O house of David! Is it too little for you to weary mortals, that you weary my God also? Therefore the LORD himself will give you a sign. Look, the young woman is with child and shall bear a son, and shall name him Immanuel. He shall eat curds and honey by the time he knows how to refuse the evil and choose the good. For before the child knows how to refuse the evil and choose the good, the land before whose two kings you are in dread will be deserted." The LORD will bring on you and on your people and on your ancestral house such days as have not come since the day that Ephraim departed from Judah — the king of Assyria."

The Psalm 24 or 24:1-7   *Domini est terra*

1   [The earth is the LORD's and all that is in it, *
        the world and all who dwell therein.

2   For it is he who founded it upon the seas *
        and made it firm upon the rivers of the deep.

3   "Who can ascend the hill of the LORD? *
        and who can stand in his holy place?"

4   "Those who have clean hands and a pure heart, *
        who have not pledged themselves to falsehood,
        nor sworn by what is a fraud.

5   They shall receive a blessing from the LORD *
        and a just reward from the God of their salvation."

6   Such is the generation of those who seek him, *
        of those who seek your face, O God of Jacob.

7   Lift up your heads, O gates;
     lift them high, O everlasting doors; *
        and the King of glory shall come in.]

8   "Who is this King of glory?" *
       "The LORD, strong and mighty,
         the LORD, mighty in battle."

9   Lift up your heads, O gates;
       lift them high, O everlasting doors; *
         and the King of glory shall come in.

10   "Who is he, this King of glory?" *
       "The LORD of hosts,
         he is the King of glory."

The Epistle   **Romans 1:1-7**

Paul, a servant of Jesus Christ, called to be an apostle, set apart for the gospel of God, which he promised beforehand through his prophets in the holy scriptures, the gospel concerning his Son, who was descended from David according to the flesh and was declared to be Son of God with power according to the spirit of holiness by resurrection from the dead, Jesus Christ our Lord, through whom we have received grace and apostleship to bring about the obedience of faith among all the Gentiles for the sake of his name, including yourselves who are called to belong to Jesus Christ, To all God's beloved in Rome, who are called to be saints: Grace to you and peace from God our Father and the Lord Jesus Christ.

The Gospel   **Matthew 1:18-25**

Now the birth of Jesus the Messiah took place in this way. When his mother Mary had been engaged to Joseph, but before they lived together, she was found to be with child from the Holy Spirit. Her husband Joseph, being a righteous man and unwilling to expose her to public disgrace, planned to dismiss her quietly. But just when he had resolved to do this, an angel of the Lord appeared to him in a dream and said, "Joseph, son of David, do not be afraid to take Mary as your wife, for the child conceived in her is from the Holy Spirit. She will bear a son, and you are to name him Jesus, for he will save his people from their sins." All this took place to fulfill what had been spoken by the Lord through the prophet: "Look, the virgin shall conceive and bear a son, and they shall name him Emmanuel," which means, "God is with us." When Joseph awoke from sleep, he did as the angel of the Lord commanded him; he took her as his wife, but had no marital relations with her until she had borne a son; and he named him Jesus.

Year B

The Lesson   **2 Samuel 7:4,8-16**

That same night the word of the LORD came to Nathan: Now therefore thus you shall say to my servant David: Thus says the LORD of hosts: I took you from the pasture, from following the sheep to be prince over my people Israel; and I have been with you wherever you went, and have cut off all your enemies from before you; and I will make for you a great name, like the name of the great ones of the earth. And I will appoint a place for my people Israel and will plant them, so that they may live in their own place, and be disturbed no more; and evildoers shall afflict them no more, as formerly, from the time that I appointed judges over my people Israel; and I will give you rest from all your enemies. Moreover the LORD declares to you that the LORD will make you a house. When your days are fulfilled and you lie down with your ancestors, I will raise up your offspring after you, who shall come forth from your body, and I will establish his kingdom. He shall build a house for my name, and I will establish the throne of his kingdom forever. I will be a father to him, and he shall be a son to me. When he commits iniquity, I will punish him with a rod such as mortals use, with blows inflicted by human beings. But I will not take my steadfast love from him, as I took it from Saul, whom I put away from before you. Your house and your kingdom shall be made sure forever before me; your throne shall be established forever.

The Psalm 132 or 132:8-15   *Memento, Domine*

1   LORD, remember David, *
         and all the hardships he endured;

2   How he swore an oath to the LORD *
         and vowed a vow to the Mighty One of Jacob:

3   "I will not come under the roof of my house, *
         nor climb up into my bed;

4   I will not allow my eyes to sleep, *
         nor let my eyelids slumber;

5   Until I find a place for the LORD, *
         a dwelling for the Mighty One of Jacob."

6   "The ark! We heard it was in Ephratah; *
         we found it in the fields of Jearim.

7   Let us go to God's dwelling place; *
         Let us fall upon our knees before his footstool."

8   [Arise, O LORD, into your resting-place, *
         you and the ark of your strength.

9   Let your priests be clothed with righteousness; *
         let your faithful people sing with joy.

10   For your servant David's sake, *
         do not turn away the face of your Anointed.

11   The LORD has sworn an oath to David; *
         in truth, he will not break it:

12   "A son, the fruit of your body *
         will I set upon your throne.

13   If your children keep my covenant
     and my testimonies that I shall teach them, *
         their children will sit upon your throne for evermore."

14   For the LORD has chosen Zion; *
        he has desired her for his habitation:

15   "This shall be my resting-place for ever; *
        here will I dwell, for I delight in her.]

16   I will surely bless her provisions, *
        and satisfy her poor with bread.

17   I will clothe her priests with salvation, *
        and her faithful people will rejoice and sing.

18   There I will make the horn of David flourish; *
        I have prepared a lamp for my Anointed.

19   As for his enemies, I will clothe them with shame; *
        but as for him, his crown will shine."

The Epistle   **Romans 16:25-27**

Now to God who is able to strengthen you according to my gospel and the proclamation of Jesus Christ, according to the revelation of the mystery that was kept secret for long ages but is now disclosed, and through the prophetic writings is made known to all the Gentiles, according to the command of the eternal God, to bring about the obedience of faith — to the only wise God, through Jesus Christ, to whom be the glory forever! Amen.

The Gospel   **Luke 1:26-38**

In the sixth month the angel Gabriel was sent by God to a town in Galilee called Nazareth, to a virgin engaged to a man whose name was Joseph, of the house of David. The virgin's name was Mary. And he came to her and said, "Greetings, favored one! The Lord is with you." But she was much perplexed by his words and pondered what sort of greeting this might be. The angel said to her, "Do not be afraid, Mary, for you have found favor with God. And now, you will conceive in your womb and bear a son, and you will name him Jesus. He will be great, and will be called the Son of the Most High, and the Lord God will give to him the throne of his ancestor David. He will reign over the house of Jacob forever, and of his kingdom there will be no end." Mary said to the angel, "How can this be, since I am a virgin?" The angel said to her, "The Holy Spirit will come upon you, and the power of the Most High will overshadow you; therefore the child to be born will be holy; he will be called Son of God. And now, your relative Elizabeth in her old age has also conceived a son; and this is the sixth month for her who was said to be barren. For nothing will be impossible with God." Then Mary said, "Here am I, the servant of the Lord; let it be with me according to your word." Then the angel departed from her.

Year C

The Lesson   **Micah 5:2-4**

You, O Bethlehem of Ephrathah, who are one of the little clans of Judah, from you shall come forth for me one who is to rule in Israel, whose origin is from of old, from ancient days. Therefore he shall give them up until the time when she who is in labor has brought forth; then the rest of his kindred shall return to the people of Israel. And he shall stand and feed his flock in the strength of the LORD, in the majesty of the name of the LORD his God. And they shall live secure, for now he shall be great to the ends of the earth.

The Psalm 80 or 80:1-7   *Qui regis Israel*

1   [Hear, O Shepherd of Israel, leading Joseph like a flock; *
        shine forth, you that are enthroned upon the cherubim.

2   In the presence of Ephraim, Benjamin, and Manasseh. *
        stir up your strength and come to help us.

3   Restore us, O God of hosts; *
        show the light of your countenance, and we shall be saved.

4   O LORD God of hosts, *
        how long will you be angered
        despite the prayers of your people?

5   You have fed them with the bread of tears; *
        you have given them bowls of tears to drink.

6   You have made us the derision of our neighbors, *
        and our enemies laugh us to scorn.

7   Restore us, O God of hosts; *
        show the light of your countenance, and we shall be saved.]

8   You have brought a vine out of Egypt; *
        you cast out the nations and planted it.

9   You prepared the ground for it; *
        it took root and filled the land.

10   The mountains were covered by its shadow *
        and the towering cedar trees by its boughs.

11   You stretched out its tendrils to the Sea *
        and its branches to the River.

12   Why have you broken down its wall, *
        so that all who pass by pluck off its grapes?

13   The wild boar of the forest has ravaged it, *
        and the beasts of the field have grazed upon it.

14   Turn now, O God of hosts, look down from heaven;
    behold and tend this vine; *
        preserve what your right hand has planted.

15   They burn it with fire like rubbish; *
        at the rebuke of your countenance let them perish.

16   Let your hand be upon the man of your right hand, *
         the son of man you have made so strong for yourself.

17   And so will we never turn away from you; *
         give us life, that we may call upon your Name.

18   Restore us, O LORD God of hosts; *
         show the light of your countenance, and we shall be saved.

The Epistle   Hebrews 10:5-10
When Christ came into the world, he said, "Sacrifices and offerings you have not
desired, but a body you have prepared for me; in burnt offerings and sin offerings you
have taken no pleasure. Then I said, 'See, God, I have come to do your will, O God'
(in the scroll of the book it is written of me)." When he said above, "You have
neither desired nor taken pleasure in sacrifices and offerings and burnt offerings and
sin offerings" (these are offered according to the law), then he added, "See, I have
come to do your will." He abolishes the first in order to establish the second. And it
is by God's will that we have been sanctified through the offering of the body of Jesus
Christ once for all.

The Gospel   Luke 1:39-49 (50-56)
In those days Mary set out and went with haste to a Judean town in the hill country,
where she entered the house of Zechariah and greeted Elizabeth. When Elizabeth
heard Mary's greeting, the child leaped in her womb. And Elizabeth was filled with
the Holy Spirit and exclaimed with a loud cry, "Blessed are you among women, and
blessed is the fruit of your womb. And why has this happened to me, that the mother
of my Lord comes to me? For as soon as I heard the sound of your greeting, the child
in my womb leaped for joy. And blessed is she who believed that there would be a
fulfillment of what was spoken to her by the Lord." And Mary said, "My soul
magnifies the Lord, and my spirit rejoices in God my Savior, for he has looked with
favor on the lowliness of his servant. Surely, from now on all generations will call me
blessed; for the Mighty One has done great things for me, and holy is his name. [His
mercy is for those who fear him from generation to generation. He has shown
strength with his arm; he has scattered the proud in the thoughts of their hearts. He
has brought down the powerful from their thrones, and lifted up the lowly; he has
filled the hungry with good things, and sent the rich away empty. He has helped his
servant Israel, in remembrance of his mercy, according to the promise he made to
our ancestors, to Abraham and to his descendants forever." And Mary remained
with her about three months and then returned to her home.]

THE NATIVITY OF OUR LORD:
CHRISTMAS DAY
DECEMBER 25

The Collect
**O God, you make us glad by the yearly festival of the birth of your only Son Jesus
Christ: Grant that we, who joyfully receive him as our Redeemer, may with sure**

confidence behold him when he comes to be our Judge; who lives and reigns with you and the Holy Spirit, one God, now and for ever. *Amen.*

O God, who makest us glad with the yearly remembrance of the birth of thy only Son Jesus Christ: Grant that as we joyfully receive him for our Redeemer, so we may with sure confidence behold him when he shall come to be our Judge; who liveth and reigneth with thee and the Holy Ghost, one God, world without end. *Amen.*

Years A, B, C

The Lesson Isaiah 9:2-4, 6-7

The people who walked in darkness have seen a great light; those who lived in a land of deep darkness — on them light has shined. You have multiplied the nation, you have increased its joy; they rejoice before you as with joy at the harvest, as people exult when dividing plunder. For the yoke of their burden, and the bar across their shoulders, the rod of their oppressor, you have broken as on the day of Midian. For a child has been born for us, a son given to us; authority rests upon his shoulders; and he is named Wonderful Counselor, Mighty God, Everlasting Father, Prince of Peace. His authority shall grow continually, and there shall be endless peace for the throne of David and his kingdom. He will establish and uphold it with justice and with righteousness from this time onward and forevermore. The zeal of the LORD of hosts will do this.

The Psalm 96 or 96:1-4, 11-12   *Cantate Domino*

1   [Sing to the LORD a new song; *
        sing to the LORD, all the whole earth.

2   Sing to the LORD and bless his Name; *
        proclaim the good news of his salvation from day to day.

3   Declare his glory among the nations *
        and his wonders among all peoples.

4   For great is the LORD and greatly to be praised; *
        he is more to be feared than all gods.]

5   As for all the gods of the nations, they are but idols; *
        but it is the LORD who made the heavens.

6   Oh, the majesty and magnificence of his presence! *
        Oh, the power and the splendor of his sanctuary!

7   Ascribe to the LORD, you families of the peoples; *
        ascribe to the LORD honor and power.

8   Ascribe to the LORD the honor due his Name; *
        bring offerings and come into his courts.

9   Worship the LORD in the beauty of holiness; *
        let the who earth tremble before him.

10   Tell it out among the nations: "The LORD is King! *
        he has made the world so firm that it cannot be moved;
        he will judge the peoples with equity."

11   [Let the heavens rejoice, and let the earth be glad;
        let the sea thunder and all that is in it; *
        let the field be joyful and all that is therein.

12   Then shall all the trees of the wood shout for joy
        before the LORD when he comes, *
        when he comes to judge the earth.]

13   He will judge the world with righteousness *
        and the peoples with his truth.

The Epistle   Titus 2:11-14

The grace of God has appeared, bringing salvation to all, training us to renounce impiety and worldly passions, and in the present age to live lives that are self-controlled, upright, and godly, while we wait for the blessed hope and the manifestation of the glory of our great God and Savior, Jesus Christ. He it is who gave himself for us that he might redeem us from all iniquity and purify for himself a people of his own who are zealous for good deeds.

The Gospel   Luke 2:1-14 (15-20)

In those days a decree went out from Emperor Augustus that all the world should be registered. This was the first registration and was taken while Quirinius was governor of Syria. All went to their own towns to be registered. Joseph also went from the town of Nazareth in Galilee to Judea, to the city of David called Bethlehem, because he was descended from the house and family of David. He went to be registered with Mary, to whom he was engaged and who was expecting a child. While they were there, the time came for her to deliver her child. And she gave birth to her firstborn son and wrapped him in bands of cloth, and laid him in a manger, because there was no place for them in the inn. In that region there were shepherds living in the fields, keeping watch over their flock by night. Then an angel of the Lord stood before them, and the glory of the Lord shone around them, and they were terrified. But the angel said to them, "Do not be afraid; for see — I am bringing you good news of great joy for all the people: to you is born this day in the city of David a Savior, who is the Messiah, the Lord. This will be a sign for you: you will find a child wrapped in bands of cloth and lying in a manger." And suddenly there was with the angel a multitude of the heavenly host, praising God and saying, "Glory to God in the highest heaven, and on earth peace among those whom he favors!" [When the angels had left them and gone into heaven, the shepherds said to one another, "Let us go now to Bethlehem and see this thing that has taken place, which the Lord has made known to us." So they went with haste and found Mary and Joseph, and the child lying in the manger. When they saw this, they made known what had been told them about this child; and all who heard it were amazed at what the shepherds told them. But Mary treasured all these words and pondered them in her heart. The shepherds

returned, glorifying and praising God for all they had heard and seen, as it had been
told them.]

CHRISTMAS DAY II
(A SECOND PROPER)

The Collect

**O God, you have caused this holy night to shine with the illumination of the true Light:
Grant that we, who have known the mystery of that Light on earth, may also enjoy him
perfectly in heaven; where with you and the Holy Spirit he lives and reigns, one God, in
glory everlasting.** *Amen.*

**O God, who hast caused this holy night to shine with the illumination of the true
Light: Grant us, we beseech thee, that as we have known the mystery of that Light
upon earth, so may we also perfectly enjoy him in heaven; where with thee and the
Holy Spirit he liveth and reigneth, one God, in glory everlasting.** *Amen.*

Years A, B, C

The Lesson   Isaiah 62:6-7,10-12

Upon your walls, O Jerusalem, I have posted sentinels; all day and all night they shall
never be silent. You who remind the LORD, take no rest, and give him no rest until
he establishes Jerusalem and makes it renowned throughout the earth. Go through,
go through the gates, prepare the way for the people; build up, build up the highway,
clear it of stones, lift up an ensign over the peoples. The LORD has proclaimed to the
end of the earth: Say to daughter Zion, "See, your salvation comes; his reward is with
him, and his recompense before him." They shall be called, "The Holy People, The
Redeemed of the LORD"; and you shall be called, "Sought Out, A City Not
Forsaken."

The Psalm 97 or 97:1-4, 11-12   *Dominus regnavit*

1   [The LORD is King;
     let the earth rejoice; *
          let the multitude of the isles be glad.

2   Clouds and darkness are round about him, *
          righteousness and justice are the foundations of his throne.

3   A fire goes before him *
          and burns up his enemies on every side.

4   His lightnings light up the world; *
          the earth sees it and is afraid.]

5   The mountains melt like wax at the presence of the LORD, *
          at the presence of the Lord of the whole earth.

6   The heavens declare his righteousness, *
          and all the peoples see his glory.

7 Confounded be all who worship carved images
   and delight in false gods! *
      Bow down before him, all you gods.

8 Zion hears and is glad, and the cities of Judah rejoice, *
      because of your judgments, O LORD.

9 For you are the LORD,
   most high over all the earth; *
      you are exalted far above all gods.

10 The LORD loves those who hate evil; *
      he preserves the lives of his saints
         and delivers them from the hand of the wicked.

11 [Light has sprung up for the righteous, *
      and joyful gladness for those who are truehearted.

12 Rejoice in the LORD, you righteous, *
      and give thanks to his holy Name.]

The Epistle
Titus 3:4-7

When the goodness and loving kindness of God our Savior appeared, he saved us, not because of any works of righteousness that we had done, but according to his mercy, through the water of rebirth and renewal by the Holy Spirit. This Spirit he poured out on us richly through Jesus Christ our Savior, so that, having been justified by his grace, we might become heirs according to the hope of eternal life.

The Gospel
Luke 2:(1-14) 15-20

[In those days a decree went out from Emperor Augustus that all the world should be registered. This was the first registration and was taken while Quirinius was governor of Syria. All went to their own towns to be registered. Joseph also went from the town of Nazareth in Galilee to Judea, to the city of David called Bethlehem, because he was descended from the house and family of David. He went to be registered with Mary, to whom he was engaged and who was expecting a child. While they were there, the time came for her to deliver her child. And she gave birth to her first-born son and wrapped him in bands of cloth, and laid him in a manger, because there was no place for them in the inn. In that region there were shepherds living in the fields, keeping watch over their flock by night. Then an angel of the Lord stood before them, and the glory of the Lord shone around them, and they were terrified. But the angel said to them, "Do not be afraid; for see — I am bringing you good news of great joy for all the people: to you is born this day in the city of David a Savior, who is the Messiah, the Lord. This will be a sign for you: you will find a child wrapped in bands of cloth and lying in a manger." And suddenly there was with the angel a multitude of the heavenly host, praising God and saying, "Glory to God in the highest heaven, and on earth peace among those whom he favors!"] When the angels had left them and gone into heaven, the shepherds said to one another, "Let us go now to Bethlehem and see this thing that has taken place, which the Lord has made known to us." So they went with haste and found Mary and Joseph, and the child lying in the manger. When they saw this, they made known what had been told them about this child; and all who heard it were amazed at what the shepherds told them. But Mary treasured all these words and pondered them in her heart. The shepherds returned, glorifying and praising God for all they had heard and seen, as it had been told them.

CHRISTMAS DAY III
(A THIRD PROPER)

The Collect

Almighty God, you have given your only-begotten Son to take our nature upon him, and to be born (this day) of a pure virgin: Grant that we, who have been born again and made your children by adoption and grace, may daily be renewed by your Holy Spirit; through our Lord Jesus Christ, to whom with you and the same Spirit be honor and glory, now and for ever. *Amen.*

Almighty God, who hast given us thy only-begotten Son to take our nature upon him and as at this time to be born of a pure virgin: Grant that we, being regenerate and made thy children by adoption and grace, may daily be renewed by thy Holy Spirit; through the same our Lord Jesus Christ, who liveth and reigneth with thee and the same Spirit ever, one God, world without end. *Amen.*

Years A, B, C

The Lesson   Isaiah 52:7-10

How beautiful upon the mountains are the feet of the messenger who announces peace, who brings good news, who announces salvation, who says to Zion, "Your God reigns." Listen! Your sentinels lift up their voices, together they sing for joy; for in plain sight they see the return of the LORD to Zion. Break forth together into singing, you ruins of Jerusalem; for the LORD has comforted his people, he has redeemed Jerusalem. The LORD has bared his holy arm before the eyes of all the nations; and all the ends of the earth shall see the salvation of our God.

The Psalm 98 or 98:1-6   *Cantate Comino*

1   [Sing to the LORD a new song, *
        for he has done marvelous things.

2   With his right hand and his holy arm *
        has he won for himself the victory.

3   The LORD has made known his victory; *
        his righteousness has he openly shown in the sight of the nations.

4   He remembers his mercy and faithfulness to the house of Israel, *
        and all the ends of the earth have seen the victory of our God.

5   Shout with joy to the LORD, all you lands; *
        lift up your voice, rejoice, and sing.

6   Sing to the LORD with the harp, *
        with the harp and the voice of song.]

7   With trumpets and the sound of the horn *
        shout with joy before the King, the LORD.

8   Let the sea make a noise and all that is in it, *
        the lands and those who dwell therein.

9   Let the rivers clap their hands, *
        and let the hills ring out with joy before the LORD,
        when he comes to judge the earth.

10   In righteousness shall he judge the world *
        and the peoples with equity.

The Epistle   **Hebrews 1:1-12**

Long ago God spoke to our ancestors in many and various ways by the prophets, but
in these last days he has spoken to us by a Son, whom he appointed heir of all things,
through whom he also created the worlds. He is the reflection of God's glory and the
exact imprint of God's very being, and he sustains all things by his powerful word.
When he had made purification for sins, he sat down at the right hand of the Majesty
on high, having become as much superior to angels as the name he has inherited is
more excellent than theirs. For to which of the angels did God ever say, "You are my
Son; today I have begotten you"? Or again, "I will be his Father, and he will be my
Son"? And again, when he brings the firstborn into the world, he says, "Let all God's
angels worship him." Of the angels he says, "He makes his angels winds, and his
servants flames of fire." But of the Son he says, "Your throne, O God, is forever and
ever, and the righteous scepter is the scepter of your kingdom. You have loved
righteousness and hated wickedness; therefore God, your God, has anointed you with
the oil of gladness beyond your companions." And, "In the beginning, Lord, you
founded the earth, and the heavens are the work of your hands; they will perish, but
you remain; they will all wear out like clothing; like a cloak you will roll them up, and
like clothing they will be changed. But you are the same, and your years will never
end."

The Gospel   **John 1:1-14**

In the beginning was the Word, and the Word was with God, and the Word was God.
He was in the beginning with God. All things came into being through him, and
without him not one thing came into being. What has come into being in him was
life, and the life was the light of all people. The light shines in the darkness, and the
darkness did not overcome it. There was a man sent from God, whose name was
John. He came as a witness to testify to the light, so that all might believe through
him. He himself was not the light, but he came to testify to the light. The true light,
which enlightens everyone, was coming into the world. He was in the world, and the
world came into being through him; yet the world did not know him. He came to
what was his own, and his own people did not accept him. But to all who received
him, who believed in his name, he gave power to become children of God, who were
born, not of blood or of the will of the flesh or of the will of man, but of God. And
the Word became flesh and lived among us, and we have seen his glory, the glory as
of a father's only son, full of grace and truth.

THE FIRST SUNDAY AFTER CHRISTMAS

The Collect

Almighty God, you have poured upon us the new light of your incarnate Word: Grant that this light, enkindled in our hearts may shine forth in our lives; through Jesus Christ our Lord, who lives and reigns with you, in the unity of the Holy Spirit, one God, now and for ever. *Amen.*

Almighty God, who hast poured upon us the new light of thine incarnate Word: Grant that the same light, enkindled in our hearts, may shine forth in our lives; through the same JesusChrist our Lord, who liveth and reigneth with thee, in the unityof the Holy Spirit, one God, now and for ever. *Amen.*

Years A, B, C

The Lesson   Isaiah 61:10-62:3

I will greatly rejoice in the LORD, my whole being shall exult in my God; for he has clothed me with the garments of salvation, he has covered me with the robe of righteousness, as a bridegroom decks himself with a garland, and as a bride adorns herself with her jewels. For as the earth brings forth its shoots, and as a garden causes what is sown in it to spring up, so the Lord GOD will cause righteousness and praise to spring up before all the nations. For Zion's sake I will not keep silent, and for Jerusalem's sake I will not rest, until her vindication shines out like the dawn, and her salvation like a burning torch. The nations shall see your vindication, and all the kings your glory; and you shall be called by a new name that the mouth of the LORD will give. You shall be a crown of beauty in the hand of the LORD, and a royal diadem in the hand of your God.

The Psalm 147 or 147:13-21   *Laudate Dominum*

1   Hallelujah!
     How good it is to sing praises to our God! *
         how pleasant it is to honor him with praise!

2   The LORD rebuilds Jerusalem; *
         he gathers the exiles of Israel.

3   He heals the brokenhearted *
         and binds up their wounds.

4   He counts the number of the stars *
         and calls them all by their names.

5   Great is our LORD and mighty in power; *
         there is no limit to his wisdom.

6   the LORD lifts up the lowly, *
         but casts the wicked to the ground.

7   Sing to the LORD with thanksgiving; *
         make music to our God upon the harp.

8   He covers the heavens with clouds *
        and prepares rain for the earth;

9   He makes grass to grow upon the mountains *
        and green plants to serve mankind.

10 He provides food for flocks and herds *
        and for the young ravens when they cry.

11 He is not impressed by the might of a horse; *
        he has no pleasure in the strength of a man;

12 But the LORD has pleasure in those who fear him, *
        in those who await his gracious favor.

13 [Worship the LORD, O Jerusalem; *
        praise your God, O Zion;

14 For he has strengthened the bars of your gates; *
        he has blessed your children within you.

15 He has established peace on your borders; *
        he satisfies you with the finest wheat.

16 He sends out his command to the earth, *
        and his word runs very swiftly.

17 He gives snow like wool; *
        he scatters hoarfrost like ashes.

18 He scatters his hail like bread crumbs; *
        who can stand against his cold?

19 He sends forth his word and melts them; *
        he blows with his wind, and the waters flow.

20 He declares his word to Jacob, *
        his statues and his judgments to Israel.

21 He has not done so to any other nation; *
        to them he has not revealed his judgments.
        Hallelujah!]

The Epistle   **Galatians 3:23-25; 4:4-7**

Now before faith came, we were imprisoned and guarded under the law until faith
would be revealed. Therefore the law was our disciplinarian until Christ came, so that
we might be justified by faith. But now that faith has come, we are no longer subject
to a disciplinarian, but when the fullness of time had come, God sent his Son, born
of a woman, born under the law, in order to redeem those who were under the law, so
that we might receive adoption as children. And because you are children, God has
sent the Spirit of his Son into our hearts, crying, "Abba! Father!" So you are no
longer a slave but a child, and if a child then also an heir, through God.

The Gospel John 1:1-18

In the beginning was the Word, and the Word was with God, and the Word was God. He was in the beginning with god. All things came into being through him, and without him not one thing came into being. What has come into being in him was life, and the life was the light of all people. The light shines in the darkness, and the darkness did not overcome it. There was a man sent from God, whose name was John. He came as a witness to testify to the light, so that all might believe through him. He himself was not the light, but he came to testify to the light. The true light, which enlightens everyone, was coming into the world. He was in the world, and the world came into being through him; yet the world did not know him. He came to what was his own, and his own people did not accept him. But to all who received him, who believed in his name, he gave power to become children of God, who were born, not of blood or of the will of the flesh or of the will of man, but of God. And the Word became flesh and lived among us, and we have seen his glory, the glory as of a father's only son, full of grace and truth. (John testified to him and cried out, "This was he of whom I said, 'He who comes after me ranks ahead of me because he was before me.'") From his fullness we have all received, grace upon grace. The law indeed was given through Moses; grace and truth came through Jesus Christ. No one has ever seen God. It is God the only Son, who is close to the Father's heart, who has made him known.

THE HOLY NAME OF OUR LORD, JESUS CHRIST
(JANUARY 1)

The Collect

Eternal Father, you gave to your incarnate Son the holy name of Jesus to be the sign of our salvation: Plant in every heart, we pray, the love of him who is the Savior of the world, our Lord Jesus Christ; who lives and reigns with you and the Holy Spirit, one God, in glory everlasting. *Amen.*

Eternal Father, who didst give to thine incarnate Son the holy name of Jesus to be the sign of our salvation: Plant in every heart, we beseech thee, the love of him who is the Savior of the world, even our Lord Jesus Christ; who liveth and reigneth with thee and the Holy Spirit, one God, in glory everlasting. *Amen.*

Years A, B, C

The Lesson Exodus 34:1-8

The LORD said to Moses, "Cut two tablets of stone like the former ones, and I will write on the tablets the words that were on the former tablets, which you broke. Be ready in the morning, and come up in the morning to Mount Sinai and present yourself there to me, on the top of the mountain. No one shall come up with you, and do not let anyone be seen throughout all the mountain; and do not let flocks or herds graze in front of that mountain." So Moses cut two tablets of stone like the former ones; and he rose early in the morning and went up on Mount Sinai, as the LORD had commanded him, and took in his hand the two tablets of stone. The LORD descended in the cloud and stood with him there, ad proclaimed the name, "The

LORD." The LORD passed before him, and proclaimed, "The LORD, the LORD, a God merciful and gracious, slow to anger, and abounding in steadfast love and faithfulness, keeping steadfast love for the thousandth generation, forgiving iniquity and transgression and sin, yet by no means clearing the guilty, but visiting the iniquity of the parents upon the children and the children's children, to the third and the fourth generation." And Moses quickly bowed his head toward the earth, and worshiped.

The Psalm 8   *Domine, Dominus noster*

1   O LORD our Governor, *
       how exalted is your Name in all the world!

2   Out of the mouths of infants and children *
       your majesty is praised above the heavens.

3   You have set up a stronghold against your adversaries, *
       to quell the enemy and the avenger.

4   When I consider your heavens, the work of your fingers, *
       the moon and the stars you have set in their courses,

5   What is man that you should be mindful of him? *
       the son of man that you should seek him out?

6   You have made him but little lower than the angels; *
       you adorn him with glory and honor;

7   You give him mastery over the works of your hands; *
       you put all things under his feet:

8   All sheep and oxen, *
       even the wild beasts of the field,

9   The birds of the air, the fish of the sea, *
       and whatsoever walks in the paths of the sea.

10   O LORD our Governor, *
       how exalted is your Name in all the world!

The Epistle   **Romans 1:1-7**

Paul, a servant of Jesus Christ, called to be an apostle, set apart for the gospel of God, which he promised beforehand through his prophets in the holy scriptures, the gospel concerning his Son, who was descended from David according to the flesh and was declared to be Son of God with power according to the spirit of holiness by resurrection from the dead, Jesus Christ our Lord, through whom we have received grace and apostleship to bring about the obedience of faith among all the Gentiles for the sake of his name, including yourselves who are called to belong to Jesus Christ, to all God's beloved in Rome, who are called to be saints: grace to you and peace from God our Father and the Lord Jesus Christ.

or, Philippians 2:9-13 (Year A only)

God also highly exalted him and gave him the name that is above every name, so that at the name of Jesus every knee should bend, in heaven and on earth and under the earth, and every tongue should confess that Jesus Christ is Lord, to the glory of God the Father. Therefore, my beloved, just as you have always obeyed me, not only in my presence, but much more now in my absence, work out your own salvation with fear and trembling; for it is God who is at work in you, enabling you both to will and to work for his good pleasure.

The Gospel   Luke 2:15-21

When the angels had left them and gone into heaven, the shepherds said to one another, "Let us go now to Bethlehem and see this thing that has taken place, which the Lord has made known to us." So they went with haste and found Mary and Joseph, and the child lying in the manger. When they saw this, they made known what had been told them about this child; and all who heard it were amazed at what the shepherds told them. But Mary treasured all these words and pondered them in her heart. The shepherds returned, glorifying and praising God for all they had heard and seen, as it had been told them. After eight days had passed, it was time to circumcise the child; and he was called Jesus, the name given by the angel before he was conceived in the womb.

THE SECOND SUNDAY AFTER CHRISTMAS

The Collect

O God, who wonderfully created, and yet more wonderfully restored, the dignity of human nature: Grant that we may share the divine life of him who humbled himself to share our humanity, your Son Jesus Christ; who lives and reigns with you, in the unity of the Holy Spirit, one God, for ever and ever. *Amen.*

O God, who didst wonderfully create, and yet more wonderfully restore, the dignity of human nature: Grant that we may share the divine life of him who humbled himself to share our humanity, thy Son Jesus Christ; who liveth and reigneth with thee, in the unity of the Holy Spirit, one God, for ever and ever. *Amen.*

Years A, B, C

The Lesson   Jeremiah 31:7-14

Thus says the LORD: Sing aloud with gladness for Jacob, and raise shouts for the chief of the nations; proclaim, give praise, and say, "Save, O LORD, your people, the remnant of Israel." See, I am going to bring them from the land of the north, and gather them from the farthest parts of the earth, among them the blind and the lame, those with child and those in labor, together; a great company, they shall return here. With weeping they shall come, and with consolations I will lead them back, I will let them walk by brooks of water, in a straight path in which they shall not stumble; for I have become a father to Israel, and Ephraim is my firstborn. Hear the word of the LORD, O nations, and declare it in the coastlands far away; say, "He who scattered Israel will gather him, and will keep him as a shepherd a flock." For the LORD has ransomed Jacob, and has redeemed him from hands too strong for him. They shall come and sing aloud on the height of Zion, and they shall be radiant over the goodness of the LORD, over the grain, the wine, and the oil, and over the young of the flock and the herd; their life shall become like a watered garden, and they shall never languish again. Then shall the young women rejoice in the dance, and the young men and the old shall be merry. I will turn their mourning into joy, I will comfort them, and give them gladness for sorrow. I will give the priests their fill of fatness, and my people shall be satisfied with my bounty, says the LORD.

The Psalm 84 or 84:1-8   *Quam dilecta!*

1   [How dear to me is your dwelling, O LORD of hosts! *
        My soul has a desire and longing for the courts of the LORD;
        my heart and my flesh rejoice in the living God.

2   The sparrow has found her a house
        and the swallow a nest where she may lay her young; *
        by the side of your altars, O LORD of hosts,
        my King and my God.

3   Happy are they who dwell in your house! *
        they will always be praising you.

4   Happy are the people whose strength is in you! *
        whose hearts are set on the pilgrims' way.

5   Those who go through the desolate valley will find it a place of springs, *
        for the early rains have covered it with pools of water.

6   They will climb from height to height, *
        and the God of gods will reveal himself in Zion.

7   LORD God of hosts, hear my prayer; *
        hearken, O God of Jacob.

8   Behold our defender, O God; *
        and look upon the face of your Anointed.]

9   For one day in your courts is better than a thousand in my own room, *
        and to stand at the threshold of the house of my God
        than to dwell in the tents of the wicked.

10   For the LORD God is both sun and shield; *
        he will give grace and glory;

11   No good thing will the LORD withhold *
        from those who walk with integrity.

12   O LORD of hosts, *
        happy are they who put their trust in you!

The Epistle   **Ephesians 1:3-6,15-19a**

Blessed be the God and Father of our Lord Jesus Christ, who has blessed us in Christ with every spiritual blessing in the heavenly places, just as he chose us in Christ before the foundation of the world to be holy and blameless before him in love. He destined us for adoption as his children through Jesus Christ, according to the good pleasure of his will, to the praise of his glorious grace that he freely bestowed on us in the Beloved. I have heard of your faith in the Lord Jesus and your love toward all the saints, and for this reason I do not cease to give thanks for you as I remember you in my prayers. I pray that the God of our Lord Jesus Christ, the Father of glory, may give you a spirit of wisdom and revelation as you come to know him, so that, with the eyes of your heart enlightened, you may know what is the hope to which he has called you, what are the riches of his glorious inheritance among the saints, and what is the immeasurable greatness of his power for us who believe.

The Gospel   **Matthew 2:13-15, 19-23**
When the wise men who had come from the East had departed, behold, an angel of the Lord appeared to Joseph in a dream and said, "Get up, take the child and his mother, and flee to Egypt, and remain there until I tell you; for Herod is about to search for the child, to destroy him." Then Joseph got up, took the child and his mother by night, and went to Egypt, and remained there until the death of Herod. This was to fulfill what had been spoken by the Lord through the prophet, "Out of Egypt I have called my son." When Herod died, an angel of the Lord suddenly appeared in a dream to Joseph in Egypt and said, "Get up, take the child and his mother, and go to the land of Israel, for those who were seeking the child's life are dead." Then Joseph got up, took the child and his mother, and went to the land of Israel. But when he heard that Archelaus was ruling over Judea in place of his father Herod, he was afraid to go there. And after being warned in a dream, he went away to the district of Galilee. There he made his home in a town called Nazareth, so that what had been spoken through the prophets might be fulfilled, "He will be called a Nazorean."

or   **Luke 2:41-52**
Every year his parents went to Jerusalem for the festival of the Passover. And when he was twelve years old, they went up as usual for the festival. When the festival was ended and they started to return, the boy Jesus stayed behind in Jerusalem, but his parents did not know it. Assuming that he was in the group of travelers, they went a day's journey. Then they started to look for him among their relatives and friends. When they did not find him, they returned to Jerusalem to search for him. After three days they found him in the temple, sitting among the teachers, listening to them and asking them questions. And all who heard him were amazed at his understanding and his answers. When his parents saw him they were astonished; and his mother said to him, "Child, why have you treated us like this? Look, your father and I have been searching for you in great anxiety." He said to them, "Why were you searching for me? Did you not know that I must be in my Father's house?" But they did not understand what he said to them. Then he went down with them and came to Nazareth, and was obedient to them. His mother treasured all these things in her heart. And Jesus increased in wisdom and in years, and in divine and human favor.

or   **Matthew 2:1-12**
In the time of King Herod, after Jesus was born in Bethlehem of Judea, wise men

from the East came to Jerusalem, asking, "Where is the child who has been born king of the Jews? For we observed his star at its rising, and have come to pay him homage." When King Herod heard this, he was frightened, and all Jerusalem with him; and calling together all the chief priests and scribes of the people, he inquired of them where the Messiah was to be born. they told him, "In Bethlehem of Judea; for so it has been written by the prophet: 'And you, Bethlehem, in the land of Judah, are by no means least among the rulers of Judah; for from you shall come a ruler who is to shepherd my people Israel.'" Then Herod secretly called for the wise men and learned from them the exact time when the star had appeared. Then he sent them to Bethlehem, saying, "Go and search diligently for the child; and when you have found him, bring me word so that I may also go and pay him homage." When they had heard the king, they set out; and there, ahead of them, went the star that they had seen at its rising, until it stopped over the place where the child was. When they saw that the star had stopped, they were overwhelmed with joy. On entering the house, they saw the child with Mary his mother; and they knelt down and paid him homage. Then, opening their treasure chests, they offered him gifts of gold, frankincense, and myrrh. And having been warned in a dream not to return to Herod, they left for their own country by another road.

THE EPIPHANY, OR THE MANIFESTATION
OF CHRIST TO THE GENTILES
JANUARY 6

The Collect

O God, by the leading of a star you manifested your only Son to the peoples of the earth: Lead us, who know you now by faith, to your presence, where we may see your glory face to face; through Jesus Christ our Lord, who lives and reigns with you and the Holy Spirit, one God, now and for ever. *Amen.*

O God, who by the leading of a star didst manifest thy only begotten Son to the peoples of the earth: Lead us, who know thee now by faith, to thy presence, where we may behold thy glory face to face; through the same Jesus Christ our Lord, who liveth and reigneth with thee and the Holy Spirit, one God, now and for ever. *Amen.*

Years A, B, C

The Lesson   Isaiah 60:1-6, 9

Arise, shine; for your light has come, and the glory of the LORD has risen upon you. For darkness shall cover the earth, and thick darkness the peoples; but the LORD will arise upon you, and his glory will appear over you. Nations shall come to your light, and kings to the brightness of your dawn. Lift up your eyes and look around; they all gather together, they come to you; your sons shall come from far away, and your daughters shall be carried on their nurses' arms. Then you shall see and be radiant; your heart shall thrill and rejoice, because the abundance of the sea shall be brought to you, the wealth of the nations shall come to you. A multitude of camels shall cover you, the young camels of Midian and Ephah; all those from Sheba shall come. They shall bring gold and frankincense, and shall proclaim the praise of the LORD. For the coastlands shall wait for me, the ships of Tarshish first, to bring your children from far away, their silver and gold with them, for the name of the Lord your God, and for the Holy One of Israel because he has glorified you.

The Psalm 72 or 72:1-2, 10-17   *Deus, judicium*

1   [Give the King your justice, O God, *
        and your righteousness to the King's Son;

2   That he may rule your people righteously *
        and the poor with justice;]

3   That the mountains may bring prosperity to the people, *
        and the little hills bring righteousness.

4   He shall defend the needy among the people; *
        he shall rescue the poor and crush the oppressor.

5   He shall live as long as the sun and moon endure, *
        from one generation to another.

6   He shall come down like rain upon the mown field, *
        like showers that water the earth.

7   In his time shall the righteous flourish; *
        there shall be abundance of peace till the moon shall be no more.

8   He shall rule from sea to sea, *
        and from the River to the ends of the earth.

9   His foes shall bow down before him, *
        and his enemies lick the dust.

10   [The kings of Tarshish and of the isles shall pay tribute, *
        and the kings of Arabia and Saba offer gifts.

11   All kings shall bow down before him, *
        and all the nations do him service.

12   For he shall deliver the poor who cries out in distress, *
        and the oppressed who has no helper.

13   He shall have pity on the lowly and poor; *
        he shall preserve the lives of the needy.

14   He shall redeem their lives from oppression and violence, *
        and dear shall their blood be in his sight.

15   Long may he live!
     and may there be given to him gold from Arabia; *
        may prayer be made for him always,
        and may they bless him all the day long.

16   May there be abundance of grain on the earth,
     growing thick even on the hilltops; *

may its fruit flourish like Lebanon,
and its grain like grass upon the earth.

17   May his Name remain for ever
and be established as long as the sun endures; *
    may all the nations bless themselves in him and call him blessed.]

18   Blessed be the Lord GOD, the God of Israel, *
    who alone does wondrous deeds!

19   And blessed be his glorious Name for ever! *
    and may all the earth be filled with his glory.
    Amen. Amen.

The Epistle   Ephesians 3:1-12

This is the reason that I Paul am a prisoner for Christ Jesus for the sake of you Gentiles — for surely you have already heard of the commission of God's grace that was given me for you, and how the mystery was made known to me by revelation, as I wrote above in a few words, a reading of which will enable you to perceive my understanding of the mystery of Christ. In former generations this mystery was not made known to humankind, as it has now been revealed to his holy apostles and prophets by the Spirit: that is, the Gentiles have become fellow heirs, members of the same body, and sharers in the promise in Christ Jesus through the gospel. Of this gospel I have become a servant according to the gift of God's grace that was given me by the working of his power. Although I am the very least of all the saints, this grace was given to me to bring to the Gentiles the news of the boundless riches of Christ, and to make everyone see what is the plan of the mystery hidden for ages in God who created all things; so that through the church the wisdom of God in its rich variety might now be made known to the rulers and authorities in the heavenly places. This was in accordance with the eternal purpose that he has carried out in Christ Jesus our Lord, in whom we have access to God in boldness and confidence through faith in him.

The Gospel   Matthew 2:1-12

In the time of King Herod, after Jesus was born in Bethlehem of Judea, wise men from the East came to Jerusalem, asking, "Where is the child who has been born king of the Jews? For we observed his star at its rising, and have come to pay him homage." When King Herod heard this, he was frightened, and all Jerusalem with him; and calling together all the chief priests and scribes of the people, he inquired of them where the Messiah was to be born. They told him, "In Bethlehem of Judea; for so it has been written by the prophet: 'And you, Bethlehem, in the land of Judah, are by no means least among the rulers of Judah; for from you shall come a ruler who is to shepherd my people Israel.'" Then Herod secretly called for the wise men and learned from them the exact time when the star had appeared. Then he sent them to Bethlehem, saying, "Go and search diligently for the child; and when you have found him, bring me word so that I may also go and pay him homage." When they had heard the king, they set out; and there, ahead of them, went the star that they had seen at its rising, until it stopped over the place where the child was. When they saw

THE EPIPHANY — Years A, B, C   41

that the star had stopped, they were overwhelmed with joy. On entering the house, they saw the child with Mary his mother; and they knelt down and paid him homage. Then, opening their treasure chests, they offered him gifts of gold, frankincense, and myrrh. And having been warned in a dream not to return to Herod, they left for their own country by another road.

THE FIRST SUNDAY AFTER EPIPHANY

The Collect
Father in heaven, who at the baptism of Jesus in the River Jordan proclaimed him your beloved Son and anointed him with the Holy Spirit: Grant that all who are baptized into his Name may keep the covenant they have made, and boldly confess him as Lord and Savior; who with you and the Holy Spirit lives and reigns, one God, in glory everlasting. *Amen.*

Father in heaven, who at the baptism of Jesus in the River Jordan didst proclaim him thy beloved Son and anoint him with the Holy Spirit: Grant that all who are baptized into his Name may keep the covenant they have made, and boldly confess him as Lord and Savior; who with thee and the same Spirit liveth and reigneth, one God, in glory everlasting. *Amen.*

Year A, B, C

The Lesson   Isaiah 42:1-9

Here is my servant, whom I uphold, my chosen, in whom my soul delights; I have put my spirit upon him; he will bring forth justice to the nations. He will not cry or lift up his voice, or make it heard in the street; a bruised reed he will not break, and a dimly burning wick he will not quench; he will faithfully bring forth justice. He will not grow faint or be crushed until he has established justice in the earth; and the coastlands wait for his teaching. Thus says God, the LORD, who created the heavens and stretched them out, who spread out the earth and what comes from it, who gives breath to the people upon it and spirit to those who walk in it: I am the LORD, I have called you in righteousness, I have taken you by the hand and kept you; I have given you as a covenant to the people, a light to the nations, to open the eyes that are blind, to bring out the prisoners from the dungeon, from the prison those who sit in darkness. I am the LORD, that is my name; my glory I give to no other, nor my praise to idols. See, the former things have come to pass, and new things I now declare; before they spring forth, I tell you of them.

The Psalm 89:1-29 or 89:20-29   *Misericordias Domini*

1   Your love, O LORD, for ever will I sing; *
         from age to age my mouth will proclaim your faithfulness.

2   For I am persuaded that your love is established for ever; *
         you have set your faithfulness firmly in the heavens.

3   "I have made a covenant with my chosen one; *
         I have sworn an oath to David my servant:

4   'I will establish your line for ever, *
       and preserve your throne for all generations.'"

5   The heavens bear witness to your wonders, O LORD, *
       and to your faithfulness in the assembly of the holy ones;

6   For who in the skies can be compared to the LORD? *
       who is like the LORD among the gods?

7   God is much to be feared in the council of the holy ones, *
       great and terrible to all those round about him.

8   Who is like you, LORD God of hosts? *
       O mighty LORD, your faithfulness is all around you.

9   You rule the raging of the sea *
       and still the surging of its waves.

10 You have crushed Rahab of the deep with a deadly wound; *
       you have scattered your enemies with your mighty arm.

11 Yours are the heavens; the earth also is yours; *
       you laid the foundations of the world and all that is in it.

12 You have made the north and the south; *
       Tabor and Hermon rejoice in your Name.

13 You have a mighty arm; *
       strong is your hand and high is your right hand.

14 Righteousness and justice are the foundations of your throne; *
       love and truth go before your face.

15 Happy are the people who know the festal shout! *
       they walk, O LORD, in the light of your presence.

16 They rejoice daily in your Name; *
       they are jubilant in your righteousness.

17 For you are the glory of their strength, *
       and by your favor our might is exalted.

18 Truly, the LORD is our ruler; *
       the Holy One of Israel is our King.

19 You spoke once in a vision and said to your faithful people: *
       "I have set the crown upon a warrior
       and have exalted one chosen out of the people.

20 [I have found David my servant; *
       with my holy oil have I anointed him.

21 My hand will hold him fast *
       and my arm will make him strong.

22   No enemy shall deceive him, *
         nor any wicked man bring him down.

23   I will crush his foes before him *
         and strike down those who hate him.

24   My faithfulness and love shall be with him, *
         and he shall be victorious through my Name.

25   I shall make his dominion extend *
         from the Great Sea to the River.

26   He will say to me, 'You are my Father, *
         my God, and the rock of my salvation.'

27   I will make him my firstborn *
         and higher than the kings of the earth.

28   I will keep my love for him for ever, *
         and my covenant will stand firm for him.

29   I will establish his line for ever *
         and his throne as the days of heaven."]

The Epistle   Acts 10:34-38
Then Peter began to speak to them: "I truly understand that God shows no partiality,
but in every nation anyone who fears him and does what is right is acceptable to
him. You know the message he sent to the people of Israel, preaching peace by Jesus
Christ — he is Lord of all. That message spread throughout Judea, beginning in
Galilee after the baptism that John announced: how God anointed Jesus of Nazareth
with the Holy Spirit and with power; how he went about doing good and healing all
who were oppressed by the devil, for God was with him."

Year A

The Gospel   Matthew 3:13-17
Then Jesus came from Galilee to John at the Jordan, to be baptized by him. John
would have prevented him, saying, "I need to be baptized by you, and do you come
to me?" But Jesus answered him, "Let it be so now; for it is proper for us in this way
to fulfill all righteousness." Then he consented. And when Jesus had been baptized,
just as he came up from the water, suddenly the heavens were opened to him and he
saw the Spirit of God descending like a dove and alighting on him. And a voice from
heaven said, "This is my Son, the Beloved, with whom I am well pleased."

Year B

The Gospel   Mark 1:7-11
John the baptizer proclaimed, "The one who is more powerful than I is coming after
me; I am not worthy to stoop down and untie the thong of his sandals. I have
baptized you with water; but he will baptize you with the Holy Spirit." In those days
Jesus came from Nazareth of Galilee and was baptized by John in the Jordan. And

just as he was coming up out of the water, he saw the heavens torn apart and the Spirit descending like dove on him. And a voice came from heaven, "You are my Son, the Beloved; with you I am well pleased."

Year C

The Gospel Luke 3:15-16, 21-22

As the people were filled with expectation, and all were questioning in their hearts concerning John, whether he might be the Messiah, John answered all of them by saying, "I baptize you with water; but one who is more powerful than I is coming; I am not worthy to untie the thong of his sandals. He will baptize you with the Holy Spirit and fire. Now when all the people were baptized, and when Jesus also had been baptized and was praying, the heaven was opened, and the Holy Spirit descended upon him in bodily form like a dove. And a voice came from heaven, "You are my Son, the Beloved; with you I am well pleased."

THE SECOND SUNDAY AFTER THE EPIPHANY

The Collect

Almighty God, whose Son our Savior Jesus Christ is the light of the world: Grant that your people, illumined by your Word and Sacraments, may shine with the radiance of Christ's glory, that he may be known, worshiped, and obeyed to the ends of the earth; through Jesus Christ our Lord, who with you and the Holy Spirit lives and reigns, one God, now and for ever. *Amen.*

Almighty God, whose Son our Savior Jesus Christ is the light of the world: Grant that thy people, illumined by thy Word and Sacraments, may shine with the radiance of Christ's glory, that he may be known, worshiped, and obeyed to the ends of the earth; through the same Jesus Christ our Lord, who with thee and the Holy Spirit liveth and reigneth, one God, now and for ever. *Amen.*

Year A

The Lesson Isaiah 49:1-7

Listen to me, O coastlands, pay attention, you peoples from far away! The LORD called me before I was born, while I was in my mother's womb he named me. He made my mouth like a sharp sword, in the shadow of his hand he hid me; he made me a polished arrow, in his quiver he hid me away. And he said to me, "You are my servant, Israel, in whom I will be glorified." But I said, "I have labored in vain, I have spent my strength for nothing and vanity; yet surely my cause is with the LORD, and my reward with my God." And now the LORD says, who formed me in the womb to be his servant, to bring Jacob back to him, and that Israel might be gathered to him, for I am honored in the sight of the LORD, and my God has become my strength — he says, "It is too light a thing that you should be my servant to raise up the tribes of Jacob and to restore the survivors of Israel; I will give you as a light to the nations, that my salvation may reach to the end of the earth." Thus says the LORD, the Redeemer of Israel and his Holy One, to one deeply despised, abhorred by the nations, the slave of rulers, "Kings shall see and stand up, princes, and they shall prostrate themselves, because of the LORD, who is faithful, the Holy One of Israel, who has chosen you."

The Psalm 40:1-10   *Expectans, expectavi*

1   I waited patiently upon the LORD; *
        he stooped to me and heard my cry.

2   He lifted me out of the desolate pit, out of the mire and clay; *
        he set my feet upon a high cliff and made my footing sure.

3   He put a new song in my mouth,
     a song of praise to our God; *
        many shall see, and stand in awe,
        and put their trust in the LORD.

4   Happy are they who trust in the LORD! *
        they do not resort to evil spirits or turn to false gods.

5   Great things are they that you have done, O LORD my God!
     How great your wonders and your plans for us! *
        there is none who can be compared with you.

6   Oh, that I could make them known and tell them! *
        but they are more than I can count.

7   In sacrifice and offering you take no pleasure *
        (you have given me ears to hear you);

8   Burnt-offering and sin-offering you have not required, *
        and so I said, "Behold, I come.

9   In the roll of the book it is written concerning me: *
        'I love to do your will, O my God;
        your law is deep in my heart.'"

10   I proclaimed righteousness in the great congregation; *
        behold, I did not restrain my lips;
        and that, O LORD, you know.

The Epistle   **1 Corinthians 1:1-9**

Paul, called to be an apostle of Christ Jesus by the will of God, and our brother
Sosthenes, to the church of God that is in Corinth, to those who are sanctified in
Christ Jesus, called to be saints, together with all those who in every place call on the
name of our Lord Jesus Christ, both their Lord and ours: Grace to you and peace
from God our Father and the Lord Jesus Christ. I give thanks to my God always for
you because of the grace of God that has been given you in Christ Jesus, for in every
way you have been enriched in him, in speech and knowledge of every kind — just as
the testimony of Christ has been strengthened among you — so that you are not
lacking in any spiritual gift as you wait for the revealing of our Lord Jesus Christ. He
will also strengthen you to the end, so that you may be blameless on the day of our
Lord Jesus Christ. God is faithful; by him you were called into the fellowship of his
Son, Jesus Christ our Lord.

The Gospel

The day after John had baptized Jesus, John saw Jesus coming toward him and declared, "Here is the Lamb of God who takes away the sin of the world! This is he of whom I said, 'After me comes a man who ranks ahead of me because he was before me.' I myself did not know him; but I came baptizing with water for this reason, that he might be revealed to Israel." And John testified, "I saw the Spirit descending from heaven like a dove, and it remained on him. I myself did not know him, but the one who sent me to baptize with water said to me, 'He on whom you see the Spirit descend and remain is the one who baptizes with the Holy Spirit.' And I myself have seen and have testified that this is the Son of God." The next day John again was standing with two of his disciples, and as he watched Jesus walk by, he exclaimed, "Look, here is the Lamb of God!" The two disciples heard him say this, and they followed Jesus. When Jesus turned and saw them following, he said to them, "What are you looking for?" They said to him, "Rabbi" (which translated means Teacher), "where are you staying?" He said to them, "Come and see." They came and saw where he was staying, and they remained with him that day. It was about four o'clock in the afternoon. One of the two who heard John speak and followed him was Andrew, Simon Peter's brother. He first found his brother Simon and said to him, "We have found the Messiah" (which is translated Anointed).

Year B

The Lesson

Now the boy Samuel was ministering to the LORD under Eli. The word of the LORD was rare in those days; visions were not widespread. At that time Eli, whose eyesight had begun to grow dim so that he could not see, was lying down in his room; the lamp of God had not yet gone out, and Samuel was lying down in the temple of the LORD, where the ark of God was. Then the LORD called, "Samuel! Samuel!" and he said, "Here I am!" and ran to Eli, and said, "Here I am, for you called me." But he said, "I did not call; lie down again." So he went and lay down. The LORD called again, "Samuel!" Samuel got up and went to Eli, and said, "Here I am, for you called me." But he said, "I did not call, my son; lie down again." Now Samuel did not yet know the LORD, and the word of the LORD had not yet been revealed to him. The LORD called Samuel again, a third time. And he got up and went to Eli, and said, "Here I am, for you called me." Then Eli perceived that the LORD was calling the boy. Therefore Eli said to Samuel, "Go, lie down; and if he calls you, you shall say, 'Speak, LORD, for your servant is listening.'" So Samuel went and lay down in his place. Now the LORD came and stood there, calling as before, "Samuel! Samuel!" And Samuel said, "Speak, for your servant is listening." [Then the LORD said to Samuel, "See, I am about to do something in Israel that will make both ears of anyone who hears of it tingle. On that day I will fulfill against Eli all that I have spoken concerning his house, from beginning to end. For I have told him that I am about to punish his house forever, for the iniquity that he knew, because his sons were blaspheming God, and he did not restrain them. Therefore I swear to the house of Eli that the iniquity of Eli's house shall not be expiated by sacrifice or offering forever." Samuel lay there until morning; then he opened the doors of the house of the LORD. Samuel was afraid to tell the vision to Eli. But Eli called Samuel and said, "Samuel, my son." He said, "Here I am." Eli said, "What was it that he told you? Do not hide it from me. May God do so to you and more also, if you hide anything from me of all that he told you." So Samuel told him everything and hid nothing from him. Then he said, "It is the LORD; let him do what seems good to him." As Samuel grew up, the LORD was with him and let none of his words fall to the ground. And all Israel from Dan to Beer-sheba knew that Samuel was a trustworthy prophet of the LORD.]

The Psalm 63:1-8　　*Deus, Deus meus*

1　　O God, you are my God; eagerly I seek you; *
　　　　my soul thirsts for you, my flesh faints for you,
　　　　as in a barren and dry land where there is no water.

2　　Therefore I have gazed upon you in your holy place, *
　　　　that I might behold your power and your glory.

3　　For your loving-kindness is better than life itself; *
　　　　my lips shall give you praise.

4　　So will I bless you as long as I live *
　　　　and lift up my hands in your Name.

5　　My soul in content, as with marrow and fatness, *
　　　　and my mouth praises you with joyful lips,

6　　When I remember you upon my bed, *
　　　　and meditate on you in the night watches.

7　　For you have been my helper, *
　　　　and under the shadow of your wings I will rejoice.

8　　My soul clings to you; *
　　　　your right hand holds me fast.

The Epistle　　　　　　　　　　　　　　　　　　　**1 Corinthians 6:11b-20**

You were washed, you were sanctified, you were justified in the name of the Lord Jesus Christ and in the Spirit of our God. "All things are lawful for me," but not all things are beneficial. "All things are lawful for me," but I will not be dominated by anything. "Food is meant for the stomach and the stomach for food," and God will destroy both one and the other. The body is meant not for fornication but for the Lord, and the Lord for the body. And God raised the Lord and will also raise us by his power. Do you not know that your bodies are members of Christ? Should I therefore take the members of Christ and make them members of a prostitute? Never! Do you not know that whoever is united to a prostitute becomes one body with her? For it is said, "The two shall be one flesh." But anyone united to the Lord becomes one spirit with him. Shun fornication! Every sin that a person commits is outside the body; but the fornicator sins against the body itself. Or do you not know that your body is a temple of the Holy Spirit within you, which you have from God, and that you are not your own? For you were bought with a price; therefore glorify God in your body.

The Gospel   John 1:43-51

The next day Jesus decided to go to Galilee. He found Philip and said to him, "Follow me." Now Philip was from Bethsaida, the city of Andrew and Peter. Philip found Nathanael and said to him, "We have found him about whom Moses in the law and also the prophets wrote, Jesus son of Joseph from Nazareth." Nathanael said to him, "Can anything good come out of Nazareth?" Philip said to him, "Come and see." When Jesus saw Nathanael coming toward him, he said of him, "Here is truly an Israelite in whom there is no deceit!" Nathanael asked him, "Where did you get to know me?" Jesus answered, "I saw you under the fig tree before Philip called you." Nathanael replied, "Rabbi, you are the Son of God! You are the King of Israel!" Jesus answered, "Do you believe because I told you that I saw you under the fig tree? You will see greater things than these." And he said to him, "Very truly, I tell you, you will see heaven opened and the angels of God ascending and descending upon the Son of Man."

Year C

The Lesson   Isaiah 62:1-5

For Zion's sake I will not keep silent, and for Jerusalem's sake I will not rest, until her vindication shines out like the dawn, and her salvation like a burning torch. The nations shall see your vindication, and all the kings your glory; and you shall be called by a new name that the mouth of the LORD will give. You shall be a crown of beauty in the hand of the LORD, and a royal diadem in the hand of your God. You shall no more be termed Forsaken, and your land shall no more be termed Desolate; but you shall be called My Delight Is in Her, and your land Married; for the LORD delights in you, and your land shall be married. For as a young man marries a young woman, so shall your builder marry you, and as the bridegroom rejoices over the bride, so shall your God rejoice over you.

The Psalm 96 or 96:1-10   *Cantate Domino*

1   [Sing to the LORD a new song; *
        sing to the LORD, all the whole earth.

2   Sing to the LORD and bless his Name; *
        proclaim the good news of his salvation from day to day.

3   Declare his glory among the nations *
        and his wonders among all peoples.

4   For great is the LORD and greatly to be praised; *
        he is more to be feared than all gods.

5   As for all the gods of the nations, they are but idols; *
        but it is the LORD who made the heavens.

6   Oh, the majesty and magnificence of his presence! *
        Oh, the power and the splendor of his sanctuary!

7   Ascribe to the LORD, you families of the peoples; *
        ascribe to the LORD honor and power.

8   Ascribe to the LORD the honor due his Name; *
         bring offerings and come into his courts.

9   Worship the LORD in the beauty of holiness; *
         let the whole earth tremble before him.

10   Tell it out among the nations: "The LORD is King! *
         he has made the world so firm that it cannot be moved;
         he will judge the peoples with equity."]

11   Let the heavens rejoice, and let the earth be glad;
         let the sea thunder and all that is in it; *
         let the field be joyful and all that is therein.

12   Then shall all the trees of the wood shout for joy
         before the LORD when he comes, *
         when he comes to judge the earth.

13   He will judge the world with righteousness *
         and the peoples with his truth.

The Epistle   **1 Corinthians 12:1-11**

Now concerning spiritual gifts, brothers and sisters, I do not want you to be
uninformed. You know that when you were pagans, you were enticed and led astray
to idols that could not speak. Therefore I want you to understand that no one
speaking by the Spirit of God ever says "Let Jesus be cursed!" and no one can say
"Jesus is Lord" except by the Holy Spirit. Now there are varieties of gifts, but the
same Spirit; and there are varieties of services, but the same Lord; and there are
varieties of activities, but it is the same God who activates all of them in everyone.
To each is given the manifestation of the Spirit for the common good. To one is given
through the Spirit the utterance of wisdom, and to another the utterance of
knowledge according to the same Spirit, to another faith by the same Spirit, to
another gifts of healing by the one Spirit, to another the working of miracles, to
another prophecy, to another the discernment of spirits, to another various kinds of
tongues, to another the interpretation of tongues. All these are activated by one and
the same Spirit, who allots to each one individually just as the Spirit chooses.

The Gospel   **John 2:1-11**

On the third day there was a wedding in Cana of Galilee, and the mother of Jesus was
there. Jesus and his disciples had also been invited to the wedding. When the wine
gave out, the mother of Jesus said to him, "They have no wine." And Jesus said to
her, "Woman, what concern is that to you and to me? My hour has not yet come."
His mother said to the servants, "Do whatever he tells you." Now standing there
were six stone water jars for the Jewish rites of purification, each holding twenty or
thirty gallons. Jesus said to them, "Fill the jars with water." And they filled them up
to the brim. He said to them, "Now draw some out, and take it to the chief steward."
So they took it. When the steward tasted the water that had become wine, and did
not know where it came from (though the servants who had drawn the water knew),
the steward called the bridegroom and said to him, "Everyone serves the good wine

first, and then the inferior wine after the guests have become drunk. But you have kept the good wine until now." Jesus did this, the first of his signs, in Cana of Galilee, and revealed his glory; and his disciples believed in him.

THE THIRD SUNDAY AFTER THE EPIPHANY

The Collect

Give us grace, O Lord, to answer readily the call of our Savior Jesus Christ and proclaim to all people the Good News of his salvation, that we and the whole world may perceive the glory of his marvelous works; who lives and reigns with you and the Holy Spirit, one God, for ever and ever. *Amen.*

Give us grace, O Lord, to answer readily the call of our Savior Jesus Christ and proclaim to all people the Good News of his salvation, that we and all the whole world may perceive the glory of his marvelous works; who liveth and reigneth with thee and the Holy Spirit, one God, for ever and ever. *Amen.*

Year A

The Lesson   Amos 3:1-8

Hear this word that the LORD has spoken against you, O people of Israel, against the whole family that I brought up out of the land of Egypt: You only have I known of all the families of the earth; therefore I will punish you for all your iniquities. Do two walk together unless they have made an appointment? Does a lion roar in the forest, when it has no prey? Does a young lion cry out from its den, if it has caught nothing? Does a bird fall into a snare on the earth, when there is no trap for it? Does a snare spring up from the ground, when it has taken nothing? Is a trumpet blown in a city, and the people are not afraid? Does disaster befall a city, unless the LORD has done it? Surely the Lord GOD does nothing, without revealing his secret to his servants the prophets. The lion has roared; who will not fear? The Lord GOD has spoken; who can but prophesy?

The Psalm 139:1-17 or 139:1-11   *Domine, probasti*

1   [LORD, you have searched me out and known me; *
        you know my sitting down and my rising up;
        you discern my thoughts from afar.

2   You trace my journeys and my resting-places *
        and are acquainted with all my ways.

3   Indeed, there is not a word on my lips, *
        but you, O LORD, know it altogether.

4   You press upon me behind and before *
        and lay your hand upon me.

5   Such knowledge is too wonderful for me; *
        it is so high that I cannot attain to it.

6   Where can I go then from your Spirit? *
        where can I flee from your presence?

7   If I climb up to heaven, you are there; *
        if I make the grave my bed, you are there also.

8   If I take the wings of the morning *
        and dwell in the uttermost parts of the sea,

9   Even there your hand will lead me *
        and your right hand hold me fast.

10   If I say, "Surely the darkness will cover me, *
        and the light around me turn to night,"

11   Darkness is not dark to you;
     the night is as bright as the day; *
        darkness and light to you are both alike.]

12   For you yourself created my inmost parts; *
        you knit me together in my mother's womb.

13   I will thank you because I am marvelously made; *
     your works are wonderful, and I know it well.

14   My body was not hidden from you, *
        while I was being made in secret
        and woven in the depths of the earth.

15   Your eyes beheld my limbs, yet unfinished in the womb;
     all of them were written in your book; *
        they were fashioned day by day,
        when as yet there was none of them.

16   How deep I find your thoughts, O God! *
        how great is the sum of them!

17   If I were to count them, they would be more in number than the sand; *
        to count them all, my life span would need to be like yours.

The Epistle   **1 Corinthians 1:10-17**

I appeal to you, brothers and sisters, by the name of our Lord Jesus Christ, that all of
you be in agreement and that there be no divisions among you, but that you be
united in the same mind and the same purpose. For it has been reported to me by
Chloe's people that there are quarrels among you, my brothers and sisters. What I
mean is that each of you says, "I belong to Paul," or "I belong to Apollos," or "I
belong to Cephas," or "I belong to Christ." Has Christ been divided? Was Paul
crucified for you? Or were you baptized in the name of Paul? I thank God that I
baptized none of you except Crispus and Gaius, so that no one can say that you were
baptized in my name. (I did baptize also the household of Stephanas; beyond that, I
do not know whether I baptized anyone else.) For Christ did not send me to baptize
but to proclaim the gospel, and not with eloquent wisdom, so that the cross of Christ
might not be emptied of its power.

The Gospel   **Matthew 4:12-23**

Now when Jesus heard that John had been arrested, he withdrew to Galilee. He left Nazareth and made his home in Capernaum by the sea, in the territory of Zebulun and Naphtali, so that what had been spoken through the prophet Isaiah might be fulfilled: "Land of Zebulun, land of Naphtali, on the road by the sea, across the Jordan, Galilee of the Gentiles — the people who sat in darkness have seen a great light, and for those who sat in the region and shadow of death light has dawned." From that time Jesus began to proclaim, "Repent, for the kingdom of heaven has come near." As he walked by the Sea of Galilee, he saw two brothers, Simon, who is called Peter, and Andrew his brother, casting a net into the sea — for they were fishermen. And he said to them, "Follow me, and I will make you fish for people." Immediately they left their nets and followed him. As he went from there, he saw two other brothers, James son of Zebedee and his brother John, in the boat with their father Zebedee, mending their nets, and he called them. Immediately they left the boat and their father, and followed him. Jesus went throughout Galilee, teaching in their synagogues and proclaiming the good news of the kingdom and curing every disease and every sickness among the people.

Year B

The Lesson   **Jeremiah 3:21-4:2**

A voice on the bare heights is heard, the plaintive weeping of Israel's children, because they have perverted their way, they have forgotten the LORD their God; Return, O faithless children, I will heal your faithlessness. "Here we come to you; for you are the LORD our God. Truly the hills are a delusion, the orgies on the mountains. Truly in the LORD our God is the salvation of Israel. "But from our youth the shameful thing has devoured all for which our ancestors had labored, their flocks and their herds, their sons and their daughters. Let us lie down in our shame, and let our dishonor cover us; for we have sinned against the LORD our God, we and our ancestors, from our youth even to this day; and we have not obeyed the voice of the LORD our God." If you return, O Israel, says the LORD, if you return to me, if you remove your abominations from my presence, and do not waver, and if you swear, "As the LORD lives!" in truth, in justice, and in uprightness, then nations shall be blessed by him, and by him they shall boast.

The Psalm 130   *De profundis*

1   Out of the depth have I called to you, O LORD;
      LORD, hear my voice; *
           let your ears consider well the voice of my supplication.

2   If you, LORD, were to note what is done amiss, *
           O Lord, who could stand?

3   For there is forgiveness with you; *
           therefore you shall be feared.

4   I wait for the LORD: my soul waits for him; *
           in his word is my hope.

5   My soul waits for the Lord,
     more than watchmen for the morning, *
        more than watchmen for the morning.

6   O Israel, wait for the Lord, *
        for with the Lord there is mercy;

7   With him there is plenteous redemption, *
        and he shall redeem Israel from all their sins.

The Epistle   **1 Corinthians 7:17-23**

Let each of you lead the life that the Lord has assigned, to which God called you.
This is my rule in all the churches. Was anyone at the time of his call already
circumcised? Let him not seek to remove the marks of circumcision. was anyone at
the time of his call uncircumcised? Let him not seek circumcision. Circumcision is
nothing, and uncircumcision is nothing; but obeying the commandment of God is
everything. Let each of you remain in the condition in which you were called. Were
you a slave when called? Do not be concerned about it. Even if you can gain your
freedom, make use of your present condition now more than ever. For whoever was
called in the Lord as a slave is a freed person belonging to the Lord, just as whoever
was free when called is a slave of Christ. You were bought with a price; do not
become slaves of human masters.

The Gospel   **Mark 1:14-20**

Now after John was arrested, Jesus came to Galilee, proclaiming the good news of
God, and saying, "The time is fulfilled, and the kingdom of God has come near;
repent, and believe in the good news." As Jesus passed along by the Sea of Galilee, he
saw Simon and his brother Andrew casting a net into the sea — for they were
fishermen. And Jesus said to them, "Follow me and I will make you fish for people."
And immediately they left their nets and followed him. As he went a little farther, he
saw James son of Zebedee and his brother John, who were in their boat mending the
nets. Immediately he called them; and they left their father Zebedee in the boat with
the hired men, and followed him.

Year C

The Lesson   **Nehemiah 8:2-10**

Accordingly, the priest Ezra brought the law before the assembly, both men and
women and all who could hear with understanding. This was on the first day of the
seventh month. He read from it facing the square before the Water Gate from early
morning until midday, in the presence of the men and the women and those who
could understand; and the ears of all the people were attentive to the book of the law.
The scribe Ezra stood on a wooden platform that had been made for the purpose;
and beside him stood Mattithiah, Shema, Anaiah, Uriah, Hilkiah, and Maaseiah on
his right hand; and Pedaiah, Mishael, Malchijah, Hashum, Hash-baddanah,
Zechariah, and Meshullam on his left hand. And Ezra opened the book in the sight
of all the people, for he was standing above all the people; and when he opened it, all
the people stood up. Then Ezra blessed the Lord, the great God, and all the people

answered, "Amen, Amen," lifting up their hands. They bowed their heads and worshiped the LORD with their faces to the ground. Also Jeshua, Bani, Sherebiah, Jamin, Akkub, Shabbethai, Hodiah, Maaseiah, Kelita, Azariah, Jozabad, Hanan, Pelaiah, the Levites, helped the people to understand the law, while the people remained in their places. So they read from the book, from the law of God, with interpretation. They gave the sense, so that the people understood the reading. And Nehemiah, who was the governor, and Ezra the priest and scribe, and the Levites who taught the people said to all the people, "This day is holy to the LORD your God; do not mourn or weep." For all the people wept when they heard the words of the law. Then he said to them, "Go your way, eat the fat and drink sweet wine and send portions of them to those for whom nothing is prepared, for this day is holy to our LORD; and do not be grieved, for the joy of the LORD is your strength."

The Psalm 113   *Laudate, pueri*

1   Hallelujah!
Give praise, you servants of the LORD; *
    praise the Name of the LORD.

2   Let the Name of the LORD be blessed, *
    from this time forth for evermore.

3   From the rising of the sun to its going down *
    let the Name of the LORD be praised.

4   The LORD is high above all nations, *
    and his glory above the heavens.

5   Who is like the LORD our God, who sits enthroned on high, *
    but stoops to behold the heavens and the earth?

6   He takes up the weak out of the dust *
    and lifts up the poor from the ashes.

7   He sets them with the princes, *
    with the princes of his people.

8   He makes the woman of a childless house *
    to be a joyful mother of children.

The Epistle   **1 Corinthians 12:12-27**

Just as the body is one and has many members, and all the members of the body, though many, are one body, so it is with Christ. For in the one Spirit we were all baptized into one body — Jews or Greeks, slaves or free — and we were all made to drink of one Spirit. Indeed, the body does not consist of one member but of many. If the foot would say, "Because I am not a hand, I do not belong to the body," that would not make it any less a part of the body. And if the ear would say, "Because I am not an eye, I do not belong to the body," that would not make it any less a part of the body. If the whole body were an eye, where would the hearing be? If the whole body were hearing, where would the sense of smell be? But as it is, God arranged the members in the body, each one of them, as he chose. If all were a single member, where would the body be? As it is, there are many members, yet one body. The eye cannot say to the hand, "I have no need of you," nor again the head to the feet, "I have no need of you." On the contrary, the members of the body that seem to be weaker are indispensable, and those members of the body that we think less honorable we clothe with greater honor, and our less respectable members are treated with greater respect; whereas our more respectable members do not need this. But God has so arranged the body, giving the greater honor to the inferior member, that there may be no dissension within the body, but the members may have the same care for one another. If one member suffers, all suffer together with it; if one member is honored, all rejoice together with it. Now you are the body of Christ and individually members of it.

The Gospel Luke 4:14-21

Jesus, filled with the power of the Spirit, returned to Galilee, and a report about him spread through all the surrounding country. He began to teach in their synagogues and was praised by everyone. When he came to Nazareth, where he had been brought up, he went to the synagogue on the sabbath day, as was his custom. He stood up to read, and the scroll of the prophet Isaiah was given to him. He unrolled the scroll and found the place where it was written: "The Spirit of the Lord is upon me, because he has anointed me to bring good news to the poor. He has sent me to proclaim release to the captives and recovery of sight to the blind, to let the oppressed go free, to proclaim the year of the Lord's favor." And he rolled up the scroll, gave it back to the attendant, and sat down. The eyes of all in the synagogue were fixed on him. Then he began to say to them, "Today this scripture has been fulfilled in your hearing."

THE FOURTH SUNDAY AFTER THE EPIPHANY

The Collect

Almighty and everlasting God, you govern all things both in heaven and on earth: Mercifully hear the supplications of your people, and in our time grant us your peace; through Jesus Christ our Lord, who lives and reigns with you and the Holy Spirit, one God, for ever and ever. *Amen.*

Almighty and everlasting God, who dost govern all things in heaven and earth: Mercifully hear the supplications of thy people, and in our time grant us thy peace; through Jesus Christ our Lord, who liveth and reigneth with thee and the Holy Spirit, one God, for ever and ever. *Amen.*

Year A

The Lesson Micah 6:1-8

Hear what the LORD says: Rise, plead your case before the mountains, and let the hills hear your voice. Hear, you mountains, the controversy of the LORD, and you enduring foundations of the earth; for the LORD has a controversy with his people, and he will contend with Israel. "O my people, what have I done to you? In what have I wearied you? Answer me! For I brought you up from the land of Egypt, and redeemed you from the house of slavery; and I sent before you Moses, Aaron, and Miriam. O my people, remember now what King Balak of Moab devised, what Balaam son of Beor answered him, and what happened from Shittim to Gilgal, that you may know the saving acts of the LORD." "With what shall I come before the

LORD, and bow myself before God on high? Shall I come before him with burnt offerings, with calves a year old? Will the LORD be pleased with thousands of rams, with ten thousands of rivers of oil? Shall I give my firstborn for my transgression, the fruit of my body for the sin of my soul?" He has told you, O mortal, what is good; and what does the LORD require of you but to do justice, and to love kindness, and to walk humbly with your God?

The Psalm 37:1-18 or 37:1-6   *Noli aemulari*

1   [Do not fret yourself because of evildoers; *
        do not be jealous of those who do wrong.

2   For they shall soon wither like the grass, *
        and like the green grass fade away.

3   Put your trust in the LORD and do good; *
        dwell in the land and feed on its riches.

4   Take delight in the LORD, *
        and he shall give you your heart's desire.

5   Commit your way to the LORD and put your trust inhim, *
        and he will bring it to pass.

6   He will make your righteousness as clear as the light *
        and your just dealing as the noonday.]

7   Be still before the LORD *
        and wait patiently for him.

8   Do not fret yourself over the one who prospers, *
        the one who succeeds in evil schemes.

9   Refrain from anger, leave rage alone; *
        do not fret yourself; it leads only to evil.

10   For evildoers shall be cut off, *
        but those who wait upon the LORD shall possess the land.

11   In a little while the wicked shall be no more; *
        you shall search out their place, but they will not be there.

12   But the lowly shall possess the land; *
        they will delight in abundance of peace.

13   The wicked plot against the righteous *
        and gnash at them with their teeth.

14   The Lord laughs at the wicked, *
        because he sees that their day will come.

15   The wicked draw their sword and bend their bow
    to strike down the poor and needy, *
        to slaughter those who are upright in their ways.

16   Their sword shall go through their own heart, *
       and their bow shall be broken.

17   The little that the righteous has *
       is better than great riches of the wicked.

18   For the power of the wicked shall be broken, *
       but the LORD upholds the righteous.

The Epistle   **1 Corinthians 1:(18-25) 26-31**

[The message about the cross is foolishness to those who are perishing, but to us who are being saved it is the power of God. For it is written, "I will destroy the wisdom of the wise, and the discernment of the discerning I will thwart." Where is the one who is wise? Where is the scribe? Where is the debater of this age? Has not God made foolish the wisdom of the world? For since, in the wisdom of God, the world did not know God through wisdom, God decided, through the foolishness of our proclamation, to save those who believe. For Jews demand signs and Greeks desire wisdom, but we proclaim Christ crucified, a stumbling block to Jews and foolishness to Gentiles, but to those who are the called, both Jews and Greeks, Christ the power of God and the wisdom of God. For God's foolishness is wiser than human wisdom, and God's weakness is stronger than human strength.] Consider your own call, brothers and sisters: not many of you were wise by human standards, not many were powerful, not many were of noble birth. But God chose what is foolish in the world to shame the wise; God chose what is weak in the world to shame the strong; God chose what is low and despised in the world, things that are not, to reduce to nothing things that are, so that no one might boast in the presence of God. He is the source of your life in Christ Jesus, who became for us wisdom from God, and righteousness and sanctification and redemption, in order that, as it is written, "Let the one who boasts, boast in the Lord."

The Gospel   **Matthew 5:1-12**

When Jesus saw the crowds, he went up the mountain; and after he sat down, his disciples came to him. Then he began to speak, and taught them, saying: "Blessed are the poor in spirit, for theirs is the kingdom of heaven. Blessed are those who mourn, for they will be comforted. Blessed are the meek, for they will inherit the earth. Blessed are those who hunger and thirst for righteousness, for they will be filled. Blessed are the merciful, for they will receive mercy. Blessed are the pure in heart, for they will see God. Blessed are the peacemakers, for they will be called children of God. Blessed are those who are persecuted for righteousness' sake, for theirs is the kingdom of heaven. Blessed are you when people revile you and persecute you and utter all kinds of evil against you falsely on my account. Rejoice and be glad, for your reward is great in heaven, for in the same way they persecuted the prophets who were before you."

The Lesson   **Deuteronomy 18:15-20**

The LORD your God will raise up for you a prophet like me from among your own people; you shall heed such a prophet. This is what you requested of the LORD your God at Horeb on the day of the assembly when you said: "If I hear the voice of the LORD my God any more, or ever again see this great fire, I will die." Then the LORD replied to me: "They are right in what they have said. I will raise up for them a prophet like you from among their own people; I will put my words in the mouth of the prophet, who shall speak to them everything that I command. Anyone who does not heed the words that the prophet shall speak in my name, I myself will hold accountable. But any prophet who speaks in the name of other gods, or who presumes to speak in my name a word that I have not commanded to prophet to speak — that prophet shall die."

The Psalm 111   *Confitebor tibi*

1   Hallelujah!
     I will give thanks to the LORD with my whole heart, *
       in the assembly of the upright, in the congregation.

2   Great are the deeds of the LORD! *
       they are studied by all who delight in them.

3   His work is full of majesty and splendor, *
       and his righteousness endures for ever.

4   He makes his marvelous works to be remembered; *
       the LORD is gracious and full of compassion.

5   He gives food to those who fear him; *
       he is ever mindful of his covenant.

6   He has shown his people the power of his works *
       in giving them the lands of the nations.

7   The works of his hands are faithfulness and justice; *
       all his commandments are sure.

8   They stand fast for ever and ever, *
       because they are done in truth and equity.

9   He sent redemption to his people;
     he commanded his covenant for ever; *
       holy and awesome is his Name.

10   The fear of the LORD is the beginning of wisdom; *
       those who act accordingly have a good understanding;
       his praise endures for ever.

The Epistle   **1 Corinthians 8:1b-13**

Knowledge puffs up, but love builds up. Anyone who claims to know something does not yet have the necessary knowledge; but anyone who loves God is known by him. Hence, as to the eating of food offered to idols, we know that "no idol in the world really exists," and that "there is no God but one." Indeed, even though there may be so-called gods in heaven or on earth — as in fact there are many gods and many lords — yet for us there is one God, the Father, from whom are all things and for whom we exist, and one Lord, Jesus Christ, through whom are all things and through whom we exist. It is not everyone, however, who has this knowledge. Since some have become so accustomed to idols until now, they still think of the food they eat as food offered to an idol; and their conscience, being weak, is defiled. "Food will not bring us close to God." We are no worse off if we do not eat, and no better off if we do. But take care that this liberty of yours does not somehow become a stumbling block to the weak. For if others see you, who possess knowledge, eating in the temple of an idol, might they not, since their conscience is weak, be encouraged to the point of eating food sacrificed to idols? So by your knowledge those weak believers for whom Christ died are destroyed. But when you thus sin against members of your family, and wound their conscience when it is weak, you sin against Christ. Therefore, if food is a cause of their falling, I will never eat meat, so that I may not cause one of them to fall.

The Gospel   **Mark 1:21-28**
Jesus and his disciples went to Capernaum; and when the sabbath came, he entered the synagogue and taught. They were astounded at his teaching, for he taught them as one having authority, and not as the scribes. Just then there was in their synagogue a man with an unclean spirit, and he cried out, "What have you to do with us, Jesus of Nazareth? Have you come to destroy us? I know who you are, the Holy One of God." But Jesus rebuked him, saying, "Be silent, and come out of him!" And the unclean spirit, convulsing him and crying with a loud voice, came out of him. They were all amazed, and they kept on asking one another, "What is this? A new teaching — with authority! He commands even the unclean spirits, and they obey him." At once his fame began to spread throughout thesurrounding region of Galilee.

Year C

The Lesson   **Jeremiah 1:4-10**
Now the word of the LORD came to me saying, "Before I formed you in the womb I knew you, and before you were born I consecrated you; I appointed you a prophet to the nations." Then I said, "Ah, Lord GOD! Truly I do not know how to speak, for I am only a boy." But the LORD said to me, "Do not say, 'I am only a boy'; for you shall go to all to whom I send you, and you shall speak whatever I command you. Do not be afraid of them, for I am with you to deliver you, says the LORD." Then the LORD put out his hand and touched my mouth; and the LORD said to me, "Now I have put my words in your mouth. See, today I appoint you over nations and over kingdoms, to pluck up and to pull down, to destroy and to overthrow, to build and to plant."

The Psalm 71:1-17 or 71:1-6, 15-17   *In te, Domine, speravi*

1   [In you, O LORD, have I taken refuge; *
     let me never be ashamed.

2   In your righteousness, deliver me and set me free; *
     incline your ear to me and save me.

3   Be my strong rock, a castle to keep me safe; *
     you are my crag and my stronghold.

4   Deliver me, my God, from the hand of the wicked, *
     from the clutches of the evildoer and the oppressor.

5   For you are my hope, O Lord GOD, *
     my confidence since I was young.

6   I have been sustained by you ever since I was born;
     from my mother's womb you have been my strength; *
     my praise shall be always of you.]

7   I have become a portent to many; *
     but you are my refuge and my strength.

8   Let my mouth be full of your praise *
     and your glory all the day long.

9   Do not cast me off in my old age; *
     forsake me not when my strength fails.

10   For my enemies are talking against me, *
     and those who lie in wait for my life take counsel together.

11   They say, "God has forsaken him;
     go after him and seize him; *
     because there is none who will save."

12   O God, be not far from me; *
     come quickly to help me, O my God.

13   Let those who set themselves against me be put to shame and be disgraced; *
     let those who seek to do me evil be covered with scorn and reproach.

14   But I shall always wait in patience, *
     and shall praise you more and more.

15   [My mouth shall recount your mighty acts and saving deeds all day long; *
     though I cannot know the number of them.

16   I will begin with the mighty works of the Lord GOD; *
     I will recall your righteousness, yours alone.

17   O God, you have taught me since I was young, *
     and to this day I tell of your wonderful works.]

The Epistle   **1 Corinthians 14:12b-20**

Since you are eager for spiritual gifts, strive to excel in them for building up the church. Therefore, one who speaks in a tongue should pray for the power to interpret. For if I pray in a tongue, my spirit prays but my mind is unproductive. What should I do then? I will pray with the spirit, but I will pray with the mind also; I will sing praise with the spirit, but I will sing praise with the mind also. Otherwise, if you say a blessing with the spirit, how can anyone in the position of an outsider say the "Amen" to your thanksgiving, since the outsider does not know what you are saying? For you may give thanks well enough, but the other person is not built up. I thank God that I speak in tongues more than all of you; nevertheless, in church I would rather speak five words with my mind, in order to instruct others also, than ten thousand words in a tongue. Brothers and sisters, do not be children in your thinking; rather be infants in evil, but in thinking be adults.

The Gospel   **Luke 4:21-32**

Jesus began to say to those in the synagogue, "Today this scripture has been fulfilled in your hearing." All spoke well of him and were amazed at the gracious words that came from his mouth. They said, "Is not this Joseph's son?" He said to them, "Doubtless you will quote to me this proverb, 'Doctor, cure yourself!' And you will say, 'Do here also in your hometown the things that we have heard you did at Capernaum.'" And he said, "Truly I tell you, no prophet is accepted in the prophet's hometown. But the truth is, there were many widows in Israel in the time of Elijah, when the heaven was shut up three years and six months, and there was a severe famine over all the land; yet Elijah was sent to none of them except to a widow at Zarephath in Sidon. There were also many lepers in Israel in the time of the prophet Elisha, and none of them was cleansed except Naaman the Syrian." When they heard this, all in the synagogue were filled with rage. They got up, drove him out of the town, and led him to the brow of the hill on which their town was built, so that they might hurl him off the cliff. But he passed through the midst of them and went on his way. He went down to Capernaum, a city in Galilee, and was teaching them on the sabbath. They were astounded at his teaching, because he spoke with authority.

THE FIFTH SUNDAY AFTER THE EPIPHANY

The Collect
Set us free, O God, from the bondage of our sins, and give us the liberty of that abundant life which you have made known to us in your Son our Savior Jesus Christ; who lives and reigns with you, in the unity of the Holy Spirit, one God, now and for ever. *Amen.*

Set us free, O God, from the bondage of our sins and give us, we beseech thee, the liberty of that abundant life which thou hast manifested to us in thy Son our Savior Jesus Christ; who liveth and reigneth with thee, in the unity of the Holy Spirit, one God, now and for ever. *Amen.*

Year A

The Lesson   **Habakkuk 3:2-6, 17-19**

O LORD, I have heard of your renown, and I stand in awe, O LORD, of your work. In our own time revive it; in our own time make it known; in wrath may you remember mercy. God came from Teman, the Holy One from Mount Paran. His glory covered the heavens, and the earth was full of his praise. The brightness was like the sun; rays came forth from his hand, where his power lay hidden. Before him went pestilence, and plague followed close behind. He stopped and shook the earth; he looked and made the nations tremble. The eternal mountains were shattered; along his ancient pathways the everlasting hills sank low. Though the fig tree does not blossom, and no fruit is on the vines; though the produce of the olive fails and the fields yield no food; though the flock is cut off from the fold and there is no herd in the stalls, yet I will rejoice in the LORD; I will exult in the God of my salvation. GOD, the Lord, is my strength; he makes my feet like the feet of a deer, and makes me tread upon the heights.

The Psalm 27 or 27:1-7   *Dominus illuminatio*

1   [The LORD is my light and my salvation;
        whom then shall I fear? *
            the LORD is the strength of my life;
            of whom then shall I be afraid?

2   When evildoers came upon me to eat up my flesh, *
            it was they, my foes and my adversaries, who stumbled and fell.

3   Though an army should encamp against me, *
            yet my heart shall not be afraid;

4   And though war should rise up against me, *
            yet will I put my trust in him.

5   One thing Have I asked of the LORD;
        one thing I seek; *
            that I may dwell in the house of the LORD all the days of my life;

6   To behold the fair beauty of the LORD *
            and to seek him in his temple.

7   For in the day of trouble he shall keep me safe in his shelter; *
            he shall hide me in the secrecy of his dwelling
            and set me high upon a rock.]

8   Even now he lifts up my head *
            above my enemies round about me.

9   Therefore I will offer in his dwelling an oblation
        with sounds of great gladness; *
            I will sing and make music to the LORD.

10   Hearken to my voice, O LORD, when I call; *
            have mercy on me and answer me.

11   You speak in my heart and say, "Seek my face." *
            Your face, LORD, will I seek.

12   Hide not your face from me, *
          Nor turn away your servant in displeasure.

13   You have been my helper;
      cast me not away; *
          do not forsake me, O God of my salvation.

14   Though my father and my mother forsake me, *
          the LORD will sustain me.

15   Show me your way, O LORD; *
          lead me on a level path, because of my enemies.

16   Deliver me not into the hand of my adversaries, *
          for false witnesses have risen up against me,
          and also those who speak malice.

17   What if I had not believed
      that I should see the goodness of the LORD *
          in the land of the living!

18   O tarry and await the LORD's pleasure;
      be strong, and he shall comfort your heart; *
          wait patiently for the LORD.

The Epistle   **1 Corinthians 2:1-11**

When I came to you, brothers and sisters, I did not come proclaiming the mystery of
God to you in lofty words or wisdom. For I decided to know nothing among you
except Jesus Christ, and him crucified. And I came to you in weakness and in fear
and in much trembling. My speech and my proclamation were not with plausible
words of wisdom, but with a demonstration of the Spirit and of power, so that your
faith might rest not on human wisdom but on the power of God. Yet among the
mature we do speak wisdom, though it is not a wisdom of this age or of the rulers of
this age, who are doomed to perish. But we speak God's wisdom, secret and hidden,
which God decreed before the ages for our glory. None of the rulers of this age
understood this; for if they had, they would not have crucified the Lord of glory. But,
as it is written, "What no eye has seen, nor ear heard, nor the human heart
conceived, what God has prepared for those who love him" — these things God has
revealed to us through the Spirit; for the Spirit searches everything, even the depths
of God. For what human being knows what is truly human except the human spirit
that is within? So also no one comprehends what is truly God's except the Spirit of
God.

The Gospel   **Matthew 5:13-20**

Jesus said, "You are the salt of the earth; but if salt has lost its taste, how can its
saltiness be restored? It is no longer good for anything, but is thrown out and
trampled under foot. You are the light of the world. A city built on a hill cannot be
hid. No one after lighting a lamp puts it under the bushel basket, but on the
lampstand, and it gives light to all in the house. In the same way, let your light shine

before others, so that they may see your good works and give glory to your Father in heaven. Do not think that I have come to abolish the law or the prophets; I have come not to abolish but to fulfill. For truly I tell you, until heaven and earth pass away, not one letter, not one stroke of a letter, will pass from the law until all is accomplished. Therefore, whoever breaks one of the least of these commandments, and teaches others to do the same, will be called least in the kingdom of heaven; but whoever does them and teaches them will be called great in the kingdom of heaven. For I tell you, unless your righteousness exceeds that of the scribes and Pharisees, you will never enter the kingdom of heaven.

Year B

The Lesson   2 Kings 4:(8-17) 18-21 (22-31) 32-37

[One day Elisha was passing through Shunem, where a wealthy woman lived, who urged him to have a meal. So whenever he passed that way, he would stop there for a meal. She said to her husband, "Look, I am sure that this man who regularly passes our way is a holy man of God. Let us make a small roof chamber with walls, and put there for him a bed, a table, a chair, and a lamp, so that he can stay there whenever he comes to us." One day when he came there, he went up to the chamber and lay down there. He said to his servant Gehazi, "Call the Shunammite woman." When he had called her, she stood before him. He said to him, "Say to her, Since you have taken all this trouble for us, what may be done for you? Would you have a word spoken on your behalf to the king or to the commander of the army?" She answered, "I live among my own people." He said, "What then may be done for her?" Gehazi answered, "Well, she has no son, and her husband is old." He said, "Call her." When he had called her, she stood at the door. He said, "At this season, in due time, you shall embrace a son." She replied, "No, my lord, O man of God; do not deceive your servant." The woman conceived and bore a son at that season, in due time, as Elisha had declare to her.] When the child was older, he went out one day to his father among the reapers. He complained to his father, "Oh, my head, my head!" The father said to his servant, "Carry him to his mother." He carried him and brought him to his mother; the child sat on her lap until noon, and he died. She went up and laid him on the bed of the man of God, closed the door oh him and left. [Then she called to her husband, and said, "Send me one of the servant and one of the donkeys, so that I may quickly go to the man of God and come back again." He said, "Why go to him today? It is neither new moon nor sabbath." She said, "It will be all right." Then she saddled the donkey and said to her servant, "Urge the animal on; do not hold back for me unless I tell you." So she set out, and came to the man of God at Mount Carmel. When the man of God saw her coming, he said to Gehazi his servant, "Look, there is the Shunammite woman; run at once to meet her, and say to her, Are you all right? Is your husband all right? Is the child all right?" She answered, "It is all right." When she came to the man of God at the mountain, she caught hold of his feet. Gehazi approached to push her away. But the man of God said, "Let her alone, for she is in bitter distress; the LORD has hidden it from me and has not told me." Then she said, "Did I ask my lord for a son? Did I not say, Do not mislead me?" He said to Gehazi, "Gird up your loins, and take my staff in your hand, and go. If you meet anyone, give no greeting, and if anyone greets you, do not answer; and lay my staff on the face of the child." Then the mother of the child said, "As the LORD lives, and as you yourself live, I will not leave without you." So he rose up and followed her. Gehazi went on ahead and laid the staff on the face of the child, but there was no sound or sign of life. He came back to meet him and told him, "The child has not awakened."] When Elisha came into the house, he saw the child lying dead on his bed. So he went in and closed the door on the two of them, and prayed to the LORD. Then he got up on the bed and lay upon the child, putting his mouth upon his mouth, his eyes upon his eyes, and his hands upon his hands; and while he lay bent over him, the flesh of the child became warm. He got down, walked once to and fro in the room, then got up again and bent over him; the child sneezed seven times, and the child opened his eyes. Elisha summoned Gehazi and said, "Call the Shunammite woman." So he called her. When she came to him, he said, "Take your son." She came and fell at his feet, bowing to the ground; then she took her son and left.

The Psalm 142   *Voce mea ad Dominum*

1   I cry to the LORD with my voice; *
           to the LORD I make loud supplication.

2   I pour out my complaint before him *
           and tell him all my trouble.

3   When my spirit languishes within me, you know my path; *
           in the way wherein I walk they have hidden a trap for me.

4   I look to my right hand and find no one who knows me; *
           I have no place to flee to, and no one cares for me.

5   I cry out to you, O LORD; *
           I say, "You are my refuge,
           my portion in the land of the living."

6   Listen to my cry for help, for I have been brought very low; *
           save me from those who pursue me,
           for they are too strong for me.

7   Bring me out of prison, that I may give thanks to your Name; *
           When you have dealt bountifully with me,
           the righteous will gather around me.

The Epistle   **1 Corinthians 9:16-23**

If I proclaim the gospel, this gives me no ground for boasting, for an obligation is laid on me, and woe to me if I do not proclaim the gospel! For if I do this of my own will, I have a reward; but if not of my own will, I am entrusted with a commission. What then is my reward? Just this: that in my proclamation I may make the gospel free of charge, so as not to make full use of my rights in the gospel. For though I am free with respect to all, I have made myself a slave to all, so that I might win more of them. To the Jews I became as a Jew, in order to win Jews. To those under the law I became as one under the law (though I myself am not under the law) so that I might win those under the law. To those outside the law I became as one outside the law (though I am not free from God's law but am under Christ's law) so that I might win those outside the law. To the weak I became weak, so that I might win the weak. I have become all things to all people, that I might by all means save some. I do it all for the sake of the gospel, so that I may share in its blessings.

The Gospel

Mark 1:29-39

Jesus left the synagogue, at Capernaum and entered the house of Simon and Andrew, with James and John. Now Simon's mother-in-law was in bed with a fever, and they told him about her at once. He came and took her by the hand and lifted her up. Then the fever left her, and she began to serve them. That evening, at sundown, they brought to him all who were sick or possessed with demons. And the whole city was gathered around the door. And he cured many who were sick with various diseases, and cast out many demons; and he would not permit the demons to speak, because they knew him. In the morning, while it was still very dark, he got up and went out to a deserted place, and there he prayed. And Simon and his companions hunted for him. When they found him, they said to him, "Everyone is searching for you." He answered, "Let us go on to the neighboring towns, so that I may proclaim the message there also; for that is what I came out to do." And he went throughout Galilee, proclaiming the message in their synagogues and casting out demons.

Year C

The Lesson

Judges 6:11-24a

Now the angel of the LORD came and sat under the oak at Ophrah, which belonged to Joash the Abiezrite, as his son Gideon was beating out wheat in the wine press, to hide it from the Midianites. The angel of the LORD appeared to him and said to him, "The LORD is with you, you mighty warrior." Gideon answered him, "But sir, if the LORD is with us, why then has all this happened to us? And where are all his wonderful deeds that our ancestors recounted to us, saying, 'Did not the LORD bring us up from Egypt?' But now the LORD has cast us off, and given us into the hand of Midian." Then the LORD turned to him and said, "Go in this might of yours and deliver Israel from the hand of Midian; I hereby commission you." He responded, "But sir, how can I deliver Israel? My clan is the weakest in Manasseh, and I am the least in my family." The LORD said to him, "But I will be with you, and you shall strike down the Midianites, every one of them." Then he said to him, "If now I have found favor with you, then show me a sign that it is you who speak with me. Do not depart from here until I come to you, and bring out my present, and set it before you." And he said, "I will stay until you return." So Gideon went into his house and prepared a kid, and unleavened cakes from an ephah of flour; the meat he put in a basket, and the broth he put in a pot, and brought them to him under the oak and presented them. The angel of God said to him, "Take the meat and the unleavened cakes, and put them on this rock, and pour out the broth." And he did so. Then the angel of the LORD reached out the tip of the staff that was in his hand, and touched the meat and the unleavened cakes; and fire sprang up from the rock and consumed the meat and the unleavened cakes; and the angel of the LORD vanished from his sight. Then Gideon perceived that it was the angel of the LORD; and Gideon said, "Help me, Lord GOD! For I have seen the angel of the LORD face to face." But the LORD said to him, "Peace be to you; do not fear, you shall not die." Then Gideon built an altar there to the LORD, and called it, The LORD is peace.

The Psalms 85 or 85:7-13   *Benedixisti, Domine*

1   You have been gracious to your land, O LORD, *
        you have restored the good fortune of Jacob.

2   You have forgiven the iniquity of your people *
        and blotted out all their sins.

3   You have withdrawn all your fury *
        and turned yourself from your wrathful indignation.

4   Restore us then, O God our Savior; *
        let your anger depart from us.

5   Will you be displeased with us for ever? *
        will you prolong your anger from age to age?

6   Will you not give us life again, *
        that your people may rejoice in you?

7   [Show us your mercy, O LORD, *
        and grant us your salvation.

8   I will listen to what the LORD God is saying, *
        for he is speaking peace to his faithful people
        and to those who turn their hearts to him.

9   Truly, his salvation is very near to those who fear him, *
        that his glory may dwell in our land.

10   Mercy and truth have met together; *
        righteousness and peace have kissed each other.

11   Truth shall spring up from the earth, *
        and righteousness shall look down from heaven.

12   The LORD will indeed grant prosperity, *
        and our land will yield its increase.

13   Righteousness shall go before him, *
        and peace shall be a pathway for his feet.]

The Epistle   **1 Corinthians 15:1-11**

Now I would remind you, brothers and sisters, of the good news that I proclaimed to you, which you in turn received, in which also you stand, through which also you are being saved, if you hold firmly to the message that I proclaimed to you — unless you have come to believe in vain. For I handed on to you as of first importance what I in turn had received: that Christ died for our sins in accordance with the scriptures, and that he was buried, and that he was raised on the third day in accordance with the scriptures, and that he appeared to Cephas, then to the twelve. Then he appeared to more than five hundred brothers and sisters at one time, most of whom are still alive, though some have died. Then he appeared to James, then to all the apostles. Last of all, as to one untimely born, he appeared also to me. For I am the least of the apostles, unfit to be called an apostle, because I persecuted the church of God. But by the grace of God I am what I am, and his grace toward me has not been in vain. On the contrary, I worked harder than any of them — though it was not I, but the grace of God that is with me. Whether then it was I or they, so we proclaim and so you have come to believe.

The Gospel   Luke 5:1-11

Once while Jesus was standing beside the lake of Gennesaret, and the crowd was pressing in on him to hear the word of God, he saw two boats there at the shore of the lake; the fishermen had gone out of them and were washing their nets. He got into one of the boats, the one belonging to Simon, and asked him to put out a little way from the shore. Then he sat down and taught the crowds from the boat. When he had finished speaking, he said to Simon, "Put out into the deep water and let down your nets for a catch." Simon answered, "Master, we have worked all night long but have caught nothing. Yet if you say so, I will let down the nets." When they had done this, they caught so many fish that their nets were beginning to break. So they signaled their partners in the other boat to come and help them. And they came and filled both boats, so that they began to sink. But when Simon Peter saw it, he fell down at Jesus' knees, saying, "Go away from me, Lord, for I am a sinful man!" For he and all who were with him were amazed at the catch of fish that they had taken; and so also were James and John, sons of Zebedee, who were partners with Simon. Then Jesus said to Simon, "Do not be afraid; from now on you will be catching people." When they had brought their boats to shore, they left everything and followed him.

THE SIXTH SUNDAY AFTER THE EPIPHANY

The Collect

O God, the strength of all who put their trust in you: Mercifully accept our prayers; and because in our weakness we can do nothing good without you, give us the help of your grace, that in keeping your commandments we may please you both in will and deed; through Jesus Christ our Lord, who lives and reigns with you and the Holy Spirit, one God, for ever and ever. *Amen.*

O God, the strength of all those who put their trust in thee: Mercifully accept our prayers; and because, through the weakness of our mortal nature, we can do not good thing without thee, grant us the help of thy grace, that in keeping thy commandments we may please thee both in will and deed; through Jesus Christ our Lord, who liveth and reigneth with thee and the Holy Spirit, one God, for ever and ever. *Amen.*

Year A

The Lesson   Ecclesiasticus (Sirach) 15:11-20

Do not say, "It was the Lord's doing that I fell away"; for he does not do what he hates. Do not say, "It was he who led me astray"; for he has no need of the sinful. The Lord hates all abominations; such things are not loved by those who fear him. It was he who created human kind in the beginning, and he left them in the power of their own free choice. If you choose, you can keep the commandments, and to act faithfully is a matter of your own choice. He has placed before you fire and water; stretch out your hand for whichever you choose. Before each person are life and death, and whichever one chooses will be given. For great is the wisdom of the Lord;

he is mighty in power and sees everything; his eyes are on those who fear him, and he knows every human action. He has not commanded anyone to be wicked, and he has not given anyone permission to sin.

The Psalm 119:1-16 or 119:9-16   *Beati immaculati*

1   Happy are they whose way is blameless, *
    who walk in the law of the LORD!

2   Happy are they who observe his decrees *
    and seek him with all their hearts!

3   Who never do any wrong, *
    but always walk in his ways.

4   You laid down your commandments, *
    that we should fully keep them.

5   Oh, that my ways were made so direct *
    that I might keep your statutes!

6   Then I should not be put to shame, *
    when I regard all your commandments.

7   I will thank you with an unfeigned heart, *
    when I have learned your righteous judgments.

8   I will keep your statutes; *
    do not utterly forsake me.

9   [How shall a young man cleanse his way? *
    By keeping to you words.

10   With my whole heart I seek you; *
    let me not stray from your commandments.

11   I treasure your promise in my heart, *
    that I may not sin against you.

12   Blessed are you, O LORD; *
    instruct me in your statutes.

13   With my lips will I recite *
    all the judgments of your mouth.

14   I have taken greater delight in the way of your decrees *
    than in all manner of riches.

15   I will meditate on your commandments *
    and give attention to your ways.

16   My delight is in your statutes; *
    I will not forget your word.]

The Epistle
1 Corinthians 3:1-9

Brothers and sisters, I could not speak to you as spiritual people, but rather as people of the flesh, as infants in Christ. I fed you with milk, not solid food, for you were not ready for solid food. Even now you are still not ready, for you are still of the flesh. For as long as there is jealousy and quarreling among you, are you not of the flesh, and behaving according to human inclinations? For when one says, "I belong to Paul," and another "I belong to Apollos," are you not merely human? What then is Apollos? What is Paul? Servants through whom you came to believe, as the Lord assigned to each. I planted, Apollos watered, but God gave the growth. So neither the one who plants nor the one who waters is anything, but only God who gives the growth. The one who plants and the one who waters have a common purpose, and each will receive wages according to the labor of each. For we are God's servants, working together; you are God's field, God's building.

The Gospel
Matthew 5:21-24, 27-30, 33-37

Jesus said, "You have heard that it was said to those of ancient times, 'You shall not murder'; and 'whoever murders shall be liable to judgment.' But I say to you that if you are angry with a brother or sister, you will be liable to judgment; and if you insult a brother or sister, you will be liable to the council; and if you say, 'You fool,' you will be liable to the hell of fire. So when you are offering your gift at the altar, if you remember that your brother or sister has something against you, leave your gift there before the altar and go; first be reconciled to your brother or sister, and then come and offer your gift. You have heard that it was said, 'You shall not commit adultery.' But I say to you that everyone who looks at a woman with lust has already committed adultery with her in his heart. If your right eye causes you to sin, tear it out and throw it away; it is better for you to lose one of your members than for your whole body to be thrown into hell. And if your right hand causes you to sin, cut it off and throw it away; it is better for you to lose one of your members than for your whole body to go into hell. Again, you have heard that it was said to those of ancient times, 'You shall not swear falsely, but carry out the vows you have made to the Lord.' But I say to you, Do not swear at all, either by heaven, for it is the throne of God, or by the earth, for it is his footstool, or by Jerusalem, for it is the city of the great King. And do not swear by your head, for you cannot make one hair white or black. Let your word be 'Yes, Yes' or 'No, No'; anything more than this comes from the evil one.

Year B

The Lesson
2 Kings 5:1-15ab

Naaman, commander of the army of the king of Aram, was a great man and in high favor with his master, because by him the Lord had given victory to Aram. The man, though a mighty warrior, suffered from leprosy. Now the Arameans on one of their raids had taken a young girl captive from the land of Israel, and she served Naaman's wife. She said to her mistress, "If only my lord were with the prophet who is in Samaria! He would cure him of his leprosy." So Naaman went in and told his lord just what the girl from the land of Israel had said. And the king of Aram said, "Go then, and I will send along a letter to the king of Israel." He went, taking with him ten talents of silver, six thousand shekels of gold, and ten sets of garments. He brought the letter to the king of Israel, which read, "When this letter reaches you, know that I have sent to you my servant Naaman, that you may cure him of his leprosy." When the king of Israel read the letter, he tore his clothes and said, "Am I God, to give death or life, that this man sends word to me to cure a man of his leprosy? Just look and see how he is trying to pick a quarrel with me." But when Elisha the man of God heard that the king of Israel had torn his clothes, he sent a message to the king, "Why have you torn your clothes? Let him come to me, that he may learn that there is a prophet in Israel." So Naaman came with his horses and chariots, and halted at the entrance of Elisha's house. Elisha sent a messenger to him, saying, "Go, wash in the Jordan seven times, and your flesh shall be restored and you shall be clean." But Naaman became angry and went away, saying, "I thought that for me he would surely come out, and stand and call on the name of the LORD his God, and would wave his hand over the spot, and cure the leprosy! Are not Abana and Pharpar, the rivers of Damascus, better than all the waters of Israel? Could I not wash in them, and be clean?" He turned and went away in a rage. But his servants approached and said to him, "Father, if the prophet had commanded you to do something difficult, would you not have done it? How much more, when all he said to you was, 'Wash, and be clean'?" So he went down and immersed himself seven times in the Jordan, according to the word of the man of God; his flesh was restored like the flesh of a young boy, and he was clean. Then he returned to the man of God, he and all his company; he came and stood before him and said, "Now I know that there is no God in all the earth except in Israel."

The Psalm 42 or 42:1-7   *Quemadmodum*

1   [As the deer longs for the water-brooks, *
        so longs my soul for you, O God.

2   My soul is athirst for God, athirst for the livingGod; *
        when shall I come to appear before the presence of God?

3   My tears have been my food day and night, *
        while all day long they say to me,
        "Where now is your God?

4   I pour out my soul when I think on these things: *
        how I went with the multitude and led them into the house of God,

5   With the voice of praise and thanksgiving, *
        among those who keep holy-day.

6   Why are you so full of heaviness, O my soul? *
        and why are you so disquieted within me?

7   Put your trust in God; *
        for I will yet give thanks to him,
        who is the help of my countenance, and my God.]

8   My soul is heavy within me; *
        therefore I will remember you from the land of Jordan,
        and from the peak of Mizar among the heights of Hermon.

9   One deep calls to another in the noise of your cataracts; *
       all your rapids and floods have gone over me.

10   The LORD grants his loving-kindness in the daytime; *
       in the night season his son is with me,
       a prayer to the God of my life.

11   I will say to the God of my strength,
       "Why have you forgotten me? *
       and why do I go so heavily while the enemy oppresses me?"

12   While my bones are being broken, *
       my enemies mock me to my face;

13   All day long they mock me *
       and say to me, "Where now is your God?"

14   Why are you so full of heaviness, O my soul? *
       and why are you so disquieted within me?

15   Put your trust in God; *
       for I will yet give thanks to him,
       who is the help of my countenance, and my God.

The Epistle   **1 Corinthians 9:24-27**

Do you not know that in a race the runners all compete, but only one receives the prize? Run in such a way that you may win it. Athletes exercise self-control in all things; they do it to receive a perishable wreath, but we an imperishable one. So I do not run aimlessly, nor do I box as though beating the air; but I punish my body and enslave it, so that after proclaiming to others I myself should not be disqualified.

The Gospel   **Mark 1:40-45**

A leper came to him begging Jesus, and kneeling he said to him, "If you choose, you can make me clean." Moved with pity, Jesus stretched out his hand and touched him, and said to him, "I do choose. Be made clean!" Immediately the leprosy left him, and he was made clean. After sternly warning him he sent him away at once,saying to him, "See that you say nothing to anyone; but go, show yourself to the priest, and offer for your cleansing what Moses commanded, as a testimony to them." But he went out and began to proclaim it freely, and to spread the word, so that Jesus could no longer go into a town openly, but stayed out in the country; and people came to him from every quarter.

Year C

The Lesson   **Jeremiah 17:5-10**

Thus says the LORD: Cursed are those who trust in mere mortals and make mere flesh their strength, whose hearts turn away from the LORD. They shall be like a shrub in the desert, and shall not see when relief comes. They shall live in the parched places of the wilderness, in an uninhabited salt land. Blessed are those who trust in the LORD, whose trust is the LORD. They shall be like a tree planted by water, sending out its roots by the stream. It shall not fear when heat comes, and its leaves shall stay green; in the year of drought it is not anxious, and it does not cease to bear fruit. The heart is devious above all else; it is perverse — who can understand it? I the LORD test the mind and search the heart, to give to all according to their ways, according to the fruit of their doings.

The Psalm 1   *Beatus vir qui non abiit*

1   Happy are they who have not walked in the counsel of the wicked, *
        nor lingered in the way of sinners,
        nor sat in the seats of the scornful!

2   Their delight is in the law of the LORD, *
        and they meditate on his law day and night.

3   They are like trees planted by streams of water,
        bearing fruit in due season, with leaves that do not wither; *
        everything they do shall prosper.

4   It is not so with the wicked; *
        they are like chaff which the wind blows away.

5   Therefore the wicked shall not stand upright when judgment comes, *
        nor the sinner in the council of the righteous.

6   For the LORD knows the way of the righteous, *
        but the way of the wicked is doomed.

The Epistle   **1 Corinthians 15:12-20**

Now if Christ is proclaimed as raised from the dead, how can some of you say there is no resurrection of the dead? If there is no resurrection of the dead, then Christ has not been raised; and if Christ has not been raised, then our proclamation has been in vain and your faith has been in vain. We are even found to be misrepresenting God, because we testified of God that he raised Christ — whom he did not raise if it is true that the dead are not raised. For if the dead are not raised, then Christ has not been raised. If Christ has not been raised, your faith is futile and you are still in your sins. Then those also who have died in Christ have perished. If for this life only we have hoped in Christ, we are of all people most to be pitied. But in fact Christ has been raised from the dead, the first fruits of those who have died.

The Gospel   **Luke 6:17-26**

Jesus came down with them and stood on a level place, with a great crowd of his disciples and a great multitude of people from all Judea, Jerusalem, and the coast of Tyre and Sidon. They had come to hear him and to be healed of their diseases; and those who were troubled with unclean spirits were cured. And all in the crowd were trying to touch him, for power came out from him and healed all of them. Then he looked up at his disciples and said: "Blessed are you who are poor, for yours is the kingdom of God. Blessed are you who are hungry now, for you will be filled. Blessed are you who weep now, for you will laugh. Blessed are you when people hate you, and when they exclude you, revile you, and defame you on account of the Son of Man.

Rejoice in that day and leap for joy, for surely your reward is great in heaven; for that is what their ancestors did to the prophets. But woe to you who are rich, for you have received your consolation. Woe to you who are full now, for you will be hungry. Woe to you who are laughing now, for you will mourn and weep. Woe to you when all speak well of you, for that is what their ancestors did to the false prophets."

THE SEVENTH SUNDAY AFTER THE EPIPHANY

The Collect

O Lord, you have taught us that without love whatever we do is worth nothing: Send your Holy Spirit and pour into our hearts your greatest gift, which is love, the true bond of peace and of all virtue, without which whoever lives is accounted dead before you. Grant this for the sake of your only Son Jesus Christ, who lives and reigns with you and the Holy Spirit, one God, now and for ever. *Amen.*

O Lord, who hast taught us that all our doings without charity are nothing worth: Send thy Holy Ghost and pour into our hearts that most excellent gift of charity, the very bond of peace and of all virtues, without which whosoever liveth is counted dead before thee. Grant this for thine only Son Jesus Christ's sake, who liveth and reigneth with thee and the same Holy Ghost, one God, now and for ever. *Amen.*

Year A

The Lesson   Leviticus 19:1-2,9-18

The LORD spoke to Moses, saying: Speak to all the congregation of the people of Israel and say to them: You shall be holy, for I the LORD your God am holy. When you reap the harvest of your land, you shall not reap to the very edges of your field, or gather the gleanings of your harvest. You shall not strip your vineyard bare, or gather the fallen grapes of your vineyard; you shall leave them for the poor and the alien: I am the LORD your God. You shall not steal; you shall not deal falsely; and you shall not lie to one another. And you shall not swear falsely by my name, profaning the name of your God; I am the LORD. You shall not defraud your neighbor; you shall not steal; and you shall not keep for yourself the wages of a laborer until morning. You shall not revile the deaf or put a stumbling block before the blind; you shall fear your God:I am the LORD. You shall not render an unjust judgment; you shall not be partial to the poor or defer to the great: with justice you shall judge your neighbor. You shall not go around as a slanderer among your people, and you shall not profit by the blood of your neighbor: I am the LORD. You shall not hate in your heart anyone of your kin; you shall reprove your neighbor, or you will incur guilt yourself. You shall not take vengeance or bear a grudge against any of your people, but you shall love your neighbor as yourself: I am the LORD.

The Psalm 71 or 71:16-24   *In te, Dominc, speravi*

1   In you, O LORD, have I taken refuge; *
        let me never be ashamed.

2   In your righteousness, deliver me and set me free; *
     incline your ear to me and save me.

3   Be my strong rock, a castle to keep me safe; *
       you are my crag and my stronghold.

4   Deliver me, my God, from the hand of the wicked, *
       from the clutches of the evildoer and the oppressor.

5   For you are my hope, O Lord GOD, *
       my confidence since I was young.

6   I have been sustained by you ever since I was born;
    from my mother's womb you have been my strength; *
       my praise shall be always of you.

7   I have become a portent to many; *
       but you are my refuge and my strength.

8   Let my mouth be full of your praise *
       and your glory all the day long.

9   Do not cast me off in my old age; *
       forsake me not when my strength fails.

10   For my enemies are talking against me, *
       and those who lie in wait for my life take counsel together.

11   They say, "God has forsaken him;
    go after him and seize him; *
       because there is none who will save."

12   O God, be not far from me; *
       come quickly to help me, O my God.

13   Let those who set themselves against me be put to shame and be disgraced; *
       let those who seek to do me evil be covered with scorn and reproach.

14   But I shall always wait in patience, *
       and shall praise you more and more.

15   My mouth shall recount your mighty acts
    and saving deeds all day long; *
       though I cannot know the number of them.

16   [I will begin with the mighty works of the Lord GOD; *
       I will recall your righteousness, yours alone.

17   O God, you have taught me since I was young, *
       and to this day I tell of your wonderful works.

18   And now that I am old and gray-headed, O God, do not forsake me, *
       till I make known your strength to this generation
       and your power to all who are to come.

19 Your righteousness, O God, reaches to the heavens; *
    you have done great things;
    who is like you, O God?

20 You have showed me great troubles and adversities, *
    but you will restore my life
    and bring me up again from the deep places of the earth.

21 You strengthen me more and more; *
    you enfold and comfort me,

22 Therefore I will praise you upon the lyre for your faithfulness, O my God; *
    I will sing to you with the harp, O Holy One of Israel.

23 My lips will sing with joy when I play to you, *
    and so will my soul, which you have redeemed.

24 My tongue will proclaim your righteousness all day long, *
    for they are ashamed and disgraced who sought to do me harm.]

The Epistle
1 Corinthians 3:10-11, 16-23

According to the grace of God given to me, like a skilled master builder I laid a foundation, and someone else is building on it. Each builder must choose with care how to build on it. For no one can lay any foundation other than the one that has been laid; that foundation is Jesus Christ. Do you not know that you are God's temple and that God's Spirit dwells in you? If anyone destroys God's temple, God will destroy that person. For God's temple is holy, and you are that temple. Do not deceive yourselves. If you think that you are wise in this age, you should become fools so that you may become wise. For the wisdom of this world is foolishness with God. For it is written, "He catches the wise in their craftiness," and again, "The Lord knows the thoughts of the wise, that they are futile." So let no one boast about human leaders. For all things are yours, whether Paul or Apollos or Cephas or the world or life or death or the present or the future — all belong to you, and you belong to Christ, and Christ belongs to God.

The Gospel
Matthew 5:38-48

Jesus said, "You have heard that it was said,'An eye for an eye and a tooth for a tooth.' But I say to you, Do not resist an evildoer. But if anyone strikes you on the right cheek, turn the other also; and if anyone wants to sue you and take your coat, give your cloak as well; and if anyone forces you to go one mile, go also the second mile. Give to everyone who begs from you, and do not refuse anyone who wants to borrow from you. You have heard that it was said, 'You shall love your neighbor and hate your enemy.' But I say to you, Love your enemies and pray for those who persecute you, so that you may be children of your Father in heaven; for he makes his sun rise on the evil and on the good, and sends rain on the righteous and on the unrighteous. For if you love those who love you, what reward do you have? Do not even the tax collectors do the same? And if you greet only your brothers and sisters, what more are you doing than others? Do not even the Gentiles do the same? Be perfect, therefore, as your heavenly Father is perfect.

The Lesson   Isaiah 43:18-25

Do not remember the former things, or consider the things of old. I am about to do a
new thing; now it springs forth, do you not perceive it? I will make a way in the
wilderness and rivers in the desert. The wild animals will honor me, the jackals and
the ostriches; for I give water in the wilderness, rivers in the desert, to give drink to
my chosen people, the people whom I formed for myself so that they might declare
my praise. Yet you did not call upon me, O Jacob; but you have been weary of me, O
Israel! You have not brought me your sheep for burnt offerings, or honored me with
your sacrifices. I have not burdened you with offerings, or wearied you with
frankincense. You have not bought me sweet cane with money, or satisfied me with
the fat of your sacrifices. But you have burdened me with your sins; you have wearied
me with your iniquities. I, I am He who blots out your transgressions for my own
sake, and I will not remember your sins.

The Psalm 32 or 32:1-8   *Beati quorum*

1   [Happy are they whose transgressions are forgiven, *
          and whose sin is put away!

2   Happy are they to whom the LORD imputes no guilt, *
          and in whose spirit there is no guile!

3   While I held my tongue, my bones withered away, *
          because of my groaning all day long.

4   For your hand was heavy upon me day and night; *
          my moisture was dried up as in the heat of summer.

5   Then I acknowledged my sin to you, *
          and did not conceal my guilt.

6   I said, "I will confess my transgressions to the LORD."
          Then you forgave me the guilt of my sin.

7   Therefore all the faithful will make their prayers to you in time of trouble; *
          when the great waters overflow, they shall not reach them.

8   You are my hiding-place;
       you preserve me from trouble; *
          you surround me with shouts of deliverance.]

9   "I will instruct you and teach you in the way that you should go; *
          I will guide you with my eye.

10   Do not be like horse or mule, which have no understanding; *
          who must be fitted with bit and bridle,
          or else they will not stay near you."

11   Great are the tribulations of the wicked; *
          but mercy embraces those who trust in the LORD.

12   Be glad, you righteous, and rejoice in the LORD; *
      shout for joy, all who are true of heart.

The Epistle   2 Corinthians 1:18-22

As surely as God is faithful, our word to you has not been "Yes and No." For the Son
of God, Jesus Christ, whom we proclaimed among you, Silvanus and Timothy and I,
was not "Yes and No"; but in him it is always "Yes." For in him every one of God's
promises is a "Yes." For this reason it is through him that we say the "Amen," to the
glory of God. But it is God who establishes us with you in Christ and has anointed
us, by putting his seal on us and giving us his Spirit in our hearts as a first
installment.

The Gospel   Mark 2:1-12

When Jesus returned to Capernaum after some days, it was reported that he was at
home. So many gathered around that there was no longer room for them, not even in
front of the door; and he was speaking the word to them. Then some people came,
bringing to him a paralyzed man, carried by four of them. And when they could not
bring him to Jesus because of the crowd, they removed the roof above him; and after
having dug through it, they let down the mat on which the paralytic lay. When Jesus
saw their faith, he said to the paralytic, "Son, your sins are forgiven." Now some of
the scribes were sitting there, questioning in their hearts, "Why does this fellow speak
in this way? It is blasphemy! Who can forgive sins but God alone?" At once Jesus
perceived in his spirit that they were discussing these questions among themselves;
and he said to them, "Why do you raise such questions in your hearts? Which is
easier, to say to the paralytic, 'Your sins are forgiven,' or to say, 'Stand up and take
your mat and walk'? But so that you may know that the Son of Man has authority on
earth to forgive sins" — he said to the paralytic — "I say to you, stand up, take your
mat and go to your home." And he stood up, and immediately took the mat and
went out before all of them; so that they were all amazed and glorified God, saying,
"We have never seen anything like this!"

Year C

The Lesson   Genesis 45:3-11, 21-28

Joseph said to his brothers, "I am Joseph. Is my father still alive?" But his brothers
could not answer him, so dismayed were they at his presence. Then Joseph said to his
brothers, "Come closer to me." And they came closer. He said, "I am your brother,
Joseph, whom you sold into Egypt. And now do not be distressed, or angry with
yourselves, because you sold me here; for God sent me before you to preserve life.
For the famine has been in the land these two years; and there are five more years in
which there will be neither plowing nor harvest. God sent me before you to preserve
for you a remnant on earth, and to keep alive for you many survivors. So it was not
you who sent me here, but God; he has made me a father to Pharaoh, and lord of all
his house and ruler over all the land of Egypt. Hurry and go up to my father and say
to him, 'Thus says your son Joseph, God has made me lord of all Egypt; come down
to me, do not delay. You shall settle in the land of Goshen, and you shall be near me,
you and your children and your children's children, as well as your flocks, your herds,

and all that you have. I will provide for you there — since there are five more years of famine to come — so that you and your household, and all that you have, will not come to poverty.'" The sons of Israel did so. Joseph gave them wagons according to the instruction of Pharaoh, and he gave them provisions for the journey. To each one of them he gave a set of garments; but to Benjamin he gave three hundred pieces of silver and five sets of garments. To his father he sent the following: ten donkeys loaded with the good things of Egypt, and ten female donkeys loaded with grain, bread, and provision for his father on the journey. Then he sent his brothers on their way, and as they were leaving he said to them, "Do not quarrel along the way." So they went up out of Egypt and came to their father Jacob in the land of Canaan. And they told him, "Joseph is still alive! He is even ruler over all the land of Egypt." He was stunned; he could not believe them. But when they told him all the words of Joseph that he had said to them, and when he saw the wagons that Joseph had sent to carry him, the spirit of their father Jacob revived. Israel said, "Enough! My son Joseph is still alive. I must go and see him before I die."

The Psalm 37:1-18 or 37:3-10   *Noli aemulari*

1   Do not fret yourself because of evildoers; *
        do not be jealous of those who do wrong.

2   For they shall soon wither like the grass, *
        and like the green grass fade away.

3   [Put your trust in the LORD and do good; *
        dwell in the land and feed on its riches.

4   Take delight in the LORD, *
        and he shall give you your heart's desire.

5   Commit your way to the LORD and put your trust in him, *
        and he will bring it to pass.

6   He will make your righteousness as clear as the light *
        and your just dealing as the noonday.

7   Be still before the LORD *
        and wait patiently for him.

8   Do not fret yourself over the one who prospers, *
        the one who succeeds in evil schemes.

9   Refrain from anger, leave rage alone; *
        do not fret yourself; it leads only to evil.

10   For evildoers shall be cut off, *
        but those who wait upon the LORD shall possess the land.]

11   In a little while the wicked shall be nomore; *
        you shall search out their place, but they will not be there.

12   But the lowly shall possess the land; *
        they will delight in abundance of peace.

13   The wicked plot against the righteous *
      and gnash at them with their teeth.

14   The Lord laughs at the wicked, *
      because he sees that their day will come.

15   The wicked draw their sword and bend their bow
    to strike down the poor and needy, *
      to slaughter those who are upright in their ways.

16   Their sword shall go through their own heart, *
      and their bow shall be broken.

17   The little that the righteous has *
      is better than great riches of the wicked.

18   For the power of the wicked shall be broken, *
      but the Lord upholds the righteous.

The Epistle   1 Corinthians 15:35-38, 42-50

But someone will ask, "How are the dead raised? With what kind of body do they come?" Fool! What you sow does not come to life unless it dies. And as for what you sow, you do not sow the body that is to be, but a bare seed, perhaps of wheat or of some other grain. But God gives it a body as he has chosen, and to each kind of seed its own body. So it is with the resurrection of the dead. What is sown is perishable, what is raised is imperishable. It is sown in dishonor, it is raised in glory. It is sown in weakness, it is raised in power. It is sown a physical body, it is raised a spiritual body. If there is a physical body, there is also a spiritual body. Thus it is written, "The first man, Adam, became a living being"; the last Adam became a life-giving spirit. But it is not the spiritual that is first, but the physical, and then the spiritual. The first man was from the earth, a man of dust; the second man is from heaven. As was the man of dust, so are those who are of the dust; and as is the man of heaven, so are those who are of heaven. Just as we have borne the image of the man of dust, we will also bear the image of the man of heaven. What I am saying, brothers and sisters, is this: flesh and blood cannot inherit the kingdom of God, nor does the perishable inherit the imperishable.

The Gospel   Luke 6:27-38

Jesus said, "I say to you that listen, Love your enemies, do good to those who hate you, bless those who curse you, pray for those who abuse you. If anyone strikes you on the cheek, offer the other also; and from anyone who takes away your coat do not withhold even your shirt. Give to everyone who begs from you; and if anyone takes away your goods, do not ask for them again. Do to others as you would have them do to you. If you love those who love you, what credit is that to you? For even sinners love those who love them.If you do good to those who do good to you, what credit is that to you? For even sinners do the same. If you lend to those from whom you hope to receive, what credit is that to you? Even sinners lend to sinners, to receive as much again. But love your enemies, do good, and lend, expecting nothing in return. Your reward will be great, and you will be children of the Most High; for he is kind to the ungrateful and the wicked. Be merciful, just as your Father is merciful. Do not judge, and you will not be judged; do not condemn, and you will not be condemned. Forgive, and you will be forgiven; give, and it will be given to you. A good measure, pressed down, shaken together, running over, will be put into your lap; for the measure you give will be the measure you get back."

THE EIGHTH SUNDAY AFTER THE EPIPHANY

The Collect
Most loving Father, whose will it is for us to give thanks for all things, to fear nothing but the loss of you, and to cast all our care on you who care for us: Preserve us from faithless fears and worldly anxieties, that no clouds of this mortal life may hide from us the light of that love which is immortal, and which you have manifested to us in your Son Jesus Christ our Lord; who lives and reigns with you, in the unity of the Holy Spirit, one God, now and for ever. *Amen.*

O most loving Father, who willest us to give thanks for all things, to dread nothing but the loss of thee, and to cast all our care on thee who carest for us: Preserve us from faithless fears and worldly anxieties, and grant that no clouds of this mortal life may hide from us the light of that love which is immortal, and which thou hast manifested unto us in thy Son Jesus Christ our Lord; who liveth and reigneth with thee, in the unity of the Holy Spirit, one God, now and for ever. *Amen.*

Year A

The Lesson   Isaiah 49:8-18
Thus says the LORD: In a time of favor I have answered you, on a day of salvation I have helped you; I have kept you and given you as a covenant to the people, to establish the land, to apportion the desolate heritages; saying to the prisoners, "Come out," to those who are in darkness, "Show yourselves." They shall feed along the ways, on all the bare heights shall be their pasture; they shall not hunger or thirst, neither scorching wind nor sun shall strike them down, for he who has pity on them will lead them, and by springs of water will guide them. And I will turn all my mountains into a road, and my highways shall be raised up. Lo, these shall come from far away, and lo, these from the north and from the west, and these from the land of Syene. Sing for joy, O heavens, and exult, O earth; break forth, O mountains, into singing! For the LORD has comforted his people, and will have compassion on his suffering ones. But Zion said, "The LORD has forsaken me, my Lord has forgotten me." Can a woman forget her nursing child, or show no compassion for the child of her womb? Even these may forget, yet I will not forget you. See, I have inscribed you on the palms of my hands; your walls are continuallybefore me. Your builders outdo your destroyers, and those who laid you waste go away from you. Lift up your eyes all around and see; they all gather, they come to you. As I live, says the LORD, you shall put all of them on like an ornament, and like a bride you shall bind them on.

The Psalm 62 or 62:6-14   *Nonne Deo?*
1   For God alone my soul in silence waits; *
         from him comes my salvation.

2   He alone is my rock and my salvation, *
     my stronghold, so that I shall not be greatly shaken.

3   How long will you assail me to crush me,
   all of you together, *
     as if you were a leaning fence, a toppling wall?

4   They seek only to bring me down from my place of honor; *
     lies are their chief delight.

5   They bless with their lips, *
     but in their hearts they curse.

6   [For God alone my soul in silence waits; *
     truly, my hope is in him.

7   He alone is my rock and my salvation, *
     my stronghold, so that I shall not be shaken.

8   In God is my safety and my honor; *
     God is my strong rock and my refuge.

9   Put your trust in him always, O people, *
     pour out your hearts before him, for God is our refuge.

10   Those of high degree are but a fleeting breath, *
     even those of low estate cannot be trusted.

11   On the scales they are lighter than a breath, *
     all of them together.

12   Put no trust in extortion;
   in robbery take no empty pride; *
     though wealth increase, set not your heart upon it.

13   God has spoken once, twice have I heard it, *
     that power belongs to God.

14   Steadfast love is yours, O Lord, *
     for you repay everyone according to his deeds.]

The Epistle   **1 Corinthians 4:1-5 (6-7) 8-13**

Think of us in this way, as servants of Christ and stewards of God's mysteries. Moreover, it is required of stewards that they be found trustworthy. But with me it is a very small thing that I should be judged by you or by any human court. I do not even judge myself. I am not aware of anything against myself, but I am not thereby acquitted. It is the Lord who judges me. Therefore do not pronounce judgment before the time, before the Lord comes, who will bring to light the things now hidden in darkness and will disclose the purposes of the heart. Then each one will receive commendation from God. [I have applied all this to Apollos and myself for your benefit, brothers and sisters, so that you may learn through us the meaning of the saying, "Nothing beyond what is written," so that none of you will be puffed up in favor of one against another. For who sees anything different in you? What do you have that you did not receive? And if you received it, why do you boast as if it were not a gift?] Already you have all you want! Already you have become rich! Quite apart from us you have become kings! Indeed, I wish that you had become kings, so that the might be kings with you! For I think that God has exhibited us apostles as last of all, as though sentenced to death, because we have become a spectacle to the world, to angels and to mortals. We are fools for the sake of Christ, but you are wise in Christ. We are weak, but you are strong. You are held in honor, but we in disrepute. To the present hour we are hungry and thirsty, we are poorly clothed and beaten and homeless, and we grow weary from the work of our own hands. When reviled, we bless; when persecuted, we endure; when slandered, we speak kindly. We have become like the rubbish of the world, the dregs of all things, to this very day.

The Gospel   Matthew 6:24-34
Jesus said, "No one can serve two masters; for a slave will either hate the one and love the other, or be devoted to the one and despise the other. You cannot serve God and wealth. Therefore I tell you, do not worry about your life, what you will eat or what you will drink, or about your body, what you will wear. Is not life more than food, and the body more than clothing? Look at the birds of the air; they neither sow nor reap nor gather into barns, and yet your heavenly Father feeds them. Are you not of more value than they? And can any of you by worrying add a single hour to your span of life? And why do you worry about clothing? Consider the lilies of the field, how they grow; they neither toil nor spin, yet I tell you, even Solomon in all his glory was not clothed like one of these. But if God so clothes the grass of the field, which is alive today and tomorrow is thrown into the oven, will he not much more clothe you — you of little faith? Therefore do not worry, saying, 'What will we eat?' or 'What will we drink?' or 'What will we wear?' For it is the Gentiles who strive for all these things; and indeed your heavenly Father knows that you need all these things. But strive first for the kingdom of God and his righteousness, and all these things will be given to you as well. So do not worry about tomorrow, for tomorrow will bring worries of its own. Today's trouble is enough for today.

Year B

The Lesson   Hosea 2:14-23
The Lord said to Hosea, "Therefore, I will now allure her, and bring her into the wilderness, and speak tenderly to her. From there I will give her vineyards, and make the Valley of Achor a door of hope. There she shall respond as in the days of her youth, as at the time when she came out of the land of Egypt. On that day, says the LORD, you will call me, "My husband," and no longer will you call me, "My Baal." For I will remove the names of the Baals from her mouth, and they shall be mentioned by name no more. I will make for you a covenant on that day with the wild animals, the birds of the air, and the creeping things of the ground; and I will abolish the bow, the sword, and war from the land; and I will make you lie down in safety. And I will take you for my wife forever; I will take you for my wife in righteousness and in justice, in steadfast love, and in mercy. I will take you for my wife in faithfulness; and you shall know the LORD. On that day I will answer, says the LORD, I will answer the heavens and they shall answer the earth; and the earth shall

answer the grain, the wine, and the oil, and they shall answer Jezreel; and I will sow him for myself in the land. And I will have pity on Loruhamah, and I will say to Loammi, "You are my people"; and he shall say, "You are my God."

The Psalm 103 or 103:1-6   *Benedic, anima mea*

1   [Bless the LORD, O my soul, *
        and all that is within me, bless his holy Name.

2   Bless the LORD, O my soul, *
        and forget not all his benefits.

3   He forgives all your sins *
        and heals all your infirmities;

4   He redeems your life from the grave *
        and crowns you with mercy and loving-kindness;

5   He satisfies you with good things, *
        and your youth is renewed like an eagle's.

6   The LORD executes righteousness *
        and judgment for all who are oppressed.]

7   He made his ways known to Moses *
        and his works to the children of Israel.

8   The LORD is full of compassion and mercy, *
        slow to anger and of great kindness.

9   He will not always accuse us, *
        nor will he keep his anger for ever.

10 He has not dealt with us according to our sins, *
        nor rewarded us according to our wickedness.

11 For as the heavens are high above the earth, *
        so is his mercy great upon those who fear him.

12 As far as the east is from the west, *
        so far has he removed our sins from us.

13 As a father cares for his children, *
        so does the LORD care for those who fear him.

14 For he himself knows whereof we are made; *
        he remembers that we are but dust.

15 Our days are like the grass; *
        we flourish like a flower of the field;

16 When the wind goes over it, it is gone, *
        and its place shall know it no more.

17　But the merciful goodness of the LORD endures for ever
on those who fear him, *
　　and his righteousness on children's children;

18　On those who keep his covenant *
　　and remember his commandments and do them.

19　The LORD has set his throne in heaven, *
　　and his kingship has dominion over all.

20　Bless the LORD, you angels of his,
you mighty ones who do his bidding, *
　　and hearken to the voice of his word.

21　Bless the LORD, all you his hosts, *
　　you ministers of his who do his will.

22　Bless the LORD, all you works of his,
in all places of his dominion; *
　　bless the LORD, O my soul.

The Epistle　　　　　　　　　　　　　**2 Corinthians 3:(4-11) 17-4:2**

[Such is the confidence that we have through Christ toward God. Not that we are
competent of ourselves to claim anything as coming from us; our competence is from
God, who has made us competent to be ministers of a new covenant, not of letter but
of spirit; for the letter kills, but the Spirit gives life. Now if the ministry of death,
chiseled in letters on stone tablets, came in glory so that the people of Israel could not
gaze at Moses' face because of the glory of his face, a glory now set aside, how much
more will the ministry of the Spirit come in glory? For if there was glory in the
ministry of condemnation, much more does the ministry of justification abound in
glory! Indeed, what once had glory has lost its glory because of the greater glory; for
if what was set aside came through glory, much more has the permanent come in
glory!] Now the Lord is the Spirit, and where the Spirit of the Lord is, there is
freedom. And all of us, with unveiled faces, seeing the glory of the Lord as though
reflected in a mirror, are being transformed into the same image from one degree of
glory to another; for this comes from the Lord, the Spirit. Therefore, since it is by
God's mercy that we are engaged in this ministry, we do not lose heart. We have
renounced the shameful things that one hides; we refuse to practice cunning or to
falsify God's word; but by the open statement of the truth we commend ourselves to
the conscience of everyone in the sight of God.

The Gospel　　　　　　　　　　　　　　　　　　**Mark 2:18-22**

Now John's disciples and the Pharisees were fasting; and people came and said to
him, "Why do John's disciples and the disciples of the Pharisees fast, but your
disciples do not fast?" Jesus said to them, "The wedding guests cannot fast while the
bridegroom is with them, can they? As long as they have the bridegroom with them,
they cannot fast. The days will come when the bridegroom is taken away from them,
and then they will fast on that day. No one sews a piece of unshrunk cloth on an old
cloak; otherwise, the patch pulls away from it, the new from the old, and a worse tear

is made. And no one puts new wine into old wineskins; otherwise, the wine will burst the skins, and the wine is lost, and so are the skins; but one puts new wine into fresh wineskins."

The Lesson Jeremiah 7:1-7 (8-15)

The word that came to Jeremiah from the LORD: Stand in the gate of the LORD's house, and proclaim there this word, and say, Hear the word of the LORD, all you people of Judah, you that enter these gates to worship the LORD. Thus says the LORD of hosts, the God of Israel: Amend your ways and your doings, and let me dwell with you in this place. Do not trust in these deceptive words: "This is the temple of the LORD, the temple of the LORD, the temple of the LORD." For if you truly amend your ways and your doings, if you truly act justly one with another, if you do not oppress the alien, the orphan, and the widow, or shed innocent blood in this place, and if you do not go after other gods to your own hurt, then I will dwell with you in this place, in the land that I have of old to your ancestors forever and ever. [Here you are, trusting in deceptive words to no avail. Will you steal, murder, commit adultery, swear falsely, make offering to Baal, and go after other gods that you have not known, and then come and stand before me in this house, which is called by my name, and say, "We are safe!"—only to go on doing all these abominations? Has this house, which is called by my name, become a den of robbers in your sight? You know, I too am watching, says the LORD. Go now to my place that was in Shiloh, where I made my name dwell at first, and see what I did to it for the wickedness of my people Israel. And now, because you have done all these things, says the LORD, and when I spoke to you persistently, you did not listen, and when I called you, you did not answer, therefore I will do to the house that is called by my name, in which you trust, and to the place that I gave to you and to your ancestors, just what I did to Shiloh. And I will cast you out of my sight, just as I cast out all your kinsfolk, all the offspring of Ephraim.]

The Psalm 92 or 92:1-5, 11-14   *Bonum est confiteri*

1 [It is a good thing to give thanks to the LORD, *
     and to sing praises to your Name, O Most High;

2 To tell of your loving-kindness early in the morning *
     and of your faithfulness in the night season;

3 On the psaltery, and on the lyre, *
     and to the melody of the harp.

4 For you have made me glad by your acts, O LORD; *
     and I shout for joy because of the works of your hands.

5 LORD, how great are your works! *
     your thoughts are very deep.]

6 The dullard does not know,
     nor does the fool understand, *

that though the wicked grow like weeds,
and all the workers of iniquity flourish,

7   They flourish only to be destroyed for ever; *
    but you, O LORD, are exalted for evermore.

8   For lo, your enemies, O LORD
    lo, your enemies shall perish, *
    and all the workers of iniquity shall be scattered.

9   But my horn you have exalted like the horns of wild bulls; *
    I am anointed with fresh oil.

10   My eyes also gloat over my enemies, *
    and my ears rejoice to hear the doom of the wicked who rise up against me.

11   [The righteous shall flourish like a palm tree, *
    and shall spread abroad like a cedar of Lebanon.

12   Those who are planted in the house of the LORD *
    shall flourish in the courts of our God;

13   They shall still bear fruit in old age; *
    they shall be green and succulent;

14   That they may show how upright the LORD is, *
    my Rock, in whom there is no fault.]

The Epistle   **1 Corinthians 15:50-58**

What I am saying, brothers and sisters, is this: flesh and blood cannot inherit the kingdom of God, nor does the perishable inherit the imperishable. Listen, I will tell you a mystery! We will not all die, but we will all be changed, in a moment, in the twinkling of an eye, at the last trumpet. For the trumpet will sound, and the dead will be raised imperishable, and we will be changed. For this perishable body must put on imperishability, and this mortal body must put on immortality. When this perishable body puts on imperishability, and this mortal body puts on immortality, then the saying that is written will be fulfilled: "Death has been swallowed up in victory. Where, O death, is your victory? Where, O death, is your sting?" The sting of death is sin, and the power of sin is the law. But thanks be to God, who gives us the victory through our Lord Jesus Christ. Therefore, my beloved, be steadfast, immovable, always excelling in the work of the Lord, because you know that in the Lord your labor is not in vain.

The Gospel   **Luke 6:39-49**

Jesus told the people a parable: "Can a blind person guide a blind person? Will not both fall into a pit? A disciple is not above the teacher, but everyone who is fully qualified will be like the teacher. Why do you see the speck in your neighbor's eye, but do not notice the log in your own eye? Or how can you say to your neighbor, 'Friend, let me take out the speck in your eye,' when you yourself do not see the log in your own eye? You hypocrite, first take the log out of your own eye, and then you will see clearly to take the speck out of your neighbor's eye. No good tree bears bad fruit, nor again does a bad tree bear good fruit; for each tree is known by its own fruit. Figs are not gathered from thorns, nor are grapes picked from a bramble bush. The good person out of the good treasure of the heart produces good, and the evil person out of evil treasure produces evil; for it is out of the abundance of the heart that the mouth speaks. Why do you call me 'Lord, Lord,' and do not do what I tell you? I will show you what someone is like who comes to me, hears my words, and acts on them. That one is like a man building a house, who dug deeply and laid the foundation on rock; when a flood arose, the river burst against that house but could not shake it, because it had been well built. But the one who hears and does not act is like a man who built a house on the ground without a foundation. When the river burst against it, immediately it fell, and great was the ruin of that house."

THE LAST SUNDAY AFTER THE EPIPHANY

The Collect

This Proper is always used on the Sunday before Ash Wednesday

O God, who before the passion of your only-begotten Son revealed his glory upon the holy mountain: Grant to us that we, beholding by faith the light of his countenance, may be strengthened to bear our cross, and be changed into his likeness from glory to glory; through Jesus Christ our Lord, who lives and reigns with you and the Holy Spirit, one God, for ever and ever. *Amen.*

O God, who before the passion of thy only-begotten Son didst reveal his glory upon the holy mount: Grant unto us that we, beholding by faith the light of his countenance, may be strengthened to bear our cross, and be changed into his likeness from glory to glory; through the same Jesus Christ our Lord, who liveth and reigneth with thee and the Holy Spirit, one God, for ever and ever. *Amen.*

Year A

The Lesson   Exodus 24:12 (13-14) 15-18

The LORD said to Moses, "Come up to me on the mountain, and wait there; and I will give you the tablets of stone, with the law and the commandment, which I have written for their instruction." [So Moses set out with his assistant Joshua, and Moses went up into the mountain of God. To the elders he had said, "Wait here for us, until we come to you again; for Aaron and Hur are with you; whoever has a dispute may go to them."] Then Moses went up on the mountain, and the cloud covered the mountain. The glory of the LORD settled on Mount Sinai, and the cloud covered it for six days; on the seventh day he called to Moses out of the cloud. Now the appearance of the glory of the LORD was like a devouring fire on the top of the mountain in the sight of the people of Israel. Moses entered the cloud, and went up on the mountain. Moses was on the mountain for forty days and forty nights.

The Psalm 99   *Dominus regnavit*

1   The LORD is King;
      let the people tremble; *
          he is enthroned upon the cherubim;
          let the earth shake.

2   The LORD is great in Zion; *
      he is high above all peoples.

3   Let them confess his Name, which is great and awesome; *
      he is the Holy One.

4   "O mighty King, lover of justice,
    you have established equity; *
      you have executed justice and righteousness in Jacob."

5   Proclaim the greatness of the LORD our God
    and fall down before his footstool; *
      he is the Holy One.

6   Moses and Aaron among his priests,
    and Samuel among those who call upon his Name, *
      they called upon the LORD, and he answered them.

7   He spoke to them out of the pillar of cloud; *
      they kept his testimonies and the decree that he gave them.

8   O LORD our God, you answered them indeed; *
    you were a God who forgave them,
      yet punished them for their evil deeds.

9   Proclaim the greatness of the LORD our God
    and worship him upon his holy hill; *
      for the LORD our God is the Holy One.

The Epistle   **Philippians 3:7-14**

Yet whatever gains I had, these I have come to regard as loss because of Christ. More than that, I regard everything as loss because of the surpassing value of knowing Christ Jesus my Lord. For his sake I have suffered the loss of all things, and I regard them as rubbish, in order that I may gain Christ and be found in him, not having a righteousness of my own that comes from the law, but one that comes through faith in Christ, the righteousness from God based on faith. I want to know Christ and the power of his resurrection and the sharing of his sufferings by becoming like him in his death, if somehow I may attain the resurrection from the dead. Not that I have already obtained this or have already reached the goal; but I press on to make it my own, because Christ Jesus has made me his own. Beloved, I do not consider that I have made it my own; but this one thing I do: forgetting what lies behind and straining forward to what lies ahead, I press on toward the goal for the prize of the heavenly call of God in Christ Jesus.

The Gospel   **Matthew 17:1-9**

Six days after Peter said that Jesus was the Christ, the Son of the living God, Jesus took with him Peter and James and his brother John and led them up a high mountain, by themselves. And he was transfigured before them, and his face shone like the sun, and his clothes became dazzling white. Suddenly there appeared to them Moses and Elijah, talking with him. Then Peter said to Jesus, "Lord, it is good for us to be here; if you wish, I will make three dwellings here, one for you, one for Moses, and one for Elijah." While he was still speaking, suddenly a bright cloud overshadowed them, and from the cloud a voice said, "This is my Son, the Beloved; with him I am well pleased; listen to him!" When the disciples heard this, they fell to the ground and were overcome by fear. But Jesus came and touched them, saying, "Get up and do not be afraid." And when they looked up, they saw no one except Jesus himself alone. As they were coming down the mountain, Jesus ordered them, "Tell no one about the vision until after the Son of Man has been raised from the dead."

Year B

The Lesson   1 Kings 19:9-18

At Horeb, the mount of God, Elijah came to a cave, and spent the night there. Then the word of the LORD came to him, saying, "What are you doing here, Elijah?" He answered, "I have been very zealous for the LORD, the God of hosts; for the Israelites have forsaken your covenant,thrown down your altars, and killed your prophets with the sword. I alone am left, and they are seeking my life, to take it away." He said, "Go out and stand on the mountain before the LORD, for the LORD is about to pass by." Now there was a great wind, so strong that it was splitting mountains and breaking rocks in pieces before the LORD, but the LORD was not in the wind; and after the wind an earthquake, but the LORD was not in the earthquake; and after the earthquake a fire, but the LORD was not in the fire; and after the fire a sound of sheer silence. When Elijah heard it, he wrapped his face in his mantle and went out and stood at the entrance of the cave. Then there came a voice to him that said, "What are you doing here, Elijah?" He answered, "I have been very zealous for the LORD, the God of hosts; for the Israelites have forsaken your covenant, thrown down your altars, and killed your prophets with the sword. I alone am left, and they are seeking my life, to take it away." Then the LORD said to him, "Go, return on your way to the wilderness of Damascus; when you arrive, you shall anoint Hazael as King over Aram. Also you shall anoint Jehu son of Nimshi as king over Israel; and you shall anoint Elisha son of Shaphat of Abel-meholah as prophet in your place. Whoever escapes from the sword of Hazael, Jehu shall kill; and whoever escapes from the sword of Jehu, Elisha shall kill. Yet I will leave seven thousand in Israel, all the knees that have not bowed to Baal, and every mouth that has not kissed him."

The Psalm 27 or 27:5-11   *Dominus illuminatio*

1   The LORD is my light and my salvation;
     whom then shall I fear? *
          the LORD is the strength of my life;
          of whom then shall I be afraid?

2   When evildoers came upon me to eat up my flesh, *
          it was they, my foes and my adversaries, who stumbled and fell.

3   Though an army should encamp against me, *
          yet my heart shall not be afraid;

4   And though war should rise up against me, *
        yet will I put my trust in him.

5   [One thing have I asked of the LORD:
     one thing I seek; *
        that I may dwell in the house of the LORD all the days of my life;

6   To behold the fair beauty of the LORD *
        and to seek him in his temple.

7   For in the day of trouble he shall keep me safe in his shelter; *
        he shall hide me in the secrecy of his dwelling
        and set me high upon a rock.

8   Even now he lifts up my head *
        above my enemies round about me.

9   Therefore I will offer in his dwelling an oblation
     with sounds of great gladness; *
        I will sing and make music to the LORD.

10   Hearken to my voice, O LORD, when I call; *
        have mercy on me and answer me.

11   You speak in my heart and say, "Seek my face." *
        Your face, LORD, will I seek.]

12   Hide not your face from me, *
        nor turn away your servant in displeasure.

13   You have been my helper;
     cast me not away; *
        do not forsake me, O God of my salvation.

14   Though my father and my mother forsake me, *
        the LORD will sustain me.

15   Show me your way, O LORD; *
        lead me on a level path, because of my enemies.

16   Deliver me not into the hand of my adversaries, *
        for false witnesses have risen up against me,
        and also those who speak malice.

17   What if I had not believed
     that I should see the goodness of the LORD *
        in the land of the living!

18   O tarry and await the LORD's pleasure;
     be strong, and he shall comfort your heart; *
        wait patiently for the LORD.

The Epistle

2 Peter 1:16-19 (20-21)

For we did not follow cleverly devised myths when we made known to you the power and coming of our Lord Jesus Christ, but we had been eyewitnesses of his majesty. For he received honor and glory from God the Father when that voice was conveyed to him by the Majestic Glory, saying, "This is my Son, my Beloved, with whom I am well pleased." We ourselves heard this voice come from heaven, while we were with him on the holy mountain. So we have the prophetic message more fully confirmed. You will do well to be attentive to this as to a lamp shining in a dark place, until the day dawns and the morning star rises in your hearts. [First of all you must understand this, that no prophecy of scripture is a matter of one's own interpretation, because no prophecy ever came by human will, but men and women moved by the Holy Spirit spoke from God.]

The Gospel

Mark 9:2-9

Six days later, Jesus took with him Peter and James and John, and led them up a high mountain apart, by themselves. And he was transfigured before them, and his clothes became dazzling white, such as no one on earth could bleach them. And there appeared to them Elijah with Moses, who were talking with Jesus. Then Peter said to Jesus, "Rabbi, it is good for us to be here; let us make three dwellings, one for you, one for Moses, and one for Elijah." He did not know what to say, for they were terrified. Then a cloud overshadowed them, and from the cloud there came a voice, "This is my Son, the Beloved; listen to him!" Suddenly when they looked around, they saw no one with them any more, but only Jesus. As they were coming down the mountain, he ordered them to tell no one about what they had seen, until after the Son of Man had risen from the dead.

Year C

The Lesson

Exodus 34:29-35

Moses came down from Mount Sinai. As he came down from the mountain with the two tablets of the covenant in his hand, Moses did not know that the skin of his face shone because he had been talking with God. When Aaron and all the Israelites saw Moses, the skin of his face was shining, and they were afraid to come near him. But Moses called to them; and Aaron and all the leaders of the congregation returned to him, and Moses spoke with them. Afterward all the Israelites came near, and he gave them in commandment all that the LORD had spoken with him on Mount Sinai. When Moses had finished speaking with them, he put a veil on his face; but whenever Moses went in before the LORD to speak with him, he would take the veil off, until he came out; and when he came out, and told the Israelites what he had been commanded, the Israelites would see the face of Moses, that the skin of his face was shining; and Moses would put the veil on his face again, until he went in to speak with him.

The Psalm 99   *Dominus regnavit*

1   The LORD is King;
     let the people tremble; *
         he is enthroned upon the cherubim;
         let the earth shake.

2   The LORD is great in Zion; *
        he is high above all peoples.

3   Let them confess his Name, which is great and awesome; *
        he is the Holy One.

4   "O mighty King, lover of justice,
    you have established equity; *
        you have executed justice ad righteousness in Jacob."

5   Proclaim the greatness of the LORD our God
    and fall down before his footstool; *
        he is the Holy One.

6   Moses and Aaron among his priests,
    and Samuel among those who call upon his Name, *
        they called upon the LORD, and he answered them.

7   He spoke to them out of the pillar of cloud; *
        they kept his testimonies and the decree that he gave them.

8   O LORD our God, you answered them indeed; *
        you were a God who forgave them,
        yet punished them for their evil deeds.

9   Proclaim the greatness of the LORD our God
    and worship him upon his holy hill; *
        for the LORD our God is the Holy One.

The Epistle   **1 Corinthians 12:27-13:13**
Now you are the body of Christ and individually members of it. And God has
appointed in the church first apostles, second prophets, third teachers; then deeds of
power,then gifts of healing, forms of assistance, forms of leadership, various kinds of
tongues. Are all apostles? Are all prophets? Are all teachers? Do all work miracles?
Do all posses gifts of healing? Do all speak in tongues? Do all interpret? But strive for
the greater gifts. And I will show you a still more excellent way. If I speak in the
tongues of mortals and of angels, but do not have love, I am a noisy gong or a
clanging cymbal. And if I have prophetic powers, and understand all mysteries and
all knowledge, and if I have all faith, so as to remove mountains, but do not have
love, I am nothing. If I give away all my possession, and if I hand over my body so
that I may boast, but do not have love, I gain nothing. Love is patient; love is kind;
love is not envious or boastful or arrogant or rude. It does not insist on its own way;
it is not irritable or resentful; it does not rejoice in wrongdoing, but rejoices in the
truth. It bears all things, believes all things, hopes all things, endures all things. Love
never ends. But as for prophecies, they will come to an end; as for tongues, they will
cease; as for knowledge, it will come to an end. For we know only in part, and we
prophesy only in part; but when the complete comes, the partial will come to an end.
When I was a child, I spoke like a child; when I became an adult, I put an end to
childish ways. For now we see in a mirror, dimly, but then we will see face to face.

Now I know only in part; then I will know fully, even as I have been fully known. And now faith, hope, and love abide, these three; and the greatest of these is love.

The Gospel Luke 9:28-36

About eight days after these sayings Jesus took with him Peter and John and James, and went up on the mountain to pray. And while he was praying, the appearance of his face changed, and his clothes became dazzling white. Suddenly they saw two men, Moses and Elijah, talking to him. They appeared in glory and were speaking of his departure, which he was about to accomplish at Jerusalem. Now Peter and his companions were weighed down with sleep; but since they had stayed awake, they saw his glory and the two men who stood with him. Just as they were leaving him, Peter said to Jesus, "Master, it is good for us to be here; let us make three dwellings, one for you, one for Moses, and one for Elijah" — not knowing what he said. While he was saying this, a cloud came and overshadowed them; and they were terrified as they entered the cloud. Then from the cloud came a voice that said, "This is my Son, my Chosen; listen to him!" When the voice had spoken, Jesus was found alone. And they kept silent and in those days told no one any of the things they had seen.

THE FIRST DAY OF LENT,
OR ASH WEDNESDAY

The Collect

Almighty and everlasting God, you hate nothing you have made and forgive the sins of all who are penitent: Create and make in us new and contrite hearts, that we, worthily lamenting our sins and acknowledging our wretchedness, may obtain of you, the god of all mercy, perfect remission and forgiveness; through Jesus Christ our Lord, who lives and reigns with you and the Holy Spirit, one God, for ever and ever. *Amen.*

Almighty and everlasting God, who hatest nothing that thou hast made and dost forgive the sins of all those who are penitent: Create and make in us new and contrite hearts, that we, worthily lamenting our sins and acknowledging our wretchedness, may obtain of thee, the God of all mercy, perfect remission and forgiveness; through Jesus Christ our Lord, who liveth and reigneth with thee and the Holy Spirit, one God, for ever and ever. *Amen.*

Years A, B, C

The Lesson Joel 2:1-2, 12-17

Blow the trumpet in Zion; sound the alarm on my holy mountain! Let all the inhabitants of the land tremble, for the day of the LORD is coming, it is near — a day of darkness and gloom, a day of clouds and thick darkness! Like blackness spread upon the mountains a great and powerful army comes; their like has never been from of old, nor will be again after them in ages to come. Yet even now, says the LORD, return to me with all your heart, with fasting, with weeping, and with mourning; rend your hearts and not your clothing. Return to the LORD, your God, for he is gracious and merciful, slow to anger, and abounding in steadfast love, and relents from punishing. Who knows whether he will not turn and relent, and leave a blessing behind him, a grain offering and a drink offering for the LORD, your God? Blow the trumpet in Zion; sanctify a fast; call a solemn assembly; gather the people. Sanctify the congregation; assemble the aged; gather the children, even infants at the breast. Let the bridegroom leave his room, and the bride her canopy. Between the vestibule and the altar let the priests, the ministers of the LORD, weep. Let them say, "Spare your people, O LORD, and do not make your heritage a mockery, a byword among the nations. Why should it be said among the peoples 'Where is their God?'"

or Isaiah 58:1-12

Shout out, do not hold back! Lift up your voice like a trumpet! Announce to my people their rebellion, to the house of Jacob their sins. Yet day after day they seek me and delight to know my ways, as if they were a nation that practiced righteousness and did not forsake the ordinance of their God; they ask of me righteous judgments, they delight to draw near to God. "Why do we fast, but you do not see? Why humble ourselves, but you do not notice?" Look, you serve your own interest on your fast day, and oppress all your workers. Look, you fast only to quarrel and to fight and to strike with a wicked fist. Such fasting as you do today will not make your voice heard on high. Is such the fast that I choose, a day to humble oneself? Is it to bow down the head like a bulrush, and to lie in sackcloth and ashes? Will you call this a fast, a day acceptable to the LORD? Is not this the fast that I choose: to loose the bonds of injustice, to undo the thongs of the yoke, to let the oppressed go free, and to break every yoke? Is it not to share your bread with the hungry, and bring the homeless poor into your house; when you see the naked, to cover them, and not to hide yourself from your own kin? Then your light shall break forth like the dawn, and your healing shall spring up quickly; your vindicator shall go before you, the glory of the LORD shall be your rear guard. Then you shall call, and the LORD will answer; you shall cry for help, and he will say, Here I am. If you remove the yoke from among you, the pointing of the finger, the speaking of evil, if you offer your food to the hungry and satisfy the needs of the afflicted, they your light shall rise in the darkness and your gloom be like the noonday. The LORD will guide you continually, and satisfy your needs in parched places, and make your bones strong; and you shall be like a watered garden, like a spring of water, whose waters never fail. Your ancient ruins shall be rebuilt; you shall raise up the foundations of many generations; you shall be called the repairer of the breach, the restorer of streets to live in.

The Psalm 103 or 103:8-14   *Benedic, anima mea*

1   Bless the LORD, O my soul, *
         and all that is within me, bless his holy Name.

2   Bless the LORD, O my soul, *
         and forget not all his benefits.

3   He forgives all your sins *
         and heals all your infirmities;

4   He redeems your life from the grave *
         and crowns you with mercy and loving-kindness;

5   He satisfies you with good things, *
         and your youth is renewed like an eagle's.

6 The LORD executes righteousness *
and judgment for all who are oppressed.

7 He made his ways known to Moses *
and his works to the children of Israel.

8 [The LORD is full of compassion and mercy, *
slow to anger and of great kindness.

9 He will not always accuse, us, *
Nor will he keep his anger for ever.

10 He has not dealt with us according to our sins, *
Nor rewarded us according to our wickedness.

11 For as the heavens are high above the earth, *
so is his mercy great upon those who fear him.

12 As far as the east is from the west, *
so far has he removed our sins from us.

13 As a father cares for his children, *
so does the LORD care for those who fear him.

14 For he himself knows whereof we are made; *
he remembers that we are but dust.]

15 Our days are like the grass; *
we flourish like a flower of the field;

16 When the wind goes over it, it is gone, *
and its place shall know it no more.

17 But the merciful goodness of the LORD endures for ever on those who fear him, *
and his righteousness on children's children;

18 On those who keep his covenant *
and remember his commandments and do them.

19 The LORD has set his throne in heaven, *
and his kingship has dominion over all.

20 Bless the LORD, you angels of his, you mighty ones who do his bidding, *
and hearken to the voice of his word.

21 Bless the LORD, all you his hosts, *
you ministers of his who do his will.

22 Bless the LORD, all you works of his,
in all places of his dominion; *
bless the LORD, O my soul.

The Epistle   **2 Corinthians 5:20b-6:10**

We entreat you on behalf of Christ, be reconciled to God. For our sake he made him to be sin who knew no sin, so that in him we might become the righteousness of God. As we work together with him, we urge you also not to accept the grace of God in vain. For he says, "At an acceptable time I have listened to you, and on a day of salvation I have helped you." See, now is the acceptable time; see, now is the day of salvation! We are putting no obstacle in anyone's way, so that no fault may be found with our ministry, but as servants of God we have commended ourselves in every way: through great endurance, in afflictions, hardships, calamities, beatings, imprisonments, riots, labors, sleepless nights, hunger; by purity, knowledge, patience, kindness, holiness of spirit, genuine love, truthful speech, and the power of God; with the weapons of righteousness for the right hand and for the left; in honor and dishonor, in ill repute and good repute. We are treated as impostors, and yet are true; as unknown, and yet are well known; as dying, and see — we are alive; as punished, and yet not killed; as sorrowful, yet always rejoicing; as poor, yet making many rich; as having nothing, and yet possessing everything.

The Gospel   **Matthew 6:1-6, 16-21**

Jesus said, "Beware of practicing your piety before others in order to be seen by them; for then you have no reward from your Father in heaven. So whenever you give alms, do not sound a trumpet before you, as the hypocrites do in the synagogues and in the streets, so that they may be praised by others. Truly I tell you, they have received their reward. But when you give alms, do not let your left hand know what your right hand is doing, so that your alms may be done in secret; and your Father who sees in secret will reward you. And whenever you pray, do not be like the hypocrites; for they love to stand and pray in the synagogues and at the street corners, so that they may be seen by others. Truly I tell you, they have received their reward. But whenever you pray, go into your room and shut the door and pray to your Father who is in secret; and your Father who sees in secret will reward you. And whenever you fast,do not look dismal, like the hypocrites, for they disfigure their faces so as to show others that they are fasting. Truly I tell you, they have received their reward. But when you fast, put oil on your head and wash your face, so that your fasting may be seennot by others but by your Father who is in secret; and your Fatherwho sees in secret will reward you. Do not store up for yourselves treasures on earth, where moth and rust consume and where thieves break in and steal; but store up for yourselves treasures in heaven, where neither moth nor rust consumes and where thieves do not break in and steal. For where your treasure is, there your heart will be also.

THE FIRST SUNDAY IN LENT

The Collect
Almighty God, whose blessed Son was led by the Spirit to be tempted by Satan: Come quickly to help us who are assaulted by many temptations; and, as you know the weaknesses of each of us, let each one find you mighty to save; through Jesus Christ your Son our Lord, who lives and reigns with you and the Holy Spirit, one God, now and for ever. *Amen.*

Almighty God, whose blessed Son was led by the Spirit to be tempted of Satan: Make speed to help thy servants who are assaulted by manifold temptations; and, as thou knowest their several infirmities, let each one find thee mighty to save; through Jesus Christ thy Son our Lord, who liveth and reigneth with thee and the Holy Spirit, one God, now and for ever. *Amen.*

Year A

The Lesson   **Genesis 2:4b-9, 15-17, 25-3:7**

In the day that the Lord God made the earth and the heavens, when no plant of the field was yet in the earth and no herb of the field had yet sprung up — for the Lord God had not caused it to rain upon the earth, and there was no one to till the ground; but a stream would rise from the earth, and water the whole face of the ground — then the Lord formed man from the dust of the ground, and breathed into his nostrils the breath of life; and the man became a living being. And the Lord God planted a garden in Eden, in the east; and there he put the man whom he had formed. Out of the ground the Lord God made to grow every tree that is pleasant to the sight and good for food, the tree of life also in the midst of the garden, and the tree of the knowledge of good and evil. The Lord God took the man and put him in the garden of Eden to till it and keep it. And the Lord God commanded the man, "You may freely eat of every tree of the garden; but of the tree of the knowledge of good and evil you shall not eat, for in the day that you eat of it you shall die." And the man and his wife were both naked, and were not ashamed. Now the serpent was more crafty than any other wild animal that the Lord God had made. He said to the woman, "Did God say, 'You shall not eat from any tree in the garden'?" The woman said to the serpent, "We may eat of the fruit of the trees in the garden; but God said, 'You shall not eat of the fruit of the tree that is in the middle of the garden, nor shall you touch it, or you shall die.'" But the serpent said to the woman. "You will not die; for God knows that when you eat of it your eyes will be opened, and you will be like God, knowing good and evil." So when the woman saw that the tree was good for food, and that it was a delight to the eyes, and that the tree was to be desired to make one wise, she took of its fruit and ate; and she also gave some to her husband, who was with her, and he ate. Then the eyes of both were opened, and they knew that they were naked; and they sewed fig leaves together and made loincloths for themselves.

The Psalm 51 or 51:1-13   *Miserere mei, Deus*

1   [Have mercy on me, O God, according to your loving-kindness; *
      in your great compassion blot out my offenses.

2   Wash me through and through from my wickedness *
      and cleanse me from my sin.

3   For I know my transgressions, *
      and my sin is ever before me.

4   Against you only have I sinned *
      and done what is evil in your sight.

5	And so you are justified when you speak * and upright in your judgment.
6	Indeed, I have been wicked from my birth, * a sinner from my mother's womb.
7	For behold, you look for truth deep within me, * and will make me understand wisdom secretly.
8	Purge me from my sin, and I shall be pure; * wash me, and I shall be clean indeed.
9	Make me hear of joy and gladness, * that the body you have broken may rejoice.
10	Hide your face from my sins * and blot out all my iniquities.
11	Create in me a clean heart, O God, * and renew a right spirit within me.
12	Cast me not away from your presence * and take not your holy Spirit from me.
13	Give me the joy of your saving help again * and sustain me with your bountiful Spirit.]
14	I shall teach your ways to the wicked, * and sinners shall return to you.

15	Deliver me from death, O God, *
	    and my tongue shall sing of your righteousness,
	    O God of my salvation.

16	Open my lips, O Lord, * and my mouth shall proclaim your praise.
17	Had you desired it, I would have offered sacrifice, * but you take no delight in burnt-offerings.
18	The sacrifice of God is a troubled spirit; * a broken and contrite heart, O God, you will not despise.
19	Be favorable and gracious to Zion, * and rebuild the walls of Jerusalem.
20	Then you will be pleased with the appointed sacrifices, with burnt-offerings and oblations; * then shall they offer young bullocks upon your altar.

The Epistle Romans 5:12-19 (20-21)

Therefore, just as sin came into the world through one man, and death came through sin, and so death spread to all because all have sinned — sin was indeed in the world before the law, but sin is not reckoned when there is no law. Yet death exercised dominion from Adam to Moses, even over those whose sins were not like the transgression of Adam, who is a type of the one who was to come. But the free gift is not like the trespass. For if the many died through the one man's trespass, much more surely have the grace of God and the free gift in the grace of the one man, Jesus Christ, abounded for the many. And the free gift is not like the effect of the one man's sin. For the judgment following one trespass brought condemnation, but the free gift following many trespasses brings justification. If, because of the one man's trespass, death exercised dominion through that one, much more surely will those who receive the abundance of grace and the free gift of righteousness exercise dominion in life through the one man, Jesus Christ. Therefore just as one man's trespass led to condemnation for all, so one man's act of righteousness leads to justification and life for all. For just as by the one man's disobedience the many were made sinners, so by the one man's obedience the many will be made righteous. [But law came in, with the result that the trespass multiplied; but where sin increased, grace abounded all the more, so that, just as sin exercised dominion in death, so grace might also exercise dominion through justification leading to eternal life through Jesus Christ our Lord.]

The Gospel
Matthew 4:1-11

After he was baptized by John, Jesus was led up by the Spirit into the wilderness to be tempted by the devil. He fasted forty days and forty nights, and afterwards he was famished. The tempter came and said to him, "If you are the Son of God, command these stones to become loaves of bread." But he answered, "It is written, 'One does not live by bread alone, but by every word that comes from the mouth of God.'" Then the devil took him to the holy city and placed him on the pinnacle of the temple, saying to him, "If you are the Son of God, throw yourself down; for it is written, 'He will command his angels concerning you.' and 'On their hands they will bear you up, so that you will not dash your foot against a stone.'" Jesus said to him, "Again it is written, 'Do not put the Lord your God to the test.'" Again, the devil took him to a very high mountain and showed him all the kingdoms of the world and their splendor; and he said to him, "All these I will give you, if you will fall down and worship me." Jesus said to him, "Away with you Satan! for it is written, 'Worship the Lord your God, and serve only him.'" Then the devil left him, and suddenly angels came and waited on him.

Year B

The Lesson
Genesis 9:8-17

Then God said to Noah and to his sons with him, "As for me, I am establishing my covenant with you and your descendants after you, and with every living creature that is with you, the birds, the domestic animals, and every animal of the earth with you, as many as came out of the ark. I establish my covenant with you, that never again shall all flesh be cut off by the waters of a flood, and never again shall there be a flood to destroy the earth." God said, "This is the sign of the covenant that I make between me and you and every living creature that is with you, for all future generations: I have set my bow in the clouds, and it shall be a sign of the covenant between me and the earth. When I bring clouds over the earth and the bow is seen in the clouds, I will remember my covenant that is between me and you and every living creature of all flesh; and the waters shall never again become a flood to destroy all flesh. When the bow is in the clouds, I will see it and remember the everlasting covenant between God and every living creature of all flesh that is on the earth." God said to Noah, "This is the sign of the covenant that I have established between me and all flesh that is on the earth."

The Psalm 25 or 25:3-9   *Ad te, Domine, levavi*

1   To you, O LORD, I lift up my soul;
      my God, I put my trust in you; *
         let me not be humiliated,
            nor let my enemies triumph over me.

2   Let none who look to you be put to shame; *
         let the treacherous be disappointed in their schemes.

3   [Show me your ways, O LORD, *
         and teach me your paths.

4   Lead me in your truth and teach me, *
         for you are the God of my salvation;
            in you have I trusted all the day long.

5   Remember, O LORD, your compassion and love, *
         for they are from everlasting.

6   Remember not the sins of my youth and my transgressions; *
         remember me according to your love
            and for the sake of your goodness, O LORD.

7   Gracious and upright is the LORD; *
         therefore he teaches sinners in his way.

8   He guides the humble in doing right *
         and teaches his way to the lowly.

9   All the paths of the LORD are love and faithfulness *
         to those who keep his covenant and his testimonies.]

10   For your Name's sake, O LORD, *
         forgive my sin, for it is great.

11   Who are they who fear the LORD? *
         he will teach them the way that they should choose.

12   They shall dwell in prosperity, *
         and their offspring shall inherit the land.

13   The LORD is a friend to those who fear him *
         and will show them his covenant.

14   My eyes are ever looking to the LORD, *
         for he shall pluck my feet out of the net.

15 Turn to me and have pity on me, *
   for I am left alone and in misery.

16 The sorrows of my heart have increased; *
   bring me out of my troubles.

17 Look upon my adversity and misery *
   and forgive me all my sin.

18 Look upon my enemies, for they are many, *
   and they bear a violent hatred against me.

19 Protect my life and deliver me; *
   let me not be put to shame, for I have trusted in you.

20 Let integrity and uprightness preserve me, *
   for my hope has been in you.

21 Deliver Israel, O God, *
   out of all his troubles.

The Epistle   **1 Peter 3:18-22**
For Christ also suffered for sins once for all, the righteous for the unrighteous, in
order to bring you to God. He was put to death in the flesh, but made alive in the
spirit, in which also he went and made a proclamation to the spirits in prison, who in
former times did not obey, when God waited patiently in the days of Noah, during
the building of the ark, in which a few, that is, eight persons, were saved through
water. And baptism, which this prefigured, now saves you — not as a removal of dirt
from the body, but as an appeal to God for a good conscience, through the
resurrection of Jesus Christ, who has gone into heaven and is at the right hand of
God, with angels, authorities, and powers made subject to him.

The Gospel   **Mark 1:9-13**
In those days Jesus came from Nazareth of Galilee and was baptized by John in the
Jordan. And just as he was coming up out of the water, he saw the heavens torn apart
and the Spirit descending like a dove on him. And a voice came from heaven, "You
are my Son, the Beloved; with you I am well pleased." And the Spirit immediately
drove him out into the wilderness. He was in the wilderness forty days, tempted by
Satan; and he was with the wild beasts; and the angels waited on him.

Year C
The Lesson   **Deuteronomy 26:(1-4) 5-11**
[Moses said, "When you have come into the land that the LORD your God is giving
you as an inheritance to possess, and you possess it, and settle in it, you shall take
some of the first of all the fruit of the ground, which you harvest from the land that
the LORD your God is giving you, and you shall put it in a basket and go to the place
that the LORD your God will choose as a dwelling for his name. You shall go to the
priest who is in office at that time, and say to him, "Today I declare to the LORD your
God that I have come into the land that the LORD swore to our ancestors to give us."

When the priest takes the basket from your hand and sets it down before the altar of the LORD your God,] you shall make this response before the LORD your God: "A wandering Aramean was my ancestor; he went down into Egypt and lived there as an alien, few in number, and there he became a great nation, mighty and populous. When the Egyptians treated us harshly and afflicted us, by imposing hard labor on us, we cried to the LORD, the God of our ancestors; the LORD heard our voice and saw our affliction, our toil, and our oppression. The LORD brought us out of Egypt with a mighty hand and an outstretched arm, with a terrifying display of power, and with signs and wonders; and he brought us into this place and gave us this land, a land flowing with milk and honey. So now I bring the first of the fruit of the ground that you, O LORD, have given me." You shall set it down before the LORD your God and bow down before the LORD your God. Then you, together with the Levites and the aliens who reside among you, shall celebrate with all the bounty that the LORD your God has given to you and to your house."

The Psalm 91 or 91:9-15   *Qui habitat*

1   He who dwells in the shelter of the Most High, *
        abides under the shadow of the Almighty.

2   He shall say to the LORD,
        "You are my refuge and my stronghold, *
        my God in whom I put my trust."

3   He shall deliver you from the snare of the hunter *
        and from the deadly pestilence.

4   He shall cover you with his pinions,
        and you shall find refuge under his wings; *
        his faithfulness shall be a shield and buckler.

5   You shall not be afraid of any terror by night, *
        nor of the arrow that flies by day;

6   Of the plague that stalks in the darkness, *
        nor of the sickness that lays waste at mid-day.

7   A thousand shall fall at your side
        and ten thousand at your right hand, *
        but it shall not come near you.

8   Your eyes have only to behold *
        to see the reward of the wicked.

9   [Because you have made the LORD your refuge, *
        and the Most High your habitation,

10   There shall no evil happen to you, *
        neither shall any plague come near your dwelling.

11   For he shall give his angels charge over you, *
        to keep you in all your ways.

12 They shall bear you in their hands, *
        lest you dash your foot against a stone.

13 You shall tread upon the lion and adder; *
        you shall trample the young lion and the serpent under your feet.

14 Because he is bound to me in love,
    therefore will I deliver him; *
        I will protect him, because he knows my Name.

15 He shall call upon me, and I will answer him; *
        I am with him in trouble;
        I will rescue him and bring him to honor.]

16 With long life will I satisfy him, *
        and show him my salvation.

The Epistle   Romans 10:(5-8a) 8b-13

[Moses writes concerning the righteousness that comes from the law, that "the person who does these things will live by them." But the righteousness that comes from faith says, "Do not say in your heart, 'Who will ascend into heaven?'" (that is, to bring Christ down) "or 'Who will descend into the abyss?'" (that is, to bring Christ up from the dead). But what does it say?] "The word is near you, on your lips and in your heart" (that is, the word of faith that we proclaim); because if you confess with your lips that Jesus is Lord and believe in your heart that God raised him from the dead, you will be saved. For one believes with the heart and so is justified, and one confesses with the mouth and so is saved. The scripture says, "No one who believes in him will be put to shame." For there is no distinction between Jew and Greek; the same Lord is Lord of all and is generous to all who call on him. For, "Everyone who calls on the name of the Lord shall be saved."

The Gospel   Luke 4:1-13

After his baptism, Jesus, full of the Holy Spirit, returned from the Jordan and was led by the Spirit in the wilderness, where for forty days he was tempted by the devil. He ate nothing at all during those days, and when they were over, he was famished. The devil said to him, "If you are the Son of God, command this stone to become a loaf of bread." Jesus answered him, "It is written, 'One does not live by bread alone.'" Then the devil led him up and showed him in an instant all the kingdoms of the world. And the devil said to him, "To you I will give their glory and all this authority; for it has been given over to me, and I give it to anyone I please. If you, then, will worship me, it will all be yours." Jesus answered him, "It is written, 'Worship the Lord your God, and serve only him.'" Then the devil took him to Jerusalem, and placed him on the pinnacle of the temple, saying to him, "If you are the Son of God, throw yourself down from here, for it is written, 'He will command his angels concerning you, to protect you,' and 'On their hands they will bear you up, so that you will not dash your foot against a stone.'" Jesus answered him, "It is said, 'Do not put the Lord your God to the test.'" When the devil had finished every test, he departed from him until an opportune time.

THE SECOND SUNDAY IN LENT

The Collect

O God, whose glory it is always to have mercy: Be gracious to all who have gone astray from your ways, and bring them again with penitent hearts and steadfast faith to embrace and hold fast the unchangeable truth of your Word, Jesus Christ your Son; who with you and the Holy Spirit lives and reigns, one God, for ever and ever. *Amen.*

O God, whose glory it is always to have mercy: Be gracious to all who have gone astray from thy ways, and bring them again with penitent hearts and steadfast faith to embrace and hold fast the unchangeable truth of your Word, Jesus Christ your Son; who with you and the Holy Spirit liveth and reigneth, one God, for ever and ever. *Amen.*

Year A

The Lesson   **Genesis 12:1-8**

Now the LORD said to Abram, "Go from your country and your kindred and your father's house to the land that I will show you. I will make of you a great nation, and I will bless you, and make your name great, so that you will be a blessing. I will bless those who bless you, and the one who curses you I will curse; and in you all the families of the earth shall be blessed." So Abram went, as the LORD had told him; and Lot went with him. Abram was seventy-five years old when he departed from Haran. Abram took his wife Sarai and his brother's son Lot, and all the possessions that they had gathered, and the persons whom they had acquired in Haran; and they set forth to go to the land of Canaan. When they had come to the land of Canaan, Abram passed through the land to the place at Shechem, to the oak of Moreh. At that time the Canaanites were in the land. Then the LORD appeared to Abram, and said, "To your offspring I will give this land." So he built there an altar to the LORD, who had appeared to him. From there he moved on to the hill country on the east of Bethel, and pitched his tent, with Bethel on the west and Ai on the east; and there he built an altar to the LORD and invoked the name of the LORD.

The Psalm 33:12-22   *Exultate, justi*

12   Happy is the nation whose God is the LORD! *
         happy the people he has chosen to be his own!

13   The LORD looks down from heaven, *
         and beholds all the people in the world.

14   From where he sits enthroned he turns his gaze *
         on all who dwell on the earth.

15   He fashions all the hearts of them *
         and understands all their works.

16   There is no king that can be saved by a mighty army; *
         a strong man is not delivered by his great strength.

17   The horse is a vain hope for deliverance; *
      for all its strength it cannot save.

18   Behold, the eye of the LORD is upon those who fear him, *
      on those who wait upon his love,

19   To pluck their lives from death, *
      and to feed them in time of famine.

20   Our soul waits for the LORD; *
      he is our help and our shield.

21   Indeed, our heart rejoices in him, *
      for in his holy Name we put our trust.

22   Let your loving-kindness, O LORD, be upon us, *
      as we have put our trust in you.

The Epistle   **Romans 4:1-5 (6-12), 13-17**

What then are we to say was gained by Abraham, our ancestor according to the flesh?
For if Abraham was justified by works, he has something to boast about, but not
before God. For what does the scripture say? "Abraham believed God, and it was
reckoned to him as righteousness." Now to one who works, wages are not reckoned as
a gift but as something due. But to one who without works trusts him who justifies
the ungodly, such faith is reckoned as righteousness. [So also David speaks of the
blessedness of those to whom God reckons righteousness apart from works: "Blessed
are those whose iniquities are forgiven, and whose sins are covered; blessed is the one
against whom the Lord will not reckon sin." Is this blessedness, then, pronounced
only on the circumcised, or also on the uncircumcised? We say, "Faith was reckoned
to Abraham as righteousness." How then was it reckoned to him? Was it before or
after he had been circumcised? It was not after, but before he was circumcised. He
received the sign of circumcision as a seal of the righteousness that he had by faith
while he was still uncircumcised. The purpose was to make him the ancestor of all
who believe without being circumcised and who thus have righteousness reckoned to
them, and likewise the ancestor of the circumcised who are not only circumcised but
who also follow the example of the faith that our ancestor Abraham had before he
was circumcised.] For the promise that he would inherit the world did not come to
Abraham or to his descendants through the law but through the righteousness of
faith. If it is the adherents of the law who are to be the heirs, faith is null and the
promise is void. For the law brings wrath; but where there is no law, neither is there
violation. For this reason it depends on faith, in order that the promise may rest on
grace and be guaranteed to all his descendants, not only to the adherents of the law
but also to those who share the faith of Abraham (for he is the father of all of us, as it
is written, "I have made you the father of many nations") — in the presence of the
God in whom he believed, who gives life to the dead and calls into existence the
things that do not exist.

The Gospel   **John 3:1-17**

Now there was a Pharisee named Nicodemus, a leader of the Jews. He came to Jesus by night and said to him, "Rabbi, we know that you are a teacher who has come from God; for no one can do these signs that you do apart from the presence of God." Jesus answered him, "Very truly, I tell you, no one can see the kingdom of God without being born from above." Nicodemus said to him, "How can anyone be born after having grown old? Can one enter a second time into the mother's womb and be born?" Jesus answered, "Very truly, I tell you, no one can enter the kingdom of God without being born of water and Spirit. What is born of the flesh is flesh, and what is born of the Spirit is spirit. Do not be astonished that I said to you 'You must be born from above.' The wind blows where it chooses, and you hear the sound of it, but you do not know where it comes from or where it goes. So it is with everyone who is born of the Spirit." Nicodemus said to him, "How can these things be?" Jesus answered him, "Are you a teacher of Israel, and yet you do not understand these things? Very truly, I tell you, we speak of what we know and testify to what we have seen; yet you do not receive our testimony. If I have told you about earthly things and you do not believe, how can you believe if I tell you about heavenly things? No one has ascended into heaven except the one who descended from heaven, the Son of Man. And just as Moses lifted up the serpent in the wilderness, so must the Son of Man be lifted up, that whoever believes in him may have eternal life. For God so loved the world that he gave his only Son, so that everyone who believes in him may not perish but may have eternal life. Indeed, God did not send the Son into the world to condemn the world, but in order that the world might be saved through him."

Year B

The Lesson   **Genesis 22:1-14**

After these things God tested Abraham. He said to him, "Abraham!" And he said, "Here I am." He said, "Take your son, your only son Isaac, whom you love, and go to the land of Moriah, and offer him there as a burnt offering on one of the mountains that I shall show you." So Abraham rose early in the morning, saddled his donkey, and took two of his young men with him, and his son Isaac; he cut the wood for the burnt offering, and set out and went to the place in the distance that God had shown him. On the third day Abraham looked up and saw the place far away. Then Abraham said to his young men, "Stay here with the donkey; the boy and I will go over there; we will worship, and then we will come back to you." Abraham took the wood of the burnt offering and laid it on his son Isaac, and he himself carried the fire and the knife. So the two of them walked on together. Isaac said to his father Abraham, "Father!" And he said, "Here I am, my son." He said, "The fire and the wood are here, but where is the lamb for a burnt offering?" Abraham said, "God himself will provide the lamb for a burnt offering, my son." So the two of them walked on together. When they came to the place that God had shown him, Abraham built an altar there and laid the wood in order. He bound his son Isaac, and laid him on the altar, on top of the wood. Then Abraham reached out his hand and took the knife to kill his son. But the angel of the LORD called to him from heaven, and said, "Abraham, Abraham!" And he said, "Here I am." He said, "Do not lay your hand on the boy or do anything to him; for now I know that you fear God, since you have not withheld your son, your only son, from me." And Abraham looked up and saw a ram, caught in a thicket by its horns. Abraham went and took the ram and offered it up as a burnt offering instead of his son. So Abraham called that place "The LORD will provide"; as it is said t this day, "On the mount of the LORD it shall be provided."

The Psalm 16 or 16:5-11   *Conserva me, Domine*

1   Protect me, O God, for I take refuge in you; *
    I have said to the LORD, "Your are my Lord,
    My good above all other."

2   All my delight is upon the godly that are in the land, *
    upon those who are noble among the people.

3   But those who run after other gods *
    shall have their troubles multiplied.

4   Their libations of blood I will not offer, *
    nor take the names of their gods upon my lips.

5   [O LORD, you are my portion and my cup; *
    it is you who uphold my lot.

6   My boundaries enclose a pleasant land; *
    indeed, I have a goodly heritage.

7   I will bless the LORD who gives me counsel; *
    my heart teaches me, night after night.

8   I have set the LORD always before me; *
    because he is at my right hand I shall not fall.

9   My heart, therefore, is glad, and my spirit rejoices; *
    my body also shall rest in hope.

10   For you will not abandon me to the grave, *
    nor let your holy one see the Pit.

11   You will show me the path of life; *
    in your presence there is fullness of joy,
    and in your right hand are pleasures for evermore.]

The Epistle   **Romans 8:31-39**

What then are we to say about these things? If God is for us, who is against us? He who did not withhold his own Son, but gave him up for all of us, will he not with him also give us everything else? Who will bring any charge against God's elect? It is God who justifies. Who is to condemn? It is Christ Jesus, who died, yes, who was raised, who is at the right hand of God, who indeed intercedes for us. Who will separate us from the love of Christ? Will hardship, or distress, or persecution, or famine, or nakedness, or peril, or sword? As it is written, "For your sake we are being killed all day long; we are accounted as sheep to be slaughtered." No, in all these things we are more than conquerors through him who loved us. For I am convinced that neither death, nor life, nor angels, nor rulers, nor things present, nor things to come, nor powers, nor height, nor depth, nor anything else in all creation, will be able to separate us from the love of God in Christ Jesus our Lord.

The Gospel   **Mark 8:31-38**

Jesus began to teach them that the Son of Man must undergo great suffering, and be rejected by the elders, the chief priests, and the scribes, and be killed, and after three days rise again. He said all this quite openly. And Peter took him aside and began to rebuke him. But turning and looking at his disciples, he rebuked Peter and said, "Get behind me, Satan! For you are setting your mind not on divine things but on human things." He called the crowd with his disciples, and said to them, "If any want to become my followers, let them deny themselves and take up their cross and follow me. For those who want to save their life will lose it, and those who lose their life for my sake, and for the sake of the gospel, will save it. For what will it profit them to gain the whole world and forfeit their life? Indeed, what can they give in return for their life? Those who are ashamed of me and of my words in this adulterous and sinful generation, of them the Son of Man will also be ashamed when he comes in the glory of his Father with the holy angels."

Year C

The Lesson   **Genesis 15:1-12, 17-18**

After these things the word of the LORD came to Abram in a vision, "Do not be afraid, Abram, I am your shield; your reward shall be very great." But Abram said, "O Lord GOD, what will you give me, for I continue childless, and the heir of my house is Eliezer of Damascus?" And Abram said, "You have given me no offspring, and so a slave born in my house is to be my heir." But the word of the LORD came to him, "This man shall not be your heir; no one but your very own issue shall be your heir." He brought him outside and said, "Look toward heaven and count the stars, if you are able to count them." Then he said to him, "So shall your descendants be." And he believed the LORD; and the LORD reckoned it to him as righteousness. Then he said to him, "I am the LORD who brought you from Ur of the Chaldeans, to give you this land to possess." But he said, "O Lord GOD, how am I to know that I shall possess it?" He said to him, "Bring me a heifer three years old, a female goat three years old, a ram three years old, a turtledove, and a young pigeon." He brought him all these and cut them in two, laying each half over against the other; but he did not cut the birds in two. And when birds of prey came down on the carcasses, Abram drove them away. As the sun was going down, a deep sleep fell upon Abram, and a deep and terrifying darkness descended upon him. When the sun had gone down and it was dark, a smoking fire pot and a flaming torch passed between these pieces. On that day the LORD made a covenant with Abram, saying, "To your descendants I give this land, from the river of Egypt to the great river, the river Euphrates."

The Psalm 27 or 27:10-18   *Dominus illuminatio*

1   The LORD is my light and my salvation;
       whom then shall I fear? *
           the LORD is the strength of my life;
           of whom then shall I be afraid?

2   When evildoers came upon me to eat up my flesh, *
           it was they, my foes and my adversaries, who stumbled and fell.

3   Though an army should encamp against me, *
       yet my heart shall not be afraid;

4   And though war should rise up against me, *
       yet will I put my trust in him.

5   One thing have I asked of the LORD;
one thing I seek; *
       that I may dwell in the house of the LORD all the days of my life;

6   To behold the fair beauty of the LORD *
       and to seek him in his temple.

7   For in the day of trouble he shall keep me safe in his shelter; *
       he shall hide me in the secrecy of his dwelling
       and set me high upon a rock.

8   Even now he lifts up my head *
       above my enemies round about me.

9   Therefore I will offer in his dwelling an oblation
with sounds of great gladness; *
       I will sing and make music to the LORD.

10   [Hearken to my voice, O LORD, when I call; *
       have mercy on me and answer me.

11   You speak in my heart and say, "Seek my face." *
       Your face, LORD, will I seek.

12   Hide not your face from me, *
       nor turn away your servant in displeasure.

13   You have been my helper;
cast me not away; *
       do not forsake me, O God of my salvation.

14   Though my father and my mother forsake me, *
       the LORD will sustain me.

15   Show me your way, O LORD; *
       lead me on a level path, because of my enemies.

16   Deliver me not into the hand of my adversaries, *
       for false witnesses have risen up against me,
       and also those who speak malice.

17   What if I had not believed
that I should see the goodness of the LORD *
       in the land of the living!

18   O tarry and await the LORD's pleasure;
be strong, and he shall comfort your heart; *
       wait patiently for the LORD.]

The Epistle   **Philippians 3:17–4:1**

Brothers and sisters, join in imitating me, and observe those who live according to the example you have in us. For many live as enemies of the cross of Christ; I have often told you of them, and now I tell you even with tears. Their end is destruction; their god is the belly; and their glory is in their shame; their minds are set on earthly things. But our citizenship is in heaven, and it is from there that we are expecting a Savior, the Lord Jesus Christ. He will transform the body of our humiliation that it may be conformed to the body of his glory, by the power that also enables him to make all things subject to himself. Therefore, my brothers and sisters, whom I love and long for, my joy and crown, stand firm in the Lord in this way, my beloved.

The Gospel   **Luke 13:(22–30) 31–35**

[Jesus went through one town and village after another, teaching as he made his way to Jerusalem. Someone asked him, "Lord, will only a few be saved?" He said to them, "Strive to enter through the narrow door; for many, I tell you, will try to enter and will not be able. When once the owner of the house has got up and shut the door, and you begin to stand outside and to knock at the door, saying, 'Lord, open to us,' then in reply he will say to you, 'I do not know where you come from.' Then you will begin to say, 'We ate and drank with you, and you taught in our streets.' But he will say, 'I do not know where you come from; go away from me, all you evildoers!' There will be weeping and gnashing of teeth when you see Abraham and Isaac and Jacob and all the prophets in the kingdom of God, and you yourselves thrown out. Then people will come from east and west, from north and south, and will eat in the kingdom of God. Indeed, some are last who will be first, and some are first who will be last."] At that very hour some Pharisees came and said to him, "Get away from here, for Herod wants to kill you." He said to them, "Go and tell that fox for me, 'Listen, I am casting out demons and performing cures today and tomorrow, and on the third day I finish my work. Yet today, tomorrow, and the next day I must be on my way, because it is impossible for a prophet to be killed outside of Jerusalem.' Jerusalem, Jerusalem, the city that kills the prophets and stones those who are sent to it! How often have I desired to gather your children together as a hen gathers her brood under her wings, and you were not willing! See, your house is left to you. And I tell you, you will not see me until the time comes when you say, 'Blessed is the one who comes in the name of the Lord.'"

THE THIRD SUNDAY IN LENT

The Collect

Almighty God, you know that we have no power in ourselves to help ourselves: Keep us both outwardly in our bodies and inwardly in our souls, that we may be defended from all adversities which may happen to the body, and from all evil thoughts which may assault and hurt the soul; through Jesus Christ our Lord, who lives and reigns with you and the Holy Spirit, one God, for ever and ever. *Amen.*

Almighty God, who seest that we have no power of ourselves to help ourselves: Keep us both outwardly in our bodies and inwardly in our souls, that we may be defended from all adversities which may happen to the body, and from all evil thoughts which may

assault and hurt the soul; through Jesus Christ our Lord, who liveth and reigneth with thee and the Holy Spirit, one God, for ever and ever. *Amen.*

Year A

The Lesson Exodus 17:1-7

From the wilderness of Sin the whole congregation of the Israelites journeyed by stages, as the LORD commanded. They camped at Rephidim, but there was no water for the people to drink. The people quarreled with Moses, and said, "Give us water to drink." Moses said to them, "Why do your quarrel with me? Why do you test the LORD?" But the people thirsted there for water; and the people complained against Moses and said, "Why did you bring us out of Egypt, to kill us and our children and livestock with thirst?" So Moses cried out to the LORD, "What shall I do with this people? They are almost ready to stone me." The LORD said to Moses, "Go on ahead of the people, and take some of the elders of Israel with you; take in your hand the staff with which you struck the Nile, and go. I will be standing there in front of you on the rock at Horeb. Strike the rock, and water will come out of it, so that the people may drink." Moses did so, in the sight of the elders of Israel. He called the place Massah and Meribah, because the Israelites quarreled and tested the LORD, saying, "Is the LORD among us or not?"

The Psalm 95 or 95:6-11   *Venite, exultemus*

1   Come, let us sing to the LORD; *
     let us shout for joy to the Rock of our salvation.

2   Let us come before his presence with thanksgiving *
     and raise a loud shout to him with psalms.

3   For the LORD is a great God, *
     and a great King above all gods.

4   In his hand are the caverns of the earth, *
     and the heights of the hills are his also.

5   The sea is his, for he made it, *
     and his hands have molded the dry land.

6   [Come, let us bow down, and bend the knee, *
     and kneel before the LORD our Maker.

7   For he is our God,
     and we are the people of his pasture and the sheep of his hand. *
       Oh, that today you would hearken to his voice!

8   Harden not your hearts,
     as your forebears did in the wilderness, *
       at Meribah, and on that day at Massah,
       when they tempted me.

9   They put me to the test, *
     though they had seen my works.

10   Forty years long I detested that generation and said, *
         "This people are wayward in their hearts;
         they do not know my ways."

11   So I swore in my wrath, *
         "They shall not enter into my rest."]

The Epistle   **Romans 5:1-11**

Since we are justified by faith, we have peace with God through our Lord Jesus
Christ, through whom we have obtained access to this grace in which we stand; and
we boast in our hope of sharing the glory of God. And not only that, but we also
boast in our sufferings, knowing that suffering produces endurance, and endurance
produces character, and character produces hope, and hope does not disappoint us,
because God's love has been poured into our hearts through the Holy Spirit that has
been given to us. For while we were still weak, at the right time Christ died for the
ungodly. Indeed, rarely will anyone die for a righteous person — though perhaps for
a good person someone might actually dare to die. But God proves his love for us in
that while we still were sinners Christ died for us. Much more surely then, now that
we have been justified by his blood, will we be saved through him from the wrath of
God. For if while we were enemies, we were reconciled to God through the death of
his Son, much more surely, having been reconciled, will we be saved by his life. But
more than that, we even boast in God through our Lord Jesus Christ, through whom
we have now received reconciliation.

The Gospel   **John 4:5-26 (27-38) 39-42**

Jesus came to a Samaritan city called Sychar, near the plot of ground that Jacob had
given to his son Joseph. Jacob's well was there, and Jesus, tired out by his journey,
was sitting by the well. It was about noon. A Samaritan woman came to draw water,
and Jesus said to her, "Give me a drink." (His disciples had gone to the city to buy
food.) The Samaritan woman said to him, "How is it that you, a Jew, ask a drink of
me, a woman of Samaria?" (Jews do not share things in common with Samaritans.)
Jesus answered her, "If you knew the gift of God, and who it is that is saying to you,
'Give me a drink,' you would have asked him, and he would have given you living
water." The woman said to him, "Sir, you have no bucket, and the well is deep.
Where do you get that living water? Are you greater than our ancestor Jacob, who
gave us the well, and with his sons and his flock drank from it?" Jesus said to her,
"Everyone who drinks of this water will be thirsty again, but those who drink of the
water that I will give them will never be thirsty. The water that I will give will become
in them a spring of water gushing up to eternal life." The woman said to him, "Sir,
give me this water, so that I may never be thirsty or have to keep coming here to draw
water." Jesus said to her, "Go, call your husband, and come back." The woman
answered him, "I have no husband." Jesus said to her, "You are right in saying, 'I
have no husband'; for you have had five husbands, and the one you have now is not
your husband. What you have said is true!" The woman said to him, "Sir, I see that
you are a prophet. Our ancestors worshiped on this mountain, but you say that the
place where people must worship is in Jerusalem." Jesus said to her, "Woman,
believe me, the hour is coming when you will worship the Father neither on this

mountain nor in Jerusalem. You worship what you do not know; we worship what we know, for salvation is from the Jews. But the hour is coming, and is now here, when the true worshipers will worship the Father in spirit and truth, for the Father seeks such as these to worship him. God is spirit, and those who worship him must worship in spirit and truth." The woman said to him, "I know that Messiah is coming" (who is called Christ). "When he comes, he will proclaim all things to us." Jesus said to her, "I am he, the one who is speaking to you." [Just then his disciples came. They were astonished that he was speaking with a woman, but no one said, "What do you want?" or, "Why are you speaking with her?" Then the woman left her water jar and went back to the city. She said to the people, "Come and see a man who told me everything I have ever done! He cannot be the Messiah, can he?" They left the city and were on their way to him. Meanwhile the disciples were urging him, "Rabbi, eat something." But he said to them, "I have food to eat that you do not know about." So the disciples said to one another, "Surely no one has brought him something to eat?" Jesus said to them, "My food is to do the will of him who sent me and to complete his work. Do you not say, 'Four months more, then comes the harvest'? But I tell you, look around you, and see how the fields are ripe for harvesting. The reaper is already receiving wages and is gathering fruit for eternal life, so that sower and reaper may rejoice together. For here the saying holds true, 'One sows and another reaps.' I sent you to reap that for which you did not labor. Others have labored, and you have entered into their labor."] Many Samaritans from that city believed in him because of the woman's testimony, "He told me everything I have ever done." So when the Samaritans came to him, they asked him to stay with them; and he stayed there two days. And many more believed because of his word. They said to the woman, "It is no longer because of what you said that we believe, for we have heard for ourselves, and we know that this is truly the Savior of the world."

Year B

The Lesson   **Exodus 20:1-17**

Then God spoke all these words: I am the LORD your God, who brought you out of the land of Egypt, out of the house of slavery; you shall have no other gods before me. You shall not make for yourself an idol, whether in the form of anything that is in heaven above, or that is on the earth beneath, or that is in the water under the earth. You shall not bow down to them or worship them; for I the LORD your God am a jealous God, punishing children for the iniquity of parents, to the third and the fourth generation of those who reject me, but showing steadfast love to the thousandth generation of those who love me and keep my commandments. You shall not make wrongful use of the name of the LORD your God, for the LORD will not acquit anyone who misuses his name. Remember the sabbath day, and keep it holy. Six days you shall labor and do all your work. But the seventh day is a sabbath to the LORD your God; you shall not do any work — you, your son or your daughter, your male or female slave, your livestock, or the alien resident in your towns. For in six days the LORD made heaven and earth, the sea, and all that is in them, but rested the seventh day; therefore the LORD blessed the sabbath day and consecrated it. Honor your father and your mother, so that your days may be long in the land that the LORD your God is giving you. You shall not murder. You shall not commit adultery.

You shall not steal. You shall not bear false witness against your neighbor. You shall not covet your neighbor's house; you shall not covet your neighbor's wife, or male or female slave, or ox, or donkey, or anything that belongs to your neighbor.

The Psalm 19:7-14   *Coeli enarrant*

7   The law of the LORD is perfect and revives the soul; *
        the testimony of the LORD is sure and give wisdom to the innocent.

8   The statutes of the LORD are just and rejoice the heart; *
        the commandment of the LORD is clear and gives light to theeyes.

9   The fear of the LORD is clean and endures for ever; *
        the judgments of the LORD are true and righteous altogether.

10   More to be desired are they than gold, more than much fine gold, *
        sweeter far than honey, than honey in the comb.

11   By them also is your servant enlightened, *
        and in keeping them there is great reward.

12   Who can tell how often he offends? *
        cleanse me from my secret faults.

13   Above all, keep your servant from presumptuous sins;
        let them not get dominion over me; *
            then shall I be whole and sound,
            and innocent of a great offense.

14   Let the words of my mouth and the meditation of my
        heart be acceptable in your sight, *
            O LORD, my strength and my redeemer.

The Epistle   **Romans 7:13-25**

Did what is good, then, bring death to me? By no means! It was sin, working death in me through what is good, in order that sin might be shown to be sin, and through the commandment might become sinful beyond measure. For we know that the law is spiritual; but I am of the flesh, sold into slavery under sin. I do not understand my own actions. For I do not do what I want, but I do the very thing I hate. Now if I do what I do not want, I agree that the law good. But in fact it is no longer I that do it, but sin that dwells within me. For I know that nothing good dwells within me, that is, in my flesh. I can will what is right, but I cannot do it. For I do not do the good I want, but the evil I do not want is what I do. Now if I do what I do not want, it is no longer I that do it, but sin that dwells within me. So I find it to be a law that when I want to do what is good, evil lies close at hand. For I delight in the law of God in my inmost self, but I see in my members another law at war with the law of my mind, making me captive to the law of sin that dwells in my members. Wretched man that I am! Who will rescue me from this body of death? Thanks be to God through Jesus Christ our Lord! So then, with my mind I am a slave to the law of God, but with my flesh I am a slave to the law of sin.

The Gospel   John 2:13-22

The Passover of the Jews was near, and Jesus went up to Jerusalem. In the temple he found people selling cattle, sheep, and doves, and the money changers seated at their tables. Making a whip of cords, he drove all of them out of the temple, both the sheep and the cattle. He also poured out the coins of the money changers and overturned their tables. He told those who were selling the doves, "Take these things out of here! Stop making my Father's house a marketplace!" His disciples remembered that it was written, "Zeal for your house will consume me." The Jews then said to him, "What sign can you show us for doing this?" Jesus answered them, "Destroy this temple, and in three days I will raise it up." The Jews then said, "This temple has been under construction for forty-six years, and will you raise it up in three days?" But he was speaking of the temple of his body. After he was raised from the dead, his disciples remembered that he had said this; and they believed the scripture and the word that Jesus had spoken.

Year C

The Lesson   Exodus 3:1-15

Moses was keeping the flock of his father-in-law Jethro, the priest of Midian; he led his flock beyond the wilderness, and came to Horeb, the mountain of God. There the angel of the LORD appeared to him in a flame of fire out of a bush; he looked, and the bush was blazing, yet it was not consumed. Then Moses said, "I must turn aside and look at this great sight, and see why the bush is not burned up." When the LORD saw that he had turned aside to see, God called to him out of the bush, "Moses, Moses!" And he said, "Here I am." Then he said, "Come no closer! Remove the sandals from your feet, for the place on which you are standing is holy ground." He said further, "I am the God of your father, the God of Abraham, the God of Isaac, and the God of Jacob." And Moses hid his face, for he was afraid to look at God. Then the LORD said, "I have observed the misery of my people who are in Egypt; I have heard their cry on account of their taskmasters. Indeed, I know their sufferings, and I have come down to deliver them from the Egyptians, and to bring them up out of that land to a good and broad land, a land flowing with milk and honey, to the country of the Canaanites, the Hittites, the Amorites, the Perizzites, the Hivites, and the Jebusites. The cry of the Israelites has now come to me; I have also seen how the Egyptians oppress them. So come, I will send you to Pharaoh to bring my people, the Israelites, out of Egypt." But Moses said to God, "Who am I that I should go to Pharaoh, and bring the Israelites out of Egypt?" He said, "I will be with you; and this shall be the sign for you that it is I who sent you: when you have brought the people out of Egypt, you shall worship God on this mountain." But Moses said to God, "If I come to the Israelites and say to them, 'The God of your ancestors has sent me to you,' and they ask me, 'What is his name?' what shall I say to them?" God said to Moses, "I AM WHO I AM." He said further, "Thus you shall say to the Israelites, 'I AM has sent me to you.'" God also said to Moses, "Thus you shall say to the Israelites, 'The LORD, the God of your ancestors, the God of Abraham, the God of Isaac, and the God of Jacob, has sent me to you': This is my name forever, and this my title for all generations."

The Psalm 103 or 103:1-11   *Benedic, anima mea*

1   [Bless the LORD, O my soul, *
         and all that is within me, bless his holy Name.

2   Bless the LORD, O my soul, *
         and forget not all his benefits.

3   He forgives all your sins *
         and heals all your infirmities;

4   He redeems your life from the grave *
         and crowns you with mercy and loving-kindness;

5   He satisfies you with good things, *
         and your youth is renewed like an eagle's.

6   The LORD executes righteousness *
         and judgment for all who are oppressed.

7   He made his ways known to Moses *
         and his works to the children of Israel.

8   The LORD is full of compassion and mercy, *
         slow to anger and of great kindness.

9   He will not always accuse us, *
         nor will he keep his anger for ever.

10 He has not dealt with us according to our sins, *
         nor rewarded us according to our wickedness.

11 For as the heavens are high above the earth, *
         so is his mercy great upon those who fear him.]

12 As far as the east is from the west, *
         so far has he removed our sins from us.

13 As a father cares for his children, *
         so does the LORD care for those who fear him.

14 For he himself knows whereof we are made; *
         he remembers that we are but dust.

15 Our days are like the grass; *
         we flourish like a flower of the field;

16 When the wind goes over it, it is gone, *
         and its place shall know it no more.

17 But the merciful goodness of the LORD endures for ever
    on those who fear him, *
         and his righteousness on children's children;

18 On those who keep his covenant *
         and remember his commandments and do them.

19   The LORD has set his throne in heaven, *
      and his kingship has dominion over all.

20   Bless the LORD, you angels of his,
      you mighty ones who do his bidding, *
      and hearken to the voice of his word.

21   Bless the LORD, all you his hosts, *
      you ministers of his who do his will.

22   Bless the LORD, all you works of his,
      in all places of his dominion; *
      bless the LORD, O my soul.

The Epistle   **1 Corinthians 10:1-13**

I do not want you to be unaware, brothers and sisters, that our ancestors were all under the cloud, and all passed through the sea, and all were baptized into Moses in the cloud and in the sea, and all ate the same spiritual food, and all drank the same spiritual drink. For they drank from the spiritual rock that followed them, and the rock was Christ. Nevertheless, God was not pleased with most of them, and they were struck down in the wilderness. Now these things occurred as examples for us, so that we might not desire evil as they did. Do not become idolaters as some of them did; as it is written, "The people sat down to eat and drink, and they rose up to play." We must not indulge in sexual immorality as some of them did, and twenty-three thousand fell in a single day. We must not put Christ to the test, as some of them did, and were destroyed by serpents. And do not complain as some of them did, and were destroyed by the destroyer. These things happened to them to serve as an example, and they were written down to instruct us, on whom the ends of the ages have come. So if you think you are standing, watch out that you do not fall. No testing has overtaken you that is not common to everyone. God is faithful, and he will not let you be tested beyond your strength, but with the testing he will also provide the way out so that you may be able to endure it.

The Gospel   **Luke 13:1-9**

At that very time there were some present who told Jesus about the Galileans whose blood Pilate had mingled with their sacrifices. He asked them, "Do you think that because these Galileans suffered in this way they were worse sinners than all other Galileans? No, I tell you; but unless you repent, you will all perish as they did. Or those eighteen who were killed when the tower of Siloam fell on them — do you think that they were worse offenders than all the others living in Jerusalem? No, I tell you; but unless you repent, you will all perish just as they did." Then he told this parable: "A man had a fig tree planted in his vineyard; and he came looking for fruit on it and found none. So he said to the gardener, 'See here! For three years I have come looking for fruit on this fig tree, and still I find none. Cut it down! Why should it be wasting the soil?' He replied, 'Sir, let it alone for one more year, until I dig around it and put manure on it. If it bears fruit next year, well and good; but if not, you can cut it down.'"

THE FOURTH SUNDAY IN LENT

The Collect

Gracious Father, whose blessed Son Jesus Christ came down from heaven to be the true bread which gives life to the world: Evermore give us this bread, that he may live in us, and we in him; who lives and reigns with you and the Holy Spirit, one God, now and for ever. *Amen.*

Gracious Father, whose blessed Son Jesus Christ came down from heaven to be the true bread, which giveth life to the world: Evermore give us this bread, that he may live in us, and we in him; who liveth and reigneth with thee and the Holy Spirit, one God, now and for ever. *Amen.*

Year A

The Lesson   **1 Samuel 16:1-13**

The LORD said to Samuel, "How long will you grieve over Saul? I have rejected him from being king over Israel. Fill your horn with oil and set out; I will send you to Jesse the Bethlehemite, for I have provided for myself a king among his sons." Samuel said, "How can I go? If Saul hears of it, he will kill me." And the LORD said, "Take a heifer with you, and say, 'I have come to sacrifice to the LORD.' Invite Jesse to the sacrifice, and I will show you what you shall do; and you shall anoint for me the one whom I name to you." Samuel did what the LORD commanded, and came to Bethlehem. The elders of the city came to meet him trembling, and said, "Do you come peaceably?" He said, "Peaceably; I have come to sacrifice to the LORD; sanctify yourselves and come with me to the sacrifice." And he sanctified Jesse and his sons and invited them to the sacrifice. When they came, he looked on Eliab and thought, "Surely the LORD's anointed is now before the LORD." But the LORD said to Samuel, "Do not look on his appearance or on the height of his stature, because I have rejected him; for the LORD does not see as mortals see; they look on the outward appearance, but the LORD looks on the heart." Then Jesse called Abinadab, and made him pass before Samuel. He said, "Neither has the LORD chosen this one." Then Jesse made Shammah pass by. And he said, "Neither has the LORD chosen this one." Jesse made seven of his sons pass before Samuel, and Samuel said to Jesse, "The LORD has not chosen any of these." Samuel said to Jesse, "Are all your sons here?" And he said, "There remains yet the youngest, but he is keeping the sheep." And Samuel said to Jesse, "Send and bring him; for we will not sit down until he comes here." He sent and brought him in. Now he was ruddy, and had beautiful eyes, and was handsome. The LORD said, "Rise and anoint him; for this is the one." Then Samuel took the horn of oil, and anointed him in the presence of his brothers; and the spirit of the LORD came mightily upon David from that day forward. Samuel then set out and went to Ramah.

The Psalm 23   *Dominus regit me*

1   The LORD is my shepherd; *
         I shall not be in want.

2   He makes me lie down in green pastures *
         and leads me beside still waters.

3   He revives my soul *
    and guides me along right pathways for his Name's sake.

4   Though I walk through the valley of the shadow of death,
    I shall fear no evil; *
        for you are with me;
        your rod and your staff, they comfort me.

5   You spread a table before me in the presence of those who trouble me; *
        you have anointed my head with oil,
        and my cup is running over.

6   Surely your goodness and mercy shall follow me all the days of my life, *
        and I will dwell in the house of the LORD for ever.

The Epistle   Ephesians 5:(1-7) 8-14

[Be imitators of God, as beloved children, and live in love, as Christ loved us and
gave himself up for us, a fragrant offering and sacrifice to God. But fornication and
impurity of any kind, or greed, must not even be mentioned among you, as is proper
among saints. Entirely out of place is obscene, silly, and vulgar talk; but instead, let
there be thanksgiving. Be sure of this, that no fornicator or impure person, or one
who is greedy (that is, an idolater), has any inheritance in the kingdom of Christ and
of God. Let no one deceive you with empty words, for because of these things the
wrath of God comes on those who are disobedient. Therefore do not be associated
with them.] For once you were darkness, but now in the Lord you are light. Live as
children of light — for the fruit of the light is found in all that is good and right and
true. Try to find out what is pleasing to the Lord. Take no part in the unfruitful works
of darkness, but instead expose them. For it is shameful even to mention what such
people do secretly; but everything exposed by the light becomes visible, for
everything that becomes visible is light. Therefore it says, "Sleeper, awake! Rise from
the dead, and Christ will shine on you."

The Gospel   John 9:1-13 (14-27) 28-38

As he walked along, Jesus saw a man blind from birth. His disciples asked him,
"Rabbi, who sinned, this man or his parents, that he was born blind?" Jesus
answered, "Neither this man nor his parents sinned; he was born blind so that God's
works might be revealed in him. We must work the works of him who sent me while
it is day; night is coming when no one can work. As long as I am in the world, I am
the light of the world." When he had said this, he spat on the ground and made mud
with the saliva and spread the mud on the man's eyes, saying to him, "Go, wash in
the pool of Siloam" (which means Sent). Then he went and washed and came back
able to see. The neighbors and those who had seen him before as a beggar began to
ask, "Is this not the man who used to sit and beg?" Some were saying, "It is he."
Others were saying, "No, but it is someone like him." He kept saying, "I am the
man." But they kept asking him, "Then how were your eyes opened?" He answered,
"The man called Jesus made mud, spread it on my eyes, and said to me, 'Go to
Siloam and wash.' Then I went and washed and received my sight." They said to
him, "Where is he?" He said, "I do not know." They brought to the Pharisees the

man who had formerly been blind. [Now it was a sabbath day when Jesus made the mud and opened his eyes. Then the Pharisees also began to ask him how he had received his sight. He said to them, "He put mud on my eyes. Then I washed, and now I see." Some of the Pharisees said, "This man is not from God, for he does not observe the sabbath." But others said, "How can a man who is a sinner perform such signs?" And they were divided. So they said again to the blind man, "What do you say about him? It was your eyes he opened." He said, "He is a prophet." The Jews did not believe that he had been blind and had received his sight until they called the parents of the man who had received his sight and asked them, "Is this your son, who you say was born blind? How then does he now see?" His parents answered, "We know that this is our son, and that he was born blind; but we do not know how it is that now he sees, nor do we know who opened his eyes. Ask him; he is of age. He will speak for himself." His parents said this because they were afraid of the Jews; for the Jews had already agreed that anyone who confessed Jesus to be the Messiah would be put out of the synagogue. Therefore his parents said, "He is of age; ask him." So for the second time they called the man who had been blind, and they said to him, "Give glory to God! We know that this man is a sinner." He answered, "I do not know whether he is a sinner. One thing I do know, that though I was blind, now I see." They said to him, "What did he do to you? How did he open your eyes?" He answered them, "I have told you already, and you would not listen. Why do you want to hear it again? Do you also want to become his disciples?"] Then they reviled him, saying, "You are his disciple, but we are disciples of Moses. We know that God has spoken to Moses, but as for this man, we do not know where he comes from." The man answered, "Here is an astonishing thing! You do not know where he comes from and yet he opened my eyes. We know that God does not listen to sinners, but he does listen to one who worships him and obeys his will. Never since the world began has it been heard that anyone opened the eyes of a person born blind. If this man were not from God, he could do nothing." They answered him, "You were born entirely in sins, and are you trying to teach us?" And they drove him out. Jesus heard that they had driven him out, and when he found him, he said, "Do you believe in the Son of Man?" He answered, "And who is he, sir? Tell me, so that I may believe in him." Jesus said to him, "You have seen him, and the one speaking with you is he." He said, "Lord, I believe." And he worshiped him. Jesus said, "I came into this world for judgment so that those who do not see may see, and those who do see may become blind." Some of the Pharisees near him heard this and said to him, "Surely we are not blind, are we?" Jesus said to them, "If you were blind, you would not have sin. But now that you say, 'We see,' your sin remains."

Year B

The Lesson   **2 Chronicles 36:14-23**

All the leading priests and the people also were exceedingly unfaithful, following all the abominations of the nations; and they polluted the house of the LORD that he had consecrated in Jerusalem. The LORD, the God of their ancestors, sent persistently to them by his messengers, because he had compassion on his people and on his dwelling place; but they kept mocking the messengers of God, despising his words, and scoffing at his prophets, until the wrath of the LORD against his people became so great that there was no remedy. Therefore he brought up against them the king of the Chaldeans, who killed their youths with the sword in the house of their sanctuary, and had no compassion on young man or young woman, the aged or the feeble; he gave them all into his hand. All the vessels of the house of God, large and small, and the treasures of the house of the LORD, and the treasures of the king and of his officials, all these he brought to Babylon. They burned the house of God, broke down the wall of Jerusalem, burned all its palaces with fire, and destroyed all its precious vessels. He took into exile in Babylon those who had escaped from the sword, and they became servants to him and to his sons until the establishment of the kingdom of Persia, to fulfill the word of the LORD by the mouth of Jeremiah, until the land had made up for its sabbaths. All the days that it lay desolate it kept sabbath, to fulfill seventy years. In the first year of King Cyrus of Persia, in fulfillment of the word of the LORD spoken by Jeremiah, the LORD stirred up the spirit of King Cyrus of Persia so that he sent a herald throughoutall his kingdom and also declared in a written edict: "Thus says King Cyrus of Persia: The LORD, the God of heaven, has given me all the kingdoms of the earth, and he has charged me to build him a house at Jerusalem, which is in Judah. Whoever is among you of all his people, may the LORD his God be with him! Let him go up."

The Psalm 122   *Laetatus sum*
1   I was glad when they said to me, *
        "Let us go to the house of the LORD."

2   Now our feet are standing *
        within your gates, O Jerusalem.

3   Jerusalem is built as a city *
        that is at unity with itself;

4   To which the tribes go up,
    the tribes of the LORD, *
        the assembly of Israel,
        to praise the Name of the LORD.

5   For there are the thrones of judgment, *
        the thrones of the house of David.

6   Pray for the peace of Jerusalem: *
        "May they prosper who love you.

7   Peace be within your walls *
        and quietness within your towers.

8   For my brethren and companions' sake, *
        I pray for your prosperity.

9   Because of the house of the LORD our God, *
        I will seek to do you good."

The Epistle   **Ephesians 2:4-10**
God, who is rich in mercy, out of the great love with which he loved us even when we were dead through our trespasses, made us alive together with Christ — by grace you

have been saved — and raised us up with him and seated us with him in the heavenly places in Christ Jesus, so that in the ages to come he might show the immeasurable riches of his grace in kindness toward us in Christ Jesus. For by grace you have been saved through faith, and this is not your own doing; it is the gift of God — not the result of works, so that no one may boast. For we are what he has made us, created in Christ Jesus for good works, which God prepared beforehand to be our way of life.

The Gospel   **John 6:4-15**

Now the Passover, the festival of the Jews, was near. When he looked up and saw a large crowd coming toward him, Jesus said to Philip, "Where are we to buy bread for these people to eat?" He said this to test him, for he himself knew what he was going to do. Philip answered him, "Six months' wages would not buy enough bread for each of them to get a little." One of his disciples, Andrew, Simon Peter's brother, said to him, "There is a boy here who has five barley loaves and two fish. But what are they among so many people?" Jesus said, "Make the people sit down." Now there was a great deal of grass in the place; so they sat down, about five thousand in all. Then Jesus took the loaves, and when he had given thanks, he distributed them to those who were seated; so also the fish, as much as they wanted. When they were satisfied, he told his disciples, "Gather up the fragments left over, so that nothing may be lost." So they gathered them up, and from the fragments of the five barley loaves, left by those who had eaten, they filled twelve baskets. When the people saw the sign that he had done, they began to say, "This is indeed the prophet who is to come into the world." When Jesus realized that they were about to come and take him by force to make him king, he withdrew again to the mountain by himself.

Year C

The Lesson   **Joshua [4:19-24]; 5:9-12**

[The people of Israel came up out of the Jordan on the tenth day of the first month, and they camped in Gilgal on the east border of Jericho. Those twelve stones, which they had taken out of the Jordan, Joshua set up in Gilgal, saying to the Israelites, "When your children ask their parents in time to come, 'What do these stones mean?' then you shall let your children know, 'Israel crossed over the Jordan here on dry ground.' For the LORD your God dried up the waters of the Jordan for you until you crossed over, as the LORD your God did to the Red Sea, which he dried up for us until we crossed over, so that all the peoples of the earth may know that the hand of the LORD is mighty, and so that you may fear the LORD your God forever."] The LORD said to Joshua, "Today I have rolled away from you the disgrace of Egypt." And so that place is called Gilgal to this day. While the Israelites were camped in Gilgal they kept the passover in the evening on the fourteenth day of the month in the plains of Jericho. On the day after the passover, on that very day, they ate the produce of the land, unleavened cakes and parched grain. The manna ceased on the day they ate the produce of the land, and the Israelites no longer had manna; they ate the crops of the land of Canaan that year.

The Psalm 34 or 34:1-8   *Benedicam Dominum*

1   [I will bless the LORD at all times; *
    his praise shall ever be in my mouth.

2   I will glory in the LORD; *
    let the humble hear and rejoice.

3   Proclaim with me the greatness of the LORD; *
    let us exalt his Name together.

4   I sought the LORD, and he answered me *
    and delivered me out of all my terror.

5   Look upon him and be radiant, *
    and let not your faces be ashamed.

6   I called in my affliction and the LORD heard me *
    and saved me from all my troubles.

7   The angel of the LORD encompasses those who fear him, *
    and he will deliver them.

8   Taste and see that the LORD is good; *
    happy are they who trust in him!]

9   Fear the LORD, you that are his saints, *
    for those who fear him lack nothing.

10   The young lions lack and suffer hunger, *
    but those who seek the LORD lack nothing that is good.

11   Come, children, and listen to me; *
    I will teach you the fear of the LORD.

12   Who among you loves life *
    and desires long life to enjoy prosperity?

13   Keep you tongue from evil-speaking *
    and your lips from lying words.

14   Turn from evil and do good; *
    seek peace and pursue it.

15   The eyes of the LORD are upon the righteous, *
    and his ears are open to their cry.

16   The face of the LORD is against those who do evil, *
    to root out the remembrance of them from the earth.

17   The righteous cry, and the LORD hears them *
    and delivers them from all their troubles.

18   The LORD is near to the brokenhearted *
    and will save those whose spirits are crushed.

19 Many are the troubles of the righteous, *
    but the LORD will deliver him out of them all.

20 He will keep safe all his bones; *
    Not one of them shall be broken.

21 Evil shall slay the wicked, *
    and those who hate the righteous will be punished.

22 The LORD ransoms the life of his servants, *
    and none will be punished who trust in him.

The Epistle   **2 Corinthians 5:17-21**

If anyone is in Christ, there is a new creation: everything old has passed away; see, everything has become new! All this is from God, who reconciled us to himself through Christ, and has given us the ministry of reconciliation; that is, in Christ God was reconciling the world to himself, not counting their trespasses against them and entrusting the message of reconciliation to us. So we are ambassadors for Christ, since God is making his appeal through us; we entreat you on behalf of Christ, be reconciled to God. For our sake he made him to be sin who knew no sin, so that in him we might become the righteousness of God.

The Gospel   **Luke 15:11-32**

Jesus said, "There was a man who had two sons. The younger of them said to his father, 'Father, give me the share of the property that will belong to me.' So he divided his property between them. A few days later the younger son gathered all he had and traveled to a distant country, and there he squandered his property in dissolute living. When he had spent everything, a severe famine took place throughout that country, and he began to be in need. So he went and hired himself out to one of the citizens of that country, who sent him to his fields to feed the pigs. He would gladly have filled himself with the pods that the pigs were eating; and no one gave him anything. But when he came to himself he said, 'How many of my father's hired hands have bread enough to spare, but here I am dying of hunger! I will get up and go to my father, and I will say to him, "Father, I have sinned against heaven and before you; I am no longer worthy to be called your son; treat me like one of your hired hands."' So he set off and went to his father. But while he was still far off, his father saw him and was filled with compassion; he ran and put his arms around him and kissed him. Then the son said to him, 'Father, I have sinned against heaven and before you; I am no longer worthy to be called your son.' But the father said to his slaves, 'Quickly, bring out a robe — the best one — and put it on him; put a ring on his finger and sandals on his feet. And get the fatted calf and kill it, and let us eat and celebrate; for this son of mine was dead and is alive again; he was lost and is found!' And they began to celebrate. Now his elder son was in the field; and when he came and approached the house, he heard music and dancing. He called one of the slaves and asked what was going on. He replied, 'Your brother has come, and your father has killed the fatted calf, because he has got him back safe and sound.' Then he became angry and refused to go in. His father came out and began to plead with him. But he answered his father, 'Listen! For all these years I have been working like a slave for you, and I have never disobeyed your command; yet you have enever given me even a young goat so that I might celebrate with my friends. But when this son of yours came back, who has devoured your property with prostitutes, you killed the fatted calf for him!' Then the father said to him, 'Son, you are always with me, and all that is mine is yours. But we had to celebrate and rejoice, because this brother of yours was dead and has come to life; he was lost and has been found.'"

THE FIFTH SUNDAY IN LENT

The Collect

Almighty God, you alone can bring into order the unruly wills and affections of sinners: Grant your people grace to love what you command and desire what you promise; that, among the swift and varied changes of the world, our hearts may surely there be fixed where true joys are to be found; through Jesus Christ our Lord, who lives and reigns with you and the Holy Spirit, one God, now and for ever. *Amen.*

O Almighty God, who alone canst order the unruly wills and affections of sinful men: Grant unto thy people that they may love the thing which thou commandest, and desire that which thou dost promise; that so, among the sundry and manifold changes of the world, our hearts may surely there be fixed where true joys are to be found; through Jesus Christ our Lord, who liveth and reigneth with thee and the Holy Spirit, one God, now and forever. *Amen.*

Year A

The Lesson   Ezekiel 37:1-3 (4-10) 11-14

The hand of the LORD came upon me, and he brought me out by the spirit of the LORD and set me down in the middle of a valley; it was full of bones. He led me all around them; there were very many lying in the valley, and they were very dry. He said to me, "Mortal, can these bones live?" I answered, "O Lord GOD, you know." [Then he said to me, "Prophesy to these bones, and say to them: O dry bones, hear the word of the LORD. Thus says the Lord GOD to these bones: I will cause breath to enter you, and you shall live. I will lay sinews on you, and will cause flesh to come upon you, and cover you with skin, and put breath in you, and you shall live; and you shall know that I am the LORD." So I prophesied as I had been commanded; and as I prophesied, suddenly there was a noise, a rattling, and the bones came together, bone to its bone. I looked, and there were sinews on them, and flesh had come upon them, and skin had covered them; but there was no breath in them. Then he said to me, "Prophesy to the breath, prophesy, mortal, and say to the breath: Thus says the Lord GOD: Come from the four winds, O breath, and breathe upon these slain, that they may live." I prophesied as he commanded me, and the breath came into them, and they lived, and stood on their feet, a vast multitude.] Then he said to me, "Mortal, these bones are the whole house of Israel. They say, 'Our bones are dried up, and our hope is lost; we are cut off completely.' Therefore prophesy, and say to them, Thus says the Lord GOD: I am going to open your graves, and bring you up from your graves, O my people; and I will bring you back to the land of Israel. And you shall know that I am the LORD, when I open your graves, and bring you up from your graves, O my people. I will put my spirit within you, and you shall live, and I will place you on your own soil; then you shall know that I, the LORD, have spoken and will act," says the LORD.

The Psalm 130   *De profundis*

1   Out of the depths have I called to you, O LORD;
    LORD, hear my voice; *
        let your ears consider well the voice of my supplication.

2   If you, LORD, were to note what is done amiss, *
        O Lord, who could stand?

3   For there is forgiveness with you; *
        therefore you shall be feared.

4   I wait for the LORD; my soul waits for him; *
        in his word is my hope.

5   My soul waits for the LORD,
    more than watchmen for the morning, *
        more than watchmen for the morning.

6   O Israel, wait for the LORD, *
        for with the LORD there is mercy;

7   With him there is plenteous redemption, *
        and he shall redeem Israel from all their sins.

The Epistle   **Romans 6:16-23**

Do you not know that if you present yourselves to anyone as obedient slaves, you are
slaves of the one whom you obey, either of sin, which leads to death, or of obedience,
which leads to righteousness? But thanks be to God that you, having once been slaves
of sin, have become obedient from the heart to the form of teaching to which you
were entrusted, and that you, having been set free from sin, have become slaves of
righteousness. I am speaking in human terms because of your natural limitations.
For just as you once presented your members as slaves to impurity and to greater and
greater iniquity, so now present your members as slaves to righteousness for
sanctification. When you were slaves of sin, you were free in regard to righteousness.
So what advantage did you then get from the things of which you now are ashamed?
The end of those things is death. But now that you have been freed from sin and
enslaved to God, the advantage you get is sanctification. The end is eternal life. For
the wages of sin is death, but the free gift of God is eternal life in Christ Jesus our
Lord.

The Gospel   **John 11:(1-16) 17-44**

[Now a certain man was ill, Lazarus of Bethany, the village of Mary and her sister
Martha. Mary was the one who anointed the Lord with perfume and wiped his feet
with her hair; her brother Lazarus was ill. So the sisters sent a message to Jesus,
"Lord, he whom you love is ill." But when Jesus heard it, he said, "This illness does
not lead to death; rather it is for God's glory, so that the Son of God may be glorified
through it." Accordingly, though Jesus loved Martha and her sister and Lazarus,
after having heard that Lazarus was ill, he stayed two days longer in the place where
he was. Then after this he said to the disciples, "Let us go to Judea again." The

disciples said to him, "Rabbi, the Jews were just now trying to stone you, and are you going there again?" Jesus answered, "Are there not twelve hours of daylight? Those who walk during the day do not stumble, because they see the light of this world. But those who walk at night stumble, because the light is not in them." After saying this, he told them, "Our friend Lazarus has fallen asleep, but I am going there to awaken him." The disciples said to him, "Lord, if he has fallen asleep, he will be all right." Jesus, however, had been speaking about his death, but they thought that he was referring merely to sleep. Then Jesus told them plainly, "Lazarus is dead. For your sake I am glad I was not there, so that you may believe. But let us go to him." Thomas, who was called the Twin, said to his fellow disciples, "Let us also go, that we may die with him."] When Jesus arrived, he found that Lazarus had already been in the tomb four days. Now Bethany was near Jerusalem, some two miles away, and many of the Jews had come to Martha and Mary to console them about their brother. When Martha heard that Jesus was coming, she went and met him, while Mary stayed at home. Martha said to Jesus, "Lord, if you had been here, my brother would not have died. But even now I know that God will give you whatever you ask of him." Jesus said to her, "Your brother will rise again." Martha said to him, "I know that he will rise again in the resurrection on the last day." Jesus said to her, "I am the resurrection and the life. Those who believe in me, even though they die, will live, and everyone who lives and believes in me will never die. Do you believe this?" She said to him, "Yes, Lord, I believe that you are the Messiah, the Son of God, the one coming into the world." When she had said this, she went back and called her sister Mary, and told her privately, "The Teacher is here and is calling for you." And when she heard it, she got up quickly and went to him. Now Jesus had not yet come to the village, but was still at the place where Martha had met him. The Jews who were with her in the house, consoling her, saw Mary get up quickly and go out. They followed her, because they thought that she was going to the tomb to weep there. When Mary came where Jesus was and saw him, she knelt at his feet and said to him, "Lord, if you had been here, my brother would not have died." When Jesus saw her weeping, and the Jews who came with her also weeping, he was greatly disturbed in spirit and deeply moved. He said, "Where have you laid him?" They said to him, "Lord, come and see." Jesus began to weep. So the Jews said, "See how he loved him!" But some of them said, "Could not he who opened the eyes of the blind man have kept this man from dying?" Then Jesus, again greatly disturbed, came to the tomb. It was a cave, and a stone was lying against it. Jesus said, "Take away the stone." Martha, the sister of the dead man, said to him, "Lord, already there is a stench because he has been dead four days." Jesus said to her, "Did I not tell you that if you believed, you would see the glory of God?" So they took away the stone. And Jesus looked upward and said, "Father, I thank you for having heard me. I knew that you always hear me, but I have said this for the sake of the crowd standing here, so that they may believe that you sent me." When he had said this, he cried with a loud voice, "Lazarus, come out!" The dead man came out, his hands and feet bound with strips of cloth, and his face wrapped in a cloth. Jesus said to them, "Unbind him, and let him go."

The Lesson Jeremiah 31:31-34

The days are surely coming, says the LORD, when I will make a new covenant with the house of Israel and the house of Judah. It will not be like the covenant that I made with their ancestors when I took them by the hand to bring them out of the land of Egypt — a covenant that they broke, though I was their husband, says the LORD. But this is the covenant that I will make with the house of Israel after those days, says the LORD: I will put my law within them, and I will write it on their hearts; and I will be their God, and they shall be my people. No longer shall they teach one another, or say to each other, "Know the LORD," for they shall all know me, from the least of them to the greatest, says the LORD; for I will forgive their iniquity, and remember their sin no more.

The Psalm 51 or 51:11-16 *Miserere mei, Deus*

1 Have mercy on me, O God, according to your loving-kindness; *
    in your great compassion blot out my offenses.

2 Wash me through and through from my wickedness *
    and cleanse me from my sin.

3 For I know my transgressions, *
    and my sin is ever before me.

4 Against you only have I sinned *
    and done what is evil in your sight.

5 And so you are justified when you speak *
    and upright in your judgment.

6 Indeed, I have been wicked from my birth, *
    a sinner from my mother's womb.

7 For behold, you look for truth deep within me, *
    and will make me understand wisdom secretly.

8 Purge me from my sin, and I shall be pure; *
    wash me, and I shall be clean indeed.

9 Make me hear of joy and gladness, *
    that the body you have broken may rejoice.

10 Hide your face from my sins *
    and blot out all my iniquities.

11 [Create in me a clean heart, O God, *
    and renew a right spirit within me.

12 Cast me not away from your presence *
    and take not your holy Spirit from me.

13 Give me the joy of your saving help again *
    and sustain me with your bountiful Spirit.

14 I shall teach your ways to the wicked, *
　　and sinners shall return to you.

15 Deliver me from death, O God, *
　　and my tongue shall sing of your righteousness,
　　O God of my salvation.

16 Open my lips, O Lord, *
　　and my mouth shall proclaim your praise.]

17 Had you desired it, I would have offered sacrifice, *
　　but you take no delight in burnt-offerings.

18 The sacrifice of God is a troubled spirit; *
　　a broken and contrite heart, O God, you will not despise.

19 Be favorable and gracious to Zion, *
　　and rebuild the walls of Jerusalem.

20 Then you will be pleased with the appointed sacrifices,
　　with burnt-offerings and oblations; *
　　then shall they offer young bullocks upon your altar.

The Epistle
Hebrews 5:(1-4) 5-10

[Every high priest chosen from among mortals is put in charge of things pertaining to God on their behalf, to offer gifts and sacrifices for sins. He is able to deal gently with the ignorant and wayward, since he himself is subject to weakness; and because of this he must offer sacrifice for his own sins as well as for those of the people. And one does not presume to take this honor, but takes it only when called by God, just as Aaron was.] So also Christ did not glorify himself in becoming a high priest, but was appointed by the one who said to him, "You are my Son, today I have begotten you"; as he says also in another place, "You are a priest forever, according to the order of Melchizedek." In the days of his flesh, Jesus offered up prayers and supplications, with loud cries and tears, to the one who was able to save him from death, and he was heard because of his reverent submission. Although he was a Son, he learned obedience through what he suffered; and having been made perfect, he became the source of eternal salvation for all who obey him, having been designated by God a high priest according to the order of Melchizedek.

The Gospel
John 12:20-33

Now among those who went up to worship at the festival were some Greeks. They came to Philip, who was from Bethsaida in Galilee, and said to him, "Sir, we wish to see Jesus." Philip went and told Andrew; then Andrew and Philip went and told Jesus. Jesus answered them, "The hour has come for the Son of Man to be glorified. Very truly, I tell you, unless a grain of wheat falls into the earth and dies, it remains just a single grain; but if it dies, it bears much fruit. Those who love their life lose it, and those who hate their life in this world will keep it for eternal life. Whoever serves me must follow me, and where I am, there will my servant be also. Whoever serves me, the Father will honor. Now my soul is troubled. And what should I say —

'Father, save me from this hour'? No, it is for this reason that I have come to this hour. Father, glorify your name." Then a voice came from heaven, "I have glorified it, and I will glorify it again." The crowd standing there heard it and said that it was thunder. Others said, "An angel has spoken to him." Jesus answered, "This voice has come for your sake, not for mine. Now is the judgment of this world; now the ruler of this world will be driven out. And I, when I am lifted up from the earth, will draw all people to myself." He said this to indicate the kind of death he was to die.

Year C

The Lesson Isaiah 43:16-21

Thus says the LORD, who makes a way in the sea, a path in the mighty waters, who brings out chariot and horse, army and warrior; they lie down, they cannot rise, they are extinguished, quenched like a wick: Do not remember the former things, or consider the things of old. I am about to do a new thing; now it springs forth, do you not perceive it? I will make a way in the wilderness and rivers in the desert. The wild animals will honor me, the jackals and the ostriches; for I give water in the wilderness, rivers in the desert, to give drink to my chosen people, the people whom I formed for myself so that they might declare my praise.

The Psalm 126   *In convertendo*

1   When the LORD restored the fortunes of Zion, *
        then were we like those who dream.

2   Then was our mouth filled with laughter, *
        and our tongue with shouts of joy.

3   Then they said among the nations, *
        "The LORD has done great things for them."

4   The LORD has done great things for us, *
        and we are glad indeed.

5   Restore our fortunes, O LORD, *
        like the watercourses of the Negev.

6   Those who sowed with tears *
        will reap with songs of joy.

7   Those who go out weeping, carrying the seed, *
        will come again with joy, shouldering their sheaves.

The Epistle Philippians 3:8-14

More than that, I regard everything as loss because of the surpassing value of knowing Christ Jesus my Lord. For his sake I have suffered the loss of all things, and I regard them as rubbish, in order that I may gain Christ and be found in him, not having a righteousness of my own that comes from the law, but one that comes through faith in Christ, the righteousness from God based on faith. I want to know Christ and the power of his resurrection and the sharing of his sufferings by becoming like him in his death, if somehow I may attain the resurrection from the dead. Not that I have already obtained this or have already reached the goal; but I press on to make it my own, because Christ Jesus has made me his own. Beloved, I do not consider that I have made it my own; but this one thing I do: forgetting what lies behind and straining forward to what lies ahead, I press on toward the goal for the prize of the heavenly call of God in Christ Jesus.

The Gospel Luke 20:9-19

Jesus began to tell the people this parable: "A man planted a vineyard, and leased it to tenants, and went to another country for a long time. When the season came, he sent a slave to the tenants in order that they might give him his share of the produce of the vineyard; but the tenants beat him and sent him away empty-handed. Next he sent another slave; that one also they beat and insulted and sent away empty-handed. And he sent still a third; this one also they wounded and threw out. Then the owner of the vineyard said, 'What shall I do? I will send my beloved son; perhaps they will respect him.' But when the tenants saw him, they discussed it among themselves and said, 'This is the heir; let us kill him so that the inheritance may be ours.' So they threw him out of the vineyard and killed him. What then will the owner of the vineyard do to them? He will come and destroy those tenants and give the vineyards to others." When they heard this, they said, "Heaven forbid!" But he looked at them and said, "What then does this text mean: 'The stone that the builders rejected has become the cornerstone'? Everyone who falls on that stone will be broken to pieces; and it will crush anyone on whom it falls." When the scribes and chief priests realized that he had told this parable against them, they wanted to lay hands on him at that very hour, but they feared the people.

THE SUNDAY OF THE PASSION:
PALM SUNDAY

The Collect
Almighty and everliving God, in your tender love for the human race you sent your Son our Savior Jesus Christ to take upon him our nature, and to suffer death upon the cross, giving us the example of his great humility: Mercifully grant that we may walk in the way of his suffering, and also share in his resurrection; through Jesus Christ our Lord, who lives and reigns with you and the Holy Spirit, one God, for ever and ever. *Amen.*

Almighty and everlasting God, who, of thy tender love towards mankind, hast sent they Son our Savior Jesus Christ to take upon him our flesh, and to suffer death upon the cross, that all mankind should follow the example of his great humility: Mercifully grant that we may both follow the example of his patience, and also be made partakers of his resurrection; through the same Jesus Christ our Lord, who liveth and reigneth with thee and the Holy Spirit, one God, for ever and ever. *Amen.*

Years A, B, C

The Lesson Isaiah 45:21-25

Declare and present your case; let them take counsel together! Who told this long ago? Who declared it of old? Was it not I, the LORD? There is no other god besides me, a righteous God and a Savior; there is no one besides me. Turn to me and be saved, all the ends of the earth! For I am God, and there is no other. By myself I have sworn, from my mouth has gone forth in righteousness a word that shall not return: "To me every knee shall bow, every tongue shall swear." Only in the LORD, it shall be said of me, are righteousness and strength; all who were incensed against him shall come to him and be ashamed. In the LORD all the offspring of Israel shall triumph and glory.

or Isaiah 52:13-53:12
See, my servant shall prosper; he shall be exalted and lifted up, and shall be very high. Just as there were many who were astonished at him — so marred was his appearance, beyond human semblance, and his form beyond that of mortals — so he shall startle many nations; kings shall shut their mouths because of him; for that which had not been told them they shall see, and that which they had not heard they shall contemplate. Who has believed what we have heard? And to whom has the arm of the LORD been revealed? For he grew up before him like a young plant, and like a root out of dry ground; he had no form or majesty that we should look at him, nothing in his appearance that we should desire him. He was despised and rejected by others; a man of suffering and acquainted with infirmity; and as one from whom others hide their faces he was despised, and we held him of no account.
Surely he has borne our infirmities and carried our diseases; yet we accounted him stricken, struck down by God, and afflicted. But he was wounded for our transgressions, crushed for our iniquities; upon him was the punishment that made us whole, and by his bruises we are healed. All we like sheep have gone astray; we have all turned to our own way, and the LORD has laid on him the iniquity of us all. He was oppressed, and he was afflicted, yet he did not open his mouth; like a lamb that is led to the slaughter, and like a sheep that before its shearers is silent, so he did not open his mouth. By a perversion of justice he was taken away. Who could have imagined his future? For he was cut off from the land of the living, stricken for the transgression of my people. They made his grave with the wicked and his tomb with the rich, although he had done no violence, and there was no deceit in his mouth. Yet it was the will of the LORD to crush him with pain. When you make his life an offering for sin, he shall see his offspring, and shall prolong his days; through him the will of the LORD shall prosper. Out of his anguish he shall see light; he shall find satisfaction through his knowledge. The righteous one, my servant, shall make many righteous, and he shall bear their iniquities. Therefore I will allot him a portion with the great, and he shall divide the spoil with the strong; because he poured out himself to death, and was numbered with the transgressors; yet he bore the sin of many, and made intercession for the transgressors.

The Psalm 22:1-21 or 22:1-11   *Deus, Deus meus*

1   [My God, my God, why have you forsaken me? *
         and are so far from my cry
         and from the words of my distress?

2   O my God, I cry in the daytime, but you do not answer; *
         by night as well, but I find no rest.

3 Yet you are the Holy One, *
    enthroned upon the praises of Israel.

4 Our forefathers put their trust in you; *
    they trusted, and you delivered them.

5 They cried out to you and were delivered; *
    they trusted in you and were not put to shame.

6 But as for me, I am a worm and no man, *
    scorned by all and despised by the people.

7 All who see me laugh me to scorn; *
    they curl their lips and wag their heads, saying,

8 "He trusted in the LORD; let him deliver him; *
    let him rescue him, if he delights in him."

9 Yet you are he who took me out of the womb, *
    and kept me safe upon my mother's breast.

10 I have been entrusted to you ever since I was born; *
    you were my God when I was still in my mother's womb.

11 Be not far from me, for trouble is near, *
    and there is none to help.]

12 Many young bulls encircle me; *
    strong bulls of Bashan surround me.

13 They open wide their jaws at me, *
    like a ravening and a roaring lion.

14 I am poured out like water;
  all my bones are out of joint; *
    my heart within my breast is melting wax.

15 My mouth is dried out like a pot-sherd;
  my tongue sticks to the roof of my mouth; *
    and you have laid me in the dust of the grave.

16 Packs of dogs close me in,
  and gangs of evildoers circle around me; *
    they pierce my hands and my feet;
    I can count all my bones.

17 They stare and gloat over me; *
    they divide my garments among them;
    they cast lots for my clothing.

18 Be not far away, O LORD; *
    you are my strength; hasten to help me.

19 Save me from the sword, *
      my life from the power of the dog.

20 Save me from the lion's mouth, *
      my wretched body from the horns of wild bulls.

21 I will declare your Name to my brethren; *
      in the midst of the congregation I will praise you.

The Epistle   **Philippians 2:5-11**
Let the same mind be in you that was in Christ Jesus, who, though he was in the
form of God, did not regard equality with God as something to be exploited, but
emptied himself, taking the form of a slave, being born in human likeness. And being
found in human form, he humbled himself and became obedient to the point of
death — even death on a cross. Therefore God also highly exalted him and gave him
the name that is above every name, so that at the name of Jesus every knee should
bend, in heaven and on earth and under the earth, and every tongue should confess
that Jesus Christ is Lord, to the glory of God the Father.

Year A

The Gospel   **Matthew (26:36-75) 27:1-54 (55-66)**
[Jesus went with his disciples to a place called Gethsemane; and he said to his
disciples, "Sit here while I go over there and pray." He took with him Peter and the
two sons of Zebedee, and began to be grieved and agitated. Then he said to them, "I
am deeply grieved, even to death; remain here, and stay awake with me." And going
a little farther, he threw himself on the ground and prayed, "My Father, if it is
possible, let this cup pass from me; yet not what I want but what you want." Then he
came to the disciples and found them sleeping; and he said to Peter, "So, could you
not stay awake with me one hour? Stay awake and pray that you may not come into
the time of trial; the spirit indeed is willing, but the flesh is weak." Again he went
away for the second time and prayed, "My Father, if this cannot pass unless I drink
it, your will be done." Again he came and found them sleeping, for their eyes were
heavy. So leaving them again, he went away and prayed for the third time, saying the
same words. Then he came to the disciples and said to them, "Are you still sleeping
and taking your rest? See, the hour is at hand, and the Son of Man is betrayed into
the hands of sinners. Get up, let us be going. See, my betrayer is at hand." While he
was still speaking, Judas, one of the twelve, arrived; with him was a large crowd with
swords and clubs, from the chief priests and the elders of the people. Now the
betrayer had given them a sign, saying, "The one I will kiss is the man; arrest him."
At once he came up to Jesus and said, "Greetings, Rabbi!" and kissed him. Jesus said
to him, "Friend, do what you are here to do." Then they came and laid hands on
Jesus and arrested him. Suddenly, one of those with Jesus put his hand on his sword,
drew it, and struck the slave of the high priest, cutting off his ear. Then Jesus said to
him, "Put your sword back into its place; for all who take the sword will perish by the
sword. Do you think that I cannot appeal to my Father, and he will at once send me
more than twelve legions of angels? But how then would the scriptures be fulfilled,
which say it must happen in this way?" At that hour Jesus said to the crowds, "Have

you come out with swords and clubs to arrest me as though I were a bandit? Day after day I sat in the temple teaching, and you did not arrest me. But all this has taken place, so that the scriptures of the prophets may be fulfilled." Then all the disciples deserted him and fled. Those who had arrested Jesus took him to Caiaphas the high priest, in whose house the scribes and the elders had gathered. But Peter was following him at a distance, as far as the courtyard of the high priest; and going inside, he sat with the guards in order to see how this would end. Now the chief priests and the whole council were looking for false testimony against Jesus so that they might put him to death, but they found none, though many false witnesses came forward. At last two came forward and said, "This fellow said, 'I am able to destroy the temple of God and to build it in three days.'" The high priest stood up and said, "Have you no answer? What is it that they testify against you?" But Jesus was silent. Then the high priest said to him, "I put you under oath before the living God, tell us if you are the Messiah, the Son of god." Jesus said to him, "You have said so. But I tell you, from now on you will see the Son of Man seated at the right hand of Power and coming on the clouds of heaven." Then the high priest tore his clothes and said, "He has blasphemed! Why do we still need witnesses? You have now heard his blasphemy. What is your verdict?" They answered, "He deserves death." Then they spat in his face and struck him; and some slapped him, saying, "Prophesy to us, you Messiah! Who is it that struck you?" Now Peter was sitting outside in the courtyard. A servant-girl came to him and said, "You also were with Jesus the Galilean." But he denied it before all of them, saying, "I do not know what you are talking about." When he went out to the porch, another servant-girl saw him, and she said to the bystanders, "This man was with Jesus of Nazareth." Again he denied it with an oath, "I do not know the man." After a little while the bystanders came up and said to Peter, "Certainly you are also one of them, for your accent betrays you." Then he began to curse, and he swore an oath, "I do not know the man!" At that moment the cock crowed. Then Peter remembered what Jesus had said: "Before the cock crows, you will deny me three times." And he went out and wept bitterly.] When morning came, all the chief priests and the elders of the people conferred together against Jesus in order to bring about his death. They bound him, led him away, and handed him over to Pilate the governor. When Judas, his betrayer, saw that Jesus was condemned, he repented and brought back the thirty pieces of silver to the chief priests and the elders. He said, "I have sinned by betraying innocent blood." But they said, "What is that to us? See to it yourself." Throwing down the pieces of silver in the temple, he departed; and he went and hanged himself. But the chief priests, taking the pieces of silver, said, "It is not lawful to put them into the treasury, since they are blood money." After conferring together, they used them to buy the potter's field as a place to bury foreigners. For this reason that field has been called the Field of Blood to this day. Then was fulfilled what had been spoken through the prophet Jeremiah, "And they took the thirty pieces of silver, the price of the one on whom a price had been set, on whom some of the people of Israel had set a price, and they gave them for the potter's field, as the Lord commanded me." Now Jesus stood before the governor; and the governor asked him, "Are you the King of the Jews?" Jesus said, "You say so." But when he was accused by the chief priests and elders, he did not answer. Then Pilate said to him, "Do you not hear how many accusations they make against you?" But he gave him no answer, not even to a single charge, so that the governor was greatly amazed. Now at the festival the governor was accustomed to release a prisoner for the crowd, anyone whom they wanted. At that time they had a notorious prisoner, called Jesus Barabbas. So after they had gathered, Pilate said to them, "Whom do you want me to release for you, Jesus Barabbas or Jesus who is called the Messiah?" For he realized that it was out of jealousy that they had handed him over. While he was sitting on the judgment seat, his wife sent word to him, "Have nothing to do with that innocent man, for today I have suffered a great deal because of a dream about him." Now the chief priests and the elders persuaded the crowds to ask for Barabbas and to have Jesus killed. The governor again said to them, "Which of the two do you want me to release for you?" And they said, "Barabbas." Pilate said to them, "Then what should I do with Jesus who is called the Messiah?" All of them said, "Let him be crucified!" Then he asked, "Why, what evil has he done?" But they shouted all the more, "Let him be crucified!" So when Pilate saw that he could do nothing, but rather that a riot was beginning, he took some water and washed his hands before the crowd, saying, "I am innocent of this man's blood; see to it yourselves." Then the people as a whole answered, "His blood be on us and on our children!" So he released Barabbas for them; and after flogging Jesus, he handed him over to be crucified. Then the soldiers of the governor took Jesus into the governor's headquarters, and they gathered the whole cohort around him. They stripped him and put a scarlet robe on him, and after twisting some thorns into a crown, they put it on his head. They put a reed in his right hand and knelt before him and mocked him, saying, "Hail, King of the Jews!" They spat on him, and took the reed and struck him on the head. After mocking him, they stripped him of the robe and put his own clothes on him. Then they led him away to crucify him. As they went out, they came upon a man from Cyrene named Simon; they compelled this man to carry his cross. And when they came to a place called Golgotha (which means Place of a Skull), they offered him wine to drink, mixed with gall; but when he tasted it, he would not drink it. And when they had crucified him, they divided his clothes among themselves by casting lots; then they sat down there and kept watch over him. Over his head they put the charge against him, which read, "This is Jesus, the King of the Jews." Then two bandits were crucified with him, one on his right and one on his left. Those who passed by derided him, shaking their heads and saying, "You who would destroy the temple and build it in three days, save yourself! If you are the Son of God, come down from the cross." In the same way the chief priests also, along with the scribes and elders, were mocking him, saying, "He saved others; he cannot save himself. He is the King of Israel; let him come down from the cross now, and we will believe in him. He trusts in God; let God deliver him now, if he wants to; for he said, 'I am God's Son.'" The bandits who were crucified with him also taunted him in the same way. From noon on, darkness came over the whole land until three in the afternoon. And about three o'clock Jesus cried with a loud voice, "Eli, Eli, lema sabachthani?" that is, "My God, my God, why have you forsaken me?" When some of the bystanders heard it, they said, "This man is calling for Elijah." At once one of them ran and got a sponge, filled it with sour wine, put it on a stick, and gave it to him to drink. But the others said, "Wait, let us see whether Elijah will come to save him." Then Jesus cried again with a loud voice and breathed his last. At that moment the curtain of the temple was torn in two, from top to bottom. The earth shook, and the rocks were split. The tombs also were opened, and many bodies of the saints who had fallen asleep were raised. After his resurrection they came out of the tombs and entered the holy city and appeared to many. Now when the centurion and those with him, who were keeping watch over Jesus, saw the earthquake and what took place, they were terrified and said, "Truly this man was God's Son!" [Many women were also there, looking on from a distance; they had followed Jesus from Galilee and had provided for him. Among them were Mary Magdalene, and Mary the mother of James and Joseph, and the mother of the sons of Zebedee. When it was evening, there came a rich man from Arimathea, named Joseph, who was also a disciple of Jesus. He went to Pilate and asked for the body of Jesus; then Pilate ordered it to be given to him. So Joseph took the body and wrapped it in a clean linen cloth and laid it in his own new tomb, which he had hewn in the rock. He then rolled a great stone to the door of the tomb and went away. Mary Magdalene and the other Mary were there, sitting opposite the tomb. The next day, that is, after the day of Preparation, the chief priests and the Pharisees gathered before Pilate and said, "Sir, we remember what that impostor said while he was still alive, 'After three days I will rise again.' Therefore command the tomb to be made secure until the third day; otherwise his disciples may go and steal him away, and tell the people, 'He has been raised from the dead,' and the last deception would be worse than the first." Pilate said to them, "You have a guard of soldiers; go, make it as secure as you can." So they went with the guard and made the tomb secure by sealing the stone.

Year B

The Gospel   Mark (14:32-72) 15:1-39 (40-47)

[They went to a place called Gethsemane; and he said to his disciples, "Sit here while I pray." He took with him Peter and James and John, and began to be distressed and agitated. And said to them, "I am deeply grieved, even to death; remain here, and keep awake." And going a little farther, he threw himself on the ground and prayed that, if it were possible, the hour might pass from him. He said, "Abba, Father, for you all things are possible; remove this cup from me; yet, not what I want, but what you want." He came and found them sleeping; and he said to Peter, "Simon, are you asleep? Could you not keep awake one hour? Keep awake and pray that you may not come into the time of trial; the spirit indeed is willing, but the flesh is weak." And again he went away and prayed, saying the same words. And once more he came and found them sleeping, for their eyes were very heavy; and they did not know what to say to him. He came a third time and said to them, "Are you still sleeping and taking your rest? Enough! The hour has come; the Son of Man is betrayed into the hands of sinners. Get up, let us be going. See, my betrayer is at hand." Immediately, while he was still speaking, Judas, one of the twelve, arrived; and with him there was a crowd with swords and clubs, from the chief priests, the scribes, and the elders. Now the betrayer had given them a sign, saying, "The one I will kiss is the man; arrest him and lead him away under guard." So when he came, he went up to him at once and said, "Rabbi!" and kissed him. Then they laid hands on him and arrested him. But one of those who stood near drew his sword and struck the slave of the high priest, cutting off his ear. Then Jesus said to them, "Have you come out with swords and clubs to arrest me as though I were a bandit? Day after day I was with you in the temple teaching, and you did not arrest me. But let the scriptures be fulfilled." All of them deserted him and fled. A certain young man was following him, wearing nothing but a linen cloth. They caught hold of him, but he left the linen cloth and ran off naked. They took Jesus to the high priest; and all the chief priests, the elders, and the scribes were assembled. Peter had followed him at a distance, right into the courtyard of the high priest; and he was sitting with the guards, warming himself at the fire. Now the chief priests and the whole council were looking for testimony against Jesus to put him to death; but they found none. For many gave false testimony against him, and their testimony did not agree. Some stood up and gave false testimony against him, saying, "We heard him say, 'I will destroy this temple that is made with hands, and in three days I will build another, not made with hands.'" But even on this point their testimony did not agree. Then the high priest stood up before them and asked Jesus, "Have you no answer? What is it that they testify against you?" But he was silent and did not answer. Again the high priest asked him, "Are you the Messiah, the Son of the Blessed One?" Jesus said, "I am; and 'you will see the Son of Man seated at the right hand of the Power,' and 'coming with the clouds of heaven.'" Then the high priest tore his clothes and said, "Why do we still need witnesses? You have heard his blasphemy! What is your decisions?" All of them condemned him as deserving death. Some began to spit on him, to blindfold him, and to strike him, saying to him, "Prophesy!" The guards also took him over and beat him. While Peter was below in the courtyard, one of the servant-girls of the high priest came by. When she saw Peter warming himself, she stared at him and said, "You also were with Jesus, the man from Nazareth." But he denied it, saying, "I do not know or understand what you are talking about." And he went out into the forecourt. Then the cock crowed. And the servant-girl, on seeing him, began again to say to the bystanders, "This man is one of them." But again he denied it. Then after a little while the bystanders again said to Peter, "Certainly you are one of them; for you are a Galilean." But he began to curse, and he swore an oath, "I do not know this man you are talking about." At that moment the cock crowed for the second time. Then Peter remembered that Jesus had said to him, "Before the cock crows twice, you will deny me three times." And he broke down and wept.] As soon as it was morning, the chief priests held a consultation with the elders and scribes and the whole council. They bound Jesus, led him away, and handed him over to Pilate. Pilate asked him, "Are you the King of the Jews?" He answered him, "You say so." Then the chief priests accused him of many things. Pilate asked him again, "Have you no answer? See how many charges they bring against you." But Jesus made no further reply, so that Pilate was amazed. Now at the festival he used to release a prisoner for them, anyone for whom they asked. Now a man called Barabbas was in prison with the rebels who had committed murder during the insurrection. So the crowd came and began to ask Pilate to do for them according to his custom. Then he answered them, "Do you want me to release for you the King of the Jews?" For he realized that it was out of jealousy that the chief priests had handed him over. But the chief priests stirred up the crowd to have him release Barabbas for them instead. Pilate spoke to them again, "Then what do you wish me to do with the man you call the King of the Jews?" They shouted back, "Crucify him!" Pilate asked them, "Why, what evil has he done?" But they shouted all the more, "Crucify him!" So Pilate, wishing to satisfy the crowd, released Barabbas for them; and after flogging Jesus, he handed him over to be crucified. Then the soldiers led him into the courtyard of the palace (that is, the governor's headquarters); and they called together the whole cohort. And they clothed him in a purple cloak; and after twisting some thorns into a crown, they put it on him. And they began saluting him, "Hail, King of the Jews!" They struck his head with a reed, spat upon him, and knelt down in homage to him. After mocking him, they stripped him of the purple cloak and put his own clothes on him. Then they led him out to crucify him. They compelled a passer-by, who was coming in from the country, to carry his cross; it was Simon of Cyrene, the father of Alexander and Rufus. Then they brought Jesus to the place called Golgotha (which means the place of a skull). And they offered him wine mixed with myrrh; but he did not take it. And they crucified him, and divided his clothes among them, casting lots to decide what each should take. It was nine o'clock in the morning when they crucified him. The inscription of the charge against him read, "The King of the Jews." And with him they crucified two bandits, one on his right and one on his left. Those who passed by derided him, shaking their heads and saying, "Aha! You who would destroy the temple and build it in three days, save yourself, and come down from the cross!" In the same way the chief priests, along with the scribes, were also mocking him among themselves and saying, "He saved others; he cannot save himself. Let the Messiah, the King of Israel, come down from the cross now, so that we may see and believe." Those who were crucified with him also taunted him. When it was noon, darkness came over the whole land until three in the afternoon. At three o'clock Jesus cried out with a loud voice, "Eloi, Eloi, lema sabachthani?" which means, "My God, my God, why have you forsaken me?" When some of the bystanders heard it, they said, "Listen, he is calling for Elijah." And someone ran, filled a sponge with sour wine, put it on a stick, and gave it to him to drink, saying, "Wait, let us see whether Elijah will come to take him down." Then Jesus gave a loud cry and breathed his last. And the curtain of the temple was torn in two, from top to bottom. Now when the centurion, who stood facing him, saw that in this way he breathed his last, he said, "Truly this man was God's Son!" [There were also women looking on from a distance; among them were Mary Magdalene, and Mary the mother of James the younger and of Joses, and Salome. These used to follow him and provided for him when he was in Galilee; and there were many other women who had come up with him to Jerusalem. When evening had come, and since it was the day of Preparation, that is, the day before the sabbath, Joseph of Arimathea, a respected member of the council, who was also himself waiting expectantly for the kingdom of God, went boldly to Pilate and asked for the body of Jesus. Then Pilate wondered if he were already dead; and summoning the centurion, he asked him whether he had been dead for some time. When he learned from the centurion that he was dead, he granted the body to Joseph. Then Joseph bought a linen cloth, and taking down the body, wrapped it in the linen cloth, and laid it in a tomb that had been hewn out of the rock. He then rolled a stone against the door of the tomb. Mary Magdalene and Mary the mother of Joses saw where the body was laid.]

Year C

The Gospel   Luke (22:39-71) 23:1-49 (50-56)

[Jesus came out and went, as was his custom, to the Mount of Olives; and the disciples followed him. When he reached the place, he said to them, "Pray that you may not come into the time of trial." Then he withdrew from them about a stone's throw, knelt down, and prayed, "Father, if you are willing, remove this cup from me; yet, not my will but yours be done." Then an angel from heaven appeared to him and gave him strength. In his anguish he prayed more earnestly, and his sweat became like great drops of blood falling down on the ground. When he got up from prayer, he came to the disciples and found them sleeping because of grief, and he said to them, "Why are you sleeping? Get up and pray that you may not come into the time of trial." While he was still speaking, suddenly a crowd came, and the one called Judas, one of the twelve, was leading them. He approached Jesus to kiss him; but Jesus said to him, "Judas, is it with a kiss that you are betraying the Son of Man?" When those who were around him saw what was coming, they asked, "Lord, should we strike with the sword?" Then one of them struck the slave of the high priest and cut off his right ear. But Jesus said, "No more of this!" And he touched his ear and healed him. Then Jesus said to the chief priests, the officer of the temple police, and the elders who had come for him, "Have you come out with swords and clubs as if I were a bandit? When I was with you day after day in the temple, you did not lay hands on me. But this is your hour, and the power of darkness!" Then they seized him and led him away, bringing him into the high priest's house. But Peter was following at a distance. When they had kindled a fire in the middle of the courtyard and sat down together, Peter sat among them. Then a servant-girl, seeing him in the firelight, stared at him and said, "This man also was with him." But he denied it, saying, "Woman, I do not know him." A little later someone else, on seeing him, said, "You also are one of them." But Peter said, "Man, I am not!" Then about an hour later still another kept insisting, "Surely this man also was with him; for he is a Galilean." But Peter said, "Man, I do not know what you are talking about!" At that moment, while he was still speaking, the cock crowed. The Lord turned and looked at Peter. Then Peter remembered the word of the Lord, how he had said to him, "Before the cock crows today, you will deny me three times." And he went out and wept bitterly. Now the men who were holding Jesus began to mock him and beat him; they also blindfolded him and kept asking him, "Prophesy! Who is it that struck you?" They kept heaping many other insults on him. When day came, the assembly of the elders of the people, both chief priests and scribes, gathered together, and they brought him to their council. They said, "If you are the Messiah, tell us." He replied, "If I tell you, you will not believe; and if I question you, you will not answer. But from now on the Son of Man will be seated at the right hand of the power of God." All of them asked, "Are you, then, the Son of God?" He said to them, "You say that I am." Then they said, "What further testimony do we need? We have heard it ourselves from his own lips!"] Then the assembly rose as a body and brought Jesus before Pilate. They began to accuse him, saying, "We found this man perverting our nation, forbidding us to pay taxes to the emperor, and saying that he himself is the Messiah, a king." Then Pilate asked him, "Are you the king of the Jews?" He answered, "You say so." Then Pilate said to the chief priests and the crowds, "I find no basis for an accusation against this man." But they were insistent and said, "He stirs up the people by teaching throughout all Judea, from Galilee where he began even to this place." When Pilate heard this, he asked whether the man was a Galilean. And when he learned that he was under Herod's jurisdiction, he sent him off to Herod, who was himself in Jerusalem at that time. When Herod saw Jesus, he was very glad, for he had been wanting to see him for a long time, because he had heard about him and was hoping to see him perform some sign. He questioned him at some length, but Jesus gave him no answer. The chief priests and the scribes stood by, vehemently accusing him. Even Herod with his soldiers treated him with contempt and mocked him, and sent him back to Pilate. That same day Herod and Pilate became friends with each other; before this they had been enemies. Pilate then called together the chief priests, the leaders, and the people, and said to them, "You brought me this man as one who was perverting the people; and here I have examined him in your presence and have not found this man guilty of any of your charges against him. Neither has Herod, for he sent him back to us. Indeed, he has done nothing to deserve death. I will therefore have him flogged and release him." Then they all shouted out together, "Away with this fellow! Release Barabbas for us!" (This was a man who had been put in prison for an insurrection that had taken place in the city, and for murder.) Pilate, wanting to release Jesus, addressed them again; but they kept shouting, "Crucify, crucify him!" A third time he said to them, "Why, what evil has he done? I have found in him no ground for the sentence of death; I will therefore have him flogged and then release him." But they kept urgently demanding with loud shouts that he should be crucified; and their voices prevailed. So Pilate gave his verdict that their demand should be granted. He released the man they asked for, the one who had been put in prison for insurrection and murder, and he handed Jesus over as they wished. As they led him away, they seized a man, Simon of Cyrene, who was coming from the country, and they laid the cross on him, and made him carry it behind Jesus. A great number of the people followed him, and among them were women who were beating their breasts and wailing for him. But Jesus turned to them and said, "Daughters of Jerusalem, do not weep for me, but weep for yourselves and for your children. For the days are surely coming when they will say, 'Blessed are the barren, and the wombs that never bore, and the breasts that never nursed.' Then they will begin to say to the mountains, 'Fall on us'; and to the hills, 'Cover us'. For if they do this when the wood is green, what will happen when it is dry?" Two others also, who were criminals, were led away to be put to death with him. When they came to the place that is called The Skull, they crucified Jesus there with the criminals, one on his right and one on his left. Then Jesus said, "Father, forgive them; for they do not know what they are doing." And they cast lots to divide his clothing. And the people stood by, watching; but the leaders scoffed at him, saying, "He saved others; let him save himself if he is the Messiah of God, his chosen one!" The soldiers also mocked him, coming up and offering him sour wine, and saying, "If you are the King of the Jews, save yourself!" There was also an inscription over him, "This is the King of the Jews." One of the criminals who were hanged there kept deriding him and saying, "Are you not the Messiah? Save yourself and us!" But the other rebuked him, saying, "Do you not fear God, since you are under the same sentence of condemnation? And we indeed have been condemned justly, for we are getting what we deserve for our deeds, but this man has done nothing wrong." Then he said, "Jesus, remember me when you come into your kingdom." He replied, "Truly I tell you, today you will be with me in Paradise." It was now about noon, and darkness came over the whole land until three in the afternoon, while the sun's light failed; and the curtain of the temple was torn in two. Then Jesus, crying with a loud voice, said, "Father, into your hands I commend my spirit." Having said this, he breathed his last. When the centurion saw what had taken place, he praised God and said, "Certainly this man was innocent." And when all the crowds who had gathered there for this spectacle saw what had taken place, they returned home, beating their breasts. But all his acquaintances, including the women who had followed him from Galilee, stood at a distance, watching these things. [Now there was a good and righteous man named Joseph, who, though a member of the council, had not agreed to their plan and action. He came from the Jewish town of Arimathea, and he was waiting expectantly for the kingdom of God. This man went to Pilate and asked for the body of Jesus. Then he took it down, wrapped it in a linen cloth, and laid it in a rock-hewn tomb where no one had ever been laid. It was the day of Preparation, and the sabbath was beginning. The women who had come with him from Galilee followed, and they saw the tomb and how his body was laid. Then they returned, and prepared spices and ointments. On the sabbath they rested according to the commandment.]

MONDAY IN HOLY WEEK

The Collect
Almighty God, whose most dear Son went not up to joy but first he suffered pain, and entered not into glory before he was crucified: Mercifully grant that we, walking in the way of the cross, may find it none other than the way of life and peace; through Jesus Christ your Son our Lord, who lives and reigns with you and the Holy Spirit, one God for ever and ever. *Amen.*

Almighty God, whose most dear Son went not up to joy but first he suffered pain, and entered not into glory before he was crucified: Mercifully grant that we, walking in the way of the cross, may find it none other than the way of life and peace; through the same thy Son Jesus Christ our Lord, who liveth and reigneth with thee and the Holy Spirit, one God, for ever and ever. *Amen.*

Years A, B, C

The Lesson   Isaiah 42:1-9
Here is my servant, whom I uphold, my chosen, in whom my soul delights; I have put my spirit upon him; he will bring forth justice to the nations. He will not cry or lift up his voice, or make it heard in the street; a bruised reed he will not break, and a dimly burning wick he will not quench; he will faithfully bring forth justice. He will not grow faint or be crushed until he has established justice in the earth; and the coastlands wait for his teaching. Thus says God, the LORD, who created the heavens and stretched them out, who spread out the earth and what comes from it, who gives breath to the people upon it and spirit to those who walk in it: I am the LORD, I have called you in righteousness, I have taken you by the hand and kept you; I have given you as a covenant to the people, a light to the nations, to open the eyes that are blind, to bring out the prisoners from the dungeon, from the prison those who sit in darkness. I am the LORD, that is my name; my glory I give to no other, nor my praise to idols. See, the former things have come to pass, and new things I now declare; before they spring forth, I tell you of them.

The Psalm 36:5-10   *Dixit Injustus*

5   Your love, O LORD, reaches to the heavens, *
    and your faithfulness to the clouds.

6   Your righteousness is like the strong mountains,
    your justice like the great deep; *
      you save both man and beast, O LORD.

7   How priceless is your love, O God! *
    your people take refuge under the shadow of your wings.

8   They feast upon the abundance of your house; *
    you give them drink from the river of your delights.

9   For with you is the well of life, *
    and in your light we see light.

10   Continue your loving-kindness to those who know you, *
    and your favor to those who are true of heart.

The Epistle   Hebrews 11:39-12:3

Yet all these, though they were commended for their faith, did not receive what was promised, since God had provided something better so that they would not, apart from us, be made perfect. Therefore, since we are surrounded by so great a cloud of witnesses, let us also lay aside every weight and the sin that clings so closely, and let us run with perseverance the race that is set before us, looking to Jesus the pioneer and perfecter of our faith, who for the sake of the joy that was set before him endured the cross, disregarding its shame, and has taken his seat at the right hand of the throne of God. Consider him who endured such hostility against himself from sinners, so that you may not grow weary or lose heart.

The Gospel   John 12:1-11

Six days before the Passover Jesus came to Bethany, the home of Lazarus, whom he had raised from the dead. There they gave a dinner for him. Martha served, and Lazarus was one of those at the table with him. Mary took a pound of costly perfume made of pure nard, anointed Jesus' feet, and wiped them with her hair. The house was filled with the fragrance of the perfume. But Judas Iscariot, one of his disciples (the one who was about to betray him), said, "Why was this perfume not sold for three hundred denarii and the money given to the poor?" (He said this not because he cared about the poor, but because he was a thief; he kept the common purse and used to steal what was put into it.) Jesus said, "Leave her alone. She bought it so that she might keep it for the day of my burial. You always have the poor with you, but you do not always have me." When the great crowd of the Jews learned that he was there, they came not only because of Jesus but also to see Lazarus, whom he had raised from the dead. So the chief priests planned to put Lazarus to death as well, since it was on account of him that many of the Jews were deserting and were believing in Jesus.

or Mark 14:3-9

While Jesus was at Bethany in the house of Simon the leper, as he sat at the table, a woman came with an alabaster jar of very costly ointment of nard, and she broke open the jar and poured the ointment on his head. But some were there who said to one another in anger, "Why was the ointment wasted in this way? For this ointment could have been sold for more than three hundred denarii, and the money given to the poor." And they scolded her. But Jesus said, "Let her alone; why do you trouble her? She has performed a good service for me. For you always have the poor with you, and you can show kindness to them whenever you wish; but you will not always have me. She has done what she could; she has anointed my body beforehand for its burial. Truly I tell you, wherever the good news is proclaimed in the whole world, what she has done will be told in remembrance of her."

TUESDAY IN HOLY WEEK

The Collect

O God, by the passion of your blessed Son you made an instrument of shameful death to be for us the means of life: Grant us so to glory in the cross of Christ, that we may gladly suffer shame and loss for the sake of your Son our Savior Jesus Christ; who lives and reigns with you and the Holy Spirit, one God, for ever and ever. *Amen.*

O God, who by the passion of thy blesses Son didst make an instrument of shameful death to be unto us the means of life: Grant us so to glory in the cross of Christ, that we may gladly suffer shame and loss for the sake of thy Son our Savior Jesus Christ; who liveth and reigneth with thee and the Holy Spirit, one God, for ever and ever. *Amen.*

Years A, B, C

The Lesson   Isaiah 49:1-6

Listen to me, O coastlands, pay attention, you peoples from far away! The LORD called me before I was born, while I was in my mother's womb he named me. He made my mouth like a sharp sword, in the shadow of his hand he hid me; he made me a polished arrow, in his quiver he hid me away. And he said to me, "You are my servant, Israel, in whom I will be glorified." But I said, "I have labored in vain, I have spent my strength for nothing and vanity; yet surely my cause is with the LORD, and my reward with my God." And now the LORD says, who formed me in the womb to be his servant, to bring Jacob back to him, and that Israel might be gathered to him, for I am honored in the sight of the LORD, and my God has become my strength — he says, "It is too light a thing that you should be my servant to raise up the tribes of Jacob and to restore the survivors of Israel; I will give you as a light to the nations, that my salvation may reach to the end of the earth."

The Psalm 71:1-12   *In te, Domine, speravi*

1   In you, O LORD, have I taken refuge; *
         let me never be ashamed.

2   In your righteousness, deliver me and set me free; *
         incline your ear to me and save me.

3 Be my strong rock, a castle to keep me safe; *
   you are my crag and my stronghold.

4 Deliver me, my God, from the hand of the wicked, *
   from the clutches of the evildoer and the oppressor.

5 For you are my hope, O Lord GOD, *
   my confidence since I was young.

6 I have been sustained by you ever since I was born;
   from my mother's womb you have been my strength; *
   my praise shall be always of you.

7 I have become a portent to many; *
   but you are my refuge and my strength.

8 Let my mouth be full of your praise *
   and your glory all the day long.

9 Do not cast me off in my old age; *
   forsake me not when my strength fails.

10 For my enemies are talking against me, *
    and those who lie in wait for my life take counsel together.

11 They say, "God has forsaken him;
    go after him and seize him; *
    because there is none who will save."

12 O God, be not far from me; *
    come quickly to help me, O my God.

The Epistle   1 Corinthians 1:18-31

For the message about the cross is foolishness to those who are perishing, but to us who are being saved it is the power of God. For it is written, "I will destroy the wisdom of the wise, and the discernment of the discerning I will thwart." Where is the one who is wise? Where is the scribe? Where is the debater of this age? Has not God made foolish the wisdom of the world? For since, in the wisdom of God, the world did not know God through wisdom, God decided, through the foolishness of our proclamation, to save those who believe. For Jews demand signs and Greeks desire wisdom, but we proclaim Christ crucified, a stumbling block to Jews and foolishness to Gentiles, but to those who are the called, both Jews and Greeks, Christ the power of God and the wisdom of God. For God's foolishness is wiser than human wisdom, and God's weakness is stronger than human strength. Consider your own call, brothers and sisters: not many of you were wise by human standards, not many were powerful, not many were of noble birth. But God chose what is foolish in the world to shame the wise; God chose what is weak in the world to shame the strong; God chose what is low and despised in the world, things that are not, to reduce to nothing things that are, so that no one might boast in the presence of God. He is the source of your life in Christ Jesus, who became for us wisdom from God, and righteousness and sanctification and redemption, in order that, as it is written, "Let the one who boasts, boast in the Lord."

The Gospel **John 12:37-38, 42-50**

Although Jesus had performed so many signs in their presence, they did not believe in him. This was to fulfill the word spoken by the prophet Isaiah: "Lord, who has believed our message, and to whom has the arm of the Lord been revealed?" Nevertheless many, even of the authorities, believed in him. But because of the Pharisees they did not confess it, for fear that they would be put out of the synagogue; for they loved human glory more than the glory that comes from God. Then Jesus cried aloud: "Whoever believes in me believes not in me but in him who sent me. And whoever sees me sees him who sent me. I have come as light into the world, so that everyone who believes in me should not remain in the darkness. I do not judge anyone who hears my words and does not keep them, for I came not to judge the world, but to save the world. The one who rejects me and does not receive my word has a judge; on the last day the word that I have spoken will serve as judge, for I have not spoken on my own, but the Father who sent me has himself given me a commandment about what to say and what to speak. And I know that his commandment is eternal life. What I speak, therefore, I speak just as the Father has told me."

or Mark 11:15-19

Then they came to Jerusalem. And Jesus entered the temple and began to drive out those who were selling and those who were buying in the temple, and he overturned the tables of the money changers and the seats of those who sold doves; and he would not allow anyone to carry anything through the temple. He was teaching and saying, "Is it not written, 'My house shall be called a house of prayer for all the nations'? But you have made it a den of robbers." And when the chief priests and the scribes heard it, they kept looking for a way to kill him; for they were afraid of him, because the whole crowd was spellbound by his teaching. And when evening came, Jesus and his disciples went out of the city.

WEDNESDAY IN HOLY WEEK

The Collect

Lord God, whose blessed Son our Savior gave his body to be whipped and his face to be spit upon: Give us grace to accept joyfully the sufferings of the present time, confident of the glory that shall be revealed; through Jesus Christ your Son our Lord, who lives and reigns with you and the Holy Spirit, one God, for ever and ever. *Amen.*

O Lord God, whose blessed Son our Savior gave his back to the smiters and hid not his face from shame: Grant us grace to take joyfully the sufferings of the present time, in full assurance of the glory that shall be revealed; through the same thy Son Jesus Christ our Lord, who liveth and reigneth with thee and the Holy Spirit, one God, for ever and ever. *Amen.*

The Lesson   Isaiah 50:4-9a

The Lord GOD has given me the tongue of a teacher, that I may know how to sustain the weary with a word. Morning by morning he wakens — wakens my ear to listen as those who are taught. The Lord GOD has opened my ear, and I was not rebellious, I did not turn backward. I gave my back to those who struck me, and my cheeks to those who pulled out the beard; I did not hide my face from insult and spitting. The Lord GOD helps me; therefore I have not been disgraced; therefore I have set my face like flint, and I know that I shall not be put to shame; he who vindicates me is near. Who will contend with me? Let us stand up together. Who are my adversaries? Let them confront me. It is the Lord GOD who helps me; who will declare me guilty?

The Psalm 69:7-15, 22-23   *Salvum me fac*

7   Let not those who hope in you be put to shame through me, Lord GOD of hosts; *

    let not those who seek you be disgraced because of me, O God of Israel.

8   Surely, for your sake have I suffered reproach, *

    and shame has covered my face.

9   I have become a stranger to my own kindred, *

    an alien to my mother's children.

10   Zeal for your house has eaten me up; *

    the scorn of those who scorn you has fallen upon me.

11   I humbled myself with fasting, *

    but that was turned to my reproach.

12   I put on sack-cloth also, *

    and became a byword among them.

13   Those who sit at the gate murmur against me, *

    and the drunkards make songs about me.

14   But as for me, this is my prayer to you, *

    at the time you have set, O LORD:

15   "In your great mercy, O God, *

    answer me with your unfailing help.

22   Reproach has broken my heart, and it cannot be healed; *

    I looked for sympathy, but there was none,

    for comforters, but I could find no one.

23   They gave me gall to eat, *

    and when I was thirsty, they gave me vinegar to drink.

The Epistle   Hebrews 9:11-15, 24-28

But when Christ came as a high priest of the good things that have come, then through the greater and perfect tent (not made with hands, that is, not of this creation), he entered once for all into the Holy Place, not with the blood of goats and calves, but with his own blood, thus obtaining eternal redemption. For if the blood of goats and bulls, with the sprinkling of the ashes of a heifer, sanctifies those who have been defiled so that their flesh is purified, how much more will the blood of Christ, who through the eternal Spirit offered himself without blemish to God, purify our conscience from dead works to worship the living God! For this reason he is the mediator of a new covenant, so that those who are called may receive the promised eternal inheritance, because a death has occurred that redeems them from the transgressions under the first covenant. For Christ did not enter a sanctuary made by human hands, a mere copy of the true one, but he entered into heaven itself, now to appear in the presence of God on our behalf. Nor was it to offer himself again and again, as the high priest enters the Holy Place year after year with blood that is not his own; for then he would have had to suffer again and again since the foundation of the world. But as it is, he has appeared once for all at the end of the age to remove sin by the sacrifice of himself. And just as it is appointed for mortals to die once, and after that the judgment, so Christ, having been offered once to bear the sins of many, will appear a second time, not to deal with sin, but to save those who are eagerly waiting for him.

The Gospel   John 13:21-35
Jesus was troubled in spirit, and declared, "Very truly, I tell you, one of you will betray me." The disciples looked at one another, uncertain of whom he was speaking. One of his disciples — the one whom Jesus loved — was reclining next to him; Simon Peter therefore motioned to him to ask Jesus of whom he was speaking. So while reclining next to Jesus, he asked him, "Lord, who is it?" Jesus answered, "It is the one to whom I give this piece of bread when I have dipped it in the dish." So when he had dipped the piece of bread, he gave it to Judas son of Simon Iscariot. After he received the piece of bread, Satan entered into him. Jesus said to him, "Do quickly what you are going to do." Now no one at the table knew why he said this to him. Some thought that, because Judas had the common purse, Jesus was telling him, "Buy what we need for the festival"; or, that he should give something to the poor. So, after receiving the piece of bread, he immediately went out. And it was night. When he had gone out, Jesus said, "Now the Son of Man has been glorified, and God has been glorified in him. If God has been glorified in him, God will also glorify him in himself and will glorify him at once. Little children, I am with you only a little longer. You will look for me; and as I said to the Jews so now I say to you, 'Where I am going, you cannot come.' I give you a new commandment, that you love one another. Just as I have loved you, you also should love one another. By this everyone will know that you are my disciples, if you have love for one another."

or Matthew 26:1-5, 14-25
When Jesus had finished saying all these things, he said to his disciples, "You know that after two days the Passover is coming, and the Son of Man will be handed over to be crucified." Then the chief priests and the elders of the people gathered in the palace of the high priest, who was called Caiaphas, and they conspired to arrest Jesus by stealth and kill him. But they said, "Not during the festival, or there may be a riot among the people." Then one of the twelve, who was called Judas Iscariot, went to the chief priests and said, "What will you give me if I betray him to you?" They paid

him thirty pieces of silver. And from that moment he began to look for an opportunity to betray him. On the first day of Unleavened Bread the disciples came to Jesus, saying, "Where do you want us to make the preparations for you to eat the Passover?" He said, "Go into the city to a certain man, and say to him, 'The Teacher says, My time is near; I will keep the Passover at your house with my disciples.'" So the disciples did as Jesus had directed them, and they prepared the Passover meal. When it was evening, he took his place with the twelve; and while they were eating, he said, "Truly I tell you, one of you will betray me." And they became greatly distressed and began to say to him one after another, "Surely not I, Lord?" He answered, "The one who has dipped his hand into the bowl with me will betray me. The Son of Man goes as it is written of him, but woe to that one by whom the Son of Man is betrayed! It would have been better for that one not to have been born." Judas, who betrayed him, said, "Surely not I, Rabbi?" He replied, "You have said so."

MAUNDY THURSDAY

The Collect

Almighty Father, whose dear Son, on the night before he suffered, instituted the Sacrament of his Body and Blood: Mercifully grant that we may receive it thankfully in remembrance of Jesus Christ our Lord, who in these holy mysteries gives us a pledge of eternal life; and who now lives and reigns with you and the Holy Spirit, one God, for ever and ever. *Amen.*

Almighty Father, whose dear Son, on the night before he suffered, did institute the Sacrament of his Body and Blood: Mercifully grant that we may thankfully receive the same in remembrance of him who in these holy mysteries giveth us a pledge of life eternal, the same thy Son Jesus Christ our Lord; who now liveth and reigneth with thee and the Holy Spirit ever, one God, world without end. *Amen.*

The Lesson   Exodus 12:1-14a

The LORD said to Moses and Aaron in the land of Egypt: This month shall mark for you the beginning of months; it shall be the first month of the year for you. Tell the whole congregation of Israel that on the tenth of this month they are to take a lamb for each family, a lamb for each household. If a household is too small for a whole lamb, it shall join its closest neighbor in obtaining one; the lamb shall be divided in proportion to the number of people who eat of it. Your lamb shall be without blemish, a year-old male; you may take it from the sheep or from the goats. You shall keep it until the fourteenth day of this month; then the whole assembled congregation of Israel shall slaughter it at twilight. They shall take some of the blood and put it on the two doorposts and the lintel of the houses in which they eat it. They shall eat the lamb that same night; they shall eat it roasted over the fire with unleavened bread and bitter herbs. Do not eat any of it raw or boiled in water, but roasted over the fire, with its head, legs, and inner organs. You shall let none of it remain until the morning; anything that remains until the morning you shall burn. This is how you shall eat it: your loins girded, your sandals on your feet, and your staff in your hand; and you shall eat it hurriedly. It is the passover of the LORD. For I will pass through the land of Egypt that night, and I will strike down every firstborn in the land of Egypt, both human beings and animals; on all the gods of Egypt I will execute judgments: I am the LORD. The blood shall be a sign for you on the houses where you live: when I see the blood, I will pass over you, and no plague shall destroy you when I strike the land of Egypt. This day shall be a day of remembrance for you. You shall celebrate it as a festival to the LORD.

The Psalm 78:14-20, 23-25   *Attendite, popule*

14   He led them with a cloud by day, *
    and all the night through with a glow of fire.

15   He split the hard rocks in the wilderness *
    and gave them drink as from the great deep.

16   He brought streams out of the cliff, *
    and the waters gushed out like rivers.

17   But they went on sinning against him, *
    rebelling in the desert against the Most High.

18   They tested God in their hearts, *
    demanding food for their craving.

19   They railed against God and said, *
    "Can God set a table in the wilderness?

20   True, he struck the rock, the waters gushed out, and the gullies overflowed; *
    but is he able to give bread
    or to provide meat for his people?"

23   So he commanded the clouds above *
    and opened the doors of heaven.

24   He rained down manna upon them to eat *
    and gave them grain from heaven.

25   So mortals ate the bread of angels; *
    he provided for them food enough.

The Epistle   **1 Corinthians 11:23-26 (27-32)**

For I received from the Lord what I also handed on to you, that the Lord Jesus on the night when he was betrayed took a loaf of bread, and when he had given thanks, he broke it and said, "This is my body that is for you. Do this in remembrance of me." In the same way he took the cup also, after supper, saying, "This cup is the new covenant in my blood. Do this, as often as you drink it, in remembrance of me." For as often as you eat this bread and drink the cup, you proclaim the Lord's death until he comes. [Whoever, therefore, eats the bread or drinks the cup of the Lord in an unworthy manner will be answerable for the body and blood of the Lord. Examine yourselves, and only then eat of the bread and drink of the cup. For all who eat and drink without discerning the body, eat and drink judgment against themselves. For this reason many of you are weak and ill, and some have died. But if we judged ourselves, we would not be judged. But when we are judged by the Lord, we are disciplined so that we may not be condemned along with the world.]

The Gospel
John 13:1-15

Before the festival of the Passover, Jesus knew that his hour had come to depart from this world and go to the Father. Having loved his own who were in the world, he loved them to the end. The devil had already put it into the heart of Judas son of Simon Iscariot to betray him. And during supper Jesus, knowing that the Father had given all things into his hands, and that he had come from God and was going to God, got up from the table, took off his outer robe, and tied a towel around him. Then he poured water into a basin and began to wash the disciples' feet and to wipe them with the towel that was tied around himself. He came to Simon Peter, who said to him, "Lord, are you going to wash my feet?" Jesus answered, "You do not know now what I am doing, but later you will understand." Peter said to him, "You will never wash my feet." Jesus answered, "Unless I wash you, you have no share with me." Simon Peter said to him, "Lord, not my feet only but also my hands and my head!" Jesus said to him, "One who has bathed does not need to wash, except for the feet, but is entirely clean. And you are clean, though not all of you." For he knew who was to betray him; for this reason he said, "Not all of you are clean." After he had washed their feet, had put on his robe, and had returned to the table, he said to them, "Do you know what I have done to you? You call me Teacher and Lord — and you are right, for that is what I am. So if I, your Lord and Teacher, have washed your feet, you also ought to wash one another's feet. For I have set you an example, that you also should do as I have done to you."

or Luke 22:14-30

When the hour came, Jesus took his place at the table, and the apostles with him. He said to them, "I have eagerly desired to eat this Passover with you before I suffer; for I tell you, I will not eat it until it is fulfilled in the kingdom of God." Then he took a cup, and after giving thanks he said, "Take this and divide it among yourselves; for I tell you that from now on I will not drink of the fruit of the vine until the kingdom of God comes." Then he took a loaf of bread, and when he had given thanks, he broke it and gave it to them, saying, "This is my body, which is given for you. Do this in remembrance of me." And he did the same with the cup after supper, saying, "This cup that is poured out for you is the new covenant in my blood. But see, the one who betrays me is with me, and his hand is on the table. For the Son of Man is going as it has been determined, but woe to that one by whom he is betrayed!" Then they began to ask one another, which one of them it could be who would do this. A dispute also arose among them as to which one of them was to be regarded as the greatest. But he said to them, "The kings of the Gentiles lord it over them; and those in authority over them are called benefactors. But not so with you; rather the greatest among you must become like the youngest, and the leader like one who serves. For who is greater, the one who is at the table or the one who serves? Is it not the one at the table? But I am among you as one who serves. "You are those who have stood by me in my trials; and I confer on you, just as my Father has conferred on me, a kingdom, so that you may eat and drink at my table in my kingdom, and you will sit on thrones judging the twelve tribes of Israel.

GOOD FRIDAY

The Collect

Almighty God, We pray you graciously to behold this your family, for whom our Lord Jesus Christ was willing to be betrayed, and given into the hands of sinners, and to suffer death upon the cross; who now lives and reigns with you and the Holy Spirit, one God, for ever and ever. *Amen.*

Almighty God, We beseech thee graciously to behold this thy family, for which our Lord Jesus Christ was contented to be betrayed, and given up into the hands of sinners, and to suffer death upon the cross; who now liveth and reigneth with thee and the Holy Ghost ever, one God, world without end. *Amen.*

Years A, B, C

The Lesson   Isaiah 52:13-53:12

See, my servant shall prosper; he shall be exalted and lifted up, and shall be very high. Just as there were many who were astonished at him — so marred was his appearance, beyond human semblance, and his form beyond that of mortals — so he shall startle many nations; kings shall shut their mouths because of him; for that which had not been told them they shall see, and that which they had not heard they shall contemplate. Who has believed what we have heard? And to whom has the arm of the LORD been revealed? For he grew up before him like a young plant, and like a root out of dry ground; he had no form or majesty that we should look at him, nothing in his appearance that we should desire him. He was despised and rejected by others; a man of suffering and acquainted with infirmity; and as one from whom others hide their faces he was despised, and we held him of no account. Surely he has borne our infirmities and carried our diseases; yet we accounted him stricken, struck down by God, and afflicted. But he was wounded for our transgressions, crushed for our iniquities; upon him was the punishment that made us whole, and by his bruises we are healed. All we like sheep have gone astray; we have all turned to our own way, and the LORD has laid on him the iniquity of us all. He was oppressed, and he was afflicted, yet he did not open his mouth; like a lamb that is led to the slaughter, and like a sheep that before its shearers is silent, so he did not open his mouth. By a perversion of justice he was taken away. Who could have imagined his future? For he was cut off from the land of the living, stricken for the transgression of my people. They made his grave with the wicked and his tomb with the rich, although he had done no violence, and there was no deceit in his mouth. Yet it was the will of the LORD to crush him with pain. When you make his life an offering for sin, he shall see his offspring, and shall prolong his days; through him the will of the LORD shall prosper. Out of his anguish he shall see light; he shall find satisfaction through his knowledge. The righteous one, my servant, shall make many righteous, and he shall bear their iniquities. Therefore I will allot him a portion with the great, and he shall divide the spoil with the strong; because he poured out himself to death, and was numbered with the transgressors; yet he bore the sin of many, and made intercession for the transgressors.

or Genesis 22:1-18

After these things God tested Abraham. He said to him, "Abraham!" And he said, "Here I am." He said, "Take your son, your only son Isaac, whom you love, and go the land of Moriah, and offer him there as a burnt offering on one of the mountains that I shall show you." So Abraham rose early in the morning, saddled his donkey, and took two of his young men with him, and his son Isaac; he cut the wood for the burnt offering, and set out and went to the place in the distance that God had shown him. On the third day Abraham looked up and saw the place far away. Then Abraham said to his young men, "Stay here with the donkey; the boy and I will go over there; we will worship, and then we will come back to you." Abraham took the wood of the burnt offering and laid it on his son Isaac, and he himself carried the fire and the knife. So the two of them walked on together. Isaac said to his father Abraham, "Father!" And he said, "Here I am, my son." He said, "The fire and the wood are here but where is the lamb for a burnt offering?" Abraham said,"God himself will provide the lamb for a burnt offering, my son." So the two of them walked on together. When they came to the place that God had shown him, Abraham built an altar there and laid the wood in order. He bound his son Isaac, and laid him on the altar, on top of the wood. Then took the knife to kill his son. But the angel of the LORD called to him from heaven, and said, "Abraham, Abraham!" And he said, "Here I am." He said, "Do not lay your hand on the boy or do anything to him; for now I know that you fear God, since you have not withheld your son, your only son, from me." And Abraham looked up and saw a ram, caught in a thicket by its horns. Abraham went and took the ram and offered it up as a burnt offering instead of his son. So Abraham called that place "The LORD will provide"; as it is said to this day, "On the mount of the LORD it shall be provided." The angel of the LORD called to Abraham a second time from heaven, and said, "By myself I have sworn, says the LORD: Because you have done this, and have not withheld your son, your only son, I will indeed bless you, and I will make your offspring as numerous as the stars of heaven and as the sand that is on the seashore. And your offspring shall possess the gate of their enemies, and by your offspring shall all the nations of the earth gain blessing for themselves, because you have obeyed my voice."

or Wisdom 2:1,12-24

For they reasoned unsoundly, saying to themselves, "Short and sorrowful is our life, and there is no remedy when a life comes to its end, and no one has been known to return from Hades. Let us lie in wait for the righteous man, because he is inconvenient to us and opposes our actions; he reproaches us for sins against the law, and accuses us of sins against our training. He professes to have knowledge of God, and calls himself a child of the Lord. He became to us a reproof of our thoughts; the very sight of him is a burden to us, because his manner of life is unlike that of others, and his ways are strange. We are considered by him as something base, and he avoids our ways as unclean; he called the last end of the righteous happy, and boasts that God is his father. Let us see if his words are true, and let us test what will happen at the end of his life; for if the righteous man is God's child, he will help him, and will deliver him from the hand of his adversaries. Let us test him with insult and torture, so that we may find out how gentle he is, and make trial of his forbearance. Let us condemn him to a shameful death, for, according to what he says, he will be protected." Thus they reasoned, but they were led astray, for their wickedness blinded them, and they did not know the secret purposes of God, nor hoped for the wages of holiness, nor discerned the prize for blameless souls; for God created us for incorruption, and made us in the image of his own eternity, but through the devil's envy death entered the world, and those who belong to his company experience it.

The Psalm 22:1-21 or 22:1-11   *Deus, Deus meus*

1   [My God, my God, why have you forsaken me? *
    and are so far from my cry
    and from the words of my distress?

2   O my God, I cry in the daytime, but you do not answer; *
    by night as well, but I find no rest.

3   Yet you are the Holy One, *
    enthroned upon the praises of Israel.

4   Our forefathers put their trust in you; *
    they trusted, and you delivered them.

5   They cried out to you and were delivered; *
    they trusted in you and were not put to shame.

6   But as for me, I am a worm and no man, *
    scorned by all and despised by the people.

7   All who see me laugh me to scorn; *
    they curl their lips and wag their heads, saying,

8   "He trusted in the LORD; let him deliver him; *
    let him rescue him, if he delights in him."

9   Yet you are he who took me out of the womb, *
    and kept me safe upon my mother's breast.

10   I have been entrusted to you ever since I was born; *
    you were my God when I was still in my mother's womb.

11   Be not far from me, for trouble is near. *
    and there is none to help.]

12   Many young bulls encircle me; *
    strong bulls of Bashan surround me.

13   They open wide their jaws at me, *
    like a ravening and a roaring lion.

14   I am poured out like water;
    all my bones are out of joint; *
    my heart within my breast is melting wax.

15   My mouth is dried out like a pot-sherd;
    my tongue sticks to the roof of my mouth; *
    and you have laid me in the dust of the grave.

16 Packs of dogs close me in,
    and gangs of evildoers circle around me; *
        they pierce my hands and my feet;
        I can count all my bones.

17 They stare and gloat over me; *
        they divide my garments among them;
        they cast lots for my clothing.

18 Be not far away, O LORD; *
        you are my strength; hasten to help me.

19 Save me from the sword, *
        my life from the power of the dog.

20 Save me from the lion's mouth, *
        my wretched body from the horns of wild bulls.

21 I will declare your Name to my brethren; *
        in the midst of the congregation I will praise you.

or Psalm 40:1-14   *Expectans, expectavi*

1   I waited patiently upon the LORD; *
        he stooped to me and heard my cry.

2   He lifted me out of the desolate pit, out of the mire and clay; *
        he set my feet upon a high cliff and made my footing sure.

3   He put a new song in my mouth,
    a song of praise to our God; *
        many shall see, and stand in awe,
        and put their trust in the LORD.

4   Happy are they who trust in the LORD! *
        they do not resort to evil spirits or turn to false gods.

5   Great things are they that you have done, O LORD my God!
    how great your wonders and your plans for us! *
        there is none who can be compared with you.

6   Oh, that I could make them known and tell them! *
        but they are more than I can count.

7   In sacrifice and offering you take no pleasure *
        (you have given me ears to hear you);

8   Burnt-offering and sin-offering you have not required, *
        and so I said, "Behold, I come.

9   In the roll of the book it is written concerning me: *
        'I love to do your will, O my God;
        your law is deep in my heart.'"

10   I proclaimed righteousness in the great congregation; *
       behold, I did not restrain my lips;
       and that, O LORD, you know.

11   Your righteousness have I not hidden in my heart;
       I have spoken of your faithfulness and your deliverance; *
       I have not concealed your love and faithfulness from the great congregation.

12   You are the LORD;
       do not withhold your compassion from me; *
       let your love and your faithfulness keep me safe for ever,

13   For innumerable troubles have crowded upon me;
       my sins have overtaken me, and I cannot see; *
       they are more in number than the hairs of my head,
       and my heart fails me.

14   Be pleased, O LORD, to deliver me; *
       O LORD, make haste to help me.

Or Psalm 69:1-23   *Salvum me fac*

1   Save me, O God, *
       for the waters have risen up to my neck.

2   I am sinking in deep mire, *
       and there is no firm ground for my feet.

3   I have come into deep waters, *
       and the torrent washes over me.

4   I have grown weary with my crying;
       my throat is inflamed; *
       my eyes have failed from looking for my God.

5   Those who hate me without a cause are more than the hairs of my head;
       my lying foes who would destroy me are mighty. *
       Must I then give back what I never stole?

6   O God, you know my foolishness, *
       and my faults are not hidden from you.

7   Let not those who hope in you be put to shame through me, Lord GOD of hosts; *
       let not those who seek you be disgraced because of me, O God of Israel.

8   Surely, for your sake have I suffered reproach, *
       and shame has covered my face.

9   I have become a stranger to my own kindred, *
       an alien to my mother's children.

10   Zeal for your house has eaten me up; *
       the scorn of those who scorn you has fallen upon me.

11   I humbled myself with fasting, *
       but that was turned to my reproach.

12   I put on sack-cloth also, *
       and became a byword among them.

13   Those who sit at the gate murmur against me, *
       and the drunkards make songs about me.

14   But as for me, this is my prayer to you, *
       at the time you have set, O LORD:

15   "In your great mercy, O God, *
       answer me with your unfailing help.

16   Save me from the mire; do not let me sink; *
       let me be rescued from those who hate me
       and out of the deep waters.

17   Let not the torrent of waters wash over me,
       neither let the deep swallow me up; *
       do not let the Pit shut its mouth upon me.

18   Answer me, O LORD, for your love is kind; *
       in your great compassion, turn to me."

19   "Hide not your face from your servant; *
       be swift and answer me, for I am in distress.

20   Draw near to me and redeem me; *
       because of my enemies deliver me.

21   You know my reproach, my shame, and my dishonor; *
       my adversaries are all in your sight."

22   Reproach has broken my heart, and it cannot be healed; *
       I looked for sympathy, but there was none,
       for comforters, but I could find no one.

23   They gave me gall to eat, *
       and when I was thirsty, they gave me vinegar to drink.

The Epistle   **Hebrews 10:1-25**

Since the law has only a shadow of the good things to come and not the true form of these realities, it can never, by the same sacrifices that are continually offered year after year, make perfect those who approach. Otherwise, would they not have ceased being offered, since the worshipers, cleansed once for all, would not longer have any consciousness of sin? But in these sacrifices there is a reminder of sin year after year. For it is impossible for the blood of bulls and goats to take away sins. Consequently, when Christ came into the world, he said, "Sacrifices and offerings you have not desired, but a body you have prepared for me; in burnt offerings and sin offerings you have taken no pleasure. Then I said, 'See, God, I have come to do your will, O God' (in the scroll of the book it is written of me)." When he said above, "You have neither desired nor taken pleasure in sacrifices and offerings and burnt offerings and sin offerings" (these are offered according to the law), then he added, "See, I have come to do your will." He abolishes the first in order to establish the second. And it is by God's will that we have been sanctified through the offering of the body of Jesus Christ once for all. And every priest stands day after day at his service, offering again and again the same sacrifices that can never take away sins. But when Christ had offered for all time a single sacrifice for sins, "he sat down at the right hand of God," and since then has been waiting "until his enemies would be made a footstool for his feet. "For by a single offering he has perfected for all time those who are sanctified. And the Holy Spirit also testifies to us, for after saying, "This is the covenant that I will make with them after those days, says the Lord: I will put my laws in their hearts, and I will write them on their minds," he also adds, "I will remember their sins and their lawless deeds no more." Where there is forgiveness of these, there is no longer any offering for sin. Therefore, my friends, since we have confidence to enter the sanctuary by the blood of Jesus, by the new and living way that he opened for us through the curtain (that is, through his flesh), and since we have a great priest over the house of God, let us approach with a true heart in full assurance of faith, with our hearts sprinkled clean from an evil conscience and our bodies washed with pure water. Let us hold fast to the confession of our hope without wavering, for he who has promised is faithful. And let us consider how to provoke one another to love and good deeds, not neglecting to meet together, as is the habit of some, but encouraging one another, and all the more as you see the Day approaching.

The Gospel   John (18:1-40) 19:1-37

[Jesus went out with his disciples across the Kidron valley to a place where there was a garden, which he and his disciples entered. Now Judas, who betrayed him, also knew the place, because Jesus often met there with his disciples. So Judas brought a detachment of soldiers together with police from the chief priests and the Pharisees, and they came there with lanterns and torches and weapons. Then Jesus, knowing all that was to happen to him, came forward and asked them, "Whom are you looking for?" They answered, "Jesus of Nazareth." Jesus replied, "I am he." Judas, who betrayed him, was standing with them. When Jesus said to them, "I am he," they stepped back and fell to the ground. Again he asked them, "Whom are you looking for?" And they said, "Jesus of Nazareth." Jesus answered, "I told you that I am he. So if you are looking for me, let these men go." This was to fulfill the word that he had spoken, "I did not lose a single one of those whom you gave me." Then Simon Peter, who had a sword, drew it, struck the high priest's slave, and cut off his right ear. The slave's name was Malchus. Jesus said to Peter, "Put your sword back into its sheath. Am I not to drink the cup that the Father has given me?" So the soldiers, their officer, and the Jewish police arrested Jesus and bound him. First they took him to Annas, who was the father-in-law of Caiaphas, the high priest that year. Caiaphas was the one who had advised the Jews that it was better to have one person die for the people. Simon Peter and another disciple followed Jesus. Since that disciple was known to the high priest, he went with Jesus into the courtyard of the high priest, but Peter was standing outside at the gate. So the other disciple, who was known to the high priest, went out, spoke to the woman who guarded the gate, and brought Peter in. The woman said to Peter, "You are not also one of this man's disciples, are you?" He said, "I am not." Now the slaves and the police had made a charcoal fire because it was cold, and they were standing around it and warming themselves. Peter also was standing with them and warming himself. Then the high priest questioned Jesus about his disciples and about his teaching. Jesus answered, "I have spoken openly to the world; I have always taught in synagogues and in the temple, where all the Jews come together. I have said nothing in secret. why do you ask me? Ask those who heard what I said to them; they know what I said." When he had said this, one of the police standing nearby struck Jesus on the face, saying, "Is that how you answer the high priest?" Jesus answered, "If I have spoken wrongly, testify to the wrong. But if I have spoken rightly, why do you strike me?" Then Annas sent him bound to Caiaphas the high priest. Now Simon Peter was standing and warming himself. They asked him, "You are not also one of his disciples, are you?" He denied it and said, "I am not." One of the slaves of the high priest, a relative of the man whose ear Peter had cut off, asked, "Did I not see you in the garden with him?" Again Peter denied it, and at that moment the cock crowed. Then they took Jesus from Caiaphas to Pilate's headquarters. It was early in the morning. They themselves did not enter the headquarters, so as to avoid ritual defilement and to be able to eat the Passover. So Pilate went out to them and said, "What accusation do you bring against this man?" They answered, "If this man were not a criminal, we would not have handed him over to you." Pilate said to them, "Take him yourselves and judge him according to your law." The Jews replied, "We are not permitted to put anyone to death." (This was to fulfill what Jesus had said when he indicated the kind of death he was to die.) Then Pilate entered the headquarters again, summoned Jesus, and asked him, "Are you the King of the Jews?" Jesus answered, "Do you ask this on your own, or did others tell you about me?" Pilate replied, "I am not a Jew, am I? Your own nation and the chief priests have handed you over to me. What have you done?" Jesus answered, "My kingdom is not from this world. If my kingdom were from this world, my followers would be fighting to keep me from being handed over to the Jews. But as it is, my kingdom is not from here." Pilate asked him, "So you are a king?" Jesus answered, "You say that I am a king. For this I was born, and for this I came into the world, to testify to the truth. Everyone who belongs to the truth listens to my voice." Pilate asked him, "What is truth?" After he had said this, he went out to the Jews again and told them, "I find no case against him. But you have a custom that I release someone for you at the Passover. Do you want me to release for you the King of the Jews?" They shouted in reply, "Not this man, but Barabbas!" Now Barabbas was a bandit.] Then Pilate took Jesus and had him flogged. And the soldiers wove a crown of thorns and put it on his head, and they dressed him in a purple robe. They kept coming up to him, saying, "Hail, King of the Jews!" and striking him on the face. Pilate went out again and said to them, "Look, I am bringing him out to you to let you know that I find no case against him." So Jesus came out, wearing the crown of thorns and the purple robe. Pilate said to them, "Here is the man!" When the chief priests and the police saw him, they shouted, "Crucify him! Crucify him!" Pilate said to them, "Take him yourselves and crucify him; I find no case against him." The Jews answered him, "We have a law, and according to that law he ought to die because he has claimed to be the Son of God." Now when Pilate heard this, he was more afraid than ever. He entered his headquarters again and asked Jesus,

"Where are you from?" But Jesus gave him no answer. Pilate therefore said to him, "Do you refuse to speak to me? Do you not know that I have power to release you, and power to crucify you?" Jesus answered him, "You would have no power over me unless it had been given you from above; therefore the one who handed me over to you is guilty of a greater sin." From then on Pilate tried to release him, but the Jews cried out, "If you release this man, you are no friend of the emperor. Everyone who claims to be a king sets himself against the emperor." When Pilate heard these words, he brought Jesus outside and sat on the judge's bench at a place called The Stone Pavement, or in Hebrew Gabbatha. Now it was the day of Preparation for the Passover; and it was about noon. He said to the Jews, "Here is your King!" They cried out, "Away with him! Away with him! Crucify him!" Pilate asked them, "Shall I crucify your King?" The chief priests answered, "We have no king but the emperor." Then he handed him over to them to be crucified. So they took Jesus; and carrying the cross by himself, he went out to what is called The Place of the Skull, which in Hebrew is called Golgotha. There they crucified him, and with him two others, one on either side, with Jesus between them. Pilate also had an inscription written and put on the cross. It read, "Jesus of Nazareth, the King of the Jews." Many of the Jews read this inscription, because the place where Jesus was crucified was near the city; and it was written in Hebrew, in Latin, and in Greek. Then the chief priests of the Jews said to Pilate, "Do not write, 'The King of the Jews,' but 'This man said, I am the King of the Jews.'" Pilate answered, "What I have written I have written." When the soldiers had crucified Jesus, they took his clothes and divided them into four parts, one for each soldier. They also took his tunic; now the tunic was seamless, woven in one piece from the top. So they said to one another, "Let us not tear it, but cast lots for it to see who will get it." This was to fulfill what the scripture says, "They divided my clothes among themselves, and for my clothing they cast lots." And that is what the soldiers did. Meanwhile, standing near the cross of Jesus were his mother, and his mother's sister, Mary the wife of Clopas, and Mary Magdalene. When Jesus saw his mother and the disciple whom he loved standing beside her, he said to his mother, "Woman, here is your son." Then he said to the disciple, "Here is your mother." And from that hour the disciple took her into his own home. After this, when Jesus knew that all was now finished, he said (in order to fulfill the scripture), "I am thirsty." A jar full of sour wine was standing there. So they put a sponge full of the wine on a branch of hyssop and held it to his mouth. When Jesus had receive the wine, he said, "It is finished." Then he bowed his head and gave up his spirit. Since it was the day of Preparation, the Jews did not want the bodies left on the cross during the sabbath, especially because that sabbath was a day of great solemnity. So they asked Pilate to have the legs of the crucified men broken and the bodies removed. Then the soldiers came and broke the legs of the first and of the other who had been crucified with him. But when they came to Jesus and saw that he was already dead, they did not break his legs. Instead, one of the soldiers pierced his side with a spear, and at once blood and water came out. (He who saw this has testified so that you also may believe. His testimony is true, and he knows that he tells the truth.) These things occurred so that the scripture might be fulfilled, "None of his bones shall be broken." And again another passage of scripture says, "They will look on the one whom they have pierced."

HOLY SATURDAY

The Collect

O God, Creator of heaven and earth: Grant that, as the crucified body of your dear Son was laid in the tomb and rested on this holy Sabbath, so we may await with him the coming of the third day, and rise with him to newness of life; who now lives and reigns with you and the Holy Spirit, one God for ever and ever. *Amen.*

O God, Creator of heaven and earth: Grant that, as the crucified body of thy dear Son was laid in the tomb and rested on this holy Sabbath, so we may await with him the coming of the third day, and rise with him to newness of life; who now liveth and reigneth with thee and the Holy Spirit, one God, for ever and ever. *Amen.*

The Lesson   Job 14:1-14

A mortal, born of woman, few of days and full of trouble, comes up like a flower and withers, flees like a shadow and does not last. Do you fix your eyes on such a one? Do you bring me into judgment with you? Who can bring a clean thing out of an unclean? No one can. Since their days are determined, and the number of their months is known to you, and you have appointed the bounds that they cannot pass, look away from them, and desist, that they may enjoy, like laborers, their days. "For there is hope for a tree, if it is cut down, that it will sprout again, and that its shoots will not cease. Though its root grows old in the earth, and its stump dies in the ground, yet at the scent of water it will bud and put forth branches like a young plant. But mortals die, and are laid low; humans expire, and where are they? As waters fail from a lake, and a river wastes away and dries up, so mortals lie down and do not rise again; until the heavens are no more, they will not awake or be roused out of their sleep. Oh that you would hide me in Sheol, that you would conceal me until your wrath is past, that you would appoint me a set time, and remember me! If mortals die, will they live again? All the days of my service I would wait until my release should come.

The Psalm 130   *De profundis*

1   Out of the depths have I called to you, O LORD;
     LORD, hear my voice; *
        let your ears consider well the voice of my supplication.

2   If you, LORD, were to note what is done amiss, *
        O LORD, who could stand?

3   For there is forgiveness with you; *
        therefore you shall be feared.

4   I wait for the LORD; my soul waits for him; *
        in his word is my hope.

5   My soul waits for the LORD,
     more than watchmen for the morning, *
        more than watchmen for the morning.

6   O Israel, wait for the Lord, *
       for with the Lord there is mercy;

7   With him there is plenteous redemption, *
       and he shall redeem Israel from all their sins.

or Psalm 31:1-5   *In te, Domine, speravi*
     In you, O Lord, have I taken refuge;
     let me never be put to shame; *
       deliver me in your righteousness.

2   Incline your ear to me; *
       make haste to deliver me.

3   Be my strong rock, a castle to keep me safe,
     for you are my crag and my stronghold; *
       for the sake of your Name, lead me and guide me.

4   Take me out of the net that they have secretly set for me, *
       for you are my tower of strength.

5   Into your hands I commend my spirit, *
       for you have redeemed me,
       O Lord, O God of truth.

The Epistle   **1 Peter 4:1-8**
Since therefore Christ suffered in the flesh, arm yourselves also with the same
intention (for whoever has suffered in the flesh has finished with sin), so as to live for
the rest of your earthly life no longer by human desires but by the will of God. You
have already spent enough time in doing what the Gentiles like to do, living in
licentiousness, passions, drunkenness, revels, carousing, and lawless idolatry. They
are surprised that you longer join them in the same excesses of dissipation, and so
they blaspheme. But they will have to given an accounting to him who stands ready
to judge the living and the dead. For this is the reason the gospel was proclaimed
even to the dead, so that, though they had been judged in the flesh as everyone is
judged, they might live in the spirit as God does. The end of all things is near;
therefore be serious and discipline yourselves for the sake of your prayers. Above all,
maintain constant love for one another, for love covers a multitude of sins.

The Gospel   **Matthew 27:57-66**
When it was evening, there came a rich man from Arimathea, named Joseph, who
was also a disciple of Jesus. He went to Pilate and asked for the body of Jesus; then
Pilate ordered it to be given to him. So Joseph took the body and wrapped it in a
clean linen cloth and laid it in his own new tomb, which he had hewn in the rock. He
then rolled a great stone to the door of the tomb and went away. Mary Magdalene
and the other Mary were there, sitting opposite the tomb. The next day, that is, after
the day of Preparation, the chief priests and the Pharisees gathered before Pilate and
said, "Sir, we remember what that impostor said while he was still alive, 'After three
days I will rise again.' Therefore command the tomb to be made secure until the

third day; otherwise his disciples may go and steal him away, and tell the people, 'He has been raised from the dead,' and the last deception would be worse than the first." Pilate said to them, "You have a guard of soldiers; go, make it as secure as you can." So they went with the guard and made the tomb secure by sealing the stone.

or John 19:38-42
After these things, Joseph of Arimathea, who was a disciple of Jesus, though a secret one because of his fear of the Jews, asked Pilate to let him take away the body of Jesus. Pilate gave him permission; so he came and removed his body. Nicodemus, who had at first come to Jesus by night, also came, bringing a mixture of myrrh and aloes, weighing about a hundred pounds. They took the body of Jesus and wrapped it with the spices in linen cloths, according to the burial custom of the Jews. Now there was a garden in the place where he was crucified, and in the garden there was a new tomb in which no one had ever been laid. And so, because it was the Jewish day of Preparation, and the tomb was nearby, they laid Jesus there.

THE GREAT VIGIL OF EASTER

At least two of the following Lessons are read, of which one is always the Lesson from Exodus. After each Lesson, the Psalm or Canticle listed, or some other suitable psalm, canticle, or hymn may be sung. A period of silence may be kept; and the Collect provided, or some other suitable Collect, may be said.

The story of Creation
Genesis 1:1-2:2
In the beginning when God created the heavens and the earth, the earth was a formless void and darkness covered the face of the deep, while a wind from God swept over the face of the waters. Then God said, "Let there be light"; and there was light. And God saw that the light was good; and God separated the light from the darkness. God called the light Day, and the darkness he called Night. And there was evening and there was morning, the first day. And God said, "Let there be a dome in the midst of the waters, and let it separate the waters from the waters." So God made the dome and separated the waters that were under the dome from the waters that were above the dome. And it was so. God called the dome Sky. And there was evening and there was morning, the second day. And God said, "Let the waters under the sky be gathered together into one place, and let the dry land appear." And it was so. God called the dry land Earth, and the waters that were gathered together he called Seas. And God saw that it was good. Then God said, "Let the earth put forth vegetation: plants yielding seed, and fruit trees of every kind on earth that bear fruit with the seed in it." And it was so. The earth brought forth vegetation: plants yielding seed of every kind, and trees of every kind bearing fruit with the seed in it. And God saw that it was good. And there was evening and there was morning, the third day. And God said, "Let there be lights in the dome of the sky to separate the day from the night; and let them be for signs and for seasons and for days and years, and let them be lights in the dome of the sky to give light upon the earth." And it was so. God made the two great lights — the greater light to rule the day and the lesser

light to rule the night — and the stars. God set them in the dome of the sky to give light upon the earth, to rule over the day and over the night, and to separate the light from the darkness. And God saw that it was good. And there was evening and there was morning, the fourth day. And God said, "Let the waters bring forth swarms of living creatures, and let birds fly above the earth across the dome of the sky." So God created the great sea monsters and every living creature that moves, of every kind, with which the waters swarm, and every winged bird of every kind. And God saw that it was good. God blessed them, saying, "Be fruitful and multiply and fill the waters in the seas, and let birds multiply on the earth." And there was evening and there was morning, the fifth day. And God said, "Let the earth bring forth living creatures of every kind: cattle and creeping things and wild animals of the earth of every kind." And it was so. God made the wild animals of the earth of every kind, and the cattle of every kind, and everything that creeps upon the ground of every kind. And God saw that it was good. Then God said, "Let us make humankind in our image, according to our likeness; and let them have dominion over the fish of the sea, and over the birds of the air, and over the cattle, and over all the wild animals of the earth, and over every creeping thing that creeps upon the earth." So God created humankind in his image, in the image of God he created them; male and female he created them. God blessed them, and God said to them, "Be fruitful and multiply, and fill the earth and subdue it; and have dominion over the fish of the sea and over the birds of the air and over every living thing that moves upon the earth." God said, "See, I have given you every plant yielding seed that is upon the face of all the earth, and every tree with seed in its fruit; you shall have them for food. And to every beast of the earth, and to every bird of the air, and to everything that creeps on the earth, everything that has the breath of life, I have given every green plant for food." And it was so. God saw everything that he had made, and indeed, it was very good. And there was evening and there was morning, the sixth day. Thus the heavens and the earth were finished, and all their multitude. And on the seventh day God finished the work that he had done, and he rested on the seventh day from all the work that he had done.

The Psalm 33:1-11 *Exultate, justi*

1 Rejoice in the LORD, you righteous; *
   it is good for the just to sing praises.

2 Praise the LORD with the harp; *
   play to him upon the psaltery and lyre.

3 Sing for him a new song; *
   sound a fanfare with all your skill upon the trumpet.

4 For the word of the LORD is right, *
   and all his works are sure.

5 He loves righteousness and justice; *
   the loving-kindness of the LORD fills the whole earth.

6 By the word of the LORD were the heavens made, *
   by the breath of his mouth all the heavenly hosts.

7 He gathers up the waters of the ocean as in a water-skin *
and stores up the depths of the sea.

8 Let all the earth fear the LORD; *
let all who dwell in the world stand in awe of him.

9 For he spoke, and it came to pass; *
he commanded, and it stood fast.

10 The LORD brings the will of the nations to naught; *
he thwarts the designs of the peoples.

11 But the LORD's will stands fast for ever, *
and the designs of his heart from age to age.

or Psalm 36:5-10   *Dixit injustus*

5 Your love, O LORD, reaches to the heavens, *
and your faithfulness to the clouds.

6 Your righteousness is like the strong mountains,
your justice like the great deep; *
you save both man and beast, O LORD.

7 How priceless is your love, O God! *
your people take refuge under the shadow of your wings.

8 They feast upon the abundance of your house; *
you give them drink from the river of your delights.

9 For with you is the well of life, *
and in your light we see light.

10 Continue your loving-kindness to those who know you, *
and your favor to those who are true of heart.

The Flood
Genesis 7:1-5, 11-18; 8:6-18; 9:8-13
Then the LORD said to Noah, "Go into the ark, you and all your household, for I
have seen that you alone are righteous before me in this generation. Take with you
seven pairs of all clean animals, the male and its mate; and a pair of the animals that
are not clean, the male and its mate; and seven pairs of the birds of the air also, male
and female, to keep their kind alive on the face of all the earth. For in seven days I
will send rain on the earth for forty days and forty nights; and every living thing that
I have made I will blot out from the face of the ground." And Noah did all that the
LORD had commanded him. In the six hundredth year of Noah's life, in the second
month, on the seventeenth day of the month, on that day all the fountains of the
great deep burst forth, and the windows of the heavens were opened. The rain fell on
the earth forty days and forty nights. On the very same day Noah with his sons,
Shem and Ham and Japheth, and Noah's wife and the three wives of his sons entered
the ark, they and every wild animal of every kind, and all domestic animals of every
kind, and every creeping thing that creeps on the earth, and every bird of every kind

— every bird, every winged creature. They went into the ark with Noah, two and two of all flesh in which there was the breath of life. And those that entered, male and female of all flesh, went in as God had commanded him; and the LORD shut him in. The flood continued forty days on the earth; and the waters increased, and bore up the ark, and it rose high above the earth. The waters swelled and increased greatly on the earth; and the ark floated on the face of the waters. At the end of forty days Noah opened the window of the ark that he had made and sent out the raven; and it went to and fro until the waters were dried up from the earth. Then he sent out the dove from him, to see if the waters had subsided from the face of the ground; but the dove found no place to set its foot, and it returned to him to the ark, for the waters were still on the face of the whole earth. So he put out his hand and took it and brought it into the ark with him. He waited another seven days, and again he sent out the dove from the ark; and the dove came back to him in the evening, and there in its beak was a freshly plucked olive leaf; so Noah knew that the waters had subsided from the earth. Then he waited another seven days, and sent out the dove; and it did not return to him anymore. In the six hundred first year, in the first month, the first day of the month, the waters were dried up from the earth; and Noah removed the covering of the ark, and looked, and saw that the face of the ground was drying. In the second month, on the twenty-seventh day of the month, the earth was dry. Then God said to Noah, "Go out of the ark, you and your wife, and your sons and your sons' wives with you. Bring out with you every living thing that is with you of all flesh — birds and animals and every creeping thing that creeps on the earth — so that they may abound on the earth, and be fruitful and multiply on the earth." So Noah went out with his sons and his wife and his sons' wives. Then God said to Noah and to his sons with him, "As for me, I am establishing my covenant with you and your descendants after you, and with every living creature that is with you, the birds, the domestic animals, and every animal of the earth with you, as many as came out of the ark. I establish my covenant with you, that never again shall all flesh be cut off by the waters of a flood, and never again shall there be a flood to destroy the earth." God said, "This is the sign of the covenant that I make between me and you and every living creature that is with you, for all future generations: I have set my bow in the clouds, and it shall be a sign of the covenant between me and the earth."

The Psalm 46   *Deus noster refugium*

1   God is our refuge and strength, *
        a very present help in trouble.

2   Therefore we will not fear, though the earth be moved, *
        and though the mountains be toppled into the depths of the sea;

3   Though its waters rage and foam, *
        and though the mountains tremble at its tumult.

4   The LORD of hosts is with us; *
        the God of Jacob is our stronghold.

5   There is a river whose streams make glad the city of God, *
        the holy habitation of the Most High.

God is in the midst of her;
she shall not be overthrown; *
    God shall help her at the break of day.

The nations make much ado, and the kingdoms are shaken; *
    God has spoken, and the earth shall melt away.

The LORD of hosts is with us; *
    the God of Jacob is our stronghold.

Come now and look upon the works of the LORD, *
    what awesome things he has done on earth.

10 It is he who makes war to cease in all the world; *
    he breaks the bow, and shatters the spear,
    and burns the shields with fire.

11 "Be still, then, and know that I am God; *
    I will be exalted among the nations;
    I will be exalted in the earth."

12 The LORD of hosts is with us; *
    the God of Jacob is our stronghold.

Abraham's sacrifice of Isaac
Genesis 22:1-18

After these things God tested Abraham. He said to him, "Abraham!" And he said,
"Here I am." He said, "Take your son, your only son Isaac, whom you love, and go to
the land of Moriah, and offer him there as a burnt offering on one of the mountains
that I shall show you." So Abraham rose early in the morning, saddled his donkey,
and took two of his young men with him, and his son Isaac; he cut the wood for the
burnt offering, and set out and went to the place in the distance that God had shown
him. On the third day Abraham looked up and saw the place far away. Then
Abraham said to his young men, "Stay here with the donkey; the boy and I will go
over there; we will worship, and then we will come back to you." Abraham took the
wood of the burnt offering and laid it on his son Isaac, and he himself carried the fire
and the knife. So the two of them walked on together. Isaac said to his father
Abraham, "Father!" And he said, "Here I am, my son." He said, "The fire and the
wood are here, but where is the lamb for a burnt offering?" Abraham said, "God
himself will provide the lamb for a burnt offering, my son." So the two of them
walked on together. When they came to the place that God had shown him, Abraham
built an altar there and laid the wood in order. He bound his son Isaac, and laid him
on the altar, on top of the wood. Then Abraham reached out his hand and took the
knife to kill his son. But the angel of the LORD called to him from heaven, and said,
"Abraham, Abraham!" And he said, "Here I am." He said, "Do not lay your hand on
the boy or do anything to him; for now I know that you fear God, since you have not
withheld your son, your only son, from me." And Abraham looked up and saw a
ram, caught in a thicket by its horns. Abraham went and took the ram and offered it
up as a burnt offering instead of his son. So Abraham called that place "The LORD

will provide"; as it is said to this day, "On the mount of the LORD it shall be provided." The angel of the LORD called to Abraham a second time from heaven, and said, "By myself I have sworn, says the LORD: Because you have done this, and have not withheld your son, your only son, I will indeed bless you, and I will make your offspring as numerous as the stars of heaven and as the sand that is on the seashore. And your offspring shall possess the gate of their enemies, and by your offspring shall all the nations of the earth gain blessing for themselves, because you have obeyed my voice."

The Psalm 33:12-22   *Exultate, justi*

12 Happy is the nation whose God is the LORD! *
     happy the people he has chosen to be his own!

13 The LORD looks down from heaven, *
     and beholds all the people in the world.

14 From where he sits enthroned he turns his gaze *
     on all who dwell on the earth.

15 He fashions all the hearts of them *
     and understands all their works.

16 There is no king that can be saved by a mighty army; *
     a strong man is not delivered by his great strength.

17 The horse is a vain hope for deliverance; *
     for all its strength it cannot save.

18 Behold, the eye of the LORD is upon those who fear him, *
     on those who wait upon his love,

19 To pluck their lives from death, *
     and to feed them in time of famine.

20 Our soul waits for the LORD; *
     he is our help and our shield.

21 Indeed, our heart rejoices in him, *
     for in his holy Name we put our trust.

22 Let your loving-kindness, O LORD, be upon us, *
     as we have put our trust in you.

or Psalm 16   *Conserva me, Domine*

1 Protect me, O God, for I take refuge in you; *
     I have said to the LORD, "You are my Lord,
         my good above all other."

2 All my delight is upon the godly that are in the land, *
     upon those who are noble among the people.

3 But those who run after other gods *
     shall have their troubles multiplied.

4   Their libations of blood I will not offer, *
        nor take the names of their gods upon my lips.

5   O LORD, you are my portion and my cup; *
        it is you who uphold my lot.

6   My boundaries enclose a pleasant land; *
        indeed, I have a goodly heritage.

7   I will bless the LORD who gives me counsel; *
        my heart teaches me, night after night.

8   I have set the LORD always before me; *
        because he is at my right hand I shall not fall.

9   My heart, therefore, is glad, and my spirit rejoices; *
        my body also shall rest in hope.

10 For you will not abandon me to the grave, *
        nor let your holy one see the Pit.

11 You will show me the path of life; *
        in your presence there is fullness of joy,
        and in your right hand are pleasures for evermore.

Israel's deliverance at the Red Sea
Exodus 14:10-15:1

As Pharaoh drew near, the Israelites looked back, and there were the Egyptians advancing on them. In great fear the Israelites cried out to the LORD. They said to Moses, "Was it because there were no graves in Egypt that you have taken us away to die in the wilderness? What have you done to us, bringing us out of Egypt? Is this not the very thing we told you in Egypt, 'Let us alone and let us serve the Egyptians'? For it would have been better for us to serve the Egyptians than to die in the wilderness." But Moses said to the people, "Do not be afraid, stand firm, and see the deliverance that the LORD will accomplish for you today; for the Egyptians whom you see today you shall never see again. The LORD will fight for you, and you have only to keep still." Then the LORD said to Moses, "Why do you cry out to me? Tell the Israelites to go forward. But you lift up your staff, and stretch out your hand over the sea and divide it, that the Israelites may go into the sea on dry ground. Then I will harden the hearts of the Egyptians so that they will go in after them; and so I will gain glory for myself over Pharaoh and all his army, his chariots, and his chariot drivers. And the Egyptians shall know that I am the LORD, when I have gained glory for myself over Pharaoh, his chariots, and his chariot drivers." The angel of God who was going before the Israelite army moved and went behind them; and the pillar of cloud moved from in front of them and took its place behind them. It came between the army of Egypt and the army of Israel. And so the cloud was there with the darkness, and it lit up the night; one did not come near the other all night. Then Moses stretched out his hand over the sea. The LORD drove the sea back by a strong east wind all night, and turned the sea into dry land; and the waters were divided. The Israelites went into the sea on dry ground, the waters forming a wall for them on their right and on their left. The Egyptians pursued, and went into the sea after them, all of Pharaoh's horses, chariots, and chariot drivers. At the morning watch the LORD in the pillar of fire and cloud looked down upon the Egyptian army, and threw the Egyptian army into panic. He clogged their chariot wheels so that they turned with difficulty. The Egyptians said, "Let us flee from the Israelites, for the LORD is fighting for them against Egypt." Then the LORD said to Moses, "Stretch out your hand over the sea, so that the water may come back upon the Egyptians, upon their chariots and chariot drivers." So Moses stretched out his hand over the sea, and at dawn the sea returned to its normal depth. As the Egyptians fled before it, the LORD tossed the Egyptians into the sea. The waters returned and covered the chariots and the chariot drivers, the entire army of Pharaoh that had followed them into the sea; not one of them remained. But the Israelites walked on dry ground through the sea, the waters forming a wall for them on their right and on their left. Thus the LORD saved Israel that day from the Egyptians; and Israel saw the Egyptians dead on the seashore. Israel saw the great work that the LORD did against the Egyptians. So the people feared the LORD and believed in the LORD and in his servant Moses. Then Moses and the Israelites sang this song to the LORD: "I will sing to the LORD, for he has triumphed gloriously; horse and rider he has thrown into the sea."

Canticle 8, *The Son of Moses Cantemus Domino*
I will sing to the Lord, for he is lofty and uplifted; *
    the horse and its rider has he hurled into the sea.
The Lord is my strength and my refuge; *
    the Lord has become my Savior.
This is my God and I will praise him, *
    the God of my people and I will exalt him.
The Lord is a mighty warrior; *
    Yahweh is his Name.
The chariots of Pharaoh and his army has he hurled into the sea; *
    the finest of those who bear armor have been drowned in the Red Sea.
The fathomless deep has overwhelmed them; *
    they sank into the depths like a stone.
Your right hand, O Lord, is glorious in might; *
    your right hand, O Lord, has overthrown the enemy.
Who can be compared with you, O Lord, among the gods? *
    who is like you, glorious in holiness,
    awesome in renown, and worker of wonders?
You stretched forth your right hand; *
    the earth swallowed them up.
With your constant love you led the people you redeemed; *
    with your might you brought them in safety to your holy dwelling.
You will bring them in and plant them *
    on the mount of your possession,
The resting-place you have made for yourself, O Lord, *
    the sanctuary, O Lord, that your hand has established.
The Lord shall reign *
    for ever and for ever.

Glory to the Father, and to the Son, and to the Holy Spirit: *
    as it was in the beginning, is now, and will be for ever. Amen.

God's Presence in a renewed Israel
Isaiah 4:2-6

On that day the branch of the LORD shall be beautiful and glorious, and the fruit of the land shall be the pride and glory of the survivors of Israel. Whoever is left in Zion and remains in Jerusalem will be called holy, everyone who has been recorded for life in Jerusalem, once the Lord has washed away the filth of the daughters of Zion and cleansed the bloodstains of Jerusalem from its midst by a spirit of judgment and by a spirit of burning. Then the LORD will create over the whole site of Mount Zion and over its places of assembly a cloud by day and smoke and the shining of a flaming fire by night. Indeed over all the glory there will be a canopy. It will serve as a pavilion, a shade by day from the heat, and a refuge and a shelter from the storm and rain.

Psalm 122 *Laetatus sum*

1   I was glad when they said to me, *
        "Let us go to the house of the LORD."

2   Now our feet are standing *
        within your gates, O Jerusalem.

3   Jerusalem is built as a city *
        that is at unity with itself;

4   To which the tribes go up,
    the tribes of the LORD, *
        the assembly of Israel,
        to praise the Name of the LORD.

5   For there are the thrones of judgment, *
        the thrones of the house of David.

6   Pray for the peace of Jerusalem: *
        "May they prosper who love you.

7   Peace be within your walls *
        and quietness within your towers.

8   For my brethren and companions' sake, *
        I pray for your prosperity.

9   Because of the house of the LORD our God, *
        I will seek to do you good."

Salvation offered freely to all
Isaiah 55:1-11

Ho, everyone who thirsts, come to the waters; and you that have no money, come, buy and eat! Come, buy wine and milk without money and without price. Why do you spend your money for that which is not bread, and your labor for that which does not satisfy? Listen carefully to me, and eat what is good, and delight yourselves in rich food. Incline your ear, and come to me; listen, so that you may live. I will make with you an everlasting covenant, my steadfast, sure love for David. See, I made him a witness to the peoples, a leader and commander for the peoples. See, you shall call nations that you do not know, and nations that do not know you shall run to you, because of the LORD your God, the Holy One of Israel, for he has glorified you. Seek the LORD while he may be found, call upon him while he is near; let the wicked forsake their way, and the unrighteous their thoughts; let them return to the LORD, that he may have mercy on them, and to our God, for he will abundantly pardon. For my thoughts are not your thoughts, nor are your ways my ways, says the LORD. For as the heavens are higher than the earth, so are my ways higher than your ways and my thoughts than your thoughts. For as the rain and the snow come down from heaven, and do not return there until they have watered the earth, making it bring forth and sprout, giving seed to the sower and bread to the eater, so shall my word be that goes out from my mouth; it shall not return to me empty, but it shall accomplish that which I purpose, and succeed in the thing for which I sent it.

Canticle 9, The First Son of Isaiah *Ecce, Deus*

Surely, it is God who saves me; *
    I will trust in him and not be afraid.
For the Lord is my stronghold and my sure defense, *
    and he will be my Savior.
Therefore you shall draw water with rejoicing *
    from the springs of salvation.
And on that day you shall say, *
    Give thanks to the Lord and call upon his Name;
Make his deeds known among the peoples; *
    see that they remember that his Name is exalted.
Sing the praises of the Lord, for he has done great things, *
    and this is known in all the world.
Cry aloud, inhabitants of Zion, ring out your joy, *
    for the great one in the midst of you is the Holy One of Israel.
Glory to the Father, and to the Son, and to the Holy Spirit: *
    as it was in the beginning, is now, and will be for ever. Amen.

or Psalm 42:1-7 *Quemadmodum*

1   As the deer longs for the water-brooks, *
      so longs my soul for you, O God.

2   My soul is athirst for God, athirst for the living God; *
      when shall I come to appear before the presence of God?

3   My tears have been my food day and night, *
      while all day long they say to me,
      "Where now is your God?"

4   I pour out my soul when I think on these things: *
      how I went with the multitude and led them into the house of God,

5   With the voice of praise and thanksgiving, *
    among those who keep holy-day.

6   Why are you so full of heaviness, O my soul? *
    and why are you so disquieted within me?

7   Put your trust in God; *
    for I will yet give thanks to him,
    who is the help of my countenance, and my God.

A new heart and a new spirit
Ezekiel 36:24-28

I will take you from the nations, and gather you from all the countries, and bring you into your own land. I will sprinkle clean water upon you, and you shall be clean from all your uncleannesses, and from all your idols I will cleanse you. A new heart I will give you, and a new spirit I will put within you; and I will remove from your body the heart of stone and give you a heart of flesh. I will put my spirit within you, and make you follow my statutes and be careful to observe my ordinances. Then you shall live in the land that I gave to your ancestors; and you shall be my people, and I will be your God.

The Psalm 42:1-7   *Quemadmodum*

1   As the deer longs for the water-brooks, *
    so longs my soul for you, O God.

2   My soul is athirst for God, athirst for the living God; *
    when shall I come to appear before the presence of God?

3   My tears have been my food day and night, *
    while all day long they say to me,
    "Where now is your God?"

4   I pour out my soul when I think on these things: *
    how I went with the multitude and led them into the house of God,

5   With the voice of praise and thanksgiving, *
    among those who keep holy-day.

6   Why are you so full of heaviness, O my soul? *
    and why are you so disquieted within me?

7   Put your trust in God; *
    for I will yet give thanks to him,
    who is the help of my countenance, and my God.

or Canticle 9, The First Son of Isaiah *Ecce, Deus*
Isaiah 12:2-6

Surely, it is God who saves me; *
    I will trust in him and not be afraid.

For the Lord is my stronghold and my sure defense, *
    and he will be my Savior.
Therefore you shall draw water with rejoicing *
    from the springs of salvation.
And on that day you shall say, *
    Give thanks to the Lord and call upon his Name;
Make his deeds known among the peoples; *
    see that they remember that his Name is exalted.
Sing the praises of the Lord, for he has done great things, *
    and this is known in all the world.
Cry aloud, inhabitants of Zion, ring out your joy, *
    for the great one in the midst of you is the Holy One of Israel.
Glory to the Father, and to the Son, and to the Holy Spirit: *
    as it was in the beginning, is now, and will be for ever. Amen.

The valley of dry bones
Ezekiel 37:1-14
The hand of the LORD came upon me, and he brought me out by the spirit of the LORD and set me down in the middle of a valley; it was full of bones. He led me all around them; there were very many lying in the valley, and they were very dry. He said to me, "Mortal, can these bones live?" I answered, "O Lord GOD, you know." Then he said to me, "Prophesy to these bones, and say to them: O dry bones, hear the word of the LORD. Thus says the Lord GOD to these bones: I will cause breath to enter you, and you shall live. I will lay sinews on you, and will cause flesh to come upon you, and cover you with skin, and put breath in you, and you shall live; and you shall know that I am the LORD." So I prophesied as I had been commanded; and as I prophesied, suddenly there was a noise, a rattling, and the bones came together, bone to its bone. I looked, and there were sinews on them, and flesh had come upon them, and skin had covered them; but there was no breath in them. Then he said to me, "Prophesy to the breath, prophesy, mortal, and say to the breath: Thus says the Lord GOD: Come from the four winds, O breath, and breathe upon these slain, that they may live." I prophesied as he commanded me, and the breath came into them, and they lived, and stood on their feet, a vast multitude. Then he said to me, "Mortal, these bones are the whole house of Israel. They say, 'Our bones are dried up, and our hope is lost; we are cut off completely.' Therefore prophesy, and say to them, Thus says the Lord GOD: I am going to open your graves, and bring you up from your graves, O my people; and I will bring you back to the land of Israel. And you shall know that I am the LORD, when I open your graves, and bring you up from your graves, O my people. I will put my spirit within you, and you shall live, and I will place you on your own soil; then you shall know that I, the LORD, have spoken and will act," says the LORD.

The Psalm 30   *Exaltabo te, Domine*
1   I will exalt you, O LORD,
    because you have lifted me up *
        and have not let my enemies triumph over me.

2   O LORD my God, I cried out to you, *
   and you restored me to health.

3   You brought me up, O LORD, from the dead; *
   you restored my life as I was going down to the grave.

4   Sing to the LORD, you servants of his; *
   give thanks for the remembrance of his holiness.

5   For his wrath endures but the twinkling of an eye, *
   his favor for a lifetime.

6   Weeping may spend the night, *
   but joy comes in the morning.

7   While I felt secure, I said,
  "I shall never be disturbed. *
   You, LORD, with your favor, made me as strong as the mountains."

8   Then you hid your face, *
   and I was filled with fear.

9   I cried to you, O LORD; *
   I pleaded with the Lord, saying,

10   "What profit is there in my blood, if I go down to the Pit? *
   will the dust praise you or declare your faithfulness?

11   Hear, O LORD, and have mercy upon me; *
   O LORD, be my helper."

12   You have turned my wailing into dancing; *
   you have put off my sack-cloth and clothed me with joy.

13   Therefore my heart sings to you without ceasing; *
   O LORD my God, I will give you thanks for ever.

or Psalm 143   *Domine, exaudi*

1   LORD, hear my prayer,
  and in your faithfulness heed my supplications; *
   answer me in your righteousness.

2   Enter not into judgment with your servant, *
   for in your sight shall no one living be justified.

3   For my enemy has sought my life;
  he has crushed me to the ground; *
   he has made me live in dark places like those who are long dead.

4   My spirit faints within me; *
   my heart within me is desolate.

5   I remember the time past;
      I muse upon all your deeds; *
         I consider the works of your hands.

6   I spread out my hands to you; *
         my soul gasps to you like a thirsty land.

7   O LORD, make haste to answer me; my spirit fails me; *
         do not hide your face from me
         or I shall be like those who go down to the Pit.

8   Let me hear of your loving-kindness in the morning,
      for I put my trust in you; *
         show me the road that I must walk,
         for I lift up my soul to you.

9   Deliver me from my enemies, O LORD, *
         for I flee to you for refuge.

10   Teach me to do what please you, for you are my God; *
         let your good Spirit lead me on level ground.

11   Revive me, O LORD, for your Name's sake; *
         for your righteousness' sake, bring me out of trouble.

12   Of your goodness, destroy my enemies
      and bring all my foes to naught, *
         for truly I am your servant.

The gathering of God's people
Zephaniah 3:12-20

For I will leave in the midst of you a people humble and lowly. They shall seek refuge in the name of the LORD — the remnant of Israel; they shall do no wrong and utter no lies, nor shall a deceitful tongue be found in their mouths. Then they will pasture and lie down, and no one shall make them afraid. Sing aloud, O daughter Zion; shout, O Israel! Rejoice and exult with all your heart, O daughter Jerusalem! The LORD has taken away the judgments against you, he has turned away your enemies. The king of Israel, the LORD, is in your midst; you shall fear disaster no more. On that day it shall be said to Jerusalem: Do not fear, O Zion; do not let your hands grow weak. The LORD, your God, is in your midst, a warrior who gives victory; he will rejoice over you with gladness, he will renew you in his love; he will exult over you with loud singing as on a day of festival. I will remove disaster from you, so that you will not bear reproach for it. I will deal with all your oppressors at that time. And I will save the lame and gather the outcast, and I will change their shame into praise and renown in all the earth. At that time I will bring you home, at the time when I gather you; for I will make you renowned and praised among all the peoples of the earth, when I restore your fortunes before your eyes, says the LORD.

Psalm 98 *Cantate Domino*

1 Sing to the LORD a new song, *
  for he has done marvelous things.

2 With his right hand and his holy arm *
  has he won for himself the victory.

3 The LORD has made known his victory; *
  his righteousness has he openly shown in the sight of the nations.

4 He remembers his mercy and faithfulness to the house of Israel, *
  and all the ends of the earth have seen the victory of our God.

5 Shout with joy to the LORD, all you lands; *
  lift up your voice, rejoice, and sing.

6 Sing to the LORD with the harp, *
  with the harp and the voice of song.

7 With trumpets and the sound of the horn *
  shout with joy before the King, the LORD.

8 Let the sea make a noise and all that is in it, *
  the lands and those who dwell therein.

9 Let the rivers clap their hands, *
  and let the hills ring out with joy before the LORD,
  when he comes to judge the earth.

10 In righteousness shall be judge the world *
  and the peoples with equity.

or Psalm 126 *In convertendo*

1 When the LORD restored the fortunes of Zion, *
  then were we like those who dream.

2 Then was our mouth filled with laughter, *
  and our tongue with shouts of joy.

3 Then they said among the nations, *
  "The LORD has done great things for them."

4 The LORD has done great things for us, *
  and we are glad indeed.

5 Restore our fortunes, O LORD, *
  like the watercourses of the Negev.

6 Those who sowed with tears *
  will reap with songs of joy.

7 Those who go out weeping, carrying the seed, *
  will come again with joy, shouldering their sheaves.

THE SUNDAY OF THE RESURRECTION,
OR EASTER DAY

The Collect

O God, who for our redemption gave your only-begotten Son to the death of the cross, and by his glorious resurrection delivered us from the power of our enemy: Grant us so to die daily to sin, that we may evermore live with him in the joy of his resurrection; through Jesus Christ your Son our Lord, who lives and reigns with you and the Holy Spirit, one God, now and for ever. *Amen.*
or,

O God, who made this most holy night to shine with the glory of the Lord's resurrection: Stir up in your Church that Spirit of adoption which is given to us in Baptism, that we, being renewed both in body and mind, may worship you in sincerity and truth; through Jesus Christ our Lord, who lives and reigns with you, in the unity of the Holy Spirit, one God, now and for ever. *Amen.*
or,

Almighty God, who through your only-begotten Son Jesus Christ overcame death and opened to us the gate of everlasting life: Grant that we, who celebrate with joy the day of the Lord's resurrection, may be raised from the death of sin by your life-giving Spirit; through Jesus Christ our Lord, who lives and reigns with you and the Holy Spirit, one God, now and for ever. *Amen.*

O God, who for our redemption didst give thine only-begotten Son to the death of the cross, and by his glorious resurrection hast delivered us from the power of our enemy: Grant us so to die daily to sin, that we may evermore live with him in the joy of his resurrection; through the same thy Son Christ our Lord, who liveth and reigneth with thee and the Holy Spirit, one God, now and for ever. *Amen.*
or,

O God, who didst make this most holy night to shine with the glory of the Lord's resurrection: Stir up in thy Church that Spirit of adoption which is given to us in Baptism, that we, being renewed both in body and mind, may worship thee in sincerity and truth; through the same Jesus Christ our Lord, who liveth and reigneth with thee in the unity of the same Spirit, one God, now and for ever. *Amen.*
or,

Almighty God, who through thine only-begotten Son Jesus Christ hast overcome death and opened unto us the gate of everlasting life: Grant that we, who celebrate with joy the day of the Lord's resurrection, may be raised from the death of sin by thy life-giving Spirit; through the same Jesus Christ our Lord, who liveth and reigneth with thee and the same Spirit ever, one God, world without end. *Amen.*

Early Service — Years A, B, C

Use one of the Old Testament Lessons from the Vigil.

The Psalm 114   *In exitu Israel*

1   Hallelujah!
      When Israel came out of Egypt, *
         the house of Jacob from a people of strange speech,

2   Judah became God's sanctuary *
    and Israel his dominion.

3   The sea beheld it and fled; *
    Jordan turned and went back.

4   The mountains skipped like rams, *
    and the little hills like young sheep.

5   What ailed you, O sea, that you fled? *
    O Jordan, that you turned back?

6   You mountains, that you skipped like rams? *
    you little hills like young sheep?

7   Tremble, O earth, at the presence of the Lord, *
    at the presence of the God of Jacob,

8   Who turned the hard rock into a pool of water *
    and flint-stone into a flowing spring.

The Epistle   **Romans 6:3-11**

Do you not know that all of us who have been baptized into Christ Jesus were
baptized into his death? Therefore we have been buried with him by baptism into
death, so that, just as Christ was raised from the dead by the glory of the Father, so
we too might walk in newness of life. For if we have been united with him in a death
like his, we will certainly be united with him in a resurrection like his. We know that
our old self was crucified with him so that the body of sin might be destroyed, and we
might no longer be enslaved to sin. For whoever has died is freed from sin. But if we
have died with Christ, we believe that we will also live with him. We know that
Christ, being raised from the dead, will never die again; death no longer has
dominion over him. the death he died, he died to sin, once for all; but the life he
lives, he lives to God. So you also must consider yourselves dead to sin and alive to
God in Christ Jesus.

The Gospel   **Matthew 28:1-10**

After the sabbath, as the first day of the week was dawning, Mary Magdalene and the
other Mary went to see the tomb. And suddenly there was a great earthquake; for an
angel of the Lord, descending from heaven, came and rolled back the stone and sat
on it. His appearance was like lightning, and his clothing white as snow. For fear of
him the guards shook and became like dead men. But the angel said to the women,
"Do not be afraid; I know that you are looking for Jesus who was crucified. He is not
here; for he has been raised, as he said. Come, see the place where he lay. Then go
quickly and tell his disciples, 'He has been raised from the dead, and indeed he is
going ahead of you to Galilee; there you will see him.' This is my message for you."
So they left the tomb quickly with fear and great joy, and ran to tell his disciples.
Suddenly Jesus met them and said, "Greetings!" And they came to him, took hold of
his feet, and worshiped him. Then Jesus said to them, "Do not be afraid; go and tell
my brothers to go to Galilee; there they will see me."

The Lesson   Acts 10:34-43

Peter began to speak to them: "I truly understand that God shows no partiality, but in every nation anyone who fears him and does what is right is acceptable to him. You know the message he sent to the people of Israel, preaching peace by Jesus Christ — he is Lord of all. That message spread throughout Judea, beginning in Galilee after the baptism that John announced: how God anointed Jesus of Nazareth with the Holy Spirit and with power; how he went about doing good and healing all who were oppressed by the devil, for God was with him. We are witnesses to all that he did both in Judea and in Jerusalem. They put him to death by hanging him on a tree; but God raised him on the third day and allowed him to appear, not to all the people but to us who were chosen by God as witnesses, and who ate and drank with him after he rose from the dead. He commanded us to preach to the people and to testify that he is the one ordained by God as judge of the living and the dead. All the prophets testify about him that everyone who believes in him receives forgiveness of sins through his name."

or Exodus 14:10-14, 21-25; 15:20-21

As Pharaoh drew near, the Israelites looked back, and there were the Egyptians advancing on them. In great fear the Israelites cried out to the LORD. They said to Moses, "Was it because there were no graves in Egypt that you have taken us away to die in the wilderness? What have you done to us, bringing us out of Egypt? Is this not the very thing we told you in Egypt, 'Let us alone and let us serve the Egyptians'? For it would have been better for us to serve the Egyptians than to die in the wilderness." But Moses said to the people, "Do not be afraid, stand firm, and see the deliverance that the LORD will accomplish for you today; for the Egyptians whom you see today you shall never see again. The LORD will fight for you, and you have only to keep still." Then Moses stretched out his hand over the sea. The LORD drove the sea back by a strong east wind all night, and turned the sea into dry land; and the waters were divided. The Israelites went into the sea on dry ground, the waters forming a wall for them on their right and on their left. The Egyptians pursued, and went into the sea after them, all of Pharaoh's horses, chariots, and chariot drivers. At the morning watch the LORD in the pillar of fire and cloud looked down upon the Egyptian army, and threw the Egyptian army into panic. He clogged their chariot wheels so that they turned with difficulty. The Egyptians said, "Let us flee from the Israelites, for the LORD is fighting for them against Egypt." Then the prophet Miriam, Aaron's sister, took a tambourine in her hand; and all the women went out after her with tambourines and with dancing. And Miriam sang to them: "Sing to the LORD, for he has triumphed gloriously; horse and rider he has thrown into the sea."

The Psalm 118:14-29 or 118:14-17, 22-24   *Confitemini Domino*

14   [The LORD is my strength and my song, *
    and he has become my salvation.

15   There is a sound of exultation and victory *
    in the tents of the righteous:

16   "The right hand of the LORD has triumphed! *
     the right hand of the LORD is exalted!
     the right hand of the LORD has triumphed!"

17   I shall not die, but live, *
     and declare the works of the LORD.]

18   The LORD has punished me sorely, *
     but he did not hand me over to death.

19   Open for me the gates of righteousness; *
     I will enter them;
     I will offer thanks to the LORD.

20   "This is the gate of the LORD; *
     he who is righteous may enter."

21   I will give thanks to you, for you answered me *
     and have become my salvation.

22   [The same stone which the builders rejected *
     has become the chief cornerstone.

23   This is the LORD's doing, *
     and it is marvelous in our eyes.

24   On this day the LORD has acted; *
     we will rejoice and be glad in it.]

25   Hosannah, LORD, hosannah! *
     LORD, send us now success.

26   Blessed is he who comes in the name of the Lord; *
     we bless you from the house of the LORD.

27   God is the LORD; he has shined upon us; *
     form a procession with branches up to the horns of the altar.

28   "You are my god, and I will thank you; *
     you are my God, and I will exalt you."

29   Give thanks to the LORD, for he is good; *
     his mercy endures for ever.

The Epistle   Colossians 3:1-4

So if you have been raised with Christ, seek the things that are above, where Christ is, seated at the right hand of God. Set your minds on things that are above, not on things that are on earth, for you have died, and your life is hidden with Christ in God. When Christ who is your life is revealed, then you also will be revealed with him in glory.

or Acts 10:34-43

Peter began to speak to them: "I truly understand that God shows no partiality, but

in every nation anyone who fears him and does what is right is acceptable to him.
You know the message he sent to the people of Israel, preaching peace by Jesus Christ
— he is Lord of all. That message spread throughout Judea, beginning in Galilee
after the baptism that John announced: how God anointed Jesus of Nazareth with
the Holy Spirit and with power; how he went about doing good and healing all who
were oppressed by the devil, for God was with him. We are witnesses to all that he
did both in Judea and in Jerusalem. They put him to death by hanging him on a tree;
but God raised him on the third day and allowed him to appear, not to all the people
but to us who were chosen by God as witnesses, and who ate and drank with him
after he rose from the dead. He commanded us to preach to the people and to testify
that he is the one ordained by God as judge of the living and the dead. All the
prophets testify about him that everyone who believes in him receives forgiveness of
sins through his name."

The Gospel   **John 20:1-10 (11-18)**

Early on the first day of the week, while it was still dark, Mary Magdalene came to
the tomb and saw that the stone had been removed from the tomb. So she ran and
went to Simon Peter and the other disciple, the one whom Jesus loved, and said to
them, "They have taken the Lord out of the tomb, and we do not know where they
have laid him." Then Peter and the other disciple set out and went toward the tomb.
The two were running together, but the other disciple outran Peter and reached the
tomb first. He bent down to look in and saw the linen wrappings lying there, but he
did not go in. Then Simon Peter came, following him, and went into the tomb. He
saw the linen wrappings lying there, and the cloth that had been on Jesus' head, not
lying with the linen wrappings but rolled up in a place by itself. Then the other
disciple, who reached the tomb first, also went in, and he saw and believed; for as yet
they did not understand the scripture, that he must rise from the dead.Then the
disciples returned to their homes. [But Mary stood weeping outside the tomb. As she
wept, she bent over to look into the tomb; and she saw two angels in white, sitting
where the body of Jesus had been lying, one at the head and the other at the feet.
They said to her, "Woman, why are you weeping?" She said to them, "They have
taken away my Lord, and I do not know where they have laid him." When she had
said this, she turned around and saw Jesus standing there, but she did not know that
it was Jesus. Jesus said to her, "Woman, why are you weeping? Whom are you
looking for?" Supposing him to be the gardener, she said to him, "Sir, if you have
carried him away, tell me where you have laid him, and I will take him away." Jesus
said to her, "Mary!" She turned and said to him in Hebrew, "Rabbouni!" (which
means Teacher). Jesus said to her, "Do not hold on to me, because I have not yet
ascended to the Father. But go to my brothers and say to them, 'I am ascending to
my Father and your Father, to my God and your God.'" Mary Magdalene went and
announced to the disciples, "I have seen the Lord"; and she told them that he had
said these things to her.]

or The Gospel   **Matthew 28:1-10**

After the sabbath, as the first day of the week was dawning, Mary Magdalene and the
other Mary went to see the tomb. And suddenly there was a great earthquake; for an
angel of the Lord, descending from heaven, came and rolled back the stone and sat

on it. His appearance was like lightning, and his clothing white as snow. For fear of him the guards shook and became like dead men. But the angel said to the women, "Do not be afraid; I know that you are looking for Jesus who was crucified. He is not here; for he has been raised, as he said. Come, see the place where he lay. Then go quickly and tell his disciples, 'He has been raised from the dead, and indeed he is going ahead of you to Galilee; there you will see him.' This is my message for you." So they left the tomb quickly with fear and great joy, and ran to tell his disciples. Suddenly Jesus met them and said, "Greetings!" And they came to him, took hold of his feet, and worshiped him. Then Jesus said to them, "Do not be afraid; go and tell my brothers to go to Galilee; there they will see me."

<h2 style="text-align:center">Principal Service — Year B</h2>

The Lesson   Acts 10:34-43

Peter began to speak to them: "I truly understand that God shows no partiality, but in every nation anyone who fears him and does what is right is acceptable to him. You know the message he sent to the people of Israel, preaching peace by Jesus Christ — he is Lord of all. That message spread throughout Judea, beginning in Galilee after the baptism that John announced: how God anointed Jesus of Nazareth with the Holy Spirit and with power; how he went about doing good and healing all who were oppressed by the devil,for God was with him. We are witnesses to all that he did both in Judea and in Jerusalem. They put him to death by hanging him on a tree; but God raised him on the third day and allowed him to appear, not to all the people but to us who were chosen by God as witnesses, and who ate and drank with him after he rose from the dead. He commanded us to preach to the people and to testify that he is the one ordained by God as judge of the living and the dead. All the prophets testify about him that everyone who believes in him receives forgiveness of sins through his name."

or Isaiah 25:6-9

On this mountain the LORD of hosts will make for all peoples a feast of rich food, a feast of well-aged wines, of rich food filled with marrow, of well-aged wines strained clear. And he will destroy on this mountain the shroud that is cast over all peoples, the sheet that is spread over all nations; he will swallow up death forever. Then the Lord GOD will wipe away the tears from all faces, and the disgrace of his people he will take away from all the earth, for the LORD has spoken. It will be said on that day, Lo, this is our God; we have waited for him, so that he might save us. This is the LORD for whom we have waited; let us be glad and rejoice in his salvation.

The Psalm 118:14-29 or 118:14-17, 22-24   *Confitemini Domino*

14   [The LORD is my strength and my song, *
        and he has become my salvation.

15   There is a sound of exultation and victory *
        in the tents of the righteous:

16   "The right hand of the LORD has triumphed! *
        the right hand of the LORD is exalted!
        the right hand of the LORD has triumphed!"

17   I shall not die, but live, *
      and declare the works of the LORD.]

18   The LORD has punished me sorely, *
      but he did not hand me over to death.

19   Open for me the gates of righteousness; *
      I will enter them;
      I will offer thanks to the LORD.

20   "This is the gate of the LORD; *
      he who is righteous may enter."

21   I will give thanks to you, for you answered me *
      and have become my salvation.

22   [The same stone which the builders rejected *
      has become the chief cornerstone.

23   This is the LORD's doing, *
      and it is marvelous in our eyes.

24   On this day the LORD has acted; *
      we will rejoice and be glad in it.]

25   Hosannah, LORD, hosannah! *
      LORD, send us now success.

26   Blessed is he who comes in the name of the Lord; *
      we bless you from the house of the LORD.

27   God is the LORD; he has shined upon us; *
      form a procession with branches up to the horns of the altar.

28   "You are my god, and I will thank you; *
      you are my God, and I will exalt you."

29   Give thanks to the LORD, for he is good; *
      his mercy endures for ever.

The Epistle   **Colossians 3:1-4**

If you have been raised with Christ, seek the things that are above, where Christ is, seated at the right hand of God. Set your minds on things that are above, not on things that are on earth, for you have died, and your life is hidden with Christ in God. When Christ who is your life is revealed, then you also will be revealed with him in glory.

or Acts 10:34-43

Peter began to speak to them: "I truly understand that God shows no partiality, but in every nation anyone who fears him and does what is right is acceptable to him. You know the message he sent to the people of Israel, preaching peace by Jesus Christ — he is Lord of all. That message spread throughout Judea, beginning in Galilee after the baptism that John announced: how God anointed Jesus of Nazareth with the Holy Spirit and with power; how he went about doing good and healing all who were oppressed by the devil, for God was with him. We are witnesses to all that he did both in Judea and in Jerusalem. They put him to death by hanging him on a tree; but God raised him on the third day and allowed him to appear, not to all the people but to us who were chosen by God as witnesses, and who ate and drank with him after he rose from the dead. He commanded us to preach to the people and to testify that he is the one ordained by God as judge of the living and the dead. All the prophets testify about him that everyone who believes in him receives forgiveness of sins through his name."

The Gospel   **Mark 16:1-8**
When the sabbath was over, Mary Magdalene, and Mary the mother of James, and Salome bought spices, so that they might go and anoint him. And very early on the first day of the week, when the sun had risen, they went to the tomb. They had been saying to one another, "Who will roll away the stone for us from the entrance to the tomb?" When they looked up, they saw that the stone, which was very large, had already been rolled back. As they entered the tomb, they saw a young man, dressed in a white robe, sitting on the right side; and they were alarmed. But he said to them, "Do not be alarmed; you are looking for Jesus of Nazareth, who was crucified. He has been raised; he is not here. Look, there is the place they laid him. But go, tell his disciples and Peter that he is going ahead of you to Galilee; there you will see him, just as he told you." So they went out and fled from the tomb, for terror and amazement had seized them; and they said nothing to anyone, for they were afraid.

Principal Service — Year C

The Lesson   **Acts 10:34-43**
Peter began to speak to them: "I truly understand that God shows no partiality, but in every nation anyone who fears him and does what is right is acceptable to him. You know the message he sent to the people of Israel, preaching peace by Jesus Christ — he is Lord of all. That message spread throughout Judea, beginning in Galilee after the baptism that John announced: how God anointed Jesus of Nazareth with the Holy Spirit and with power; how he went about doing good and healing all who were oppressed by the devil, for God was with him. We are witnesses to all that he did both in Judea and in Jerusalem. They put him to death by hanging him on a tree; but God raised him on the third day and allowed him to appear, not to all the people but to us who were chosen by God as witnesses, and who ate and drank with him after he rose from the dead. He commanded us to preach to the people and to testify that he is the one ordained by God as judge of the living and the dead. All the prophets testify about him that everyone who believes in him receives forgiveness of sins through his name."

or Isaiah 51:9-11
Awake, awake, put on strength, O arm of the LORD! Awake, as in days of old, the generations of long ago! Was it not you who cut Rahab in pieces, who pierced the dragon? Was it not you who dried up the sea, the waters of the great deep; who made the depths of the sea a way for the redeemed to cross over? So the ransomed of the

Lord shall return, and come to Zion with singing; everlasting joy shall be upon their heads; they shall obtain joy and gladness, and sorrow and sighing shall flee away.

The Psalm 118:14-29 or 118:14-17, 22-24   *Confitemini Domino*

14   [The Lord is my strength and my song, *
          and he has become my salvation.

15   There is a sound of exultation and victory *
          in the tents of the righteous:

16   "The right hand of the Lord has triumphed! *
          the right hand of the Lord is exalted!
          the right hand of the Lord has triumphed!"

17   I shall not die, but live, *
          and declare the works of the Lord.]

18   The Lord has punished me sorely, *
          but he did not hand me over to death.

19   Open for me the gates of righteousness; *
          I will enter them;
          I will offer thanks to the Lord.

20   "This is the gate of the Lord; *
          he who is righteous may enter."

21   I will give thanks to you, for you answered me *
          and have become my salvation.

22   [The same stone which the builders rejected *
          has become the chief cornerstone.

23   This is the Lord's doing, *
          and it is marvelous in our eyes.

24   On this day the Lord has acted; *
          we will rejoice and be glad in it.]

25   Hosannah, Lord, hosannah! *
          Lord, send us now success.

26   Blessed is he who comes in the name of the Lord; *
          we bless you from the house of the Lord.

27   God is the Lord; he has shined upon us; *
          form a procession with branches up to the horns of the altar.

28   "You are my god, and I will thank you; *
          you are my God, and I will exalt you."

29   Give thanks to the Lord, for he is good; *
          his mercy endures for ever.

The Epistle   **Colossians 3:1-4**

f you have been raised with Christ, seek the things that are above, where Christ is, seated at the right hand of God. Set your minds on things that are above, not on things that are on earth, for you have died, and your life is hidden with Christ in God. When Christ who is your life is revealed, then you also will be revealed with him in glory.

or Acts 10:34-43

Peter began to speak to them: "I truly understand that God shows no partiality, but in every nation anyone who fears him and does what is right is acceptable to him. You know the message he sent to the people of Israel, preaching peace by Jesus Christ — he is Lord of all. That message spread throughout Judea, beginning in Galilee after the baptism that John announced: how God anointed Jesus of Nazareth with the Holy Spirit and with power; how he went about doing good and healing all who were oppressed by the devil, for God was with him. We are witnesses to all that he did both in Judea and in Jerusalem. They put him to death by hanging him on a tree; but God raised him on the third day and allowed him to appear, not to all the people but to us who were chosen by God as witnesses, and who ate and drank with him after he rose from the dead. He commanded us to preach to the people and to testify that he is the one ordained by God as judge of the living and the dead. All the prophets testify about him that everyone who believes in him receives forgiveness of sins through his name."

The Gospel   **Luke 24:1-10**

On the first day of the week, at early dawn, they came to the tomb, taking the spices that they had prepared. They found the stone rolled away from the tomb, but when they went in, they did not find the body. While they were perplexed about this, suddenly two men in dazzling clothes stood beside them. The women were terrified and bowed their faces to the ground, but the men said to them, "Why do you look for the living among the dead? He is not here, but has risen. Remember how he told you, while he was still in Galilee, that the Son of Man must be handed over to sinners, and be crucified, and on the third day rise again." Then they remembered his words, and returning from the tomb, they told all this to the eleven and to all the rest. Now it was Mary Magdalene, Joanna, Mary the mother of James, and the other women with them who told this to the apostles.

Evening Service — Years A, B, C

The Lesson   **Acts 5:29a, 30-32**

But Peter and the apostles answered the high priest, "The God of our ancestors raised up Jesus, whom you had killed by hanging him on a tree. God exalted him at his right hand as Leader and Savior that he might give repentance to Israel and forgiveness of sins. And we are witnesses to these things, and so is the Holy Spirit whom God has given to those who obey him."

or Daniel 12:1-3

"At that time Michael, the great prince, the protector of your people, shall arise. There shall be a time of anguish, such as has never occurred since nations first came into existence. But at that time your people shall be delivered, everyone who is found written in the book. Many of those who sleep in the dust of the earth shall awake, some to everlasting life, and some to shame and everlasting contempt. Those who are wise shall shine like the brightness of the sky, and those who lead many to righteousness, like the stars forever and ever."

The Psalm 114   *In exitu Israel*

1   Hallelujah!
    When Israel came out of Egypt, *
      the house of Jacob from a people of strange speech,

2   Judah became God's sanctuary *
      and Israel his dominion.

3   The sea beheld it and fled; *
      Jordan turned and went back.

4   The mountains skipped like rams, *
      and the little hills like young sheep.

5   What ailed you, O sea, that you fled? *
      O Jordan, that you turned back?

6   You mountains, that you skipped like rams? *
      you little hills like young sheep?

7   Tremble, O earth, at the presence of the Lord, *
      at the presence of the God of Jacob,

8   Who turned the hard rock into a pool of water *
      and flint-stone into a flowing spring.

or Psalm 136   *Confitemini*

1   Give thanks to the LORD, for he is good, *
      for his mercy endures for ever.

2   Give thanks to the God of gods, *
      for his mercy endures for ever.

3   Give thanks to the Lord of lords, *
      for his mercy endures for ever.

4   Who only does great wonders, *
      for his mercy endure for ever;

5   Who by wisdom made the heavens, *
      for his mercy endures for ever;

6   Who spread out the earth upon the waters, *
      for his mercy endures for ever;

7   Who created great lights, *
      for his mercy endures for ever;

8 The sun to rule the day, *
      for his mercy endures for ever;

9 The moon and the stars to govern the night, *
      for his mercy endures for ever.

10 Who struck down the firstborn of Egypt, *
      for his mercy endures for ever;

11 And brought out Israel from among them, *
      for his mercy endures for ever;

12 With a might hand and a stretched-out arm, *
      for his mercy endures for ever;

13 Who divided the Red Sea in two, *
      for his mercy endures for ever;

14 And made Israel to pass through the midst of it, *
      for his mercy endures for ever;

15 But swept Pharaoh and his army into the Red Sea, *
      for his mercy endures for ever;

16 Who led his people through the wilderness, *
      for his mercy endures for ever.

17 Who struck down great kings, *
      for his mercy endures for ever;

18 And slew mighty kings, *
      for his mercy endures for ever;

19 Sihon, king of the Amorites, *
      for his mercy endures for ever;

20 And Og, the king of Bashan, *
      for his mercy endures for ever;

21 And gave away their lands for an inheritance, *
      for his mercy endures for ever;

22 An inheritance for Israel his servant, *
      for his mercy endures for ever;

23 Who remembered us in our low estate, *
      for his mercy endures for ever;

24 And delivered us from our enemies, *
      for his mercy endures for ever;

25 Who gives food to all creatures, *
      for his mercy endures for ever;

26   Give thanks to the God of heaven, *
        for his mercy endures for ever;

or Psalm 118:14-17, 22-24   *Confitemini Domino*

14   The LORD is my strength and my song, *
        and he has become my salvation.

15   There is a sound of exultation and victory *
        in the tents of the righteous:

16   "The right hand of the LORD has triumphed! *
        the right hand of the LORD is exalted!
        the right hand of the LORD has triumphed!"

17   I shall not die, but live, *
        and declare the works of the LORD.

22   The same stone which the builders rejected *
        has become the chief cornerstone.

23   This is the LORD's doing, *
        and it is marvelous in our eyes.

24   On this day the LORD has acted; *
        we will rejoice and be glad in it.

The Epistle   1 Corinthians 5:6b-8

Do you not know that a little yeast leavens the whole batch of dough? Clean out the old yeast so that you may be a new batch, as you really are unleavened. For our paschal lamb, Christ, has been sacrificed. Therefore, let us celebrate the festival, not with the old yeast, the yeast of malice and evil, but with the unleavened bread of sincerity and truth.

or Acts 5:29a, 30-32

Peter and the apostles answered the high priest, "The God of our ancestors raised up Jesus, whom you had killed by hanging him on a tree. God exalted him at his right hand as Leader and Savior that he might give repentance to Israel and forgiveness of sins. And we are witnesses to these things, and so is the Holy Spirit whom God has given to those who obey him."

The Gospel   Luke 24:13-35

On the first day of the week, two of Jesus' followers were going to a village called Emmaus, about seven miles from Jerusalem, and talking with each other about all these things that had happened. While they were talking and discussing, Jesus himself came near and went with them, but their eyes were kept from recognizing him. And he said to them, "What are you discussing with each other while you walk along?" They stood still, looking sad. Then one of them, whose name was Cleopas, answered him, "Are you the only stranger in Jerusalem who does not know the things that have taken place there in these days?" He asked them, "What things?" They replied, "The things about Jesus of Nazareth, who was a prophet mighty in deed and word before God and all the people, and how our chief priests and leaders handed him over to be condemned to death and crucified him. But we had hoped that he was the one to redeem Israel. Yes, and besides all this, it is now the third day since these things took place. Moreover, some women of our group astounded us. They were at the tomb early this morning, and when they did not find his body there, they came back and told us that they had indeed seen a vision of angels who said that he was alive. Some of those who were with us went to the tomb and found it just as the women had said; but they did not see him." Then he said to them, "Oh, how foolish you are, and how slow of heart to believe all that the prophets have declared! Was it not necessary that the Messiah should suffer these things and then enter into his glory?" Then beginning with Moses and all the prophets, he interpreted to them the things about himself in all the scriptures. As they came near the village to which they were going, he walked ahead as if he were going on. But they urged him strongly, saying, "Stay with us, because it is almost evening and the day is now nearly over." So he went in to stay with them. When he was at the table with them, he took bread, blessed and broke it, and gave it to them. Then their eyes were opened, and they recognized him; and he vanished from their sight. They said to each other, "Were not our hearts burning within us while he was talking to us on the road, while he was opening the scriptures to us?" That same hour they got up and returned to Jerusalem; and they found the eleven and their companions gathered together. They were saying, "The Lord has risen indeed, and he has appeared to Simon!" Then they told what had happened on the road, and how he had been made known to them in the breaking of the bread.

MONDAY IN EASTER WEEK

The Collect
Grant, we pray, Almighty God, that we who celebrate with awe the Paschal feast may be found worthy to attain to everlasting joys; through Jesus Christ our Lord, who lives and reigns with you and the Holy Spirit, one God, now and for ever. *Amen.*

Grant, we beseech thee, Almighty God, that we who celebrate with reverence the Paschal feast may be found worthy to attain to everlasting joys; through Jesus Christ our Lord, who liveth and reigneth with thee and the Holy Spirit, one God, now and for ever. *Amen.*

Years A, B, C

The Lesson   Acts 2:14, 22b-32
But Peter, standing with the eleven, raised his voice and addressed them, "Men of Judea and all who live in Jerusalem, let this be known to you, and listen to what I say. You that are Israelites, listen to what I have to say: Jesus of Nazareth, a man attested to you by God with deeds of power, wonders, and signs that God did through him among you, as you yourselves know — this man, handed over to you according to the definite plan and foreknowledge of God, you crucified and killed by the hands of those outside the law. But God raised him up, having freed him from death, because it was impossible for him to be held in its power. For David says concerning him, 'I saw the Lord always before me, for he is at my right hand so that I will not be shaken; therefore my heart was glad, and my tongue rejoiced; moreover

my flesh will live in hope. For you will not abandon my soul to Hades, or let your Holy One experience corruption. You have made known to me the ways of life; you will make me full of gladness with your presence.' Fellow Israelites, I may say to you confidently of our ancestor David that he both died and was buried, and his tomb is with us to this day. Since he was a prophet, he knew that God had sworn with an oath to him that he would put one of his descendants on his throne. Foreseeing this, David spoke of the resurrection of the Messiah, saying, 'He was not abandoned to Hades, nor did his flesh experience corruption.' This Jesus God raised up, and of that all of us are witnesses."

The Psalm 16:8-11   *Conserva me, Domine*
8   I have set the LORD always before me; *
            because he is at my right hand I shall not fall.

9   My heart, therefore, is glad, and my spirit rejoices; *
            my body also shall rest in hope.

10   For you will not abandon me to the grave, *
            nor let your holy one see the Pit.

11   You will show me the path of life; *
            in your presence there is fullness of joy,
            and in your right hand are pleasures for evermore.

or Psalm 118:19-24   *Confitemini Domino*
19   Open for me the gates of righteousness; *
            I will enter them;
            I will offer thanks to the LORD.

20   "This is the gate of the LORD; *
            he who is righteous may enter."

21   I will give thanks to you, for you answered me *
            and have become my salvation.

22   The same stone which the builders rejected *
            has become the chief cornerstone.

23   This is the LORD's doing, *
            and it is marvelous in our eyes.

24   On this day the LORD has acted; *
            we will rejoice and be glad in it.

The Gospel   **Matthew 28:9-15**
Suddenly Jesus met Mary Magdalene and the other Mary and said, "Greetings!" And they came to him, took hold of his feet, and worshiped him. Then Jesus said to them, "Do not be afraid; go and tell my brothers to go to Galilee; there they will see me." While they were going, some of the guard went into the city and told the chief priests everything that had happened. After the priests had assembled with the elders, they devised a plan to give a large sum of money to the soldiers, telling them, "You must

say, 'His disciples came by night and stole him away while we were asleep.' If this comes to the governor's ears, we will satisfy him and keep you out of trouble." So they took the money and did as they were directed. And this story is still told among the Jews to this day.

TUESDAY IN EASTER WEEK

The Collect
O God, who by the glorious resurrection of your Son Jesus Christ destroyed death and brought life and immortality to light: Grant that we, who have been raised with him, may abide in his presence and rejoice in the hope of eternal glory; through Jesus Christ our Lord, to whom, with you and the Holy Spirit, be dominion and praise for ever and ever. *Amen.*

O God, who by the glorious resurrection of thy Son Jesus Christ didst destroy death and bring life and immortality to light: Grant that we, who have been raised with him, may abide in his presence and rejoice in the hope of eternal glory; through Jesus Christ our Lord, to whom, with thee and the Holy Spirit, be dominion and praise for ever and ever. *Amen.*

Years A, B, C

The Lesson   Acts 2:36-41
Peter said, "Therefore let the entire house of Israel know with certainty that God has made him both Lord and Messiah, this Jesus whom you crucified." Now when they heard this, they were cut to the heart and said to Peter and to the other apostles, "Brothers, what should we do?" Peter said to them, "Repent, and be baptized every one of you in the name of Jesus Christ so that your sins may be forgiven; and you will receive the gift of the Holy Spirit. For the promise is for you, for your children, and for all who are far away, everyone whom the Lord our God calls to him." And he testified with many other arguments and exhorted them, saying, "Save yourselves from this corrupt generation." So those who welcomed his message were baptized, and that day about three thousand persons were added.

The Psalm 33:18-22   *Exultate, justi*
18   Behold, the eye of the LORD is upon those who fear him, *
         on those who wait upon his love,

19   To pluck their lives from death, *
         and to feed them in time of famine.

20   Our soul waits for the LORD; *
         he is our help and our shield.

21   Indeed, our heart rejoices in him, *
         for in his holy Name we put our trust.

22   Let your loving-kindness, O LORD, be upon us, *
         as we have put our trust in you.

or Psalm 118:19-24　　*Confitemini Domino*

19　　Open for me the gates of righteousness; *
　　　　I will enter them;
　　　　I will offer thanks to the LORD.

20　　"This is the gate of the LORD; *
　　　　he who is righteous may enter."

21　　I will give thanks to you, for you answered me *
　　　　and have become my salvation.

22　　The same stone which the builders rejected *
　　　　has become the chief cornerstone.

23　　This is the LORD's doing, *
　　　　and it is marvelous in our eyes.

24　　On this day the LORD has acted; *
　　　　we will rejoice and be glad in it.

The Gospel　　　　　　　　　　　　　　　　　　　　**John 20:11-18**

Mary Magdalene stood weeping outside the tomb. As she wept, she bent over to look into the tomb; and she saw two angels in white, sitting where the body of Jesus had been lying, one at the head and the other at the feet. They said to her, "Woman, why are you weeping?" She said to them, "They have taken away my Lord, and I do not know where they have laid him." When she had said this, she turned around and saw Jesus standing there, but she did not know that it was Jesus. Jesus said to her, "Woman, why are you weeping? Whom are you looking for?" Supposing him to be the gardener, she said to him, "Sir, if you have carried him away, tell me where you have laid him, and I will take him away." Jesus said to her, "Mary!" She turned and said to him in Hebrew, "Rabbouni!" (which means Teacher). Jesus said to her, "Do not hold on to me, because I have not yet ascended to the Father. But go to my brothers and say to them, 'I am ascending to my Father and your Father, to my God and your God.'" Mary Magdalene went and announced to the disciples, "I have seen the Lord"; and she told them that he had said these things to her.

WEDNESDAY IN EASTER WEEK

The Collect

O God, whose blessed Son made himself known to his disciples in the breaking of bread: Open the eyes of our faith, that we may behold him in all his redeeming work; who lives and reigns with you, in the unity of the Holy Spirit, one God, now and for ever. *Amen.*

O God, whose blessed Son did manifest himself to his disciples in the breaking of the bread: Open, we pray thee, the eyes of our faith, that we may behold him in all his redeeming work; through the same thy Son Jesus Christ our Lord, who liveth and reigneth with thee, in the unity of the Holy Spirit, one God, now and for ever. *Amen.*

The Lesson Acts 3:1-10

One day Peter and John were going up to the temple at the hour of prayer, at three o'clock in the afternoon. And a man lame from birth was being carried in. People would lay him daily at the gate of the temple called the Beautiful Gate so that he could ask for alms from those entering the temple. When he saw Peter and John about to go into the temple, he asked them for alms. Peter looked intently at him, as did John, and said, "Look at us." And he fixed his attention on them, expecting to receive something from them. But Peter said, "I have no silver or gold, but what I have I give you; in the name of Jesus Christ of Nazareth, stand up and walk." And he took him by the right hand and raised him up; and immediately his feet and ankles were made strong. Jumping up, he stood and began to walk, and he entered the temple with them, walking and leaping and praising God. All the people saw him walking and praising God, and they recognized him as the one who used to sit and ask for alms at the Beautiful Gate of the temple; and they were filled with wonder and amazement at what had happened to him.

The Psalm 105:1-8   *Confitemini Domino*

1   Give thanks to the LORD and call upon his Name; *
     make known his deeds among the peoples.

2   Sing to him, sing praises to him, *
     and speak of all his marvelous works.

3   Glory in his holy Name; *
     let the hearts of those who seek the LORD rejoice.

4   Search for the LORD and his strength; *
     continually seek his face.

5   Remember the marvels he has done, *
     his wonders and the judgments of his mouth,

6   O offspring of Abraham his servant, *
     O children of Jacob his chosen.

7   He is the LORD our God; *
     his judgments prevail in all the world.

8   He has always been mindful of his covenant, *
     the promise he made for a thousand generations:

or Psalm 118:19-24   *Confitemini Domino*

19   Open for me the gates of righteousness; *
     I will enter them;
     I will offer thanks to the LORD.

20   "This is the gate of the LORD; *
     he who is righteous may enter."

21   I will give thanks to you, for you answered me *
        and have become my salvation.

22   The same stone which the builders rejected *
        has become the chief cornerstone.

23   This is the LORD's doing, *
        and it is marvelous in our eyes.

24   On this day the LORD has acted; *
        we will rejoice and be glad in it.

The Gospel   Luke 24:13-35

On the first day of the week, two of Jesus' follwers were going to a village called
Emmaus, about seven miles from Jerusalem, and talking with each other about all
these things that had happened. While they were talking and discussing, Jesus himself
came near and went with them, but their eyes were kept from recognizing him. And
he said to them, "What are you discussing with each other while you walk along?"
They stood still, looking sad. Then one of them, whose name was Cleopas, answered
him, "Are you the only stranger in Jerusalem who does not know the things that have
taken place there in these days?" He asked them, "What things?" They replied, "The
things about Jesus of Nazareth, who was a prophet mighty in deed and word before
God and all the people, and how our chief priests and leaders handed him over to be
condemned to death and crucified him. But we had hoped that he was the one to
redeem Israel. Yes, and besides all this, it is now the third day since these things took
place. Moreover, some women of our group astounded us. They were at the tomb
early this morning, and when they did not find his body there, they came back and
told us that they had indeed seen a vision of angels who said that he was alive. Some
of those who were with us went to the tomb and found it just as the women had said;
but they did not see him." Then he said to them, "Oh, how foolish you are, and how
slow of heart to believe all that the prophets have declared! Was it not necessary that
the Messiah should suffer these things and then enter into his glory?" Then beginning
with Moses and all the prophets, he interpreted to them the things about himself in
all the scriptures. As they came near the village to which they were going, he walked
ahead as if he were going on. But they urged him strongly, saying, "Stay with us,
because it is almost evening and the day is now nearly over." So he went in to stay
with them. When he was at the table with them, he took bread, blessed and broke it,
and gave it to them. Then their eyes were opened, and they recognized him; and he
vanished from their sight. They said to each other, "Were not our hearts burning
within us while he was talking to us on the road, while he was opening the scriptures
to us?" That same hour they got up and returned to Jerusalem; and they found the
eleven and their companions gathered together. They were saying, "The Lord has
risen indeed, and he has appeared to Simon!" Then they told what had happened on
the road, and how he had been made known to them in the breaking of the bread.

THURSDAY IN EASTER WEEK

The Collect

Almighty and everlasting God, who in the Paschal mystery established the new covenant of reconciliation: Grant that all who have been reborn into the fellowship of Christ's Body may show forth in their lives what they profess by their faith; through Jesus Christ our Lord, who lives and reigns with you and the Holy Spirit, one God, for ever and ever. *Amen.*

Almighty and everlasting God who in the Paschal mystery hast established the new covenant of reconciliation: Grant that all who have been reborn into the fellowship of Christ's Body may show forth in their lives what they profess by their faith; through the same Jesus Christ our Lord, who liveth and reigneth with thee and the Holy Spirit, one God for ever and ever. *Amen.*

Years A, B, C

The Lesson   Acts 3:11-26

While the lame man clung to Peter and John, all the people ran together to them in the portico called Solomon's Portico, utterly astonished. When Peter saw it, he addressed the people, "You Israelites, why do you wonder at this, or why do you stare at us, as though by our own power or piety we had made him walk? The God of Abraham, the God of Isaac, and the God of Jacob, the God of our ancestors has glorified his servant Jesus, whom you handed over and rejected in the presence of Pilate, though he had decided to release him. But you rejected the Holy and Righteous One and asked to have a murderer given to you, and you killed the Author of life, whom God raised from the dead. To this we are witnesses. And by faith in his name, his name itself has made this man strong, whom you see and know; and the faith that is through Jesus has given him this perfect health in the presence of all of you. And now, friends, I know that you acted in ignorance, as did also your rulers. In this way God fulfilled what he had foretold through all the prophets, that his Messiah would suffer. Repent therefore, and turn to God so that your sins may be wiped out, so that times of refreshing may come from the presence of the Lord, and that he may send the Messiah appointed for you, that is, Jesus, who must remain in heaven until the time of universal restoration that God announced long ago through his holy prophets. Moses said, 'The Lord your God will raise up for you from your own people a prophet like me. You must listen to whatever he tells you. And it will be that everyone who does not listen to that prophet will be utterly rooted out of the people.' And all the prophets, as many as have spoken, from Samuel and those after him, also predicted these days. You are the descendants of the prophets and of the covenant that God gave to your ancestors, saying to Abraham, 'And in your descendants all the families of the earth shall be blessed.' When God raised up his servant, he sent him first to you, to bless you by turning each of you from your wicked ways."

The Psalm 8   *Domine, Dominus noster*

1   O LORD our Governor, *
        how exalted is your Name in all the world!

2   Out of the mouths of infants and children *
       your majesty is praised above the heavens.

3   You have set up a stronghold against your adversaries, *
       to quell the enemy and the avenger.

4   When I consider your heavens, the work of your fingers, *
       the moon and the stars you have set in their courses,

5   What is man that you should be mindful of him? *
       the son of man that you should seek him out?

6   You have made him but little lower than the angels: *
       you adorn him with glory and honor;

7   You give him mastery over the works of your hands; *
       you put all things under his feet:

8   All sheep and oxen, *
       even the wild beasts of the field,

9   The birds of the air, the fish of the sea, *
       and whatsoever walks in the paths of the sea.

10   O LORD our Governor, *
       how exalted is your Name in all the world!

or Psalm 114   *In exitu Israel*

1   Hallelujah!
    When Israel came out of Egypt, *
       the house of Jacob from a people of strange speech,

2   Judah became God's sanctuary *
       and Israel his dominion.

3   The sea beheld it and fled; *
       Jordan turned and went back.

4   The mountains skipped like rams, *
       and the little hills like young sheep.

5   What ailed you, O sea, that you fled? *
       O Jordan, that you turned back?

6   You mountains, that you skipped like rams? *
       you little hills like young sheep?

7   Tremble, O earth, at the presence of the Lord, *
       at the presence of the God of Jacob,

8   Who turned the hard rock into a pool of water *
       and flint-stone into a flowing spring.

19   Open for me the gates of righteousness; *
        I will enter them;
        I will offer thanks to the LORD.

20   "This is the gate of the LORD; *
        he who is righteous may enter."

21   I will give thanks to you, for you answered me *
        and have become my salvation.

22   The same stone which the builders rejected *
        has become the chief cornerstone.

23   This is the LORD's doing, *
        and it is marvelous in our eyes.

24   On this day the LORD has acted; *
        we will rejoice and be glad in it.

The Gospel   Luke 24:36b-48

Jesus himself appeared and stood among the eleven and said to them, "Peace be with you." They were startled and terrified, and thought that they were seeing a ghost. He said to them, "Why are you frightened, and why do doubts arise in your hearts? Look at my hands and my feet; see that it is I myself. Touch me and see; for a ghost does not have flesh and bones as you see that I have." And when he had said this, he showed them his hands and his feet. While in their joy they were disbelieving and still wondering, he said to them, "Have you anything here to eat?" They gave him a piece of broiled fish, and he took it and ate in their presence. Then he said to them, "These are my words that I spoke to you while I was still with you — that everything written about me in the law of Moses, the prophets, and the psalms must be fulfilled." Then he opened their minds to understand the scriptures, and he said to them, "Thus it is written, that the Messiah is to suffer and to rise from the dead on the third day, and that repentance and forgiveness of sins is to be proclaimed in his name to all nations, beginning from Jerusalem. You are witnesses of these things."

FRIDAY IN EASTER WEEK

The Collect

Almighty Father, who gave your only Son to die for our sins, and to rise for our justification: Give us grace so to put away the leaven of malice and wickedness, that we may always serve you in pureness of living and truth; through Jesus Christ your Son our Lord, who lives and reigns with you and the Holy Spirit, one God, now and for ever. *Amen.*

Almighty Father, who hast given thine only Son to die for our sins and to rise again for our justification: Grant us so to put away the leaven of malice and wickedness, that we may always serve thee in pureness of living and truth; through the same thy Son Jesus Christ our Lord, who liveth and reigneth with thee and the Holy Spirit, one God, now and for ever. *Amen.*

The Lesson   Acts 4:1-12

While Peter and John were speaking to the people, the priests, the captain of the temple, and the Sadducees came to them, much annoyed because they were teaching the people and proclaiming that in Jesus there is the resurrection of the dead. So they arrested them and put them in custody until the next day, for it was already evening. But many of those who heard the word believed; and they numbered about five thousand. The next day their rulers, elders, and scribes assembled in Jerusalem, with Annas the high priest, Caiaphas, John, and Alexander, and all who were of the high-priestly family. When they had made the prisoners stand in their midst, they inquired, "By what power or by what name did you do this?" Then Peter, filled with the Holy Spirit, said to them, "Rulers of the people and elders, if we are questioned today because of a good deed done to someone who was sick and are asked how this man has been healed, let it be known to all of you, and to all the people of Israel, that this man is standing before you in good health by the name of Jesus Christ of Nazareth, whom you crucified, whom God raised from the dead. This Jesus is 'the stone that was rejected by you, the builders; it has become the cornerstone.' There is salvation in no one else, for there is no other name under heaven given among mortals by which we must be saved."

The Psalm 116:1-8   *Dilexi, quoniam*

1   I love the LORD, because he has heard the voice of my supplication, *
        because he has inclined his ear to me whenever I called upon him.

2   The cords of death entangled me;
     the grip of the grave took hold of me; *
        I came to grief and sorrow.

3   Then I called upon the Name of the LORD: *
        "O LORD, I pray you, save my life."

4   Gracious is the LORD and righteous; *
        our God is full of compassion.

5   The LORD watches over the innocent; *
        I was brought very low, and he helped me.

6   Turn again to your rest, O my soul, *
        for the LORD has treated you well.

7   For you have rescued my life from death, *
        my eyes from tears, and my feet from stumbling.

8   I will walk in the presence of the LORD *
        in the land of the living.

or Psalm 118:19-24   *Confitemini Domino*

19   Open for me the gates of righteousness; *
        I will enter them;
        I will offer thanks to the LORD.

20   "This is the gate of the LORD; *
    he who is righteous may enter."

21   I will give thanks to you, for you answered me *
    and have become my salvation.

22   The same stone which the builders rejected *
    has become the chief cornerstone.

23   This is the LORD's doing, *
    and it is marvelous in our eyes.

24   On this day the LORD has acted; *
    we will rejoice and be glad in it.

The Gospel   **John 21:1-14**

Jesus showed himself again to the disciples by the Sea of Tiberias; and he showed himself in this way. Gathered there together were Simon Peter, Thomas called the Twin, Nathanael of Cana in Galilee, the sons of Zebedee, and two others of this disciples. Simon Peter said to them, "I am going fishing." They said to him, "We will go with you." They went out and got into the boat, but that night they caught nothing. Just after daybreak, Jesus stood on the beach; but the disciples did not know that it was Jesus. Jesus said to them, "Children, you have no fish, have you?" They answered him, "No." He said to them, "Cast the net to the right side of the boat, and you will find some." So they cast it, and now they were not able to haul it in because there were so many fish. That disciple whom Jesus loved said to Peter, "It is the Lord!" When Simon Peter heard that it was the Lord, he put on some clothes, for he was naked, and jumped into the sea. But the other disciples came in the boat, dragging the net full of fish, for they were not far from the land, only about a hundred yards off. When they had gone ashore, they saw a charcoal fire there, with fish on it, and bread. Jesus said to them, "Bring some of the fish that you have just caught." So Simon Peter went aboard and hauled the net ashore, full of large fish, a hundred fifty-three of them; and though there were so many, the net was not torn. Jesus said to them, "Come and have breakfast." Now none of the disciples dared to ask him, "Who are you?" because they knew it was the Lord. Jesus came and took the bread and gave it to them, and did the same with the fish. This was now the third time that Jesus appeared to the disciples after he as raised from the dead.

SATURDAY IN EASTER WEEK

The Collect

We thank you, heavenly Father, that you have delivered us from the dominion of sin and death and brought us into the kingdom of your Son; and we pray that, as by his death he has recalled us to life, so by his love me may raise us to eternal joys; who lives and reigns with you, in the unity of the Holy Spirit, one God, now and for ever. *Amen.*

We thank thee, heavenly Father, for that thou hast delivered us from the dominion of sin and death and hast brought us into the kingdom of thy Son; and we pray thee that, as by his death he hath recalled us to life, so by his love he may raise us to joys eternal;

who liveth and reigneth with thee, in the unity of the Holy Spirit, one God, now and for ever. *Amen.*

Years A, B, C

The Lesson   Acts 4:13-21

Now when the rulers and elders saw the boldness of Peter and John and realized that they were uneducated and ordinary men, they were amazed and recognized them as companions of Jesus. When they saw the man who had been cured standing beside them, they had nothing to say in opposition. So they ordered them to leave the council while they discussed the matter with one another. They said, "What will we do with them? For it is obvious to all who live in Jerusalem that a notable sign has been done through them; we cannot deny it. But to keep it from spreading further among the people, let us warn them to speak no more to anyone in this name." So they called them and ordered them not to speak or teach at all in the name of Jesus. But Peter and John answered the, "Whether it is right in God's sight to listen to you rather than to God, you must judge; for we cannot keep from speaking about what we have seen and heard." After threatening them again, they let them go, finding no way to punish them because of the people, for all of them praised God for what had happened.

The Psalm 118:14-18   *Confitemini Domino*

14   The LORD is my strength and my song, *
          and he has become my salvation.

15   There is a sound of exultation and victory *
          in the tents of the righteous:

16   "The right hand of the LORD has triumphed! *
          the right hand of the LORD is exalted!
          the right hand of the LORD has triumphed!"

17   I shall not die, but live, *
          and declare the works of the LORD.

18   The LORD has punished me sorely, *
          but he did not hand me over to death.

or Psalm 118:19-24   *Confitemini Domino*

19   Open for me the gates of righteousness; *
          I will enter them;
          I will offer thanks to the LORD.

20   "This is the gate of the LORD; *
          he who is righteous may enter."

21   I will give thanks to you, for you answered me *
          and have become my salvation.

22   The same stone which the builders rejected *
          has become the chief cornerstone.

23 This is the LORD's doing, *
      and it is marvelous in our eyes.

24 On this day the LORD has acted; *
      we will rejoice and be glad in it.

The Gospel   Mark 16:9-15, 20

After Jesus rose early on the first day of the week, he appeared first to Mary
Magdalene, from whom he had cast out seven demons. She went out and told those
who had been with him, while they were mourning and weeping. But when they
heard that he was alive and had been seen by her, they would not believe it. After this
he appeared in another form to two of them, as they were walking into the country.
And they went back and told the rest, but they did not believe them. Later he
appeared to the eleven themselves as they were sitting at the table; and he upbraided
them for their lack of faith and stubbornness, because they had not believed those
who saw him after he had risen. And he said to them, "Go into all the world and
proclaim the good news to the whole creation. And they went out and proclaimed the
good news everywhere, while the Lord worked with them and confirmed the message
by the signs that accompanied it.

THE SECOND SUNDAY OF EASTER

The Collect

**Almighty and everlasting God, who in the Paschal mystery established the new
covenant of reconciliation: Grant that all who have been reborn into the fellowship of
Christ's Body may show forth in their lives what they profess by their faith; through
Jesus Christ our Lord, who lives and reigns with you and the Holy Spirit, one God, for
ever and ever.** *Amen.*

**Almighty and everlasting God, who in the Paschal mystery hast established the new
covenant of reconciliation: Grant that all who have been reborn into the fellowship of
Christ's Body may show forth in their lives what they profess by their faith; through
the same Jesus Christ our Lord, who liveth and reigneth with thee and the Holy Spirit,
one God, for ever and ever.** *Amen.*

Year A

The Lesson   Acts 2:14a, 22-32

Peter, standing with the eleven, raised his voice and addressed them, "You that are
Israelites, listen to what I have to say: Jesus of Nazareth, a man attested to you by
God with deeds of power, wonders, and signs that God did through him among you,
as you yourselves know — this man, handed over to you according to the definite
plan and foreknowledge of God, you crucified and killed by the hands of those
outside the law. But God raised him up, having freed him from death, because it was
impossible for him to be held in its power. For David says concerning him, 'I saw the
Lord always before me, for he is at my right hand so that I will not be shaken;
therefore my heart was glad, and my tongue rejoiced; moreover my flesh will live in
hope. For you will not abandon my soul to Hades, or let your Holy One experience
corruption. You have made known to me the ways of life; you will make me full of
gladness with your presence.' Fellow Israelites, I may say to you confidently of our

ancestor David that he both died and was buried, and his tomb is with us to this day. Since he was a prophet, he knew that God had sworn with an oath to him that he would put one of his descendants on his throne. Foreseeing this, David spoke of the resurrection of the Messiah, saying, 'He was not abandoned to Hades, nor did his flesh experience corruption.' This Jesus God raised up, and of that all of us are witnesses."

or Genesis 8:6-16; 9:8-16

At the end of forty days Noah opened the window of the ark that he had made and sent out the raven; and it went to and fro until the waters were dried up from the earth. Then he sent out the dove from him, to see if the waters had subsided from the face of the ground; but the dove found no place to set its foot, and it returned to him to the ark, for the waters were still on the face of the whole earth. So he put out his hand and took it and brought it into the ark with him. He waited another seven days, and again he sent out the dove from the ark; and the dove came back to him in the evening, and there in its beak was a freshly plucked olive leaf; so Noah knew that the waters had subsided from the earth. Then he waited another seven days, and sent out the dove; and it did not return to him any more. In the six hundred first year, in the first month, the first day of the month, the waters were dried up from the earth; and Noah removed the covering of the ark, and looked, and saw that the face of the ground was drying. In the second month, on the twenty-seventh day of the month, the earth was dry." Then God said to Noah, "Go out of the ark, you and your wife, and your sons and your sons' wives with you. Then God said to Noah and to his sons with him, "As for me, I am establishing my covenant with you and your descendants after you, and with every living creature that is with you, the birds, the domestic animals, and every animal of the earth with you, as many as came out of the ark, I establish my covenant with you, that never again shall all flesh be cut off by the waters of a flood, and never again shall there be a flood to destroy the earth." God said, "This is the sign of the covenant that I make between me and you and every living creature that is with you, for all future generations: I have set my bow in the clouds, and it shall be a sign of the covenant between me and the earth. When I bring clouds over and the bow is seen in the clouds, I will remember by covenant that is between me and you and every living creature of all flesh; and the waters shall never again become a flood to destroy all flesh. When the bow is in the clouds, I will see it and remember the everlasting covenant between God and every living creature of all flesh that is on the earth."

The Psalm 111   *Confitebor tibi*

1   Hallelujah!
       I will give thanks to the LORD with my whole heart, *
          in the assembly of the upright, in the congregation.

2   Great are the deeds of the LORD! *
          they are studied by all who delight in them.

3   His work is full of majesty and splendor, *
          and his righteousness endures for ever.

4   He makes his marvelous works to be remembered; *
        the LORD is gracious and full of compassion.

5   He gives food to those who fear him; *
        he is ever mindful of his covenant.

6   He has shown his people the power of his works *
        in giving them the lands of the nations.

7   The works of his hands are faithfulness and justice; *
        all his commandments are sure.

8   They stand fast for ever and ever, *
        because they are done in truth and equity.

9   He sent redemption to his people;
    he commanded his covenant for ever; *
        holy and awesome is his Name.

10 The fear of the LORD is the beginning of wisdom; *
        those who act accordingly have a good understanding;
        his praises endures for ever.

or Psalm 118:19-24   *Confitemini Domino*
19 Open for me the gates of righteousness; *
        I will enter them;
        I will offer thanks to the LORD.

20 "This is the gate of the LORD; *
        he who is righteous may enter."

21 I will give thanks to you, for you answered me *
        and have become my salvation.

22 The same stone which the builders rejected *
        has become the chief cornerstone.

23 This is the LORD's doing, *
        and it is marvelous in our eyes.

24 On this day the LORD has acted; *
        we will rejoice and be glad in it.

The Epistle   **1 Peter 1:3-9**
Blessed be the God and Father of our Lord Jesus Christ! By his great mercy he has
given us a new birth into a living hope through the resurrection of Jesus Christ from
the dead, and into an inheritance that is imperishable, undefiled, and unfading, kept
in heaven for you, who are being protected by the power of God through faith for a
salvation ready to be revealed in the last time. In this you rejoice, even if now for a
little while you have had to suffer various trials, so that the genuineness of your faith
— being more precious than gold that, though perishable, is tested by fire — may be
found to result in praise and glory and honor when Jesus Christ is revealed. Although

you have not seen him, you love him; and even though you do not see him now, you believe in him and rejoice with an indescribable and glorious joy, for you are receiving the outcome of your faith, the salvation of your souls.

or Acts 2:14a, 22-32

Peter, standing with the eleven, raised his voice and addressed them, "You that are Israelites, listen to what I have to say: Jesus of Nazareth, a man attested to you by God with deeds of power, wonders, and signs that God did through him among you, as you yourselves know — this man, handed over to you according to the definite plan and foreknowledge of God, you crucified and killed by the hands of those outside the law. But God raised him up, having freed him from death, because it was impossible for him to be held in its power. For David says concerning him, 'I saw the Lord always before me, for he is at my right hand so that I will not be shaken; therefore my heart was glad, and my tongue rejoiced; moreover my flesh will live in hope. For you will not abandon my soul to Hades, or let your Holy One experience corruption. You have made known to me the ways of life; you will make me full of gladness with your presence.' Fellow Israelites, I may say to you confidently of our ancestor David that he both died and was buried, and his tomb is with us to this day. Since he was a prophet, he knew that God had sworn with an oath to him that he would put one of his descendants on his throne. Foreseeing this, David spoke of the resurrection of the Messiah, saying, 'He was not abandoned to Hades, nor did his flesh experience corruption.' This Jesus God raised up, and of that all of us are witnesses."

The Gospel   **John 20:19-31**

When it was evening on that day, the first day of the week, and the doors of the house where the disciples had met were locked for fear of the Jews, Jesus came and stood among them and said, "Peace be with you." After he said this, he showed them his hands and his side. Then the disciples rejoiced when they saw the Lord. Jesus said to them again, "Peace be with you. As the Father has sent me, so I send you." When he had said this, he breathed on them and said to them, "Receive the Holy Spirit. If you forgive the sins of any, they are forgiven them; if you retain the sins of any, they are retained." But Thomas (who was called the Twin), one of the twelve, was not with them when Jesus came. So the other disciples told him, "We have seen the Lord." But he said to them, "Unless I see the mark of the nails in his hands, and put my finger in the mark of the nails and my hand in his side, I will not believe." A week later his disciples were again in the house, and Thomas was with them. Although the doors were shut, Jesus came and stood among them and said, "Peace be with you." Then he said to Thomas, "Put your finger here and see my hands. Reach out your hand and put it in my side. Do not doubt but believe." Thomas answered him, "My Lord and my God!" Jesus said to him, "Have you believed because you have seen me? Blessed are those who have not seen and yet have come to believe." Now Jesus did many other signs in the presence of his disciples, which are not written in this book. But these are written so that you may come to believe that Jesus is the Messiah, the Son of God, and that through believing you may have life in his name.

The Lesson   Acts 3:12a, 13-15, 17-26

When Peter saw it, he addressed the people, "The God of Abraham, the God of Isaac, and the God of Jacob, the God of our ancestors has glorified his servant Jesus, whom you handed over and rejected in the presence of Pilate, though he had decided to release him. But you rejected the Holy and Righteous One and asked to have a murderer given to you, and you killed the Author of life, whom God raised from the dead. To this we are witnesses. "And now, friends, I know that you acted in ignorance, as did also your rulers. In this way God fulfilled what he had foretold through all the prophets, that his Messiah would suffer. Repent therefore, and turn to God so that your sins may be wiped out, so that times of refreshing may come from the presence of the Lord, and that he may send the Messiah appointed for you, that is, Jesus, who must remain in heaven until the time of universal restoration that God announced long ago through his holy prophets. Moses said, 'The Lord your God will raise up for you from your own people a prophet like me. You must listen to whatever he tells you. And it will be that everyone who does not listen to that prophet will be utterly rooted out of the people.' And all the prophets, as many as have spoken, from Samuel and those after him, also predicted these days. You are the descendants of the prophets and of the covenant that God gave to your ancestors, saying to Abraham, 'And in your descendants all the families of the earth shall be blessed.' When God raised up his servant, he sent him first to you, to bless you by turning each of you from your wicked ways."

or Isaiah 26:2-9, 19

Open the gates, so that the righteous nation that keeps faith may enter in. Those of steadfast mind you keep in peace — in peace because they trust in you. Trust in the LORD forever, for in the LORD GOD you have an everlasting rock. For he has brought low the inhabitants of the height; the lofty city he lays low. He lays it low to the ground, casts it to the dust. The foot tramples it, the feet of the poor, the steps of the needy. The way of the righteous is level; O Just One, you make smooth the path of the righteous. In the path of your judgments, O LORD, we wait for you; your name and your renown are the soul's desire. My soul yearns for you in the night, my spirit within me earnestly seeks you. For when your judgments are in the earth, the inhabitants of the world learn righteousness. Your dead shall live, their corpses shall rise. O dwellers in the dust, awake and sing for joy! For your dew is radiant dew, and the earth will give birth to those long dead.

The Psalm 111   *Confitebor tibi*

1   Hallelujah!
       I will give thanks to the LORD with my whole heart, *
          in the assembly of the upright, in the congregation.

2   Great are the deeds of the LORD! *
          they are studied by all who delight in them.

3   His work is full of majesty and splendor, *
          and his righteousness endures for ever.

4   He makes his marvelous works to be remembered; *
       the LORD is gracious and full of compassion.

5   He gives food to those who fear him; *
       he is ever mindful of his covenant.

6   He has shown his people the power of his works *
       in giving them the lands of the nations.

7   The works of his hands are faithfulness and justice; *
       all his commandments are sure.

8   They stand fast for ever and ever, *
       because they are done in truth and equity.

9   He sent redemption to his people;
    he commanded his covenant for ever; *
       holy and awesome is his Name.

10   The fear of the LORD is the beginning of wisdom; *
       those who act accordingly have a good understanding;
       his praises endures for ever.

or Psalm 118:19-24   *Confitemini Domino*

19   Open for me the gates of righteousness; *
       I will enter them;
       I will offer thanks to the LORD.

20   "This is the gate of the LORD; *
       he who is righteous may enter."

21   I will give thanks to you, for you answered me *
       and have become my salvation.

22   The same stone which the builders rejected *
       has become the chief cornerstone.

23   This is the LORD's doing, *
       and it is marvelous in our eyes.

24   On this day the LORD has acted; *
       we will rejoice and be glad in it.

The Epistle   **1 John 5:1-6**

Everyone who believes that Jesus is the Christ has been born of God, and everyone who loves the parent loves the child. By this we know that we love the children of God, when we love God and obey his commandments. For the love of God is this, that we obey his commandments. And his commandments are not burdensome, for whatever is born of God conquers the world. And this is the victory that conquers the world, our faith. Who is it that conquers the world but the one who believes that Jesus is the Son of God? This is the one who came by water and blood, Jesus Christ, not with the water only but with the water and the blood. And the Spirit is the one that testifies, for the Spirit is the truth.

or Acts 3:12a, 13-15, 17-26

The healed man clung to Peter and John and when Peter saw their astonishment, he addressed the people, "The God of Abraham, the God of Isaac, and the God of Jacob, the God of our ancestors has glorified his servant Jesus, whom you handed over and rejected in the presence of Pilate, though he had decided to release him. But you rejected the Holy and Righteous One and asked to have a murderer given to you, and you killed the Author of life, whom God raised from the dead. To this we are witnesses. And now, friends, I know that you acted in ignorance, as did also your rulers. In this way God fulfilled what he had foretold through all the prophets, that his Messiah would suffer. Repent therefore, and turn to God so that your sins may be wiped out, so that times of refreshing may come from the presence of the Lord, and that he may send the Messiah appointed for you, that is, Jesus, who must remain in heaven until the time of universal restoration that God announced long ago through his holy prophets. Moses said, 'The Lord your God will raise up for you from your own people a prophet like me. You must listen to whatever he tells you. And it will be that everyone who does not listen to that prophet will be utterly rooted out of the people.' And all the prophets, as many as have spoken, from Samuel and those after him, also predicted these days. You are the descendants of the prophets and of the covenant that God gave to your ancestors, saying to Abraham, 'And in your descendants all the families of the earth shall be blessed.' When God raised up his servant, he sent him first to you, to bless you by turning each of you from your wicked ways."

The Gospel
John 20:19-31

When it was evening of Easter day, the first day of the week, and the doors of the house where the disciples had met were locked for fear of the Jews, Jesus came and stood among them and said, "Peace be with you." After he said this, he showed them his hands and his side. Then the disciples rejoiced when they saw the Lord. Jesus said to them again, "Peace be with you. As the Father has sent me, so I send you." When he had said this, he breathed on them and said to them, "Receive the Holy Spirit. If you forgive the sins of any, they are forgiven them; if you retain the sins of any, they are retained." But Thomas (who was called the Twin), one of the twelve, was not with them when Jesus came. So the other disciples told him, "We have seen the Lord." But he said to them, "Unless I see the mark of the nails in his hands, and put my finger in the mark of the nails and my hand in his side, I will not believe." A week later his disciples were again in the house, and Thomas was with them. Although the doors were shut, Jesus came and stood among them and said, "Peace be with you." Then he said to Thomas, "Put your finger here and see my hands. Reach out your hand and put it in my side. Do not doubt but believe." Thomas answered him, "My Lord and my God!" Jesus said to him, "Have you believed because you have seen me? Blessed are those who have not seen and yet have come to believe." Now Jesus did many other signs in the presence of his disciples, which are not written in this book. But these are written so that you may come to believe that Jesus is the Messiah, the Son of God, and that through believing you may have life in his name.

The Lesson   Acts 5:12a, 17-22, 25-29

Now many signs and wonders were done among the people through the apostles. Then the high priest took action; he and all who were with him (that is, the sect of the Sadducees), being filled with jealousy, arrested the apostles and put them in the public prison. But during the night an angel of the Lord opened the prison doors, brought them out, and said, "Go, stand in the temple and tell the people the whole message about this life." When they heard this, they entered the temple at daybreak and went on with their teaching. When the high priest and those with him arrived, they called together the council and the whole body of the elders of Israel, and sent to the prison to have them brought. But when the temple police went there, they did not find them in the prison; so they returned and reported. Then someone arrived and announced, "Look, the men whom you put in prison are standing in the temple and teaching the people!" Then the captain went with the temple police and brought them, but without violence, for they were afraid of being stoned by the people. When they had brought them, they had them stand before the council. The high priest questioned them, saying, "We gave you strict orders not to teach in this name, yet here you have filled Jerusalem with your teaching and you are determined to bring this man's blood on us." But Peter and the apostles answered, "We must obey God rather than any human authority."

or Job 42:1-6

Then Job answered the LORD: "I know that you can do all things, and that no purpose of yours can be thwarted. 'Who is this that hides counsel without knowledge?' Therefore I have uttered what I did not understand, things too wonderful for me, which I did not know. 'Hear, and I will speak; I will question you, and you declare to me.' I had heard of you by the hearing of the ear, but now my eye sees you; therefore I despise myself, and repent in dust and ashes."

The Psalm 111 *Confitebor tibi*

1 Hallelujah!
  I will give thanks to the LORD with my whole heart, *
   in the assembly of the upright, in the congregation.

2 Great are the deeds of the LORD! *
   they are studied by all who delight in them.

3 His work is full of majesty and splendor, *
   and his righteousness endures for ever.

4 He makes his marvelous works to be remembered; *
   the LORD is gracious and full of compassion.

5 He gives food to those who fear him; *
   he is ever mindful of his covenant.

6 He has shown his people the power of his works *
   in giving them the lands of the nations.

7　　The works of his hands are faithfulness and justice; *
　　　　all his commandments are sure.

8　　They stand fast for ever and ever, *
　　　　because they are done in truth and equity.

9　　He sent redemption to his people;
　　　　he commanded his covenant for ever; *
　　　　holy and awesome is his Name.

10　　The fear of the LORD is the beginning of wisdom; *
　　　　those who act accordingly have a good understanding;
　　　　his praises endures for ever.

or Psalm 118:19-24　　　*Confitemini Domino*

19　　Open for me the gates of righteousness; *
　　　　I will enter them;
　　　　I will offer thanks to the LORD.

20　　"This is the gate of the LORD; *
　　　　he who is righteous may enter."

21　　I will give thanks to you, for you answered me *
　　　　and have become my salvation.

22　　The same stone which the builders rejected *
　　　　has become the chief cornerstone.

23　　This is the LORD's doing, *
　　　　and it is marvelous in our eyes.

24　　On this day the LORD has acted; *
　　　　we will rejoice and be glad in it.

The Epistle　　　　　　　　　　　　　　　Revelation 1:(1-8) 9—19

[The revelation of Jesus Christ, which God gave him to show his servants what must soon take place; he made it known by sending his angel to his servant John, who testified to the word of God and to the testimony of Jesus Christ, even to all that he saw. Blessed is the one who reads aloud the words of the prophecy, and blessed are those who hear and who keep what is written in it; for the time is near. John to the seven churches that are in Asia: Grace to you and peace from him who is and who was and who is to come, and from the seven spirits who are before his throne, and from Jesus Christ, the faithful witness, the firstborn of the dead, and the ruler of the kings of the earth. To him who loves us and freed us from our sins by his blood, and made us to be a kingdom, priests serving his God and Father, to him be glory and dominion forever and ever. Amen. Look! He is coming with the clouds; every eye will see him, even those who pierced him; and on his account all the tribes of the earth will wail. So it is to be. Amen. "I am the Alpha and the Omega," says the Lord God, who is and who was and who is to come, the Almighty.] I, John, your brother who share with you in Jesus the persecution and the kingdom and the patient endurance, was on the island called Patmos because of the word of God and the testimony of Jesus. I was in the spirit on the Lord's day, and I heard behind me a loud voice like a trumpet saying, "Write in a book what you see and send it to the seven churches, to Ephesus, to Smyrna, to Pergamum, to Thyatira, to Sardis, to Philadelphia, and to Laodicea." Then I turned to see whose voice it was that spoke to me, and on turning I saw seven golden lampstands, and in the midst of the lampstands I saw one like the Son of Man, clothed with a long robe and with a golden sash across his chest. His head and his hair were white as white wool, white as snow; his eyes were like a flame of fire, his feet were like burnished bronze, refined as in a furnace, and his voice was like the sound of many waters. In his right hand he held seven stars, and from his mouth came a sharp, two-edged sword, and his face was like the sun shining with full force. When I saw him, I fell at his feet as though dead. But he placed his right hand on me, saying, "Do not be afraid; I am the first and the last, and the living one. I was dead, and see, I am alive forever and ever; and I have the keys of Death and of Hades. Now write what you have seen, what is, and what is to take place after this."

or Acts 5:12a, 17-22, 25-29
Now many signs and wonders were done among the people through the apostles. Then the high priest took action; he and all who were with him (that is, the sect of the Sadducees), being filled with jealousy, arrested the apostles and put them in the public prison. But during the night an angel of the Lord opened the prison doors, brought them out, and said, "Go, stand in the temple and tell the people the whole message about this life." When they heard this, they entered the temple at daybreak and went on with their teaching. When the high priest and those with him arrived, they called together the council and the whole body of the elders of Israel, and sent to the prison to have them brought. But when the temple police went there, they did not find them in the prison; so they returned and reported. Then someone arrived and announced, "Look, the men whom you put in prison are standing in the temple and teaching the people!" Then the captain went with the temple police and brought them, but without violence, for they were afraid of being stoned by the people. When they had brought them, they had them stand before the council. The high priest questioned them, saying, "We gave you strict orders not to teach in this name, yet here you have filled Jerusalem with your teaching and you are determined to bring this man's blood on us." But Peter and the apostles answered, "We must obey God rather than any human authority."

The Gospel   **John 20:19-31**
When it was evening of Easter, the first day of the week, and the doors of the house where the disciples had met were locked for fear of the Jews, Jesus came and stood among them and said, "Peace be with you." After he said this, he showed them his hands and his side. Then the disciples rejoiced when they saw the Lord. Jesus said to them again, "Peace be with you. As the Father has sent me, so I send you." When he had said this, he breathed on them and said to them, "Receive the Holy Spirit. If you forgive the sins of any, they are forgiven them; if you retain the sins of any, they are retained." But Thomas (who was called the Twin), one of the twelve, was not with them when Jesus came. So the other disciples told him, "We have seen the Lord."

But he said to them, "Unless I see the mark of the nails in his hands, and put my finger in the mark of the nails and my hand in his side, I will not believe." A week later his disciples were again in the house, and Thomas was with them. Although the doors were shut, Jesus came and stood among them and said, "Peace be with you." Then he said to Thomas, "Put your finger here and see my hands. Reach out your hand and put it in my side. Do not doubt but believe." Thomas answered him, "My Lord and my God!" Jesus said to him, "Have you believed because you have seen me? Blessed are those who have not seen and yet have come to believe." Now Jesus did many other signs in the presence of his disciples, which are not written in this book. But these are written so that you may come to believe that Jesus is the Messiah, the Son of God, and that through believing you may have life in his name.

THE THIRD SUNDAY OF EASTER

The Collect

O God, whose blessed Son made himself known to his disciples in the breaking of bread: Open the eyes of our faith, that we may behold him in all his redeeming work; who lives and reigns with you, in the unity of the Holy Spirit, one God, now and for ever. *Amen.*

O God, whose blessed Son did manifest himself to his disciples in the breaking of bread: Open, we pray thee, the eyes of our faith, that we may behold him in all his redeeming work; through the same thy Son Jesus Christ our Lord, who liveth and reigneth with thee, in the unity of the Holy Spirit, one God, now and for ever. *Amen.*

Year A

The Lesson

Acts 2:14a, 36-47

But Peter, standing with the eleven, raised his voice and addressed them, "Therefore let the entire house of Israel know with certainty that God has made him both Lord and Messiah, this Jesus whom you crucified." Now when they heard this, they were cut to the heart and said to Peter and to the other apostles, "Brothers, what should we do?" Peter said to them, "Repent, and be baptized every one of you in the name of Jesus Christ so that your sins may be forgiven; and you will receive the gift of the Holy Spirit. For the promise is for you, for your children, and for all who are far away, everyone whom the Lord our God calls to him." And he testified with many other arguments and exhorted them, saying, "Save yourselves from this corrupt generation." So those who welcomed his message were baptized, and that day about three thousand persons were added. They devoted themselves to the apostles' teaching and fellowship, to the breaking of bread and the prayers. Awe came upon everyone, because many wonders and signs were being done by the apostles. All who believed were together and had all things in common; they would sell their possessions and goods and distribute the proceeds to all, as any had need. Day by day, as they spent much time together in the temple, they broke bread at home and ate their food with glad and generous hearts, praising God and having the goodwill of all the people. And day by day the Lord added to their number those who were being saved.

or Isaiah 43:1-12

But now thus says the LORD, he who created you, O Jacob, he who formed you, O Israel: Do not fear for I have redeemed you; I have called you by name, you are mine. When you pass through the waters, I will be with you; and through the rivers, they shall not overwhelm you; when you walk through fire you shall not be burned, and the flame shall not consume you. For I am the LORD your God, the Holy One of Israel, your Savior. I give Egypt as your ransom, Ethiopia and Seba in exchange for you. Because you are precious in my sight, and honored, and I love you, I give people in return for you, nations in exchange for your life. Do not fear, for I am with you; I will bring your offspring from the east, and from the west I will gather you; I will say to the north, "Give them up," and to the south, "Do not withhold; bring my sons from far away and my daughters from the end of the earth — everyone who is called by my name, whom I created for my glory, whom I formed and made." Bring forth the people who are blind, yet have eyes, who are deaf, yet have ears! Let all the nations gather together, and let the peoples assemble. Who among them declared this, and foretold to us the former things? Let them bring their witnesses to justify them, and let them hear and say, "It is true." You are my witnesses, says the LORD, and my servant whom I have chosen, so that you may know and believe me and understand that I am he. Before me no god was formed, nor shall there be any after me. I, I am the LORD, and besides me there is no savior. I declared and saved and proclaimed, when there was no strange god among you; and you are my witnesses, says the LORD.

The Psalm 116 or 116:10-17   *Dilexi, quoniam*

1   I love the LORD, because he has heard the voice of my supplication, *
      because he has inclined his ear to me whenever I called upon him.

2   The cords of death entangled me;
      the grip of the grave took hold of me; *
      I came to grief and sorrow.

3   Then I called upon the Name of the LORD: *
      "O LORD, I pray you, save my life."

4   Gracious is the LORD and righteous; *
      our God is full of compassion.

5   The LORD watches over the innocent; *
      I was brought very low, and he helped me.

6   Turn again to your rest, O my soul, *
      for the LORD has treated you well.

7   For you have rescued my life from death, *
      my eyes from tears, and my feet from stumbling.

8   I will walk in the presence of the LORD *
      in the land of the living.

9   I believed, even when I said,
    "I have been brought very low." *
       In my distress I said, "No one can be trusted."

10   [How shall I repay the LORD *
       for all the good things he has done for me?

11   I will lift up the cup of salvation *
       and call upon the Name of the LORD.

12   I will fulfill my vows to the LORD *
       in the presence of all his people.

13   Precious in the sight of the LORD *
       is the death of his servants.

14   O LORD, I am your servant; *
       I am your servant and the child of your handmaid;
       you have freed me from my bonds.

15   I will offer you the sacrifice of thanksgiving *
       and call upon the Name of the LORD.

16   I will fulfill my vows to the LORD *
       in the presence of all his people,

17   In the courts of the LORD'S house, *
       in the midst of you, O Jerusalem.
       Hallelujah!]

The Epistle   **1 Peter 1:17-23**

If you invoke as Father the one who judges all people impartially according to their deeds, live in reverent fear during the time of your exile. You know that you were ransomed from the futile ways inherited from your ancestors, not with perishable things like silver or gold, but with the precious blood of Christ, like that of a lamb without defect or blemish. He was destined before the foundation of the world, but was revealed at the end of the ages for your sake. Through him you have come to trust in God, who raised him from the dead and gave him glory, so that your faith and hope are set on God. Now that you have purified your souls by your obedience to the truth so that you have genuine mutual love, love one another deeply from the heart. You have been born anew, not of perishable but of imperishable seed, through the living and enduring word of God.

or Acts 2:14a, 36-47

Peter, standing with the eleven, raised his voice and addressed them, "Therefore let the entire house of Israel know with certainty that God has made him both Lord and Messiah, this Jesus whom you crucified." Now when they heard this, they were cut to the heart and said to Peter and to the other apostles, "Brothers, what should we do?" Peter said to them, "Repent, and be baptized every one of you in the name of Jesus Christ so that your sins may be forgiven; and you will receive the gift of the Holy

Spirit. For the promise is for you, for your children, and for all who are far away, everyone whom the Lord our God calls to him." And he testified with many other arguments and exhorted them, saying, "Save yourselves from this corrupt generation." So those who welcomed his message were baptized, and that day about three thousand persons were added. They devoted themselves to the apostles' teaching and fellowship, to the breaking of bread and the prayers. Awe came upon everyone, because many wonders and signs were being done by the apostles. All who believed were together and had all things in common; they would sell their possessions and goods and distribute the proceeds to all, as any had need. Day by day, as they spent much time together in the temple, they broke bread at home and ate their food with glad and generous hearts, praising God and having the goodwill of all the people. And day by day the Lord added to their number those who were being saved.

The Gospel   **Luke 24:13-35**
On the first day of the week, two of Jesus' followers were going to a village called Emmaus, about seven miles from Jerusalem, and talking with each other about all these things that had happened. While they were talking and discussing, Jesus himself came near and went with them, but their eyes were kept from recognizing him. And he said to them, "What are you discussing with each other while you walk along?" They stood still, looking sad. Then one of them, whose name was Cleopas, answered him, "Are you the only stranger in Jerusalem who does not know the things that have taken place there in these days?" He asked them, "What things?" They replied, "The things about Jesus of Nazareth, who was a prophet mighty in deed and word before God and all the people, and how our chief priests and leaders handed him over to be condemned to death and crucified him. But we had hoped that he was the one to redeem Israel. Yes, and besides all this, it is now the third day since these things took place. Moreover, some women of our group astounded us. They were at the tomb early this morning, and when they did not find his body there, they came back and told us that they had indeed seen a vision of angels who said that he was alive. Some of those who were with us went to the tomb and found it just as the women had said; but they did not see him." Then he said to them, "Oh, how foolish you are, and how slow of heart to believe all that the prophets have declared! Was it not necessary that the Messiah should suffer these things and then enter into his glory?" Then beginning with Moses and all the prophets, he interpreted to them the things about himself in all the scriptures. As they came near the village to which they were going, he walked ahead as if he were going on. But they urged him strongly, saying, "Stay with us, because it is almost evening and the day is now nearly over." So he went in to stay with them. When he was at the table with them, he took bread, blessed and broke it, and gave it to them. Then their eyes were opened, and they recognized him; and he vanished from their sight. They said to each other, "Were not our hearts burning within us while he was talking to us on the road, while he was opening the scriptures to us?" That same hour they got up and returned to Jerusalem; and they found the eleven and their companions gathered together. They were saying, "The Lord has risen indeed, and he has appeared to Simon!" Then they told what had happened on the road, and how he had been made known to them in the breaking of the bread.

The Lesson   Acts 4:5-12

The next day their rulers, elders, and scribes assembled in Jerusalem, with Annas the high priest, Caiaphas, John, and Alexander, and all who were of the high-priestly family. When they had made the prisoners stand in their midst, they inquired, "By what power or by what name did you do this?" Then Peter, filled with the Holy Spirit, said to them, "Rulers of the people and elders, if we are questioned today because of a good deed done to someone who was sick and are asked how this man has been healed, let it be known to all of you, and to all the people of Israel, that this man is standing before you in good health by the name of Jesus Christ of Nazareth, whom you crucified, whom God raised from the dead. This Jesus is 'the stone that was rejected by you, the builders; it has become the cornerstone.' There is salvation in no one else, for there is no other name under heaven given among mortals by which we must be saved."

or Micah 4:1-5

In days to come the mountain of the LORD'S house shall be established as the highest of the mountains, and shall be raised up above the hills. Peoples shall stream to it, and many nations shall come and say: "Come, let us go up to the mountain of the LORD, to the house of the God of Jacob; that he may teach us his ways and that we may walk in his paths." For out of Zion shall go forth instruction, and the word of the LORD from Jerusalem. He shall judge between many peoples, and shall arbitrate between strong nations far away; they shall beat their swords into plowshares, and their spears into pruning hooks; nation shall not lift up sword against nation, neither shall they learn war any more; but they shall all sit under their own vines and under their own fig trees, and no one shall make them afraid; for the mouth of the LORD of hosts has spoken. For all the peoples walk, each in the name of its god, but we will walk in the name of the LORD our God forever and ever.

The Psalm 98 or 98:1-5   *Cantate Domino*

1   [Sing to the LORD a new song, *
        for he has done marvelous things.

2   With his right hand and his holy arm *
        has he won for himself the victory.

3   The LORD has made known his victory; *
        his righteousness has he openly shown in the sight of the nations.

4   He remembers his mercy and faithfulness to the house of Israel, *
        and all the ends of the earth have seen the victory of our God.

5   Shout with joy to the LORD, all you lands; *
        lift up your voice, rejoice, and sing.]

6   Sing to the LORD with the harp, *
        with the harp and the voice of song.

7   With trumpets and the sound of the horn *
        shout with joy before the King, the LORD.

8   Let the sea make a noise and all that is in it, *
       the lands and those who dwell therein.

9   Let the rivers clap their hands, *
       and let the hills ring out with joy before the LORD,
       when he comes to judge the earth.

10   In righteousness shall be judge the world *
       and the peoples with equity.

The Epistle   **1 John 1:1-2:2**
We declare to you what was from the beginning, what we have heard, what we have
seen with our eyes, what we have looked at and touched with our hands, concerning
the word of life — this life was revealed, and we have seen it and testify to it, and
declare to you the eternal life that was with the Father and was revealed to us — we
declare to you what we have seen and heard so that you also may have fellowship
with us; and truly our fellowship is with the Father and with his Son Jesus Christ. We
are writing these things so that our joy may be complete. This is the message we have
heard from him and proclaim to you, that God is light and in him there is no
darkness at all. If we say that we have fellowship with him while we are walking in
darkness, we lie and do not do what is true; but if we walk in the light as he himself is
in the light, we have fellowship with one another, and the blood of Jesus his Son
cleanses us from all sin. If we say that we have no sin, we deceive ourselves, and the
truth is not in us. If we confess our sins, he who is faithful and just will forgive us our
sins and cleanse us from all unrighteousness. If we say that we have not sinned, we
make him a liar, and his word is not in us. My little children, I am writing these
things to you so that you may not sin. But if anyone does sin, we have an advocate
with the Father, Jesus Christ the righteous; and he is the atoning sacrifice for our sins
and not for ours only but also for the sins of the whole world.

or Acts 4:5-12
The next day their rulers, elders, and scribes assembled in Jerusalem, with Annas the
high priest, Caiaphas, John, and Alexander, and all who were of the high-priestly
family. When they had made the prisoners stand in their midst, they inquired, "By
what power or by what name did you do this?" Then Peter, filled with the Holy
Spirit, said to them, "Rulers of the people and elders, if we are questioned today
because of a good deed done to someone who was sick and are asked how this man
has been healed, let it be known to all of you, and to all the people of Israel, that this
man is standing before you in good health by the name of Jesus Christ of Nazareth,
whom you crucified, whom God raised from the dead. This Jesus is 'the stone that
was rejected by you, the builders; it has become the cornerstone.' There is salvation
in no one else, for there is no other name under heaven given among mortals by
which we must be saved."

The Gospel   **Luke 24:36b-48**
While the disciples were telling how they had seen Jesus risen from the dead, Jesus
himself stood among them and said to them, "Peace be with you." They were startled

and terrified, and thought that they were seeing a ghost. He said to them, "Why are you frightened, and why do doubts arise in your hearts? Look at my hands and my feet; see that it is I myself. Touch me and see; for a ghost does not have flesh and bones as you see that I have." And when he had said this, he showed them his hands and his feet. While in their joy they were disbelieving and still wondering, he said to them, "Have you anything here to eat?" They gave him a piece of broiled fish, and he took it and ate in their presence. Then he said to them, "These are my words that I spoke to you while I was still with you — that everything written about me in the law of Moses, the prophets, and the psalms must be fulfilled." Then he opened their minds to understand the scriptures, and he said to them, "Thus it is written, that the Messiah is to suffer and to rise from the dead on the third day, and that repentance and forgiveness of sins is to be proclaimed in his name to all nations, beginning from Jerusalem. You are witnesses of these things."

Year C

The Lesson

Acts 9:1-19a

Saul, still breathing threats and murder against the disciples of the Lord, went to the high priest and asked him for letters to the synagogues at Damascus, so that if he found any who belonged to the Way, men or women, he might bring them bound to Jerusalem. Now as he was going along and approaching Damascus, suddenly a light from heaven flashed around him. He fell to the ground and heard a voice saying to him, "Saul, Saul, why do you persecute me?" He asked, "Who are you, Lord?" The reply came, "I am Jesus, whom you are persecuting. But get up and enter the city, and you will be told what you are to do." The men who were traveling with him stood speechless because they heard the voice but saw no one. Saul got up from the ground, and though his eyes were open, he could see nothing; so they led him by the hand and brought him into Damascus. For three days he was without sight, and neither ate nor drank. Now there was a disciple in Damascus named Ananias. The Lord said to him in a vision, "Ananias." He answered, "Here I am, Lord." The Lord said to him, "Get up and go to the street called Straight, and at the house of Judas look for a man of Tarsus named Saul. At this moment he is praying, and he has seen in a vision a man named Ananias come in and lay his hands on him so that he might regain his sight." But Ananias answered, "Lord, I have heard from many about this man, how much evil he has done to your saints in Jerusalem; and here he has authority from the chief priests to bind all who invoke your name." But the Lord said to him, "Go, for he is an instrument whom I have chosen to bring my name before Gentiles and kings and before the people of Israel; I myself will show him how much he must suffer for the sake of my name." So Ananias went and entered the house. He laid his hands on Saul and said, "Brother Saul, the Lord Jesus, who appeared to you on your way here, has sent me so that you may regain your sight and be filled with the Holy Spirit." And immediately something like scales fell from his eyes, and his sight was restored. Then he got up and was baptized, and after taking some food, he regained his strength.

or Jeremiah 32:36-41

Thus says the LORD, the God of Israel, concerning this city of which you say, "It is being given into the hand of the king of Babylon by the sword, by famine, and by pestilence": See, I am going to gather them from all the lands to which I drove them in my anger and my wrath and in great indignation; I will bring them back to this place, and I will settle them in safety. They shall be my people, and I will be their God. I will give them one heart and one way, that they may fear me for all time, for their own good and the good of their children after them. I will make an everlasting covenant with them, never to draw back from doing good to them; and I will put the fear of me in their hearts, so that they may not turn from me. I will rejoice in doing good to them, and I will plant them in this land in faithfulness, with all my heart and all my soul.

The Psalm 33 or 33:1-11   *Exultate, justi*

1   [Rejoice in the LORD, you righteous; *
          it is good for the just to sing praises.

2   Praise the LORD with the harp; *
          play to him upon the psaltery and lyre.

3   Sing for him a new song; *
          sound a fanfare with all your skill upon the trumpet.

4   For the word of the LORD is right, *
          and all his works are sure.

5   He loves righteousness and justice; *
          the loving-kindness of the LORD fills the whole earth.

6   By the word of the LORD were the heavens made, *
          by the breath of his mouth all the heavenly hosts.

7   He gathers up the waters of the ocean as in a water-skin *
          and stores up the depths of the sea.

8   Let all the earth fear the LORD; *
          let all who dwell in the world stand in awe of him.

9   For he spoke, and it came to pass; *
          he commanded, and it stood fast.

10   The LORD brings the will of the nations to naught; *
          he thwarts the designs of the peoples.

11   But the LORD'S will stands fast for ever, *
          and the designs of his heart from age to age.]

12   Happy is the nation whose God is the LORD! *
          happy the people he has chosen to be his own!

13   The LORD looks down from heaven, *
          and beholds all the people in the world.

14   From where he sits enthroned he turns his gaze *
          on all who dwell on the earth.

15   He fashions all the hearts of them *
       and understands all their works.

16   There is no king that can be saved by a mighty army; *
       a strong man is not delivered by his great strength.

17   The horse is a vain hope for deliverance; *
       for all its strength it cannot save.

18   Behold, the eye of the LORD is upon those who fear him, *
       on those who wait upon his love,

19   To pluck their lives from death, *
       and to feed them in time of famine.

20   Our soul waits for the LORD; *
       he is our help and our shield.

21   Indeed, our heart rejoices in him, *
       for in his holy Name we put our trust.

22   Let your loving-kindness, O LORD, be upon us, *
       as we have put our trust in you.

The Epistle   **Revelation 5:6-14**

Then I saw between the throne and the four living creatures and among the elders a Lamb standing as if it had been slaughtered, having seven horns and seven eyes, which are the seven spirits of God sent out into all the earth. He went and took the scroll from the right hand of the one who was seated on the throne. When he had taken the scroll, the four living creatures and the twenty-four elders fell before the Lamb, each holding a harp and golden bowls full of incense, which are the prayers of the saints. They sing a new song: "You are worthy to take the scroll and to open its seals, for you were slaughtered and by your blood you ransomed for God saints from every tribe and language and people and nation; you have made them to be a kingdom and priests serving our God, and they will reign on earth." Then I looked, and I heard the voice of many angels surrounding the throne and the living creatures and the elders; they numbered myriads of myriads and thousands of thousands, singing with full voice, "Worthy is the Lamb that was slaughtered to receive power and wealth and wisdom and might and honor and glory and blessing!" Then I heard every creature in heaven and on earth and under the earth and in the sea, and all that is in them, singing, "To the one seated on the throne and to the Lamb be blessing and honor and glory and might forever and ever!" And the four living creatures said, "Amen!" And the elders fell down and worshiped.

or Acts 9:1-19a

Saul, still breathing threats and murder against the disciples of the Lord, went to the high priest and asked him for letters to the synagogues at Damascus, so that if he found any who belonged to the Way, men or women, he might bring them bound to Jerusalem. Now as he was going along and approaching Damascus, suddenly a light from heaven flashed around him. He fell to the ground and heard a voice saying to him, "Saul, Saul, why do you persecute me?" He asked, "Who are you, Lord?" The reply came, "I am Jesus, whom you are persecuting. But get up and enter the city, and you will be told what you are to do." The men who were traveling with him stood speechless because they heard the voice but saw no one. Saul got up from the ground, and though his eyes were open, he could see nothing; so they led him by the hand and brought him into Damascus. For three days he was without sight, and neither ate nor drank. Now there was a disciple in Damascus named Ananias. The Lord said to him in a vision, "Ananias." He answered, "Here I am, Lord." The Lord said to him, "Get up and go to the street called Straight, and at the house of Judas look for a man of Tarsus named Saul. At this moment he is praying, and he has seen in a vision a man named Ananias come in and lay his hands on him so that he might regain his sight." But Ananias answered, "Lord, I have heard from many about this man, how much evil he has done to your saints in Jerusalem; and here he has authority from the chief priests to bind all who invoke your name." But the Lord said to him, "Go, for he is an instrument whom I have chosen to bring my name before Gentiles and kings and before the people of Israel; I myself will show him how much he must suffer for the sake of my name." So Ananias went and entered the house. He laid his hands on Saul and said, "Brother Saul, the Lord Jesus, who appeared to you on your way here, has sent me so that you may regain your sight and be filled with the Holy Spirit." And immediately something like scales fell from his eyes, and his sight was restored. Then he got up and was baptized, and after taking some food, he regained his strength.

The Gospel   **John 21:1-14**

Jesus showed himself again to the disciples by the Sea of Tiberias; and he showed himself in this way. Gathered there together were Simon Peter, Thomas called the Twin, Nathanael of Cana in Galilee, the sons of Zebedee, and two others of his disciples. Simon Peter said to them, "I am going fishing." They said to him, "We will go with you." They went out and got into the boat, but that night they caught nothing. Just after daybreak, Jesus stood on the beach; but the disciples did not know that it was Jesus. Jesus said to them, "Children, you have no fish, have you?" They answered him, "No." He said to them, "Cast the net to the right side of the boat, and you will find some." So they cast it, and now they were not able to haul it in because there were so many fish. That disciple whom Jesus loved said to Peter, "It is the Lord!" When Simon Peter heard that it was the Lord, he put on some clothes, for he was naked, and jumped into the sea. But the other disciples came in the boat, dragging the net full of fish, for they were not far from the land, only about a hundred yards off. When they had gone ashore, they saw a charcoal fire there, with fish on it, and bread. Jesus said to them, "Bring some of the fish that you have just caught." So Simon Peter went aboard and hauled the net ashore, full of large fish, a hundred fifty-three of them; and though there were so many, the net was not torn. Jesus said to them, "Come and have breakfast." Now none of the disciples dared to ask him, "Who are you?" because they knew it was the Lord. Jesus came and took the bread and gave it to them, and did the same with the fish. This was now the third time that Jesus appeared to the disciples after he was raised from the dead.

THE FOURTH SUNDAY OF EASTER

The Collect

O God, whose Son Jesus is the good shepherd of your people: Grant that when we hear his voice we may know him who calls us each by name, and follow were he leads; who, with you and the Holy Spirit, lives and reigns, one God, for ever and ever. *Amen.*

O God, whose Son Jesus is the good shepherd of thy people: Grant that when we hear his voice we may know him who calleth us each by name, and follow where he doth lead; who, with thee and the Holy Spirit, liveth and reigneth, one God, for ever and ever. *Amen.*

Year A

The Lesson

Acts 6:1-9, 7:2a, 51-60

Now during those days, when the disciples were increasing in number, the Hellenists complained against the Hebrews because their widows were being neglected in the daily distribution of food. And the twelve called together the whole community of the disciples and said, "It is not right that we should neglect the word of God in order to wait on tables. Therefore, friends, select from among yourselves seven men of good standing, full of the Spirit and of wisdom, whom we may appoint to this task, while we, for our part, will devote ourselves to prayer and to serving the word." What they said pleased the whole community, and they chose Stephen, a man full of faith and the Holy Spirit, together with Phillip, Prochorus, Nicanor, Timon, Parmenas, and Nicolaus, a proselyte of Antioch. They had these men stand before the apostles, who prayed and laid their hands on them. The word of God continued to spread; the number of the disciples increased greatly in Jerusalem, and a great many of the priests became obedient to the faith. Stephen, full of grace and power, did great wonders and signs among the people. Then some of those who belonged to the synagogue of the Freedmen (as it was called), Cyrenians, Alexandrians, and others of those from Cilicia and Asia, stood up and argued with Stephen. And Stephen replied: "Brothers and fathers, listen to me. You stiff-necked people, uncircumcised in heart and ears, you are forever opposing the Holy Spirit, just as your ancestors used to do. Which of the prophets did your ancestors not persecute? They killed those who foretold the coming of the Righteous One, and now you have become his betrayers and murderers. You are the ones that received the law as ordained by angels, and yet you have not kept it." When they heard these things, they became enraged and ground their teeth at Stephen. But filled with the Holy Spirit, he gazed into heaven and saw the glory of God and Jesus standing at the right hand of God. "Look," he said, "I see the heavens opened and the Son of Man standing at the right hand of God!" But they covered their ears, and with a loud shout all rushed together against him. Then they dragged him out of the city and began to stone him; and the witnesses laid their coats at the feet of a young man named Saul. While they were stoning Stephen, he prayed, "Lord Jesus, receive my spirit." Then he knelt down and cried out in a loud voice, "Lord, do not hold this sin against them." When he had said this, he died.

or Nehemiah 9:6-15

And Ezra said: "You are the LORD, you alone; you have made heaven, the heaven of heavens, with all their host, the earth and all that is on it, the seas and all that is in them. To all of them you give life, and the host of heaven worships you. You are the LORD, the God who chose Abram and brought him out of Ur of the Chaldeans and gave him the name Abraham; and you found his heart faithful before you, and made with him a covenant to give to his descendants the land of the Canaanite, the Hittite, the Amorite, the Perizzite, the Jebusite, and the Girgashite; and you have fulfilled your promise, for you are righteous. And you saw the distress of our ancestors in Egypt and heard their cry at the Red Sea. You performed signs and wonders against Pharaoh and all his servants and all the people of his land, for you knew that they acted insolently against our ancestors. You made a name for yourself, which remains to this day. And you divided the sea before them, so that they passed through the sea on dry land, but you threw their pursuers into the depths, like a stone into mighty waters. Moreover, you led them by day with a pillar of cloud, and by night with a pillar of fire, to give them light on the way in which they should go. You came down also upon Mount Sinai, and spoke with them from heaven, and gave them right ordinances and true laws, good statutes and commandments, and you made known your holy sabbath to them and gave them commandments and statutes and a law through your servant Moses. For their hunger you gave them bread from heaven, and for their thirst you brought water for them out of the rock, and you told them to go in to possess the land that you swore to give them."

The Psalm 23   *Dominus regit me*
1   The LORD is my shepherd; *
       I shall not be in want.

2   He makes me lie down in green pastures *
       and leads me beside still waters.

3   He revives my soul *
       and guides me along right pathways for his Name's sake.

4   Though I walk through the valley of the shadow of death,
     I shall fear no evil; *
         for you are with me;
         your rod and your staff, they comfort me.

5   You spread a table before me in the presence of those who trouble me; *
       you have anointed my head with oil,
       and my cup is running over.

6   Surely your goodness and mercy shall follow me all the days of my life, *
       and I will dwell in the house of the LORD for ever.

The Epistle   **1 Peter 2:19-25**
For it is a credit to you if, being aware of God, you endure pain while suffering unjustly. If you endure when you are beaten for doing wrong, what credit is that? But if you endure when you do right and suffer for it, you have God's approval. For to this you have been called, because Christ also suffered for you, leaving you an example, so that you should follow in his steps. "He committed no sin, and no deceit

was found in his mouth." When he was abused, he did not return abuse; when he suffered, he did not threaten; but he entrusted himself to the one who judges justly. He himself bore our sins in his body on the cross, so that, free from sins, we might live for righteousness; by his wounds you have been healed. For you were going astray like sheep, but now you have returned to the shepherd and guardian of your souls.

or Acts 6:1-9, 7:2a, 51-60 (see above — page 225)

The Gospel

John 10:1-10

Jesus said, "Very truly, I tell you, anyone who does not enter the sheepfold by the gate but climbs in by another way is a thief and a bandit. The one who enters by the gate is the shepherd of the sheep. The gatekeeper opens the gate for him, and the sheep hear his voice. He calls his own sheep by name and leads them out. When he has brought out all his own, he goes ahead of them, and the sheep follow him because they know his voice. They will not follow a stranger, but they will run from him because they do not know the voice of strangers." Jesus used this figure of speech with them, but they did not understand what he was saying to them. So again Jesus said to them, "Very truly, I tell you, I am the gate for the sheep. All who came before me are thieves and bandits; but the sheep did not listen to them. I am the gate. Whoever enters by me will be saved, and will come in and go out and find pasture. The thief comes only to steal and kill and destroy. I came that they may have life, and have it abundantly."

Year B

The Lesson

Acts 4:(23-31) 32-37

[After Peter and John were released, they went to their friends and reported what the chief priests and the elders had said to them. When they heard it, they raised their voices together to God and said, "Sovereign Lord, who made the heaven and the earth, the sea, and everything in them, it is you who said by the Holy Spirit through our ancestor David, your servant: 'Why did the Gentiles rage, and the peoples imagine vain things? The kings of the earth took their stand, and the rulers have gathered together against the Lord and against his Messiah.' For in this city, in fact, both Herod and Pontius Pilate, with the Gentiles and the peoples of Israel, gathered together against your holy servant Jesus, whom you anointed, to do whatever your hand and your plan had predestined to take place. And now, Lord, look at their threats, and grant to your servants to speak your word with all boldness, while you stretch out your hand to heal, and signs and wonders are performed through the name of your holy servant Jesus." When they had prayed, the place in which they were gathered together was shaken; and they were all filled with the Holy Spirit and spoke the word of God with boldness.] Now the whole group of those who believed were of one heart and soul, and no one claimed private ownership of any possessions, but everything they owned was held in common. With great power the apostles gave their testimony to the resurrection of the Lord Jesus, and great grace was upon them all. There was not a needy person among them, for as many as owned lands or houses sold them and brought the proceeds of what was sold. They laid it at the apostles' feet, and it was distributed to each as any had need. There was a Levite, a native of Cyprus, Joseph, to whom the apostles gave the name Barnabas (which means "son of encouragement'). He sold a field that belonged to him, then brought the money, and laid it at the apostles' feet.

or Ezekiel 34:1-10
The word of the LORD came to me: Mortal, prophesy against the shepherds of Israel: prophesy, and say to them — to the shepherds: Thus says the Lord GOD: Ah, you shepherds of Israel who have been feeding yourselves! Should not shepherds feed the sheep? You eat the fat, you clothe yourselves with the wool, you slaughter the fatlings; but you do not feed the sheep. You have not strengthened the weak, you have not healed the sick, you have not bound up the injured, you have not brought back the strayed, you have not sought the lost, but with force and harshness you have ruled them. So they were scattered, because there was no shepherd; and scattered, they became food for all the wild animals. My sheep were scattered, they wandered over all the mountains and on every high hill; my sheep were scattered over all the face of the earth, with no one to search or seek for them. Therefore, you shepherds, hear the word of the LORD: As I live, says the Lord GOD, because my sheep have become a prey, and my sheep have become food for all the wild animals, since there was no shepherd; and because my shepherds have not searched for my sheep, but the shepherds have fed themselves, and have not fed my sheep; therefore, you shepherds, hear the word of the LORD: Thus says the Lord GOD, I am against the shepherds; and I will demand my sheep at their hand, and put a stop to their feeding the sheep; no longer shall the shepherds feed themselves. I will rescue my sheep from their mouths, so that they may not be food for them.

The Psalm 23   *Dominus regit me*
1   The LORD is my shepherd; *
        I shall not be in want.

2   He makes me lie down in green pastures *
        and leads me beside still waters.

3   He revives my soul *
        and guides me along right pathways for his Name's sake.

4   Though I walk through the valley of the shadow of death,
      I shall fear no evil; *
          for you are with me;
          your rod and your staff, they comfort me.

5   You spread a table before me in the presence of those who trouble me; *
          you have anointed my head with oil,
          and my cup is running over.

6   Surely your goodness and mercy shall follow me all the days of my life, *
        and I will dwell in the house of the LORD for ever.

or Psalm 100   *Jubilate Deo*
1   Be joyful in the LORD, all you lands; *

serve the LORD with gladness
and come before his presence with a song.

2 Know this: The LORD himself is God; *
   he himself has made us, and we are his;
      we are his people and the sheep of his pasture.

3 Enter his gates with thanksgiving;
   go into his courts with praise; *
      give thanks to him and call upon his Name.

4 For the LORD is good;
   his mercy is everlasting; *
      and his faithfulness endures from age to age.

The Epistle   1 John 3:1-8

See what love the Father has given us, that we should be called children of God; and
that is what we are. The reason the world does not know us is that it did not know
him. Beloved, we are God's children now; what we will be has not yet been revealed.
What we do know is this: when he is revealed, we will be like him, for we will see him
as he is. And all who have this hope in him purify themselves, just as he is pure.
Everyone who commits sin is guilty of lawlessness; sin is lawlessness. You know that
he was revealed to take away sins, and in him there is no sin. No one who abides in
him sins; no one who sins has either seen him or known him. Little children, let no
one deceive you. Everyone who does what is right is righteous, just as he is righteous.
Everyone who commits sin is a child of the devil; for the devil has been sinning from
the beginning. The Son of God was revealed for this purpose, to destroy the works of
the devil.

or Acts 4:(23-31) 32-37 (see above — page 227)

The Gospel   John 10:11-16

Jesus said, "I am the good shepherd. The good shepherd lays down his life for the
sheep. The hired hand, who is not the shepherd and does not own the sheep, sees the
wolf coming and leaves the sheep and runs away — and the wolf snatches them and
scatters them. The hired hand runs away because a hired hand does not care for the
sheep. I am the good shepherd. I know my own and my own know me, just as the
Father knows me and I know the Father. And I lay down my life for the sheep. I have
other sheep that do not belong to this fold. I must bring them also, and they will
listen to my voice. So there will be one flock, one shepherd."

Year C

The Lesson   Acts 13:15-16, 26-33 (34-39)

After the reading of the law and the prophets, the officials of the synagogue sent Paul
and Barnabas a message, saying, "Brothers, if you have any word of exhortation for
the people, give it." So Paul stood up and with a gesture began to speak: "My
brothers, you descendants of Abraham's family, and others who fear God, to us the
message of this salvation has been sent. Because the residents of Jerusalem and their

leaders did not recognize him or understand the words of the prophets that are read every sabbath, they fulfilled those words by condemning him. Even though they found no cause for a sentence of death, they asked Pilate to have him killed. When they had carried out everything that was written about him, they took him down from the tree and laid him in a tomb. But God raised him from the dead; and for many days he appeared to those who came up with him from Galilee to Jerusalem, and they are now his witnesses to the people. And we bring you the good news that what God promised to our ancestors he has fulfilled for us, their children, by raising Jesus; as also it is written in the second psalm, 'You are my Son; today I have begotten you.'" [As to his raising him from the dead, no more to return to corruption, he has spoken in this way, 'I will give you the holy promises made to David.' Therefore he has also said in another psalm, 'You will not let your Holy One experience corruption.' For David, after he had served the purpose of God in his own generation, died, was laid beside his ancestors, and experienced corruption; but he whom God raised up experienced no corruption. Let it be known to you therefore, my brothers, that through his man forgiveness of sins is proclaimed to you; by this Jesus everyone who believes is set free from all those sins from which you could not be freed by the law of Moses."]

or Numbers 27:12-23
The LORD said to Moses, " Go up this mountain of the Abarim range, and see the land that I have given to the Israelites. When you have seen it, you also shall be gathered to your people, as your brother Aaron was, because you rebelled against my word in the wilderness of Zin when the congregation quarreled with me. You did not show my holiness before their eyes at the waters." (These are the waters of Meribah of Kadesh in the wilderness of Zin.) Moses spoke to the LORD, saying, "Let the LORD, the God of the spirits of all flesh, appoint someone over the congregation who shall go out before them and come in before them, who shall lead them out and bring them in, so that the congregation of the LORD may not be like sheep without a shepherd." So the LORD said to Moses, "Take Joshua son of Nun, a man in whom is the spirit, and lay your hand upon him; have him stand before Eleazar the priest and all the congregation, and commission him in their sight. You shall give him some of your authority, so that all the congregation of the Israelites may obey. But he shall stand before Eleazar the priest, who shall inquire for him by the decision of the Urim before the LORD; at his word they shall go out, and at his word they shall come in, both he and all the Israelites with him, the whole congregation." So Moses did as the LORD commanded him. He took Joshua and had him stand before Eleazar the priest and the whole congregation; he laid his hands on him and commissioned him — as the LORD had directed through Moses.

The Psalm 100   *Jubilate Deo*
1   Be joyful in the LORD, all you lands; *
          serve the LORD with gladness
          and come before his presence with a song.

2   Know this: The LORD himself is God; *
     he himself has made us, and we are his;
     we are his people and the sheep of his pasture.

3   Enter his gates with thanksgiving;
     go into his courts with praise; *
     give thanks to him and call upon his Name.

4   For the LORD is good;
     his mercy is everlasting; *
     and his faithfulness endures from age to age.

The Epistle   **Revelation 7:9-17**

After this I looked, and there was a great multitude that no one could count, from every nation, from all tribes and peoples and languages, standing before the throne and before the Lamb, robed in white, with palm branches in their hands. They cried out in a loud voice, saying, "Salvation belongs to our God who is seated on the throne, and to the Lamb!" And all the angels stood around the throne and around the elders and the four living creatures, and they fell on their faces before the throne and worshiped God, singing, "Amen! Blessing and glory and wisdom and thanksgiving and honor and power and might be to our God forever and ever! Amen." Then one of the elders addressed me, saying, "Who are these, robed in white, and where have they come from?" I said to him, "Sir, you are the one that knows." Then he said to me, "These are they who have come out of the great ordeal; they have washed their robes and made them white in the blood of the Lamb. For this reason they are before the throne of God, and worship him day and night within his temple, and the one who is seated on the throne will shelter them. They will hunger no more, and thirst no more; the sun will not strike them, nor any scorching heat; for the Lamb at the center of the throne will be their shepherd, and he will guide them to springs of the water of life, and God will wipe away every tear from their eyes."

or Acts 13:15-16, 26-33 (34-39) (see above — page 229)

The Gospel   **John 10:22-30**

It was the festival of the Dedication at Jerusalem. It was winter, and Jesus was walking in the temple, in the portico of Solomon. So the Jews gathered around him and said to him, "How long will you keep us in suspense? If you are the Messiah, tell us plainly." Jesus answered, "I have told you, and you do not believe. The works that I do in my Father's name testify to me; but you do not believe, because you do not belong to my sheep. My sheep hear my voice. I know them, and they follow me. I give them eternal life, and they will never perish. No one will snatch them out of my hand. What my Father has given me is greater than all else, and no one can snatch it out of the Father's hand. The Father and I are one."

THE FIFTH SUNDAY OF EASTER

The Collect

Almighty God, whom truly to know is everlasting life: Grant us so perfectly to know your Son Jesus Christ to be the way, the truth, and the life, that we may steadfastly follow his steps in the way that leads to eternal life; through Jesus Christ your Son our Lord, who lives and reigns with you, in the unity of the Holy Spirit, one God, for ever and ever. *Amen.*

O Almighty God, whom truly to know is everlasting life: Grant us so perfectly to know thy Son Jesus Christ to be the way, the truth, and the life, that we may steadfastly follow his steps in the way that leadeth to eternal life; through the same thy Son Jesus Christ our Lord, who liveth and reigneth with thee, in the unity of the Holy Spirit, one God, for ever and ever. *Amen.*

Year A

The Lesson   Acts 17:1-15

After Paul and Silas had passed through Amphipolis and Apollonia, they came to Thessalonica, where there was a synagogue of the Jews. And Paul went in, as was his custom, and on three sabbath days argued with them from the scriptures, explaining and proving that it was necessary for the Messiah to suffer and to rise from the dead, and saying, "This is the Messiah, Jesus whom I am proclaiming to you." Some of them were persuaded and joined Paul and Silas, as did a great many of the devout Greeks and not a few of the leading women. But the Jews became jealous, and with the help of some ruffians in the marketplaces they formed a mob and set the city in an uproar. While they were searching for Paul and Silas to bring them out to the assembly, they attacked Jason's house. When they could not find them, they dragged Jason and some believers before the city authorities, shouting, "These people who have been turning the world upside down have come here also, and Jason has entertained them as guests. They are all acting contrary to the decrees of the emperor, saying that there is another king named Jesus." The people and the city officials were disturbed when they heard this, and after they had taken bail from Jason and the others, they let them go. That very night the believers sent Paul and Silas off to Beroea; and when they arrived, they went to the Jewish synagogue. These Jews were more receptive than those in Thessalonica, for they welcomed the message very eagerly and examined the scriptures every day to see whether these things were so. Many of them therefore believed, including not a few Greek women and men of high standing. But when the Jews of Thessalonica learned that the word of God had been proclaimed by Paul in Beroea as well, they came there too, to stir up and incite the crowds. Then the believers immediately sent Paul away to the coast, but Silas and Timothy remained behind. Those who conducted Paul brought him as far as Athens; and after receiving instructions to have Silas and Timothy join him as soon as possible, they left him.

or Deuteronomy 6:20-25

When your children ask you in time to come, "What is the meaning of the decrees and the statutes and the ordinances that the LORD our God has commanded you?" then you shall say to your children, "We were Pharaoh's slaves in Egypt, but the

LORD brought us out of Egypt with a mighty hand. The LORD displayed before our eyes great and awesome signs and wonders against Egypt, against Pharaoh and all his household. He brought us out from there in order to bring us in, to give us the land that he promised on oath to our ancestors. Then the LORD commanded us to observe all these statutes, to fear the LORD our God, for our lasting good, so as to keep us alive, as is now the case. If we diligently observe this entire commandment before the LORD our God, as he has commanded us, we will be in the right."

The Psalm 66:1-11 or 66:1-8 *Jubilate Deo*

1   [Be joyful in God, all you lands; *
        sing the glory of his Name;
        sing the glory of his praise.

2   Say to God, "How awesome are your deeds! *
        because of your great strength your enemies cringe before you.

3   All the earth bows down before you, *
        sings to you, sings out your Name."

4   Come now and see the works of God, *
        how wonderful he is in his doing toward all people.

5   He turned the sea into dry land,
        so that they went through the water on foot, *
        and there we rejoiced in him.

6   In his might he rules for ever;
        his eyes keep watch over the nations; *
        let no rebel rise up against him.

7   Bless our God, you peoples; *
        make the voice of his praise to be heard;

8   Who holds our souls in life, *
        and will not allow our feet to slip.]

9   For you, O God, have proved us; *
        you have tried us just as silver is tried.

10 You brought us into the snare; *
        you laid heavy burdens upon our backs.

11 You let enemies ride over our heads; *
        we went through fire and water; *
        but you brought us out into a place of refreshment.

The Epistle   **1 Peter 2:1-10**
Rid yourselves, of all malice, and all guile, insincerity, envy, and all slander. Like newborn infants, long for the pure, spiritual milk, so that by it you may grow into salvation — if indeed you have tasted that the Lord is good. Come to him, a living stone, though rejected by mortals yet chosen and precious in God's sight, and like living stones, let yourselves be built into a spiritual house, to be a holy priesthood, to

offer spiritual sacrifices acceptable to God through Jesus Christ. For it stands in scripture: "See, I am laying in Zion a stone, a cornerstone chosen and precious; and whoever believes in him will not be put to shame." To you then who believe, he is precious; but for those who do not believe, "The stone that the builders rejected has become the very head of the corner," and "A stone that makes them stumble, and a rock that makes them fall." They stumble because they disobey the word, as they were destined to do. But you are a chosen race, a royal priesthood, a holy nation, God's own people, in order that you may proclaim the mighty acts of him who called you out of darkness into his marvelous light. Once you were not a people, but now you are God's people; once you had not received mercy, but now you have received mercy.

or Acts 17:1-15 (see above — page 232)

The Gospel John 14:1-14

Jesus said, "Do not let your hearts be troubled. Believe in God, believe also in me. In my Father's house there are many dwelling places. If it were not so, would I have told you that I go to prepare a place for you? And if I go and prepare a place for you, I will come again and will take you to myself, so that where I am, there you may be also. And you know the way to the place where I am going." Thomas said to him, "Lord, we do not know where you are going. How can we know the way?" Jesus said to him, "I am the way, and the truth, and the life. No one comes to the Father except through me. If you know me,you will know my Father also. From now on you do know him and have seen him." Philip said to him, "Lord, show us the Father, and we will be satisfied." Jesus said to him, "Have I been with you all this time, Philip, and you still do not know me? Whoever has seen me has seen the Father. How can you say, 'Show us the Father'? Do you not believe that I am in the Father and the Father is in me? The words that I say to you I do not speak on my own; but the Father who dwells in me does his works. Believe me that I am in the Father and the Father is in me; but if you do not, then believe me because of the works themselves. Very truly, I tell you, the one who believes in me will also do the works that I do and, in fact, will do greater works than these, because I am going to the Father. I will do whatever you ask in my name, so that the Father may be glorified in the Son. If in my name you ask me for anything, I will do it."

Year B

The Lesson Acts 8:26-40

Then an angel of the Lord said to Philip, "Get up and go toward the south to the road that goes down from Jerusalem to Gaza." (This is a wilderness road.) So he got up and went. Now there was an Ethiopian eunuch, a court official of the Candace, queen of the Ethiopians, in charge of her entire treasury. He had come to Jerusalem to worship and was returning home; seated in his chariot, he was reading the prophet Isaiah. Then the Spirit said to Philip, "Go over to this chariot and join it." So Philip ran up to it and heard him reading the prophet Isaiah. He asked, "Do you understand what you are reading?" He replied, "How can I, unless someone guides me?" And he invited Philip to get in and sit beside him. Now the passage of the scripture that he was reading was this: "Like a sheep he was led to the slaughter, and like a lamb silent before its shearer, so he does not open his mouth. In his humiliation justice was denied him. Who can describe his generation? For his life is taken away from the earth." The eunuch asked Philip, "About whom, may I ask you, does the prophet say this, about himself or about someone else?" Then Philip began to speak, and starting with this scripture, he proclaimed to him the good news about Jesus. As they were going along the road, they came to some water; and the eunuch said, "Look, here is water! What is to prevent me from being baptized?" He commanded the chariot to stop, and both of them, Philip and the eunuch, went down into the water, and Philip baptized him. When they came up out of the water, the Spirit of the Lord snatched Philip away; the eunuch saw him no more, and went on his way rejoicing. But Philip found himself at Azotus, and as he was passing through the region, he proclaimed the good news to all the towns until he came to Caesarea.

or Deuteronomy 4:32-40

Ask now about former ages, long before your own, ever since the day that God created human beings on the earth; ask from one end of heaven to the other: has anything so great as this ever happened or has its like ever been heard of? Has any people ever heard the voice of a god speaking out of a fire, as you have heard, and lived? Or has any god ever attempted to go and take a nation for himself from the midst of another nation, by trials, by signs and wonders, by war, by a mighty hand and an outstretched arm, and by terrifying displays of power, as the LORD your God did for you in Egypt before your very eyes? To you it was shown so that you would acknowledge that the LORD is God; there is no other besides him. from heaven he made you hear his voice to discipline you. On earth he showed you his great fire, while you heard his words coming out of the fire. And because he loved your ancestors, he chose their descendants after them. He brought you out of Egypt with his own presence, by his great power, driving out before you nations greater and mightier than yourselves, to bring you in, giving you their land for a possession, as it is still today. So acknowledge today and take to heart that the LORD is God in heaven above and on the earth beneath; there is no other. Keep his statutes and his commandments, which I am commanding you today for your own well-being and that of your descendants after you, so that you may long remain in the land that the LORD your God is giving you for all time.

The Psalm 66:1-11 or 66:1-8   *Jubilate Deo*

1   [Be joyful in God, all you lands; *
    sing the glory of his Name;
    sing the glory of his praise.

2   Say to God, "How awesome are your deeds! *
    because of your great strength your enemies cringe before you.

3   All the earth bows down before you, *
    sings to you, sings out your Name."

4   Come now and see the works of God, *
    how wonderful he is in his doing toward all people.

5   He turned the sea into dry land,
so that they went through the water on foot, *
    and there we rejoiced in him.

6   In his might he rules for ever;
his eyes keep watch over the nations; *
    let no rebel rise up against him.

7   Bless our God, you peoples; *
    make the voice of his praise to be heard;

8   Who holds our souls in life, *
    and will not allow our feet to slip.]

9   For you, O God, have proved us; *
    you have tried us just as silver is tried.

10   You brought us into the snare; *
    you laid heavy burdens upon our backs.

11   You let enemies ride over our heads;
we went through fire and water; *
    but you brought us out into a place of refreshment.

The Epistle   **1 John 3:(14-17) 18-24**

[We know that we have passed from death to life because we love one another. Whoever does not love abides in death. All who hate a brother or sister are murderers, and you know that murderers do not have eternal life abiding in them. We know love by this, that he laid down his life for us — and we ought to lay down our lives for one another. How does God's love abide in anyone who has the world's goods and sees a brother or sister in need and yet refuses help?] Little children, let us love, not in word or speech, but in truth and action. And by this we will know that we are from the truth and will reassure our hearts before him whenever our hearts condemn us; for God is greater than our hearts, and he knows everything. Beloved, if our hearts do not condemn us, we have boldness before God; and we receive from him whatever we ask, because we obey his commandments and do what pleases him. And this is his commandment, that we should believe in the name of his Son Jesus Christ and love one another, just as he has commanded us. All who obey his commandments abide in him, and he abides in them. And by this we know that he abides in us, by the Spirit that he has given us.

or Acts 8:26-40 (see above — page 234)

The Gospel   **John 14:15-21**

Jesus said to his disciples, "If you love me, you will keep my commandments. And I will ask the Father, and he will give you another Advocate, to be with you forever. This is the Spirit of truth, whom the world cannot receive, because it neither sees him nor knows him. You know him, because he abides with you, and he will be in you. I will not leave you orphaned; I am coming to you. In a little while the world will no longer see me, but you will see me; because I live, you also will live. On that day you will know that I am in my Father, and you in me, and I in you. They who have my commandments and keep them are those who love me; and those who love me will be loved by my Father, and I will love them and reveal myself to them."

Year C

The Lesson   Acts 13:44-52

The next sabbath almost the whole city gathered to hear the word of the Lord. But when the Jews saw the crowds, they were filled with jealousy; and blaspheming, they contradicted what was spoken by Paul. Then both Paul and Barnabas spoke out boldly, saying, "It was necessary that the word of God should be spoken first to you. Since you reject it and judge yourselves to be unworthy of eternal life, we are now turning to the Gentiles. For so the Lord has commanded us, saying, 'I have set you to be a light for the Gentiles, so that you may bring salvation to the ends of the earth.'" When the Gentiles heard this, they were glad and praised the word of the Lord; and as many as had been destined for eternal life became believers. Thus the word of the Lord spread throughout the region. But the Jews incited the devout women of high standing and the leading men of the city, and stirred up persecution against Paul and Barnabas, and drove them out of their region. So they shook the dust off their feet in protest against them, and went to Iconium. And the disciples were filled with joy and with the Holy Spirit.

or Leviticus 19:1-2, 9-18

The LORD spoke to Moses, saying: Speak to all the congregation of the people of Israel and say to them: You shall be holy, for I the LORD your God am holy. When you reap the harvest of your land, you shall not reap to the very edges of your field, or gather the gleanings of your harvest. You shall not strip your vineyard bare, or gather the fallen grapes of your vineyard; you shall leave them for the poor and the alien: I am the LORD your God. You shall not steal; you shall not deal falsely; and you shall not lie to one another. And you shall not swear falsely by my name, profaning the name of your God: I am the LORD. You shall not defraud your neighbor; you shall not steal; and you shall not keep for yourself the wages of a laborer until morning. You shall not revile the deaf or put a stumbling block before the blind; you shall fear your God: I am the LORD. You shall not render an unjust judgment; you shall not be partial to the poor or defer to the great: with justice you shall judge your neighbor. You shall not go around as a slanderer among your people, and you shall not profit by the blood of your neighbor: I am the LORD. You shall not hate in your heart anyone of your kin; you shall reprove your neighbor, or you will incur guilt yourself. You shall not take vengeance or bear a grudge against any of your people, but you shall love your neighbor as yourself: I am the LORD.

The Psalm 145 or 145:1-9   *Exaltabo te, Deus*

1   [I will exalt you, O God my King, *
        and bless your Name for ever and ever.

2   Every day will I bless you *
        and praise your Name for ever and ever.

3   Great is the Lord and greatly to be praised; *
        there is no end to his greatness.

4   One generation shall praise your works to another *
        and shall declare your power.

5   I will ponder the glorious splendor of your majesty *
        and all your marvelous works.

6   They shall speak of the might of your wondrous acts, *
        and I will tell of your greatness.

7   They shall publish the remembrance of your great goodness; *
        they shall sing of your righteous deeds.

8   The Lord is gracious and full of compassion, *
        slow to anger and of great kindness.

9   The Lord is loving to everyone *
        and his compassion is over all his works.]

10 All your works praise you, O Lord, *
        and your faithful servants bless you.

11 They make known the glory of your kingdom *
        and speak of your power;

12 That the peoples may know of your power *
        and the glorious splendor of your kingdom.

13 Your kingdom is an everlasting kingdom; *
        your dominion endures throughout all ages.

14 The Lord is faithful in all his words *
        and merciful in all his deeds.

15 The Lord upholds all those who fall; *
        he lifts up those who are bowed down.

16 The eyes of all wait upon you, O Lord, *
        and you give them their food in dues season.

17 You open wide your hand *
        and satisfy the needs of every living creature.

18 The Lord is righteous in hall his ways *
        and loving in all his works.

19 The Lord is near to those who call upon him, *
        to all who call upon him faithfully.

20 He fulfills the desire of those who fear him; *
        he hears their cry and helps them.

21 The LORD preserves all those who love him, *
    but he destroys all the wicked.

22 My mouth shall speak the praise of the LORD; *
    let all flesh bless his holy Name for ever and ever.

The Epistle   Revelation 19:1, 4-9

After this I heard what seemed to be the loud voice of a great multitude in heaven, saying, "Hallelujah! Salvation and glory and power to our God. And the twenty-four elders and the four living creatures fell down and worshiped God who is seated on the throne, saying, "Amen. Hallelujah!" And from the throne came a voice saying, "Praise our God, all you his servants, and all who fear him, small and great." Then I heard what seemed to be the voice of a great multitude, like the sound of many waters and like the sound of mighty thunderpeals, crying out, "Hallelujah! For the Lord our God the Almighty reigns. Let us rejoice and exult and give him the glory, for the marriage of the Lamb has come, and his bride has made herself ready; to her it has been granted to be clothed with fine linen, bright and pure" — for the fine linen is the righteous deeds of the saints. And the angel said to me, "Write this: Blessed are those who are invited to the marriage supper of the Lamb." And he said to me, "These are true words of God."

or Acts 13:44-52 (see above — page 237)

The Gospel   John 13:31-35

At the last supper, when Judas had gone out, Jesus said, "Now the Son of Man has been glorified, and God has been glorified in him. If God has been glorified in him, God will also glorify him in himself and will glorify him at once. Little children, I am with you only a little longer. You will look for me; and as I said to the Jews so now I say to you, 'Where I am going, you cannot come.' I give you a new commandment, that you love one another. Just as I have loved you, you also should love one another. By this everyone will know that you are my disciples, if you have love for one another."

THE SIXTH SUNDAY OF EASTER

The Collect

O God, you have prepared for those who love you such good things as surpass our understanding; Pour into our hearts such love towards you, that we, loving you in all things and above all things, may obtain your promises, which exceed all that we can desire; through Jesus Christ our Lord, who lives and reigns with you and the Holy Spirit, one God, for ever and ever. *Amen.*

O God, who has prepared for those who love thee such good things as pass man's understanding; Pour into our hearts such love toward thee, that we, loving thee in all things and above all things, may obtain thy promises, which exceed all that we can desire; through Jesus Christ our Lord, who liveth and reigneth with thee and the Holy Spirit, one God, for ever and ever. *Amen.*

The Lesson Acts 17:22-31

Paul stood in front of the Areopagus and said, "Athenians, I see how extremely religious you are in every way. For as I went through the city and looked carefully at the objects of your worship, I found among them an altar with the inscription, 'To an unknown god.' What therefore you worship as unknown, this I proclaim to you. The God who made the world and everything in it, he who is Lord of heaven and earth, does not live in shrines made by human hands, nor is he served by human hands, as though he needed anything, since he himself gives to all mortals life and breath and all things. From one ancestor he made all nations to inhabit the whole earth, and he allotted the times of their existence and the boundaries of the places where they would live, so that they would search for God and perhaps grope for him and find him — though indeed he is not far from each one of us. For 'In him we live and move and have our being'; as even some of your own poets have said, 'For we too are his offspring.' Since we are God's offspring, we ought not to think that the deity is like gold, or silver, or stone, an image formed by the art and imagination of mortals. While God has overlooked the times of human ignorance, nowhe commands all people everywhere to repent, because he has fixed a day on which he will have the world judged in righteousness by a man whom he has appointed, and of this he has given assurance to all by raising him from the dead."

or Isaiah 41:17-20

When the poor and needy seek water, and there is none, and their tongue is parched with thirst, I the LORD will answer them, I the God of Israel will not forsake them. I will open rivers on the bare heights, and fountains in the midst of the valleys; I will make the wilderness a pool of water, and the dry land springs of water. I will put in the wilderness the cedar, the acacia, the myrtle, and the olive; I will set in the desert the cypress, the plane and the pine together, so that all may see and know, all may consider and understand, that the hand of the LORD has done this, the Holy One of Israel has created it.

Psalm 148 or 148:7-14   *Laudate Dominum*

1   Hallelujah!
      Praise the LORD from the heavens; *
         praise him in the heights.

2   Praise him, all you angels of his; *
         praise him, all his host.

3   Praise him, sun and moon; *
         praise him, all you shining stars.

4   Praise him, heaven of heavens, *
         and you waters above the heavens.

5   Let them praise the Name of the LORD; *
         for he commanded, and they were created.

6 He made them stand fast for ever and ever; *
    he gave them a law which shall not pass away.

7 [Praise the LORD from the earth, *
    you sea-monsters and all deeps;

8 Fire and hail, snow and fog, *
    tempestuous wind, doing his will;

9 Mountains and all hills, *
    fruit trees and all cedars;

10 Wild beasts and all cattle, *
    creeping things and winged birds;

11 Kings of the earth and all peoples, *
    princes and all rulers of the world;

12 Young men and maidens, *
    old and young together.

13 Let them praise the Name of the LORD, *
    for his Name only is exalted,
    his splendor is over earth and heaven.

14 He has raised up strength for his people
    and praise for all his loyal servants, *
    the children of Israel, a people who are near him.
    Hallelujah!]

The Epistle   **1 Peter 3:8-18**
All of you, have unity of spirit, sympathy, love for one another, a tender heart, and a
humble mind. Do not repay evil for evil or abuse for abuse; but, on the contrary,
repay with a blessing. It is for this that you were called — that you might inherit a
blessing. For "Those who desire life and desire to see good days, let them keep their
tongues from evil and their lips from speaking deceit; let them turn away from evil
and do good; let them seek peace and pursue it. For the eyes of the Lord are on the
righteous, and his ears are open to their prayer. But the face of the Lord is against
those who do evil." Now who will harm you if you are eager to do what is good? But
even if you do suffer for doing what is right, you are blessed. Do not fear what they
fear, and do not be intimidated, but in your hearts sanctify Christ as Lord. Always be
ready to make your defense to anyone who demands from you an accounting for the
hope that is in you; yet do it with gentleness and reverence. Keep your conscience
clear, so that, when you are maligned, those who abuse you for your good conduct in
Christ may be put to shame. For it is better to suffer for doing good, if suffering
should be God's will, than to suffer for doing evil. For Christ also suffered for sins
once for all, the righteous for the unrighteous, in order to bring you to God. He was
put to death in the flesh, but made alive in the spirit.

or Acts 17:22-31 (see above — page 240)

The Gospel
John 15:1-8

Jesus said, "I am the true vine, and my Father is the vinegrower. He removes every branch in me that bears no fruit. Every branch that bears fruit he prunes to make it bear more fruit. You have already been cleansed by the word that I have spoken to you. Abide in me as I abide in you. Just as the branch cannot bear fruit by itself unless it abides in the vine, neither can you unless you abide in me. I am the vine, you are the branches. Those who abide in me and I in them bear much fruit, because apart from me you can do nothing. Whoever does not abide in me is thrown away like a branch and withers; such branches are gathered, thrown into the fire, and burned. If you abide in me, and my words abide in you, ask for whatever you wish, and it will be done for you. My Father is glorified by this, that you bear much fruit and become my disciples.

Year B

The Lesson
Acts 11:19-30

Now those who were scattered because of the persecution that took place over Stephen traveled as far as Phoenicia, Cyprus, and Antioch, and they spoke the word to no one except Jews. But among them were some men of Cyprus and Cyrene who, on coming to Antioch, spoke to the Hellenists also, proclaiming the Lord Jesus. The hand of the Lord was with them, and a great number became believers and turned to the Lord. News of this came to the ears of the church in Jerusalem, and they sent Barnabas to Antioch. When he came and saw the grace of God, he rejoiced, and he exhorted them all to remain faithful to the Lord with steadfast devotion; for he was a good man, full of the Holy Spirit and of faith. And a great many people were brought to the Lord. Then Barnabas went to Tarsus to look for Saul, and when he had found him, he brought him to Antioch. So it was that for an entire year they met with the church and taught a great many people, and it was in Antioch that the disciples were first called "Christians." At that time prophets came down from Jerusalem to Antioch. One of them named Agabus stood up and predicted by the Spirit that there would be a severe famine over all the world; and this took place during the reign of Claudius. The Disciples determined that according to their ability, each would send relief to the believers living in Judea; this they did, sending it to the elders by Barnabas and Saul.

or Isaiah 45:11-13, 18-19

Thus says the LORD, the Holy One of Israel, and its Maker: Will you question me about my children, or command me concerning the work of my hands? I made the earth, and created humankind upon it; it was my hands that stretched out the heavens, and I commanded all their host. I have aroused Cyrus in righteousness, and I will make all his paths straight; he shall build my city and set my exiles free, not for price or reward, says the LORD of hosts. For thus says the LORD, who created the heavens (he is God!), who formed the earth and made it (he established it; he did not create it a chaos, he formed it to be inhabited!): I am the LORD, and there is no other.

I did not speak in secret, in a land of darkness; I did not say to the offspring of Jacob, "Seek me in chaos." I the LORD speak the truth, I declare what is right.

The Psalm 33 or 33:1-8, 18-22   *Exultate, justi*

1   [Rejoice in the LORD, you righteous; *
    it is good for the just to sing praises.

2   Praise the LORD with the harp; *
    play to him upon the psaltery and lyre.

3   Sing for him a new song; *
    sound a fanfare with all your skill upon the trumpet.

4   For the word of the LORD is right, *
    and all his works are sure.

5   He loves righteousness and justice; *
    the loving-kindness of the LORD fills the whole earth.

6   By the word of the LORD were the heavens made, *
    by the breath of his mouth all the heavenly hosts.

7   He gathers up the waters of the ocean as in a water-skin *
    and stores up the depths of the sea.

8   Let all the earth fear the LORD; *
    let all who dwell in the world stand in awe of him.]

9   For he spoke, and it came to pass; *
    he commanded, and it stood fast.

10   The LORD brings the will of the nations to naught; *
    he thwarts the designs of the peoples.

11   But the LORD'S will stands fast for ever, *
    and the designs of his heart from age to age.

12   Happy is the nation whose God is the LORD! *
    happy the people he has chosen to be his own!

13   The LORD looks down from heaven, *
    and beholds all the people in the world.

14   From where he sits enthroned he turns his gaze *
    on all who dwell on the earth.

15   He fashions all the hearts of them *
    and understands all their works.

16   There is no king that can be saved by a mighty army; *
    a strong man is not delivered by his great strength.

17   The horse is a vain hope for deliverance; *
    for all its strength it cannot save.

18 [Behold, the eye of the LORD is upon those who fear him, *
        on those who wait upon his love,

19 To pluck their lives from death, *
        and to feed them in time of famine.

20 Our soul waits for the LORD; *
        he is our help and our shield.

21 Indeed, our heart rejoices in him, *
        for in his holy Name we put our trust.

22 Let your loving-kindness, O LORD, be upon us, *
        as we have put our trust in you.]

The Epistle   1 John 4:7-21

Beloved, let us love one another, because love is from God; everyone who loves is born of God and knows God. Whoever does not love does not know God, for God is love. God's love was revealed among us in this way: God sent his only Son into the world so that we might live through him. In his is love, not that we loved God but that he loved us and sent his Son to be the atoning sacrifice for our sins. Beloved, since God loved us so much, we also ought to love one another. No one has ever seen God; if we love one another, God lives in us, and his love is perfected in us. By this we know that we abide in him and he in us, because he has given us of his Spirit. And we have seen and do testify that the Father has sent his Son as the Savior of the world. God abides in those who confess that Jesus is the Son of God, and they abide in God. So we have known and believe the love that God has for us. God is love, and those who abide in love abide in God, and God abides in them. Love has been perfected among us in this: that we may have boldness on the day of judgment, because as he is, so are we in this world. There is no fear in love, but perfect love casts out fear; for fear has to do with punishment, and whoever fears has not reached perfection in love. We love because he first loved us. Those who say, "I love God," and hate their brothers or sisters, are liars; for those who do not love a brother or sister whom they have seen, cannot love God whom they have not seen. The commandment we have from him is this: those who love God must love their brother sand sisters also.

or Acts 11:19-30 (see above - page 242)

The Gospel   John 15:9-17

Jesus said to his disciples, "As the Father has loved me, so I have loved you; abide in my love. If you keep my commandments, you will abide in my love, just as I have kept my Father's commandments and abide in his love. I have said these things to you so that my joy may be in you, and that your joy may be complete. This is my commandment, that you love one another as I have loved you. No one has greater love than this, to lay down one's life for one's friends. You are my friends if you do what I command you. I do not call you servants any longer, because the servant does not know what the master is doing; but I have called you friends, because I have made known to you everything that I have heard from my Father. You did not choose me but I chose you. And I appointed you to go and bear fruit, fruit that will last, so that the Father will give you whatever you ask him in my name. I am giving you these commands so that you may love one another."

Year C

The Lesson

Acts 14:8-18

In Lystra there was a man sitting who could not use his feet and had never walked, for he had been crippled from birth. He listened to Paul as he was speaking. And Paul, looking at him intently and seeing that he had faith to be healed, said in a loud voice, "Stand upright on your feet." And the man sprang up and began to walk. When the crowds saw what Paul had done, they shouted in the Lycaonian language, "The gods have come down to us in human form!" Barnabas they called Zeus, and Paul they called Hermes, because he was the chief speaker. The priest of Zeus, whose temple was just outside the city, brought oxen and garlands to the gates; he and the crowds wanted to offer sacrifice. When the apostles Barnabas and Paul heard of it, they tore their clothes and rushed out into the crowd, shouting, "Friends, why are you doing this? We are mortals just like you, and we bring you good news, that you should turn from these worthless things to the living God, who made the heaven and the earth and the sea and all that is in them. In past generations he allowed all the nations to follow their own ways; yet he has not left himself without a witness in doing good — giving you rains from heaven and fruitful seasons, and filling you with food and your hearts with joy." Even with these words, they scarcely restrained the crowds from offering sacrifice to them.

or Joel 2:21-27

Do not fear, O soil; be glad and rejoice, for the LORD has done great things! Do not fear, you animals of the field, for the pastures of the wilderness are green; the tree bears its fruit, the fig tree and vine give their full yield. O children of Zion, be glad and rejoice in the LORD your God; for he has given the early rain for your vindication, he has poured down for you abundant rain, the early and the later rain, as before. The threshing floors shall be full of grain, the vats shall overflow with wine and oil. I will repay you for the years that the swarming locust has eaten, the hopper, the destroyer, and the cutter, my great army, which I sent against you. You shall eat in plenty and be satisfied, and praise the name of the LORD your God, who has dealt wondrously with you. And my people shall never again be put to shame. You shall know that I am in the midst of Israel, and that I, the LORD, am your God and there is no other. And my people shall never again be put to shame.

The Psalm 67 *Deus misereatur*

1 May God be merciful to us and bless us, *
      show us the light of his countenance and come to us.

2 Let your ways be known upon earth, *
      your saving health among all nations.

3 Let the peoples praise you, O God; *
      let all the peoples praise you.

4   Let the nations be glad and sing for joy, *
          for you judge the peoples with equity
          and guide all the nations upon earth.

5   Let the peoples praise you, O God; *
          let all the peoples praise you.

6   The earth has brought forth her increase; *
          may God, our own God, give us his blessing.

7   May God give us his blessing, *
          and may all the ends of the earth stand in awe of him.

The Epistle   **Revelation 21:22-22:5**

I saw no temple in the city, for its temple is the Lord God the Almighty and the Lamb. And the city has no need of sun or moon to shine on it, for the glory of God is its light, and its lamp is the Lamb. The nations will walk by its light, and the kings of the earth will bring their glory into it. Its gates will never be shut by day — and there will be no night there. People will bring into it the glory and the honor of the nations. But nothing unclean will enter it, nor anyone who practices abomination or falsehood, but only those who are written in the Lamb's book of life. Then the angel showed me the river of the water of life, bright as crystal, flowing from the throne of God and of the Lamb through the middle of the street of the city. On either side of the river, is the tree of life with its twelve kinds of fruit, producing its fruit each month; and the leaves of the tree are for the healing of the nations. Nothing accursed will be found there any more. But the throne of God and of the Lamb will be in it, and his servants will worship him; they will see his face, and his name will be on their foreheads. And there will be no more night; they need no light of lamp or sun, for the Lord God will be their light, and they will reign forever and ever.

or Acts 14:8-18 (see above - page 245)

The Gospel   **John 14:23-29**

Jesus said to Judas (not Iscariot), "Those who love me will keep my word, and my Father will love them, and we will come to them and make our home with them. Whoever does not love me does not keep my words; and the word that you hear is not mine, but is from the Father who sent me. I have said these things to you while I am still with you. But the Advocate, the Holy Spirit, whom the Father will send in my name, will teach you everything, and remind you of all that I have said to you. Peace I leave with you; my peace I give to you. I do not give to you as the world gives. Do not let your hearts be troubled, and do not let them be afraid. You heard me say to you, 'I am going away, and I am coming to you.' If you loved me, you would rejoice that I am going to the Father, because the Father is greater than I. And now I have told you this before it occurs, so that when it does occur, you may believe."

ASCENSION DAY

The Collect

Almighty God, whose blessed Son our Savior Jesus Christ ascended far above all heavens that he might fill all things: Mercifully give us faith to perceive that, according to his promise, he abides with his Church on earth, even to the end of the ages; through Jesus Christ our Lord, who lives and reigns with you and the Holy Spirit, one God, in glory everlasting. *Amen.*

or this (Contemporary)

Grant, we pray, Almighty God, that as we believe your only-begotten Son our Lord Jesus Christ to have ascended into heaven, so we may also in heart and mind there ascend, and with him continually dwell; who lives and reigns with you and the Holy Spirit, one God, for ever and ever. *Amen.*

O Almighty God, whose blessed Son our Savior Jesus Christ ascended far above all heavens that he might fill all things: Mercifully give us faith to perceive that, according to his promise, he abideth with his Church on earth, even unto the end of the ages; through the same Jesus Christ our Lord, who liveth and reigneth with thee and the Holy Spirit, one God, in glory everlasting. *Amen.*

or this (Traditional)

Grant, we beseech thee, Almighty God, that like as we do believe thy only-begotten Son our Lord Jesus Christ to have ascended into the heavens, so we may also in heart and mind thither ascend, and with him continually dwell; who liveth and reigneth with thee and the Holy Ghost, one God, world without end. *Amen.*

Years A, B, C

The Lesson Acts 1:1-11

In the first book, Theophilus, I wrote about all that Jesus did and taught from the beginning until the day when he was taken up to heaven, after giving instructions through the Holy Spirit to the apostles whom he had chosen. After his suffering he presented himself alive to them by many convincing proofs, appearing to them during forty days and speaking about the kingdom of God. While staying with them, he ordered them not to leave Jerusalem, but to wait there for the promise of the Father. "This," he said, "is what you have heard from me; for John baptized with water, but you will be baptized with the Holy Spirit not many days from now." So when they had come together, they asked him, "Lord, is this the time when you will restore the kingdom to Israel?" He replied, "It is not for you to know the times or periods that the Father has set by his own authority. But you will receive power when the Holy Spirit has come upon you; and you will be my witnesses in Jerusalem, in all Judea and Samaria, and to the end of the earth." When he had said this, as they were watching, he was lifted up, and a cloud took him out of their sight. While he was going and they were gazing up toward heaven, suddenly two men in white robes stood by them. They said, "Men of Galilee, why do you stand looking up toward heaven? This Jesus, who has been taken up from you into heaven, will come in the same way as you saw him go into heaven."

or, Year A — Daniel 7:9-14

As I watched, thrones were set in place, and an Ancient One took his throne, his clothing was white as snow, and the hair of his head like pure wool; his throne was fiery flames, and its wheels were burning fire. A stream of fire issued and flowed out from his presence. A thousand thousands served him, and ten thousand times ten thousand stood attending him. The court sat in judgment, and the books were opened. I watched then because of the noise of the arrogant words that the horn was speaking. And as I watched, the beast was put to death, and its body destroyed and given over to be burned with fire. As for the rest of the beasts, their dominion was taken away, but their lives were prolonged for a season and a time. As I watched in the night visions, I saw one like a human being coming with the clouds of heaven. And he came to the Ancient One and was presented before him. To him was given dominion and glory and kingship, that all peoples, nations, and languages should serve him. His dominion is an everlasting dominion that shall not pass away, and his kingship is one that shall never be destroyed.

or, Year B — Ezekiel 1:3-5a, 15-22, 26-28

The word of the LORD came to the priest Ezekiel son of Buzi, in the land of the Chaldeans by the river Chebar; and the hand of the LORD was on him there. As I looked, a stormy wind came out of the north: a great cloud with brightness around it and fire flashing forth continually, and in the middle of the fire, something like gleaming amber. In the middle of it was something like four living creatures. As I looked at the living creatures, I saw a wheel on the earth beside the living creatures, one for each of the four of them. As for the appearance of the wheels and their construction: their appearance was like the gleaming of beryl; and the four had the same form, their construction being something like a wheel within a wheel. When they moved, they moved in any of the four directions without veering as they moved. Their rims were tall and awesome, for the rims of all four were full of eyes all around. When the living creatures moved, the wheels moved beside them; and when the living creatures rose from the earth, the wheels rose. Wherever the spirit would go, they went, and the wheels rose along with them; for the spirit of the living creatures was in the wheels. When they moved, the others moved; when they stopped, the others stopped; and when they rose from the earth, the wheels rose along with them; for the spirit of the living creatures was in the wheels. Over the heads of the living creatures there was something like a dome, shining like crystal, spread out above their heads. And above the dome over their heads there was something like a throne, in appearance like sapphire; and seated above the likeness of a throne was something that seemed like a human form. Upward from what appeared like the loins I saw something like gleaming amber, something that looked like fire enclosed all around; and downward from what looked like the loins I saw something that looked like fire, and there was a splendor all around. Like the bow in a cloud on a rainy day, such was the appearance of the splendor all around. This was the appearance of the likeness of the glory of the LORD. When I saw it, I fell on my face, and I heard the voice of someone speaking.

or, Year C — 2 Kings 2:1-15

Now when the LORD was about to take Elijah up to heaven by a whirlwind, Elijah and Elisha were on their way from Gilgal. Elijah said to Elisha, "Stay here; for the LORD has sent me as far as Bethel." But Elisha said, "As the LORD lives, and as you yourself live, I will not leave you." So they went down to Bethel. The company prophets who were in Bethel came out to Elisha, and said to him, "Do you know that today the LORD will take your master away from you?" And he said, "Yes, I know; keep silent." Elijah said to him, "Elisha, stay here; for the LORD has sent me to Jericho." But he said, "As the LORD lives, and as you yourself live, I will not leave you." So they came to Jericho. The company of prophets who were at Jericho drew near to Elisha, and said to him, "Do you know that today the LORD will take your master away from you?" And he answered, "Yes, I know; be silent." Then Elijah said to him, "Stay here; for the LORD has sent me to the Jordan." But he said, "As the LORD lives, and as you yourself live, I will not leave you." So the two of them went on. Fifty men of the company of prophets also went, and stood at some distance from them, as they both were standing by the Jordan. Then Elijah took his mantle and rolled it up, and struck the water; the water was parted to the one side and to the other, until the two of them crossed on dry ground. When they had crossed, Elijah said to Elisha, "Tell me what I may do for you, before I am taken from you." Elisha said, "Please let me inherit a double share of your spirit." He responded, "You have asked a hard thing; yet, if you see me as I am being taken from you, it will be granted you; if not, it will not." As they continued walking and talking, a chariot of fire and horses of fire separated the two of them, and Elijah ascended in a whirlwind into heaven. Elisha kept watching and crying out, "Father, father! The chariots of Israel and its horsemen!" But when he could no longer see him, he grasped his own clothes and tore them in two pieces. He picked up the mantle of Elijah that had fallen from him, and went back and stood on the bank of the Jordan. He took the mantle of Elijah that had fallen from him, and struck the water, saying, "Where is the LORD, the God of Elijah?" When he had struck the water, the water was parted to the one side and to the other, and Elisha went over. When the company of prophets who were at Jericho saw him at a distance, they declared, "The spirit of Elijah rests on Elisha." They came to meet him and bowed to the ground before him.

The Psalm 47   *Omnes gentes, plaudite*

1   Clap your hands, all you peoples; *
        shout to God with a cry of joy.

2   For the LORD Most High is to be feared; *
        he is the great King over all the earth.

3   He subdues the peoples under us, *
        and the nations under our feet.

4   He chooses our inheritance for us, *
        the pride of Jacob whom he loves.

5   God has gone up with a shout, *
        the LORD with the sound of the ram's-horn.

6   Sing praises to God, sing praises; *
        sing praises to our King, sing praises.

7   For God is King of all the earth; *
         sing praises with all your skill.

8   God reigns over the nations; *
         God sits upon his holy throne.

9   The nobles of the peoples have gathered together *
         with the people of the God of Abraham.

10   The rulers of the earth belong to God, *
         and he is highly exalted.

or Psalm 110:1-5   *Dixit Dominus*
1   The LORD said to my Lord, "Sit at my right hand, *
         until I make your enemies your footstool."

2   The LORD will send the scepter of your power out of Zion, *
         saying, "Rule over your enemies round about you.

3   Princely state has been yours from the day of your birth; *
         in the beauty of holiness have I begotten you,
         like dew from the womb of the morning."

4   The LORD has sworn and he will not recant: *
         "You are a priest for ever after the order of Melchizedek."

5   The Lord who is at your right hand
     will smite kings in the day of his wrath; *
         he will rule over the nations.

The Epistle   **Ephesians 1:15-23**
I have heard of your faith in the Lord Jesus and your love toward all the saints, and
for this reason I do not cease to give thanks for you as I remember you in my prayers.
I pray that the God of our Lord Jesus Christ, the Father of glory, may give you a
spirit of wisdom and revelation as you come to know him, so that, with the eyes of
your heart enlightened, you may know what is the hope to which he has called you,
what are the riches of his glorious inheritance among the saints, and what is the
immeasurable greatness of his power for us who believe, according to the working of
his great power. God put this power to work in Christ when he raised him from the
dead and seated him at his right hand in the heavenly places, far above all rule and
authority and power and dominion, and above every name that is named, not only in
this age but also in the age to come. And he has put all things under his feet and has
made him the head over all things for the church, which is his body, the fullness of
him who fills all in all.

or Acts 1:1-11 (see above - page 247)

The Gospel   **Luke 24:49-53)**
Jesus to his disciples, "And see, I am sending upon you what my Father promised; so
stay here in the city until you have been clothed with power from on high." Then he

250   **ASCENSION DAY — Years A, B, C**

led them out as far as Bethany, and, lifting up his hands, he blessed them. While he was blessing them, he withdrew from them and was carried up into heaven. And they worshiped him, and returned to Jerusalem with great joy; and they were continually in the temple blessing God.

or Mark 16:9-15, 19-20
Now after Jesus rose early on the first day of the week, he appeared first to Mary Magdalene, from whom he had cast out seven demons. She went out and told those who had been with him, while they were mourning and weeping. But when they heard that he was alive and had been seen by her, they would not believe it. After this he appeared in another form to two of them, as they were walking into the country. And they went back and told the rest, but they did not believe them. Later he appeared to the eleven themselves as they were sitting at the table; and he upbraided them for their lack of faith and stubbornness, because they had not believed those who saw him after he had risen. And he said to them, "Go into all the world and proclaim the good news to the whole creation." So then the Lord Jesus, after he had spoken to them, was taken up into heaven and sat down at the right hand of God. And they went out and proclaimed the good news everywhere, while the Lord worked with them and confirmed the message by the signs that accompanied it.

THE SEVENTH SUNDAY OF EASTER: THE SUNDAY AFTER ASCENSION DAY

The Collect
O God, the King of glory, you have exalted your only Son Jesus Christ with great triumph to your kingdom in heaven: Do not leave us comfortless, but send us your Holy Spirit to strengthen us, and exalt us to that place where our Savior Christ has gone before; who lives and reigns with you and the Holy Spirit, one God, in glory everlasting. *Amen.*

O God, the King of glory, who hast exalted thine only Son Jesus Christ with great triumph unto thy kingdom in heaven: We beseech thee, leave us not comfortless, but send to us thine Holy Ghost to comfort us, and exalt us unto the same place whither our Savior Christ is gone before; who liveth and reigneth with thee and the same Holy Ghost, one God, world without end. *Amen.*

Year A

The Lesson   Acts 1:(1-7) 8-14
[In the first book, Theophilus, I wrote about all that Jesus did and taught from the beginning until the day when he was taken up to heaven, after giving instructions through the Holy Spirit to the apostles whom he had chosen. After his suffering he presented himself alive to them by many convincing proofs, appearing to them during forty days and speaking about the kingdom of God. While staying with them, he ordered them not to leave Jerusalem, but to wait there for the promise of the Father. "This," he said, "is what you have heard from me; for John baptized with water, but you will be baptized with the Holy Spirit not many days from now." So when they had come together, they asked him, "Lord, is this the time when you will restore the kingdom to Israel?" He replied, "It is not for you to know the times or

periods that the Father has set by his own authority.] But you will receive power when the Holy Spirit has come upon you; and you will be my witnesses in Jerusalem, in all Judea and Samaria, and to the ends of the earth." When he had said this, as they were watching, he was lifted up, and a cloud took him out of their sight. While he was going and they were gazing up toward heaven, suddenly two men in white robes stood by them. They said, "Men of Galilee, why do you stand looking up toward heaven? This Jesus, who has been taken up from you into heaven, will come in the same way as you saw him go into heaven." Then they returned to Jerusalem from the mount called Olivet, which is near Jerusalem, a sabbath day's journey away. When they had entered the city, they went to the room upstairs where they were staying, Peter, and John, and James, and Andrew, Philip and Thomas, Bartholomew and Matthew, James son of Alphaeus, and Simon the Zealot, and Judas son of James. All these were constantly devoting themselves to prayer, together with certain women, including Mary the mother of Jesus, as well as his brothers.

or Ezekiel 39:21-29

I will display my glory among the nations; and all the nations shall see my judgment that I have executed, and my hand that I have laid on them. The house of Israel shall know that I am the LORD their God, from that day forward. And the nations shall know that the house of Israel went into captivity for their iniquity, because they dealt treacherously with me. So I hid my face from them and gave them into the hand of their adversaries, and they all fell by the sword. I dealt with them according to their uncleanness and their transgressions, and hid my face from them. Therefore thus says the Lord GOD: Now I will restore the fortunes of Jacob, and have mercy on the whole house of Israel; and I will be jealous for my holy name. They shall forget their shame, and all the treachery they have practiced against me, when they live securely in their land with no one to make them afraid, when I have brought them back from the peoples and gathered them from their enemies' lands, and through them have displayed my holiness in the sight of many nations. Then they shall know that I am the LORD their God because I sent them into exile among the nations, and then gathered them into their own land. I will leave none of them behind; and I will never again hide my face from them, when I pour out my spirit upon the house of Israel, says the Lord GOD.

The Psalm 68:1-20   *Exsurgat Deus*

1   Let God arise, and let his enemies be scattered; *
     let those who hate him flee before him.

2   Let them vanish like smoke when the wind drives it away; *
     as the wax melts at the fire, so let the wicked perish at the presence of God.

3   But let the righteous be glad and rejoice before God; *
     let them also be merry and joyful.

4   Sing to God, sing praises to his Name;
     exalt him who rides upon the heavens; *
     YAHWEH is his Name, rejoice before him!

5   Father of orphans, defender of widows, *
         God in his holy habitation!

6   God gives the solitary a home and brings forth prisoners into freedom; *
         but the rebels shall live in dry places.

7   O God, when you went forth before your people, *
         when you marched through the wilderness.

8   The earth shook, and the skies poured down rain,
     at the presence of God, the God of Sinai, *
         at the presence of God, the God of Israel.

9   You sent a gracious rain, O God, upon your inheritance; *
         you refreshed the land when it was weary.

10   Your people found their home in it; *
         in your goodness, O God, you have made provision for the poor.

11   The Lord gave the word; *
         great was the company of women who bore the tidings:

12   "Kings with their armies are fleeing away; *
         the women at home are dividing the spoils."

13   Though you lingered among the sheepfolds, *
         you shall be like a dove whose wings are covered with silver,
         whose feathers are like green gold.

14   When the Almighty scattered kings, *
         it was like snow falling in Zalmon.

15   O mighty mountain, O hill of Bashan! *
         O rugged mountain, O hill of Bashan!

16   Why do you look with envy, O rugged mountain,
     at the hill which god chose for his resting place? *
         truly, the LORD will dwell there for ever.

17   The chariots of God are twenty thousand,
     even thousands of thousands; *
         the Lord comes in holiness from Sinai.

18   You have gone up on high and led captivity captive;
     you have received gifts even from your enemies, *
         that the LORD God might dwell among them.

19   Blessed be the Lord day by day, *
         the God of our salvation, who bears our burdens.

20   He is our God, the God of our salvation; *
         God is the LORD, by whom we escape death.

or Psalm 47   *Omnes gentes, plaudite*

1   Clap your hands, all you peoples; *
        shout to God with a cry of joy.

2   For the LORD Most High is to be feared; *
        he is the great King over all the earth.

3   He subdues the peoples under us, *
        and the nations under our feet.

4   He chooses our inheritance for us, *
        the pride of Jacob whom he loves.

5   God has gone up with a shout, *
        the LORD with the sound of the ram's-horn.

6   Sing praises to God, sing praises; *
        sing praises to our King, sing praises.

7   For God is King of all the earth; *
        sing praises with all your skill.

8   God reigns over the nations; *
        God sits upon his holy throne.

9   The nobles of the peoples have gathered together *
        with the people of the God of Abraham.

10   The rulers of the earth belong to God, *
        and he is highly exalted.

The Epistle   **1 Peter 4:12-19**
Beloved, do not be surprised at the fiery ordeal that is taking place among you to test
you, as though something strange were happening to you. But rejoice insofar as you
are sharing Christ's sufferings, so that you may also be glad and shout for joy when
his glory is revealed. If you are reviled for the name of Christ, you are blessed,
because the spirit of glory, which is the Spirit of God, is resting on you. but let none
of you suffer as a murderer, a thief, a criminal, or even as a mischief maker. Yet if
any of you suffers as a Christian, do not consider it a disgrace, but glorify God
because you bear this name. For the time has come for judgment to begin with us,
what will be the end for those who do not obey the gospel of God? And "If it is hard
for the righteous to be saved, what will become of the ungodly and the sinners?"
Therefore, let those suffering in accordance with God's will entrust themselves to a
faithful Creator, while continuing to do good.

or Acts 1:(1-7) 8-14 (see above - page 251)

The Gospel   **John 17:1-11**
Jesus looked up to heaven and said, "Father, the hour has come; glorify your Son so
that the Son may glorify you, since you have given him authority over all people, to
give eternal life to all whom you have given him. And this is eternal life, that they

may know you, the only true God, and Jesus Christ whom you have sent. I glorified you on earth by finishing the work that you gave me to do. So now, Father, glorify me in your own presence with the glory that I had in your presence before the world existed. I have made your name known to those whom you gave me from the world. They were yours, and you gave them to me, and they have kept your word. Now they know that everything you have given me is from you; for the words that you gave to me I have given to them, and they have received them and know in truth that I came from you; and they have believed that you sent me. I am asking on their behalf; I am not asking on behalf of the world, but on behalf of those whom you gave me, because they are yours. All mine are yours, and yours are mine; and I have been glorified in them. And now I am no longer in the world, but they are in the world, and I am coming to you. Holy Father, protect them in your name that you have given me, so that they may be one, as we are one."

Year B

The Lesson   Acts 1:15-26

In those days Peter stood up among the believers (together the crowd numbered about one hundred twenty persons) and said, "Friends, the scripture had to be fulfilled, which the Holy Spirit through David foretold concerning Judas, who became a guide for those who arrested Jesus — for he was numbered among us and was allotted his share in this ministry. (Now this man acquired a field with the reward of his wickedness; and falling headlong, he burst open in the middle and all his bowels gushed out. This became known to all the residents of Jerusalem, so that the field was called in their language Hakeldama, that is, Field of Blood.) "For it is written in the book of Psalms, 'Let his homestead become desolate, and let there be no one to live in it'; and 'Let another take his position of overseer.' So one of the men who have accompanied us during all the time that the Lord Jesus went in and out among us, beginning from the baptism of John until the day when he was taken up from us — one of these must become a witness with us to his resurrection." So they proposed two, Joseph called Barsabbas, who was also known as Justus, and Matthias. Then they prayed and said, "Lord, you know everyone's heart. Show us which one of these two you have chosen to take the place in this ministry and apostleship from which Judas turned aside to go to his own place." And they cast lots for them, and the lot fell on Matthias; and he was added to the eleven apostles.

or Exodus 28:1-4, 9-10, 29-30

Then bring near to you your brother Aaron, and his sons with him, from among the Israelites, to serve me as priests — Aaron and Aaron's sons, Nadab and Abihu, Eleazar and Ithamar. You shall make sacred vestments for the glorious adornment of your brother Aaron. And you shall speak to all who have ability, whom I have endowed with skill, that they make Aaron's vestments to consecrate him for my priesthood. These are the vestments that they shall make: a breastpiece, an ephod, a robe, a checkered tunic, a turban, and a sash. When they make these sacred vestments for your brother Aaron and his sons to serve me as priests. You shall take two onyx stones, and engrave on them the names of the sons of Israel, six of their names on the one stone, and the names of the remaining six on the other stone, in the order of their birth. So Aaron shall bear the names of the sons of Israel in the breastpiece of judgment on his heart when he goes into the holy place, for a continual remembrance before the LORD. In the breastpiece of judgment you shall put the Urim and the Thummim, and they shall be on Aaron's heart when he goes in before the LORD; thus Aaron shall bear the judgment of the Israelites on his heart before the LORD continually.

The Psalm 68:1-20   *Exsurgat Deus*

1   Let God arise, and let his enemies be scattered; *
      let those who hate him flee before him.

2   Let them vanish like smoke when the wind drives it away; *
      as the wax melts at the fire, so let the wicked perish at the presence of God.

3   But let the righteous be glad and rejoice before God; *
      let them also be merry and joyful.

4   Sing to God, sing praises to his Name;
      exalt him who rides upon the heavens; *
      YAHWEH is his Name, rejoice before him!

5   Father of orphans, defender of widows, *
      God in his holy habitation!

6   God gives the solitary a home and brings forth prisoners into freedom; *
      but the rebels shall live in dry places.

7   O God, when you went forth before your people, *
      when you marched through the wilderness.

8   The earth shook, and the skies poured down rain,
      at the presence of God, the God of Sinai, *
      at the presence of God, the God of Israel.

9   You sent a gracious rain, O God, upon your inheritance; *
      you refreshed the land when it was weary.

10   Your people found their home in it; *
      in your goodness, O God, you have made provision for the poor.

11   The Lord gave the word; *
      great was the company of women who bore the tidings:

12   "Kings with their armies are fleeing away; *
      the women at home are dividing the spoils."

13   Though you lingered among the sheepfolds, *
      you shall be like a dove whose wings are covered with silver,
      whose feathers are like green gold.

14   When the Almighty scattered kings, *
      it was like snow falling in Zalmon.

15   O mighty mountain, O hill of Bashan! *
      O rugged mountain, O hill of Bashan!

16   Why do you look with envy, O rugged mountain,
at the hill which god chose for his resting place? *
    truly, the LORD will dwell there for ever.

17   The chariots of God are twenty thousand,
even thousands of thousands; *
    the Lord comes in holiness from Sinai.

18   You have gone up on high and led captivity captive;
you have received gifts even from your enemies, *
    that the LORD God might dwell among them.

19   Blessed be the Lord day by day, *
    the God of our salvation, who bears our burdens.

20   He is our God, the God of our salvation; *
    God is the LORD, by whom we escape death.

or Psalm 47   *Omnes gentes, plaudite*

1   Clap your hands, all you peoples; *
    shout to God with a cry of joy.

2   For the LORD Most High is to be feared; *
    he is the great King over all the earth.

3   He subdues the peoples under us, *
    and the nations under our feet.

4   He chooses our inheritance for us, *
    the pride of Jacob whom he loves.

5   God has gone up with a shout, *
    the LORD with the sound of the ram's-horn.

6   Sing praises to God, sing praises; *
    sing praises to our King, sing praises.

7   For God is King of all the earth; *
    sing praises with all your skill.

8   God reigns over the nations; *
    God sits upon his holy throne.

9   The nobles of the peoples have gathered together *
    with the people of the God of Abraham.

10   The rulers of the earth belong to God, *
    and he is highly exalted.

The Epistle   **1 John 5:9-15**

If we receive human testimony, the testimony of God is greater; for this is the testimony of God that he has testified to his Son. Those who believe in the Son of God have the testimony in their hearts. Those who do not believe in God have made him a liar by not believing in the testimony that God has given concerning his Son. And this is the testimony: God gave us eternal life, and this life is in his Son. Whoever has the Son has life; whoever does not have the Son of God does not have life. I write these things to you who believe in the name of the Son of God, so that you may know that you have eternal life. And this is the boldness we have in him, that if we ask anything according to his wile, he hears us. And if we know that he hears us in whatever we ask, we know that we have obtained the requests made of him.

or Acts 1:15-26 (see above - page 255)

The Gospel John 17:11b-19

Jesus prayed for his disciples, "Holy Father, protect them in your name that you have given me, so that they may be one, as we are one. While I was with them, I protected them in your name that you have given me. I guarded them, and not one of them was lost except the one destined to be lost, so that the scripture might befulfilled. But now I am coming to you, and I speak these things in the world so that they may have my joy made complete in themselves. I have given them your word, and the world has hated them because they do not belong to the world, just as I do not belong to the world. I am not asking you to take them out of the world, but I ask you to protect them from the evil one. They do not belong to the world, just as I do not belong to the world. Sanctify them in the truth; your word is truth. As you have sent me into the world, so I have sent them into the world. And for their sakes I sanctify myself, so that they also may be sanctified in truth."

Year C

The Lesson Acts 16:16-34

One day, as we (Paul and his traveling companions) were going to the place of prayer, we met a slave girl who had a spirit of divination and brought her owners a great deal of money by fortune-telling. While she followed Paul and us, she would cry out, "These men are slaves of the Most High God, who proclaim to you a way of salvation." She kept doing this for many days. But Paul, very much annoyed, turned and said to the spirit, "I order you in the name of Jesus Christ to come out of her." And it came out that very hour. But when her owners saw that their hope of making money was gone, they seized Paul and Silas and dragged them into the marketplace before the authorities. When they had brought them before the magistrates, they said, "These men are disturbing our city; they are Jews and are advocating customs that are not lawful for us as Romans to adopt or observe." The crowd joined in attacking them, and the magistrates had them stripped of their clothing and ordered them to be beaten with rods. After they had given them a severe flogging, they threw them into prison and ordered the jailer to keep them securely. Following these instructions, he put them in the innermost cell and fastened their feet in the stocks. About midnight Paul and Silas were praying and singing hymns to God, and the prisoners were listening to them. Suddenly there was an earthquake, so violent that the foundations of the prison were shaken; and immediately all the doors were opened and everyone's chains were unfastened. When the jailer woke up and saw the prison doors wide open, he drew his sword and was about to kill himself, since he supposed that the prisoners had escaped. But Paul shouted in a loud voice, "Do not harm yourself, for we are all here." The jailer called for lights, and rushing in, he fell down trembling before Paul and Silas. Then he brought them outside and said, "Sirs, what must I do to be saved?" They answered, "Believe on the Lord Jesus, and you will be saved, you and your household." They spoke the word of the Lord to him and to all who were in his house. At the same hour of the night he took them and washed their wounds; then he and his entire family were baptized without delay. He brought them up into the house and set food before them; and he and his entire household rejoiced that he had become a believer in God.

or I Samuel 12:19-24

All the people said to Samuel, "Pray to the LORD your God for your servants, so that we may not die; for we have added to all our sins the evil of demanding a king for ourselves." And Samuel said to the people, "Do not be afraid; you have done all this evil, yet do not turn aside from following the LORD, but serve the LORD with all your heart; and do not turn aside after useless things that cannot profit or save, for they are useless. For the LORD will not cast away his people, for his great name's sake, because it has pleased the LORD to make you a people for himself. Moreover as for me, far be it from me that I should sin against the LORD by ceasing to pray for you; and I will instruct you in the good and the right way. Only fear the LORD, and serve him faithfully with all your heart; for consider what great things he has done for you.

The Psalm 68:1-20   *Exsurgat Deus*

1   Let God arise, and let his enemies be scattered; *
        let those who hate him flee before him.

2   Let them vanish like smoke when the wind drives it away; *
        as the wax melts at the fire, so let the wicked perish at the presence of God.

3   But let the righteous be glad and rejoice before God; *
        let them also be merry and joyful.

4   Sing to God, sing praises to his Name;
     exalt him who rides upon the heavens; *
        YAHWEH is his Name, rejoice before him!

5   Father of orphans, defender of widows, *
        God in his holy habitation!

6   God gives the solitary a home and brings forth prisoners into freedom; *
        but the rebels shall live in dry places.

7   O God, when you went forth before your people, *
        when you marched through the wilderness.

8   The earth shook, and the skies poured down rain,
     at the presence of God, the God of Sinai, *
        at the presence of God, the God of Israel.

9   You sent a gracious rain, O God, upon your inheritance; *
        you refreshed the land when it was weary.

10   Your people found their home in it; *
    in your goodness, O God, you have made provision for the poor.

11   The Lord gave the word; *
    great was the company of women who bore the tidings:

12   "Kings with their armies are fleeing away; *
    the women at home are dividing the spoils."

13   Though you lingered among the sheepfolds, *
    you shall be like a dove whose wings are covered with silver,
    whose feathers are like green gold.

14   When the Almighty scattered kings, *
    it was like snow falling in Zalmon.

15   O mighty mountain, O hill of Bashan! *
    O rugged mountain, O hill of Bashan!

16   Why do you look with envy, O rugged mountain,
    at the hill which god chose for his resting place? *
    truly, the LORD will dwell there for ever.

17   The chariots of God are twenty thousand,
    even thousands of thousands; *
    the Lord comes in holiness from Sinai.

18   You have gone up on high and led captivity captive;
    you have received gifts even from your enemies, *
    that the LORD God might dwell among them.

19   Blessed be the Lord day by day, *
    the God of our salvation, who bears our burdens.

20   He is our God, the God of our salvation; *
    God is the LORD, by whom we escape death.

or Psalm 47   *Omnes gentes, plaudite*

1   Clap your hands, all you peoples; *
    shout to God with a cry of joy.

2   For the LORD Most High is to be feared; *
    he is the great King over all the earth.

3   He subdues the peoples under us, *
    and the nations under our feet.

4   He chooses our inheritance for us, *
    the pride of Jacob whom he loves.

5   God has gone up with a shout, *
    the LORD with the sound of the ram's-horn.

Sing praises to God, sing praises; *
  sing praises to our King, sing praises.

For God is King of all the earth; *
  sing praises with all your skill.

God reigns over the nations; *
  God sits upon his holy throne.

The nobles of the peoples have gathered together *
  with the people of the God of Abraham.

10 The rulers of the earth belong to God, *
  and he is highly exalted.

The Epistle   Revelation 22:12-14, 16-17, 20

Jesus said, "See, I am coming soon; my reward is with me, to repay according to everyone's work. I am the Alpha and the Omega, the first and the last, the beginning and the end." Blessed are those who wash their robes, so that they will have the right to the tree of life and may enter the city by the gates. "It is I, Jesus, who sent my angel to you with this testimony for the churches. I am the root and the descendant of David, the bright morning star." The Spirit and the bride say, "Come." And let everyone who hears say, "Come." And let everyone who is thirsty come. Let anyone who wishes take the water of life as a gift. The one who testifies to these things says, "Surely I am coming soon." Amen. Come, Lord Jesus!

or Acts 16:16-34 (see above - page 258)

The Gospel   John 17:20-26

Jesus prayed for his disciples and then he said, "I ask not only on behalf of these, but also on behalf of those who will believe in me through their word, that they may all be one. As you, Father, are in me and I am in you, may they also be in us, so that the world may believe that you have sent me. The glory that you have given me I have given them, so that they may be one, as we are one, I in them and you in me, that they may become completely one, so that the world may know that you have sent me and have loved them even as you have loved me. Father, I desire that those also, whom you have given me, may be with me where I am, to see my glory, which you have given me because you loved me before the foundation of the world. "Righteous Father, the world does not know you, but I know you; and these know that you have sent me. I made your name known to them, and I will make it known, so that the love with which you have loved me may be in them, and I in them."

THE DAY OF PENTECOST:
WHITSUNDAY

The Collect
Almighty God, on this day you opened the way of eternal life to every race and nation by the promised gift of your Holy Spirit: Shed abroad this gift throughout the world by the preaching of the Gospel, that it may reach to the ends of the earth; through Jesus

Christ our Lord, who lives and reigns with you, in the unity of the Holy Spirit, one God, for ever and ever. *Amen.*

or this (Contemporary)

O God, who on this day taught the hearts of your faithful people by sending to them the light of your Holy Spirit: Grant us by the same Spirit to have a right judgment in all things, and evermore to rejoice in his holy comfort; through Jesus Christ your Son our Lord, who lives and reigns with you, in the unity of the Holy Spirit, one God, for ever and ever. *Amen.*

Almighty God, who on this day didst open the way of eternal life to every race and nation by the promised gift of thy Holy Spirit: Shed abroad this gift throughout the world by the preaching of the Gospel, that it may reach to the ends of the earth; through Jesus Christ our Lord, who liveth and reigneth with thee, in the unity of the same Spirit, one God, for ever and ever. *Amen.*

or this (Traditional)

O God, who on this day didst teach the hearts of thy faithful people by sending to them the light of thy Holy Spirit: Grant us by the same Spirit to have a right judgment in all things, and evermore to rejoice in his holy comfort; through the merits of Christ Jesus our Savior, who liveth and reigneth with thee, in the unity of the same Spirit, one God, world without end. *Amen.*

Years A, B, C

The Lesson Acts 2:1-11 When the day of Pentecost had come, they were all together in one place. And suddenly from heaven there came a sound like the rush of a violent wind, and it filled the entire house where they were sitting. Divided tongues, as of fire, appeared among them, and a tongue rested on each of them. All of them were filled with the Holy Spirit and began to speak in other languages, as the Spirit gave them ability. Now there were devout Jews from every nation under heaven living in Jerusalem. And at this sound the crowd gathered and was bewildered, because each one heard them speaking in the native language of each. Amazed and astonished, they asked, "Are not all these who are speaking Galileans? And how is it that we hear, each of us, in our own native language? Parthians, Medes, Elamites, and residents of Mesopotamia, Judea and Cappadocia, Pontus and Asia, Phrygia and Pamphylia, Egypt and the parts of Libya belonging to Cyrene, and visitors from Rome, both Jews and proselytes, Cretans and Arabs — in our own languages we hear them speaking about God's deeds of power."

or, Year A — Ezekiel 11:17-20

Therefore say: Thus says the Lord GOD: I will gather you from the peoples, and assemble you out of the countries where you have been scattered, and I will give you the land of Israel. When they come there, they will remove from it all its detestable things and all its abominations. I will give them one heart, and put a new spirit within them; I will remove the heart of stone from their flesh and give them a heart of flesh, so that they may follow my statutes and keep my ordinances and obey them. Then they shall be my people, and I will be their God.

or, Year B — Isaiah 44:1-8

But now hear, O Jacob my servant, Israel whom I have chosen! Thus says the LORD who made you, who formed you in the womb and will help you: Do not fear, O Jacob my servant, Jeshurun whom I have chosen. For I will pour water on the thirsty land, and streams on the dry ground; I will pour my spirit upon your descendants, and my blessing on your offspring. They shall spring up like a green tamarisk, like willows by flowing streams. This one will say, "I am the LORD's," another will be called by the name of Jacob, yet another will write on the hand, "The LORD's," and adopt the name of Israel. Thus says the LORD, the King of Israel, and his Redeemer, the LORD of hosts: I am the first and I am the last; besides me there is no god. Who is like me? Let them proclaim it, let them declare and set it forth before me. Who has announced from of old the things to come? Let them tell us what is yet to be. Do not fear, or be afraid; have I not told you from of old and declared it? You are my witnesses! Is there any God besides me? There is no other rock; I know not one.

or, Year C — Joel 2:28-32

Then afterward I will pour out my spirit on all flesh; your sons and your daughters shall prophesy, your old men shall dream dreams, and your young men shall see visions. Even on the male and female slaves, in those days, I will pour out my spirit. I will show portents in the heavens and one the earth, blood and fire and columns of smoke. The sun shall be turned to darkness, and the moon to blood, before the great and terrible day of the LORD comes. Then everyone who calls on the name of the LORD shall be saved; for in Mount Zion and in Jerusalem there shall be those who escape, as the LORD has said, and among the survivors shall be those whom the LORD calls.

The Psalm 104:25-37 or 104:25-32   *Benedic, anima mea*

25   [O LORD, how manifold are your works! *

26   Yonder is the great and wide sea
      with its living things too many to number, *
          creatures both small and great.

27   There move the ships,
      and there is that Leviathan, *
          which you have made for the sport of it.

28   All of them look to you *
      to give them their food in due season.

29   You give it to them; they gather it; *
      you open your hand, and they are filled with good things.

30   You hide your face, and they are terrified; *
      you take away their breath,
      and they die and return to their dust.

31   You send forth your Spirit, and they are created; *
      and so you renew the face of the earth.

32   May the glory of the LORD endure for ever; *
      may the LORD rejoice in all his works.]

33   He looks at the earth and it trembles; *
      he touches the mountains and they smoke.

34   I will sing to the LORD as long as I live; *
      I will praise my God while I have my being.

35   May these words of mine please him; *
      I will rejoice in the LORD.

36   Let sinners be consumed out of the earth, *
      and the wicked be no more.

37   Bless the LORD, O my soul. *
      Hallelujah!

or Psalm 33:12-15, 18-22   *Exulte, justi*

12   Happy is the nation whose God is the LORD! *
      happy the people he has chosen to be his own!

13   The LORD looks down from heaven, *
      and beholds all the people in the world.

14   From where he sits enthroned he turns his gaze *
      on all who dwell on the earth.

15   He fashions all the hearts of them *
      and understands all their works.

18   Behold, the eye of the LORD is upon those who fear him, *
      on those who wait upon his love,

19   To pluck their lives from death, *
      and to feed them in time of famine.

20   Our soul waits for the LORD; *
      he is our help and our shield.

21   Indeed, our heart rejoices in him, *
      for in his holy Name we put our trust.

22   Let your loving-kindness, O LORD, be upon us, *
      as we have put our trust in you.

The Epistle   **1 Corinthians 12:4-13**

Now there are varieties of gifts, but the same Spirit; and there are varieties of services, but the same Lord; and there are varieties of activities, but it is the same God who activates all of them in everyone. To each is given the manifestation of the Spirit for the common good. To one is given through the Spirit the utterance of wisdom, and to another the utterance of knowledge according to the same Spirit, to another faith by the same Spirit, to another gifts of healing by the one Spirit, to another the working of miracles, to another prophecy, to another the discernment of spirits, to another various kinds of tongues, to another the interpretation of tongues. All these are activated by one and the same Spirit, who allots to each one individually just as the Spirit chooses. For just as the body is one and has many members, and all the members of body, though many, are one body, so it is with Christ. For in the one Spirit we were all baptized into one body — Jews or Greeks, slaves or free — and we were all made to drink of one Spirit.

or Acts 2:1-11 (see above - page 262)

The Gospel   John 20:19-23

When it was evening on that day, the first day of the week, and the doors of the house where the disciples had met were locked for fear of the Jews, Jesus came and stood among them and said, "Peace be with you." After he said this, he showed them his hands and his side. Then the disciples rejoiced when they saw the Lord. Jesus said to them again, "Peace be with you. As the Father has sent me, so I send you." When he had said this, he breathed on them and said to them, "Receive the Holy Spirit. If you forgive the sins of any, they are forgiven them; if you retain the sins of any, they are retained."

or John 14:8-17

Philip said to Jesus, "Lord, show us the Father, and we will be satisfied." Jesus said to him, "Have I been with you all this time, Philip, and you still do not know me? Whoever has seen me has seen the Father. How can you say, 'Show us the Father'? Do you not believe that I am in the Father and the Father is in me? The words that I say to you I do not speak on my own; but the Father who dwells in me does his works. Believe me that I am in the Father and the Father is in me; but if you do not, then believe me because of the works themselves. "Very truly, I tell you, the one who believes in me will also do the works that I do and, in fact, will do greater works than these, because I am going to the Father. I will do whatever you ask in my name, so that the Father may be glorified in the Son. If in my name you ask me for anything, I will do it. "If you love me, you will keep my commandments. And I will ask the Father, and he will give you another Advocate, to be with you forever. This is the Spirit of truth, whom the world cannot receive, because it neither sees him nor knows him. You know him, because he abides with you, and he will be in you.

THE FIRST SUNDAY AFTER PENTECOST: TRINITY SUNDAY

The Collect

Almighty and everlasting God, you have given to us your servants grace, by the confession of a true faith, to acknowledge the glory of the eternal Trinity, and in the power of your divine Majesty to worship the Unity: Keep us steadfast in this faith and worship, and bring us at last to see you in your one and eternal glory, O Father; who with the Son and the Holy Spirit live and reign, one God, for ever and ever. *Amen.*

Almighty and everlasting God, who hast given unto us thy servants grace, by the confession of a true faith, to acknowledge the glory of the eternal Trinity, and in the power of the Divine Majesty to worship the Unity: We beseech thee that thou wouldest keep us steadfast in this faith and worship, and bring us at last to see thee in thy one and eternal glory, O Father; who with the Son and the Holy Spirit livest and reignest, one God, for ever and ever. *Amen.*

Year A

The Lesson   **Genesis 1:1-2:3**

In the beginning when God created the heavens and the earth, the earth was a formless void and darkness covered the face of the deep, while a wind from God swept over the face of the waters. Then God said, "Let there be light"; and there was light. And God saw that the light was good; and God separated the light from the darkness. God called the light Day, and the darkness he called Night. And there was evening and there was morning, the first day. And God said, "Let there be a dome in the midst of the waters, and let it separate the waters from the waters." So God made the dome and separated the waters that were under the dome from the waters that were above the dome. And it was so. God called the dome Sky. And there was evening and there was morning, the second day. And God said, "Let the waters under the sky be gathered together into one place, and let the dry land appear." And it was so. God called the dry land Earth, and the waters that were gathered together he called Seas. And God saw that it was good. Then God said, "Let the earth put forth vegetation: plants yielding seed, and fruit trees of every kind on earth that bear fruit with the seed in it." And it was so. The earth brought forth vegetation: plants yielding seed of every kind, and trees of every kind bearing fruit with the seed in it. And God saw that it was good. And there was evening and there was morning, the third day. And God said, "Let there be lights in the dome of the sky to separate the day from the night; and let them be for signs and for seasons and for days and years, and let them be lights in the dome of the sky to give light upon the earth." And it was so. God made the two great lights — the greater light to rule the day and the lesser light to rule the night — and the stars. God set them in the dome of the sky to give light upon the earth, to rule over the day and over the night, and to separate the light from the darkness. And God saw that it was good. And there was evening and there was morning, the fourth day. And God said, "Let the waters bring forth swarms of living creatures, and let birds fly above the earth across the dome of the sky." So God created the great sea monsters and every living creature that moves, of every kind, with which the waters swarm, and every winged bird of every kind. And God saw that it was good. God blessed them, saying, "Be fruitful and multiply and fill the waters in the seas, and let birds multiply on the earth." And there was evening and the was morning, the fifth day. And God said, "Let the earth bring forth living creatures of every kind: cattle and creeping things and wild animals of the earth of every kind." And it was so. God made the wild animals of the earth of every kind, and the cattle of every kind, and everything that creeps upon the ground of every kind. And God saw that it was good. Then God said,"Let us make humankind in our image, according to our likeness; and let them have dominion over the fish of the sea, and over the birds of the air, and over the cattle, and over all the wild animals of the earth, and over every creeping thing that creeps upon the earth." So God created humankind in his image, in the image of God he created them; male and female he created them. God blessed them, and God said to them, "Be fruitful and multiply, and fill the earth and subdue it; and have dominion over the fish of the sea and over the birds of the air and over every living thing that moves upon the earth." God said, "See, I have given you every plant yielding seed that is upon the face of all the earth, and every tree with seed in its fruit; you shall have them for food. And to every beast of the earth, and to every bird of the air, and to everything that creeps on the earth, everything that has the breath of life, I have given every green plant for food." And it was so. God saw everything that he had made, and indeed, it was very good. And there was evening and there was morning, the sixth day. Thus the heavens and the earth were finished, and all their multitude. And on the seventh day God finished the work that he had done, and he rested on the seventh day from all the work that he had done. So God blessed the seventh day and hallowed it, because on it God rested from all the work that he had done in creation.

The Psalm 150   *Laudate Dominum*

1   Hallelujah!
    Praise God in his holy temple; *
        praise him in the firmament of his power.

2   Praise him for his mighty acts; *
        praise him for his excellent greatness.

3   Praise him with the blast of the ram's-horn; *
        praise him with lyre and harp.

4   Praise him with timbrel and dance; *
        praise him with strings and pipe.

5   Praise him with resounding cymbals; *
        praise him with loud-clanging cymbals.

6   Let everything that has breath *
        praise the LORD.
        Hallelujah!

or Canticle 2 *Benedictus es, Domine*
Blessed art thou, O Lord god of our fathers; *
    praised and exalted above all for ever.
Blessed art thou for the Name of thy Majesty; *
    praised and exalted above all for ever.
Blessed art thou in the temple of thy holiness; *
    praised and exalted above all for ever.
Blessed art thou that beholdest the depths,
and dwellest between the Cherubim; *
    praised and exalted above all for ever.
Blessed art thou on the glorious throne of thy kingdom; *
    praised and exalted above all for ever.
Blessed art thou in the firmament of heaven; *
    praised and exalted above all for ever.

Blessed art thou, O Father, Son, and Holy Spirit; *
    praised and exalted above all for ever.

or Canticle 13 *Benedictus es, Domine*
Glory to you, Lord God of our fathers; *
    you are worthy of praise; glory to you.
Glory to you for the radiance of your holy Name; *
    we will praise you and highly exalt you for ever.
Glory to you in the splendor of your temple; *
    on the throne of your majesty, glory to you.
Glory to you, seated between the Cherubim; *
    we will praise you and highly exalt you for ever.
Glory to you, beholding the depth; *
    in the high vault of heaven, glory to you.
Glory to you, Father, Son, and Holy Spirit; *
    we will praise you and highly exalt you for ever.

The Epistle   **2 Corinthians 13:(5-10) 11-13**
[Examine yourselves to see whether you are living in the faith. Test yourselves. Do
you not realize that Jesus Christ is in you? — unless, indeed, you fail to meet the test!
I hope you will find out that we have not failed. But we pray to God that you may not
do anything wrong — not that we may appear to have met the test, but that you may
do what is right, though we may seem to have failed. For we cannot do anything
against the truth, but only for the truth. For we rejoice when we are weak and you are
strong. This is what we pray for, that you may become perfect. So I write these things
while I am away from you, so that when I come, I may not have to be severe in using
the authority that the Lord has given me for building up and not for tearing down.]
Finally, brothers and sisters, farewell. Put things in order, listen to my appeal, agree
with one another, live in peace; and the God of love and peace will be with you.
Greet one another with a holy kiss. All the saints greet you. The grace of the Lord
Jesus Christ, the love of God, and the communion of the Holy Spirit be with all of
you.

The Gospel   **Matthew 28:16-20**
The eleven disciples went to Galilee, to the mountain to which Jesus had directed
them. When they saw him, they worshiped him; but some doubted. And Jesus came
and said to them, "All authority in heaven and on earth has been given to me. Go
therefore and make disciples of all nations, baptizing them in the name of the Father
and of the Son and of the Holy Spirit, and teaching them to obey everything that I
have commanded you. And remember, I am with you always, to the end of the age."

Year B

The Lesson   **Exodus 3:1-6**
Moses was keeping the flock of his father-in-law Jethro, the priest of Midian; he led
his flock beyond the wilderness, and came to Horeb, the mountain of God. There the
angel of the LORD appeared to him in a flame of fire out of a bush; he looked, and
the bush was blazing, yet it was not consumed. Then Moses said, "I must turn aside

and look at this great sight, and see why the bush is not burned up." When the LORD saw that he had turned aside to see, God called to him out of the bush, "Moses, Moses!" And he said, "Here I am." Then he said, "Come no closer! Remove the sandals from you feet, for the place on which you are standing is holy ground." He said further, "I am the God of your father, the God of Abraham, the God of Isaac, and the God of Jacob." And Moses hid his face, for he was afraid to look at God.

The Psalm 93 *Dominus regnavit*

1 The LORD is King;
   he has put on splendid apparel; *
      the LORD has put on his apparel
      and girded himself with strength.

2 He has made the whole world so sure *
      that it cannot be moved;

3 Ever since the world began, your throne has been established; *
      you are from everlasting.

4 The waters have lifted up, O LORD,
   the waters have lifted up their voice; *
      the waters have lifted up their pounding waves.

5 Mightier than the sound of many waters,
   mightier than the breakers of the sea, *
      mightier is the LORD who dwells on high.

6 Your testimonies are very sure, *
      and holiness adorns your house, O LORD,
      for ever and for evermore.

or Canticle 2 *Benedictus es, Domine* **(see above - page 267)**

or Canticle 13 *Benedictus es, Domine* **(see above - page 268)**

The Epistle   Romans 8:12-17

So then, brothers and sisters, we are debtors, not to the flesh, to live according to the flesh — for if you live according to the flesh, you will die; but if by the Spirit you put to death the deeds of the body, you will live. For all who are led by the Spirit of God are children of God. For you did not receive a spirit of slavery to fall back into fear, but you have received a spirit of adoption. When we cry, "Abba! Father!" it is that very Spirit bearing witness with our spirit that we are children of God, and if children, then heirs, heirs of God and joint heirs with Christ — if, in fact, we suffer with him so that we may also be glorified with him.

The Gospel   John 3:1-16

Now there was a Pharisee named Nicodemus, a leader of the Jews. He came to Jesus by night and said to him, "Rabbi, we know that you are a teacher who has come from God; for no one can do these signs that you do apart from the presence of

God." Jesus answered him, "Very truly, I tell you, no one can see the kingdom of God without being born from above." Nicodemus said to him, "How can anyone be born after having grown old? Can one enter a second time into the mother's womb and be born?" Jesus answered, "Very truly, I tell you, no one can enter the kingdom of God without being born of water and Spirit. What is born of the flesh is flesh, and what is born of the Spirit is spirit. Do not be astonished that I said to you, 'You must be born from above.' The wind blows where it chooses, and you hear the sound of it, but you do not know where it comes from or where it goes. So it is with everyone who is born of the Spirit." Nicodemus said to him, "How can these things be?" Jesus answered him, "Are you a teacher of Israel, and yet you do not understand these things? Very truly, I tell you, we speak of what we know and testify to what we have seen; yet you do not receive our testimony. If I have told you about earthly things and you do not believe, how can you believe if I tell you about heavenly things? No one has ascended into heaven except the one who descended from heaven, the Son of Man. And just as Moses lifted up the serpent in the wilderness, so must the Son of Man be lifted up, that whoever believes in him may have eternal life. For God so loved the world that he gave his only Son, so that everyone who believes in him may not perish but may have eternal life."

Year C

The Lesson   Isaiah 6:1-8

In the year that King Uzziah died, I saw the Lord sitting on a throne, high and lofty; and the hem of his robe filled the temple. Seraphs were in attendance above him; each had six wings: with two they covered their faces, and with two they covered their feet, and with two they flew. And one called to another and said: "Holy, holy, holy is the LORD of hosts; they whole earth is full of his glory." The pivots on the thresholds shook at the voices of those who called, and the house filled with smoke. And I said: "Woe is me! I am lost, for I am a man of unclean lips, and I live among a people of unclean lips; yet my eyes have seen the King, the LORD of hosts!" Then one of the seraphs flew to me, holding a live coal that had been taken from the altar with a pair of tongs. The seraph touched my mouth with it and said: "Now that this has touched your lips, your guilt has departed and your sin is blotted out." Then I heard the voice of the Lord saying, "Whom shall I send, and who will go for us?" And I said, "Here am I; send me!"

The Psalm 29   *Afferte Domino*

1   Ascribe to the LORD, you gods, *
        ascribe to the LORD glory and strength.

2   Ascribe to the LORD the glory due his Name; *
        worship the LORD in the beauty of holiness.

3   The voice of the LORD is upon the waters;
     the God of glory thunders; *
        the LORD is upon the mighty waters.

4   The voice of the LORD is a powerful voice; *
        the voice of the LORD is a voice of splendor.

5   The voice of the Lord breaks the cedar trees; *
     the voice of the Lord breaks the cedars of Lebanon;

6   He makes Lebanon skip like a calf, *
     and Mount Hermon like a young wild ox.

7   The voice of the Lord splits the flames of fire;
   the voice of the Lord shakes the wilderness; *
     the Lord shakes the wilderness of Kadesh.

8   The voice of the Lord makes the oak trees write *
     and strips the forests bare.

9   And in the temple of the Lord *
     all are crying, "Glory!"

10 The Lord sits enthroned above the flood; *
     the Lord sits enthroned as King for evermore.

11 The Lord shall give strength to his people; *
     the Lord shall give his people the blessing of peace.

or Canticle 2 *Benedictus es, Domine* **(see above - page 267)**

or Canticle 13 *Benedictus es, Domine* **(see above - page 268)**

The Epistle

Revelation 4:1-11

After this I looked, and there in heaven a door stood open! And the first voice, which I had heard speaking to me like a trumpet, said, "Come up here, and I will show you what must take place after this." At once I was in the spirit, and there in heaven stood a throne, with one seated on the throne! And the one seated there looks like jasper and carnelian, and around the throne is a rainbow that looks like an emerald. Around the throne are twenty-four thrones, and seated on the thrones are twenty-four elders, dressed in white robes, with golden crowns on their heads. Coming from the throne are flashes of lightning, and rumblings and peals of thunder, and in front of the throne burn seven flaming torches, which are the seven spirits of God; and in front of the throne there is something like a sea of glass, like crystal. Around the throne, and on each side of the throne, are four living creatures, full of eyes in front and behind: the first living creature like a lion, the second living creature like an ox, the third living creature with a face like a human face, and the fourth living creature like a flying eagle. And the four living creatures, each of them with six wings, are full of eyes all around and inside. Day and night without ceasing they sing, "Holy, holy, holy, the Lord God the Almighty, who was and is and is to come." And whenever the living creatures give glory and honor and thanks to the one who is seated on the throne, who lives forever and ever, the twenty-four elders fall before the one who is seated on the throne and worship the one who lives forever and ever; they cast their crowns before the throne, singing, "You are worthy, our Lord and God, to receive glory and honor and power, for you created all things, and by your will they existed and were created."

The Gospel   **John 16:(5-11) 12-15**

["Now I am going to him who sent me; yet none of you asks me, 'Where are you going?' But because I have said these things to you, sorrow has filled your hearts. Nevertheless I tell you the truth: it is to your advantage that I go away, for if I do not go away, the Advocate will not come to you; but if I go, I will send him to you. And when he comes, he will prove the world wrong about sin and righteousness and judgment: about sin, because they do not believe in me; about righteousness, because I am going to the Father and you will see me no longer; about judgment, because the ruler of this world has been condemned.] "I still have many things to say to you, but you cannot bear them now. When the Spirit of truth comes, he will guide you into all the truth; for he will not speak on his own, but will speak whatever he hears, and he will declare to you the things that are to come. He will glorify me, because he will take what is mine and declare it to you. All that the Father has is mine. For this reason I said that he will take what is mine and declare it to you."

THE SEASON AFTER PENTECOST

Proper 1 *The Sunday closest to May 11*

The Collect

Remember, O Lord, what you have wrought in us and not what we deserve; and, as you have called us to your service, make us worthy of our calling; through Jesus Christ our Lord, who lives and reigns with you and the Holy Spirit, one God, now and for ever. *Amen.*

Remember, O Lord, what thou hast wrought in us and not what we deserve; and, as thou hast called us to thy service, make us worthy of our calling; through Jesus Christ our Lord, who liveth and reigneth with thee and the Holy Spirit, one God, now and for ever. *Amen.*

Year A

The Lesson   **Ecclesiasticus (Sirach) 15:11-20**

Do not say, "It was the Lord's doing that I fell away"; for he does not do what he hates. Do not say, "It was he who led me astray"; for he has no need of the sinful. The Lord hates all abominations; such things are not loved by those who fear him. It was he who created humankind in the beginning, and he left them in the power of their own free choice. If you choose, you can keep the commandments, and to act faithfully is a matter of your own choice. He has placed before you fire and water; stretch out your hand for whichever you choose. Before each person are life and death, and whichever one chooses will be given. For great is the wisdom of the Lord; he is mighty in power and sees everything; his eyes are one those who fear him, and he knows every human action. He has not commanded anyone to be wicked, and he has not given anyone permission to sin.

The Psalm 119:1-16 or 119:9-16   *Beati immaculati*

1   Happy are they whose way is blameless, *
          who walk in the law of the LORD!

2   Happy are they who observe his decrees *
      and seek him with all their hearts!

3   Who never do any wrong, *
      but always walk in his ways.

4   You laid down your commandments, *
      that we should fully keep them.

5   Oh, that my ways were made so direct *
      that I might keep your statutes!

6   Then I should not be put to shame, *
      when I regard all your commandments.

7   I will thank you with an unfeigned heart, *
      when I have learned your righteous judgments.

8   I will keep your statutes; *
      do not utterly forsake me.

9   [How shall a young man cleanse his way? *
      By keeping to your words.

10   With my whole heart I seek you; *
      let me not stray from your commandments.

11   I treasure your promise in my heart, *
      that I may not sin against you.

12   Blessed are you, O LORD; *
      instruct me in your statutes.

13   With my lips will I recite *
      all the judgments of your mouth.

14   I have taken greater delight in the way of your decrees *
      than in all manner of riches.

15   I will meditate on your commandments *
      and give attention to your ways.

16   My delight is in your statutes; *
      I will not forget your word.]

The Epistle   **1 Corinthians 3:1-9**

And so, brothers and sisters, I could not speak to you as spiritual people, but rather as people of the flesh, as infants in Christ. I fed you with milk, not solid food, for you were not ready for solid food. Even now you are still not ready, for you are still of the flesh. For as long as there is jealousy and quarreling among you, are you not of the flesh, and behaving according to human inclinations? For when one says, "I belong to Apollos," are you not merely human? What then is Apollos? What is Paul? Servants through whom you came to believe, as the Lord assigned to each. I planted, Apollos watered, but God gave the growth. So neither the one who plants nor the one who waters is anything, but only God who gives the growth. The one who plants and the one who waters have a common purpose, and each will receive wages according to the labor or each. For we are God's servants, working together; you are God's field, God's building.

The Gospel   Matthew 5:21-24, 27-30, 33-37

Jesus said, "You have heard that it was said to those of ancient times, 'You shall not murder'; and 'whoever murders shall be liable to judgment.' But I say to you that if you are angry with a brother or sister, you will be liable to judgment; and if you insult a brother or sister, you will be liable to the council; and if you say, 'You fool,' you will be liable to the hell of fire. So when you are offering your gift at the altar, if you remember that your brother or sister has something against you, leave your gift there before the altar and go; first be reconciled to your brother or sister, and then come and offer your gift. You have heard that it was said, 'You shall not commit adultery.' But I say to you that everyone who looks at a woman with lust has already committed adultery with her in his heart. If your right eye causes you to sin, tear it out and throw it away; it is better for you to lose one of your members than for your whole body to be thrown into hell. And if your right hand causes you to sin, cut it off and throw it away; it is better for you to lose one of your members than for your whole body to go into hell. Again, you have heard that it was said to those of ancient times, 'You shall not swear falsely, but carry out the vows you have made to the Lord.' But I say to you, Do not swear at all, either by heaven, for it is the throne of God, or by the earth, for it is his footstool, or by Jerusalem, for it is the city of the great King. And do not swear by your head, for you cannot make one hair white or black. Let your word be 'Yes, Yes' or 'No, No'; anything more than this comes from the evil one.

Year B

The Lesson   2 Kings 5:1-15ab

Naaman, commander of the army of the king of Aram, was a great man and in high favor with his master, because by him the LORD had given victory to Aram. The man, though a mighty warrior, suffered from leprosy. Now the Arameans on one of their raids had taken a young girl captive from the land of Israel, and she served Naaman's wife. She said to her mistress, "If only my lord were with the prophet who is in Samaria! He would cure him of his leprosy." So Naaman went in and told his lord just what the girl from the land of Israel had said. And the king of Aram said, "Go then, and I will send along a letter to the king of Israel." He went, taking with him ten talents of silver, six thousand shekels of gold, and ten sets of garments. He brought the letter to the king of Israel, which read, "When this letter reaches you, know that I have sent to you my servant Naaman, that you may cure him of his leprosy." When the king of Israel read the letter, he tore his clothes and said, "Am I God, to give death or life, that this man sends word to me to cure a man of his leprosy? Just look and see how he is trying to pick a quarrel with me." But when Elisha the man of God heard that the king of Israel had torn his clothes, he sent a message to the king, "Why have you torn you clothes? Let him come to me, that he may learn that there is a prophet in Israel." So Naaman came with his horses and chariots, and halted at the entrance of Elisha's house. Elisha sent a messenger to him, saying, "Go, wash in the Jordan seven times, and your flesh shall be restored and you shall be clean." But Naaman became angry and went away, saying, "I thought that for me he would surely come out, and stand and call on the name of the LORD his God, and would wave his hand over the spot, and cure the leprosy! Are not Abana and Pharpar, the rivers of Damascus, better than all the waters of Israel? Could I not wash in them, and be clean?" He turned and went away in a rage. But his servants approached and said to him, "Father, if the prophet had commanded you to do something difficult, would you not have done it? How much more, when all he said to you was, 'Wash, and be clean'?" So he went down and immersed himself seven times in the Jordan, according to the word of the man of God; his flesh was restored like the flesh of a young boy, and he was clean. Then he returned to the man of God, he and all his company; he came and stood before him and said, "Now I know that there is no God in all the earth except in Israel."

The Psalm 42 or 42:1-7   *Quemadmodum*

1   [As the deer longs for the water- brooks, *
         so longs my soul for you, O God.

2   My soul is athirst for God, athirst for the living God; *
         when shall I come to appear before the presence of God?

3   My tears have been my food day and night, *
         while all day long they say to me,
         "Where now is your God?"

4   I pour out my soul when I think on these things: *
         how I went with the multitude and led them into the house of God,

5   With the voice of praise and thanksgiving, *
         among those who keep holy-day.

6   Why are you so full of heaviness, O my soul? *
         and why are you so disquieted within me?

7   Put your trust in God; *
         for I will yet give thanks to him,
         who is the help of my countenance, and my God.]

8   My soul is heavy within me; *
         therefore I will remember you from the land of Jordan,
         and from the peak of Mizar among the heights of Hermon.

9   One deep calls to another in the noise of your cataracts; *
         all your rapids and floods have gone over me.

10   The LORD grants his loving-kindness in the daytime; *
         in the night season his song is with me,
         a prayer to the God of my life.

11   I will say to the God of my strength,
           "Why have you forgotten me? *
             and why do I go so heavily while the enemy oppresses me?"

12   While my bones are being broken, *
           my enemies mock me to my face;

13   All day long they mock me *
           and say to me, "Where now is your God?"

14   Why are you so full of heaviness, O my soul? *
           and why are you so disquieted within me?

15   Put your trust in God; *
           for I will yet give thanks to him,
           who is the help of my countenance, and my God.

The Epistle   **1 Corinthians 9:24-27**

Do you not know that in a race the runners all compete, but only one receives the prize? Run in such a way that you may win it. Athletes exercise self-control in all things; they do it to receive a perishable wreath, but we an imperishable one. So I do not run aimlessly, nor do I box as though beating the air; but I punish my body and enslave it, so that after proclaiming to others I myself should not be disqualified.

The Gospel   **Mark 1:40-45**

A leper came to Jesus begging him, and kneeling he said to him, "If you choose, you can make me clean." Moved with pity, Jesus stretched out his hand and touched him, and said to him, "I do choose. Be made clean!" Immediately the leprosy left him, and he was made clean. After sternly warning him he sent him away at once, saying to him, "See that you say nothing to anyone; but go, show yourself to the priest, and offer for your cleansing what Moses commanded, as a testimony to them." But he went out and began to proclaim it freely, and to spread the word, so that Jesus could not longer go into a town openly, but stayed out in the country; and people came to him from every quarter.

Year C

The Lesson   **Jeremiah 17:5-10**

Thus says the LORD: Cursed are those who trust in mere mortals and make mere flesh their strength, whose hearts turn away from the LORD. They shall be like a shrub in the desert, and shall not see when relief comes. They shall live in the parched places of the wilderness, in an uninhabited salt land. Blessed are those who trust in the LORD, whose trust is the LORD. They shall be like a tree planted by water, sending out its roots by the stream. It shall not fear when heat comes, and its leaves shall stay green; in the year of drought it is not anxious, and it does not cease to bear fruit. The heart is devious above all else; it is perverse — who can understand it? I the LORD test the mind and search the heart, to give to all according to their ways, according to the fruit of their doings.

The Psalm 1   *Beatus vir qui non abiit*

1   Happy are they who have not walked in the counsel of the wicked, *
       nor lingered in the way of sinners,
       nor sat in the seats of the scornful!

2   Their delight is in the law of the LORD, *
       and they meditate on his law day and night.

3   They are like trees planted by streams of water,
       bearing fruit in due season, with leaves that do not wither; *
       everything they do shall prosper.

4   It is not so with the wicked; *
       they are like chaff which the wind blows away.

5   Therefore the wicked shall not stand upright when judgment comes, *
       nor the sinner in the council of the righteous.

6   For the LORD knows the way of the righteous, *
       but the way of the wicked is doomed.

The Epistle   1 Corinthians 15:12-20

Now if Christ is proclaimed as raised from the dead, how can some of you say there is no resurrection of the dead? If there is no resurrection of the dead, then Christ has not been raised; and if Christ has not been raised, then our proclamation has been in vain and your faith has been in vain. We are even found to be misrepresenting God, because we testified of God that he raised Christ — whom he did not raise if it is true that the dead are not raised. For if the dead are not raised, then Christ has not been raised. If Christ has not been raised, your faith is futile and you are still in your sins. Then those also who have died in Christ have perished. If for this life only we have hoped in Christ, we are of all people most to be pitied. But in fact Christ has been raised from the dead, the first fruits of those who have died.

The Gospel   Luke 6:17-26

Jesus came down with the twelve apostles and stood on a level place, with a great crowd of his disciples and a great multitude of people from all Judea, Jerusalem, and the coast of Tyre and Sidon. They had come to hear him and to be healed of their diseases; and those who were troubled with unclean spirits were cured. And all in the crowd were trying to touch him, for power came out from him and healed all of them. Then he looked up at his disciples and said: "Blessed are you who are poor, for yours is the kingdom of God. Blessed are you who are hungry now, for you will be filled. Blessed are you who weep now, for you will laugh. Blessed are you when people hate you, and when they exclude you, revile you, and defame you on account of the Son of Man. Rejoice in that day and leap for joy, for surely your reward is great in heaven; for that is what their ancestors did to the prophets. But woe to you who are rich, for you have received your consolation. Woe to you who are full now, for you will be hungry. Woe to you who are laughing now, for you will mourn and weep. Woe to you when all speak well of you, for that is what their ancestors did to the false prophets.

Proper 2 *The Sunday closest to May 18*

The Collect

Almighty and merciful God, in your goodness keep us, we pray, from all things that may hurt us, that we, being ready both in mind and body, may accomplish with free hearts those things which belong to your purpose; through Jesus Christ our Lord, who lives and reigns with you and the Holy Spirit, one God, now and for ever. *Amen.*

O Almighty and most merciful God, of thy bountiful goodness keep us, we beseech thee, from all things that may hurt us, that we, being ready both in body and soul, may with free hearts accomplish those things which belong to thy purpose; through Jesus Christ our Lord, who liveth and reigneth with thee and the Holy Spirit, one God, now and for ever. *Amen.*

Year A

The Lesson   Leviticus 19:1-2, 9-18

The LORD spoke to Moses, saying: Speak to all the congregation of the people of Israel and say to them: You shall be holy, for I the LORD your God am holy. When you reap the harvest of your land, you shall not reap to the very edges of your field, or gather the gleanings of your harvest. You shall not strip your vineyard bare, or gather the fallen grapes of your vineyard; you shall leave them for the poor and the alien: I am the LORD your God. You shall not steal; you shall not deal falsely; and you shall not lie to one another. And you shall not swear falsely by my name, profaning the name of your God: I am the LORD. You shall not defraud your neighbor; you shall not steal; and you shall not keep for yourself the wages of a laborer until morning. You shall not revile the deaf or put a stumbling block before the blind; you shall fear your God: I am the LORD. You shall not render an unjust judgment; you shall not be partial to the poor or defer to the great: with justice you shall judge your neighbor. You shall not go around as a slanderer among your people, and you shall not profit by the blood of your neighbor: I am the LORD. You shall not hate in your heart anyone of your kin; you shall reprove your neighbor, or you will incur guilt yourself. You shall not take vengeance or bear a grudge against any of your people, but you shall love your neighbor as yourself: I am the LORD.

The Psalm 71 or 71:16-24   *In te, Domine, speravi*

1   In you, O LORD, have I taken refuge; *
         let me never be ashamed.

2   In your righteousness, deliver me and set me free; *
         incline your ear to me and save me.

3   Be my strong rock, a castle to keep me safe; *
         you are my crag and my stronghold.

4   Deliver me, my God, from the hand of the wicked, *
         from the clutches of the evildoer and the oppressor.

5   For you are my hope, O Lord GOD, *
         my confidence since I was young.

6 I have been sustained by you ever since I was born;
from my mother's womb you have been my strength; *
  my praise shall be always of you.

7 I have become a portent to many; *
  but you are my refuge and my strength.

8 Let my mouth be full of your praise *
  and your glory all the day long.

9 Do not cast me off in my old age; *
  forsake me not when my strength fails.

10 For my enemies are talking against me, *
  and those who lie in wait for my life take counsel together.

11 They say, "God has forsaken him;
go after him and seize him; *
  because there is none who will save."

12 O God, be not far from me; *
  come quickly to help me, O my God.

13 Let those who set themselves against me be put to shame and be disgraced; *
  let those who seek to do me evil be covered with scorn and reproach.

14 But I shall always wait in patience, *
  and shall praise you more and more.

15 My mouth shall recount your mighty acts
and saving deeds all day long; *
  though I cannot know the number of them.

16 [I will begin with the mighty works of the Lord GOD; *
  I will recall your righteousness, yours alone.

17 O God, you have taught me since I was young, *
  and to this day I tell of your wonderful works.

18 And now that I am old and gray-headed, O God, do not forsake me, *
  till I make known your strength to this generation
  and your power to all who are to come.

19 Your righteousness, O God, reaches to the heavens; *
  you have done great things;
  who is like you, O God?

20 You have showed me great troubles and adversities, *
  but you will restore my life
  and bring me up again from the deep places of the earth.

21 You strengthen me more and more; *
  you enfold and comfort me,

22   Therefore I will praise you upon the lyre for your faithfulness, O my God; *
         I will sing to you with the harp, O Holy One of Israel.

23   My lips will sing with joy when I play to you, *
         and so will my soul, which you have redeemed.

24   My tongue will proclaim your righteousness all day long, *
         for they are ashamed and disgraced who sought to do me harm.]

The Epistle   1 Corinthians 3:10-11, 16-23

According to the grace of God given to me, like a skilled master builder I laid a foundation, and someone else is building on it. Each builder must choose with care how to build on it. For no one can lay any foundation other than the one that has been laid; that foundation is Jesus Christ. Do you not know that you are God's temple and that God's Spirit dwells in you? If anyone destroys God's temple, God will destroy that person. For God's temple is holy, and you are that temple. Do not deceive yourselves. If you think that you are wise in this age, you should become fools so that you may become wise. For the wisdom of this world is foolishness with God. For it is written, "He catches the wise in their craftiness," and again, "The Lord knows the thoughts of the wise, that they are futile." So let no one boast about human leaders. For all things are yours, whether Paul or Apollos or Cephas or the world or life or death or the present or the future — all belong to you, and you belong to Christ, and Christ belongs to God.

The Gospel   Matthew 5:38-48

Jesus said, "You have heard that it was said, 'An eye for an eye and a tooth for a tooth.' But I say to you, Do not resist an evildoer. But if anyone strikes you on the right cheek, turn the other also; and if anyone wants to sue you and take your coat, give your cloak as well; and if anyone forces you to go one mile, go also the second mile. Give to everyone who begs from you, and do not refuse anyone who want to borrow from you. You have heard that it was said, 'You shall love your neighbor and hate your enemy.' But I say to you, Love your enemies and pray for those who persecute you, so that you may be children of your Father in heaven; for he makes his sun rise on the evil and on the good, and sends rain on the righteous and on the unrighteous. For if you love those who love you, what reward do you have? Do not even the tax collectors do the same? And if you greet only your brothers and sisters, what more are you doing than others? Do not even the Gentiles do the same? Be perfect, therefore, as your heavenly Father is perfect.

Year B

The Lesson   Isaiah 43:18-25

Do not remember the former things, or consider the things of old. I am about to do a new thing; now it springs forth, do you not perceive it? I will make a way in the wilderness and rivers in the desert. The wild animals will honor me, the jackals and the ostriches; for I give water in the wilderness, rivers in the desert, to give drink to my chosen people, the people whom I formed for myself so that they might declare my praise. Yet you did not call upon me, O Jacob; but you have been weary of me, O

Israel! You have not brought me your sheep for burnt offerings, or honored me with your sacrifices. I have not burdened you with offerings, or wearied you with frankincense. You have not bought me sweet cane with money, or satisfied me with the fat of your sacrifices. But you have burdened with your sins; you have wearied me with your iniquities. I, I am He who blots out your transgressions for my own sake, and I will not remember your sins.

The Psalm 32 or 32:1-8   *Beati quorum*

1   [Happy are they whose transgressions are forgiven, *
         and whose sin is put away!

2   Happy are they to whom the LORD imputes no guilt, *
         and in whose spirit there is no guile!

3   While I held my tongue, my bones withered away, *
         because of my groaning all day long.

4   For your hand was heavy upon me day and night; *
         my moisture was dried up as in the heat of summer.

5   Then I acknowledged my sin to you, *
         and did not conceal my guilt.

6   I said, "I will confess my transgressions to the LORD." *
         Then you forgave me the guilt of my sin.

7   Therefore all the faithful will make their prayers to you in time of trouble; *
         when the great waters overflow, they shall not reach them.

8   You are my hiding-place;
       you preserve me from trouble; *
         you surround me with shouts of deliverance.]

9   "I will instruct you and teach you in the way that you should go; *
         I will guide you with my eye.

10   Do not be like horse or mule, which have no understanding; *
         who must be fitted with bit and bridle,
         or else they will not stay near you.

11   Great are the tribulations of the wicked; *
         but mercy embraces those who trust in the LORD.

12   Be glad, you righteous, and rejoice in the LORD; *
         shout for joy, all who are true of heart.

The Epistle   **2 Corinthians 1:18-22**

As surely as God is faithful, our word to you has not been "Yes and No." For the Son of God, Jesus Christ, whom we proclaimed among you, Silvanus and Timothy and I, was not "Yes and No"; but in him it is always "Yes." For in him every one of God's promises is a "Yes." For this reason it is through him that we say the "Amen," to the glory of God. But it is God who establishes us with you in Christ and has anointed us, by putting his seal on us and giving us his Spirit in our hearts as a first installment.

The Gospel   Mark 2:1-12
When Jesus returned to Capernaum after some days, it was reported that he was at home. So many gathered around that there was no longer room for them, not even in front of the door; and he was speaking the word to them. Then some people came, bringing to him a paralyzed man, carried by four of them. And when they could not bring him to Jesus because of the crowd, they removed the roof above him; and after having dug through it, they let down the mat on which the paralytic lay. When Jesus saw their faith, he said to the paralytic, "Son, your sins are forgiven." Now some of the scribes were sitting there, questioning in their hearts, "Why does this fellow speak in this way? It is blasphemy! Who can forgive sins but God alone?" At once Jesus perceived in his spirit that they were discussing these questions among themselves; and he said to them, "Why do you raise such questions in your hearts? Which is easier, to say to the paralytic, 'Your sins are forgiven,' or to say, 'Stand up and take your mat and walk'? But so that you may know that the Son of Man has authority on earth to forgive sins" — he said to the paralytic — "I say to you, stand up, take your mat and go to your home." And he stood up, and immediately took the mat and went out before all of them; so that they were all amazed and glorified God, saying, "We have never seen anything like this!"

Year C

The Lesson   Genesis 45:3-11, 21-28
Joseph said to his brothers, "I am Joseph. Is my father still alive?" But his brothers could not answer him, so dismayed were they at his presence. Then Joseph said to his brothers, "Come closer to me." And they came closer. He said, "I am your brother, Joseph, whom you sold into Egypt. And now do not be distressed, or angry with yourselves, because you sold me here; for God sent me before you to preserve life. For the famine has been in the land these two years; and there are five more years in which there will be neither plowing nor harvest. God sent me before you to preserve for you a remnant on earth, and to keep alive for you many survivors. So it was not you who sent me here, but God; he has made me a father to Pharaoh, and lord of all his house and ruler over all the land of Egypt. Hurry and go up to my father and say to him, 'Thus says your son Joseph, God has made me lord of all Egypt; come down to me, do not delay. You shall settle in the land of Goshen, and you shall be near me, you and your children and your children's children, as well as your flocks, your herds, and all that you have. I will provide for you there — since there are five more years of famine to come — so that you and your household, and all that you have, will not come to poverty.' The sons of Israel did so. Joseph gave them wagons according to the instruction of Pharaoh, and he gave them provisions for the journey. To each one of them he gave a set of garments; but to Benjamin he gave three hundred pieces of silver and five sets of garments. To his father he sent the following: ten donkeys loaded with the good things of Egypt, and ten female donkeys loaded with grain, bread, and provision for his father on the journey. Then he sent his brothers on their way, and as they were leaving he said to them, "Do not quarrel along the way." So they went up out of Egypt and came to their father Jacob in the land of Canaan. And

they told him, "Joseph is still alive! He is even ruler over all the land of Egypt." He was stunned; he could not believe them. But when they told him all the words of Joseph that he had said to them, and when he saw the wagons that Joseph had sent to carry him, the spirit of their father Jacob revived. Israel said, "Enough! My son Joseph is still alive. I must go and see him before I die."

The Psalm 37:1-18 or 37:3-10   *Noli aemulari*

1   Do not fret yourself because of evildoers; *
        do not be jealous of those who do wrong.

2   For they shall soon wither like the grass, *
        and like the green grass fade away.

3   [Put your trust in the LORD and do good; *
        dwell in the land and feed on its riches.

4   Take delight in the LORD, *
        and he shall give you your heart's desire.

5   Commit your way to the LORD and put your trust in him, *
        and he will bring it to pass.

6   He will make your righteousness as clear as the light *
        and your just dealing as the noonday.

7   Be still before the LORD *
        and wait patiently for him.

8   Do not fret yourself over the one who prospers, *
        the one who succeeds in evil schemes.

9   Refrain from anger, leave rage alone; *
        do not fret yourself; it leads only to evil.

10   For evildoers shall be cut off, *
        but those who wait upon the LORD shall possess the land.]

11   In a little while the wicked shall be no more; *
        you shall search out their place, but they will not be there.

12   But the lowly shall possess the land; *
        they will delight in abundance of peace.

13   The wicked plot against the righteous *
        and gnash at them with their teeth.

14   The Lord laughs at the wicked, *
        because he sees that their day will come.

15   The wicked draw their sword and bend their bow
     to strike down the poor and needy, *
        to slaughter those who are upright in their ways.

16   Their sword shall go through their own heart, *
      and their bow shall be broken.

17   The little that the righteous has *
      is better than great riches of the wicked.

18   For the power of the wicked shall be broken, *
      but the LORD upholds the righteous.

The Epistle   1 Corinthians 15:35-38, 42-50

But someone will ask, "How are the dead raised? With what kind of body do they
come?" Fool! What you sow does not come to life unless it dies. And as for what you
sow, you do not sow the body that is to be, but a bare seed, perhaps of wheat or of
some other grain. But God gives it a body as he has chosen, and to each kind of seed
its own body. So it is with the resurrection of the dead. What is sown is perishable,
what is raised is imperishable. It is sown in dishonor, it is raised in glory. It is sown
in weakness, it is raised in power. It is sown a physical body, it is raised a spiritual
body. If there is a physical body, there is also a spiritual body. Thus it is written,
"The first man, Adam, became a living being"; the last Adam became a life-giving
spirit. But it is not the spiritual that is first, but the physical, and then the spiritual.
The first man was from the earth, a man of dust; the second man is from heaven. As
was the man of dust, so are those who are of the dust; and as is the man of heaven, so
are those who are of heaven. Just as we have borne the image of the man of dust, we
will also bear the image of the man of heaven. What I am saying, brothers and sisters,
is this: flesh and blood cannot inherit the kingdom of God, nor does the perishable
inherit the imperishable.

The Gospel   Luke 6:27-38

Jesus said, "I say to you that listen, Love your enemies, do good to those who hate
you, bless those who curse you, pray for those who abuse you. If anyone strikes you
on the cheek, offer the other also; and from anyone who takes away your coat do not
withhold even your shirt. Give to everyone who begs from you; and if anyone takes
away your goods, do not ask for them again. Do to others as you would have them do
to you. If you love those who love you, what credit is that to you? For even sinners
love those who love them. If you do good to those who do good to you, what credit is
that to you? For even sinners do the same. If you lend to those from whom you hope
to receive, what credit is that to you? Even sinners lend to sinners, to receive as much
again. But love your enemies, do good, and lend, expecting nothing in return. Your
reward will be great, and you will be children of the Most High; for he is kind to the
ungrateful and the wicked. Be merciful, just as your Father is merciful. Do not judge,
and you will not be judged; do not condemn, and you will not be condemned.
Forgive, and you will be forgiven; give, and it will be given to you. A good measure,
pressed down, shaken together, running over, will be put into your lap; for the
measure you give will be the measure you get back."

Proper 3 *The Sunday closest to May 25*

The Collect

Grant, O Lord, that the course of this world may be peaceably governed by your providence; and that your Church may joyfully serve you in confidence and serenity; through Jesus Christ our Lord, who lives and reigns with you and the Holy Spirit, one God, for ever and ever. *Amen.*

Grant, O Lord, we beseech thee, that the course of this world may be peaceably governed by thy providence, and that thy Church may joyfully serve thee in confidence and serenity; through Jesus Christ our Lord, who liveth and reigneth with thee and the Holy Spirit, one God, for ever and ever. *Amen.*

Year A

The Lesson   Isaiah 49:8-18

Thus says the LORD: In a time of favor I have answered you, on a day of salvation I have helped you; I have kept you and given you as a covenant to the people, to establish the land, to apportion the desolate heritages; saying to the prisoners, "Come out," to those who are in darkness, "Show yourselves." They shall feed along the ways, on all the bare heights shall be their pasture; they shall not hunger or thirst, neither scorching wind nor sun shall strike them down, for he who has pity on them will lead them, and by springs of water will guide them. And I will turn all my mountains into a road, and my highways shall be raised up. Lo, these shall come from far away, and lo, these from the north and from the west, and these from the land of Syene. Sing for joy, O heavens, and exult, O earth; break forth, O mountains, into singing! For the LORD has comforted his people, and will have compassion on his suffering ones. But Zion said, "The LORD has forsaken me, my Lord has forgotten me." Can a woman forget her nursing child, or show no compassion for the child of her womb? Even these may forget, yet I will not forget you. See, I have inscribed you on the palms of my hands; your walls are continually before me. Your builders outdo your destroyers, and those who laid you waste go away from you. Lift up your eyes all around and see; they all gather, they come to you. As I live, says the LORD, you shall put all of them on like an ornament, and like a bride you shall bind them on.

The Psalm 62 or 62:6-14   *Nonne Deo?*

1   For God alone my soul in silence waits; *
        from him comes my salvation.

2   He alone is my rock and my salvation, *
        my stronghold, so that I shall not be greatly shaken.

3   How long will you assail me to crush me,
     all of you together, *
        as if you were a leaning fence, a toppling wall?

4   They seek only to bring me down from my place of honor; *
        lies are their chief delight.

5   They bless with their lips, *
        but in their hearts they curse.

6   [For God alone my soul in silence waits; *
        truly, my hope is in him.

7   He alone is my rock and my salvation, *
        my stronghold, so that I shall not be shaken.

8   In God is my safety and my honor; *
        God is my strong rock and my refuge.

9   Put your trust in him always, O people, *
        pour out your hearts before him, for God is our refuge.

10   Those of high degree are but a fleeting breath, *
        even those of low estate cannot be trusted.

11   On the scales they are lighter than a breath, *
        all of them together.

12   Put no trust in extortion;
     in robbery take no empty pride; *
        though wealth increase, set not your heart upon it.

13   God has spoken once, twice have I heard it, *
        that power belongs to God.

14   Steadfast love is yours, O Lord, *
        for you repay everyone according to his deeds.]

The Epistle   **1 Corinthians 4:1-5, (6-7) 8-13**
Think of us in this way, as servants of Christ and stewards of God's mysteries.
Moreover, it is required of stewards that they be found trustworthy. But with me it is
a very small thing that I should be judged by your or by any human court. I do not
even judge myself. I am not aware of anything against myself, but I am not thereby
acquitted. It is the Lord who judges me. Therefore do not pronounce judgment
before the time, before the Lord comes, who will bring to light the things now hidden
in darkness and will disclose the purposes of the heart. Then each one will receive
commendation from God. [I have applied all this to Apollos and myself for your
benefit, brothers and sisters, so that you may learn through us the meaning of the
saying, "Nothing beyond what is written," so that none of you will be puffed up in
favor of one against another. For who sees anything different in you? What do you
have that you did not receive? And if you received it, why do you boast as if it were
not a gift?] Already you have all you want! Already you have become rich! Quite
apart from us you have become kings! Indeed, I wish that you had become kings, so
that we might be kings with you! For I think that God has exhibited us apostles as
last of all, as though sentenced to death, because we have become a spectacle to the
world, to angels and to mortals. We are fools for the sake of Christ, but you are wise
in Christ. We are weak, but you are strong. You are held in honor, but we in
disrepute. To the present hour we are hungry and thirsty, we are poorly clothed and

beaten and homeless, and we grow weary from the work of our own hands. When reviled, we bless; when persecuted, we endure; when slandered, we speak kindly. We have become like the rubbish of the world, the dregs of all things, to this very day.

The Gospel   Matthew 6:24-34

Jesus said, "No one can serve two masters; for a slave will either hate the one and love the other, or be devoted to the one and despise the other. You cannot serve God and wealth. Therefore I tell you, do not worry about your life, what you will eat or what you will drink, or about your body, what you will wear. Is not life more than food, and the body more than clothing? Look at the birds of the air; they neither sow nor reap nor gather into barns, and yet your heavenly Father feeds them. Are you not of more value than they? And can any of you by worrying add a single hour to your span of life? And why do you worry about clothing? Consider the lilies of the field, how they grow; they neither toil nor spin, yet I tell you, even Solomon in all his glory was not clothed like one of these. But if God so clothes the grass of the field, which is alive today and tomorrow is thrown into the oven, will he not much more clothe you — you of little faith? Therefore do not worry, saying, 'What will we eat?' or 'What will we drink?' or 'What will we wear?' For it is the Gentiles who strive for all these things; and indeed your heavenly Father knows that you need all these things. But strive first for the kingdom of God and his righteousness, and all these things will be given to you as well. So do not worry about tomorrow, for tomorrow will bring worries of its own. Today's trouble is enough for today."

Year B

The Lesson   Hosea 2:14-23

Therefore, I will now allure her, and bring her into the wilderness, and speak tenderly to her. From there I will give her her vineyards, and make the Valley of Achor a door of hope. There she shall respond as in the days of her youth, as at the time when she came out of the land of Egypt. On that day, says the LORD, you will call me, "My husband," and no longer will you call me, "My Baal." For I will remove the names of the Baals from her mouth, and they shall be mentioned by name no more. I will make for you a covenant on that day with the wild animals, the birds of the air, and the creeping things of the ground; and I will abolish the bow, the sword, and war from the land; and I will make you lie down in safety. And I will take you for my wife forever; I will take you for my wife in righteousness and in justice, in steadfast love, and in mercy. I will take you for my wife in faithfulness; and you shall know the LORD. On that day I will answer, says the LORD, I will answer the heavens and they shall answer the earth; and the earth shall answer the grain, the wine, and the oil, and they shall answer Jezreel; and I will sow him for myself in the land. And I will have pity on Lo-ruhamah, and I will say to Lo-ammi, "You are my people"; and he shall say, "You are my God."

The Psalm 103 or 103:1-6   *Benedic, anima mea*

1   [Bless the LORD, O my soul, *
        and all that is within me, bless his holy Name.

2   Bless the LORD, O my soul, *
         and forget not all his benefits.

3   He forgives all your sins *
         and heals all your infirmities;

4   He redeems your life from the grave *
         and crowns you with mercy and loving-kindness;

5   He satisfies you with good things, *
         and your youth is renewed like an eagle's.

6   The LORD executes righteousness *
         and judgment for all who are oppressed.]

7   He made his ways known to Moses *
         and his works to the children of Israel.

8   The LORD is full of compassion and mercy, *
         slow to anger and of great kindness.

9   He will not always accuse us, *
         nor will he keep his anger for ever.

10   He has not dealt with us according to our sins, *
         nor rewarded us according to our wickedness.

11   For as the heavens are high above the earth, *
         so is his mercy great upon those who fear him.

12   As far as the east is from the west, *
         so far has he removed our sins from us.

13   As a father cares for his children, *
         so does the LORD care for those who fear him.

14   For he himself knows whereof we are made; *
         he remembers that we are but dust.

15   Our days are like the grass; *
         we flourish like a flower of the field;

16   When the wind goes over it, it is gone, *
         and its place shall know it no more.

17   But the merciful goodness of the LORD endures for
                         ever on those who fear him, *
         and his righteousness on children's children;

18   On those who keep his covenant *
         and remember his commandments and do them.

19   The LORD has set his throne in heaven, *
         and his kingship has dominion over all.

20   Bless the LORD, you angels of his,
                  you mighty ones who do his bidding, *
      and hearken to the voice of his word.

21   Bless the LORD, all you his hosts, *
      you ministers of his who do his will.

22   Bless the LORD, all you works of his,
                  in all places of his dominion; *
      bless the LORD, O my soul.

The Epistle   2 Corinthians 3:(4-11) 17-4:2

[Such is the confidence that we have through Christ toward God. Not that we are competent of ourselves to claim anything as coming from us; our competence is from God, who has made us competent to be ministers of a new covenant, not of letter but of spirit; for the letter kills, but the Spirit gives life. Now if the ministry of death, chiseled in letters on stone tablets, came in glory so that the people of Israel could not gaze at Moses' face because of the glory of his face, a glory now set aside, how much more will the ministry of the Spirit come in glory? For if there was glory in the ministry of condemnation, much more does the ministry of justification abound in glory! Indeed, what once had glory has lost its glory because of the greater glory; for if what was set aside came through glory, much more has the permanent come in glory!] Now the Lord is the Spirit, and where the Spirit of the Lord is, there is freedom. And all of us, with unveiled faces, seeing the glory of the Lord as though reflected in a mirror, are being transformed into the same image from one degree of glory to another; for this comes from the Lord, the Spirit. Therefore, since it is by God's mercy that we are engaged in this ministry, we do not lose heart. We have renounced the shameful things that one hides; we refuse to practice cunning or to falsify God's word; but by the open statement of the truth we commend ourselves to the conscience of everyone in the sight of God.

The Gospel   Mark 2:18-22

Now John's disciples and the Pharisees were fasting; and people came and said to him, "Why do John's disciples and the disciples of the Pharisees fast, but your disciples do not fast?" Jesus said to them, "The wedding guests cannot fast while the bridegroom is with them, can they? As long as they have the bridegroom with them, they cannot fast. The days will come when the bridegroom is taken away from them, and then they will fast on that day. "No one sews a piece of unshrunk cloth on an old cloak; otherwise, the patch pulls away from it, the new from the old, and a worse tear is made. And no one puts new wine into old wineskins; otherwise, the wine will burst the skins, and the wine is lost, and so are the skins; but one puts new wine into fresh wineskins."

Year C

The Lesson   Jeremiah 7:1-7 (8-15)

The word that came to Jeremiah from the LORD: Stand in the gate of the LORD's house, and proclaim there this word, and say, Hear the word of the LORD, all you people of Judah, you that enter these gates to worship the LORD. Thus says the LORD of hosts, the God of Israel: Amend your ways and your doings, and let me dwell with you in this place. Do not trust in these deceptive words: "This is the temple of the LORD, the temple of the LORD, the temple of the LORD." For if you truly amend your ways and your doings, if you truly act justly one with another, if you do not oppress the alien, the orphan, and the widow, or shed innocent blood in this place, and if you do not go after other gods to your own hurt, then I will dwell with you in this place, in the land that I gave of old to your ancestors forever and ever. [Here you are, trusting in deceptive words to no avail. Will you steal, murder, commit adultery, swear falsely, make offerings to Baal, and go after other gods that you have not known, and then come and stand before me in this house, which is called by my name, and say, "We are safe!" — only to go on doing all these abominations? Has this house, which is called by my name, become a den of robbers in your sight? You know, I too am watching, says the LORD. Go now to my place that was in Shiloh, where I made my name dwell at first, and see what I did to it for the wickedness of my people Israel. And now, because you have done all these things, says the LORD, and when I spoke to you persistently, you did not listen, and when I called you, you did not answer, therefore I will do to the house that is called by my name, in which you trust, and to the place that I gave to you and to your ancestors, just what I did to Shiloh. And I will cast you out of my sight, just as I cast out all your kinsfolk, all the offspring of Ephraim.]

The Psalm 92 or 92:1-5, 11-14   *Bonum est confiteri*

1   [It is a good thing to give thanks to the LORD, *
     and to sing praises to your Name, O Most High;

2   To tell of your loving-kindness early in the morning *
     and of your faithfulness in the night season;

3   On the psaltery, and on the lyre, *
     and to the melody of the harp.

4   For you have made me glad by your acts, O LORD; *
     and I shout for joy because of the works of your hands.

5   LORD, how great are your works! *
     your thoughts are very deep.]

6   The dullard does not know,
    nor does the fool understand, *
      that though the wicked grow like weeds,
      and all the workers of iniquity flourish,

7   They flourish only to be destroyed for ever; *
     but you, O LORD, are exalted for evermore.

8   For lo, your enemies, O LORD,
    lo, your enemies shall perish, *
      and all the workers of iniquity shall be scattered.

9   But my horn you have exalted like the horns of wild bulls; *
        I am anointed with fresh oil.

10   My eyes also gloat over my enemies, *
        and my ears rejoice to hear the doom of the wicked who rise up against me.

11   [The righteous shall flourish like a palm tree, *
        and shall spread abroad like a cedar of Lebanon.

12   Those who are planted in the house of the LORD *
        shall flourish in the courts of our God;

13   They shall still bear fruit in old age; *
        they shall be green and succulent;

14   That they may show how upright the LORD is, *
        my Rock, in whom there is no fault.]

The Epistle   1 Corinthians 15:50-58

What I am saying, brothers and sisters, is this: flesh and blood cannot inherit the kingdom of God, nor does the perishable inherit the imperishable. Listen, I will tell you a mystery! We will not all die, but we will all be changed, in a moment, in the twinkling of an eye, at the last trumpet. For the trumpet will sound, and the dead will be raised imperishable, and we will be changed. For this perishable body must put on imperishability, and this mortal body must put on immortality. When this perishable body puts on imperishability, and this mortal body puts on immortality, then the saying that is written will be fulfilled: "Death has been swallowed up in victory." "Where, O death, is your victory? Where, O death, is your sting?" The sting of death is sin, and the power of sin is the law. But thanks be to God, who gives us the victory through our Lord Jesus Christ. Therefore, my beloved, be steadfast, immovable, always excelling in the work of the Lord, because you know that in the Lord you labor is not in vain.

The Gospel   Luke 6:39-49

Jesus told the people a parable: "Can a blind person guide a blind person? Will not both fall into a pit? A disciple is not above the teacher, but everyone who is fully qualified will be like the teacher. Why do you see the speck in your neighbor's eye, but do not notice the log in your own eye? Or how can you say to your neighbor, 'Friend, let me take out the speck in your eye,' when you yourself do not see the log in your own eye? You hypocrite, first take the log out of your own eye, and then you will see clearly to take the speck out of your neighbor's eye. No good tree bears bad fruit, nor again does a bad tree bear good fruit; for each tree is known by its own fruit. Figs are not gathered from thorns, nor are grapes picked from a bramble bush. The good person out of the good treasure of the heart produces good, and the evil person out of evil treasure produces evil; for it is out of the abundance of the heart that the mouth speaks. "Why do you call me 'Lord, Lord,' and do not do what I tell you? I will show you what someone is like who comes to me, hears my words, and acts on them. That one is like a man building a house, who dug deeply and laid the foundation on rock; when a flood arose, the river burst against that house but could not shake it, because it had been well built. But the one who hears and does not act is like a man who built a house on the ground without a foundation. When the river burst against it, immediately it fell, and great was the ruin of that house."

Proper 4 *The Sunday closest to June 1*

The Collect

O God, your never-failing providence sets in order all things both in heaven and earth: Put away from us, we entreat you, all hurtful things, and give us those things which are profitable for us; through Jesus Christ our Lord, who lives and reigns with you and the Holy Spirit, one God, for ever and ever. *Amen.*

O God, whose never-failing providence ordereth all things both in heaven and earth: We humbly beseech thee to put away from us all hurtful things, and to give us those things which are profitable for us; through Jesus Christ our Lord, who liveth and reigneth with thee and the Holy Spirit, one God, for ever and ever. *Amen.*

Year A

The Lesson   Deuteronomy 11:18-21, 26-28

You shall put these words of mine in your heart and soul, and you shall bind them as a sign on your hand, and fix them as an emblem on your forehead. Teach them to your children, talking about them when you are at home and when you are away, when you lie down and when you rise. Write them on the doorposts of your house and on your gates, so that your days and the days of your children may be multiplied in the land that the LORD swore to your ancestors to give them, as long as the heavens are above the earth. See, I am setting before you today a blessing and a curse: the blessing, if you obey the commandments of the LORD your God that I am commanding you today; and the curse, if you do not obey the commandments of the LORD your God, but turn from the way that I am commanding you today, to follow other gods that you have not known.

The Psalm 31 or 31:1-5, 19-24   *In te, Domine, speravi*

1   [In you, O LORD, have I taken refuge;
     let me never be put to shame; *
         deliver me in your righteousness.

2   Incline your ear to me; *
         make haste to deliver me.

3   Be my strong rock, a castle to keep me safe,
     for you are my crag and my stronghold; *
         for the sake of your Name, lead me and guide me.

4   Take me out of the net that they have secretly set for me, *
         for you are my tower of strength.

5   Into your hands I commend my spirit, *
         for you have redeemed me,
         O LORD, O God of truth.]

6   I hate those who cling to worthless idols, *
        and I put my trust in the LORD.

7   I will rejoice and be glad because of your mercy; *
        for you have seen my affliction;
        you know my distress.

8   You have not shut me up in the power of the enemy; *
        you have set my feet in an open place.

9   Have mercy on me, O LORD, for I am in trouble; *
        my eye is consumed with sorrow,
        and also my throat and my belly.

10 For my life is wasted with grief,
    and my years with sighing; *
        my strength fails me because of affliction,
        and my bones are consumed.

11 I have become a reproach to all my enemies and even to my neighbors,
    a dismay to those of my acquaintance; *
        when they see me in the street they avoid me.

12 I am forgotten like a dead man, out of mind; *
        I am as useless as a broken pot.

13 For I have heard the whispering of the crowd;
    fear is all around; *
        they put their heads together against me;
        they plot to take my life.

14 But as for me, I have trusted in you, O LORD. *
        I have said, "You are my God.

15 My times are in your hand; *
        rescue me from the hand of my enemies,
        and from those who persecute me.

16 Make your face to shine upon your servant, *
        and in your loving-kindness save me."

17 LORD, let me not be ashamed for having called upon you; *
        rather, let the wicked be put to shame;
        let them be silent in the grave.

18 Let the lying lips be silenced which speak against the righteous, *
        haughtily, disdainfully, and with contempt.

19 [How great is your goodness, O LORD!
    which you have laid up for those who fear you; *
        which you have done in the sight of all
        for those who put their trust in you.

20   You hide them in the covert of your presence from those who slander them; *
     you keep them in your shelter from the strife of tongues.

21   Blessed be the LORD! *
     for he has shown me the wonders of his love in a besieged city.

22   Yet I said in my alarm,
     "I have been cut off from the sight of your eyes."
     Nevertheless, you heard the sound of my entreaty
     when I cried out to you.

23   Love the LORD, all you who worship him; *
     the LORD protects the faithful,
     but repays to the full those who act haughtily.

24   Be strong and let your heart take courage, *
     all you who wait for the LORD.]

The Epistle   Romans 3:21-25a, 28

Apart from law, the righteousness of God has been disclosed, and is attested by the
law and the prophets, the righteousness of God through faith in Jesus Christ for all
who believe. For there is no distinction, since all have sinned and fall short of the
glory of God; they are now justified by his grace as a gift, through the redemption
that is in Christ Jesus, whom God put forward as a sacrifice of atonement by his
blood, effective through faith. For we hold that a person is justified by faith apart
from works prescribed by the law.

The Gospel   Matthew 7:21-27

Jesus said, "Not everyone who says to me, 'Lord, Lord,' will enter the kingdom of
heaven, but only the one who does the will of my Father in heaven. On that day
many will say to me, 'Lord, Lord, did we not prophesy in your name, and cast out
demons in your name, and do many deeds of power in your name?' Then I will
declare to them, 'I never knew you; go away from me, you evildoers.' Everyone then
who hears these words of mine and acts on them will be like a wise man who built
his house on rock. The rain fell, the floods came, and the winds blew and beat on that
house, but it did not fall, because it had been founded on rock. And everyone who
hears these words of mine and does not act on them will be like a foolish man who
built his house on sand. The rain fell, and the floods came, and the winds blew and
beat against that house, and it fell — and great was its fall!"

Year B

The Lesson   Deuteronomy 5:6-21

I am the LORD your God, who brought you out of the land of Egypt, out of the house
of slavery; you shall have no other gods before me. You shall not make for yourself an
idol, whether in the form of anything that is in heaven above, or that is on the earth
beneath, or that is in the water under the earth. You shall not bow down to them or
worship them; for I the LORD your God am a jealous God, punishing children for the
iniquity of parents, to the third and fourth generation of those who reject me, but

showing steadfast love to the thousandth generation of those who love me and keep my commandments. You shall not make wrongful use of the name of the LORD your God, for the LORD will not acquit anyone who misuses his name. Observe the sabbath day and keep it holy, as the LORD your God commanded you. Six days you shall labor and do all your work. But the seventh day is a sabbath to the LORD your God; you shall not do any work — you, or your son or your daughter, or your male or female slave, or your ox or your donkey, or any of your livestock, or the resident alien in your towns, so that your male and female slave may rest as well as you. Remember that you were a slave in the land of Egypt, and the LORD your God brought you out from there with a mighty hand and an outstretched arm; therefore the LORD your God commanded you to keep the sabbath day. Honor your father and your mother, as the LORD your God commanded you, so that your days may be long and that it may go well with you in the land that the LORD your God is giving you. You shall not murder. Neither shall you commit adultery. Neither shall you steal. Neither shall you bear false witness against your neighbor. Neither shall you covet your neighbor's wife. Neither shall you desire your neighbor's house, or field, or male or female slave, or ox, or donkey, or anything that belongs to your neighbor.

The Psalm 81 or 81:1-10   *Exultate Deo*

1   [Sing with joy to God our strength *
        and raise a loud shout to the God of Jacob.

2   Raise a song and sound the timbrel, *
        the merry harp, and the lyre.

3   Blow the ram's-horn at the new moon, *
        and at the full moon, the day of our feast.

4   For this is a statute for Israel, *
        a law of the God of Jacob.

5   He laid it as a solemn charge upon Joseph, *
        when he came out the land of Egypt.

6   I heard an unfamiliar voice saying, *
        "I eased his shoulder from the burden;
        his hands were set free from bearing the load."

7   You called on me in trouble, and I saved you; *
        I answered you from the secret place of thunder
        and tested you at the waters of Meribah.

8   Hear, O my people, and I will admonish you: *
        O Israel, if you would but listen to me!

9   There shall be no strange god among you; *
        you shall not worship a foreign god.

10   I am the LORD your God,
        who brought you out of the land of Egypt and said, *
        "Open your mouth wide, and I will fill it."]

11   And yet my people did not hear my voice, *
        and Israel would not obey me.

12   So I gave them over to the stubbornness of their hearts, *
        to follow their own devices.

13   Oh, that my people would listen to me! *
        that Israel would walk in my ways!

14   I should soon subdue their enemies *
        and turn my hand against their foes.

15   Those who hate the LORD would cringe before him, *
        and their punishment would last for ever.

16   But Israel would I feed with the finest wheat *
        and satisfy him with honey from the rock.

The Epistle   2 Corinthians 4:5-12

We do not proclaim ourselves; we proclaim Jesus Christ as Lord and ourselves as your slaves for Jesus' sake. For it is the God who said, "Let light shine out of darkness," who has shone in our hearts to give the light of the knowledge of the glory of God in the face of Jesus Christ. But we have this treasure in clay jars, so that it may be made clear that this extraordinary power belongs to God and does not come from us. We are afflicted in every way, but not crushed; perplexed, but not driven to despair; persecuted, but not forsaken; struck down, but not destroyed; always carrying in the body the death of Jesus, so that the life of Jesus may also be made visible in our bodies. For while we live, we are always being given up to death for Jesus' sake, so that the life of Jesus may be made visible in our mortal flesh. So death is at work in us, but life in you.

The Gospel   Mark 2:23-28

On a sabbath day, Jesus and his disciples were going through the grainfields; and as they made their way his disciples began to pluck heads of grain. The Pharisees said to him, "Look, why are they doing what is not lawful on the sabbath?" And he said to them, "Have you never read what David did when he and his companions were hungry and in need of food? He entered the house of God, when Abiathar was high priest, and ate the bread of the Presence, which it is not lawful for any but the priests to eat, and he gave some to his companions." Then he said to them, "The sabbath was made for humankind, and not humankind for the sabbath; so the Son of Man is lord even of the sabbath."

Year C

The Lesson   1 Kings 8:22-23, 27-30, 41-43

Then Solomon stood before the altar of the LORD in the presence of all the assembly of Israel, and spread out his hands to heaven. He said, "O LORD, God of Israel, there is no God like you in heaven above or on earth beneath, keeping covenant and steadfast love for your servants who walk before you with all their heart. But will God indeed dwell on the earth? Even heaven and the highest heaven cannot contain you, much less this house that I have built! Regard your servant's prayer and his plea,

O Lord my God, heeding the cry and the prayer that your servant prays to you today; that your eyes may be open night and day toward this house, the place of which you said, 'My name shall be there,' that you may heed the prayer that your servant prays toward this place. Hear the plea of your servant and of your people Israel when they pray toward this place; O hear in heaven your dwelling place; heed and forgive. Likewise when a foreigner, who is not of your people Israel, comes from a distant land because of your name — for they shall hear of your great name, your mighty hand, and your outstretched arm — when a foreigner comes and prays toward this house, then hear in heaven your dwelling place, and do according to all that the foreigner calls to you, so that all the peoples of the earth may know your name and fear you, as do your people Israel, and so that they may know that your name has been invoked on this house that I have built.

The Psalm 96 or 96:1-9   *Cantate Domino*

1   [Sing to the Lord a new song; *
        sing to the Lord, all the whole earth.

2   Sing to the Lord and bless his Name; *
        proclaim the good news of his salvation from day to day.

3   Declare his glory among the nations *
        and his wonders among all peoples.

4   For great is the Lord and greatly to be praised; *
        he is more to be feared than all gods.

5   As for all the gods of the nations, they are but idols; *
        but it is the Lord who made the heavens.

6   Oh, the majesty and magnificence of his presence! *
        Oh, the power and the splendor of his sanctuary!

7   Ascribe to the Lord, you families of the peoples; *
        ascribe to the Lord honor and power.

8   Ascribe to the Lord the honor due his Name; *
        bring offerings and come into his courts.

9   Worship the Lord in the beauty of holiness; *
        let the whole earth tremble before him.]

10   Tell it out among the nations: "The Lord is King! *
        he has made the world so firm that it cannot be moved;
        he will judge the peoples with equity."

11   Let the heaven rejoice, and let the earth be glad;
        let the sea thunder and all that is in it; *
        let the field be joyful and all that is therein.

12   Then shall all the trees of the wood shout for joy
        before the Lord when he comes, *
        when he comes to judge the earth.

13 He will judge the world with righteousness *
    and the peoples with his truth.

The Epistle   **Galatians 1:1-10**

Paul an apostle — sent neither by human commission nor from human authorities,
but through Jesus Christ and God the Father, who raised him from the dead — and
all the members of God's family who are with me, To the churches of Galatia: Grace
to you and peace from God our Father and the Lord Jesus Christ, who gave himself
for our sins to set us free from the present evil age, according to the will of our God
and Father, to whom be the glory forever and ever. Amen. I am astonished that you
are so quickly deserting the one who called you in the grace of Christ and are turning
to a different gospel — not that there is another gospel, but there are some who are
confusing you and want to pervert the gospel of Christ. But even if we or an angel
from heaven should proclaim to you a gospel contrary to what we proclaimed to you,
let that one be accursed! As we have said before, so now I repeat, if anyone proclaims
to you a gospel contrary to what you received, let that one be accursed! Am I now
seeking human approval, or God's approval? Or am I trying to please people? If I
were still pleasing people, I would not be a servant of Christ.

The Gospel   **Luke 7:1-10**

After Jesus had finished all his sayings in the hearing of the people, he entered
Capernaum. A centurion there had a slave whom he valued highly, and who was ill
and close to death. When he heard about Jesus, he sent some Jewish elders to him,
asking him to come and heal his slave. When they came to Jesus, they appealed to
him earnestly, saying, "He is worthy of having you do this for him, for he loves our
people, and it is he who built our synagogue for us." And Jesus went with them, but
when he was not far from the house, the centurion sent friends to say to him, "Lord,
do not trouble yourself, for I am not worthy to have you come under my roof;
therefore I did not presume to come to you. But only speak the word, and let my
servant be healed. For I also am a man set under authority, with soldiers under me;
and I say to one, 'Go,' and he goes, and to another, 'Come,' and he comes, and to my
slave, 'Do this,' and the slave does it." When Jesus heard this he was amazed at him,
and turning to the crowd that followed him, he said, "I tell you, not even in Israel
have I found such faith." When those who had been sent returned to the house, they
found the slave in good health.

Proper 5 *The Sunday closest to June 8*

The Collect

**O God, from whom all good proceeds: Grant that by your inspiration we may think
those things that are right, and by your merciful guiding may do them; through Jesus
Christ our Lord, who lives and reigns with you and the Holy Spirit, one God, for ever
and ever.** *Amen.*

**O God, from whom all good doth come: Grant that by thy inspiration we may think
those things that are right, and by thy merciful guiding may perform the same; through
Jesus Christ our Lord, who liveth and reigneth with thee and the Holy Spirit, one God,
for ever and ever.** *Amen.*

The Lesson   Hosea 5:15-6:6

I will return again to my place until they acknowledge their guilt and seek my face. In their distress they will beg my favor: "Come, let us return to the LORD; for it is he who has torn, and he will heal us; he has struck down, and he will bind us up. After two days he will revive us; on the third day he will raise us up, that we may live before him. Let us know, let us press on to know the LORD; his appearing is as sure as the dawn; he will come to us like the showers, like the spring rains that water the earth." What shall I do with you, O Ephraim? What shall I do with you, O Judah? Your love is like a morning cloud, like the dew that goes away early. Therefore I have hewn them by the prophets, I have killed them by the words of my mouth, and my judgment goes forth as the light. For I desire steadfast love and not sacrifice, the knowledge of God rather than burnt offerings.

The Psalm 50 or 50:7-15   *Deus deorum*

1   The LORD, the God of gods, has spoken; *
       he has called the earth from the rising of the sun to its setting.

2   Out of Zion, perfect in its beauty, *
       God reveals himself in glory.

3   Our God will come and will not keep silence; *
       before him there is a consuming flame,
       and round about him a raging storm.

4   He calls the heavens and the earth from above *
       to witness the judgment of his people.

5   "Gather before me my loyal followers, *
       those who have made a covenant with me
       and sealed it with sacrifice."

6   Let the heavens declare the rightness of his cause; *
       for God himself is judge.

7   [Hear, O my people, and I will speak:
       "O Israel, I will bear witness against you; *
       for I am God, your God.

8   I do not accuse you because of your sacrifices; *
       your offerings are always before me.

9   I will take no bull-calf from your stalls, *
       nor he-goats out of your pens;

10   For all the beasts of the forest are mine, *
       the herds in their thousands upon the hills.

11   I know every bird in the sky, *
       and the creatures of the fields are in my sight.

12   If I were hungry, I would not tell you, *
       for the whole world is mine and all that is in it.

13   Do you think I eat the flesh of bulls, *
       or drink the blood of goats?

14   Offer to God a sacrifice of thanksgiving *
       and make good your vows to the Most High.

15   Call upon me in the day of trouble; *
       I will deliver you, and you shall honor me."]

16   But to the wicked God says: *
       "Why do you recite my statutes,
       and take my covenant upon your lips;

17   Since you refuse discipline, *
       and toss my words behind your back?

18   When you see a thief, you make him your friend, *
       and you cast in your lot with adulterers.

19   You have loosed your lips for evil, *
       and harnessed your tongue to a lie.

20   You are always speaking evil of your brother *
       and slandering your own mother's son.

21   These things you have done, and I kept still, *
       and you thought that I am like you."

22   "I have made my accusation; *
       I have put my case in order before your eyes.

23   Consider this well, you who forget God, *
       lest I rend you and there be none to deliver you.

24   Whoever offers me the sacrifice of thanksgiving honors me; *
       but to those who keep in my way will I show the salvation of God."

The Epistle   **Romans 4:13-18**

For the promise that he would inherit the world did not come to Abraham or to his descendants through the law but through the righteousness of faith. If it is the adherents of the law who are to be the heirs, faith is null and the promise is void. For the law brings wrath; but where there is no law, neither is there violation. For this reason it depends on faith, in order that the promise may rest on grace and be guaranteed to all his descendants, not only to the adherents of the law but also to those who share the faith of Abraham (for he is the father of all of us, as it is written, "I have made you the father of many nations") — in the presence of the God in whom he believed, who gives life to the dead and calls into existence the things that do not exist. Hoping against hope, he believed that he would become "the father of many nations," according to what was said, "So numerous shall your descendants be."

The Gospel

Matthew 9:9-13

Jesus saw a man called Matthew sitting at the tax booth; and he said to him, "Follow me." And he got up and followed him. And as he sat at dinner in the house, many tax collectors and sinners came and were sitting with him and his disciples. When the Pharisees saw this, they said to his disciples, "Why does your teacher eat with tax collectors and sinners?" But when he heard this, he said, "Those who are well have no need of a physician, but those who are sick. Go and learn what this means,'I desire mercy, not sacrifice.' For I have come to call not the righteous but sinners."

Year B

The Lesson

Genesis 3:(1-7) 8-21

[Now the serpent was more crafty than any other wild animal that the LORD God had made. He said to the woman, "Did God say, 'You shall not eat from any tree in the garden'?" The woman said to the serpent, "We may eat of the fruit of the trees in the garden; but God said, 'You shall not eat of the fruit of the tree that is in the middle of the garden, nor shall you touch it, or you shall die.'" But the serpent said to the woman, "You will not die; for God knows that when you eat of it your eyes will be opened, and you will be like God, knowing good and evil." So when the woman saw that the tree was good for food, and that it was a delight to the eyes, and that the tree was to be desired to make one wise, she took of its fruit and ate; and she also gave some to her husband, who was with her, and he ate. Then the eyes of both were opened, and they knew that they were naked; and they sewed fig leaves together and made loincloths for themselves.] They heard the sound of the LORD God walking in the garden at the time of the evening breeze, and the man and his wife hid themselves from the presence of the LORD God among the trees of the garden. But the LORD God called to the man, and said to him, "Where are you?" He said, "I heard the sound of you in the garden, and I was afraid, because I was naked; and I hid myself." He said, "Who told you that you were naked? Have you eaten from the tree of which I commanded you not to eat?" The man said, "The woman whom you gave to be with me, she gave me fruit from the tree, and I ate." Then the LORD God said to the woman, "What is this that you have done?" The woman said, "The serpent tricked me, and I ate." The LORD God said to the serpent, "Because you have done this, cursed are you among all animals and among all wild creatures; upon your belly you shall go, and dust you shall eat all the days of your life. I will put enmity between you and the woman, and between your offspring and hers; he will strike your head, and you will strike his heel." To the woman he said, "I will greatly increase your pangs in childbearing; in pain you shall bring forth children, yet your desire shall be for your husband, and he shall rule over you." And to the man he said, "Because you have listened to the voice of your wife, and have eaten of the tree about which I commanded you, 'You shall not eat of it,' cursed is the ground because of you; in toil you shall eat of it all the days of your life; thorns and thistles it shall bring forth for you; and you shall eat the plants of the field. By the sweat of your face you shall eat bread until you return to the ground, for out of it you were taken; you are dust, and to dust you shall return." The man named his wife Eve, because she was the mother of all living. And the LORD God made garments of skins for the man and for his wife, and clothed them.

The Psalm 130   *De profundis*

1   Out of the depths have I called to you, O LORD;
     LORD, hear my voice; *
        let your ears consider well the voice of my supplication.

2   If you, LORD, were to note what is done amiss, *
        O Lord, who could stand?

3   For there is forgiveness with you; *
        therefore you shall be feared.

4   I wait for the LORD; my soul waits for him; *
        in his word is my hope.

5   My soul waits for the LORD,
     more than watchmen for the morning, *
        more than watchmen for the morning.

6   O Israel, wait for the LORD, *
        for with the LORD there is mercy;

7   With him there is plenteous redemption, *
        and he shall redeem Israel from all their sins.

The Epistle   **2 Corinthians 4:13-18**
Just as we have the same spirit of faith that is in accordance with scripture — "I believed, and so I spoke" — we also believe, and so we speak, because we know that the one who raised the Lord Jesus will raise us also with Jesus, and will bring us with you into his presence. Yes, everything is for your sake, so that grace, as it extends to more and more people, may increase thanksgiving, to the glory of God. So we do not lose heart. Even though our outer nature is wasting away, our inner nature is being renewed day by day. For this slight momentary affliction is preparing us for an eternal weight of glory beyond all measure, because we look not at what can be seen but at what cannot be seen; for what can be seen is temporary, but what cannot be seen is eternal.

The Gospel   **Mark 3:20-35**
The crowd came together again, so that Jesus and his disciples could not even eat. When his family heard it, they went out to restrain him, for people were saying, "He has gone out of his mind." And the scribes who came down from Jerusalem said, "He has Beelzebul, and by the ruler of the demons he casts out demons." And he called them to him, and spoke to them in parables, "How can Satan cast out Satan? If a kingdom is divided against itself, that kingdom cannot stand. And if a house is divided against itself, that house will not be able to stand. And if Satan has risen up against himself and is divided, he cannot stand, but his end has come. But no one can enter a strong man's house and plunder his property without first tying up the strong man; then indeed the house can be plundered. Truly I tell you, people will be

forgiven for their sins and whatever blasphemies they utter; but whoever blasphemes against the Holy Spirit can never have forgiveness, but is guilty of an eternal sin" — for they had said, "He has an unclean spirit." Then his mother and his brothers came; and standing outside, they sent to him and called him. A crowd was sitting around him; and they said to him, "Your mother and your brothers and sisters are outside, asking for you." And he replied, "Who are my mother and my brothers?" And looking at those who sat around him, he said, "Here are my mother and my brothers! Whoever does the will of God is my brother and sister and mother."

Year C

The Lesson   **1 Kings 17:17-24**

After this the son of the woman, the mistress of the house, became ill; his illness was so severe that there was no breath left in him. She then said to Elijah, "What have you against me, O man of God? You have come to me to bring my sin to remembrance, and to cause the death of my son!" But he said to her, "Give me your son." He took him from her bosom, carried him up into the upper chamber where he was lodging, and laid him on his own bed. He cried out to the LORD, "O LORD my God, have you brought calamity even upon the widow with whom I am staying, by killing her son?" Then he stretched himself upon the child three times, and cried out to the LORD, "O LORD my God, let this child's life come into him again." The LORD listened to the voice of Elijah; the life of the child came into him again, and he revived. Elijah took the child, brought him down from the upper chamber into the house, and gave him to his mother; then Elijah said, "See, your son is alive." So the woman said to Elijah, "Now I know that you are a man of God, and that the word of the LORD in your mouth is truth."

The Psalm 30 or 30:1-6, 12-13   *Exaltabo te, Domine*

1   [I will exalt you, O LORD,
    because you have lifted me up *
        and have not let my enemies triumph over me.

2   O LORD my God, I cried out to you, *
        and you restored me to health.

3   You brought me up, O LORD, from the dead; *
        you restored my life as I was going down to the grave.

4   Sing to the LORD, you servants of his; *
        give thanks for the remembrance of his holiness.

5   For his wrath endures but the twinkling of an eye, *
        his favor for a lifetime.

6   Weeping may spend the night, *
        but joy comes in the morning.]

7   While I felt secure, I said,
    "I shall never be disturbed. *
        You, LORD, with your favor, made me as strong as the mountains."

8   Then you hid your face, *
         and I was filled with fear.

9   I cried to you, O LORD; *
         I pleaded with the Lord, saying,

10   "What profit is there in my blood, if I go down to the Pit? *
         will the dust praise you or declare your faithfulness?

11   Hear, O LORD, and have mercy upon me; *
         O LORD, be my helper."

12   [You have turned my wailing into dancing; *
         you have put off my sack-cloth and clothed me with joy.

13   Therefore my heart sings to you without ceasing; *
         O LORD my God, I will give you thanks for ever.]

The Epistle   **Galatians 1:11-24**

For I want you to know, brothers and sisters, that the gospel that was proclaimed by me is not of human origin; for I did not receive it from a human source, nor was I taught it, but I received it through a revelation of Jesus Christ. You have heard, no doubt, of my earlier life in Judaism. I was violently persecuting the church of God and was trying to destroy it. I advanced in Judaism beyond many among my people of the same age, for I was far more zealous for the traditions of my ancestors. But when God, who had set me apart before I was born and called me through his grace, was pleased to reveal his Son to me, so that I might proclaim him among the Gentiles, I did not confer with any human being, nor did I go up to Jerusalem to those who were already apostles before me, but I went away at once into Arabia, and afterwards I returned to Damascus. Then after three years I did go up to Jerusalem to visit Cephas and stayed with him fifteen days; but I did not see any other apostle except James the Lord's brother. In what I am writing to you, before God, I do not lie! Then I went into the regions of Syria and Cilicia, and I was still unknown by sight to the churches of Judea that are in Christ; they only heard it said, "The one who formerly was persecuting us is now proclaiming the faith he once tried to destroy." And they glorified God because of me.

The Gospel   **Luke 7:11-17**

Soon after healing the centurion's slave, Jesus went to a town called Nain, and his disciples and a large crowd went with him. As he approached the gate of the town, a man who had died was being carried out. He was his mother's only son, and she was a widow; and with her was a large crowd from the town. When the Lord saw her, he had compassion for her and said to her, "Do not weep." Then he came forward and touched the bier, and the bearers stood still. And he said, "Young man, I say to you, rise!" The dead man sat up and began to speak, and Jesus gave him to his mother. Fear seized all of them; and they glorified God, saying, "A great prophet has risen among us!" and "God has looked favorably on his people!" This word about him spread throughout Judea and all the surrounding country.

Proper 6 *The Sunday closest to June 15*

The Collect

Keep, O Lord, your household the Church in your steadfast faith and love, that through your grace we may proclaim your truth with boldness, and minister your justice with compassion; for the sake of our Savior Jesus Christ, who lives and reigns with you and the Holy Spirit, one God, now and for ever. *Amen.*

Keep, O Lord, we beseech thee, thy household the Church in thy steadfast faith and love, that by the help of thy grace we may proclaim thy truth with boldness, and minister thy justice with compassion; for the sake of our Savior Jesus Christ, who liveth and reigneth with thee and the Holy Spirit, one God, now and for ever. *Amen.*

Year A

The Lesson

Exodus 19:2-8a

The people of Israel had journeyed from Rephidim, entered the wilderness of Sinai, and camped in the wilderness; Israel camped there in front of the mountain. Then Moses went up to God; the LORD called to him from the mountain, saying, "Thus you shall say to the house of Jacob, and tell the Israelites: You have seen what I did to the Egyptians, and how I bore you on eagles' wings and brought you to myself. Now therefore, if you obey my voice and keep my covenant, you shall be my treasured possession out of all the peoples. Indeed, the whole earth is mine, but you shall be for me a priestly kingdom and a holy nation. These are the words that you shall speak to the Israelites." So Moses came, summoned the elders of the people, and set before them all these words that the LORD had commanded him. The people all answered as one: "Everything that the LORD has spoken we will do."

The Psalm 100   *Jubilate Deo*

1   Be joyful in the LORD, all you lands; *
        serve the LORD with gladness
        and come before his presence with a song.

2   Know this: The LORD himself is God; *
        he himself has made us, and we are his;
        we are his people and the sheep of his pasture.

3   Enter his gates with thanksgiving;
    go into his courts with praise; *
        give thanks to him and call upon his Name.

4   For the LORD is good;
    his mercy is everlasting; *
        and his faithfulness endures from age to age.

The Epistle

Romans 5:6-11

For while we were still weak, at the right time Christ died for the ungodly. Indeed, rarely will anyone die for a righteous person — though perhaps for a good person someone might actually dare to die. But God proves his love for us in that while we still were sinners Christ died for us. Much more surely then, now that we have been justified by his blood, will we be saved through him from the wrath of God. For if while we were enemies, we were reconciled to God through the death of his Son, much more surely, having been reconciled, will we be saved by his life. But more than that, we even boast in God through our Lord Jesus Christ, through whom we have now received reconciliation.

The Gospel   Matthew 9:35-10:8 (9-15)

Jesus went about all the cities and villages, teaching in their synagogues, and proclaiming the good news of the kingdom, and curing every disease and every sickness. When he saw the crowds, he had compassion for them, because they were harassed and helpless, like sheep without a shepherd. Then he said to his disciples, "The harvest is plentiful, but the laborers are few; therefore ask the Lord of the harvest to send out laborers into his harvest." Then Jesus summoned his twelve disciples and gave them authority over unclean spirits, to cast them out, and to cure every disease and every sickness. These are the names of the twelve apostles: first, Simon, also known as Peter, and his brother Andrew; James son of Zebedee, and his brother John; Philip and Bartholomew; Thomas and Matthew the tax collector; James son of Alphaeus, and Thaddaeus; Simon the Cananaean, and Judas Iscariot, the one who betrayed him. These twelve Jesus sent out with the following instructions: "Go nowhere among the Gentiles, and enter no town of the Samaritans, but go rather to the lost sheep of the house of Israel. As you go, proclaim the good news, 'The kingdom of heaven has come near.' Cure the sick, raise the dead, cleanse the lepers, cast out demons. You received without payment; give without payment. [Take no gold, or silver, or copper in your belts, no bag for your journey, or two tunics, or sandals, or a staff; for laborers deserve their food. Whatever town or village you enter, find out who in it is worthy, and stay there until you leave. As you enter the house, greet it. If the house is worthy, let your peace come upon it; but if it is not worthy, let your peace return to you. If anyone will not welcome you or listen to your words, shake off the dust from your feet as you leave that house or town. Truly I tell you, it will be more tolerable for the land of Sodom and Gomorrah on the day of judgment than for that town."]

Year B

The Lesson   Ezekiel 31:1-6, 10-14

In the eleventh year, in the third month, on the first day of the month, the word of the LORD came to me: Mortal, say to Pharaoh king of Egypt and to his hordes: Whom are you like in your greatness? Consider Assyria, a cedar of Lebanon, with fair branches and forest shade, and of great height, its top among the clouds. The waters nourished it, the deep made it grow tall, making its rivers flow around the place it was planted, sending forth its streams to all the trees of the field. So it towered high above all the trees of the field; its boughs grew large and its branches long, from abundant water in its shoots. All the birds of the air made their nests in its boughs; under its branches all the animals of the field gave birth to their young; and in its shade all great nations lived. Therefore thus says the Lord GOD: Because it towered high and set its top among the clouds, and its heart was proud of its height, I gave it into the hand of the prince of the nations; he has dealt with it as its wickedness deserves. I have cast it out. Foreigners from the most terrible of the nations have cut it down and left it. On the mountains and in all the valleys its branches have fallen, and its boughs lie broken in all the watercourses of the land; and all the peoples of the earth went away from its shade and left it. On its fallen trunk settle all the birds of the air, and among its boughs lodge all the wild animals. All this is in order that no trees by the waters may grow to lofty height or set their tops among the clouds, and that no trees that drink water may reach up to them in height. For all of them are handed over to death, to the world below; along with all mortals, with those who go down to the Pit.

The Psalm 92 or 92:1-4, 11-14   *Bonum est confiteri*

1   [It is a good thing to give thanks to the LORD, *
        and to sing praises to your Name, O Most High;

2   To tell of your loving-kindness early in the morning *
        and of your faithfulness in the night season;

3   On the psaltery, and on the lyre, *
        and to the melody of the harp.

4   For you have made me glad by your acts, O LORD; *
        and I shout for joy because of the works of your hands.]

5   LORD, how great are your works! *
        your thoughts are very deep.

6   The dullard does not know,
    nor does the fool understand, *
        that though the wicked grow like weeds,
        and all the workers of iniquity flourish.

7   They flourish only to be destroyed for ever; *
        but you, O LORD, are exalted for evermore.

8   For lo, your enemies, O LORD,
    lo, your enemies shall perish, *
        and all the workers of iniquity shall be scattered.

9   But my horn you have exalted like the horns of wild bulls; *
        I am anointed with fresh oil.

10   My eyes also gloat over my enemies, *
        and my ears rejoice to hear the doom of the wicked who rise up against me.

11   [The righteous shall flourish like a palm tree, *
        and shall spread abroad like a cedar of Lebanon.

12   Those who are planted in the house of the LORD *
        shall flourish in the courts of our God;

13   They shall still bear fruit in old age; *
        they shall be green and succulent;

14   That they may show how upright the LORD is, *
        my Rock, in whom there is no fault.]

The Epistle   **2 Corinthians 5:1-10**

For we know that if the earthly tent we live in is destroyed, we have a building from God, a house not made with hands, eternal in the heavens. For in this tent we groan, longing to be clothed with our heavenly dwelling — if indeed, when we have taken it off we will not be found naked. For while we are still in this tent, we groan under our burden, because we wish not to be unclothed but to be further clothed, so that what is mortal may be swallowed up by life. He who has prepared us for this very thing is God, who has given us the Spirit as a guarantee. So we are always confident; even though we know that while we are at home in the body we are away from the Lord — for we walk by faith, not by sight. Yes, we do have confidence, and we would rather be away from the body and at home with the Lord. So whether we are at home or away, we make it our aim to please him. For all of us must appear before the judgment seat of Christ, so that each may receive recompense for what has been done in the body, whether good or evil.

The Gospel   **Mark 4:26-34**

Jesus said, "The kingdom of God is as if someone would scatter seed on the ground, and would sleep and rise night and day, and the seed would sprout and grow, he does not know how. The earth produces of itself, first the stalk, then the head, then the full grain in the head. But when the grain is ripe, at once he goes in with his sickle, because the harvest has come." He also said, "With what can we compare the kingdom of God, or what parable will we use for it? It is like a mustard seed, which, when sown upon the ground, is the smallest of all the seeds on earth; yet when it is sown it grows up and becomes the greatest of all shrubs, and puts forth large branches, so that the birds of the air can make nests in its shade." With many such parables he spoke the word to them, as they were able to hear it; he did not speak to them except in parables, but he explained everything in private to his disciples.

Year C

The Lesson   **2 Samuel 11:26-12:10, 13-15**

When the wife of Uriah heard that her husband was dead, she made lamentation for him. When the mourning was over, David sent and brought her to his house, and she became his wife, and bore him a son. But the thing that David had done displeased the LORD, and the LORD sent Nathan to David. He came to him, and said to him, "There were two men in a certain city, the one rich and the other poor. The rich man had very many flocks and herds; but the poor man had nothing but one little ewe lamb, which he had bought. He brought it up, and it grew up with him and with his children; it used to eat of his meager fare, and drink from his cup, and lie in his bosom, and it was like a daughter to him. Now there came a traveler to the rich man, and he was loath to take one of his own flock or herd to prepare for the wayfarer who had come to him, but he took the poor man's lamb, and prepared that for the guest who had come to him." Then David's anger was greatly kindled against the man. He said to Nathan, "As the LORD lives, the man who has done this deserves to die; he shall restore the lamb fourfold, because he did this thing, and because he had not pity." Nathan said to David, "You are the man! Thus says the LORD, the God of Israel: I anointed you king over Israel, and I rescued you from the hand of Saul; I gave you your master's house, and your master's wives into your bosom, and gave you the house of Israel and of Judah; and if that had been too little, I would have added as much more. Why have you despised the word of the LORD, to do what is evil in his sight? You have struck down Uriah the Hittite with the sword, and have taken his wife to be your wife, and have killed him with the sword of the Ammonites. Now therefore the sword shall never depart from your house, for you have despised me, and have taken the wife of Uriah the Hittite to be your wife. David said to Nathan, "I have sinned against the LORD." Nathan said to David, "Now the LORD has put away your sin; you shall not die. Nevertheless, because by this deed you have utterly scorned the LORD, the child that is born to you shall die." Then Nathan went to his house. The Lord struck the child that Uriah's wife bore to David and it became very ill.

The Psalm 32 or 32:1-8   *Beati quorum*

1   [Happy are they whose transgressions are forgiven, *
        and whose sin is put away!

2   Happy are they to whom the LORD imputes no guilt, *
        and in whose spirit there is no guile!

3   While I held my tongue, my bones withered away, *
        because of my groaning all day long.

4   For your hand was heavy upon me day and night; *
        my moisture was dried up as in the heat of summer.

5   Then I acknowledged my sin to you, *
        and did not conceal my guilt.

6   I said, "I will confess my transgressions to the LORD." *
        Then you forgave me the guilt of my sin.

7   Therefore all the faithful will make their prayers to you in time of trouble; *
        when the great waters overflow, they shall not reach them.

8   You are my hiding-place;
    you preserve me from trouble; *
        you surround me with shouts of deliverance.]

9   "I will instruct you and teach you in the way that you should go; *
        I will guide you with my eye.

10 Do not be like horse or mule, which have no understanding; *
        who must be fitted with bit and bridle,
        or else they will not stay near you.

11 Great are the tribulations of the wicked; *
        but mercy embraces those who trust in the LORD.

12 Be glad, you righteous, and rejoice in the LORD; *
    shout for joy, all who are true of heart.

The Epistle   **Galatians 2:11-21**

When Cephas came to Antioch, I opposed him to his face, because he stood self-condemned; for until certain people came from James, he used to eat with the Gentiles. But after they came, he drew back and kept himself separate for fear of the circumcision faction. And the other Jews joined him in this hypocrisy, so that even Barnabas was led astray by their hypocrisy. But when I saw that they were not acting consistently with the truth of the gospel, I said to Cephas before them all, "If you, though a Jew, live like a Gentile and not like a Jew, how can you compel the Gentiles to live like Jews?" We ourselves are Jews by birth and not Gentile sinners; yet we know that a person is justified not by the works of the law but through faith in Jesus Christ. And we have come to believe in Christ Jesus, so that we might be justified by faith in Christ, and not by doing the works of the law, because no one will be justified by the works of the law. But if, in our effort to be justified in Christ, we ourselves have been found to be sinners, is Christ then a servant of sin? Certainly not! But if I build up again the very things that I once tore down, then I demonstrate that I am a transgressor. For through the law I died to the law, so that I might live to God. I have been crucified with Christ; and it is no longer I who live, but it is Christ who lives in me. And the life I now live in the flesh I live by faith in the Son of God, who loved me and gave himself for me. I do not nullify the grace of God; for if justification comes through the law, then Christ died for nothing.

The Gospel   **Luke 7:36-50**

One of the Pharisees asked Jesus to eat with him, and he went into the Pharisee's house and took his place at the table. And a woman in the city, who was a sinner, having learned that he was eating in the Pharisee's house, brought an alabaster jar of ointment. She stood behind him at his feet, weeping, and began to bathe his feet with her tears and to dry them with her hair. Then she continued kissing his feet and anointing them with the ointment. Now when the Pharisee who had invited him saw it, he said to himself, "If this man were a prophet, he would have known who and what kind of woman this is who is touching him — that she is a sinner." Jesus spoke up and said to him, "Simon, I have something to say to you." "Teacher," he replied, "Speak." "A certain creditor had two debtors; one owed five hundred denarii, and the other fifty. When they could not pay, he canceled the debts for both of them. Now which of them will love him more?" Simon answered, "I suppose the one for whom he canceled the greater debt." And Jesus said to him, "You have judged rightly." Then turning toward the woman, he said to Simon, "Do you see this woman? I entered your house; you gave me no water for my feet, but she has bathed my feet with her tears and dried them with her hair. You gave me no kiss, but from the time I came in she has not stopped kissing my feet. You did not anoint my head with oil, but she has anointed my feet with ointment. Therefore, I tell you, her sins, which were many, have been forgiven; hence she has shown great love. But the one to whom little is forgiven, loves little." Then he said to her, "Your sins are forgiven." But those who were at the table with him began to say among themselves, "Who is this who even forgives sins?" And he said to the woman, "Your faith has saved you; go in peace."

Proper 7 *The Sunday closest to June 22*

The Collect

O Lord, make us have perpetual love and reverence for your holy Name, for you never fail to help and govern those whom you have set upon the sure foundation of your loving-kindness; through Jesus Christ our Lord, who lives and reigns with you and the Holy Spirit, one God, for ever and ever. *Amen.*

O Lord, we beseech thee, make us to have a perpetual fear and love of thy holy Name, for thou never failest to help and govern those whom thou has set upon the sure foundation of thy loving-kindness; through Jesus Christ our Lord, who liveth and reigneth with thee and the Holy Spirit, one God, for ever and ever. *Amen.*

Year A

The Lesson   Jeremiah 20:7-13

O LORD, you have enticed me, and I was enticed; you have overpowered me, and you have prevailed. I have become a laughingstock all day long; everyone mocks me. For whenever I speak, I must cry out, I must shout, "Violence and destruction!" For the word of the LORD has become for me a reproach and derision all day long. If I say, "I will not mention him, or speak any more in his name," then within me there is something like a burning fire shut up in my bones; I am weary with holding it in, and I cannot. For I hear many whispering: "Terror is all around! Denounce him! Let us denounce him!" All my close friends are watching for me to stumble. "Perhaps he can be enticed, and we can prevail against him, and take our revenge on him." But the LORD is with me like a dread warrior; therefore my persecutors will stumble, and they will not prevail. They will be greatly shamed, for they will not succeed. Their eternal dishonor will never be forgotten. O LORD of hosts, you test the righteous, you see the heart and the mind; let me see your retribution upon them, for to you I have committed my cause. Sing to the LORD; praise the LORD! For he has delivered the life of the needy from the hands of evildoers.

The Psalm 69:1-18 or 69:7-10, 16-18   *Salvum me fac*

1   Save me, O God, *
        for the waters have risen up to my neck.

2   I am sinking in deep mire, *
        and there is no firm ground for my feet.

3   I have come into deep waters, *
        and the torrent washes over me.

4   I have grown weary with my crying;
    my throat is inflamed; *
        my eyes have failed from looking for my God.

5   Those who hate me without a cause are more than the hairs of my head;
my lying foes who would destroy me are mighty. *
    Must I then give back what I never stole?

6   O God, you know my foolishness, *
and my faults are not hidden from you.

7   [Let not those who hope in you be put to shame through me, Lord GOD of hosts; *
    let not those who seek you be disgraced because of me, O God of Israel.

8   Surely, for your sake have I suffered reproach, *
and shame has covered my face.

9   I have become a stranger to my own kindred, *
an alien to my mother's children.

10   Zeal for your house has eaten me up; *
the scorn of those who scorn you has fallen upon me.]

11   I humbled myself with fasting, *
but that was turned to my reproach.

12   I put on sack-cloth also, *
and became a byword among them.

13   Those who sit at the gate murmur against me, *
and the drunkards make songs about me.

14   But as for me, this is my prayer to you, *
at the time you have set, O LORD:

15   "In your great mercy, O God, *
answer me with your unfailing help.

16   [Save me from the mire; do not let me sink; *
let me be rescued from those who hate me
and out of the deep waters.

17   Let not the torrent of waters wash over me,
neither let the deep swallow me up; *
do not let the Pit shut its mouth upon me.

18   Answer me, O LORD, for you love is kind; *
in your great compassion, turn to me."]

The Epistle   Romans 5:15b-19

If the many died through the one man's trespass, much more surely have the grace of God and the free gift in the grace of the one man, Jesus Christ, abounded for the many. And the free gift is not like the effect of the one man's sin. For the judgment following one trespass brought condemnation, but the free gift following many trespasses brings justification. If, because of the one man's trespass, death exercised dominion through that one, much more surely will those who receive the abundance of grace and the free gift of righteousness exercise dominion in life through the one man, Jesus Christ. Therefore just as one man's trespass led to condemnation for all, so one man's act of righteousness leads to justification and life for all. For just as by the one man's disobedience the many were made sinners, so by the one man's obedience the many will be made righteous.

The Gospel   **Matthew 10:(16-23) 24-33**

[Jesus sent out his twelve disciples, saying to them, "See, I am sending you out like sheep into the midst of wolves; so be wise as serpents and innocent as doves. Beware of them, for they will hand you over to councils and flog you in their synagogues; and you will be dragged before governors and kings because of me, as a testimony to them and the Gentiles. When they hand you over, do not worry about how you are to speak or what you are to say; for what you are to say will be given to you at that time; for it is not you who speak, but the Spirit of your Father speaking through you. Brother will betray brother to death, and a father his child and children will rise against parents and have them put to death; and you will be hated by all because of my name. But the one who endures to the end will be saved. When they persecute you in one town, flee to the next; for truly I tell you, you will not have gone through all the towns of Israel before the Son of Man comes.] A disciple is not above the teacher, nor a slave above the master; it is enough for the disciple to be like the teacher, and the slave like the master. If they have called the master of the house Beelzebul, how much more will they malign those of his household! So have no fear of them; for nothing is covered up that will not be uncovered, and nothing secret that will not become known. What I say to you in the dark, tell in the light; and what you hear whispered, proclaim from the housetops. Do not fear those who kill the body but cannot kill the soul; rather fear him who can destroy both soul and body in hell. Are not two sparrows sold for a penny? Yet not one of them will fall to the ground apart from your Father. And even the hairs of your head are all counted. So do not be afraid; you are of more value than many sparrows. Everyone therefore who acknowledges me before others, I also will acknowledge before my Father in heaven; but whoever denies me before others, I also will deny before my Father in heaven."

Year B

The Lesson   **Job 38:1-11, 16-18**

Then the LORD answered Job out of the whirlwind: "Who is this that darkens counsel by words without knowledge? Gird up your loins like a man, I will question you, and you shall declare to me. "Where were you when I laid the foundation of the earth? Tell me, if you have understanding. Who determined its measurements — surely you know! Or who stretched the line upon it? On what were its bases sunk, or who laid its cornerstone when the morning stars sang together and all the heavenly beings shouted for joy? Or who shut in the sea with doors when it burst out from the womb? — when I made the clouds its garment, and thick darkness its swaddling band, and prescribed bounds for it, and set bars and doors, and said, 'Thus far shall you come, and no farther, and here shall your proud waves be stopped"? Have you entered into the springs of the sea, or walked in the recesses of the deep? Have the gates of death been revealed to you, or have you seen the gates of deep darkness? Have you comprehended the expanse of the earth? Declare, if you know all this."

The Psalm 107:1-32 or 107:1-3, 23-32   *Confitemini Domino*

1   [Give thanks to the LORD, for he is good, *
          and his mercy endures for ever.

2   Let all those whom the LORD has redeemed proclaim *
          that he redeemed them from the hand of the foe.

3   He gathered them out of the lands; *
          from the east and from the west,
          from the north and from the south.]

4   Some wandered in desert wastes; *
          they found no way to a city where they might dwell.

5   They were hungry and thirsty; *
          their spirits languished within them.

6   Then they cried to the LORD in their trouble, *
          and he delivered them from their distress.

7   He put their feet on a straight path *
          to go to a city where they might dwell.

8   Let them give thanks to the LORD for his mercy *
          and the wonders he does for his children.

9   For he satisfies the thirsty *
          and fills the hungry with good things.

10   Some sat in darkness and deep gloom, *
          bound fast in misery and iron;

11   Because they rebelled against the words of God *
          and despised the counsel of the Most High.

12   So he humbled their spirits with hard labor; *
          they stumbled, and there was none to help.

13   Then they cried to the LORD in their trouble, *
          and he delivered them from their distress.

14   He led them out of darkness and deep gloom *
          and broke their bonds asunder.

15   Let them give thanks to the LORD for his mercy *
          and the wonders he does for his children.

16   For he shatters the doors of bronze *
          and breaks in two the iron bars.

17   Some were fools and took to rebellious ways; *
          they were afflicted because of their sins.

18   They abhorred all manner of food *
       and drew near to death's door.

19   Then they cried to the LORD in their trouble, *
       and he delivered them from their distress.

20   He sent forth his word and healed them *
       and saved them from the grave.

21   Let them give thanks to the LORD for his mercy *
       and the wonders he does for his children.

22   Let them offer a sacrifice of thanksgiving *
       and tell of his acts with shouts of joy.

23   [Some went down to the sea in ships *
       and plied their trade in deep waters;

24   They beheld the works of the LORD *
       and his wonders in the deep.

25   Then he spoke, and a stormy wind arose, *
       which tossed high the waves of the sea.

26   They mounted up to the heavens and fell back to the depths; *
       their hearts melted because of their peril.

27   They reeled and staggered like drunkards *
       and were at their wits' end.

28   Then they cried to the LORD in their trouble, *
       and he delivered them from their distress.

29   He stilled the storm to a whisper *
       and quieted the waves of the sea.

30   Then were they glad because of the calm, *
       and he brought them to the harbor they were bound for.

31   Let them give thanks to the LORD for his mercy *
       and the wonders he does for his children.

32   Let them exalt him in the congregation of the people *
       and praise him in the council of the elders.]

The Epistle   **2 Corinthians 5:14-21**

For the love of Christ urges us on, because we are convinced that one has died for all; therefore all have died. And he died for all, so that those who live might live no longer for themselves, but for him who died and was raised for them. From now on, therefore, we regard no one from a human point of view; even though we once knew Christ from a human point of view, we know him no longer in that way. So if anyone is in Christ, there is a new creation: everything old has passed away; see, everything has become new! All this is from God, who reconciled us to himself through Christ, and has given us the ministry of reconciliation; that is, in Christ God was reconciling the world to himself, not counting their trespasses against them, and entrusting the message of reconciliation to us. So we are ambassadors for Christ, since God is making his appeal through us; we entreat you on behalf of Christ, be reconciled to God. For our sake he made him to be sin who knew no sin, so that in him we might become the righteousness of God.

The Gospel   Mark 4:35-41 (5:1-20)
When evening had come, Jesus said to his disciples, "Let us go across to the other side." And leaving the crowd behind, they took him with them in the boat, just as he was. Other boats were with him. A great windstorm arose, and the waves beat into the boat, so that the boat was already being swamped. But he was in the stern, asleep on the cushion; and they woke him up and said to him, "Teacher, do you not care that we are perishing?" He woke up and rebuked the wind, and said to the sea, "Peace! Be still!" Then the wind ceased, and there was a dead calm. He said to them, "Why are you afraid? Have you still no faith?" And they were filled with great awe and said to one another, "Who then is this, that even the wind and the sea obey him?" [They came to the other side of the sea, to the country of the Gerasenes. And when he had stepped out of the boat, immediately a man out of the tombs with an unclean spirit met him. He lived among the tombs; and no one could restrain him any more, even with a chain; for he had often been restrained with shackles and chains, but the chains he wrenched apart, and the shackles he broke in pieces; and no one had the strength to subdue him. Night and day among the tombs and on the mountains he was always howling and bruising himself with stones. When he saw Jesus from a distance, he ran and bowed down before him; and he shouted at the top of his voice, "What have you to do with me, Jesus, Son of the Most High God? I adjure you by God, do not torment me." For he had said to him, "Come out of the man, you unclean spirit!" Then Jesus asked him, "What is your name?" He replied, "My name is Legion; for we are many." He begged him earnestly not to send them out of the country. Now there on the hillside a great herd of swine was feeding; and the unclean spirits begged him, "Send us into the swine; let us enter them." So he gave them permission. And the unclean spirits came out and entered the swine; and the herd, numbering about two thousand, rushed down the steep bank into the sea, and were drowned in the sea. The swineherds ran off and told it in the city and in the country. Then people came to see what it was that had happened. They came to Jesus and saw the demoniac sitting there, clothed and in his right mind, the very man who had had the legion; and they were afraid. Those who had seen what had happened to the demoniac and to the swine reported it. Then they began to beg Jesus to leave their neighborhood. As he was getting into the boat, the man who had been possessed by demons begged him that he might be with him. But Jesus refused, and said to him, "Go home to your friends, and tell them how much the Lord has done for you, and what mercy he has shown you." And he went away and began to proclaim in the Decapolis how much Jesus had done for him; and everyone was amazed.]

Year C

The Lesson   Zechariah 12:8-10; 13:1
Thus says the Lord, "On that day the Lord will shield the inhabitants of Jerusalem

so that the feeblest among them on that day shall be like David, and the house of David shall be like God, like the angel of the LORD, at their head. And on that day I will seek to destroy all the nations that come against Jerusalem. And I will pour out a spirit of compassion and supplication on the house of David and the inhabitants of Jerusalem, so that, when they look on the one whom they have pierced, they shall mourn for him, as one mourns for an only child, and weep bitterly over him, as one weeps over a firstborn. On that day a fountain shall be opened for the house of David and the inhabitants of Jerusalem, to cleanse them from sin and impurity."

The Psalm 63:1-8   *Deus, Deus meus*

1   O God, you are my God; eagerly I seek you; *
     my soul thirsts for you, my flesh faints for you,
     as in a barren and dry land where there is no water.

2   Therefore I have gazed upon you in your holy place, *
     that I might behold your power and your glory.

3   For your loving-kindness is better than life itself; *
     my lips shall give you praise.

4   So will I bless you as long as I live *
     and lift up my hands in your Name.

5   My soul is content, as with marrow and fatness, *
     and my mouth praises you with joyful lips,

6   When I remember you upon my bed, *
     and meditate on you in the night watches.

7   For you have been my helper, *
     and under the shadow of your wings I will rejoice.

8   My soul clings to you; *
     your right hand holds me fast.

The Epistle   Galatians 3:23-29

Now before faith came, we were imprisoned and guarded under the law until faith would be revealed. Therefore the law was our disciplinarian until Christ came, so that we might be justified by faith. But now that faith has come, we are no longer subject to a disciplinarian, for in Christ Jesus you are all children of God through faith. As many of you as were baptized into Christ have clothed yourselves with Christ. There is no longer Jew or Greek, there is no longer slave or free, there is no longer male and female; for all of you are one in Christ Jesus. And if you belong to Christ, then you are Abraham's offspring, heirs according to the promise.

The Gospel   Luke 9:18-24

Once when Jesus was praying alone, with only the disciples near him, he asked them, "Who do the crowds say that I am?" They answered, "John the Baptist; but others, Elijah; and still others, that one of the ancient prophets has arisen." He said to them, "But who do you say that I am?" Peter answered, "The Messiah of God." He sternly ordered and commanded them not to tell anyone, saying, "The Son of Man must undergo great suffering, and be rejected by the elders, chief priests, and scribes, and be killed, and on the third day be raised." Then he said to them all, "If any want to become my followers, let them deny themselves and take up their cross daily and follow me. For those who want to save their life will lose it, and those who lose their life for my sake will save it."

Proper 8 *The Sunday closest to June 29*

The Collect

Almighty God, you have built your Church upon the foundation of the apostles and prophets, Jesus Christ himself being the chief cornerstone: Grant us so to be joined together in unity of spirit by their teaching, that we may be made a holy temple acceptable to you; through Jesus Christ our Lord, who lives and reigns with you and the Holy Spirit, one God, for ever and ever. *Amen.*

O Almighty God, who hast built thy Church upon the foundation of the apostles and prophets, Jesus Christ himself being the chief cornerstone: Grant us so to be joined together in unity of spirit by their doctrine, that we may be made an holy temple acceptable unto thee; through the same Jesus Christ our Lord, who liveth and reigneth with thee and the Holy Spirit, one God, for ever and ever. *Amen.*

Year A

The Lesson   Isaiah 2:10-17

Enter into the rock, and hide in the dust from the terror of the Lord, and from the glory of his majesty. The haughty eyes of people shall be brought low, and the pride of everyone shall be humbled; and the Lord alone will be exalted in that day. For the Lord of hosts has a day against all that is proud and lofty, against all that is lifted up and high; against all the cedars of Lebanon, lofty and lifted up; and against all the oaks of Bashan; against all the high mountains, and against all the lofty hills; against every high tower, and against every fortified wall; against all the ships of Tarshish, and against all the beautiful craft. The haughtiness of people shall be humbled, and the pride of everyone shall be brought low; and the Lord alone will be exalted on that day.

The Psalm 89:1-18 or 89:1-4, 15-18   *Misericordias Domini*

1   [Your love, O Lord, for ever will I sing; *
         from age to age my mouth will proclaim your faithfulness.

2   For I am persuaded that your love is established for ever; *
         you have set your faithfulness firmly in the heavens.

3   "I have made a covenant with my chosen one; *
         I have sworn an oath to David my servant:

4   'I will establish your line for ever, *
         and preserve your throne for all generations.'"]

5   The heavens bear witness to your wonders, O Lord, *
         and to your faithfulness in the assembly of the holy ones;

6   For who in the skies can be compared to the LORD? *
     who is like the LORD among the gods

7   God is much to be feared in the council of the holy ones, *
     great and terrible to all those round about him.

8   Who is like you, LORD God of hosts? *
     O mighty LORD, your faithfulness is all around you.

9   You rule the raging of the sea *
     and still the surging of its waves.

10   You have crushed Rahab of the deep with a deadly wound; *
     you have scattered your enemies with your mighty arm.

11   Yours are the heavens; the earth also is yours; *
     you laid the foundations of the world and all that is in it.

12   You have made the north and the south; *
     Tabor and Hermon rejoice in your Name.

13   You have a mighty arm; *
     strong is your hand and high is your right hand.

14   Righteousness and justice are the foundations of your throne; *
     love and truth go before your face.

15   [Happy are the people who know the festal shout! *
     they walk, O LORD, in the light of your presence.

16   They rejoice daily in your Name; *
     they are jubilant in your righteousness.

17   For you are the glory of their strength, *
     and by your favor our might is exalted.

18   Truly, the LORD is our ruler; *
     the Holy One of Israel is our King.]

The Epistle   **Romans 6:3-11**

Do you not know that all of us who have been baptized into Christ Jesus were baptized into his death? Therefore we have been buried with him by baptism into death, so that, just as Christ was raised from the dead by the glory of the Father, so we too might walk in newness of life. For if we have been united with him in a death like his, we will certainly be united with him in a resurrection like his. We know that our old self was crucified with him so that the body of sin might be destroyed, and we might no longer be enslaved to sin. For whoever has died is freed from sin. But if we have died with Christ, we believe that we will also live with him. We know that Christ, being raised from the dead, will never die again; death no longer has dominion over him. The death he died, he died to sin, once for all; but the life he lives, he lives to God. So you also must consider yourselves dead to sin and alive to God in Christ Jesus.

The Gospel   **Matthew 10:34-42**

Jesus said, "Do not think that I have come to bring peace to the earth; I have not
come to bring peace, but a sword. For I have come to set a man against his father,
and a daughter against her mother, and a daughter-in-law against her mother-in-law;
and one's foes will be members of one's own household. Whoever loves father or
mother more than me is not worthy of me; and whoever loves son or daughter more
than me is not worthy of me; and whoever does not take up the cross and follow me
is not worthy of me. Those who find their life will lose it, and those who lose their life
for my sake will find it. Whoever welcomes you welcomes me, and whoever
welcomes me welcomes the one who sent me. Whoever welcomes a prophet in the
name of a prophet will receive a prophet's reward; and whoever welcomes a righteous
person in the name of a righteous person will receive the reward of the righteous; and
whoever gives even a cup of cold water to one of these little ones in the name of a
disciple — truly I tell you, none of these will lose their reward."

Year B

The Lesson   **Deuteronomy 15:7-11**

If there is among you anyone in need, a member of your community in any of your
towns within the land that the LORD your God is giving you, do not be hard-hearted
or tight-fisted toward your needy neighbor. You should rather open your hand,
willingly lending enough to meet the need, whatever it may be. Be careful that you do
not entertain a mean thought, thinking, "The seventh year, the year of remission, is
near," and therefore view your needy neighbor with hostility and give nothing; your
neighbor might cry to the LORD against you, and you would incur guilt. Give
liberally and be ungrudging when you do so, for on this account the LORD your God
will bless you in all your work and in all that you undertake. Since there will never
cease to be some in need on the earth, I therefore command you, "Open your hand
to the poor and needy neighbor in your land."

The Psalm 112   *Beatus vir*

1   Hallelujah!
     Happy are they who fear the Lord *
          and have great delight in his commandments!

2   Their descendants will be mighty in the land; *
          the generation of the upright will be blessed.

3   Wealth and riches will be in their house, *
          and their righteousness will last for ever.

4   Light shines in the darkness for the upright; *
          the righteous are merciful and full of compassion.

5   It is good for them to be generous in lending *
          and to manage their affairs with justice.

6   For they will never be shaken; *
          the righteous will be kept in everlasting remembrance.

7   They will not be afraid of any evil rumors; *
        their heart is right;
        they put their trust in the Lord.

8   Their heart is established and will not shrink, *
        until they see their desire upon their enemies.

9   They have given freely to the poor, *
        and their righteousness stands fast for ever;
        they will hold up their head with honor.

10 The wicked will see it and be angry;
        they will gnash their teeth and pine away; *
        the desires of the wicked will perish.

The Epistle
2 Corinthians 8:1-9, 13-15

We want you to know, brothers and sisters, about the grace of God that has been granted to the churches of Macedonia; for during a severe ordeal of affliction, their abundant joy and their extreme poverty have overflowed in a wealth of generosity on their part. For, as I can testify, they voluntarily gave according to their means, and even beyond their means, begging us earnestly for the privilege of sharing in this ministry to the saints — and this, not merely as we expected; they gave themselves first to the Lord and, by the will of God, to us, so that we might urge Titus that, as he had already made a beginning, so he should also complete this generous undertaking among you. Now as you excel in everything — in faith, in speech, in knowledge, in utmost eagerness, and in our love for you — so we want you to excel also in this generous undertaking. I do not say this as a command, but I am testing the genuineness of your love against the earnestness of others. For you know the generous act of our Lord Jesus Christ, that though he was rich, yet for your sakes he became poor, so that by his poverty you might become rich. I do not mean that there should be relief for others and pressure on you, but it is a question of a fair balance between your present abundance and their need, so that their abundance may be for your need, in order that there may be a fair balance. As it is written, "The one who had much did not have too much, and the one who had little did not have too little."

The Gospel
Mark 5:22-24, 35b-43

Then one of the leaders of the synagogue named Jairus came and, when he saw Jesus, fell at his feet and begged him repeatedly, "My little daughter is at the point of death. Come and lay your hands on her, so that she may be made well, and live." So he went with him. And a large crowd followed him and pressed in on him. Some people came from the leader's house to say, "Your daughter is dead. Why trouble the teacher any further?" But overhearing what they said, Jesus said to the leader of the synagogue, "Do not fear, only believe." He allowed no one to follow him except Peter, James, and John, the brother of James. When they came to the house of the leader of the synagogue, he saw a commotion, people weeping and wailing loudly. When he had entered, he said to them, "Why do you make a commotion and weep? The child is not dead but sleeping." And they laughed at him. Then he put them all outside, and took the child's father and mother and those who were with him, and went in where the child was. He took her by the hand and said to her, "Talitha cum," which means "Little girl, get up!" And immediately the girl got up and began to walk about (she was twelve years of age). At this they were overcome with amazement. He strictly ordered them that no one should know this, and told them to give her something to eat.

Year C

The Lesson   1 Kings 19:15-16, 19-21

Then the LORD said to Elijah, "Go, return on your way to the wilderness of Damascus; when you arrive, you shall anoint Hazael as king over Aram. Also you shall anoint Jehuson of Nimshi as king over Israel; and you shall anoint Elisha son of Shaphat of Abel-meholah as prophet in your place. So he set out from there, and found Elisha son of Shaphat, who was plowing. There were twelve yoke of oxen ahead of him, and he was with the twelfth. Elijah passed by him and threw his mantle over him. He left the oxen, ran after Elijah, and said, "Let me kiss my father and my mother, and then I will follow you." Then Elijah said to him, "Go back again; for what have I done to you?" He returned from following him, took the yoke of oxen, and slaughtered them; using the equipment from the oxen, he boiled their flesh, and gave it to the people, and they ate. Then he set out and followed Elijah, and became his servant.

The Psalm 16 or 16:5-11   *Conserva me, Domine*

1   Protect me, O God, for I take refuge in you; *
         I have said to the LORD, "You are my Lord,
         my good above all other."

2   All my delight is upon the godly that are in the land, *
         upon those who are noble among the people.

3   But those who run after other gods *
         shall have their troubles multiplied.

4   Their libations of blood I will not offer, *
         nor take the names of their gods upon my lips.

5   [O LORD, you are my portion and my cup; *
         it is you who uphold my lot.

6   My boundaries enclose a pleasant land; *
         indeed, I have a goodly heritage.

7   I will bless the LORD who gives me counsel; *
         my heart teaches me, night after night.

8   I have set the LORD always before me; *
         because he is at my right hand I shall not fall.

9   My heart, therefore, is glad, and my spirit rejoices; *
         my body also shall rest in hope.

10   For you will not abandon me to the grave, *
         nor let your holy one see the Pit.

11   You will show me the path of life; *
         in your presence there is fullness of joy,
         and in your right hand are pleasures for evermore.]

The Epistle   **Galatians 5:1, 13-25**
For freedom Christ has set us free. Stand firm, therefore, and do not submit again to
a yoke of slavery. For you were called to freedom, brothers and sisters; only do not
use your freedom as an opportunity for self-indulgence, but through love become
slaves to one another. For the whole law is summed up in a single commandment,
"You shall love your neighbor as yourself." If, however, you bite and devour one
another, take care that you are not consumed by one another. Live by the Spirit, I
say, and do not gratify the desires of the flesh. For what the flesh desires is opposed to
the Spirit, and what the Spirit desires is opposed to the flesh; for these are opposed to
each other, to prevent you from doing what you want. But if you are led by the Spirit,
you are not subject to the law. Now the works of the flesh are obvious: fornication,
impurity, licentiousness, idolatry, sorcery, enmities, strife, jealousy, anger, quarrels,
dissensions, factions, envy, drunkenness, carousing, and things like these. I am
warning you, as I warned you before: those who do such things will not inherit the
kingdom of God. By contrast, the fruit of the Spirit is love, joy, peace, patience,
kindness, generosity, faithfulness, gentleness, and self-control. There is no law against
such things. And those who belong to Christ Jesus have crucified the flesh with its
passions and desires. If we live by the Spirit, let us also be guided by the Spirit.

The Gospel   **Luke 9:51-62**
When the days drew near for Jesus to be taken up, he set his face to go to Jerusalem.
And he sent messengers ahead of him. On their way they entered a village of the
Samaritans to make ready for him; but they did not receive him, because his face was
set toward Jerusalem. When his disciples James and John saw it, they said, "Lord, do
you want us to command fire to come down from heaven and consume them?" But
he turned and rebuked them. Then they went on to another village. As they were
going along the road, someone said to him, "I will follow you wherever you go." And
Jesus said to him, "Foxes have holes, and birds of the air have nests; but the Son of
Man has nowhere to lay his head." To another he said, "Follow me." But he said,
"Lord, first let me go and bury my father." But Jesus said to him, "Let the dead bury
their own dead; but as for you, go and proclaim the kingdom of God." Another said,
"I will follow you, Lord; but let me first say farewell to those at my home." Jesus said
to him, "No one who puts a hand to the plow and looks back is fit for the kingdom of
God."

Proper 9 *The Sunday closest to July 6*

The Collect
**O God, you have taught us to keep all your commandments by loving you and our
neighbor: Grant us the grace of your Holy Spirit, that we may be devoted to you with**

our whole heart, and united to one another with pure affection; through Jesus Christ our Lord, who lives and reigns with you and the Holy Spirit, one God, for ever and ever. *Amen.*

O God, who hast taught us to keep all thy commandments by loving thee and our neighbor: Grant us the grace of thy Holy Spirit, that we may be devoted to thee with our whole heart, and united to one another with pure affection; through Jesus Christ our Lord, who liveth and reigneth with thee and the same Spirit, one God, for ever and ever. *Amen.*

Year A

The Lesson   Zechariah 9:9-12

Rejoice greatly, O daughter Zion! Shout aloud, O daughter Jerusalem! Lo, your king comes to you; triumphant and victorious is he, humble and riding on a donkey, on a colt, the foal of a donkey. He will cut off the chariot from Ephraim and the war horse from Jerusalem; and the battle bow shall be cut off, and he shall command peace to the nations; his dominion shall be from sea to sea, and from the River to the ends of the earth. As for you also, because of the blood of my covenant with you, I will set your prisoners free from the waterless pit. Return to your stronghold, O prisoners of hope; today I declare that I will restore to you double.

The Psalm 145 or 145:8-14   *Exaltabo te, Deus*

1   I will exalt you, O God my King, *
          and bless your Name for ever and ever.

2   Every day will I bless you *
          and praise your Name for ever and ever.

3   Great is the LORD and greatly to be praised; *
          there is no end to his greatness.

4   One generation shall praise your works to another *
          and shall declare your power.

5   I will ponder the glorious splendor of your majesty *
          and all your marvelous works.

6   They shall speak of the might of your wondrous acts, *
          and I will tell of your greatness.

7   They shall publish the remembrance of your great goodness; *
          they shall sing of your righteous deeds.

8   [The LORD is gracious and full of compassion, *
          slow to anger and of great kindness.

9   The LORD is loving to everyone *
          and his compassion is over all his works.

10   All your works praise you, O LORD, *
          and your faithful servants bless you.

11 They make known the glory of your kingdom *
    and speak of your power;

12 That the peoples may know of your power *
    and the glorious splendor of your kingdom.

13 Your kingdom is an everlasting kingdom; *
    your dominion endures throughout all ages.

14 The LORD is faithful in all his words *
    and merciful in all his deeds.]

15 The LORD upholds all those who fall; *
    he lifts up those who are bowed down.

16 The eyes of all wait upon you, O LORD, *
    and you give them their food in due season.

17 You open wide your hand *
    and satisfy the needs of every living creature.

18 The LORD is righteous in all his ways *
    and loving in all his works.

19 The LORD is near to those who call upon him, *
    to all who call upon him faithfully.

20 He fulfills the desire of those who fear him; *
    he hears their cry and helps them.

21 The LORD preserves all those who love him, *
    but he destroys all the wicked.

22 My mouth shall speak the praise of the LORD; *
    let all flesh bless his holy Name for ever and ever.

The Epistle
Romans 7:21-8:6

I find it to be a law that when I want to do what is good, evil lies close at hand. For I delight in the law of God in my inmost self, but I see in my members another law at war with the law of my mind, making me captive to the law of sin that dwells in my members. Wretched man that I am! Who will rescue me from this body of death? Thanks be to God through Jesus Christ our Lord! So then, with my mind I am a slave to the law of God, but with my flesh I am a slave to the law of sin. There is therefore now no condemnation for those who are in Christ Jesus. For the law of the Spirit of life in Christ Jesus has set you free from the law of sin and of death. For God has done what the law, weakened by the flesh, could not do: by sending his own Son in the likeness of sinful flesh, and to deal with sin, he condemned sin in the flesh, so that the just requirement of the law might be fulfilled in us, who walk not according to the flesh but according to the Spirit. For those who live according to the flesh set their minds on the things of the flesh, but those who live according to the Spirit set their minds on the things of the Spirit. To set the mind on the flesh is death, but to set the mind on the Spirit is life and peace.

The Gospel Matthew 11:25-30

Jesus said, "I thank you, Father, Lord of heaven and earth, because you have hidden these things from the wise and the intelligent and have revealed them to infants; yes, Father, for such was your gracious will. All things have been handed over to me by my Father; and no one knows the Son except the Father, and no one knows the Father except the Son and anyone to whom the Son chooses to reveal him. Come to me, all you that are weary and are carrying heavy burdens, and I will give you rest. Take my yoke upon you, and learn from me; for I am gentle and humble in heart, and you will find rest for your souls. For my yoke is easy, and my burden is light."

Year B

The Lesson Ezekiel 2:1-7

The Lord said to me: O mortal, stand up on your feet, and I will speak with you. And when he spoke to me, a spirit entered into me and set me on my feet; and I heard him speaking to me. He said to me, Mortal, I am sending you to the people of Israel, to a nation of rebels who have rebelled against me; they and their ancestors have transgressed against me to this very day. The descendants are impudent and stubborn. I am sending you to them, and you shall say to them, "Thus says the Lord GOD." Whether they hear or refuse to hear (for they are a rebellious house), they shall know that there has been a prophet among them. And you, O mortal, do not be afraid of them, and do not be afraid of their words, though briers and thorns surround you and you live among scorpions; do not be afraid of their words, and do not be dismayed at their looks, for they are a rebellious house. You shall speak my words to them, whether they hear or refuse to hear; for they are a rebellious house.

The Psalm 123 *Ad te levavi oculos meos*

1   To you I lift up my eyes, *
   to you enthroned in the heavens.

2   As the eyes of servants look to the hand of their masters, *
   and the eyes of a maid to the hand of her mistress,

3   So our eyes look to the LORD our God, *
   until he shows us his mercy.

4   Have mercy upon us, O LORD, have mercy, *
   for we have had more than enough of contempt,

5   Too much of the scorn of the indolent rich, *
   and of the derision of the proud.

The Epistle 2 Corinthians 12:2-10

I know a person in Christ who fourteen years ago was caught up to the third heaven — whether in the body or out of the body I do not know; God knows. And I know that such a person — whether in the body or out of the body I do not know; God knows — was caught up into Paradise and heard things that are not to be told, that no mortal is permitted to repeat. On behalf of such a one I will boast, but on my own behalf I will not boast, except of my weaknesses. But if I wish to boast, I will not be a fool, for I will be speaking the truth. But I refrain from it, so that no one may think better of me than what is seen in me or heard from me, even considering the exceptional character of the revelations. Therefore, to keep me from being too elated, a thorn was given me in the flesh, a messenger of Satan to torment me, to keep me from being too elated. Three times I appealed to the Lord about this, that it would leave me, but he said to me, "My grace is sufficient for you, for power is made perfect in weakness." So, I will boast all the more gladly of my weaknesses, so that the power of Christ may dwell in me. Therefore I am content with weaknesses, insults, hardships, persecutions, and calamities for the sake of Christ; for whenever I am weak, then I am strong.

The Gospel
Mark 6:1-6

Jesus came to his hometown, and his disciples followed him. On the sabbath he began to teach in the synagogue, and many who heard him were astounded. They said, "Where did this man get all this? What is this wisdom that has been given to him? What deeds of power are being done by his hands! Is not this the carpenter, the son of Mary and brother of James and Joses and Judas and Simon, and are not his sisters here with us?" And they took offense at him. Then Jesus said to them, "Prophets are not without honor, except in their hometown, and among their own kin, and in their own house." And he could do no deed of power there, except that he laid his hands on a few sick people and cured them. And he was amazed at their unbelief. Then he went about among the villages teaching.

Year C

The Lesson
Isaiah 66:10-16

Thus said the Lord, rejoice with Jerusalem, and be glad for her, all you who love her; rejoice with her in joy, all you who mourn over her — that you may nurse and be satisfied from her consoling breast; that you may drink deeply with delight from her glorious bosom. For thus says the LORD: I will extend prosperity to her like a river, and the wealth of the nations like an overflowing stream; and you shall nurse and be carried on her arm, and dandled on her knees. As a mother comforts her child, so I will comfort you; you shall be comforted in Jerusalem. You shall see, and your heart shall rejoice; your bodies shall flourish like the grass; and it shall be known that the hand of the LORD is with his servants, and his indignation is against his enemies. For the LORD will come in fire, and his chariots like the whirlwind, to pay back his anger in fury, and his rebuke in flames of fire. For by fire will the LORD execute judgment, and by his sword, on all flesh; and those slain by the LORD shall be many.

The Psalm 66 or 66:1-8   *Jubilate Deo*

1   [Be joyful in God, all you lands; *
    sing the glory of his Name;
    sing the glory of his praise.

2   Say to God, "How awesome are your deeds! *
    because of your great strength your enemies cringe before you.

3   All the earth bows down before you, *
    sings to you, sings out your Name."

4 Come now and see the works of God, *
  how wonderful he is in his doing toward all people.

5 He turned the sea into dry land,
 so that they went through the water on foot, *
  and there we rejoiced in him.

6 In his might he rules for ever;
 his eyes keep watch over the nations; *
  let no rebel rise up against him.

7 Bless our God, you peoples; *
  make the voice of his praise to be heard;

8 Who holds our souls in life, *
  and will not allow our feet to slip.]

9 For you, O God, have proved us; *
  you have tried us just as silver is tried.

10 You brought us into the snare; *
  you laid heavy burdens upon our backs.

11 You let enemies ride over our heads;
 we went through fire and water; *
  but you brought us out into a place of refreshment.

12 I will enter your house with burnt-offerings
 and will pay you my vows, *
  which I promised with my lips
  and spoke with my mouth when I was in trouble.

13 I will offer you sacrifices of fat beasts
 with the smoke of rams; *
  I will give you oxen and goats.

14 Come and listen, all you who fear God, *
  and I will tell you what he has done for me.

15 I called out to him with my mouth, *
  and his praise was on my tongue.

16 If I had found evil in my heart, *
  the Lord would not have heard me;

17 But in truth God has heard me; *
  he has attended to the voice of my prayer.

18 Blessed be God, who has not rejected my prayer, *
  nor withheld his love from me.

The Epistle   **Galatians 6:(1-10) 14-18**

[My friends, if anyone is detected in a transgression, you who have received the
Spirit should restore such a one in a spirit of gentleness. Take care that you yourselves

are not tempted. Bear one another's burdens, and in this way you will fulfill the law of Christ. For if those who are nothing think they are something, they deceive themselves. All must test their own work; then that work, rather than their neighbor's work, will become a cause for pride. For all must carry their own loads. Those who are taught the word must share in all good things with their teacher. Do not be deceived; God is not mocked, for you reap whatever you sow. If you sow to your own flesh, you will reap corruption from the flesh; but if you sow to the Spirit, you will reap eternal life from the Spirit. So let us not grow weary in doing what is right, for we will reap at harvest-time, if we do not give up. So then, whenever we have an opportunity, let us work for the good of all, and especially for those of the family of faith.] May I never boast of anything except the cross of our Lord Jesus Christ, by which the world has been crucified to me, and I to the world. For neither circumcision nor uncircumcision is anything; but a new creation is everything! As for those who will follow this rule — peace be upon them, and mercy, and upon the Israel of God. From now on, let no one make trouble for me; for I carry the marks of Jesus branded on my body. May the grace of our Lord Jesus Christ be with your spirit, brothers and sisters. Amen.

The Gospel   Luke 10:1-12, 16-20

The Lord appointed seventy others and sent them on ahead of him in pairs to every town and place where he himself intended to go. He said to them, "The harvest is plentiful, but the laborers are few; therefore ask the Lord of the harvest to send out laborers into his harvest. Go on your way. See, I am sending you out like lambs into the midst of wolves. Carry no purse, no bag, no sandals; and greet no one on the road. Whatever house you enter, first say, 'Peace to this house!' And if anyone is there who shares in peace, your peace will rest on that person; but if not, it will return to you. Remain in the same house, eating and drinking whatever they provide, for the laborer deserves to be paid. Do not move about from house to house. Whenever you enter a town and its people welcome you, eat what is set before you; cure the sick who are there, and say to them, 'The kingdom of God has come near to you.' But whenever you enter a town and they do not welcome you, go out into its streets and say, 'Even the dust of your town that clings to our feet, we wipe off in protest against you. Yet know this: the kingdom of God has come near.' I tell you, on that day it will be more tolerable for Sodom than for that town. Whoever listens to you listens to me, and whoever rejects you rejects me, and whoever rejects me rejects the one who sent me." The seventy returned with joy, saying, "Lord, in your name even the demons submit to us!" He said to them, "I watched Satan fall from heaven like a flash of lightning. See, I have given you authority to tread on snakes and scorpions, and over all the power of the enemy; and nothing will hurt you. Nevertheless, do not rejoice at this, that the spirits submit to you, but rejoice that your names are written in heaven."

Proper 10 *The Sunday closest to July 13*

The Collect

O Lord, mercifully receive the prayers of your people who call upon you, and grant that they may know and understand what things they ought to do, and also may have grace

and power faithfully to accomplish them; through Jesus Christ our Lord, who lives and reigns with you and the Holy Spirit, one God, now and for ever. *Amen.*

O Lord, we beseech thee mercifully to receive the prayers of thy people who call upon thee, and grant that they may both perceive and know what things they ought to do, and also may have grace and power faithfully to fulfill the same; through Jesus Christ our Lord, who liveth and reigneth with thee and the Holy Spirit, one God, now and for ever. *Amen.*

Year A

The Lesson Isaiah 55:1-5, 10-13

Ho, everyone who thirsts, come to the waters; and you that have no money, come, buy and eat! Come, buy wine and milk without money and without price. Why do you spend your money for that which is not bread, and your labor for that which does not satisfy? Listen carefully to me, and eat what is good, and delight yourselves in rich food. Incline your ear, and come to me; listen, so that you may live. I will make with you an everlasting covenant, my steadfast, sure love for David. See, I made him a witness to the peoples, a leader and commander for the peoples. See, you shall call nations that you do not know, and nations that do not know you shall run to you, because of the LORD your God, the Holy One of Israel, for he has glorified you. For as the rain and the snow come down from heaven, and do not return there until they have watered the earth, making it bring forth and sprout, giving seed to the sower and bread to the eater, so shall my word be that goes out from my mouth; it shall not return to me empty, but it shall accomplish that which I purpose, and succeed in the thing for which I sent it. For you shall go out in joy, and be led back in peace; the mountains and the hills before you shall burst into song, and all the trees of the field shall clap their hands. Instead of the thorn shall come up the cypress; instead of the brier shall come up the myrtle; and it shall be to the LORD for a memorial, for an everlasting sign that shall not be cut off.

The Psalm 65 or 65:9-14 *Te decet hymnus*

1   You are to be praised, O God, in Zion; *
        to you shall vows be performed in Jerusalem.

2   To you that hear prayer shall all flesh come, *
        because of their transgressions.

3   Our sins are stronger than we are, *
        but you will blot them out.

4   Happy are they whom you choose
    and draw to your courts to dwell there! *
        they will be satisfied by the beauty of your house,
        by the holiness of your temple.

5   Awesome things will you show us in your righteousness,
    O God of our salvation, *
        O Hope of all the ends of the earth
        and of the seas that are far away.

6   You make fast the mountains by your power; *
        they are girded about with might.

7   You still the roaring of the seas, *
        the roaring of their waves,
        and the clamor of the peoples.

8   Those who dwell at the ends of the earth will tremble at your marvelous signs; *
        you make the dawn and the dusk to sing for joy.

9   [You visit the earth and water it abundantly;
    you make it very plenteous; *
        the river of God is full of water.

10   You prepare the grain, *
        for so you provide for the earth.

11   You drench the furrows and smooth out the ridges; *
        with heavy rain you soften the ground and bless its increase.

12   You crown the year with your goodness, *
        and your paths overflow with plenty.

13   May the fields of the wilderness be rich for grazing, *
        and the hills be clothed with joy.

14   May the meadows cover themselves with flocks,
    and the valleys cloak themselves with grain; *
        let them shout for joy and sing.]

The Epistle

Romans 8:9-17

But you are not in the flesh; you are in the Spirit, since the Spirit of God dwells in you. Anyone who does not have the Spirit of Christ does not belong to him. But if Christ is in you, though the body is dead because of sin, the Spirit is life because of righteousness. If the Spirit of him who raised Jesus from the dead dwells in you, he who raised Christ from the dead will give life to your mortal bodies also through his Spirit that dwells in you. So then, brothers and sisters, we are debtors, not to the flesh, to live according to the flesh — for if you live according to the flesh, you will die; but if by the Spirit you put to death the deeds of the body, you will live. For all who are led by the Spirit of God are children of God. For you did not receive a spirit of slavery to fall back into fear, but you have received a spirit of adoption. When we cry, "Abba! Father!" it is that very Spirit bearing witness with our spirit that we are children of God, and if children, then heirs, heirs of God and joint heirs with Christ — if, in fact, we suffer with him so that we may also be glorified with him.

The Gospel

Matthew 13:1-9, 18-23

Jesus went out of the house and sat beside the sea. Such great crowds gathered around him that he got into a boat and sat there, while the whole crowd stood on the beach. And he told them many things in parables, saying: "Listen! A sower went out to sow. And as he sowed, some seeds fell on the path, and the birds came and ate them up. Other seeds fell on rocky ground, where they did not have much soil, and they sprang up quickly, since they had no depth of soil. But when the sun rose, they were scorched; and since they had no root, they withered away. Other seeds fell among thorns, and the thorns grew up and choked them. Other seeds fell on good soil and brought forth grain, some a hundredfold, some sixty, some thirty. Let anyone with ears listen! Hear then the parable of the sower. When anyone hears the word of the kingdom and does not understand it, the evil one comes and snatches away what is sown in the heart; this is what was sown on the path. As for what was sown on rocky ground, this is the one who hears the word and immediately receives it with joy; yet such a person has no root, but endures only for a while, and when trouble or persecution arises on account of the word, that person immediately falls away. As for what was sown among thorns, this is the one who hears the word, but the cares of the world and the lure of wealth choke the word, and it yields nothing. But as for what was sown on good soil, this is the one who hears the word and understands it, who indeed bears fruit and yields, in one case a hundredfold, in another sixty, and in another thirty."

Year B

The Lesson Amos 7:7-15

This is what he showed me: the Lord was standing beside a wall built with a plumb line, with a plumb line in his hand. And the LORD said to me, "Amos, what do you see?" And I said, "A plumb line." Then the Lord said, "See, I am setting a plumb line in the midst of my people Israel; I will never again pass them by; the high places of Isaac shall be made desolate, and the sanctuaries of Israel shall be laid waste, and I will rise against the house of Jeroboam with the sword." Then Amaziah, the priest of Bethel, sent to King Jeroboam of Israel, saying, "Amos has conspired against you in the very center of the house of Israel; the land is not able to bear all his words. For thus Amos has said, 'Jeroboam shall die by the sword, and Israel must go into exile away from his land.'" And Amaziah said to Amos, "O seer, go, flee away to the land of Judah, earn your bread there, and prophesy there; but never again prophesy at Bethel, for it is the king's sanctuary, and it is a temple of the kingdom." Then Amos answered Amaziah, "I am no prophet, nor a prophet's son; but I am a herdsman, and a dresser of sycamore trees, and the LORD took me from following the flock, and the LORD said to me, 'Go, prophesy to my people Israel.'

The Psalm 85 or 85:7-13 *Benedixisti, Domine*

1   You have been gracious to your land, O LORD, *
       you have restored the good fortune of Jacob.

2   You have forgiven the iniquity of your people *
       and blotted out all their sins.

3   You have withdrawn all your fury *
       and turned yourself from your wrathful indignation.

4   Restore us then, O God our Savior; *
       let your anger depart from us.

5   Will you be displeased with us for ever? *
       will you prolong your anger from age to age?

6   Will you not give us life again, *
       that your people may rejoice in you?

7   [Show us your mercy, O LORD, *
       and grant us your salvation.

8   I will listen to what the LORD God is saying, *
       for he is speaking peace to his faithful people
       and to those who turn their hearts to him.

9   Truly, his salvation is very near to those who fear him, *
       that his glory may dwell in our land.

10 Mercy and truth have met together; *
       righteousness and peace have kissed each other.

11 Truth shall spring up from the earth, *
       and righteousness shall look down from heaven.

12 The LORD will indeed grant prosperity, *
       and our land will yield its increase.

13 Righteousness shall go before him, *
       and peace shall be a pathway for his feet.]

The Epistle   **Ephesians 1:1-14**

Paul, an apostle of Christ Jesus by the will of God, To the saints who are in Ephesus and are faithful in Christ Jesus: Grace to you and peace from God our Father and the Lord Jesus Christ. Blessed be the God and Father of our Lord Jesus Christ, who has blessed us in Christ with every spiritual blessing in the heavenly places, just as he chose us in Christ before the foundation of the world to be holy and blameless before him in love. He destined us for adoption as his children through Jesus Christ, according to the good pleasure of his will, to the praise of his glorious grace that he freely bestowed on us in the Beloved. In him we have redemption through his blood, the forgiveness of our trespasses, according to the riches of his grace that he lavished on us. With all wisdom and insight he has made known to us the mystery of his will, according to his good pleasure that he set forth in Christ, as a plan for the fullness of time, to gather up all things in him, things in heaven and things on earth. In Christ we have also obtained an inheritance, having been destined according to the purpose of him who accomplishes all things according to his counsel and will, so that we, who were the first to set our hope on Christ, might live for the praise of his glory. In him you also, when you had heard the word of truth, the gospel of your salvation, and had believed in him, were marked with the seal of the promised Holy Spirit; this is the pledge of our inheritance toward redemption as God's own people, to the praise of his glory.

The Gospel Mark 6:7-13

Jesus called the twelve and began to send them out two by two, and gave them authority over the unclean spirits. He ordered them to take nothing for their journey except a staff; no bread, no bag, no money in their belts; but to wear sandals and not to put on two tunics. He said to them, "Wherever you enter a house, stay there until you leave the place. If any place will not welcome you and they refuse to hear you, as you leave, shake off the dust that is on your feet as a testimony against them." So they went out and proclaimed that all should repent. They cast out many demons, and anointed with oil many who were sick and cured them.

Year C

The Lesson Deuteronomy 30:9-14

The LORD your God will make you abundantly prosperous in all your undertakings, in the fruit of your body, in the fruit of your livestock, and in the fruit of your soil. For the LORD will again take delight in prospering you, just as he delighted in prospering your ancestors, when you obey the LORD your God by observing his commandments and decrees that are written in this book of the law, because you turn to the LORD your God with all your heart and with all your soul. Surely, this commandment that I am commanding you today is not too hard for you, nor is it too far away. It is not in heaven, that you should say, "Who will go up to heaven for us, and get it for us so that we may hear it and observe it?" Neither is it beyond the sea, that you should say, "Who will cross to the other side of the sea for us, and get it for us so that we may hear it and observe it?" No, the word is very near to you; it is in your mouth and in your heart for you to observe.

The Psalm 25 or 25:3-9 *Ad te, Domine, levavi*

1   To you, O LORD, I lift up my soul;
     my God, I put my trust in you; *
        let me not be humiliated,
        nor let my enemies triumph over me.

2   Let none who look to you be put to shame; *
        let the treacherous be disappointed in their schemes.

3   [Show me your ways, O LORD, *
        and teach me your paths.

4   Lead me in your truth and teach me, *
        for you are the God of my salvation;
        in you have I trusted all the day long.

5   Remember, O LORD, your compassion and love, *
        for they are from everlasting.

6   Remember not the sins of my youth and my transgressions; *
        remember me according to your love
        and for the sake of your goodness, O LORD.

7   Gracious and upright is the LORD; *
        therefore he teaches sinners in his way.

8   He guides the humble in doing right *
     and teaches his way to the lowly.

9   All the paths of the LORD are love and faithfulness *
     to those who keep his covenant and his testimonies.]

10   For your Name's sake, O LORD, *
     forgive my sin, for it is great.

11   Who are they who fear the LORD? *
     he will teach them the way that they should choose.

12   They shall dwell in prosperity, *
     and their offspring shall inherit the land.

13   The LORD is a friend to those who fear him *
     and will show them his covenant.

14   My eyes are ever looking to the LORD, *
     for he shall pluck my feet out of the net.

15   Turn to me and have pity on me, *
     for I am left alone and in misery.

16   The sorrows of my heart have increased; *
     bring me out of my troubles.

17   Look upon my adversity and misery *
     and forgive me all my sin.

18   Look upon my enemies, for they are many, *
     and they bear a violent hatred against me.

19   Protect my life and deliver me; *
     let me not be put to shame, for I have trusted in you.

20   Let integrity and uprightness preserve me, *
     for my hope has been in you.

21   Deliver Israel, O God, *
     out of all his troubles.

The Epistle
Colossians 1:1-14

Paul, an apostle of Christ Jesus by the will of God, and Timothy our brother, to the saints and faithful brothers and sisters in Christ in Colossae: grace to you and peace from God our Father. In our prayers for you we always thank God, the Father of our Lord Jesus Christ, for we have heard of your faith in Christ Jesus and of the love that you have for all the saints, because of the hope laid up for you in heaven. You have heard of this hope before in the word of the truth, the gospel that has come to you. Just as it is bearing fruit and growing in the whole world, so it has been bearing fruit among yourselves from the day you heard it and truly comprehended the grace of God. This you learned from Epaphras, our beloved fellow servant. He is a faithful minister of Christ on your behalf, and he has made known to us your love in the

Spirit. For this reason, since the day we heard it, we have not ceased praying for you and asking that you may be filled with the knowledge of God's will in all spiritual wisdom and understanding, so that you may lead lives worthy of the Lord, fully pleasing to him, as you bear fruit in every good work and as you grow in the knowledge of God. May you be made strong with all the strength that comes from his glorious power, and may you be prepared to endure everything with patience, while joyfully giving thanks to the Father, who has enabled you to share in the inheritance of the saints in the light. He has rescued us from the power of darkness and transferred us into the kingdom of his beloved Son, in whom we have redemption, the forgiveness of sins.

The Gospel   Luke 10:25-37

A lawyer stood up to test Jesus. "Teacher," he said, "what must I do to inherit eternal life?" Jesus said to him, "What is written in the law? What do you read there?" He answered, "You shall love the Lord your God with all your heart, and with all your soul, and with all your strength, and with all your mind; and your neighbor as yourself." And Jesus said to him, "You have given the right answer; do this, and you will live." But wanting to justify himself, he asked Jesus, "And who is my neighbor?" Jesus replied, "A man was going down from Jerusalem to Jericho, and fell into the hands of robbers, who stripped him, beat him, and went away, leaving him half dead. Now by chance a priest was going down that road; and when he saw him, he passed by on the other side. So likewise a Levite, when he came to the place and saw him, passed by on the other side. But a Samaritan while traveling came near him; and when he saw him, he was moved with pity. He went to him and bandaged his wounds, having poured oil and wine on them. Then he put him on his own animal, brought him to an inn, and took care of him. The next day he took out two denarii, gave them to the innkeeper, and said, 'Take care of him; and when I come back, I will repay you whatever more you spend.' Which of these three, do you think, was a neighbor to the man who fell into the hands of the robbers?" He said, "The one who showed him mercy." Jesus said to him, "Go and do likewise."

Proper 11 *The Sunday closest to July 20*

The Collect

Almighty God, the fountain of all wisdom, you know our necessities before we ask and our ignorance in asking: Have compassion on our weakness, and mercifully give us those things which for our unworthiness we dare not, and for our blindness we cannot ask; through the worthiness of your Son Jesus Christ our Lord, who lives and reigns with you and the Holy Spirit, one God, now and for ever. *Amen.*

Almighty God, the fountain of all wisdom, who knowest our necessities before we ask and our ignorance in asking: Have compassion, we beseech thee, upon our infirmities, and those things which for our unworthiness we dare not, and for our blindness we cannot ask, mercifully give us for the worthiness of thy Son Jesus Christ our Lord; who liveth and reigneth with thee and the Holy Spirit, one God, now and for ever. *Amen.*

The Lesson   Wisdom 12:13, 16-19

There is no god besides you, whose care is for all people, to whom you should prove
that you have not judged unjustly; For your strength is the source of righteousness,
and your sovereignty over all causes you to spare all. For you show your strength
when people doubt the completeness of your power, and you rebuke any insolence
among those who know it. Although you are sovereign in strength, you judge with
mildness, and with great forbearance you govern us; for you have power to act
whenever you choose. Through such works you have taught your people that the
righteous must be kind, and you have filled your children with good hope, because
you give repentance for sins.

The Psalm 86 or 86:11-17   *Inclina, Domine*

1   Bow down your ear, O LORD, and answer me, *
         for I am poor and in misery.

2   Keep watch over my life, for I am faithful; *
         save your servant who puts his trust in you.

3   Be merciful to me, O LORD, for you are my God; *
         I call upon you all the day long.

4   Gladden the soul of your servant, *
         for to you, O LORD, I lift up my soul.

5   For you, O LORD, are good and forgiving, *
         and great is your love toward all who call upon you.

6   Give ear, O LORD, to my prayer, *
         and attend to the voice of my supplications.

7   In the time of my trouble I will call upon you, *
         for you will answer me.

8   Among the gods there is none like you, O LORD, *
         nor anything like your works.

9   All nations you have made will come and worship you, O LORD, *
         and glorify your Name.

10   For you are great;
     you do wondrous things; *
         and you alone are God.

11   [Teach me your way, O LORD,
     and I will walk in your truth; *
         knit my heart to you that I may fear your Name.

12   I will thank you, O LORD my God, with all my heart, *
         and glorify your Name for evermore.

13   For great is your love toward me; *
         you have delivered me from the nethermost Pit.

14 The arrogant rise up against me, O God,
  and a band of violent men seeks my life; *
    they have not set you before their eyes.

15 But you, O LORD, are gracious and full of compassion, *
    slow to anger, and full of kindness and truth.

16 Turn to me and have mercy upon me; *
    give your strength to your servant;
    and save the child of your handmaid.

17 Show me a sign of your favor,
    so that those who hate me may see it and be ashamed; *
    because you, O LORD, have helped me and comforted me.]

The Epistle   **Romans 8:18-25**

I consider that the sufferings of this present time are not worth comparing with the
glory about to be revealed to us. For the creation waits with eager longing for the
revealing of the children of God; for the creation was subjected to futility, not of its
own will but by the will of the one who subjected it, in hope that the creation itself
will be set free from its bondage to decay and will obtain the freedom of the glory of
the children of God. We know that the whole creation has been groaning in labor
pains until now; and not only the creation, but we ourselves, who have the first fruits
of the Spirit, groan inwardly while we wait for adoption, the redemption of our
bodies. For in hope we were saved. Now hope that is seen is not hope. For who hopes
for what is seen? But if we hope for what we do not see, we wait for it with patience.

The Gospel   **Matthew 13:24-30, 36-43**

Jesus put before them another parable: "The kingdom of heaven may be compared to
someone who sowed good seed in his field; but while everybody was asleep, an enemy
came and sowed weeds among the wheat, and then went away. So when the plants
came up and bore grain, then the weeds appeared as well. And the slaves of the
householder came and said to him, 'Master, did you not sow good seed in your field?
Where, then, did these weeds come from?' He answered, 'An enemy has done this.'
The slaves said to him, 'Then do you want us to go and gather them?' But he replied,
'No; for in gathering the weeds you would uproot the wheat along with them. Let
both of them grow together until the harvest; and at harvest time I will tell the
reapers, Collect the weeds first and bind them in bundles to be burned, but gather the
wheat into my barn.'" Then he left the crowds and went into the house. And his
disciples approached him, saying, "Explain to us the parable of the weeds of the
field." He answered, "The one who sows the good seed is the Son of Man; the field is
the world, and the good seed are the children of the kingdom; the weeds are the
children of the evil one, and the enemy who sowed them is the devil; the harvest is
the end of the age, and the reapers are angels. Just as the weeds are collected and
burned up with fire, so will it be at the end of the age. The Son of Man will send his
angels, and they will collect out of his kingdom all causes of sin and all evildoers, and
they will throw them into the furnace of fire, where there will be weeping and

gnashing of teeth. Then the righteous will shine like the sun in the kingdom of their Father. Let anyone with ears listen!"

Year B

The Lesson   Isaiah 57:14b-21

"Build up, build up, prepare the way, remove every obstruction from my people's way." For thus says the high and lofty one who inhabits eternity, whose name is Holy: I dwell in the high and holy place, and also with those who are contrite and humble in spirit, to revive the spirit of the humble, and to revive the heart of the contrite. For I will not continually accuse, nor will I always be angry; for then the spirits would grow faint before me, even the souls that I have made. Because of their wicked covetousness I was angry; I struck them, I hid and was angry; but they kept turning back to their own ways. I have seen their ways, but I will heal them; I will lead them and repay them with comfort, creating for their mourners the fruit of the lips. Peace, peace, to the far and the near, says the LORD; and I will heal them. But the wicked are like the tossing sea that cannot keep still; its waters toss up mire and mud. There is no peace, says my God, for the wicked.

The Psalm 22:22-30   *Deus, Deus Meus*

22 Praise the LORD, you that fear him; *
    stand in awe of him, O offspring of Israel;
    all you of Jacob's line, give glory.

23 For he does not despise nor abhor the poor in their poverty;
    neither does he hide his face from them; *
    but when they cry to him he hears them.

24 My praise is of him in the great assembly; *
    I will perform my vows in the presence of those who worship him.

25 The poor shall eat and be satisfied,
    and those who seek the LORD shall praise him: *
    "May your heart live for ever!"

26 All the ends of the earth shall remember and turn to the LORD, *
    and all the families of the nations shall bow before him.

27 For kingship belongs to the LORD; *
    he rules over the nations.

28 To him alone all who sleep in the earth bow down in worship; *
    all who go down to the dust fall before him.

29 My soul shall live for him;
    my descendants shall serve him; *
    they shall be known as the LORD's for ever.

30 They shall come and make known to a people yet unborn *
    the saving deeds that he has done.

The Epistle   Ephesians 2:11-22

Remember that at one time you Gentiles by birth, called "the uncircumcision" by
those who are called "the circumcision" — a physical circumcision made in the flesh
by human hands — remember that you were at that time without Christ, being aliens
from the commonwealth of Israel, and strangers to the covenants of promise, having
no hope and without God in the world. But now in Christ Jesus you who once were
far off have been brought near by the blood of Christ. For he is our peace; in his flesh
he has made both groups into one and has broken down the dividing wall, that is, the
hostility between us. He has abolished the law with its commandments and
ordinances, that he might create in himself one new humanity in place of the two,
thus making peace, and might reconcile both groups to God in one body through the
cross, thus putting to death that hostility through it. So he came and proclaimed
peace to you who were far off and peace to those who were near; for through him
both of us have access in one Spirit to the Father. So then you are no longer strangers
and aliens, but you are citizens with the saints and also members of the household of
God, built upon the foundation of the apostles and prophets, with Christ Jesus
himself as the cornerstone. In him the whole structure is joined together and grows
into a holy temple in the LORD; in whom you also are built together spiritually into a
dwelling place for God.

The Gospel   Mark 6:30-44

The apostles gathered around Jesus, and told him all that they had done and taught.
He said to them, "Come away to a deserted place all by yourselves and rest a while."
For many were coming and going, and they had no leisure even to eat. And they went
away in the boat to a deserted place by themselves. Now many saw them going and
recognized them, and they hurried there on foot from all the towns and arrived
ahead of them. As he went ashore, he saw a great crowd; and he had compassion for
them, because they were like sheep without a shepherd; and he began to teach them
many things. When it grew late, his disciples came to him and said, "This is a
deserted place, and the hour is now very late; send them away so that they may go
into the surrounding country and villages and buy something for themselves to eat."
But he answered them, "You give them something to eat." They said to him, "Are we
to go and buy two hundred denarii worth of bread, and give it to them to eat?" And
he said to them, "How many loaves have you? Go and see." When they had found
out, they said, "Five, and two fish." Then he ordered them to get all the people tó sit
down in groups on the green grass. So they sat down in groups of hundreds and of
fifties. Taking the five loaves and the two fish, he looked up to heaven, and blessed
and broke the loaves, and gave them to his disciples to set before the people; and he
divided the two fish among them all. And all ate and were filled; and they took up
twelve baskets full of broken pieces and of the fish. Those who had eaten the loaves
numbered five thousand men.

Year C

The Lesson   Genesis 18:1-10a (10b-14)

The LORD appeared to Abraham by the oaks of Mamre, as he sat at the entrance of
his tent in the heat of the day. He looked up and saw three men standing near him.
When he saw them, he ran from the tent entrance to meet them, and bowed down to

the ground. He said, "My lord, if I find favor with you, do not pass by your servant. Let a little water be brought, and wash your feet, and rest yourselves under the tree. Let me bring a little bread, that you may refresh yourselves, and after that you may pass on — since you have come to your servant." So they said, "Do as you have said." And Abraham hastened into the tent to Sarah, and said, "Make ready quickly three measures of choice flour, knead it, and make cakes." Abraham ran to the herd, and took a calf, tender and good, and gave it to the servant, who hastened to prepare it. Then he took curds and milk and the calf that he had prepared, and set it before them; and he stood by them under the tree while they ate. They said to him, "Where is your wife Sarah?" And he said, "There, in the tent." Then one said, "I will surely return to you in due season, and your wife Sarah shall have a son." [And Sarah was listening at the tent entrance behind him. Now Abraham and Sarah were old, advanced in age; it had ceased to be with Sarah after the manner of women. So Sarah laughed to herself, saying, "After I have grown old, and my husband is old, shall I have pleasure?" The LORD said to Abraham, "Why did Sarah laugh, and say, 'Shall I indeed bear a child, now that I am old?' Is anything too wonderful for the LORD? At the set time I will return to you, in due season, and Sarah shall have a son."]

The Psalm 15   *Domine, quis habitabit?*

1   LORD, who may dwell in your tabernacle? *
       who may abide upon your holy hill?

2   Whoever leads a blameless life and does what is right, *
       who speaks the truth from his heart.

3   There is no guile upon his tongue;
     he does no evil to his friend; *
       he does not heap contempt upon his neighbor.

4   In his sight the wicked is rejected, *
       but he honors those who fear the LORD.

5   He has sworn to do no wrong *
       and does not take back his word.

6   He does not give his money in hope of gain, *
       nor does he take a bribe against the innocent.

7   Whoever does these things *
       shall never be overthrown.

The Epistle   Colossians 1:21-29

You who were once estranged and hostile in mind, doing evil deeds, he has now reconciled in his fleshly body through death, so as to present you holy and blameless and irreproachable before him — provided that you continue securely established and steadfast in the faith, without shifting from the hope promised by the gospel that you heard, which has been proclaimed to every creature under heaven. I, Paul, became a servant of this gospel. I am now rejoicing in my sufferings for your sake, and in my flesh I am completing what is lacking in Christ's afflictions for the sake of his body, that is, the church. I became its servant according to God's commission that was given to me for you, to make the word of God fully known, the mystery that has been hidden throughout the ages and generations but has now been revealed to his saints. To them God chose to make known how great among the Gentiles are the riches of the glory of this mystery, which is Christ in you, the hope of glory. It is he whom we proclaim, warning everyone and teaching everyone in all wisdom, so that we may present everyone mature in Christ. For this I toil and struggle with all the energy that he powerfully inspires within me.

The Gospel   Luke 10:38-42

As Jesus and his disciples went on their way, Jesus entered a certain village, where a woman named Martha welcomed him into her home. She had a sister named Mary, who sat at the Lord's feet and listened to what he was saying. But Martha was distracted by her many tasks; so she came to him and asked, "Lord, do you not care that my sister has left me to do all the work by myself? Tell her then to help me." But the Lord answered her, "Martha, Martha, you are worried and distracted by many things; there is need of only one thing. Mary has chosen the better part, which will not be taken away from her."

Proper 12 *The Sunday closest to July 27*

The Collect

O God, the protector of all who trust in you, without whom nothing is strong, nothing is holy: Increase and multiply upon us your mercy; that, with you as our ruler and guide, we may so pass through things temporal, that we lose not the things eternal; through Jesus Christ our Lord, who lives and reigns with you and the Holy Spirit, one God, for ever and ever. *Amen.*

O God, the protector of all that trust in thee, without whom nothing is strong, nothing is holy: Increase and multiply upon us thy mercy, that, thou being our ruler and guide, we may so pass through things temporal, that we finally lose not the things eternal; through Jesus Christ our Lord, who liveth and reigneth with thee and the Holy Spirit, one God, for ever and ever. *Amen.*

Year A

The Lesson   1 Kings 3:5-12

At Gibeon the LORD appeared to Solomon in a dream by night; and God said, "Ask what I should give you." And Solomon said, "You have shown great and steadfast love to your servant my father David, because he walked before you in faithfulness, in righteousness, and in uprightness of heart toward you; and you have kept for him this great and steadfast love, and have given him a son to sit on his throne today. And now, O LORD my God, you have made your servant king in place of my father David, although I am only a little child; I do not know how to go out or come in. And your servant is in the midst of the people whom you have chosen, a great people, so numerous they cannot be numbered or counted. Give your servant therefore an understanding mind to govern your people, able to discern between good and evil; for who can govern this your great people?" It pleased the Lord that Solomon had asked this. God said to him, "Because you have asked this, and have not asked for yourself long life or riches, or for the life of your enemies, but have asked for yourself understanding to discern what is right, I now do according to your word. Indeed I give you a wise and discerning mind; no one like you has been before you and no one like you shall arise after you."

The Psalm 119:121-136 or 119:129-136   *Feci judicium*

121   I have done what is just and right; *
      do not deliver me to my oppressors.

122   Be surety for your servant's good; *
      let not the proud oppress me.

123   My eyes have failed from watching for your salvation *
      and for your righteous promise.

124   Deal with your servant according to your loving-kindness *
      and teach me your statues.

125   I am your servant; grant me understanding, *
      that I may know your decrees.

126   It is time for you to act, O LORD, *
      for they have broken your law.

127   Truly, I love your commandments *
      more than gold and precious stones.

128   I hold all your commandments to be right for me; *
      all paths of falsehood I abhor.

129   [Your decrees are wonderful; *
      therefore I obey them with all my heart.

130   When your word goes forth it gives light; *
      it gives understanding to the simple.

131   I open my mouth and pant; *
      I long for your commandments.

132   Turn to me in mercy, *
      as you always do to those who love your Name.

133   Steady my footsteps in your word; *
      let no iniquity have dominion over me.

134   Rescue me from those who oppress me, *
      and I will keep your commandments.

135   Let your countenance shine upon your servant *
      and teach me your statutes.

136   My eyes shed streams of tears, *
      because people do not keep your law.]

The Epistle **Romans 8:26-34**

Likewise the Spirit helps us in our weakness; for we do not know how to pray as we ought, but that very Spirit intercedes with sighs too deep for words. And God, who searches the heart, knows what is the mind of the Spirit, because the Spirit intercedes for the saints according to the will of God. We know that all things work together for good for those who love God, who are called according to his purpose. For those whom he foreknew he also predestined to be conformed to the image of his Son, in order that he might be the firstborn within a large family. And those whom he predestined he also called; and those whom he called he also justified; and those whom he justified he also glorified. What then are we to say about these things? If God is for us, who is against us? He who did not withhold his own Son, but gave him up for all of us, will he not with him also give us everything else? Who will bring any charge against God's elect? It is God who justifies. Who is to condemn? It is Christ Jesus, who died, yes, who was raised, who is at the right hand of God, who indeed intercedes for us.

The Gospel **Matthew 13:31-33, 44-49a**

Jesus put before them another parable: "The kingdom of heaven is like a mustard seed that someone took and sowed in his field; it is the smallest of all the seeds, but when it has grown it is the greatest of shrubs and becomes a tree, so that the birds of the air come and make nests in its branches." He told them another parable: "The kingdom of heaven is like yeast that a woman took and mixed in with three measures of flour until all of it was leavened. The kingdom of heaven is like treasure hidden in a field, which someone found and hid; then in his joy he goes and sells all that he has and buys that field. Again, the kingdom of heaven is like a merchant in search of fine pearls; on finding one pearl of great value, he went and sold all that he had and bought it. Again, the kingdom of heaven is like a net that was thrown into the sea and caught fish of every kind; when it was full, they drew it ashore, sat down, and put the good into baskets but threw out the bad. So it will be at the end of the age."

Year B

The Lesson **2 Kings 2:1-15**

Now when the LORD was about to take Elijah up to heaven by a whirlwind, Elijah and Elisha were on their way from Gilgal. Elijah said to Elisha, "Stay here; for the LORD has sent me as far as Bethel." But Elisha said, "As the LORD lives, and as you yourself live, I will not leave you." So they went down to Bethel. The company of prophets who were in Bethel came out to Elisha, and said to him, "Do you know that today the LORD will take your master away from you?" And he said, "Yes, I know; keep silent." Elijah said to him, "Elisha, stay here; for the LORD has sent me to Jericho." But he said, "As the LORD lives, and as you yourself live, I will not leave you." So they came to Jericho. The company of prophets who were at Jericho drew near to Elisha, and said to him, "Do you know that today the LORD will take your master away from you?" And he answered, "Yes, I know; be silent." Then Elijah said to him, "Stay here; for the LORD has sent me to the Jordan." But he said, "As the LORD lives, and as you yourself live, I will not leave you." So the two of them went on. Fifty men of the company of prophets also went, and stood at some distance from them, as they both were standing by the Jordan. Then Elijah took his mantle and rolled it up, and struck the water; the water was parted to the one side and to the other, until the two of them crossed on dry ground. When they had crossed, Elijah said to Elisha, "Tell me what I may do for you, before I am taken from you." Elisha said, "Please let me inherit a double share of your spirit." He responded, "You have asked a hard thing; yet, if you see me as I am being taken from you, it will be granted you; if not, it will not." As they continued walking and talking, a chariot of fire and horses of fire separated the two of them, and Elijah ascended in a whirlwind into heaven. Elisha kept watching and crying out, "Father, father! The chariots of Israel and its horsemen!" But when he could no longer see him, he grasped his own clothes and tore them in two pieces. He picked up the mantle of Elijah that had fallen from him, and went back and stood on the bank of the Jordan. He took the mantle of Elijah that had fallen from him, and struck the water, saying, "Where is the LORD, the God of Elijah?" When he had struck the water, the water was parted to the one side and to the other, and Elisha went over. When the company of prophets who were at Jericho saw him at a distance, they declared, "The spirit of Elijah rests on Elisha." They came to meet him and bowed to the ground before him.

The Psalm 114   *In exitu Israel*

1   Hallelujah!
     When Israel came out of Egypt, *
        the house of Jacob from a people of strange speech,

2   Judah became God's sanctuary *
        and Israel his dominion.

3   The sea beheld it and fled; *
        Jordan turned and went back.

4   The mountains skipped like rams, *
        and the little hills like young sheep.

5   What ailed you, O sea, that you fled? *
        O Jordan, that you turned back?

6   You mountains, that you skipped like rams? *
        you little hills like young sheep?

7   Tremble, O earth, at the presence of the Lord, *
        at the presence of the God of Jacob,

8   Who turned the hard rock into a pool of water *
        and flint-stone into a flowing spring.

The Epistle   **Ephesians 4:1-7, 11-16**

I therefore, the prisoner in the Lord, beg you to lead a life worthy of the calling to which you have been called, with all humility and gentleness, with patience, bearing with one another in love, making every effort to maintain the unity of the Spirit in the bond of peace. There is one body and one Spirit, just as you were called to the one hope of your calling, one Lord, one faith, one baptism, one God and Father of all, who is above all and through all and in all. But each of us was given grace according to the measure of Christ's gift. The gifts he gave were that some would be apostles, some prophets, some evangelists, some pastors and teachers, to equip the saints for the work of ministry, for building up the body of Christ, until all of us come to the unity of the faith and of the knowledge of the Son of God, to maturity, to the measure of the full stature of Christ. We must no longer be children, tossed to and fro and blown about by every wind of doctrine, by people's trickery, by their craftiness in deceitful scheming. But speaking the truth in love, we must grow up in every way into him who is the head, into Christ, from whom the whole body, joined and knit together by every ligament with which it is equipped, as each part is working properly, promotes the body's growth in building itself up in love.

The Gospel   **Mark 6:45-52**

Immediately after the feeding of the five thousand, Jesus made his disciples get into the boat and go on ahead to the other side, to Bethsaida, while he dismissed the crowd. After saying farewell to them, he went up on the mountain to pray. When evening came, the boat was out on the sea, and he was alone on the land. When he saw that they were straining at the oars against an adverse wind, he came towards them early in the morning, walking on the sea. He intended to pass them by. But when they saw him walking on the sea, they thought it was a ghost and cried out; for they all saw him and were terrified. But immediately he spoke to them and said, "Take heart, it is I; do not be afraid." Then he got into the boat with them and the wind ceased. And they were utterly astounded, for they did not understand about the loaves, but their hearts were hardened.

Year C

The Lesson   **Genesis 18:20-33**

Then the LORD said, "How great is the outcry against Sodom and Gomorrah and how very grave their sin! I must go down and see whether they have done altogether according to the outcry that has come to me; and if not, I will know." So the men turned from there, and went toward Sodom, while Abraham remained standing before the LORD. Then Abraham came near and said, "Will you indeed sweep away the righteous with the wicked? Suppose there are fifty righteous within the city; will you then sweep away the place and not forgive it for the fifty righteous who are in it? Far be it from you to do such a thing, to slay the righteous with the wicked, so that the righteous fare as the wicked! Far be that from you! Shall not the Judge of all the earth do what is just?" And the LORD said, "If I find at Sodom fifty righteous in the city, I will forgive the whole place for their sake." Abraham answered, "Let me take it upon myself to speak to the Lord, I who am but dust and ashes. Suppose five of the fifty righteous are lacking? Will you destroy the whole city for lack of five?" And he said, "I will not destroy it if I find forty-five there." Again he spoke to him, "Suppose forty are found there." He answered, "For the sake of forty I will not do it." Then he said, "Oh do not let the Lord be angry if I speak. Suppose thirty are found there." He answered, "I will not do it, if I find thirty there." He said, "Let me take it upon myself to speak to the Lord. Suppose twenty are found there." He answered, "For the sake of twenty I will not destroy it." Then he said, "Oh do not let the Lord be angry if I speak just once more. Suppose ten are found there." He answered, "For the sake of ten I will not destroy it." And the LORD went his way, when he had finished speaking to Abraham; and Abraham returned to his place.

The Psalm 138   *Confitebor tibi*

1   I will give thanks to you, O LORD, with my whole heart; *
        before the gods I will sing your praise.

2   I will bow down toward your holy temple
     and praise your Name, *
        because of your love and faithfulness;

3   For you have glorified your Name *
        and your word above all things.

4   When I called, you answered me; *
        you increased my strength within me.

5   All the kings of the earth will praise you, O LORD, *
        when they have heard the words of your mouth.

6   They will sing of the ways of the LORD, *
        that great is the glory of the LORD.

7   Though the LORD be high, he cares for the lowly; *
        he perceives the haughty from afar.

8   Though I walk in the midst of trouble, you keep me safe; *
        you stretch forth your hand against the fury of my enemies;
        your right hand shall save me.

9   The LORD will make good his purpose for me; *
        O LORD, your love endures for ever;
        do not abandon the works of your hands.

The Epistle   Colossians 2:6-15

As you therefore have received Christ Jesus the Lord, continue to live your lives in him, rooted and built up in him and established in the faith, just as you were taught, abounding in thanksgiving. See to it that no one takes you captive through philosophy and empty deceit, according to human tradition, according to the elemental spirits of the universe, and not according to Christ. For in him the whole fullness of deity dwells bodily, and you have come to fullness in him, who is the head of every ruler and authority. In him also you were circumcised with a spiritual circumcision, by putting off the body of the flesh in the circumcision of Christ; when you were buried with him in baptism, you were also raised with him through faith in the power of God, who raised him from the dead. And when you were dead in trespasses and the uncircumcision of your flesh, God made you alive together with him, when he forgave us all our trespasses, erasing the record that stood against us with its legal demands. He set this aside, nailing it to the cross. He disarmed the rulers and authorities and made a public example of them, triumphing over them in it.

The Gospel Luke 11:1-13

Jesus was praying in a certain place, and after he had finished, one of his disciples said to him, "Lord, teach us to pray, as John taught his disciples." He said to them, "When you pray, say: Father, hallowed be your name. Your kingdom come. Give us each day our daily bread. And forgive us our sins, for we ourselves forgive everyone indebted to us. And do not bring us to the time of trial." And he said to them, "Suppose one of you has a friend, and you go to him at midnight and say to him, 'Friend, lend me three loaves of bread; for a friend of mine has arrived, and I have nothing to set before him.' And he answers from within, 'Do not bother me; the door has already been locked, and my children are with me in bed; I cannot get up and give you anything.' I tell you, even though he will not get up and give him anything because he is his friend, at least because of his persistence he will get up and give him whatever he needs. So I say to you, Ask, and it will be given you; search, and you will find; knock, and the door will be opened for you. For everyone who asks receives, and everyone who searches finds, and for everyone who knocks, the door will be opened. Is there anyone among you who, if your child asks for a fish, will give a snake instead of a fish? Or if the child asks for an egg, will give a scorpion? If you then, who are evil, know how to give good gifts to your children, how much more will the heavenly Father give the Holy Spirit to those who ask him!"

Proper 13 *The Sunday closest to August 3*

The Collect

Let your continual mercy, O Lord, cleanse and defend your Church; and, because it cannot continue in safety without your help, protect and govern it always by your goodness; through Jesus Christ our Lord, who lives and reigns with you and the Holy Spirit, one God, for ever and ever. *Amen.*

O Lord, we beseech thee, let thy continual pity cleanse and defend thy Church, and, because it cannot continue in safety without thy succor, preserve it evermore by thy help and goodness; through Jesus Christ our Lord, who liveth and reigneth with thee and the Holy Spirit, one God, for ever and ever. *Amen.*

Year A

The Lesson Nehemiah 9:16-20

Ezra said, "O Lord God they and our ancestors acted presumptuously and stiffened their necks and did not obey your commandments; they refused to obey, and were not mindful of the wonders that you performed among them; but they stiffened their necks and determined to return to their slavery in Egypt. But you are a God ready to forgive, gracious and merciful, slow to anger and abounding in steadfast love, and you did not forsake them. Even when they had cast an image of a calf for themselves and said, 'This is your God who brought you up out of Egypt,' and had committed great blasphemies, you in your great mercies did not forsake them in the wilderness; the pillar of cloud that led them in the way did not leave them by day, nor the pillar of fire by night that gave them light on the way by which they should go. You gave your good spirit to instruct them, and did not withhold your manna from their mouths, and gave them water for their thirst."

The Psalm 78:1-29 or (78:14-20, 23-25)   *Attendite, popule*

1   Hear my teaching, O my people; *
        incline your ears to the words of my mouth.

2   I will open my mouth in a parable; *
        I will declare the mysteries of ancient times.

3   That which we have heard and known,
    and what our forefathers have told us, *
        we will not hide from their children.

4   We will recount to generations to come
    the praiseworthy deeds and the power of the LORD, *
        and the wonderful works he has done.

5   He gave his decrees to Jacob
    and established a law for Israel, *
        which he commanded them to teach their children;

6   That the generations to come might know,
    and the children yet unborn; *
        that they in their turn might tell it to their children;

7   So that they might put their trust in God, *
        and not forget the deeds of God,
        but keep his commandments;

8   And not be like their forefathers,
    a stubborn and rebellious generation, *
        a generation whose heart was not steadfast,
        and whose spirit was not faithful to God.

9   The people of Ephraim, armed with the bow, *
        turned back in the day of battle;

10 They did not keep the covenant of God, *
        and refused to walk in his law;

11 They forgot what he had done, *
        and the wonders he had shown them.

12 He worked marvels in the sight of their forefathers, *
        in the land of Egypt, in the field of Zoan.

13 He split open the sea and let them pass through; *
        he made the waters stand up like walls.

14 [He led them with a cloud by day, *
        and all the night through with a glow of fire.

15 He split the hard rocks in the wilderness *
        and gave them drink as from the great deep.

16 He brought streams out of the cliff, *
   and the waters gushed out like rivers.

17 But they went on sinning against him, *
   rebelling in the desert against the Most High.

18 They tested God in their hearts, *
   demanding food for their craving.

19 They railed against God and said, *
   "Can God set a table in the wilderness?

20 True, he struck the rock, the waters gushed out, and the
            gullies overflowed; *
   but is he able to give bread
   or to provide meat for his people?"]

21 When the LORD heard this, he was full of wrath; *
   a fire was kindled against Jacob,
   and his anger mounted against Israel;

22 For they had no faith in God, *
   nor did they put their trust in his saving power.

23 [So he commanded the clouds above *
   and opened the doors of heaven.

24 He rained down manna upon them to eat *
   and gave them grain from heaven.

25 So mortals ate the bread of angels; *
   he provided for them food enough.]

26 He caused the east wind to blow in the heavens *
   and led out the south wind by his might.

27 He rained down flesh upon them like dust *
   and winged birds like the sand of the sea.

28 He let it fall in the midst of their camp *
   and round about their dwellings.

29 So they ate and were well filled *
   for he gave them what they craved.

The Epistle   **Romans 8:35-39**

Who will separate us from the love of Christ? Will hardship, or distress, or
persecution, or famine, or nakedness, or peril, or sword? As it is written, "For your
sake we are being killed all day long; we are accounted as sheep to be slaughtered."
No, in all these things we are more than conquerors through him who loved us. For I
am convinced that neither death, nor life, nor angels, nor rulers, nor things present,
nor things to come, nor powers, nor height, nor depth, nor anything else in all
creation, will be able to separate us from the love of God in Christ Jesus our Lord.

The Gospel   Matthew 14:13-21

Jesus withdrew in a boat to a deserted place by himself. But when the crowds heard
it, they followed him on foot from the towns. When he went ashore, he saw a great
crowd; and he had compassion for them and cured their sick. When it was evening,
the disciples came to him and said, "This is a deserted place, and the hour is now
late; send the crowds away so that they may go into the villages and buy food for
themselves." Jesus said to them, "They need not go away; you give them something
to eat." They replied, "We have nothing here but five loaves and two fish." And he
said, "Bring them here to me." Then he ordered the crowds to sit down on the grass.
Taking the five loaves and the two fish, he looked up to heaven, and blessed and
broke the loaves, and gave them to the disciples, and the disciples gave them to the
crowds. And all ate and were filled; and they took up what was left over of the broken
pieces, twelve baskets full. And those who ate were about five thousand men, besides
women and children.

Year B

The Lesson   Exodus 16:2-4, 9-15

The whole congregation of the Israelites complained against Moses and Aaron in the
wilderness. The Israelites said to them, "If only we had died by the hand of the LORD
in the land of Egypt, when we sat by the fleshpots and ate our fill of bread; for you
have brought us out into this wilderness to kill this whole assembly with hunger."
Then the LORD said to Moses, "I am going to rain bread from heaven for you, and
each day the people shall go out and gather enough for that day. In that way I will test
them, whether they will follow my instruction or not. Then Moses said to Aaron,
"Say to the whole congregation of the Israelites, 'Draw near to the LORD, for he has
heard your complaining.'" And as Aaron spoke to the whole congregation of the
Israelites, they looked toward the wilderness, and the glory of the LORD appeared in
the cloud. The LORD spoke to Moses and said, "I have heard the complaining of the
Israelites; say to them, 'At twilight you shall eat meat, and in the morning you shall
have your fill of bread; then you shall know that I am the LORD your God.'" In the
evening quails came up and covered the camp; and in the morning there was a layer
of dew around the camp. When the layer of dew lifted, there on the surface of the
wilderness was a fine flaky substance, as fine as frost on the ground. When the
Israelites saw it, they said to one another, "What is it?" For they did not know what
it was. Moses said to them, "It is the bread that the LORD has given you to eat."

The Psalm 78:1-25 or 78:14-20, 23-25   *Attendite, popule*

1   Hear my teaching, O my people; *
            incline your ears to the words of my mouth.

2   I will open my mouth in a parable; *
            I will declare the mysteries of ancient times.

3   That which we have heard and known,
            and what our forefathers have told us, *
                  we will not hide from their children.

4   We will recount to generations to come
the praiseworthy deeds and the power of the LORD, *
  and the wonderful works he has done.

5   He gave his decrees to Jacob
and established a law for Israel, *
  which he commanded them to teach their children;

6   That the generations to come might know,
and the children yet unborn; *
  that they in their turn might tell it to their children;

7   So that they might put their trust in God, *
and not forget the deeds of God,
  but keep his commandments;

8   And not be like their forefathers,
a stubborn and rebellious generation, *
  a generation whose heart was not steadfast,
  and whose spirit was not faithful to God.

9   The people of Ephraim, armed with the bow, *
  turned back in the day of battle;

10   They did not keep the covenant of God, *
  and refused to walk in his law;

11   They forgot what he had done, *
  and the wonders he had shown them.

12   He worked marvels in the sight of their forefathers, *
  in the land of Egypt, in the field of Zoan.

13   He split open the sea and let them pass through; *
  he made the waters stand up like walls.

14   [He led them with a cloud by day, *
  and all the night through with a glow of fire.

15   He split the hard rocks in the wilderness *
  and gave them drink as from the great deep.

16   He brought streams out of the cliff, *
  and the waters gushed out like rivers.

17   But they went on sinning against him, *
  rebelling in the desert against the Most High.

18   They tested God in their hearts, *
  demanding food for their craving.

19   They railed against God and said, *
  "Can God set a table in the wilderness?

20   True, he struck the rock, the waters gushed out, and the
                gullies overflowed; *
      but is he able to give bread
      or to provide meat for his people?"]

21   When the LORD heard this, he was full of wrath; *
      a fire was kindled against Jacob,
      and his anger mounted against Israel;

22   For they had not faith in God, *
      nor did they put their trust in his saving power.

23   [So he commanded the clouds above *
      and opened the doors of heaven.

24   He rained down manna upon them to eat *
      and gave them grain from heaven.

25   So mortals ate the bread of angels; *
      he provided for them food enough.]

The Epistle   **Ephesians 4:17-25**

Now this I affirm and insist on in the Lord: you must no longer live as the Gentiles live, in the futility of their minds. They are darkened in their understanding, alienated from the life of God because of their ignorance and hardness of heart. They have lost all sensitivity and have abandoned themselves to licentiousness, greedy to practice every kind of impurity. That is not the way you learned Christ! For surely you have heard about him and were taught in him, as truth is in Jesus. You were taught to put away your former way of life, your old self, corrupt and deluded by its lusts, and to be renewed in the spirit of your minds, and to clothe yourselves with the new self, created according to the likeness of God in true righteousness and holiness. So then, putting away falsehood, let all of us speak the truth to our neighbors, for we are members of one another.

The Gospel   **John 6:24-35**

On the next day, when the people who remained after the feeding of the five thousand saw that Jesus was not there, nor his disciples, they themselves got into the boats and went to Capernaum looking for Jesus. When they found him on the other side of the sea, they said to him, "Rabbi, when did you come here?" Jesus answered them, "Very truly, I tell you, you are looking for me, not because you saw signs, but because you ate your fill of the loaves. Do not work for the food that perishes, but for the food that endures for eternal life, which the Son of Man will give you. For it is on him that God the Father has set his seal." Then they said to him, "What must we do to perform the works of God?" Jesus answered them, "This is the work of God, that you believe in him whom he has sent." So they said to him, "What sign are you going to give us then, so that we may see it and believe you? What work are you performing? Our ancestors ate the manna in the wilderness; as it is written, 'He gave them bread from heaven to eat.'" Then Jesus said to them, "Very truly, I tell you, it was not Moses who gave you the bread from heaven, but it is my Father who gives you the true bread from heaven. For the bread of God is that which comes down from heaven and gives life to the world." They said to him, "Sir, give us this bread always." Jesus said to them, "I am the bread of life. Whoever comes to me will never be hungry, and whoever believes in me will never be thirsty."

Year C

The Lesson   Ecclesiastes 1:12-14; 2:(1-7, 11) 18-23

I, the Teacher, when king over Israel in Jerusalem, applied my mind to seek and to search out by wisdom all that is done under heaven; it is an unhappy business that God has given to human beings to be busy with. I saw all the deeds that are done under the sun; and see, all is vanity and a chasing after wind. [I said to myself, "Come now, I will make a test of pleasure; enjoy yourself." But again, this also was vanity. I said of laughter, "It is mad," and of pleasure, "What use is it?" I searched with my mind how to cheer my body with wine — my mind still guiding me with wisdom — and how to lay hold on folly, until I might see what was good for mortals to do under heaven during the few days of their life. I made great works; I built houses and planted vineyards for myself; I made myself gardens and parks, and planted in them all kinds of fruit trees. I made myself pools from which to water the forest of growing trees. I bought male and female slaves, and had slaves who were born in my house; I also had great possessions of herds and flocks, more than any who had been before me in Jerusalem. Then I considered all that my hands had done and the toil I had spent in doing it, and again, all was vanity and a chasing after wind, and there was nothing to be gained under the sun.] I hated all my toil in which I had toiled under the sun, seeing that I must leave it to those who come after me — and who knows whether they will be wise or foolish? Yet they will be master of all for which I toiled and used my wisdom under the sun. This also is vanity. So I turned and gave my heart up to despair concerning all the toil of my labors under the sun, because sometimes one who has toiled with wisdom and knowledge and skill must leave all to be enjoyed by another who did not toil for it. This also is vanity and a great evil. What do mortals get from all the toil and strain with which they toil under the sun? For all their days are full of pain, and their work is a vexation; even at night their minds do not rest. This also is vanity.

The Psalm 49 or 49:1-11   *Audite haec, omnes*

1   [Hear this, all you peoples;
       hearken, all you who dwell in the world, *
          you of high degree and low, rich and poor together.

2   My mouth shall speak of wisdom, *
          and my heart shall meditate on understanding.

3   I will incline my ear to a proverb *
          and set forth my riddle upon the harp.

4   Why should I be afraid in evil days, *
          when the wickedness of those at my heels surrounds me,

5   The wickedness of those who put their trust in their goods, *
          and boast of their great riches?

6   We can never ransom ourselves, *
      or deliver to God the price of our life;

7   For the ransom of our life is so great, *
      that we should never have enough to pay it,

8   In order to live for ever and ever, *
      and never see the grave.

9   For we see that the wise die also;
    like the dull and stupid they perish *
      and leave their wealth to those who come after them.

10   Their graves shall be their homes for ever,
    their dwelling places from generation to generation, *
      though they call the lands after their own names.

11   Even though honored, they cannot live for ever; *
      they are like the beasts that perish.]

12   Such is the way of those who foolishly trust in themselves, *
      and the end of those who delight in their own words.

13   Like a flock of sheep they are destined to die;
    Death is their shepherd; *
      they go down straightway to the grave.

14   Their form shall waste away, *
      and the land of the dead shall be their home.

15   But God will ransom my life; *
      he will snatch me from the grasp of death.

16   Do not be envious when some become rich, *
      or when the grandeur of their house increases;

17   For they will carry nothing away at their death, *
      nor will their grandeur follow them.

18   Though they thought highly of themselves while they lived, *
      and were praised for their success,

19   They shall join the company of their forebears, *
      who will never see the light again.

20   Those who are honored, but have no understanding, *
      are like the beasts that perish.

The Epistle   **Colossians 3:(5-11) 12-17**
[Put to death, therefore, whatever in you is earthly: fornication, impurity, passion,
evil desire, and greed (which is idolatry). On account of these the wrath of God is
coming on those who are disobedient. These are the ways you also once followed,
when you were living that life. But now you must get rid of all such things — anger,

wrath, malice, slander, and abusive language from your mouth. Do not lie to one another, seeing that you have stripped off the old self with its practices and have clothed yourselves with the new self, which is being renewed in knowledge according to the image of its creator. In that renewal there is no longer Greek and Jew, circumcised and uncircumcised, barbarian, Scythian, slave and free; but Christ is all and in all!] As God's chosen ones, holy and beloved, clothe yourselves with compassion, kindness, humility, meekness, and patience. Bear with one another and, if anyone has a complaint against another, forgive each other; just as the Lord has forgiven you, so you also must forgive. Above all, clothe yourselves with love, which binds everything together in perfect harmony. And let the peace of Christ rule in your hearts, to which indeed you were called in the one body. And be thankful. Let the word of Christ dwell in you richly; teach and admonish one another in all wisdom; and with gratitude in your hearts sing psalms, hymns, and spiritual songs to God. And whatever you do, in word or deed, do everything in the name of the Lord Jesus, giving thanks to God the Father through him.

The Gospel
Luke 12:13-21

Someone in the crowd said to Jesus, "Teacher, tell my brother to divide the family inheritance with me." But he said to him, "Friend, who set me to be a judge or arbitrator over you?" And he said to them, "Take care! Be on your guard against all kinds of greed; for one's life does not consist in the abundance of possessions." Then he told them a parable: "The land of a rich man produced abundantly. And he thought to himself, 'What should I do, for I have no place to store my crops?' Then he said, 'I will do this: I will pull down my barns and build larger ones, and there I will store all my grain and my goods. And I will say to my soul, 'Soul, you have ample goods laid up for many years; relax, eat, drink, be merry.' But God said to him, 'You fool! This very night your life is being demanded of you. And the things you have prepared, whose will they be?' So it is with those who store up treasures for themselves but are not rich toward God."

Proper 14 *The Sunday closest to August 10*

The Collect
Grant to us, Lord, we pray, the spirit to think and do always those things that are right, that we, who cannot exist without you, may by you be enabled to live according to your will; through Jesus Christ our Lord, who lives and reigns with you and the Holy Spirit, one God, for ever and ever. *Amen.*

Grant to us, Lord, we beseech thee, the spirit to think and do always such things as are right, that we, who cannot exist without thee, may by thee be enabled to live according to thy will; through Jesus Christ our Lord, who liveth and reigneth with thee and the Holy Spirit, one God, for ever and ever. *Amen.*

Year A

The Lesson
Jonah 2:1-9

Then Jonah prayed to the LORD his God from the belly of the fish, saying, "I called to the LORD out of my distress, and he answered me; out of the belly of Sheol I cried, and you heard my voice. You cast me into the deep, into the heart of the seas, and the flood surrounded me; all your waves and your billows passed over me. Then I said, 'I am driven away from your sight; how shall I look again upon your holy temple?' The waters closed in over me; the deep surrounded me; weeds were wrapped around my head at the roots of the mountains. I went down to the land whose bars closed upon me forever; yet you brought up my life from the Pit, O LORD my God. As my life was ebbing away, I remembered the LORD; and my prayer came to you, into your holy temple. Those who worship vain idols forsake their true loyalty. But I with the voice of thanksgiving will sacrifice to you; what I have vowed I will pay. Deliverance belongs to the LORD!'"

The Psalm 29 *Afferte Domino*

1 Ascribe to the LORD, you gods, *
        ascribe to the LORD glory and strength.

2 Ascribe to the LORD the glory due his Name; *
        worship the LORD in the beauty of holiness.

3 The voice of the LORD is upon the waters;
   the God of glory thunders; *
        the LORD is upon the mighty waters.

4 The voice of the LORD is a powerful voice; *
        the voice of the LORD is a voice of splendor.

5 The voice of the LORD breaks the cedar trees; *
        the LORD breaks the cedars of Lebanon;

6 He makes Lebanon skip like a calf, *
        and Mount Hermon like a young wild ox.

7 The voice of the LORD splits the flames of fire;
   the voice of the LORD shakes the wilderness; *
        the LORD shakes the wilderness of Kadesh.

8 The voice of the LORD makes the oak trees writhe *
        and strips the forests bare.

9 And in the temple of the LORD *
        all are crying, "Glory!"

10 The LORD sits enthroned above the flood; *
        the LORD sits enthroned as King for evermore.

11 The LORD shall give strength to his people; *
        the LORD shall give his people the blessing of peace.

The Epistle   **Romans 9:1-5**
I am speaking the truth in Christ — I am not lying; my conscience confirms it by the Holy Spirit — I have great sorrow and unceasing anguish in my heart. For I could wish that I myself were accursed and cut off from Christ for the sake of my own people, my kindred according to the flesh. They are Israelites, and to them belong the adoption, the glory, the covenants, the giving of the law, the worship, and the

promises; to them belong the patriarchs, and from them, according to the flesh, comes the Messiah, who is over all, God blessed forever. Amen.

The Gospel   Matthew 14:22-33

Jesus made the disciples get into the boat and go on ahead to the other side, while he dismissed the crowds. And after he had dismissed the crowds, he went up the mountain by himself to pray. When evening came, he was there alone, but by this time the boat, battered by the waves, was far from the land, for the wind was against them. And early in the morning he came walking toward them on the sea. But when the disciples saw him walking on the sea, they were terrified, saying, "It is a ghost!" And they cried out in fear. But immediately Jesus spoke to them and said, "Take heart, it is I; do not be afraid." Peter answered him, "Lord, if it is you, command me to come to you on the water." He said, "Come." So Peter got out of the boat, started walking on the water, and came toward Jesus. But when he noticed the strong wind, he became frightened, and beginning to sink, he cried out, "Lord, save me!" Jesus immediately reached out his hand and caught him, saying to him, "You of little faith, why did you doubt?" When they got into the boat, the wind ceased. And those in the boat worshiped him, saying, "Truly you are the Son of God."

Year B

The Lesson   Deuteronomy 8:1-10

This entire commandment that I command you today you must diligently observe, so that you may live and increase, and go in and occupy the land that the LORD promised on oath to your ancestors. Remember the long way that the LORD your God has led you these forty years in the wilderness, in order to humble you, testing you to know what is in your heart, whether or not you would keep his commandments. He humbled you by letting you hunger, then by feeding you with manna, with which neither you nor your ancestors were acquainted, in order to make you understand that one does not live by bread alone, but by every word that comes from the mouth of the LORD. The clothes on your back did not wear out and your feet did not swell these forty years. Know then in your heart that as a parent disciplines a child so the LORD your God disciplines you. Therefore keep the commandments of the LORD your God, by walking in his ways and by fearing him. For the LORD your God is bringing you into a good land, a land with flowing streams, with springs and underground waters welling up in valleys and hills, a land of wheat and barley, of vines and fig trees and pomegranates, a land of olive trees and honey, a land where you may eat bread without scarcity, where you will lack nothing, a land whose stones are iron and from whose hills you may mine copper. You shall eat your fill and bless the LORD your God for the good land that he has given you.

The Psalm 34 or 34:1-8   *Benedicam Dominum*

1   [I will bless the LORD at all times; *
        his praise shall ever be in my mouth.

2   I will glory in the LORD; *
        let the humble hear and rejoice.

3 Proclaim with me the greatness of the LORD; *
    let us exalt his Name together.

4 I sought the LORD, and he answered me *
    and delivered me out of all my terror.

5 Look upon him and be radiant, *
    and let not your faces be ashamed.

6 I called in my affliction and the LORD heard me *
    and saved me from all my troubles.

7 The angel of the LORD encompasses those who fear him, *
    and he will deliver them.

8 Taste and see that the LORD is good; *
    happy are they who trust in him!]

9 Fear the LORD, you that are his saints, *
    for those who fear him lack nothing.

10 The young lions lack and suffer hunger, *
    but those who seek the LORD lack nothing that is good.

11 Come, children, and listen to me; *
    I will teach you the fear of the LORD.

12 Who among you loves life *
    and desires long life to enjoy prosperity?

13 Keep your tongue from evil-speaking *
    and your lips from lying words.

14 Turn from evil and do good; *
    seek peace and pursue it.

15 The eyes of the LORD are upon the righteous, *
    and his ears are open to their cry.

16 The face of the LORD is against those who do evil, *
    to root out the remembrance of them from the earth.

17 The righteous cry, and the LORD hears them *
    and delivers them from all their troubles.

18 The LORD is near to the brokenhearted *
    and will save those whose spirits are crushed.

19 Many are the troubles of the righteous, *
    but the LORD will deliver him out of them all.

20 He will keep safe all his bones; *
    not one of them shall be broken.

21   Evil shall slay the wicked, *
      and those who hate the righteous will be punished.

22   The LORD ransoms the life of his servants, *
      and none will be punished who trust in him.

The Epistle   **Ephesians 4:(25-29) 30-5:2**

[Putting away falsehood, let all of us speak the truth to our neighbors, for we are members of one another. Be angry but do not sin; do not let the sun go down on your anger, and do not make room for the devil. Thieves must give up stealing; rather let them labor and work honestly with their own hands, so as to have something to share with the needy. Let no evil talk come out of your mouths, but only what is useful for building up, as there is need, so that your words may give grace to those who hear.] And do not grieve the Holy Spirit of God, with which you were marked with a seal for the day of redemption. Put away from you all bitterness and wrath and anger and wrangling and slander, together with all malice, and be kind to one another, tenderhearted, forgiving one another, as God in Christ has forgiven you. Therefore be imitators of God, as beloved children, and live in love, as Christ loved us and gave himself up for us, a fragrant offering and sacrifice to God.

The Gospel   **John 6:37-51**

Jesus said to the people, "Everything that the Father gives me will come to me, and anyone who comes to me I will never drive away; for I have come down from heaven, not to do my own will, but the will of him who sent me. And this is the will of him who sent me, that I should lose nothing of all that he has given me, but raise it up on the last day. This is indeed the will of my Father, that all who see the Son and believe in him may have eternal life; and I will raise them up on the last day." Then the Jews began to complain about him because he said, "I am the bread that came down from heaven." They were saying, "Is not this Jesus, the son of Joseph, whose father and mother we know? How can he now say, 'I have come down from heaven'?" Jesus answered them, "Do not complain among yourselves. No one can come to me unless drawn by the Father who sent me; and I will raise that person up on the last day. It is written in the prophets, 'And they shall all be taught by God.' Everyone who has heard and learned from the Father comes to me. Not that anyone has seen the Father except the one who is from God; he has seen the Father. Very truly, I tell you, whoever believes has eternal life. I am the bread of life. Your ancestors ate the manna in the wilderness, and they died. This is the bread that comes down from heaven, so that one may eat of it and not die. I am the living bread that came down from heaven. Whoever eats of this bread will live forever; and the bread that I will give for the life of the world is my flesh."

Year C

The Lesson   **Genesis 15:1-6**

After these things the word of the LORD came to Abram in a vision, "Do not be afraid, Abram, I am your shield; your reward shall be very great." But Abram said, "O Lord GOD, what will you give me, for I continue childless, and the heir of my house is Eliezer of Damascus?" And Abram said, "You have given me no offspring, and so a slave born in my house is to be my heir." But the word of the LORD came to him, "This man shall not be your heir; no one but your very own issue shall be your heir." He brought him outside and said, "Look toward heaven and count the stars, if you are able to count them." Then he said to him, "So shall your descendants be." And he believed the LORD; and the LORD reckoned it to him as righteousness.

The Psalm 33 or 33:12-15, 18-22   *Exultate, justi*

1   Rejoice in the LORD, you righteous; *
          it is good for the just to sing praises.

2   Praise the LORD with the harp; *
          play to him upon the psaltery and lyre.

3   Sing for him a new song; *
          sound a fanfare with all your skill upon the trumpet.

4   For the word of the LORD is right, *
          and all his works are sure.

5   He loves righteousness and justice; *
          the loving-kindness of the LORD fills the whole earth.

6   By the word of the LORD were the heavens made, *
          by the breath of his mouth all the heavenly hosts.

7   He gathers up the waters of the ocean as in a water-skin *
          and stores up the depths of the sea.

8   Let all the earth fear the LORD; *
          let all who dwell in the world stand in awe of him.

9   For he spoke, and it came to pass; *
          he commanded, and it stood fast.

10   The LORD brings the will of the nations to naught; *
          he thwarts the designs of the peoples.

11   But the LORD'S will stands fast for ever, *
          and the designs of his heart from age to age.

12   [Happy is the nation whose God is the LORD! *
          happy the people he has chosen to be his own!

13   The LORD looks down from heaven, *
          and beholds all the people in the world.

14   From where he sits enthroned he turns his gaze *
          on all who dwell on the earth.

15   He fashions all the hearts of them *
          and understands all their works.]

16   There is no king that can be saved by a mighty army; *
          a strong man is not delivered by his great strength.

17   The horse is a vain hope for deliverance; *
        for all its strength it cannot save.

18   [Behold, the eye of the LORD is upon those who fear him, *
        on those who wait upon his love,

19   To pluck their lives from death, *
        and to feed them in time of famine.

20   Our soul waits for the LORD; *
        he is our help and our shield.

21   Indeed, our heart rejoices in him, *
        for in his holy Name we put our trust.

22   Let your loving-kindness, O LORD, be upon us, *
        as we have put our trust in you.]

The Epistle   Hebrews 11:1-3 (4-7) 8-16

Now faith is the assurance of things hoped for, the conviction of things not seen. Indeed, by faith our ancestors received approval. By faith we understand that the worlds were prepared by the word of God, so that what is seen was made from things that are not visible. [By faith Abel offered to God a more acceptable sacrifice than Cain's. Through this he received approval as righteous, God himself giving approval to his gifts; he died, but through his faith he still speaks. By faith Enoch was taken so that he did not experience death; and "he was not found, because God had taken him." For it was attested before he was taken away that "he had pleased God." And without faith it is impossible to please God, for whoever would approach him must believe that he exists and that he rewards those who seek him. By faith Noah, warned by God about events as yet unseen, respected the warning and built an ark to save his household; by this he condemned the world and became an heir to the righteousness that is in accordance with faith.] By faith Abraham obeyed when he was called to set out for a place that he was to receive as an inheritance; and he set out, not knowing where he was going. By faith he stayed for a time in the land he had been promised, as in a foreign land, living in tents, as did Isaac and Jacob, who were heirs with him of the same promise. For he looked forward to the city that has foundations, whose architect and builder is God. By faith he received power of procreation, even though he was too old — and Sarah herself was barren — because he considered him faithful who had promised. Therefore from one person, and this one as good as dead, descendants were born, "as many as the stars of heaven and as the innumerable grains of sand by the seashore." All of these died in faith without having received the promises, but from a distance they saw and greeted them. They confessed that they were strangers and foreigners on the earth, for people who speak in this way make it clear that they are seeking a homeland. If they had been thinking of the land that they had left behind, they would have had opportunity to return. But as it is, they desire a better country, that is, a heavenly one. Therefore God is not ashamed to be called their God; indeed, he has prepared a city for them.

The Gospel   **Luke 12:32-40**

Jesus said to his disciples, "Do not be afraid, little flock, for it is your Father's good pleasure to give you the kingdom. Sell your possessions, and give alms. Make purses for yourselves that do not wear out, an unfailing treasure in heaven, where no thief comes near and no moth destroys. For where your treasure is, there your heart will be also. Be dressed for action and have your lamps lit; be like those who are waiting for their master to return from the wedding banquet, so that they may open the door for him as soon as he comes and knocks. Blessed are those slaves whom the master finds alert when he comes; truly I tell you, he will fasten his belt and have them sit down to eat, and he will come and serve them. If he comes during the middle of the night, or near dawn, and finds them so, blessed are those slaves. But know this: if the owner of the house had known at what hour the thief was coming, he would not have let his house be broken into. You also must be ready, for the Son of Man is coming at an unexpected hour."

Proper 15 *The Sunday closest to August 17*

The Collect

Almighty God, you have given your only Son to be for us a sacrifice for sin, and also an example of godly life: Give us grace to receive thankfully the fruits of his redeeming work, and to follow daily in the blessed steps of his most holy life; through Jesus Christ your Son our Lord, who lives and reigns with you and the Holy Spirit, one God, now and for ever. *Amen.*

Almighty God, who hast given thy only Son to be unto us both a sacrifice for sin and also an example of godly life: Give us grace that we may always most thankfully receive that his inestimable benefit, and also daily endeavor ourselves to follow the blessed steps of his most holy life; through the same thy Son Jesus Christ our Lord, who liveth and reigneth with thee and the Holy Spirit, one God, now and for ever. *Amen.*

Year A

The Lesson   **Isaiah 56:1 (2-5) 6-7**

Thus says the LORD: Maintain justice, and do what is right, for soon my salvation will come, and my deliverance be revealed. [Happy is the mortal who does this, the one who holds it fast, who keeps the sabbath, not profaning it, and refrains from doing any evil. Do not let the foreigner joined to the LORD say, "The LORD will surely separate me from his people"; and do not let the eunuch say, "I am just a dry tree." For thus says the LORD: To the eunuchs who keep my sabbaths, who choose the things that please me and hold fast my covenant, I will give, in my house and within my walls, a monument and a name better than sons and daughters; I will give them an everlasting name that shall not be cut off.] And the foreigners who join themselves to the LORD, to minister to him, to love the name of the LORD, and to be his servants, all who keep the sabbath, and do not profane it, and hold fast my covenant — these I will bring to my holy mountain, and make them joyful in my house of prayer; their burnt offerings and their sacrifices will be accepted on my altar; for my house shall be called a house of prayer for all peoples.

The Psalm 67   *Deus misereatur*

1   May God be merciful to us and bless us, *
     show us the light of his countenance and come to us.

2   Let your ways be known upon earth, *
     your saving health among all nations.

3   Let the peoples praise you, O God; *
     let all the peoples praise you.

4   Let the nations be glad and sing for joy, *
     for you judge the peoples with equity
     and guide all the nations upon earth.

5   Let the peoples praise you, O God; *
     let all the peoples praise you.

6   The earth has brought forth her increase; *
     may God, our own God, give us his blessing.

7   May God give us his blessing, *
     and may all the ends of the earth stand in awe of him.

The Epistle   Romans 11:13-15, 29-32

Now I am speaking to you Gentiles. Inasmuch then as I am an apostle to the Gentiles, I glorify my ministry in order to make my own people jealous, and thus save some of them. For if their rejection is the reconciliation of the world, what will their acceptance be but life from the dead! For the gifts and the calling of God are irrevocable. Just as you were once disobedient to God but have now received mercy because of their disobedience, so they have now been disobedient in order that, by the mercy shown to you, they too may now receive mercy. For God has imprisoned all in disobedience so that he may be merciful to all.

The Gospel   Matthew 15:21-28

Jesus left that place and went away to the district of Tyre and Sidon. Just then a Canaanite woman from that region came out and started shouting, "Have mercy on me, Lord, Son of David; my daughter is tormented by a demon." But he did not answer her at all. And his disciples came and urged him, saying, "Send her away, for she keeps shouting after us." He answered, "I was sent only to the lost sheep of the house of Israel." But she came and knelt before him, saying, "Lord, help me." He answered, "It is not fair to take the children's food and throw it to the dogs." She said, "Yes, Lord, yet even the dogs eat the crumbs that fall from their masters' table." Then Jesus answered her, "Woman, great is your faith! Let it be done for you as you wish." And her daughter was healed instantly.

Year B

The Lesson   Proverbs 9:1-6

Wisdom has built her house, she has hewn her seven pillars. She has slaughtered her animals, she has mixed her wine, she has also set her table. She has sent out her servant girls, she calls from the highest places in the town, "You that are simple, turn in here!" To those without sense she says, "Come, eat of my bread and drink of the wine I have mixed. Lay aside immaturity, and live, and walk in the way of insight."

The Psalm 147   *Laudate Dominum*

1   Hallelujah!
     How good it is to sing praises to our God! *
        how pleasant it is to honor him with praise!

2   The LORD rebuilds Jerusalem; *
        he gathers the exiles of Israel.

3   He heals the brokenhearted *
        and binds up their wounds.

4   He counts the number of the stars *
        and calls them all by their names.

5   Great is our LORD and mighty in power; *
        there is no limit to his wisdom.

6   The LORD lifts up the lowly, *
        but casts the wicked to the ground.

7   Sing to the LORD with thanksgiving; *
        make music to our God upon the harp.

8   He covers the heavens with clouds *
        and prepares rain for the earth;

9   He makes grass to grow upon the mountains *
        and green plants to serve mankind.

10   He provides food for flocks and herds *
        and for the young ravens when they cry.

11   He is not impressed by the might of a horse; *
        he has no pleasure in the strength of a man;

12   But the LORD has pleasure in those who fear him, *
        in those who await his gracious favor.

13   Worship the LORD, O Jerusalem; *
        praise your God, O Zion;

14   For he has strengthened the bars of your gates; *
        he has blessed your children within you.

15   He has established peace on your borders; *
        he satisfies you with the finest wheat.

16   He sends out his command to the earth, *
        and his word runs very swiftly.

17   He gives snow like wool; *
        he scatters hoarfrost like ashes.

18   He scatters his hail like bread crumbs; *
        who can stand against his cold?

19   He sends forth his word and melts them; *
        he blows with his wind, and the waters flow.

20   He declares his word to Jacob, *
        his statutes and his judgments to Israel.

21   He has not done so to any other nation; *
        to them he has not revealed his judgments.
     Hallelujah!

or Psalm 34:9-14   *Benedicam Dominum*

9   Fear the LORD, you that are his saints, *
        for those who fear him lack nothing.

10   The young lions lack and suffer hunger, *
        but those who seek the LORD lack nothing that is good.

11   Come, children, and listen to me; *
        I will teach you the fear of the LORD.

12   Who among you loves life *
        and desires long life to enjoy prosperity?

13   Keep your tongue from evil-speaking *
        and your lips from lying words.

14   Turn from evil and do good; *
        seek peace and pursue it.

The Epistle   **Ephesians 5:15-20**

Be careful then how you live, not as unwise people but as wise, making the most of
the time, because the days are evil. So do not be foolish, but understand what the will
of the Lord is. Do not get drunk with wine, for that is debauchery; but be filled with
the Spirit, as you sing psalms and hymns and spiritual songs among yourselves,
singing and making melody to the Lord in your hearts, giving thanks to God the
Father at all times and for everything in the name of our Lord Jesus Christ.

The Gospel   **John 6:53-59**

Jesus said, "Very truly, I tell you, unless you eat the flesh of the Son of Man and
drink his blood, you have no life in you. Those who eat my flesh and drink my blood
have eternal life, and I will raise them up on the last day; for my flesh is true food
and my blood is true drink. Those who eat my flesh and drink my blood abide in me,
and I in them. Just as the living Father sent me, and I live because of the Father, so
whoever eats me will live because of me. This is the bread that came down from
heaven, not like that which your ancestors ate, and they died. But the one who eats
this bread will live forever." He said these things while he was teaching in the
synagogue at Capernaum.

The Lesson   Jeremiah 23:23-29

Am I a God near by, says the LORD, and not a God far off? Who can hide in secret places so that I cannot see them? says the LORD. Do I not fill heaven and earth? says the LORD. I have heard what the prophets have said who prophesy lies in my name, saying, "I have dreamed, I have dreamed!" How long? Will the hearts of the prophets ever turn back — those who prophesy lies, and who prophesy the deceit of their own heart? They plan to make my people forget my name by their dreams that they tell one another, just as their ancestors forgot my name for Baal. Let the prophet who has a dream tell the dream, but let the one who has my word speak my word faithfully. What has straw in common with wheat? says the LORD. Is not my word like fire, says the LORD, and like a hammer that breaks a rock in pieces?

The Psalm 82   *Deus stetit*

1   God takes his stand in the council of heaven; *
         he gives judgment in the midst of the gods:

2   "How long will you judge unjustly, *
         and show favor to the wicked?

3   Save the weak and the orphan; *
         defend the humble and needy;

4   Rescue the weak and the poor; *
         deliver them from the power of the wicked.

5   They do not know, neither do they understand;
     they go about in darkness; *
         all the foundations of the earth are shaken.

6   Now I say to you, 'You are gods, *
         and all of you children of the Most High;

7   Nevertheless, you shall die like mortals, *
         and fall like any prince.'"

8   Arise, O God, and rule the earth, *
         for you shall take all nations for your own.

The Epistle   Hebrews 12:1-7 (8-10) 11-14

Since we are surrounded by so great a cloud of witnesses, let us also lay aside every weight and the sin that clings so closely, and let us run with perseverance the race that is set before us, looking to Jesus the pioneer and perfecter of our faith, who for the sake of the joy that was set before him endured the cross, disregarding its shame, and has taken his seat at the right hand of the throne of God. Consider him who endured such hostility against himself from sinners, so that you may not grow weary or lose heart. In your struggle against sin you have not yet resisted to the point of shedding your blood. And you have forgotten the exhortation that addresses you as children — "My child, do not regard lightly the discipline of the Lord, or lose heart when you are punished by him; for the Lord disciplines those whom he loves, and chastises every child whom he accepts." Endure trials for the sake of discipline. God is treating you as children; for what child is there whom a parent does not discipline? [If you do not have that discipline in which all children share, then you are illegitimate and not his children. Moreover, we had human parents to discipline us, and we respected them. Should we not be even more willing to be subject to the Father of spirits and live? For they disciplined us for a short time as seemed best to them, but he disciplines us for our good, in order that we may share his holiness.] Now, discipline always seems painful rather than pleasant at the time, but later it yields the peaceful fruit of righteousness to those who have been trained by it. Therefore lift your drooping hands and strengthen your weak knees, and make straight paths for your feet, so that what is lame may not be put out of joint, but rather be healed. Pursue peace with everyone, and the holiness without which no one will see the Lord.

The Gospel
Luke 12:49-56

Jesus said, "I came to bring fire to the earth, and how I wish it were already kindled! I have a baptism with which to be baptized, and what stress I am under until it is completed! Do you think that I have come to bring peace to the earth? No, I tell you, but rather division! From now on five in one household will be divided, three against two and two against three; they will be divided: father against son and son against father, mother against daughter and daughter against mother, mother-in-law against her daughter-in-law and daughter-in-law against mother-in-law." He also said to the crowds, "When you see a cloud rising in the west, you immediately say, 'It is going to rain'; and so it happens. And when you see the south wind blowing, you say, 'There will be scorching heat'; and it happens. You hypocrites! You know how to interpret the appearance of earth and sky, but why do you not know how to interpret the present time?"

Proper 16 *The Sunday closest to August 24*

The Collect
Grant, O merciful God, that your Church, being gathered together in unity by your Holy Spirit, may show forth your power among all peoples, to the glory of your Name; through Jesus Christ our Lord, who lives and reigns with you and the Holy Spirit, one God, for ever and ever. *Amen.*

Grant, we beseech thee, merciful God, that thy Church, being gathered together in unity by thy Holy Spirit, may manifest thy power among all peoples, to the glory of thy Name; through Jesus Christ our Lord, who liveth and reigneth with thee and the same Spirit, one God, world without end. *Amen.*

Year A

The Lesson
Isaiah 51:1-6

Listen to me, you that pursue righteousness, you that seek the LORD. Look to the rock from which you were hewn, and to the quarry from which your were dug. Look to Abraham your father and to Sarah who bore you; for he was but one when I called him, but I blessed him and made him many. For the LORD will comfort Zion; he will comfort all her waste places, and will make her wilderness like Eden, her desert like the garden of the LORD; joy and gladness will be found in her, thanksgiving and the voice of song. Listen to me, my people, and give heed to me, my nation; for a teaching will go out from me, and my justice for a light to the peoples. I will bring near my deliverance swiftly, my salvation has gone out and my arms will rule the peoples; the coastlands wait for me, and for my arm they hope. Lift up your eyes to the heavens, and look at the earth beneath; for the heavens will vanish like smoke, the earth will wear out like a garment, and those who live on it will die like gnats; but my salvation will be forever, and my deliverance will never be ended.

The Psalm 138   *Confitebor tibi*

1   I will give thanks to you, O LORD, with my whole heart; *
         before the gods I will sing your praise.

2   I will bow down toward your holy temple
     and praise your Name, *
         because of your love and faithfulness;

3   For you have glorified your Name *
         and your word above all things.

4   When I called, you answered me; *
         you increased my strength within me.

5.   All the kings of the earth will praise you, O LORD, *
         when they have heard the words of your mouth.

6   They will sing of the ways of the LORD, *
         that great is the glory of the LORD.

7   Though the LORD be high, he cares for the lowly; *
         he perceives the haughty from afar.

8   Though I walk in the midst of trouble, you keep me safe; *
         you stretch forth your hand against the fury of my enemies;
         your right hand shall save me.

9   The LORD will make good his purpose for me; *
         O LORD, your love endures for ever;
         do not abandon the works of your hands.

The Epistle   Romans 11:33-36

O the depth of the riches and wisdom and knowledge of God! How unsearchable are his judgments and how inscrutable his ways! "For who has known the mind of the Lord?" "Or who has been his counselor?" "Or who has given a gift to him, to receive a gift in return?" For from him and through him and to him are all things. To him be the glory forever. Amen.

The Gospel   Matthew 16:13-20

When Jesus came into the district of Caesarea Philippi, he asked his disciples, "Who do people say that the Son of Man is?" And they said, "Some say John the Baptist, but others Elijah, and still others Jeremiah or one of the prophets." He said to them, "But who do you say that I am?" Simon Peter answered, "You are the Messiah, the Son of the living God." And Jesus answered him, "Blessed are you, Simon son of Jonah! For flesh and blood has not revealed this to you, but my Father in heaven. And I tell you, you are Peter, and on this rock I will build my church, and the gates of Hades will not prevail against it. I will give you the keys of the kingdom of heaven, and whatever you bind on earth will be bound in heaven, and whatever you loose on earth will be loosed in heaven." Then he sternly ordered the disciples not to tell anyone that he was the Messiah.

Year B

The Lesson   Joshua 24:1-2a, 14-25

Joshua gathered all the tribes of Israel to Shechem, and summoned the elders, the heads, the judges, and the officers of Israel; and they presented themselves before God. And Joshua said to all the people, "Thus says the LORD, the God of Israel: Now therefore revere the LORD, and serve him in sincerity and in faithfulness; put away the gods that your ancestors served beyond the River and in Egypt, and serve the LORD. Now if you are unwilling to serve the LORD, choose this day whom you will serve, whether the gods your ancestors served in the region beyond the River or the gods of the Amorites in whose land you are living; but as for me and my household, we will serve the LORD." Then the people answered, "Far be it from us that we should forsake the LORD to serve other gods; for it is the LORD our God who brought us and our ancestors up from the land of Egypt, out of the house of slavery, and who did those great signs in our sight. He protected us along all the way that we went, and among all the peoples through whom we passed; and the LORD drove out before us all the peoples, the Amorites who lived in the land. Therefore we also will serve the LORD, for he is our God." But Joshua said to the people, "You cannot serve the LORD, for he is a holy God. He is a jealous God; he will not forgive your transgressions or your sins. If you forsake the LORD and serve foreign gods, then he will turn and do you harm, and consume you, after having done you good." And the people said to Joshua, "No, we will serve the LORD!" Then Joshua said to the people, "You are witnesses against yourselves that you have chosen the LORD, to serve him." And they said, "We are witnesses." He said, "Then put away the foreign gods that are among you, and incline your hearts to the LORD, the God of Israel." The people said to Joshua, "The LORD our God we will serve, and him we will obey." So Joshua made a covenant with the people that day, and made statutes and ordinances for them at Shechem.

The Psalm 16   *Conserva me, Domine*

1   Protect me, O God, for I take refuge in you; *
         I have said to the LORD, "You are my Lord,
         my good above all other."

2   All my delight is upon the godly that are in the land, *
         upon those who are noble among the people.

3   But those who run after other gods *
         shall have their troubles multiplied.

4   Their libations of blood I will not offer, *
        nor take the names of their gods upon my lips.

5   O LORD, you are my portion and my cup; *
        it is you who uphold my lot.

6   My boundaries enclose a pleasant land; *
        indeed, I have a goodly heritage.

7   I will bless the LORD who gives me counsel; *
        my heart teaches me, night after night.

8   I have set the LORD always before me; *
        because he is at my right hand I shall not fall.

9   My heart, therefore, is glad, and my spirit rejoices; *
        my body also shall rest in hope.

10   For you will not abandon me to the grave, *
        nor let your holy one see the Pit.

11   You will show me the path of life; *
        in your presence there is fullness of joy,
        and in your right hand are pleasures for evermore.

Or Psalm 34:15-22   *Benedicam Donimum*
15   The eyes of the LORD are upon the righteous, *
        and his ears are open to their cry.

16   The face of the LORD is against those who do evil, *
        to root out the remembrance of them from the earth.

17   The righteous cry, and the LORD hears them *
        and delivers them from all their troubles.

18   The LORD is near to the brokenhearted *
        and will save those whose spirits are crushed.

19   Many are the troubles of the righteous, *
        but the LORD will deliver him out of them all.

20   He will keep safe all his bones; *
        not one of them shall be broken.

21   Evil shall slay the wicked, *
        and those who hate the righteous will be punished.

22   The LORD ransoms the life of his servants, *
        and none will be punished who trust in him.

The Epistle   **Ephesians 5:21-33**
Be subject to one another out of reverence for Christ. Wives, be subject to your
husbands as you are to the Lord. For the husband is the head of the wife just as

Christ is the head of the church, the body of which he is the Savior. Just as the church is subject to Christ, so also wives ought to be, in everything, to their husbands. Husbands, love your wives, just as Christ loved the church and gave himself up for her, in order to make her holy by cleansing her with the washing of water by the word, so as to present the church to himself in splendor, without a spot or wrinkle or anything of the kind — yes, so that she may be holy and without blemish. In the same way, husbands should love their wives as they do their own bodies. He who loves his wife loves himself. For no one ever hates his own body, but he nourishes and tenderly cares for it, just as Christ does for the church, because we are members of his body. "For this reason a man will leave his father and mother and be joined to his wife, and the two will become one flesh." This is a great mystery, and I am applying it to Christ and the church. Each of you, however, should love his wife as himself, and a wife should respect her husband.

The Gospel   John 6:60-69

Jesus said, "I am the living bread which came down from heaven... he who eats this bread will live forever." When many of his disciples heard this, they said, "This teaching is difficult; who can accept it?" But Jesus, being aware that his disciples were complaining about it, said to them, "Does this offend you? Then what if you were to see the Son of Man ascending to where he was before? It is the spirit that gives life; the flesh is useless. The words that I have spoken to you are spirit and life. But among you there are some who do not believe." For Jesus knew from the first who were the ones that did not believe, and who was the one that would betray him. And he said, "For this reason I have told you that no one can come to me unless it is granted by the Father." Because of this many of his disciples turned back and no longer went about with him. So Jesus asked the twelve, "Do you also wish to go away?" Simon Peter answered him, "Lord, to whom can we go? You have the words of eternal life. We have come to believe and know that you are the Holy One of God."

Year C

The Lesson   Isaiah 28:14-22

Hear the word of the LORD, you scoffers who rule this people in Jerusalem. Because you have said, "We have made a covenant with death, and with Sheol we have an agreement; when the overwhelming scourge passes through it will not come to us; for we have made lies our refuge, and in falsehood we have taken shelter"; therefore thus says the Lord GOD, See, I am laying in Zion a foundation stone, a tested stone, a precious cornerstone, a sure foundation: "One who trusts will not panic." And I will make justice the line, and righteousness the plummet; hail will sweep away the refuge of lies, and waters will overwhelm the shelter. Then your covenant with death will be annulled, and your agreement with Sheol will not stand; when the overwhelming scourge passes through you will be beaten down by it. As often as it passes through, it will take you; for morning by morning it will pass through, by day and by night; and it will be sheer terror to understand the message. For the bed is too short to stretch oneself on it, and the covering too narrow to wrap oneself in it. For the LORD will rise up as on Mount Perazim, he will rage as in the valley of Gibeon; to do his deed — strange is his deed! and to work his work — alien is his work! Now therefore do not scoff, or your bonds will be made stronger; for I have heard a decree of destruction from the Lord GOD of hosts upon the whole land.

The Psalm 46   *Deus noster refugium*

1   God is our refuge and strength, *
        a very present help in trouble.

2   Therefore we will not fear, though the earth be moved, *
        and though the mountains be toppled into the depths of the sea;

3   Though its waters rage and foam, *
        and though the mountains tremble at its tumult.

4   The LORD of hosts is with us; *
        the God of Jacob is our stronghold.

5   There is a river whose streams make glad the city of God, *
        the holy habitation of the Most High.

6   God is in the midst of her;
     she shall not be overthrown; *
        God shall help her at the break of day.

7   The nations make much ado, and the kingdoms are shaken; *
        God has spoken, and the earth shall melt away.

8   The LORD of hosts is with us; *
        the God of Jacob is our stronghold.

9   Come now and look upon the works of the LORD, *
        what awesome things he has done on earth.

10   It is he who makes war to cease in all the world; *
        he breaks the bow, and shatters the spear,
        and burns the shields with fire.

11   "Be still, then, and know that I am God; *
        I will be exalted among the nations;
        I will be exalted in the earth."

12   The LORD of hosts is with us; *
        the God of Jacob is our stronghold.

The Epistle   Hebrews 12:18-19, 22-29

You have not come to something that can be touched, a blazing fire, and darkness, and gloom, and a tempest, and the sound of a trumpet, and a voice whose words made the hearers beg that not another word be spoken to them. But you have come to Mount Zion and to the city of the living God, the heavenly Jerusalem, and to innumerable angels in festal gathering, and to the assembly of the firstborn who are enrolled in heaven, and to God the judge of all, and to the spirits of the righteous made perfect, and to Jesus, the mediator of a new covenant, and to the sprinkled blood that speaks a better word than the blood of Abel. See that you do not refuse the one who is speaking; for if they did not escape when they refused the one who warned them on earth, how much less will we escape if we reject the one who warns from heaven! At that time his voice shook the earth; but now he has promised, "Yet once more I will shake not only the earth but also the heaven." This phrase, "Yet once more," indicates the removal of what is shaken — that is, created things — so that what cannot be shaken may remain. Therefore, since we are receiving a kingdom that cannot be shaken, let us give thanks, by which we offer to God an acceptable worship with reverence and awe; for indeed our God is a consuming fire.

The Gospel **Luke 13:22-30**

Jesus went through one town and village after another, teaching as he made his way to Jerusalem. Someone asked him, "Lord, will only a few be saved?" He said to them, "Strive to enter through the narrow door; for many, I tell you, will try to enter and will not be able. When once the owner of the house has got up and shut the door, and you begin to stand outside and to knock at the door, saying, 'Lord, open to us,' then in reply he will say to you, 'I do not know where you come from.' Then you will begin to say, 'We ate and drank with you, and you taught in our streets.' But he will say, 'I do not know where you come from; go away from me, all you evildoers!' There will be weeping and gnashing of teeth when you see Abraham and Isaac and Jacob and all the prophets in the kingdom of God, and you yourselves thrown out. Then people will come from east and west, from north and south, and will eat in the kingdom of God. Indeed, some are last who will be first, and some are first who will be last."

Proper 17 *The Sunday closest to August 31*

The Collect

Lord of all power and might, the author and giver of all good things: Graft in our hearts the love of your Name; increase in us true religion, nourish us with all goodness; and bring forth in us the fruit of good works; through Jesus Christ our Lord, who lives and reigns with you and the Holy Spirit, one God for ever and ever. *Amen.*

Lord of all power and might, who art the author and giver of all good things: Graft in our hearts the love of thy Name, increase in us true religion, nourish us with all goodness, and bring forth in us the fruit of good works; through Jesus Christ our Lord, who liveth and reigneth with thee and the Holy Spirit, one God, for ever and ever. *Amen.*

Year A

The Lesson **Jeremiah 15:15-21**

O LORD, you know; remember me and visit me, and bring down retribution for me on my persecutors. In your forbearance do not take me away; know that on your account I suffer insult. Your words were found, and I ate them, and your words became to me a joy and the delight of my heart; for I am called by your name, O LORD, God of hosts. I did not sit in the company of merrymakers, nor did I rejoice; under the weight of your hand I sat alone, for you had filled me with indignation. Why is my pain unceasing, my wound incurable, refusing to be healed? Truly, you are to me like a deceitful brook, like waters that fail. Therefore thus says the LORD: If you turn back, I will take you back, and you shall stand before me. If you utter what is precious, and not what is worthless, you shall serve as my mouth. It is they who will turn to you, not you who will turn to them. And I will make you to this people a fortified wall of bronze; they will fight against you, but they shall not prevail over you, for I am with you to save you and deliver you, says the LORD. I will deliver you out of the hand of the wicked, and redeem you from the grasp of the ruthless."

The Psalm 26 or 26:1-8 *Judica me, Domine*

1   [Give judgment for me, O LORD,
      for I have lived with integrity; *
         I have trusted in the Lord and have not faltered.

2   Test me, O LORD, and try me; *
         examine my heart and my mind.

3   For your love is before my eyes; *
         I have walked faithfully with you.

4   I have not sat with the worthless, *
         nor do I consort with the deceitful.

5   I have hated the company of evildoers; *
         I will not sit down with the wicked.

6   I will wash my hands in innocence, O LORD, *
         that I may go in procession round your altar,

7   Singing aloud a song of thanksgiving *
         and recounting all your wonderful deeds.

8   LORD, I love the house in which you dwell *
         and the place where your glory abides.]

9   Do not sweep me away with sinners, *
         nor my life with those who thirst for blood,

10   Whose hands are full of evil plots, *
         and their right hand full of bribes.

11   As for me, I will live with integrity; *
         redeem me, O LORD, and have pity on me.

12   My foot stands on level ground; *
         in the full assembly I will bless the LORD.

The Epistle   **Romans 12:1-8**
I appeal to you therefore, brothers and sisters, by the mercies of God, to present your bodies as a living sacrifice, holy and acceptable to God, which is your spiritual worship. Do not be conformed to this world, but be transformed by the renewing of your minds, so that you may discern what is the will of God — what is good and acceptable and perfect. For by the grace given to me I say to everyone among you not to think of yourself more highly than you ought to think, but to think with sober

judgment, each according to the measure of faith that God has assigned. For as in one body we have many members, and not all the members have the same function, so we, who are many, are one body in Christ, and individually we are members one of another. We have gifts that differ according to the grace given to us: prophecy, in proportion to faith; ministry, in ministering; the teacher, in teaching; the exhorter, in exhortation; the giver, in generosity; the leader, in diligence; the compassionate, in cheerfulness.

The Gospel   Matthew 16:21-27

Jesus began to show his disciples that he must go to Jerusalem and undergo great suffering at the hands of the elders and chief priests and scribes, and be killed, and on the third day be raised. And Peter took him aside and began to rebuke him, saying, "God forbid it, Lord! This must never happen to you." But he turned and said to Peter, "Get behind me, Satan! You are a stumbling block to me; for you are setting your mind not on divine things but on human things." Then Jesus told his disciples, "If any want to become my followers, let them deny themselves and take up their cross and follow me. For those who want to save their life will lose it, and those who lose their life for my sake will find it. For what will it profit them if they gain the whole world but forfeit their life? Or what will they give in return for their life? For the Son of Man is to come with his angels in the glory of his Father, and then he will repay everyone for what has been done."

Year B

The Lesson   Deuteronomy 4:1-9

Moses said, "So now, Israel, give heed to the statutes and ordinances that I am teaching you to observe, so that you may live to enter and occupy the land that the LORD, the God of your ancestors, is giving you. You must neither add anything to what I command you nor take away anything from it, but keep the commandments of the LORD your God with which I am charging you. You have seen for yourselves what the LORD did with regard to the Baal of Peor — how the LORD your God destroyed from among you everyone who followed the Baal of Peor, while those of you who held fast to the LORD your God are all alive today. See, just as the LORD my God has charged me, I now teach you statutes and ordinances for you to observe in the land that you are about to enter and occupy. You must observe them diligently, for this will show your wisdom and discernment to the peoples, who, when they hear all these statutes, will say, "Surely this great nation is a wise and discerning people!" For what other great nation has a god so near to it as the LORD our God is whenever we call to him? And what other great nation has statutes and ordinances as just as this entire law that I am setting before you today? But take care and watch yourselves closely, so as neither to forget the things that your eyes have seen nor to let them slip from your mind all the days of your life; make them known to your children and your children's children."

The Psalm 15   *Domine, quis habitabit?*

1   LORD, who may dwell in your tabernacle? *
         who may abide upon your holy hill?

2   Whoever leads a blameless life and does what is right, *
      who speaks the truth from his heart.

3   There is no guile upon his tongue;
    he does no evil to his friend; *
      he does not heap contempt upon his neighbor.

4   In his sight the wicked is rejected, *
      but he honors those who fear the LORD.

5   He has sworn to do no wrong *
      and does not take back his word.

6   He does not give his money in hope of gain, *
      nor does he take a bribe against the innocent.

7   Whoever does these things *
      shall never be overthrown.

The Epistle   **Ephesians 6:10-20**

Be strong in the Lord and in the strength of his power. Put on the whole armor of God, so that you may be able to stand against the wiles of the devil. For our struggle is not against enemies of blood and flesh, but against the rulers, against the authorities, against the cosmic powers of this present darkness, against the spiritual forces of evil in the heavenly places. Therefore take up the whole armor of God, so that you may be able to withstand on that evil day, and having done everything, to stand firm. Stand therefore, and fasten the belt of truth around your waist, and put on the breastplate of righteousness. As shoes for your feet put on whatever will make you ready to proclaim the gospel of peace. With all of these, take the shield of faith, with which you will be able to quench all the flaming arrows of the evil one. Take the helmet of salvation, and the sword of the Spirit, which is the word of God. Pray in the Spirit at all times in every prayer and supplication. To that end keep alert and always persevere in supplication for all the saints. Pray also for me, so that when I speak, a message may be given to me to make known with boldness the mystery of the gospel, for which I am an ambassador in chains. Pray that I may declare it boldly, as I must speak.

The Gospel   **Mark 7:1-8, 14-15, 21-23**

Now when the Pharisees and some of the scribes who had come from Jerusalem gathered around Jesus, they noticed that some of his disciples were eating with defiled hands, that is, without washing them. (For the Pharisees, and all the Jews, do not eat unless they thoroughly wash their hands, thus observing the tradition of the elders; and they do not eat anything from the market unless they wash it; and there are also many other traditions that they observe, the washing of cups, pots, and bronze kettles.) So the Pharisees and the scribes asked him, "Why do your disciples not live according to the tradition of the elders, but eat with defiled hands?" He said to them, "Isaiah prophesied rightly about you hypocrites, as it is written, 'This people honors me with their lips, but their hearts are far from me; in vain do they worship me, teaching human precepts as doctrines.' You abandon the commandment of God and hold to human tradition." Then he called the crowd again and said to them, "Listen to me, all of you, and understand: there is nothing outside a person that by going in can defile, but the things that come out are what defile. For it is from within, from the human heart, that evil intentions come: fornication, theft, murder, adultery, avarice, wickedness, deceit, licentiousness, envy, slander, pride, folly. All these evil things come from within, and they defile a person."

Year C

The Lesson   **Ecclesiasticus (Sirach) 10:(7-11) 12-18**

[Arrogance is hateful to the Lord and to mortals, and injustice is outrageous to both. Sovereignty passes from nation to nation on account of injustice and insolence and wealth. How can dust and ashes be proud? Even in life the human body decays. A long illness baffles the physician; the king of today will die tomorrow. For when one is dead he inherits maggots and vermin and worms.] The beginning of human pride is to forsake the Lord; the heart has withdrawn from its Maker. For the beginning of pride is sin, and the one who clings to it pours out abominations. Therefore the Lord brings upon them unheard-of calamities, and destroys them completely. The Lord overthrows the thrones of rulers, and enthrones the lowly in their place. The Lord plucks up the roots of the nations and plants the humble in their place. The Lord lays waste the lands of the nations, and destroys them to the foundations of the earth. He removes some of them and destroys them, and erases the memory of them from the earth. Pride was not created for human beings, or violent anger for those born of women.

The Psalm 112   *Beatus vir*

1   Hallelujah!
     Happy are they who fear the Lord *
          and have great delight in his commandments!

2   Their descendants will be mighty in the land; *
          the generation of the upright will be blessed.

3   Wealth and riches will be in their house, *
          and their righteousness will last for ever.

4   Light shines in the darkness for the upright; *
          the righteous are merciful and full of compassion.

5   It is good for them to be generous in lending *
          and to manage their affairs with justice.

6   For they will never be shaken; *
          the righteous will be kept in everlasting remembrance.

7   They will not be afraid of any evil rumors; *
          their heart is right;
          they put their trust in the Lord.

8   Their heart is established and will not shrink, *
          until they see their desire upon their enemies.

9   They have given freely to the poor, *
           and their righteousness stands fast for ever;
           they will hold up their head with honor.

10   The wicked will see it and be angry;
           they will gnash their teeth and pine away; *
           the desires of the wicked will perish.

The Epistle
Hebrews 13:1-8

Let mutual love continue. Do not neglect to show hospitality to strangers, for by doing that some have entertained angels without knowing it. Remember those who are in prison, as though you were in prison with them; those who are being tortured, as though you yourselves were being tortured. Let marriage be held in honor by all, and let the marriage bed be kept undefiled; for God will judge fornicators and adulterers. Keep your lives free from the love of money, and be content with what you have; for he has said, "I will never leave you or forsake you." So we can say with confidence, "The Lord is my helper; I will not be afraid. What can anyone do to me?" Remember your leaders, those who spoke the word of God to you; consider the outcome of their way of life, and imitate their faith. Jesus Christ is the same yesterday and today and forever.

The Gospel
Luke 14:1,7-14

On one occasion when Jesus was going to the house of a leader of the Pharisees to eat a meal on the sabbath, they were watching him closely. When he noticed how the guests chose the places of honor, he told them a parable. "When you are invited by someone to a wedding banquet, do not sit down at the place of honor, in case someone more distinguished than you has been invited by your host; and the host who invited both of you may come and say to you, 'Give this person your place,' and then in disgrace you would start to take the lowest place. But when you are invited, go and sit down at the lowest place, so that when your host comes, he may say to you, 'Friend, move up higher'; then you will be honored in the presence of all who sit at the table with you. For all who exalt themselves will be humbled, and those who humble themselves will be exalted." He said also to the one who had invited him, "When you give a luncheon or a dinner, do not invite your friends or your brothers or your relatives or rich neighbors, in case they may invite you in return, and you would be repaid. But when you give a banquet, invite the poor, the crippled, the lame, and the blind. And you will be blessed, because they cannot repay you, for you will be repaid at the resurrection of the righteous."

Proper 18 *The Sunday closest to September 7*

The Collect

Grant us, O Lord, to trust in you with all our hearts; for, as you always resist the proud who confide in their own strength, so you never forsake those who make their boast of your mercy; through Jesus Christ our Lord, who lives and reigns with you and the Holy Spirit, one God, now and for ever. *Amen.*

Grant us, O Lord, we pray thee, to trust in thee with all our heart; seeing that, as thou dost always resist the proud who confide in their own strength, so thou dost not forsake

those who make their boast of thy mercy; through Jesus Christ our Lord, who liveth and reigneth with thee and the Holy Spirit, one God, now and for ever. *Amen.*

Year A

The Lesson   **Ezekiel 33:(1-6) 7-11**

[The word of the LORD came to me: O Mortal, speak to your people and say to them, If I bring the sword upon a land, and the people of the land take one of their number as their sentinel; and if the sentinel sees the sword coming upon the land and blows the trumpet and warns the people; then if any who hear the sound of the trumpet do not take warning, and the sword comes and takes them away, their blood shall be upon their own heads. They heard the sound of the trumpet and did not take warning; their blood shall be upon themselves. But if they had taken warning, they would have saved their lives. But if the sentinel sees the sword coming and does not blow the trumpet, so that the people are not warned, and the sword comes and takes any of them, they are taken away in their iniquity, but their blood I will require at the sentinel's hand.] So you, mortal, I have made a sentinel for the house of Israel; whenever you hear a word from my mouth, you shall give them warning from me. If I say to the wicked, "O wicked ones, you shall surely die," and you do not speak to warn the wicked to turn from their ways, the wicked shall die in their iniquity, but their blood I will require at your hand. But if you warn the wicked to turn from their ways, and they do not turn from their ways, the wicked shall die in their iniquity, but you will have saved your life. Now you, mortal, say to the house of Israel, Thus you have said: "Our transgressions and our sins weigh upon us, and we waste away because of them; how then can we live?" Say to them, As I live, says the Lord GOD, I have no pleasure in the death of the wicked, but that the wicked turn from their ways and live; turn back, turn back from your evil ways; for why will you die, O house of Israel?

The Psalm 119:33-48 or 119:33-40   *Legem pone*

33   [Teach me, O LORD, the way of your statutes, *
          and I shall keep it to the end.

34   Give me understanding, and I shall keep your law; *
          I shall keep it with all my heart.

35   Make me go in the path of your commandments, *
          for that is my desire.

36   Incline my heart to your decrees *
          and not to unjust gain.

37   Turn my eyes from watching what is worthless; *
          give me life in your ways.

38   Fulfill your promise to your servant, *
          which you make to those who fear you.

39   Turn away the reproach which I dread, *
          because your judgments are good.

40   Behold, I long for your commandments; *
      in your righteousness preserve my life.]

41   Let your loving-kindness come to me, O LORD, *
      and your salvation, according to your promise.

42   Then shall I have a word for those who taunt me, *
      because I trust in your words.

43   Do not take the word of truth out of my mouth, *
      for my hope is in your judgments.

44   I shall continue to keep your law; *
      I shall keep it for ever and ever.

45   I will walk at liberty, *
      because I study your commandments.

46   I will tell of your decrees before kings *
      and will not be ashamed.

47   I delight in your commandments, *
      which I have always loved.

48   I will lift up my hands to your commandments, *
      and I will meditate on your statutes.

The Epistle   **Romans 12:9-21**

Let love be genuine; hate what is evil, hold fast to what is good; love one another
with mutual affection; outdo one another in showing honor. Do not lag in zeal, be
ardent in spirit, serve the Lord. Rejoice in hope, be patient in suffering, persevere in
prayer. Contribute to the needs of the saints; extend hospitality to strangers. Bless
those who persecute you; bless and do not curse them. Rejoice with those who
rejoice, weep with those who weep. Live in harmony with one another; do not be
haughty, but associate with the lowly; do not claim to be wiser than you are. Do not
repay anyone evil for evil, but take thought for what is noble in the sight of all. If it is
possible, so far as it depends on you, live peaceably with all. Beloved, never avenge
yourselves, but leave room for the wrath of God; for it is written, "Vengeance is
mine, I will repay, says the Lord." No, "if your enemies are hungry, feed them; if they
are thirsty, give them something to drink; for by doing this you will heap burning
coals on their heads." Do not be overcome by evil, but overcome evil with good.

The Gospel   **Matthew 18:15-20**

Jesus said, "If another member of the church sins against you, go and point out the
fault when the two of you are alone. If the member listens to you, you have regained
that one. But if you are not listened to, take one or two others along with you, so that
every word may be confirmed by the evidence of two or three witnesses. If the
member refuses to listen to them, tell it to the church; and if the offender refuses to
listen even to the church, let such a one be to you as a Gentile and a tax collector.
Truly I tell you, whatever you bind on earth will be bound in heaven, and whatever

you loose on earth will be loosed in heaven. Again, truly I tell you, if two of you agree on earth about anything you ask, it will be done for you by my Father in heaven. For where two or three are gathered in my name, I am there among them."

Year B

The Lesson   Isaiah 35:4-7a

Say to those who are of a fearful heart, "Be strong, do not fear! Here is your God. He will come with vengeance, with terrible recompense. He will come and save you." Then the eyes of the blind shall be opened, and the ears of the deaf unstopped; then the lame shall leap like a deer, and the tongue of the speechless sing for joy. For waters shall break forth in the wilderness, and streams in the desert; the burning sand shall become a pool, and the thirsty ground springs of water.

The Psalm 146 or 146:4-9   *Lauda, anima mea*

1   Hallelujah!
       Praise the LORD, O my soul! *
           I will praise the LORD as long as I live;
           I will sing praises to my God while I have my being.

2   Put not your trust in rulers, nor in any child of earth, *
           for there is no help in them.

3   When they breathe their last, they return to earth, *
           and in that day their thoughts perish.

4   [Happy are they who have the God of Jacob for their help! *
           whose hope is in the LORD their God;

5   Who made heaven and earth, the seas, and all that is in them; *
           who keeps his promise for ever;

6   Who gives justice to those who are oppressed, *
           and food to those who hunger.

7   The LORD sets the prisoners free;
       the LORD opens the eyes of the blind; *
           the LORD lifts up those who are bowed down;

8   The LORD loves the righteous;
       the LORD cares for the stranger; *
           he sustains the orphan and widow,
           but frustrates the way of the wicked.

9   The LORD shall reign for ever, *
           your God, O Zion, throughout all generations.
           Hallelujah!]

The Epistle   James 1:17-27

Every generous act of giving, with every perfect gift, is from above, coming down from the Father of lights, with whom there is no variation or shadow due to change. In fulfillment of his own purpose he gave us birth by the word of truth, so that we would become a kind of first fruits of his creatures. You must understand this, my beloved: let everyone be quick to listen, slow to speak, slow to anger; for your anger does not produce God's righteousness. Therefore rid yourselves of all sordidness and rank growth of wickedness, and welcome with meekness the implanted word that has the power to save your souls. But be doers of the word, and not merely hearers who deceive themselves. For if any are hearers of the word and not doers, they are like those who look at themselves in a mirror; for they look at themselves and, on going away, immediately forget what they were like. But those who look into the perfect law, the law of liberty, and persevere, being not hearers who forget but doers who act — they will be blessed in their doing. If any think they are religious, and do not bridle their tongues but deceive their hearts, their religion is worthless. Religion that is pure and undefiled before God, the Father, is this: to care for orphans and widows in their distress, and to keep oneself unstained by the world.

The Gospel
Mark 7:31-37

Jesus returned from the region of Tyre, and went by way of Sidon towards the Sea of Galilee, in the region of the Decapolis. They brought to him a deaf man who had an impediment in his speech; and they begged him to lay his hand on him. He took him aside in private, away from the crowd, and put his fingers into his ears, and he spat and touched his tongue. Then looking up to heaven, he sighed and said to him, "Ephphatha," that is, "Be opened." And immediately his ears were opened, his tongue was released, and he spoke plainly. Then Jesus ordered them to tell no one; but the more he ordered them, the more zealously they proclaimed it. They were astounded beyond measure, saying, "He has done everything well; he even makes the deaf to hear and the mute to speak."

Year C

The Lesson
Deuteronomy 30:15-20

Moses said, "See, I have set before you today life and prosperity, death and adversity. If you obey the commandments of the LORD your God that I am commanding you today, by loving the LORD your God, walking in his ways, and observing his commandments, decrees, and ordinances, then you shall live and become numerous, and the LORD your God will bless you in the land that you are entering to possess. But if your heart turns away and you do not hear, but are led astray to bow down to other gods and serve them, I declare to you today that you shall perish; you shall not live long in the land that you are crossing the Jordan to enter and possess. I call heaven and earth to witness against you today that I have set before you life and death, blessings and curses. Choose life so that you and your descendants may live, loving the LORD your God, obeying him, and holding fast to him; for that means life to you and length of days, so that you may live in the land that the LORD swore to give to your ancestors, to Abraham, to Isaac, and to Jacob."

The Psalm 1   *Beatus vir qui non abiit*

1   Happy are they who have not walked in the counsel of the wicked, *
       nor lingered in the way of sinners,
       nor sat in the seats of the scornful!

2   Their delight is in the law of the LORD, *
        and they meditate on his law day and night.

3   They are like trees planted by streams of water,
        bearing fruit in due season, with leaves that do not wither; *
        everything they do shall prosper.

4   It is not so with the wicked; *
        they are like chaff which the wind blows away.

5   Therefore the wicked shall not stand upright when judgment comes, *
        nor the sinner in the council of the righteous.

6   For the LORD knows the way of the righteous, *
        but the way of the wicked is doomed.

The Epistle   **Philemon 1-20**

Paul, a prisoner of Christ Jesus, and Timothy our brother, To Philemon our dear friend and co-worker, to Apphia our sister, to Archippus our fellow soldier, and to the church in your house: Grace to you and peace from God our Father and the Lord Jesus Christ. When I remember you in my prayers, I always thank my God because I hear of your love for all the saints and your faith toward the Lord Jesus. I pray that the sharing of your faith may become effective when you perceive all the good that we may do for Christ. I have indeed received much joy and encouragement from your love, because the hearts of the saints have been refreshed through you, my brother. For this reason, though I am bold enough in Christ to command you to do your duty, yet I would rather appeal to you on the basis of love — and I, Paul, do this as an old man, and now also as a prisoner of Christ Jesus. I am appealing to you for my child, Onesimus, whose father I have become during my imprisonment. Formerly he was useless to you, but now he is indeed useful both to you and to me. I am sending him, that is, my own heart, back to you. I wanted to keep him with me, so that he might be of service to me in your place during my imprisonment for the gospel; but I preferred to do nothing without your consent, in order that your good deed might be voluntary and not something forced. Perhaps this is the reason he was separated from you for a while, so that you might have him back forever, no longer as a slave but more than a slave, a beloved brother — especially to me but how much more to you, both in the flesh and in the Lord. So if you consider me your partner, welcome him as you would welcome me. If he has wronged you in any way, or owes you anything, charge that to my account. I, Paul, am writing this with my own hand: I will repay it. I say nothing about your owing me even your own self. Yes, brother, let me have this benefit from you in the Lord! Refresh my heart in Christ.

The Gospel   **Luke 14:25-33**

Large crowds were traveling with Jesus; and he turned and said to them, "Whoever comes to me and does not hate father and mother, wife and children, brothers and sisters, yes, and even life itself, cannot be my disciple. Whoever does not carry the cross and follow me cannot be my disciple. For which of you, intending to build a tower, does not first sit down and estimate the cost, to see whether he has enough to complete it? Otherwise, when he has laid a foundation and is not able to finish, all who see it will begin to ridicule him, saying, 'This fellow began to build and was not able to finish.' Or what king, going out to wage war against another king, will not sit down first and consider whether he is able with ten thousand to oppose the one who comes against him with twenty thousand? If he cannot, then, while the other is still far away, he sends a delegation and asks for the terms of peace. So therefore, none of you can become my disciple if you do not give up all your possessions."

Proper 19 *The Sunday closest to September 14*

The Collect

O God, because without you we are not able to please you, mercifully grant that your Holy Spirit may in all things direct and rule our hearts; through Jesus Christ our Lord, who lives and reigns with you and the Holy Spirit, one God, now and for ever. *Amen.*

O God, forasmuch as without thee we are not able to please thee, mercifully grant that thy Holy Spirit may in all things direct and rule our hearts; through Jesus Christ our Lord, who with thee and the same Spirit liveth and reigneth, one God, now and for ever. *Amen.*

Year A

The Lesson
Ecclesiasticus (Sirach) 27:30-28:7

Anger and wrath, these also are abominations, yet a sinner holds on to them. The vengeful will face the Lord's vengeance, for he keeps a strict account of their sins. Forgive you neighbor the wrong he has done, and then your sins will be pardoned when you pray. Does anyone harbor anger against another, and expect healing from the Lord? If one has no mercy toward another like himself, can he then seek pardon for his own sins? If a mere mortal harbors wrath, who will make an atoning sacrifice for his sins? Remember the end of your life, and set enmity aside; remember corruption and death, and be true to the commandments. Remember the commandments, and do not be angry with your neighbor; remember the covenant of the Most High, and overlook faults.

The Psalm 103 or 103:8-13 *Benedic, anima mea*

1   Bless the LORD, O my soul, *
        and all that is within me, bless his holy Name.

2   Bless the LORD, O my soul, *
        and forget not all his benefits.

3   He forgives all your sins *
        and heals all your infirmities;

4   He redeems your life from the grave *
        and crowns you with mercy and loving-kindness;

5   He satisfies you with good things, *
        and your youth is renewed like an eagle's.

6   The LORD executes righteousness *
        and judgment for all who are oppressed.

7   He made his ways known to Moses *
        and his works to the children of Israel.

8   [The LORD is full of compassion and mercy, *
        slow to anger and of great kindness.

9   He will not always accuse us, *
        nor will he keep his anger for ever.

10   He has not dealt with us according to our sins, *
        nor rewarded us according to our wickedness.

11   For as the heavens are high above the earth, *
        so is his mercy great upon those who fear him.

12   As far as the east is from the west, *
        so far has he removed our sins from us.

13   As a father cares for his children, *
        so does the LORD care for those who fear him.]

14   For he himself knows whereof we are made; *
        he remembers that we are but dust.

15   Our days are like the grass; *
        we flourish like a flower of the field;

16   When the wind goes over it, it is gone, *
        and its place shall know it no more.

17   But the merciful goodness of the LORD endures for ever
                on those who fear him, *
        and his righteousness on children's children;

18   On those who keep his covenant *
        and remember his commandments and do them.

19   The LORD has set his throne in heaven, *
        and his kingship has dominion over all.

20   Bless the LORD, you angels of his,
        you mighty ones who do his bidding, *
        and hearken to the voice of his word.

21   Bless the LORD, all you his hosts, *
        you ministers of his who do his will.

22   Bless the LORD, all you works of his,
        in all places of his dominion; *
        bless the LORD, O my soul.

The Epistle   **Romans 14:5-12**

Some judge one day to be better than another, while others judge all days to be alike.
Let all be fully convinced in their own minds. Those who observe the day, observe it
in honor of the Lord. Also those who eat, eat in honor of the Lord, since they give
thanks to God; while those who abstain, abstain in honor of the Lord and give
thanks to God. We do not live to ourselves, and we do not die to ourselves. If we live,
we live to the Lord, and if we die, we die to the Lord; so then, whether we live or
whether we die, we are the Lord's. For to this end Christ died and lived again, so that
he might be Lord of both the dead and the living. Why do you pass judgment on
your brother or sister? Or you, why do you despise your brother or sister? For we will
all stand before the judgment seat of God. For it is written, "As I live, says the Lord,
every knee shall bow to me, and every tongue shall give praise to God." So then, each
of us will be accountable to God.

The Gospel   **Matthew 18:21-35**

Peter came and said to Jesus, "Lord, if another member of the church sins against
me, how often should I forgive? As many as seven times?" Jesus said to him, "Not
seven times, but, I tell you, seventy-seven times. For this reason the kingdom of
heaven may be compared to a king who wished to settle accounts with his slaves.
When he began the reckoning, one who owed him ten thousand talents was brought
to him; and, as he could not pay, his lord ordered him to be sold, together with his
wife and children and all his possessions, and payment to be made. So the slave fell
on his knees before him, saying, 'Have patience with me, and I will pay you
everything.' And out of pity for him, the lord of that slave released him and forgave
him the debt. But that same slave, as he went out, came upon one of his fellow slaves
who owed him a hundred denarii; and seizing him by the throat, he said, 'Pay what
you owe.' Then his fellow slave fell down and pleaded with him, 'Have patience with
me, and I will pay you.' But he refused; then he went and threw him into prison until
he would pay the debt. When his fellow slaves saw what had happened, they were
greatly distressed, and they went and reported to their lord all that had taken place.
Then his lord summoned him and said to him, 'You wicked slave! I forgave you all
that debt because you pleaded with me. Should you not have had mercy on your
fellow slave, as I had mercy on you?' And in anger his lord handed him over to be
tortured until he would pay his entire debt. So my heavenly Father will also do to
every one of you, if you do not forgive your brother or sister from your heart."

Year B

The Lesson   **Isaiah 50:4-9**

The Lord GOD has given me the tongue of a teacher, that I may know how to sustain
the weary with a word. Morning by morning he wakens — wakens my ear to listen as
those who are taught. The Lord GOD has opened my ear, and I was not rebellious, I
did not turn backward. I gave my back to those who struck me, and my cheeks to
those who pulled out the beard; I did not hide my face from insult and spitting. The
Lord GOD helps me; therefore I have not been disgraced; therefore I have set my
face like flint, and I know that I shall not be put to shame; he who vindicates me is
near. Who will contend with me? Let us stand up together. Who are my adversaries?

Let them confront me. It is the Lord GOD who helps me; who will declare me guilty?
All of them will wear out like a garment; the moth will eat them up.

The Psalm 116 or 116:1-8   *Dilexi, quoniam*

1   [I love the LORD, because he has heard the voice of my supplication, *
    because he has inclined his ear to me whenever I called upon him.

2   The cords of death entangled me;
    the grip of the grave took hold of me; *
      I came to grief and sorrow.

3   Then I called upon the Name of the LORD: *
    "O LORD, I pray you, save my life."

4   Gracious is the LORD and righteous; *
    our God is full of compassion.

5   The LORD watches over the innocent; *
    I was brought very low, and he helped me.

6   Turn again to your rest, O my soul, *
    for the LORD has treated you well.

7   For you have rescued my life from death, *
    my eyes from tears, and my feet from stumbling.

8   I will walk in the presence of the LORD *
    in the land of the living.]

9   I believed, even when I said,
    "I have been brought very low." *
      In my distress I said, "No one can be trusted."

10   How shall I repay the LORD *
    for all the good things he has done for me?

11   I will lift up the cup of salvation *
    and call upon the Name of the LORD.

12   I will fulfill my vows to the LORD *
    in the presence of all his people.

13   Precious in the sight of the LORD *
    is the death of his servants.

14   O LORD, I am your servant; *
    I am your servant and the child of your handmaid;
    you have freed me from my bonds.

15   I will offer you the sacrifice of thanksgiving *
    and call upon the Name of the LORD.

16   I will fulfill my vows to the LORD *
    in the presence of all his people,

17   In the courts of the LORD's house, *
       in the midst of you, O Jerusalem.
       Hallelujah!

The Epistle   **James 2:1-5, 8-10, 14-18**

My brothers and sisters, do you with your acts of favoritism really believe in our glorious Lord Jesus Christ? For if a person with gold rings and in fine clothes comes into your assembly, and if a poor person in dirty clothes also comes in, and if you take notice of the one wearing the fine clothes and say, "Have a seat here, please," while to the one who is poor you say, "Stand there," or, "Sit at my feet," have you not made distinctions among yourselves, and become judges with evil thoughts? Listen, my beloved brothers and sisters. Has not God chosen the poor in the world to be rich in faith and to be heirs of the kingdom that he has promised to those who love him? You do well if you really fulfill the royal law according to the scripture, "You shall love your neighbor as yourself." But if you show partiality, you commit sin and are convicted by the law as transgressors. For whoever keeps the whole law but fails in one point has become accountable for all of it. What good is it, my brothers and sisters, if you say you have faith but do not have works? Can faith save you? If a brother or sister is naked and lacks daily food, and one of you says to them, "Go in peace; keep warm and eat your fill," and yet you do not supply their bodily needs, what is the good of that? So faith by itself, if it has no works, is dead. But someone will say, "You have faith and I have works." Show me your faith apart from your works, and I by my works will show you my faith.

The Gospel   **Mark 8:27-38**

Jesus went on with his disciples to the villages of Caesarea Philippi; and on the way he asked his disciples, "Who do people say that I am?" And they answered him, "John the Baptist; and others, Elijah; and still others, one of the prophets." He asked them, "But who do you say that I am?" Peter answered him, "You are the Messiah." And he sternly ordered them not to tell anyone about him. Then he began to teach them that the Son of Man must undergo great suffering, and be rejected by the elders, the chief priests, and the scribes, and be killed, and after three days rise again. He said all this quite openly. And Peter took him aside and began to rebuke him. But turning and looking at his disciples, he rebuked Peter and said, "Get behind me, Satan! For you are setting your mind not on divine things but on human things." He called the crowd with his disciples, and said to them, "If any want to become my followers, let them deny themselves and take up their cross and follow me. For those who want to save their life will lose it, and those who lose their life for my sake, and for the sake of the gospel will save it. For what will it profit them to gain the whole world and forfeit their life? Indeed, what can they give in return for their life? Those who are ashamed of me and of my words in this adulterous and sinful generation, of them the Son of Man will also be ashamed when he comes in the glory of his Father with the holy angels."

or Mark 9:14-29

When Jesus with Peter and James and John came to the disciples, they saw a great crowd around them, and some scribes arguing with them. When the whole crowd saw him, they were immediately overcome with awe, and they ran forward to greet him. He asked them, "What are you arguing about with them?" Someone from the crowd answered him, "Teacher, I brought you my son; he has a spirit that makes him unable to speak; and whenever it seizes him, it dashes him down; and he foams and grinds his teeth and becomes rigid; and I asked your disciples to cast it out, but they could not do so." He answered them, "You faithless generation, how much longer must I be among you? How much longer must I put up with you? Bring him to me." And they brought the boy to him. When the spirit saw him, immediately it convulsed the boy, and he fell on the ground and rolled about, foaming at the mouth. Jesus asked the father, "How long has this been happening to him?" And he said, "From childhood. It has often cast him into the fire and into the water, to destroy him; but if you are able to do anything, have pity on us and help us." Jesus said to him, "If you are able! — All things can be done for the one who believes." Immediately the father of the child cried out, "I believe; help my unbelief!" When Jesus saw that a crowd came running together, he rebuked the unclean spirit, saying to it, "You spirit that keeps this boy from speaking and hearing, I command you, come out of him, and never enter him again!" After crying out and convulsing him terribly, it came out, and the boy was like a corpse, so that most of them said, "He is dead." But Jesus took him by the hand and lifted him up, and he was able to stand. When he had entered the house, his disciples asked him privately, "Why could we not cast it out?" He said to them, "This kind can come out only through prayer."

Year C

The Lesson   Exodus 32:1, 7-14

When the people saw that Moses delayed to come down from the mountain, the people gathered around Aaron, and said to him, "Come, make gods for us, who shall go before us; as for this Moses, the man who brought us up out of the land of Egypt, we do not know what has become of him." The LORD said to Moses, "Go down at once! Your people, whom you brought up out of the land of Egypt, have acted perversely; they have been quick to turn aside from the way that I commanded them; they have cast for themselves an image of a calf, and have worshiped it and sacrificed to it, and said, 'These are your gods, O Israel, who brought you up out of the land of Egypt!'" The LORD said to Moses, "I have seen this people, how stiff-necked they are. Now let me alone, so that my wrath may burn hot against them and I may consume them; and of you I will make a great nation." But Moses implored the LORD his God, and said, "O LORD, why does your wrath burn hot against your people, whom you brought out of the land of Egypt with great power and with a mighty hand? Why should the Egyptians say, 'It was with evil intent that he brought them out to kill them in the mountains, and to consume them from the face of the earth'? Turn from your fierce wrath; change your mind and do not bring disaster on your people. Remember Abraham, Isaac, and Israel, your servants, how you swore to them by your own self, saying to them, 'I will multiply your descendants like the stars of heaven, and all this land that I have promised I will give to your descendants, and they shall inherit it forever.'" And the LORD changed his mind about the disaster that he planned to bring on his people.

The Psalm 51:1-18 or 51:1-11   *Miserere mei, Deus*

1 [Have mercy on me, O God, according to your
       loving-kindness; *
    in your great compassion blot out my offenses.

2 Wash me through and through from my wickedness *
    and cleanse me from my sin.

3 For I know my transgressions, *
    and my sin is ever before me.

4 Against you only have I sinned *
    and done what is evil in your sight.

5 And so you are justified when you speak *
    and upright in your judgment.

6 Indeed, I have been wicked from my birth, *
    a sinner from my mother's womb.

7 For behold, you look for truth deep within me, *
    and will make me understand wisdom secretly.

8 Purge me from my sin, and I shall be pure; *
    wash me, and I shall be clean indeed.

9 Make me hear of joy and gladness, *
    that the body of you have broken may rejoice.

10 Hide your face from my sins *
    and blot out all my iniquities.

11 Create in me a clean heart, O God, *
    and renew a right spirit within me.]

12 Cast me not away from your presence *
    and take not your holy Spirit from me.

13 Give me the joy of your saving help again *
    and sustain me with your bountiful Spirit.

14 I shall teach your ways to the wicked, *
    and sinners shall return to you.

15 Deliver me from death, O God, *
    and my tongue shall sing of your righteousness,
       O God of my salvation.

16 Open my lips, O Lord, *
    and my mouth shall proclaim your praise.

17 Had you desired it, I would have offered sacrifice, *
    but you take no delight in burnt-offerings.

18 The sacrifice of God is a troubled spirit; *
     a broken and contrite heart, O God, you will not despise.

The Epistle
1 Timothy 1:12-17

I am grateful to Christ Jesus our Lord, who has strengthened me, because he judged me faithful and appointed me to his service, even though I was formerly a blasphemer, a persecutor, and a man of violence. But I received mercy because I had acted ignorantly in unbelief, and the grace of our Lord overflowed for me with the faith and love that are in Christ Jesus. The saying is sure and worthy of full acceptance, that Christ Jesus came into the world to save sinners — of whom I am the foremost. But for that very reason I received mercy, so that in me, as the foremost, Jesus Christ might display the utmost patience, making me an example to those who would come to believe in him for eternal life. To the King of the ages, immortal, invisible, the only God, be honor and glory forever and ever. Amen.

The Gospel
Luke 15:1-10

Now all the tax collectors and sinners were coming near to listen to Jesus. And the Pharisees and the scribes were grumbling and saying, "This fellow welcomes sinners and eats with them." So he told them this parable: "Which one of you, having a hundred sheep and losing one of them, does not leave the ninety-nine in the wilderness and go after the one that is lost until he finds it? When he has found it, he lays it on his shoulders and rejoices. And when he comes home, he calls together his friends and neighbors, saying to them, 'Rejoice with me, for I have found my sheep that was lost.' Just so, I tell you, there will be more joy in heaven over one sinner who repents than over ninety-nine righteous persons who need no repentance. Or what woman having ten silver coins, if she loses one of them, does not light a lamp, sweep the house, and search carefully until she finds it? When she has found it, she calls together her friends and neighbors, saying, 'Rejoice with me, for I have found the coin that I had lost.' Just so, I tell you, there is joy in the presence of the angels of God over one sinner who repents."

Proper 20 *The Sunday closest to September 21*

The Collect

Grant us, Lord, not to be anxious about earthly things, but to love things heavenly; and even now, while we are placed among things that are passing away, to hold fast to those that shall endure; through Jesus Christ our Lord, who lives and reigns with you and the Holy Spirit, one God, for ever and ever. *Amen.*

Grant us, O Lord, not to mind earthly things, but to love things heavenly; and even now, while we are placed among things that are passing away, to cleave to those that shall abide; through Jesus Christ our Lord, who liveth and reigneth with thee and the Holy Spirit, one God, for ever and ever. *Amen.*

Year A

The Lesson
Jonah 3:10-4:11

When God saw what the Ninevites did, how they turned from their evil ways, God changed his mind about the calamity that he had said he would bring upon them; and he did not do it. But this was very displeasing to Jonah, and he became angry. He prayed to the LORD and said, "O LORD! Is not this what I said while I was still in my own country? That is why I fled to Tarshish at the beginning; for I knew that you are a gracious God and merciful, slow to anger, and abounding in steadfast love, and ready to relent from punishing. And now, O LORD, please take my life from me, for it is better for me to die than to live." And the LORD said, "Is it right for you to be angry?" Then Jonah went out of the city and sat down east of the city, and made a booth for himself there. He sat under it in the shade, waiting to see what would become of the city. The LORD God appointed a bush, and made it come up over Jonah, to give shade over his head, to save him from his discomfort; so Jonah was very happy about the bush. But when dawn came up the next day, God appointed a worm that attacked the bush, so that it withered. When the sun rose, God prepared a sultry east wind, and the sun beat down on the head of Jonah so that he was faint and asked that he might die. He said, "It is better for me to die than to live." But God said to Jonah, "Is it right for you to be angry about the bush?" And he said, "Yes, angry enough to die." Then the LORD said, "You are concerned about the bush, for which you did not labor and which you did not grow; it came into being in a night and perished in a night. And should I not be concerned about Nineveh, that great city, in which there are more than a hundred and twenty thousand persons who do not know their right hand from their left, and also many animals?"

The Psalm 145 or 145:1-8   *Exaltabo te, Deus*

1   [I will exalt you, O God my King, *
        and bless your Name for ever and ever.

2   Every day will I bless you *
        and praise your Name for ever and ever.

3   Great is the LORD and greatly to be praised; *
        there is no end to his greatness.

4   One generation shall praise your works to another *
        and shall declare your power.

5   I will ponder the glorious splendor of your majesty *
        and all your marvelous works.

6   They shall speak of the might of your wondrous acts, *
        and I will tell of your greatness.

7   They shall publish the remembrance of your great goodness; *
        they shall sing of your righteous deeds.

8   The LORD is gracious and full of compassion, *
        slow to anger and of great kindness.]

9   The LORD is loving to everyone *
        and his compassion is over all his works.

10   All your works praise you, O LORD, *
        and your faithful servants bless you.

11   They make known the glory of your kingdom *
        and speak of your power;

12   That the peoples may know of your power *
        and the glorious splendor of your kingdom.

13   Your kingdom is an everlasting kingdom; *
        your dominion endures throughout all ages.

14   The LORD is faithful in all his words *
        and merciful in all his deeds.

15   The LORD upholds all those who fall; *
        he lifts up those who are bowed down.

16   The eyes of all wait upon you, O LORD, *
        and you give them their food in due season.

17   You open wide your hand *
        and satisfy the needs of every living creature.

18   The LORD is righteous in all his ways *
        and loving in all his works.

19   The LORD is near to those who call upon him, *
        to all who call upon him faithfully.

20   He fulfills the desire of those who fear him; *
        he hears their cry and helps them.

21   The LORD preserves all those who love him, *
        but he destroys all the wicked.

22   My mouth shall speak the praise of the LORD; *
        let all flesh bless his holy Name for ever and ever.

The Epistle   **Philippians 1:21-27**

For to me, living is Christ and dying is gain. If I am to live in the flesh, that means fruitful labor for me; and I do not know which I prefer. I am hard pressed between the two: my desire is to depart and be with Christ, for that is far better; but to remain in the flesh is more necessary for you. Since I am convinced of this, I know that I will remain and continue with all of you for your progress and joy in faith, so that I may share abundantly in your boasting in Christ Jesus when I come to you again. Only, live your life in a manner worthy of the gospel of Christ, so that, whether I come and see you or am absent and hear about you, I will know that you are standing firm in one spirit, striving side by side with one mind for the faith of the gospel.

The Gospel   **Matthew 20:1-16**

Jesus said, "For the kingdom of heaven is like a landowner who went out early in the morning to hire laborers for his vineyard. After agreeing with the laborers for the usual daily wage, he sent them into his vineyard. When he went out about nine o'clock, he saw others standing idle in the marketplace; and he said to them, 'You also go into the vineyard, and I will pay you whatever is right.' So they went. When he went out again about noon and about three o'clock, he did the same. And about five o'clock he went out and found others standing around; and he said to them, 'Why are you standing here idle all day?' They said to him, 'Because no one has hired us.' He said to them, 'You also go into the vineyard.' When evening came, the owner of the vineyard said to his manager, 'Call the laborers and give them their pay, beginning with the last and then going to the first.' When those hired about five o'clock came, each of them received the usual daily wage. Now when the first came, they thought they would receive more; but each of them also received the usual daily wage. And when they received it, they grumbled against the landowner, saying, 'These last worked only one hour, and you have made them equal to us who have borne the burden of the day and the scorching heat.' But he replied to one of them, 'Friend, I am doing you no wrong; did you not agree with me for the usual daily wage? Take what belongs to you and go; I choose to give to this last the same as I give to you. Am I not allowed to do what I choose with what belongs to me? Or are you envious because I am generous?' So the last will be first, and the first will be last."

Year B

The Lesson   Wisdom 1:16-2:1 (6-11) 12-22

But the ungodly by their words and deeds summoned death; considering him a friend, they pined away and made a covenant with him, because they are fit to belong to his company. For they reasoned unsoundly, saying to themselves, "Short and sorrowful is our life, and there is no remedy when a life comes to its end, and no one has been known to return from Hades. [Come, therefore, let us enjoy the good things that exist, and make use of the creation to the full as in youth. Let us take our fill of costly wine and perfumes, and let no flower of spring pass us by. Let us crown ourselves with rosebuds before they wither. Let none of us fail to share in our revelry; everywhere let us leave signs of enjoyment, because this is our portion, and this our lot. Let us oppress the righteous poor man; let us not spare the widow or regard the gray hairs of the aged. But let our might be our law of right, for what is weak proves itself to be useless.] Let us lie in wait for the righteous man, because he is inconvenient to us and opposes our actions; he reproaches us for sins against the law, and accuses us of sins against our training. He professes to have knowledge of God, and calls himself a child of the Lord. He became to us a reproof of our thoughts; the very sight of him is a burden to us, because his manner of life is unlike that of others, and his ways are strange. We are considered by him as something base, and he avoids our ways as unclean; he calls the last end of the righteous happy, and boasts that God is his father. Let us see if his words are true, and let us test what will happen at the end of his life; for if the righteous man is God's child, he will help him, and will deliver him from the hand of his adversaries. Let us test him with insult and torture, so that we may find out how gentle he is, and make trial of his forbearance. Let us condemn him to a shameful death, for, according to what he says, he will be protected." Thus they reasoned, but they were led astray, for their wickedness blinded them, and they did not know the secret purposes of God, nor hoped for the wages of holiness, nor discerned the prize for blameless souls.

The Psalm 54   *Deus, in nomine*

1   Save me, O God, by your Name; *
          in your might, defend my cause.

2   Hear my prayer, O God; *
          give ear to the words of my mouth.

3   For the arrogant have risen up against me,
     and the ruthless have sought my life, *
          those who have no regard for God.

4   Behold, God is my helper; *
          it is the Lord who sustains my life.

5   Render evil to those who spy on me; *
          in your faithfulness, destroy them.

6   I will offer you a freewill sacrifice *
          and praise your Name, O LORD, for it is good.

7   For you have rescued me from every trouble, *
          and my eye has seen the ruin of my foes.

The Epistle   James 3:16-4:6

For where there is envy and selfish ambition, there will also be disorder and wickedness of every kind. But the wisdom from above is first pure, then peaceable, gentle, willing to yield, full of mercy and good fruits, without a trace of partiality or hypocrisy. And a harvest of righteousness is sown in peace for those who make peace. Those conflicts and disputes among you, where do they come from? Do they not come from your cravings that are at war within you? You want something and do not have it; so you commit murder. And you covet something and cannot obtain it; so you engage in disputes and conflicts. You do not have, because you do not ask. You ask and do not receive, because you ask wrongly, in order to spend what you get on your pleasures. Adulterers! Do you not know that friendship with the world is enmity with God? Therefore whoever wishes to be a friend of the world becomes an enemy of God. Or do you suppose that it is for nothing that the scripture says, "God yearns jealously for the spirit that he has made to dwell in us"? But he gives all the more grace; therefore it says, "God opposes the proud, but gives grace to the humble."

The Gospel   Mark 9:30-37

Jesus and his disciples went on from there and passed through Galilee. He did not want anyone to know it; for he was teaching his disciples, saying to them, "The Son of Man is to be betrayed into human hands, and they will kill him, and three days after being killed, he will rise again." But they did not understand what he was saying and were afraid to ask him. Then they came to Capernaum; and when he was in the house he asked them, "What were you arguing about on the way?" But they were silent, for on the way they had argued with one another who was the greatest. He sat down, called the twelve, and said to them, "Whoever wants to be first must be last of all and servant of all." Then he took a little child and put it among them; and taking it in his arms, he said to them, "Whoever welcomes one such child in my name welcomes me, and whoever welcomes me welcomes not me but the one who sent me."

Year C

The Lesson   Amos 8:4-7 (8-12)

Hear this, you that trample on the needy, and bring to ruin the poor of the land, saying, "When will the new moon be over so that we may sell grain; and the sabbath, so that we may offer wheat for sale? We will make the ephah small and the shekel great, and practice deceit with false balances, buying the poor for silver and the needy for a pair of sandals, and selling the sweepings of the wheat." The LORD has sworn by the pride of Jacob: Surely I will never forget any of their deeds. [Shall not the land tremble on this account, and everyone mourn who lives in it, and all of it rise like the Nile, and be tossed about and sink again, like the Nile of Egypt? On that day, says the Lord GOD, I will make the sun go down at noon, and darken the earth in broad daylight. I will turn your feasts into mourning, and all your songs into lamentation; I will bring sackcloth on all loins, and baldness on every head; I will make it like the mourning for an only son, and the end of it like a bitter day. The time is surely coming, says the Lord GOD, when I will send a famine on the land; not a famine of bread, or a thirst for water, but of hearing the words of the LORD. They shall wander from sea to sea, and from north to east; they shall run to and fro, seeking the word of the LORD, but they shall not find it.]

The Psalm 138   *Confitebor tibi*

1   I will give thanks to you, O LORD, with my whole heart; *
         before the gods I will sing your praise.

2   I will bow down toward your holy temple
     and praise your Name, *
         because of your love and faithfulness;

3   For you have glorified your Name *
         and your word above all things.

4   When I called, you answered me; *
         you increased my strength within me.

5   All the kings of the earth will praise you, O LORD, *
         when they have heard the words of your mouth.

6   They will sing of the ways of the LORD, *
         great is the Glory of the LORD.

7   Though the LORD be high, he cares for the lowly; *
         he perceives the haughty from afar.

8   Though I walk in the midst of trouble, you keep me safe; *
          you stretch forth your hand against the fury of my enemies;
          your right hand shall save me.

9   The LORD will make good his purpose for me; *
          O LORD, your love endures for ever;
          do not abandon the works of your hands.

The Epistle   **1 Timothy 2:1-8**

First of all, then, I urge that supplications, prayers, intercessions, and thanksgivings
be made for everyone, for kings and all who are in high positions, so that we may
lead a quiet and peaceable life in all godliness and dignity. This is right and is
acceptable in the sight of God our Savior, who desires everyone to be saved and to
come to the knowledge of the truth. For there is one God; there is also one mediator
between God and humankind, Christ Jesus, himself human, who gave himself a
ransom for all — this was attested at the right time. For this I was appointed a herald
and an apostle (I am telling the truth, I am not lying), a teacher of the Gentiles in
faith and truth. I desire, then, that in every place the men should pray, lifting up holy
hands without anger or argument.

The Gospel   **Luke 16:1-13**

Jesus said to the disciples, "There was a rich man who had a manager, and charges
were brought to him that this man was squandering his property. So he summoned
him and said to him, 'What is this that I hear about you? Give me an accounting of
your management, because you cannot be my manager any longer.' Then the
manager said to himself, 'What will I do, now that my master is taking the position
away from me? I am not strong enough to dig, and I am ashamed to beg. I have
decided what to do so that, when I am dismissed as manager, people may welcome
me into their homes.' So, summoning his master's debtors one by one, he asked the
first, 'How much do you owe my master?' He answered, 'A hundred jugs of olive oil.'
He said to him, 'Take your bill, sit down quickly, and make it fifty.' Then he asked
another, 'And how much do you owe?' He replied, 'A hundred containers of wheat.'
He said to him, 'Take your bill and make it eighty.' And his master commended the
dishonest manager because he had acted shrewdly; for the children of this age are
more shrewd in dealing with their own generation than are the children of light. And
I tell you, make friends for yourselves by means of dishonest wealth so that when it is
gone, they may welcome you into the eternal homes. Whoever is faithful in a very
little is faithful also in much; and whoever is dishonest in a very little is dishonest
also in much. If then you have not been faithful with the dishonest wealth, who will
entrust to you the true riches? And if you have not been faithful with what belongs to
another, who will give you what is your own? No slave can serve two masters; for a
slave will either hate the one and love the other, or be devoted to the one and despise
the other. You cannot serve God and wealth."

Proper 21 *The Sunday closest to September 28*

The Collect

O God, you declare your almighty power chiefly in showing mercy and pity: Grant us the fullness of your grace, that we, running to obtain your promises, may become partakers of your heavenly treasure; through Jesus Christ our Lord, who lives and reigns with you and the Holy Spirit, one God, for ever and ever. *Amen.*

O God, who declarest thy almighty power chiefly in showing mercy and pity: Mercifully grant unto us such a measure of thy grace, that we, running to obtain thy promises, may be made partakers of thy heavenly treasure; through Jesus Christ our Lord, who liveth and reigneth with thee and the Holy Spirit, one God, for ever and ever. *Amen.*

Year A

The Lesson   **Ezekiel 18:1-4, 25-32**

The word of the LORD came to me: What do you mean by repeating this proverb concerning the land of Israel, "The parents have eaten sour grapes, and the children's teeth are set on edge"? As I live, says the Lord GOD, this proverb shall no more be used by you in Israel. Know that all lives are mine; the life of the parent as well as the life of the child is mine: it is only the person who sins that shall die. Yet you say, "The way of the Lord is unfair." Hear now, O house of Israel: Is my way unfair? Is it not your ways that are unfair? When the righteous turn away from their righteousness and commit iniquity, they shall die for it; for the iniquity that they have committed they shall die. Again, when the wicked turn away from the wickedness they have committed and do what is lawful and right, they shall save their life. Because they considered and turned away from all the transgressions that they had committed, they shall surely live; they shall not die. Yet the house of Israel says, "The way of the Lord is unfair." O house of Israel, are my ways unfair? Is it not your ways that are unfair? Therefore I will judge you, O house of Israel, all of you according to your ways, says the Lord GOD. Repent and turn from all your transgressions; otherwise iniquity will be your ruin. Cast away from you all the transgressions that you have committed against me, and get yourselves a new heart and a new spirit! Why will you die, O house of Israel? For I have no pleasure in the death of anyone, says the Lord GOD. Turn, then, and live.

The Psalm 25:1-14 or 25:3-9   *Ad te, Domine, levavi*

1   To you, O LORD, I lift up my soul;
      my God, I put my trust in you; *
         let me not be humiliated,
            nor let my enemies triumph over me.

2   Let none who look to you be put to shame; *
         let the treacherous be disappointed in their schemes.

3   [Show me your ways, O LORD, *
         and teach me your paths.

4   Lead me in your truth and teach me, *
       for you are the God of my salvation;
       in you have I trusted all the day long.

5   Remember, O Lord, your compassion and love, *
       for they are from everlasting.

6   Remember not the sins of my youth and my transgressions; *
       remember me according to your love
       and for the sake of your goodness, O Lord.

7   Gracious and upright is the Lord; *
       therefore he teaches sinners in his way.

8   He guides the humble in doing right *
       and teaches his way to the lowly.

9   All the paths of the Lord are love and faithfulness *
       to those who keep his covenant and his testimonies.]

10   For your Name's sake, O Lord, *
       forgive my sin, for it is great.

11   Who are they who fear the Lord? *
       he will teach them the way that they should choose.

12   They shall dwell in prosperity, *
       and their offspring shall inherit the land.

13   The Lord is a friend to those who fear him *
       and will show them his covenant.

14   My eyes are ever looking to the Lord, *
       for he shall pluck my feet out of the net.

The Epistle   **Philippians 2:1-13**

If there is any encouragement in Christ, any consolation from love, any sharing in the Spirit, any compassion and sympathy, make my joy complete: be of the same mind, having the same love, being in full accord and of one mind. Do nothing from selfish ambition or conceit, but in humility regard others as better than yourselves. Let each of you look not to your own interests, but to the interests of others. Let the same mind be in you that was in Christ Jesus, who, though he was in the form of God, did not regard equality with God as something to be exploited, but emptied himself, taking the form of a slave, being born in human likeness. And being found in human form, he humbled himself and became obedient to the point of death — even death on a cross. Therefore God also highly exalted him and gave him the name that is above every name, so that at the name of Jesus every knee should bend, in heaven and on earth and under the earth, and every tongue should confess that Jesus Christ is Lord, to the glory of God the Father. Therefore, my beloved, just as you have always obeyed me, not only in my presence, but much more now in my absence, work out your own salvation with fear and trembling; for it is God who is at work in you, enabling you both to will and to work for his good pleasure.

The Gospel **Matthew 21:28-32**

Jesus said, "What do you think? A man had two sons; he went to the first and said, 'Son, go and work in the vineyard today.' He answered, 'I will not'; but later he changed his mind and went. The father went to the second and said the same; and he answered, 'I go, sir'; but he did not go. Which of the two did the will of his father?" They said, "The first." Jesus said to them, "Truly I tell you, the tax collectors and the prostitutes are going into the kingdom of God ahead of you. For John came to you in the way of righteousness and you did not believe him, but the tax collectors and the prostitutes believed him; and even after you saw it, you did not change your minds and believe him."

<h2 style="text-align:center">Year B</h2>

The Lesson **Numbers 11:4-6, 10-16, 24-29**

The rabble among them had a strong craving; and the Israelites also wept again, and said, "If only we had meat to eat! We remember the fish we used to eat in Egypt for nothing, the cucumbers, the melons, the leeks, the onions, and the garlic; but now our strength is dried up, and there is nothing at all but this manna to look at." Moses heard the people weeping throughout their families, all at the entrances of their tents. Then the LORD became very angry, and Moses was displeased. So Moses said to the LORD, "Why have you treated your servant so badly? Why have I not found favor in your sight, that you lay the burden of all this people on me? Did I conceive all this people? Did I give birth to them, that you should say to me, 'Carry them in your bosom, as a nurse carries a sucking child,' to the land that you promised on oath to their ancestors? Where am I to get meat to give to all this people? For they come weeping to me and say, 'Give us meat to eat!' I am not able to carry all this people alone, for they are too heavy for me. If this is the way you are going to treat me, put me to death at once — if I have found favor in your sight — and do not let me see my misery." So the LORD said to Moses, "Gather for me seventy of the elders of Israel, whom you know to be the elders of the people and officers over them; bring them to the tent of meeting, and have them take their place there with you." So Moses went out and told the people the words of the LORD; and he gathered seventy elders of the people, and placed them all around the tent. Then the LORD came down in the cloud and spoke to him, and took some of the spirit that was on him and put it on the seventy elders; and when the spirit rested upon them, they prophesied. But they did not do so again. Two men remained in the camp, one named Eldad, and the other named Medad, and the spirit rested on them; they were among those registered, but they had not gone out to the tent, and so they prophesied in the camp. And a young man ran and told Moses, "Eldad and Medad are prophesying in the camp." And Joshua son of Nun, the assistant of Moses, one of his chosen men, said, "My lord Moses, stop them!" But Moses said to him, "Are you jealous for my sake? Would that all the LORD's people were prophets, and that the LORD would put his spirit on them!"

The Psalm 19 or 19:7-14   *Coeli enarrant*

1 The heavens declare the glory of God, *
   and the firmament shows his handiwork.

2 One day tells its tale to another, *
   and one night imparts knowledge to another.

3 Although they have no words or language, *
   and their voices are not heard,

4 Their sound has gone out into all lands, *
   and their message to the ends of the world.

5 In the deep has he set a pavilion for the sun; *
   it comes forth like a bridegroom out of his chamber;
   it rejoices like a champion to run its course.

6 It goes forth from the uttermost edge of the heavens
   and runs about to the end of it again; *
   nothing is hidden from its burning heat.

7 [The law of the Lord is perfect and revives the soul; *
   the testimony of the Lord is sure and gives wisdom to the innocent.

8 The statutes of the Lord are just and rejoice the heart; *
   the commandment of the Lord is clear and gives light to the eyes.

9 The fear of the Lord is clean and endures for ever; *
   the judgments of the Lord are true and righteous altogether.

10 More to be desired are they than gold, more than much fine gold, *
   sweeter far than honey, than honey in the comb.

11 By them also is your servant enlightened, *
   and in keeping them there is great reward.

12 Who can tell how often he offends? *
   cleanse me from my secret faults.

13 Above all, keep your servant from presumptuous sins;
   let them not get dominion over me; *
   then shall I be whole and sound,
   and innocent of a great offense.

14 Let the words of my mouth and the meditation of my heart be acceptable in
   your sight, *
   O Lord, my strength and my redeemer.]

The Epistle   **James 4:7-12 (13-5:6)**

Submit yourselves therefore to God. Resist the devil, and he will flee from you. Draw
near to God, and he will draw near to you. Cleanse your hands, you sinners, and
purify your hearts, you double-minded. Lament and mourn and weep. Let your
laughter be turned into mourning and your joy into dejection. Humble yourselves

before the Lord, and he will exalt you. Do not speak evil against one another, brothers and sisters. Whoever speaks evil against another or judges another, speaks evil against the law and judges the law; but if you judge the law, you are not a doer of the law but a judge. There is one lawgiver and judge who is able to save and to destroy. So who, then, are you to judge your neighbor? [Come now, you who say, "Today or tomorrow we will go to such and such a town and spend a year there, doing business and making money." Yet you do not even know what tomorrow will bring. What is your life? For you are a mist that appears for a little while and then vanishes. Instead you ought to say, "If the Lord wishes, we will live and do this or that." As it is, you boast in your arrogance; all such boasting is evil. Anyone, then, who knows the right thing to do and fails to do it, commits sin. Come now, you rich people, weep and wail for the miseries that are coming to you. Your riches have rotted, and your clothes are moth-eaten. Your gold and silver have rusted, and their rust will be evidence against you, and it will eat your flesh like fire. You have laid up treasures for the last days. Listen! The wages of the laborers who mowed your fields, which you kept back by fraud, cry out, and the cries of the harvesters have reached the ears of the Lord of hosts. You have lived on the earth in luxury and in pleasure; you have fattened your hearts in a day of slaughter. You have condemned and murdered the righteous one, who does not resist you.]

The Gospel
Mark 9:38-43, 45, 47-48

John said to Jesus, "Teacher, we saw someone casting out demons in your name, and we tried to stop him, because he was not following us." But Jesus said, "Do not stop him; for no one who does a deed of power in my name will be able soon afterward to speak evil of me. Whoever is not against us is for us. For truly I tell you, whoever gives you a cup of water to drink because you bear the name of Christ will by no means lose the reward. If any of you put a stumbling block before one of these little ones who believe in me, it would be better for you if a great millstone were hung around your neck and you were thrown into the sea. If your hand causes you to stumble, cut it off; it is better for you to enter life maimed than to have two hands and to go to hell, to the unquenchable fire. And if your foot causes you to stumble, cut it off; it is better for you to enter life lame than to have two feet and to be thrown into hell. And if your eye causes you to stumble, tear it out; it is better for you to enter the kingdom of God with one eye than to have two eyes and to be thrown into hell, where their worm never dies, and the fire is never quenched."

Year C

The Lesson
Amos 6:1-7

Alas for those who are at ease in Zion, and for those who feel secure on Mount Samaria, the notables of the first of the nations, to whom the house of Israel resorts! Cross over to Calneh, and see; from there go to Hamath the great; then go down to Gath of the Philistines. Are you better than these kingdoms? Or is your territory greater than their territory, O you that put away the evil day, and bring near a reign of violence? Alas for those who lie on beds of ivory, and lounge on their couches, and eat lambs from the flock, and calves from the stall; who sing idle songs to the sound of the harp, and like David improvise on instruments of music; who drink wine from bowls, and anoint themselves with the finest oils, but are not grieved over the ruin of

Proper 21 — Year C 403

Joseph! Therefore they shall now be the first to go into exile, and the revelry of the loungers shall pass away.

The Psalm 146 or 146:4-9   *Lauda, anima mea*

1   Hallelujah!
Praise the LORD, O my soul! *
      I will praise the LORD as long as I live;
      I will sing praises to my God while I have my being.

2   Put not your trust in rulers, nor in any child of earth, *
      for there is no help in them.

3   When they breathe their last, they return to earth, *
      and in that day their thoughts perish.

4   [Happy are they who have the God of Jacob for their help! *
      whose hope is in the LORD their God;

5   Who made heaven and earth, the seas, and all that is in them; *
      who keeps his promise for ever;

6   Who gives justice to those who are oppressed, *
      and food to those who hunger.

7   The LORD sets the prisoners free;
the LORD opens the eyes of the blind; *
      the LORD lifts up those who are bowed down;

8   The LORD loves the righteous;
the LORD cares for the stranger; *
      he sustains the orphan and widow,
      but frustrates the way of the wicked.

9   The LORD shall reign for ever, *
      your God, O Zion, throughout all generations.
      Hallelujah!]

The Epistle   1 Timothy 6:11-19
As for you, man of God, shun all this; pursue righteousness, godliness, faith, love, endurance, gentleness. Fight the good fight of the faith; take hold of the eternal life, to which you were called and for which you made the good confession in the presence of many witnesses. In the presence of God, who gives life to all things, and of Christ Jesus, who in his testimony before Pontius Pilate made the good confession, I charge you to keep the commandment without spot or blame until the manifestation of our Lord Jesus Christ, which he will bring about at the right time — he who is the blessed and only Sovereign, the King of kings and Lord of lords. It is he alone who has immortality and dwells in unapproachable light, whom no one has ever seen or can see; to him be honor and eternal dominion. Amen. As for those who in the present age are rich, command them not to be haughty, or to set their hopes on the uncertainty of riches, but rather on God who richly provides us with everything for our enjoyment. They are to do good, to be rich in good works, generous, and ready to

share, thus storing up for themselves the treasure of a good foundation for the future, so that they may take hold of the life that really is life.

The Gospel   Luke 16:19-31

Jesus said, "There was a rich man who was dressed in purple and fine linen and who feasted sumptuously every day. And at his gate lay a poor man named Lazarus, covered with sores, who longed to satisfy his hunger with what fell from the rich man's table; even the dogs would come and lick his sores. The poor man died and was carried away by the angels to be with Abraham. The rich man also died and was buried. In Hades, where he was being tormented, he looked up and saw Abraham far away with Lazarus by his side. He called out, 'Father Abraham, have mercy on me, and send Lazarus to dip the tip of his finger in water and cool my tongue; for I am in agony in these flames.' But Abraham said, 'Child, remember that during your lifetime you received your good things, and Lazarus in like manner evil things; but now he is comforted here, and you are in agony. Besides all this, between you and us a great chasm has been fixed, so that those who might want to pass from here to you cannot do so, and no one can cross from there to us.' He said, 'Then, father, I beg you to send him to my father's house — for I have five brothers — that he may warn them, so that they will not also come into this place of torment.' Abraham replied, 'They have Moses and the prophets; they should listen to them.' He said, 'No, father Abraham; but if someone goes to them from the dead, they will repent.' He said to him, 'If they do not listen to Moses and the prophets, neither will they be convinced even if someone rises from the dead.'"

Proper 22 *The Sunday closest to October 5*

The Collect

Almighty and everlasting God, you are always more ready to hear than we to pray, and to give more than we either desire or deserve: Pour upon us the abundance of your mercy, forgiving us those things of which our conscience is afraid, and giving us those good things for which we are not worthy to ask, except through the merits and mediation of Jesus Christ our Savior; who lives and reigns with you and the Holy Spirit, one God, for ever and ever. *Amen.*

Almighty and everlasting God, who art always more ready to hear than we to pray, and art wont to give more than either we desire or deserve: Pour down upon us the abundance of thy mercy, forgiving us those things whereof our conscience is afraid, and giving us those good things which we are not worthy to ask, but through the merits and mediation of Jesus Christ thy Son our Lord; who liveth and reigneth with thee and the Holy Spirit, one God, for ever and ever. *Amen.*

Year A

The Lesson   Isaiah 5:1-7

Let me sing for my beloved my love-song concerning his vineyard: My beloved had a vineyard on a very fertile hill. He dug it and cleared it of stones, and planted it with choice vines; he built a watchtower in the midst of it, and hewed out a wine vat in it; he expected it to yield grapes, but it yielded wild grapes. And now, inhabitants of Jerusalem and people of Judah, judge between me and my vineyard. What more was there to do for my vineyard that I have not done in it? When I expected it to yield grapes, why did it yield wild grapes? And now I will tell you what I will do to my vineyard. I will remove its hedge, and it shall be devoured; I will break down its wall, and it shall be trampled down. I will make it a waste; it shall not be pruned or hoed, and it shall be overgrown with briers and thorns; I will also command the clouds that they rain no rain upon it. For the vineyard of the LORD of hosts is the house of Israel, and the people of Judah are his pleasant planting; he expected justice, but saw bloodshed; righteousness, but heard a cry!

The Psalm 80 or 80:7-14   *Qui regis Israel*

1   Hear, O Shepherd of Israel, leading Joseph like a flock; *
    shine forth, you that are enthroned upon the cherubim.

2   In the presence of Ephraim, Benjamin, and Manasseh. *
    stir up your strength and come to help us.

3   Restore us, O God of hosts; *
    show the light of your countenance, and we shall be saved.

4   O LORD God of hosts, *
    how long will you be angered
    despite the prayers of your people?

5   You have fed them with the bread of tears; *
    you have given them bowls of tears to drink.

6   You have made us the derision of our neighbors, *
    and our enemies laugh us to scorn.

7   [Restore us, O God of hosts; *
    show the light of your countenance, and we shall be saved.

8   You have brought a vine out of Egypt; *
    you cast out the nations and planted it.

9   You prepared the ground for it; *
    it took root and filled the land.

10   The mountains were covered by its shadow *
    and the towering cedar trees by its boughs.

11   You stretched out its tendrils to the Sea *
    and its branches to the River.

12   Why have you broken down its wall, *
    so that all who pass by pluck off its grapes?

13   The wild boar of the forest has ravaged it, *
    and the beasts of the field have grazed upon it.

14   Turn now, O God of hosts, look down from heaven;
    behold and tend this vine; *
       preserve what your right hand has planted.]

15   They burn it with fire like rubbish; *
     at the rebuke of your countenance let them perish.

16   Let your hand be upon the man of your right hand, *
     the son of man you have made so strong for yourself.

17   And so will we never turn away from you; *
     give us life, that we may call upon your Name.

18   Restore us, O LORD God of hosts; *
     show the light of your countenance, and we shall be saved.

The Epistle   **Philippians 3:14-21**

I press on toward the goal for the prize of the heavenly call of God in Christ Jesus. Let those of us then who are mature be of the same mind; and if you think differently about anything, this too God will reveal to you. Only let us hold fast to what we have attained. Brothers and sisters, join in imitating me, and observe those who live according to the example you have in us. For many live as enemies of the cross of Christ; I have often told you of them, and now I tell you even with tears. Their end is destruction; their god is the belly; and their glory is in their shame; their minds are set on earthly things. But our citizenship is in heaven, and it is from there that we are expecting a Savior, the Lord Jesus Christ. He will transform the body of our humiliation that it may be conformed to the body of his glory, by the power that also enables him to make all things subject to himself.

The Gospel   **Matthew 21:33-43**

Jesus said, "Listen to another parable. There was a landowner who planted a vineyard, put a fence around it, dug a wine press in it, and built a watchtower. Then he leased it to tenants and went to another country. When the harvest time had come, he sent his slaves to the tenants to collect his produce. But the tenants seized his slaves and beat one, killed another, and stoned another. Again he sent other slaves, more than the first; and they treated them in the same way. Finally he sent his son to them, saying, 'They will respect my son.' But when the tenants saw the son, they said to themselves, 'This is the heir; come, let us kill him and get his inheritance.' So they seized him, threw him out of the vineyard, and killed him. Now when the owner of the vineyard comes, what will he do to those tenants?" They said to him, "He will put those wretches to a miserable death, and lease the vineyard to other tenants who will give him the produce at the harvest time." Jesus said to them, "Have you never read in the scriptures: 'The stone that the builders rejected has become the cornerstone; this was the Lord's doing, and it is amazing in our eyes'? Therefore I tell you, the kingdom of God will be taken away from you and given to a people that produces the fruits of the kingdom."

Year B

The Lesson   **Genesis 2:18-24**

Then the LORD God said, "It is not good that the man should be alone; I will make him a helper as his partner." So out of the ground the LORD God formed every animal of the field and every bird of the air, and brought them to the man to see what he would call them; and whatever the man called every living creature, that was its name. The man gave names to all cattle, and to the birds of the air, and to every animal of the field; but for the man there was not found a helper as his partner. So the LORD God caused a deep sleep to fall upon the man, and he slept; then he took one of his ribs and closed up its place with flesh. And the rib that the LORD God had taken from the man he made into a woman and brought her to the man. Then the man said, "This at last is bone of my bones and flesh of my flesh; this one shall be called Woman, for out of Man this one was taken." Therefore a man leaves his father and his mother and clings to his wife, and they become one flesh.

The Psalm 8   *Domine, Dominus noster*

1   O LORD our Governor, *
        how exalted is your Name in all the world!

2   Out of the mouths of infants and children *
        your majesty is praised above the heavens.

3   You have set up a stronghold against your adversaries, *
        to quell the enemy and the avenger.

4   When I consider your heavens, the work of your fingers, *
        the moon and the stars you have set in their courses,

5   What is man that you should be mindful of him? *
        the son of man that you should seek him out?

6   You have made him but little lower than the angels; *
        you adorn him with glory and honor;

7   You give him mastery over the works of your hands; *
        you put all things under his feet:

8   All sheep and oxen, *
        even the wild beasts of the field,

9   The birds of the air, the fish of the sea, *
        and whatsoever walks in the paths of the sea.

10   O LORD our Governor, *
        how exalted is your Name in all the world!

or Psalm 128   *Beati omnes*

1   Happy are they all who fear the LORD, *
        and who follow in his ways!

2   You shall eat the fruit of your labor; *
        happiness and prosperity shall be yours.

3   Your wife shall be like a fruitful vine within your house, *
        your children like olive shoots round about your table.

4   The man who fears the LORD *
        shall thus indeed be blessed.

5   The LORD bless you from Zion, *
      and may you see the prosperity of Jerusalem all the days
          of your life.

6   May you live to see your children's children; *
      may peace be upon Israel.

The Epistle   **Hebrews 2:(1-8) 9-18**

[We must pay greater attention to what we have heard, so that we do not drift away from it. For if the message declared through angels was valid, and every transgression or disobedience received a just penalty, how can we escape if we neglect so great a salvation? It was declared at first through the Lord, and it was attested to us by those who heard him, while God added his testimony by signs and wonders and various miracles, and by gifts of the Holy Spirit, distributed according to his will. Now God did not subject the coming world, about which we are speaking, to angels. But someone has testified somewhere, "What are human beings that you are mindful of them, or mortals, that you care for them? You have made them for a little while lower than the angels; you have crowned them with glory and honor, subjecting all things under their feet." Now in subjecting all things to them, God left nothing outside their control. As it is, we do not yet see everything in subjection to them,] but we do see Jesus, who for a little while was made lower than the angels, now crowned with glory and honor because of the suffering of death, so that by the grace of God he might taste death for everyone. It was fitting that God, for whom and through whom all things exist, in bringing many children to glory, should make the pioneer of their salvation perfect through sufferings. For the one who sanctifies and those who are sanctified all have one Father. For this reason Jesus is not ashamed to call them brothers and sisters, saying, "I will proclaim your name to my brothers and sisters, in the midst of the congregation I will praise you." And again, "I will put my trust in him." And again, "Here am I and the children whom God has given me." Since, therefore, the children share flesh and blood, he himself likewise shared the same things, so that through death he might destroy the one who has the power of death, that is, the devil, and free those who all their lives were held in slavery by the fear of death. For it is clear that he did not come to help angels, but the descendants of Abraham. Therefore he had to become like his brothers and sisters in every respect, so that he might be a merciful and faithful high priest in the service of God, to make a sacrifice of atonement for the sins of the people. Because he himself was tested by what he suffered, he is able to help those who are being tested.

The Gospel   **Mark 10:2-9**

Some Pharisees came, and to test Jesus they asked, "Is it lawful for a man to divorce his wife?" He answered them, "What did Moses command you?" They said, "Moses allowed a man to write a certificate of dismissal and to divorce her." But Jesus said to them, "Because of your hardness of heart he wrote this commandment for you. But from the beginning of creation, 'God made them male and female.' 'For this reason a man shall leave his father and mother and be joined to his wife, and the two shall become one flesh.' So they are no longer two, but one flesh. Therefore what God has joined together, let no one separate."

Year C

The oracle that the prophet Habakkuk saw. O LORD, how long shall I cry for help, and you will not listen? Or cry to you "Violence!" and you will not save? Why do you make me see wrong-doing and look at trouble? Destruction and violence are before me; strife and contention arise. So the law becomes slack and justice never prevails. The wicked surround the righteous — therefore judgment comes forth perverted. Look at the nations, and see! Be astonished! Be astounded! For a work is being done in your days that you would not believe if you were told. For I am rousing the Chaldeans, that fierce and impetuous nation, who march through the breadth of the earth to seize dwellings not their own. [Dread and fearsome are they; their justice and dignity proceed from themselves. Their horses are swifter than leopards, more menacing than wolves at dusk; their horses charge. Their horsemen come from far away; they fly like an eagle swift to devour. They all come for violence, with faces pressing forward; they gather captives like sand. At kings they scoff, and of rulers they make sport. They laugh at every fortress, and heap up earth to take it. Then they sweep by like the wind; they transgress and become guilty; their own might is their god!] Are you not from of old, O LORD my God, my Holy One? You shall not die. O LORD, you have marked them for judgment; and you, O Rock, have established them for punishment. Your eyes are too pure to behold evil, and you cannot look on wrongdoing; why do you look on the treacherous, and are silent when the wicked swallow those more righteous than they? I will stand at my watchpost, and station myself on the rampart; I will keep watch to see what he will say to me, and what he will answer concerning my complaint. Then the LORD answered me and said: Write the vision; make it plain on tablets, so that a runner may read it. For there is still a vision for the appointed time; it speaks of the end, and does not lie. If it seems to tarry, wait for it; it will surely come, it will not delay. Look at the proud! Their spirit is not right in them, but the righteous live by their faith.

The Psalm 37:1-18 or 37:3-10   *Noli oemulari*

1   Do not fret yourself because of evildoers; *
         do not be jealous of those who do wrong.

2   For they shall soon wither like the grass, *
         and like the green grass fade away.

3   [Put your trust in the LORD and do good; *
         dwell in the land and feed on its riches.

4   Take delight in the LORD, *
         and he shall give you your heart's desire.

5   Commit your way to the LORD and put your trust in him, *
         and he will bring it to pass.

6   He will make your righteousness as clear as the light *
         and your just dealing as the noonday.

7　Be still before the LORD *
　　and wait patiently for him.

8　Do not fret yourself over the one who prospers, *
　　the one who succeeds in evil schemes.

9　Refrain from anger, leave rage alone; *
　　do not fret yourself; it leads only to evil.

10　For evildoers shall be cut off, *
　　but those who wait upon the LORD shall possess the land.]

11　In a little while the wicked shall be no more; *
　　you shall search out their place, but they will not be there.

12　But the lowly shall possess the land; *
　　they will delight in abundance of peace.

13　The wicked plot against the righteous *
　　and gnash at them with their teeth.

14　The Lord laughs at the wicked, *
　　because he sees that their day will come.

15　The wicked draw their sword and bend their bow
　　to strike down the poor and needy, *
　　to slaughter those who are upright in their ways.

16　Their sword shall go through their own heart, *
　　and their bow shall be broken.

17　The little that the righteous has *
　　is better than great riches of the wicked.

18　For the power of the wicked shall be broken, *
　　but the LORD upholds the righteous.

The Epistle　　　　　　　　　　　　　　　　　　　**2 Timothy 1:(1-5) 6-14**

[Paul, an apostle of Christ Jesus by the will of God, for the sake of the promise of life that is in Christ Jesus, To Timothy, my beloved child: Grace, mercy, and peace from God the Father and Christ Jesus our Lord. I am grateful to God — whom I worship with a clear conscience, as my ancestors did — when I remember you constantly in my prayers night and day. Recalling your tears, I long to see you so that I may be filled with joy. I am reminded of your sincere faith, a faith that lived first in your grandmother Lois and your mother Eunice and now, I am sure, lives in you.] For this reason I remind you to rekindle the gift of God that is within you through the laying on of my hands; for God did not give us a spirit of cowardice, but rather a spirit of power and of love and of self-discipline. Do not be ashamed, then, of the testimony about our Lord or of me his prisoner, but join with me in suffering for the gospel, relying on the power of God, who saved us and called us with a holy calling, not according to our works but according to his own purpose and grace. This grace was given to us in Christ Jesus before the ages began, but it has now been revealed through the appearing of our Savior Christ Jesus, who abolished death and brought life and immortality to light through the gospel. For this gospel I was appointed a herald and an apostle and a teacher, and for this reason I suffer as I do. But I am not ashamed, for I know the one in whom I have put my trust, and I am sure that he is able to guard until that day what I have entrusted to him. Hold to the standard of sound teaching that you have heard from me, in the faith and love that are in Christ Jesus. Guard the good treasure entrusted to you, with the help of the Holy Spirit living in us.

The Gospel Luke 17:5-10

The apostles said to the Lord, "Increase our faith!" The Lord replied, "If you had faith the size of a mustard seed, you could say to this mulberry tree, 'Be uprooted and planted in the sea,' and it would obey you. Who among you would say to your slave who has just come in from plowing or tending sheep in the field, 'Come here at once and take your place at the table'? Would you not rather say to him, 'Prepare supper for me, put on your apron and serve me while I eat and drink; later you may eat and drink'? Do you thank the slave for doing what was commanded? So you also, when you have done all that you were ordered to do, say, 'We are worthless slaves; we have done only what we ought to have done!'"

Proper 23 *The Sunday closest to October 12*

The Collect

Lord, we pray that your grace may always precede and follow us, that we may continually be given to good works; through Jesus Christ our Lord, who lives and reigns with you and the Holy Spirit, one God, now and for ever. *Amen.*

Lord, we pray thee that thy grace may always precede and follow us, and make us continually to be given to all good works; through Jesus Christ our Lord, who liveth and reigneth with thee and the Holy Spirit, one God, now and for ever. *Amen.*

Year A

The Lesson Isaiah 25:1-9

O LORD, you are my God; I will exalt you, I will praise your name; for you have done wonderful things, plans formed of old, faithful and sure. For you have made the city a heap, the fortified city a ruin; the palace of aliens is a city no more, it will never be rebuilt. Therefore strong peoples will glorify you; cities of ruthless nations will fear you. For you have been a refuge to the poor, a refuge to the needy in their distress, a shelter from the rainstorm and a shade from the heat. When the blast of the ruthless was like a winter rainstorm, the noise of aliens like heat in a dry place, you subdued the heat with the shade of clouds; the song of the ruthless was stilled. On this mountain the LORD of hosts will make for all peoples a feast of rich food, a feast of well-aged wines, of rich food filled with marrow, of well-aged wines strained clear. And he will destroy on this mountain the shroud that is cast over all peoples, the sheet that is spread over all nations; he will swallow up death forever. Then the Lord GOD will wipe away the tears from all faces, and the disgrace of his people he will take away from all the earth, for the LORD has spoken. It will be said on that day, Lo, this is our God; we have waited for him, so that he might save us. This is the LORD for whom we have waited; let us be glad and rejoice in his salvation.

The Psalm 23   *Dominus regit me*

1   The LORD is my shepherd; *
       I shall not be in want.

2   He makes me lie down in green pastures *
       and leads me beside still waters.

3   He revives my soul *
       and guides me along right pathways for his Name's sake.

4   Though I walk through the valley of the shadow of death,
     I shall fear no evil; *
         for you are with me;
         your rod and your staff, they comfort me.

5   You spread a table before me in the presence of those
                       who trouble me; *
         you have anointed my head with oil,
         and my cup is running over.

6   Surely your goodness and mercy shall follow me all the days
                       of my life, *
         and I will dwell in the house of the LORD for ever.

The Epistle   **Philippians 4:4-13**

Rejoice in the Lord always; again I will say, Rejoice. Let your gentleness be known to everyone. The Lord is near. Do not worry about anything, but in everything by prayer and supplication with thanksgiving let your requests be made known to God. And the peace of God, which surpasses all understanding, will guard your hearts and your minds in Christ Jesus. Finally, beloved, whatever is true, whatever is honorable, whatever is just, whatever is pure, whatever is pleasing, whatever is commendable, if there is any excellence and if there is anything worthy of praise, think about these things. Keep on doing the things that you have learned and received and heard and seen in me, and the God of peace will be with you. I rejoice in the Lord greatly that now at last you have revived your concern for me; indeed, you were concerned for me, but had no opportunity to show it. Not that I am referring to being in need; for I have learned to be content with whatever I have. I know what it is to have little, and I know what it is to have plenty. In any and all circumstances I have learned the secret of being well-fed and of going hungry, of having plenty and of being in need. I can do all things through him who strengthens me.

The Gospel   **Matthew 22:1-14**

Once more Jesus spoke to them in parables, saying: "The kingdom of heaven may be compared to a king who gave a wedding banquet for his son. He sent his slaves to call those who had been invited to the wedding banquet, but they would not come. Again he sent other slaves, saying, 'Tell those who have been invited: Look, I have prepared my dinner, my oxen and my fat calves have been slaughtered, and everything is ready; come to the wedding banquet.' But they made light of it and went away, one to his farm, another to his business, while the rest seized his slaves, mistreated them, and killed them. The king was enraged. He sent his troops, destroyed those murderers, and burned their city. Then he said to his slaves, 'The wedding is ready, but those invited were not worthy. Go therefore into the main streets, and invite everyone you find to the wedding banquet.' Those slaves went out into the streets and gathered all whom they found, both good and bad; so the wedding hall was filled with guests. But when the king came in to see the guests, he noticed a man there who was not wearing a wedding robe, and he said to him, 'Friend, how did you get in here without a wedding robe?' And he was speechless. Then the king said to the attendants, 'Bind him hand and foot, and throw him into the outer darkness, where there will be weeping and gnashing of teeth.' For many are called, but few are chosen."

Year B

The Lesson   **Amos 5:6-7, 10-15**

Seek the LORD and live, or he will break out against the house of Joseph like fire, and it will devour Bethel, with no one to quench it. Ah, you that turn justice to wormwood, and bring righteousness to the ground! They hate the one who reproves in the gate, and they abhor the one who speaks the truth. Therefore because you trample on the poor and take from them levies of grain, you have built houses of hewn stone, but you shall not live in them; you have planted pleasant vineyards, but you shall not drink their wine. For I know how many are your transgressions, and how great are your sins — you who afflict the righteous, who take a bribe, and push aside the needy in the gate. Therefore the prudent will keep silent in such a time; for it is an evil time. Seek good and not evil, that you may live; and so the LORD, the God of hosts, will be with you, just as you have said. Hate evil and love good, and establish justice in the gate; it may be that the LORD, the God of hosts, will gracious to the remnant of Joseph.

The Psalm 90 or 90:1-8, 12   *Domine, refugium*

1   [Lord, you have been our refuge *
         from one generation to another.

2   Before the mountains were brought forth,
      or the land and the earth were born, *
         from age to age you are God.

3   You turn us back to the dust and say, *
         "Go back, O child of earth."

4   For a thousand years in your sight are like yesterday when it is past *
         and like a watch in the night.

5   You sweep us away like a dream; *
         we fade away suddenly like the grass.

6   In the morning it is green and flourishes; *
      in the evening it is dried up and withered.

7   For we consume away in your displeasure; *
      we are afraid because of your wrathful indignation.

8   Our iniquities you have set before you, *
      and our secret sins in the light of your countenance.]

9   When you are angry, all our days are gone; *
      we bring our years to an end like a sigh.

10   The span of our life is seventy years,
      perhaps in strength even eighty; *
         yet the sum of them is but labor and sorrow,
         for they pass away quickly and we are gone.

11   Who regards the power of your wrath? *
      who rightly fears your indignation?

12   [So teach us to number our days *
      that we may apply our hearts to wisdom.]

13   Return, O LORD; how long will you tarry? *
      be gracious to your servants.

14   Satisfy us by your loving-kindness in the morning; *
      so shall we rejoice and be glad all the days of our life.

15   Make us glad by the measure of the days that you afflicted us *
      and the years in which we suffered adversity.

16   Show your servants your works *
      and your splendor to their children.

17   May the graciousness of the LORD our God be upon us; *
      prosper the work of our hands;
      prosper our handiwork.

The Epistle   Hebrews 3:1-6
Brothers and sisters, holy partners in a heavenly calling, consider that Jesus, the
apostle and high priest of our confession, was faithful to the one who appointed him,
just as Moses also "was faithful in all God's house." Yet Jesus is worthy of more
glory than Moses, just as the builder of a house has more honor than the house itself.
(For every house is built by someone, but the builder of all things is God.) Now
Moses was faithful in all God's house as a servant, to testify to the things that would
be spoken later. Christ, however, was faithful over God's house as a son, and we are
his house if we hold firm the confidence and the pride that belong to hope.

The Gospel   Mark 10:17-27 (28-31)
As Jesus was setting out on a journey, a man ran up and knelt before Jesus, and
asked him, "Good Teacher, what must I do to inherit eternal life?" Jesus said to him,

"Why do you call me good? No one is good but God alone. You know the commandments: 'You shall not murder; You shall not commit adultery; You shall not steal; You shall not bear false witness; You shall not defraud; Honor your father and mother.'" He said to him, "Teacher, I have kept all these since my youth." Jesus, looking at him, loved him and said, "You lack one thing; go, sell what you own, and give the money to the poor, and you will have treasure in heaven; then come, follow me." When he heard this, he was shocked and went away grieving, for he had many possessions. Then Jesus looked around and said to his disciples, "How hard it will be for those who have wealth to enter the kingdom of God!" And the disciples were perplexed at these words. But Jesus said to them again, "Children, how hard it is to enter the kingdom of God! It is easier for a camel to go through the eye of a needle than for someone who is rich to enter the kingdom of God." They were greatly astounded and said to one another, "Then who can be saved?" Jesus looked at them and said, "For mortals it is impossible, but not for God; for God all things are possible." [Peter began to say to him, "Look, we have left everything and followed you." Jesus said, "Truly I tell you, there is no one who has left house or brothers or sisters or mother or father or children or fields, for my sake and for the sake of the good news, who will not receive a hundredfold now in this age — houses, brothers and sisters, mothers and children, and fields with persecutions — and in the age to come eternal life. But many who are first will be last, and the last will be first."]

Year C

The Lesson Ruth 1:(1-7) 8-19a

[In the days when the judges ruled, there was a famine in the land, and a certain man of Bethlehem in Judah went to live in the country of Moab, he and his wife and two sons. The name of the man was Elimelech and the name of his wife Naomi, and the names of his two sons were Mahlon and Chilion; they were Ephrathites from Bethlehem in Judah. They went into the country of Moab and remained there. But Elimelech, the husband of Naomi, died, and she was left with her two sons. These took Moabite wives; the name of the one was Orpah and the name of the other Ruth. When they had lived there about ten years, both Mahlon and Chilion also died, so that the woman was left without her two sons and her husband. Then she started to return with her daughters-in-law from the country of Moab, for she had heard in the country of Moab that the LORD had considered his people and given them food. So she set out from the place where she had been living, she and her two daughters-in-law, and they went on their way to go back to the land of Judah.] But Naomi said to her two daughters-in-law, "Go back each of you to your mother's house. May the LORD deal kindly with you, as you have dealt with the dead and with me. The LORD grant that you may find security, each of you in the house of your husband." Then she kissed them, and they wept aloud. They said to her, "No, we will return with you to your people." But Naomi said, "Turn back, my daughters, why will you go with me? Do I still have sons in my womb that they may become your husbands? Turn back, my daughters, go your way, for I am too old to have a husband. Even if I thought there was hope for me, even if I should have a husband tonight and bear sons, would you then wait until they were grown? Would you then refrain from marrying? No, my daughters, it has been far more bitter for me than for you, because the hand of the LORD has turned against me." Then they wept aloud again. Orpah kissed her mother-in-law, but Ruth clung to her. So she said, "See, your sister-in-law has gone back to her people and to her gods; return after your sister-in-law." But Ruth said, "Do not press me to leave you or to turn back from following you! Where you go, I will go; Where you lodge, I will lodge; your people shall be my people, and your God my God. Where you die, I will die — there will I be buried. May the LORD do thus and so to me, and more as well, if even death parts me from you!" When Naomi saw that she was determined to go with her, she said no more to her. So the two of them went on until they came to Bethlehem.

The Psalm 113 *Laudate, pueri*

1 Hallelujah!
Give praise, you servants of the LORD; *
    praise the Name of the LORD.

2 Let the Name of the LORD be blessed, *
    from this time forth for evermore.

3 From the rising of the sun to its going down *
    let the Name of the LORD be praised.

4 The LORD is high above all nations, *
    and his glory above the heavens.

5 Who is like the LORD our God, who sits enthroned on high, *
    but stoops to behold the heavens and the earth?

6 He takes up the weak out of the dust *
    and lifts up the poor from the ashes.

7 He sets them with the princes, *
    with the princes of his people.

8 He makes the woman of a childless house *
    to be a joyful mother of children.

The Epistle   2 Timothy 2:(3-7) 8-15

[Share in suffering like a good soldier of Christ Jesus. No one serving in the army gets entangled in everyday affairs; the soldier's aim is to please the enlisting officer. And in the case of an athlete, no one is crowned without competing according to the rules. It is the farmer who does the work who ought to have the first share of the crops. Think over what I say, for the Lord will give you understanding in all things.] Remember Jesus Christ, raised from the dead, a descendant of David — that is my gospel, for which I suffer hardship, even to the point of being chained like a criminal. But the word of God is not chained. Therefore I endure everything for the sake of the elect, so that they may also obtain the salvation that is in Christ Jesus, with eternal glory. The saying is sure: If we have died with him, we will also live with him; if we endure, we will also reign with him; if we deny him, he will also deny us; if we are faithless, he remains faithful — for he cannot deny himself. Remind them of this, and warn them before God that they are to avoid wrangling over words, which does no good but only ruins those who are listening. Do your best to present yourself to

God as one approved by him, a worker who has no need to be ashamed, rightly explaining the word of truth.

The Gospel Luke 17:11-19

On the way to Jerusalem Jesus was going through the region between Samaria and Galilee. As he entered a village, ten lepers approached him. Keeping their distance, they called out, saying, "Jesus, Master, have mercy on us!" When he saw them, he said to them, "Go and show yourselves to the priests." And as they went, they were made clean. Then one of them, when he saw that he was healed, turned back, praising God with a loud voice. He prostrated himself at Jesus' feet and thanked him. And he was a Samaritan. Then Jesus asked, "Were not ten made clean? But the other nine, where are they? Was none of them found to return and give praise to God except this foreigner?" Then he said to him, "Get up and go on your way; your faith has made you well."

Proper 24 *The Sunday closest to October 19*

The Collect

Almighty and everlasting God, in Christ you have revealed your glory among the nations: Preserve the works of your mercy, that your Church throughout the world may persevere with steadfast faith in the confession of your Name; through Jesus Christ our Lord, who lives and reigns with you and the Holy Spirit, one God, for ever and ever. *Amen.*

Almighty and everlasting God, who in Christ hast revealed thy glory among the nations: Preserve the works of thy mercy, that thy Church throughout the world may persevere with steadfast faith in the confession of thy Name; through the same Jesus Christ our Lord, who liveth and reigneth with thee and the Holy Spirit, one God, for ever and ever. *Amen.*

Year A

The Lesson Isaiah 45:1-7

Thus says the LORD to his anointed, to Cyrus, whose right hand I have grasped to subdue nations before him and strip kings of their robes, to open doors before him — and the gates shall not be closed: I will go before you and level the mountains, I will break in pieces the doors of bronze and cut through the bars of iron, I will give you the treasures of darkness and riches hidden in secret places, so that you may know that it is I, the LORD, the God of Israel, who call you by your name. For the sake of my servant Jacob, and Israel my chosen, I call you by your name, I surname you, though you do not know me. I am the LORD, and there is no other; besides me there is no god. I arm you, though you do not know me, so that they may know, from the rising of the sun and from the west, that there is no one besides me; I am the LORD, and there is no other. I form light and create darkness, I make weal and create woe; I the LORD do all these things.

The Psalm 96 or 96:1-9   *Cantate Domino*

1   [Sing to the LORD a new song; *
      sing to the LORD, all the whole earth.

2 Sing to the LORD and bless his Name; *
        proclaim the good news of his salvation from day to day.

3 Declare his glory among the nations *
        and his wonders among all peoples.

4 For great is the LORD and greatly to be praised; *
        he is more to be feared than all gods.

5 As for all the gods of the nations, they are but idols; *
        but it is the LORD who made the heavens.

6 Oh, the majesty and magnificence of his presence! *
        Oh, the power and the splendor of his sanctuary!

7 Ascribe to the LORD, you families of the peoples; *
        ascribe to the LORD honor and power.

8 Ascribe to the LORD the honor due his Name; *
        bring offerings and come into his courts.

9 Worship the LORD in the beauty of holiness; *
        let the whole earth tremble before him.]

10 Tell it out among the nations: "The LORD is King! *
        he has made the world so firm that it cannot be moved;
        he will judge the peoples with equity."

11 Let the heavens rejoice, and let the earth be glad;
        let the sea thunder and all that is in it; *
        let the field be joyful and all that is therein.

12 Then shall all the trees of the wood shout for joy
        before the LORD when he comes, *
        when he comes to judge the earth.

13 He will judge the world with righteousness *
        and the peoples with his truth.

The Epistle   **1 Thessalonians 1:1-10**

Paul, Silvanus, and Timothy, To the church of the Thessalonians in God the Father
and the Lord Jesus Christ: Grace to you and peace. We always give thanks to God for
all of you and mention you in our prayers, constantly remembering before our God
and Father your work of faith and labor of love and steadfastness of hope in our
Lord Jesus Christ. For we know, brothers and sisters beloved by God, that he has
chosen you, because our message of the gospel came to you not in word only, but also
in power and in the Holy Spirit and with full conviction; just as you know what kind
of persons we proved to be among you for your sake. And you became imitators of us
and of the Lord, for in spite of persecution you received the word with joy inspired
by the Holy Spirit, so that you became an example to all the believers in Macedonia
and in Achaia. For the word of the Lord has sounded forth from you not only in
Macedonia and Achaia, but in every place your faith in God has become known, so

that we have no need to speak about it. For the people of those regions report about us what kind of welcome we had among you, and how you turned to God from idols, to serve a living and true God, and to wait for his Son from heaven, whom he raised from the dead — Jesus, who rescues us from the wrath that is coming.

The Gospel   Matthew 22:15-22

The Pharisees went and plotted to entrap Jesus in what he said. So they sent their disciples to him, along with the Herodians, saying, "Teacher, we know that you are sincere, and teach the way of God in accordance with truth, and show deference to no one; for you do not regard people with partiality. Tell us, then, what you think. Is it lawful to pay taxes to the emperor, or not?" But Jesus, aware of their malice, said, "Why are you putting me to the test, you hypocrites? Show me the coin used for the tax." And they brought him a denarius. Then he said to them, "Whose head is this, and whose title?" They answered, "The emperor's." Then he said to them, "Give therefore to the emperor the things that are the emperor's, and to God the things that are God's." When they heard this, they were amazed; and they left him and went away.

Year B

The Lesson   Isaiah 53:4-12

Surely he has borne our infirmities and carried our diseases; yet we accounted him stricken, struck down by God, and afflicted. But he was wounded for our transgressions, crushed for our iniquities; upon him was the punishment that made us whole, and by his bruises we are healed. All we like sheep have gone astray; we have all turned to our own way, and the LORD has laid on him the iniquity of us all. He was oppressed, and he was afflicted, yet he did not open his mouth; like a lamb that is led to the slaughter, and like a sheep that before its shearers is silent, so he did not open his mouth. By a perversion of justice he was taken away. Who could have imagined his future? For he was cut off from the land of the living, stricken for the transgression of my people. They made his grave with the wicked and his tomb with the rich, although he had done no violence, and there was no deceit in his mouth. Yet it was the will of the LORD to crush him with pain. When you make his life an offering for sin, he shall see his offspring, and shall prolong his days; through him the will of the LORD shall prosper. Out of his anguish he shall see light; he shall find satisfaction through his knowledge. The righteous one, my servant, shall make many righteous, and he shall bear their iniquities. Therefore I will allot him a portion with the great, and he shall divide the spoil with the strong; because he poured out himself to death, and was numbered with the transgressors; yet he bore the sin of many, and made intercession for the transgressors.

The Psalm 91 or 91:9-16   *Qui habitat*

1   He who dwells in the shelter of the Most High, *
        abides under the shadow of the Almighty.

2   He shall say to the LORD,
     "You are my refuge and my stronghold, *
        my God in whom I put my trust."

3   He shall deliver you from the snare of the hunter *
     and from the deadly pestilence.

4   He shall cover you with his pinions,
     and you shall find refuge under his wings; *
        his faithfulness shall be a shield and buckler.

5   You shall not be afraid of any terror by night, *
        nor of the arrow that flies by day;

6   Of the plague that stalks in the darkness, *
        nor of the sickness that lays waste at mid-day.

7   A thousand shall fall at your side
     and ten thousand at your right hand, *
        but it shall not come near you.

8   Your eyes have only to behold *
        to see the reward of the wicked.

9   [Because you have made the LORD your refuge, *
        and the Most High your habitation,

10   There shall no evil happen to you, *
        neither shall any plague come near your dwelling.

11   For he shall give his angels charge over you, *
        to keep you in all your ways.

12   They shall bear you in their hands, *
        lest you dash your foot against a stone.

13   You shall tread upon the lion and adder; *
        you shall trample the young lion and the serpent under your feet.

14   Because he is bound to me in love,
     therefore will I deliver him; *
        I will protect him, because he knows my Name.

15   He shall call upon me, and I will answer him; *
        I am with him in trouble;
        I will rescue him and bring him to honor.

16   With long life will I satisfy him, *
        and show him my salvation.]

The Epistle   **Hebrews 4:12-16**
The word of God is living and active, sharper than any two-edged sword, piercing until it divides soul from spirit, joints from marrow; it is able to judge the thoughts and intentions of the heart. And before him no creature is hidden, but all are naked and laid bare to the eyes of the one to whom we must render an account. Since, then, we have a great high priest who has passed through the heavens, Jesus, the Son of God, let us hold fast to our confession. For we do not have a high priest who is

unable to sympathize with our weaknesses, but we have one who in every respect has been tested as we are, yet without sin. Let us therefore approach the throne of grace with boldness, so that we may receive mercy and find grace to help in time of need.

The Gospel Mark 10:35-45

James and John, the sons of Zebedee, came forward to Jesus and said to him, "Teacher, we want you to do for us whatever we ask of you." And he said to them, "What is it you want me to do for you?" And they said to him, "Grant us to sit, one at your right hand and one at your left, in your glory." But Jesus said to them, "You do not know what you are asking. Are you able to drink the cup that I drink, or be baptized with the baptism that I am baptized with?" They replied, "We are able." Then Jesus said to them, "The cup that I drink you will drink; and with the baptism with which I am baptized, you will be baptized; but to sit at my right hand or at my left is not mine to grant, but it is for those for whom it has been prepared." When the ten heard this, they began to be angry with James and John. So Jesus called them and said to them, "You know that among the Gentiles those whom they recognize as their rulers lord it over them, and their great ones are tyrants over them. But it is not so among you; but whoever wishes to become great among you must be your servant, and whoever wishes to be first among you must be slave of all. For the Son of Man came not to be served but to serve, and to give his life a ransom for many."

Year C

The Lesson Genesis 32:3-8, 22-30

Jacob sent messengers before him to his brother Esau in the land of Seir, the country of Edom, instructing them, "Thus you shall say to my lord Esau: Thus says your servant Jacob, 'I have lived with Laban as an alien, and stayed until now; and I have oxen, donkeys, flocks, male and female slaves; and I have sent to tell my lord, in order that I may find favor in your sight.'" The messengers returned to Jacob, saying, "We came to your brother Esau, and he is coming to meet you, and four hundred men are with him." Then Jacob was greatly afraid and distressed; and he divided the people that were with him, and the flocks and herds and camels, into two companies, thinking, "If Esau comes to the one company and destroys it, then the company that is left will escape." The same night he got up and took his two wives, his two maids, and his eleven children, and crossed the ford of the Jabbok. He took them and sent them across the stream, and likewise everything that he had. Jacob was left alone; and a man wrestled with him until daybreak. When the man saw that he did not prevail against Jacob, he struck him on the hip socket; and Jacob's hip was put out of joint as he wrestled with him. Then he said, "Let me go, for the day is breaking." But Jacob said, "I will not let you go, unless you bless me." So he said to him, "What is your name?" And he said, "Jacob." Then the man said, "You shall no longer be called Jacob, but Israel, for you have striven with God and with humans, and have prevailed." Then Jacob asked him, "Please tell me your name?" But he said, "Why is it that you ask my name?" And there he blessed him. So Jacob called the place Peniel, saying, "For I have seen God face to face, and yet my life is preserved."

The Psalm 121   *Levavi oculos*

1   I lift up my eyes to the hills; *
        from where is my help to come?

2   My help comes from the LORD, *
        the maker of heaven and earth.

3   He will not let your foot be moved *
        and he who watches over you will not fall asleep.

4   Behold, he who keeps watch over Israel *
        shall neither slumber nor sleep;

5   The LORD himself watches over you; *
        the LORD is your shade at your right hand,

6   So that the sun shall not strike you by day, *
        nor the moon by night.

7   The LORD shall preserve you from all evil; *
        it is he who shall keep you safe.

8   The LORD shall watch over your going out and your coming in, *
        from this time forth for evermore.

The Epistle   2 Timothy 3:14-4:5

As for you, continue in what you have learned and firmly believed, knowing from
whom you learned it, and how from childhood you have known the sacred writings
that are able to instruct you for salvation through faith in Christ Jesus. All scripture
is inspired by God and is useful for teaching, for reproof, for correction, and for
training in righteousness, so that everyone who belongs to God may be proficient,
equipped for every good work. In the presence of God and of Christ Jesus, who is to
judge the living and the dead, and in view of his appearing and his kingdom, I
solemnly urge you: proclaim the message; be persistent whether the time is favorable
or unfavorable; convince, rebuke, and encourage, with the utmost patience in
teaching. For the time is coming when people will not put up with sound doctrine,
but having itching ears, they will accumulate for themselves teachers to suit their own
desires, and will turn away from listening to the truth and wander away to myths. As
for you, always be sober, endure suffering, do the work of an evangelist, carry out
your ministry fully.

The Gospel   Luke 18:1-8a

Jesus told the diciples a parable about their need to pray always and not to lose heart.
He said, "In a certain city there was a judge who neither feared God nor had respect
for people. In that city there was a widow who kept coming to him and saying, 'Grant
me justice against my opponent.' For a while he refused; but later he said to himself,
'Though I have no fear of God and no respect for anyone, yet because this widow
keeps bothering me, I will grant her justice, so that she may not wear me out by
continually coming.'" And the Lord said, "Listen to what the unjust judge says. And

will not God grant justice to his chosen ones who cry to him day and night? Will he delay long in helping them? I tell you, he will quickly grant justice to them."

Proper 25 *The Sunday closest to October 26*

The Collect

Almighty and everlasting God, increase in us the gifts of faith, hope, and charity; and, that we may obtain what you promise, make us love what you command; through Jesus Christ our Lord, who lives and reigns with you and the Holy Spirit, one God, for ever and ever. *Amen.*

Almighty and everlasting God, give unto us the increase of faith, hope, and charity; and, that we may obtain that which thou dost promise, make us to love that which thou dost command; through Jesus Christ our Lord, who liveth and reigneth with thee and the Holy Spirit, one God, for ever and ever. *Amen.*

Year A

The Lesson   Exodus 22:21-27

You shall not wrong or oppress a resident alien, for you were aliens in the land of Egypt. You shall not abuse any widow or orphan. If you do abuse them, when they cry out to me, I will surely heed their cry; my wrath will burn, and I will kill you with the sword, and your wives shall become widows and your children orphans. If you lend money to my people, to the poor among you, you shall not deal with them as a creditor; you shall not exact interest from them. If you take your neighbor's cloak in pawn, you shall restore it before the sun goes down; for it may be your neighbor's only clothing to use as cover; in what else shall that person sleep? And if your neighbor cries out to me, I will listen, for I am compassionate.

The Psalm 1   *Beatus vir qui non abiit*

1   Happy are they who have not walked in the counsel of the wicked, *
        nor lingered in the way of sinners,
        nor sat in the seats of the scornful!

2   Their delight is in the law of the LORD, *
        and they meditate on his law day and night.

3   They are like trees planted by streams of water,
    bearing fruit in due season, with leaves that do not wither; *
        everything they do shall prosper.

4   It is not so with the wicked; *
        they are like chaff which the wind blows away.

5   Therefore the wicked shall not stand upright when judgment comes, *
        nor the sinner in the council of the righteous.

6   For the LORD knows the way of the righteous, *
        but the way of the wicked is doomed.

The Epistle   **1 Thessalonians 2:1-8**

You yourselves know, brothers and sisters, that our coming to you was not in vain, but though we had already suffered and been shamefully mistreated at Philippi, as you know, we had courage in our God to declare to you the gospel of God in spite of great opposition. For our appeal does not spring from deceit or impure motives or trickery, but just as we have been approved by God to be entrusted with the message of the gospel, even so we speak, not to please mortals, but to please God who tests our hearts. As you know and as God is our witness, we never came with words of flattery or with a pretext for greed; nor did we seek praise from mortals, whether from you or from others, though we might have made demands as apostles of Christ. But we were gentle among you, like a nurse tenderly caring for her own children. So deeply do we care for you that we are determined to share with you not only the gospel of God but also our own selves, because you have become very dear to us.

The Gospel   Matthew 22:34-46

When the Pharisees heard that Jesus had silenced the Sadducees, they gathered together, and one of them, a lawyer, asked him a question to test him. "Teacher, which commandment in the law is the greatest?" He said to him, "'You shall love the Lord your God with all your heart, and with all your soul, and with all your mind.' This is the greatest and first commandment. And a second is like it: 'You shall love your neighbor as yourself.' On these two commandments hang all the law and the prophets." Now while the Pharisees were gathered together, Jesus asked them this question: "What do you think of the Messiah? Whose son is he?" They said to him, "The son of David." He said to them, "How is it then that David by the Spirit calls him Lord, saying, 'The Lord said to my Lord, "Sit at my right hand, until I put your enemies under your feet"'? If David thus calls him Lord, how can he be his son?" No one was able to give him an answer, nor from that day did anyone dare to ask him any more questions.

Year B

Lesson   **Isaiah 59:(1-4) 9-19**

[See, the LORD's hand is not too short to save, nor his ear too dull to hear. Rather, your iniquities have been barriers between you and your God, and your sins have hidden his face from you so that he does not hear. For your hands are defiled with blood, and your fingers with iniquity; your lips have spoken lies, your tongue mutters wickedness. No one brings suit justly, no one goes to law honestly; they rely on empty pleas, they speak lies, conceiving mischief and begetting iniquity.] Therefore justice is far from us, and righteousness does not reach us; we wait for light, and lo! there is darkness; and for brightness, but we walk in gloom. We grope like the blind along a wall, groping like those who have no eyes; we stumble at noon as in the twilight, among the vigorous as though we were dead. We all growl like bears; like doves we moan mournfully. We wait for justice, but there is none; for salvation, but it is far from us. For our transgressions before you are many, and our sins testify against us. Our transgressions indeed are with us, and we know our iniquities: transgressing, and denying the LORD, and turning away from following our God, talking oppression and revolt, conceiving lying words and uttering them from the heart. Justice is turned back, and righteousness stands at a distance; for truth stumbles in the public square, and uprightness cannot enter. Truth is lacking, and whoever turns from evil is despoiled. The LORD saw it, and it displeased him that there was no justice. He saw that there was no one, and was appalled that there was no one to intervene; so his own arm brought him victory, and his righteousness upheld him. He put on righteousness like a breastplate, and a helmet of salvation on his head; he put on garments of vengeance for clothing, and wrapped himself in fury as in a mantle. According to their deeds, so will he repay; wrath to his adversaries, requital to his enemies; to the coastlands he will render requital. So those in the west shall fear the name of the LORD, and those in the east, his glory; for he will come like a pent-up stream that the wind of the LORD drives on.

The Psalm 13   *Usquequo, Domine?*

1   How long, O LORD?
     will you forget me for ever? *
        how long will you hide your face from me?

2   How long shall I have perplexity in my mind,
     and grief in my heart, day after day? *
        how long shall my enemy triumph over me?

3   Look upon me and answer me, O LORD my God; *
        give light to my eyes, lest I sleep in death;

4   Lest my enemy say, "I have prevailed over him," *
        and my foes rejoice that I have fallen.

5   But I put my trust in your mercy; *
        my heart is joyful because of your saving help.

6   I will sing to the LORD, for he has dealt with me richly; *
        I will praise the Name of the Lord Most High.

The Epistle   **Hebrews 5:12-6:1, 9-12**

For though by this time you ought to be teachers, you need someone to teach you again the basic elements of the oracles of God. You need milk, not solid food; for everyone who lives on milk, being still an infant, is unskilled in the word of righteousness. But solid food is for the mature, for those whose faculties have been trained by practice to distinguish good from evil. Therefore let us go on toward perfection, leaving behind the basic teaching about Christ, and not laying again the foundation: repentance from dead works and faith toward God. Even though we speak in this way, beloved, we are confident of better things in your case, things that belong to salvation. For God is not unjust; he will not overlook your work and the love that you showed for his sake in serving the saints, as you still do. And we want each one of you to show the same diligence so as to realize the full assurance of hope to the very end, so that you may not become sluggish, but imitators of those who through faith and patience inherit the promises.

The Gospel   **Mark 10:46-52**

Jesus and his disciples came to Jericho. As he and his disciples and a large crowd were leaving Jericho, Bartimaeus son of Timaeus, a blind beggar, was sitting by the roadside. When he heard that it was Jesus of Nazareth, he began to shout out and say, "Jesus, Son of David, have mercy on me!" Many sternly ordered him to be quiet, but he cried out even more loudly, "Son of David, have mercy on me!" Jesus stood still and said, "Call him here." And they called the blind man, saying to him, "Take heart; get up, he is calling you." So throwing off his cloak, he sprang up and came to Jesus. Then Jesus said to him, "What do you want me to do for you?" The blind man said to him, "My teacher, let me see again." Jesus said to him, "Go; your faith has made you well." Immediately he regained his sight and followed him on the way.

Year C

The Lesson   **Jeremiah 14:(1-6) 7-10, 19-22**

[The word of the LORD that came to Jeremiah concerning the drought: "Judah mourns and her gates languish; they lie in gloom on the ground, and the cry of Jerusalem goes up. Her nobles send their servants for water; they come to the cisterns, they find no water, they return with their vessels empty. They are ashamed and dismayed and cover their heads, because the ground is cracked. Because there has been no rain on the land the farmers are dismayed; they cover their heads. Even the doe in the field forsakes her newborn fawn because there is no grass. The wild asses stand on the bare heights, they pant for air like jackals; their eyes fail because there is no herbage.] Although our iniquities testify against us, act, O LORD, for your name's sake; our apostasies indeed are many, and we have sinned against you. O hope of Israel, its savior in time of trouble, why should you be like a stranger in the land, like a traveler turning aside for the night? Why should you be like someone confused, like a mighty warrior who cannot give help? Yet you, O LORD, are in the midst of us, and we are called by your name; do not forsake us! Thus says the LORD concerning this people: Truly they have loved to wander, they have not restrained their feet; therefore the LORD does not accept them, now he will remember their iniquity and punish their sins. Have you completely rejected Judah? Does your heart loathe Zion? Why have you struck us down so that there is no healing for us? We look for peace, but find no good; for a time of healing, but there is terror instead. We acknowledge our wickedness, O LORD, the iniquity of our ancestors, for we have sinned against you. Do not spurn us, for your name's sake; do not dishonor your glorious throne; remember and do not break your covenant with us. Can any idols of the nations bring rain? Or can the heavens give showers? Is it not you, O LORD our God? We set our hope on you, for it is you who do all this."

The Psalm 84 or 84:1-6   *Quam dilecta!*

1   [How dear to me is your dwelling, O LORD of hosts! *
    My soul has a desire and longing for the courts of the LORD;
    my heart and my flesh rejoice in the living God.

2   The sparrow has found her a house
   and the swallow a nest where she may lay her young; *
    by the side of your altars, O LORD of hosts,
    my King and my God.

3   Happy are they who dwell in your house! *
       they will always be praising you.

4   Happy are the people whose strength is in you! *
       whose hearts are set on the pilgrims' way.

5   Those who go through the desolate valley will find it a place of springs, *
       for the early rains have covered it with pools of water.

6   They will climb from height to height, *
       and the God of gods will reveal himself in Zion.]

7   LORD God of hosts, hear my prayer; *
       hearken, O God of Jacob.

8   Behold our defender, O God; *
       and look upon the face of your Anointed.

9   For one day in your courts is better than a thousand in my own room, *
       and to stand at the threshold of the house of my God
       than to dwell in the tents of the wicked.

10   For the LORD God is both sun and shield; *
       he will give grace and glory;

11   No good thing will the LORD withhold *
       from those who walk with integrity.

12   O LORD of hosts, *
       happy are they who put their trust in you!

The Epistle   **2 Timothy 4:6-8, 16-18**

As for me, I am already being poured out as a libation, and the time of my departure has come. I have fought the good fight, I have finished the race, I have kept the faith. From now on there is reserved for me the crown of righteousness, which the Lord, the righteous judge, will give me on that day, and not only to me but also to all who have longed for his appearing. At my first defense no one came to my support, but all deserted me. May it not be counted against them! But the Lord stood by me and gave me strength, so that through me the message might be fully proclaimed and all the Gentiles might hear it. So I was rescued from the lion's mouth. The Lord will rescue me from every evil attack and save me for his heavenly kingdom. To him be the glory forever and ever. Amen.

The Gospel   **Luke 18:9-14**

Jesus also told this parable to some who trusted in themselves that they were righteous and regarded others with contempt: "Two men went up to the temple to pray, one a Pharisee and the other a tax collector. The Pharisee, standing by himself, was praying thus, 'God, I thank you that I am not like other people: thieves, rogues, adulterers, or even like this tax collector. I fast twice a week; I give a tenth of all my income.' But the tax collector, standing far off, would not even look up to heaven, but was beating his breast and saying, 'God, be merciful to me, a sinner!' I tell you, this man went down to his home justified rather than the other; for all who exalt themselves will be humbled, but all who humble themselves will be exalted."

Proper 26 *The Sunday closest to November 2*

The Collect
Almighty and merciful God, it is only by your gift that your faithful people offer you true and laudable service: Grant that we may run without stumbling to obtain your heavenly promises; through Jesus Christ our Lord, who lives and reigns with you and the Holy Spirit, one God, now and for ever. *Amen.*

Almighty and merciful God, of whose only gift it cometh that thy faithful people do unto thee true and laudable service: Grant, we beseech thee, that we may run without stumbling to obtain thy heavenly promises; through Jesus Christ our Lord, who liveth and reigneth with thee and the Holy Spirit, one God, now and for ever. *Amen.*

Year A

The Lesson   Micah 3:5-12
Thus says the LORD concerning the prophets who lead my people astray, who cry "Peace" when they have something to eat, but declare war against those who put nothing into their mouths. Therefore it shall be night to you, without vision, and darkness to you, without revelation. The sun shall go down upon the prophets, and the day shall be black over them; the seers shall be disgraced, and the diviners put to shame; they shall all cover their lips, for there is no answer from God. But as for me, I am filled with power, with the spirit of the LORD, and with justice and might, to declare to Jacob his transgression and to Israel his sin. Hear this, you rulers of the house of Jacob and chiefs of the house of Israel, who abhor justice and pervert all equity, who build Zion with blood and Jerusalem with wrong! Its rulers give judgment for a bribe, its priests teach for a price, its prophets give oracles for money; yet they lean upon the LORD and say, "Surely the LORD is with us! No harm shall come upon us." Therefore because of you Zion shall be plowed as a field; Jerusalem shall become a heap of ruins, and the mountain of the house a wooded height.

The Psalm 43   *Judica me, Deus*
1   Give judgment for me, O God,
         and defend my cause against an ungodly people; *
             deliver me from the deceitful and the wicked.

2   For you are the God of my strength;
         why have you put me from you? *
             and why do I go so heavily while the enemy oppresses me?

3   Send out your light and your truth, that they may lead me, *
             and bring me to your holy hill
             and to your dwelling;

4   That I may go to the altar of God,
         to the God of my joy and gladness; *
             and on the harp I will give thanks to you, O God my God.

5   Why are you so full of heaviness, O my soul? *
      and why are you so disquieted within me?

6   Put your trust in God; *
      for I will yet give thanks to him,
      who is the help of my countenance, and my God.

The Epistle   1 Thessalonians 2:9-13, 17-20

You remember our labor and toil, brothers and sisters; we worked night and day, so
that we might not burden any of you while we proclaimed to you the gospel of God.
You are witnesses, and God also, how pure, upright, and blameless our conduct was
toward you believers. As you know, we dealt with each one of you like a father with
his children, urging and encouraging you and pleading that you lead a life worthy of
God, who calls you into his own kingdom and glory. We also constantly give thanks
to God for this, that when you received the word of God that you heard from us, you
accepted it not as a human word but as what it really is, God's word, which is also at
work in you believers. As for us, brothers and sisters, when, for a short time, we were
made orphans by being separated from you — in person, not in heart — we longed
with great eagerness to see you face to face. For we wanted to come to you —
certainly I, Paul, wanted to again and again — but Satan blocked our way. For what
is our hope or joy or crown of boasting before our Lord Jesus at his coming? Is it not
you? Yes, you are our glory and joy!

The Gospel   Matthew 23:1-12

Jesus said to the crowds and to his disciples, "The scribes and the Pharisees sit on
Moses' seat; therefore, do whatever they teach you and follow it; but do not do as
they do, for they do not practice what they teach. They tie up heavy burdens, hard to
bear, and lay them on the shoulders of others; but they themselves are unwilling to
lift a finger to move them. They do all their deeds to be seen by others; for they make
their phylacteries broad and their fringes long. They love to have the place of honor
at banquets and the best seats in the synagogues, and to be greeted with respect in the
marketplaces, and to have people call them rabbi. But you are not to be called rabbi,
for you have one teacher, and you are all students. And call no one your father on
earth, for you have one Father — the one in heaven. Nor are you to be called
instructors, for you have one instructor, the Messiah. The greatest among you will be
your servant. All who exalt themselves will be humbled, and all who humble
themselves will be exalted."

Year B

The Lesson   Deuteronomy 6:1-9

Moses said, "Now this is the commandment — the statutes and the ordinances —
that the LORD your God charged me to teach you to observe in the land that you are
about to cross into and occupy, so that you and your children and your children's
children, may fear the LORD your God all the days of your life, and keep all his
decrees and his commandments that I am commanding you, so that your days may
be long. Hear therefore, O Israel, and observe them diligently, so that it may go well
with you, and so that you may multiply greatly in a land flowing with milk and

honey, as the LORD, the God of your ancestors, has promised you. Hear, O Israel: The LORD is our God, the LORD alone. You shall love the LORD your God with all your heart, and with all your soul, and with all your might. Keep these words that I am commanding you today in your heart. Recite them to your children and talk about them when you are at home and when you are away, when you lie down and when you rise. Bind them as a sign on your hand, fix them as an emblem on your forehead, and write them on the doorposts of your house and on your gates."

The Psalm 119:1-16 or 119:1-8   *Beati immaculati*

1   [Happy are they whose way is blameless, *
          who walk in the law of the LORD!

2   Happy are they who observe his decrees *
          and seek him with all their hearts!

3   Who never do any wrong, *
          but always walk in his ways.

4   You laid down your commandments, *
          that we should full keep them.

5   Oh, that my ways were made so direct *
          that I might keep your statutes!

6   Then I should not be put to shame, *
          when I regard all your commandments.

7   I will thank you with an unfeigned heart, *
          when I have learned your righteous judgments.

8   I will keep your statutes; *
          do not utterly forsake me.]

9   How shall a young man cleanse his way? *
          By keeping to your words.

10   With my whole heart I seek you; *
          let me not stray from your commandments.

11   I treasure your promise in my heart, *
          that I may not sin against you.

12   Blessed are you, O LORD; *
          instruct me in your statutes.

13   With my lips will I recite *
          all the judgments of your mouth.

14   I have taken greater delight in the way of your decrees *
          than in all manner of riches.

15   I will meditate on your commandments *
          and give attention to your ways.

16 My delight is in your statutes; *
    I will not forget your word.

The Epistle   **Hebrews 7:23-28**
The former priests were many in number, because they were prevented by death
from continuing in office; but he holds his priesthood permanently, because he
continues forever. Consequently he is able for all time to save those who approach
God through him, since he always lives to make intercession for them. For it was
fitting that we should have such a high priest, holy, blameless, undefiled, separated
from sinners, and exalted above the heavens. Unlike the other high priests, he has no
need to offer sacrifices day after day, first for his own sins, and then for those of the
people; this he did once for all when he offered himself. For the law appoints as high
priests those who are subject to weakness, but the word of the oath, which came later
than the law, appoints a Son who has been made perfect forever.

The Gospel   **Mark 12:28-34**
One of the scribes came near and heard the Sadducees disputing with one another,
and seeing that Jesus answered them well, he asked him, "Which commandment is
the first of all?" Jesus answered, "The first is 'Hear, O Israel: the Lord our God, the
Lord is one; you shall love the Lord your God with all your heart, and with all your
soul, and with all your mind, and with all your strength.' The second is this, 'You
shall love your neighbor as yourself.' There is no other commandment greater than
these." Then the scribe said to him, "You are right, Teacher; you have truly said that
'he is one, and besides him there is no other'; and 'to love him with all the heart, and
with all the understanding, and with all the strength', and 'to love one's neighbor as
oneself,' — this is much more important than all whole burnt offerings and
sacrifices." When Jesus saw that he answered wisely, he said to him, "You are not far
from the kingdom of God." After that no one dared to ask him any question.

Year C

The Lesson   **Isaiah 1:10-20**
Hear the word of the LORD, you rulers of Sodom! Listen to the teaching of our God,
you people of Gomorrah! What to me is the multitude of your sacrifices? says the
LORD; I have had enough of burnt offerings of rams and the fat of fed beasts; I do not
delight in the blood of bulls, or of lambs, or of goats. When you come to appear
before me, who asked this from your hand? Trample my courts no more; bringing
offerings is futile; incense is an abomination to me. New moon and sabbath and
calling of convocation — I cannot endure solemn assemblies with iniquity. Your new
moons and your appointed festivals my soul hates; they have become a burden to
me, I am weary of bearing them. When you stretch out your hands, I will hide my
eyes from you; even though you make many prayers, I will not listen; your hands are
full of blood. Wash yourselves; make yourselves clean; remove the evil of your doings
from before my eyes; cease to do evil, learn to do good; seek justice, rescue the
oppressed, defend the orphan, plead for the widow. Come now, let us argue it out,
says the LORD: though your sins are like scarlet, they shall be like snow; though they
are red like crimson, they shall become like wool. If you are willing and obedient, you

shall eat the good of the land; but if you refuse and rebel, you shall be devoured by the sword; for the mouth of the LORD has spoken.

The Psalm 32 or 32:1-8   *Beati quorum*

1 [Happy are they whose transgressions are forgiven, *
    and whose sin is put away!

2 Happy are they to whom the LORD imputes no guilt, *
    and in whose spirit there is no guile!

3 While I held my tongue, my bones withered away, *
    because of my groaning all day long.

4 For your hand was heavy upon me day and night; *
    my moisture was dried up as in the heat of summer.

5 Then I acknowledged my sin to you, *
    and did not conceal my guilt.

6 I said, "I will confess my transgressions to the LORD."
    Then you forgave me the guilt of my sin.

7 Therefore all the faithful will make their prayers to you in time of trouble; *
    when the great waters overflow, they shall not reach them.

8 You are my hiding-place;
    you preserve me from trouble; *
    you surround me with shouts of deliverance.]

9 "I will instruct you and teach you in the way that you should go; *
    I will guide you with my eye.

10 Do not be like horse or mule, which have no understanding; *
    who must be fitted with bit and bridle,
    or else they will not stay near you.

11 Great are the tribulations of the wicked; *
    but mercy embraces those who trust in the LORD.

12 Be glad, you righteous, and rejoice in the LORD; *
    shout for joy, all who are true of heart.

The Epistle   **2 Thessalonians 1:1-5 (6-10) 11-12**

Paul, Silvanus, and Timothy, To the church of the Thessalonians in God our Father and the Lord Jesus Christ: Grace to you and peace from God our Father and the Lord Jesus Christ. We must always give thanks to God for you, brothers and sisters, as is right, because your faith is growing abundantly, and the love of everyone of you for one another is increasing. Therefore we ourselves boast of you among the churches of God for your steadfastness and faith during all your persecutions and the afflictions that you are enduring. This is evidence of the righteous judgment of God, and is intended to make you worthy of the kingdom of God, for which you are also suffering. [For it is indeed just of God to repay with affliction those who afflict you, and to give relief to the afflicted as well as to us, when the Lord Jesus is revealed from heaven with his mighty angels in flaming fire, inflicting vengeance on those who do not know God and on those who do not obey the gospel of our Lord Jesus. These will suffer the punishment of eternal destruction, separated from the presence of the Lord and from the glory of his might, when he comes to be glorified by his saints and to be marveled at on that day among all who have believed, because our testimony to you was believed.] To this end we always pray for you, asking that our God will make you worthy of his call and will fulfill by his power every good resolve and work of faith, so that the name of our Lord Jesus may be glorified in you, and you in him, according to the grace of our God and the Lord Jesus Christ.

The Gospel   Luke 19:1-10

Jesus entered Jericho and was passing through it. A man was there named Zacchaeus; he was a chief tax collector and was rich. He was trying to see who Jesus was, but on account of the crowd he could not, because he was short in stature. So he ran ahead and climbed a sycamore tree to see him, because he was going to pass that way. When Jesus came to the place, he looked up and said to him, "Zacchaeus, hurry and come down; for I must stay at your house today." So he hurried down and was happy to welcome him. All who saw it began to grumble and said, "He has gone to be the guest of one who is a sinner." Zacchaeus stood there and said to the LORD, "Look, half of my possessions, Lord, I will give to the poor; and if I have defrauded anyone of anything, I will pay back four times as much." Then Jesus said to him, "Today salvation has come to this house, because he too is a son of Abraham. For the Son of Man came to seek out and to save the lost."

Proper 27 *The Sunday closest to November 9*

The Collect

O God, whose blessed Son came into the world that he might destroy the works of the devil and make us children of God and heirs of eternal life: Grant that, having this hope, we may purify ourselves as he is pure; that, when he comes again with power and great glory, we may be made like him in his eternal and glorious kingdom; where he lives and reigns with you and the Holy Spirit, one God, for ever and ever. *Amen.*

O God, whose blessed Son was manifested that he might destroy the works of the devil and make us the children of God and heirs of eternal life: Grant us, we beseech thee, that, having this hope, we may purify ourselves even as he is pure; that, when he shall appear again with power and great glory, we may be made like unto him in his eternal and glorious kingdom; where with thee, O Father, and thee, O Holy Ghost, he liveth and reigneth ever, one God, world without end. *Amen.*

Year A

The Lesson   Amos 5:18-24

Alas for you who desire the day of the LORD! Why do you want the day of the LORD? It is darkness, not light; as if someone fled from a lion, and was met by a bear; or went into the house and rested a hand against the wall, and was bitten by a snake. Is not the day of the LORD darkness, not light, and gloom with no brightness in it? I hate, I despise your festivals, and I take no delight in your solemn assemblies. Even though you offer me your burnt offerings and grain offerings, I will not accept them; and the offerings of well-being of your fatted animals I will not look upon. Take away from me the noise of your songs; I will not listen to the melody of your harps. But let justice roll down like waters, and righteousness like an everflowing stream.

The Psalm 70   *Deus, in adjutorium*

1   Be pleased, O God, to deliver me; *
      O LORD, make haste to help me.

2   Let those who seek my life be ashamed
and altogether dismayed; *
      let those who take pleasure in my misfortune
      draw back and be disgraced.

3   Let those who say to me "Aha!" and gloat over me turn back, *
      because they are ashamed.

4   Let all who seek you rejoice and be glad in you; *
      let those who love your salvation say for ever,
      "Great is the LORD!"

5   But as for me, I am poor and needy; *
      come to me speedily, O God.

6   You are my helper and my deliverer; *
      O LORD, do not tarry.

The Epistle   1 Thessalonians 4:13-18

We do not want you to be uninformed, brothers and sisters, about those who have died, so that you may not grieve as others do who have no hope. For since we believe that Jesus died and rose again, even so, through Jesus, God will bring with him those who have died. For this we declare to you by the word of the Lord, that we who are alive, who are left until the coming of the Lord, will by no means precede those who have died. For the Lord himself, with a cry of command, with the archangel's call and with the sound of God's trumpet, will descend from heaven, and the dead in Christ will rise first. Then we who are alive, who are left, will be caught up in the clouds together with them to meet the Lord in the air; and so we will be with the Lord forever. Therefore encourage one another with these words.

The Gospel   Matthew 25:1-13

Jesus said, "Then the kingdom of heaven will be like this. Ten bridesmaids took their lamps and went to meet the bridegroom. Five of them were foolish, and five were wise. When the foolish took their lamps, they took no oil with them; but the wise took flasks of oil with their lamps. As the bridegroom was delayed, all of them became drowsy and slept. But at midnight there was a shout, 'Look! Here is the bridegroom! Come out to meet him.' Then all those bridesmaids got up and trimmed their lamps. The foolish said to the wise, 'Give us some of your oil, for our lamps are going out.' But the wise replied, 'No! there will not be enough for you and for us; you had better go to the dealers and buy some for yourselves.' And while they went to buy it, the bridegroom came, and those who were ready went with him into the wedding banquet; and the door was shut. Later the other bridesmaids came also, saying, 'Lord, lord, open to us.' But he replied, 'Truly I tell you, I do not know you.' Keep awake therefore, for you know neither the day nor the hour."

Year B

The Lesson   **1 Kings 17:8-16**

The word of the LORD came to Elijah, saying, "Go now to Zarephath, which belongs to Sidon, and live there; for I have commanded a widow there to feed you." So he set out and went to Zarephath. When he came to the gate of the town, a widow was there gathering sticks; he called to her and said, "Bring me a little water in a vessel, so that I may drink." As she was going to bring it, he called to her and said, "Bring me a morsel of bread in your hand." But she said, "As the LORD your God lives, I have nothing baked, only a handful of meal in a jar, and a little oil in a jug; I am now gathering a couple of sticks, so that I may go home and prepare it for myself and my son, that we may eat it, and die." Elijah said to her, "Do not be afraid; go and do as you have said; but first make me a little cake of it and bring it to me, and afterwards make something for yourself and your son. For thus says the LORD the God of Israel: The jar of meal will not be emptied, and the jug of oil will not fail until the day that the LORD sends rain on the earth." She went and did as Elijah said, so that she as well as he and her household ate for many days. The jar of meal was not emptied, neither did the jug of oil fail, according to the word of the LORD that he spoke by Elijah.

The Psalm 146 or 146:4-9   *Lauda, anima mea*

1   Hallelujah!
     Praise the LORD, O my soul! *
          I will praise the LORD as long as I live;
          I will sing praises to my God while I have my being.

2   Put not your trust in rulers, nor in any child of earth, *
          for there is no help in them.

3   When they breathe their last, they return to earth, *
          and in that day their thoughts perish.

4   [Happy are they who have the God of Jacob for their help! *
          whose hope is in the LORD their God;

5   Who made heaven and earth, the seas, and all that is in them; *
          who keeps his promise for ever;

6   Who gives justice to those who are oppressed, *
          and food to those who hunger.

7   The LORD sets the prisoners free;
     the LORD opens the eyes of the blind; *
          the LORD lifts up those who are bowed down;

8   The LORD loves the righteous;
    the LORD cares for the stranger; *
        he sustains the orphan and widow,
        but frustrates the way of the wicked.

9   The LORD shall reign for ever, *
        your God, O Zion, throughout all generations.
        Hallelujah!]

The Epistle

Hebrews 9:24-28

Christ did not enter a sanctuary made by human hands, a mere copy of the true one, but he entered into heaven itself, now to appear in the presence of God on our behalf. Nor was it to offer himself again and again, as the high priest enters the Holy Place year after year with blood that is not his own; for then he would have had to suffer again and again since the foundation of the world. But as it is, he has appeared once for all at the end of the age to remove sin by the sacrifice of himself. And just as it is appointed for mortals to die once, and after that the judgment, so Christ, having been offered once to bear the sins of many will appear a second time, not to deal with sin, but to save those who are eagerly waiting for him.

The Gospel

Mark 12:38-44

Teaching in the temple, Jesus said, "Beware of the scribes, who like to walk around in long robes, and to be greeted with respect in the marketplaces, and to have the best seats in the synagogues and places of honor at banquets! They devour widows' houses and for the sake of appearance say long prayers. They will receive the greater condemnation." He sat down opposite the treasury, and watched the crowd putting money into the treasury. Many rich people put in large sums. A poor widow came and put in two small copper coins, which are worth a penny. Then he called his disciples and said to them, "Truly I tell you, this poor widow has put in more than all those who are contributing to the treasury. For all of them have contributed out of their abundance; but she out of her poverty has put in everything she had, all she had to live on."

Year C

The Lesson

Job 19:23-27a

"O that my words were written down! O that they were inscribed in a book! O that with an iron pen and with lead they were engraved on a rock forever! For I know that my Redeemer lives, and that at the last he will stand upon the earth; and after my skin has been thus destroyed, then in my flesh I shall see God, whom I shall see on my side, and my eyes shall behold, and not another.

The Psalm 17 or 17:1-8   *Exaudi, Domine*

1   [Hear my plea of innocence, O LORD;
    give heed to my cry; *
        listen to my prayer, which does not come from lying lips.

2 Let my vindication come forth from your presence; *
    let your eyes be fixed on justice.

3 Weigh my heart, summon me by night, *
    melt me down; you will find no impurity in me.

4 I give no offense with my mouth as others do; *
    I have heeded the words of your lips.

5 My footsteps hold fast to the ways of your law; *
    in your paths my feet shall not stumble.

6 I call upon you, O God, for you will answer me; *
    incline your ear to me and hear my words.

7 Show me your marvelous loving-kindness, *
    O Savior of those who take refuge at your right hand
    from those who rise up against them.

8 Keep me as the apple of your eye; *
    hide me under the shadow of your wings,]

9 From the wicked who assault me, *
    from my deadly enemies who surround me.

10 They have closed their heart to pity, *
    and their mouth speaks proud things.

11 They press me hard,
now they surround me, *
    watching how they may cast me to the ground,

12 Like a lion, greedy for its prey, *
    and like a young lion lurking in secret places.

13 Arise, O LORD; confront them and bring them down; *
    deliver me from the wicked by your sword.

14 Deliver me, O LORD, by your hand *
    from those whose portion in life is this world;

15 Whose bellies you fill with your treasure, *
    who are well supplied with children
    and leave their wealth to their little ones.

16 But at my vindication I shall see your face; *
    when I awake, I shall be satisfied, beholding your likeness.

The Epistle   2 Thessalonians 2:13-3:5

We must always give thanks to God for you, brothers and sisters beloved by the Lord, because God chose you as the first fruits for salvation through sanctification by the Spirit and through belief in the truth. For this purpose he called you through our proclamation of the good news, so that you may obtain the glory of our Lord Jesus

Christ. So then, brothers and sisters, stand firm and hold fast to the traditions that you were taught by us, either by word of mouth or by our letter. Now may our Lord Jesus Christ himself and God our Father, who loved us and through grace gave us eternal comfort and good hope, comfort your hearts and strengthen them in every good work and word. Finally, brothers and sisters, pray for us, so that the word of the Lord may spread rapidly and be glorified everywhere, just as it is among you, and that we may be rescued from wicked and evil people; for not all have faith. But the Lord is faithful; he will strengthen you and guard you from the evil one. And we have confidence in the Lord concerning you, that you are doing and will go on doing the things that we command. May the Lord direct your hearts to the love of God and to the steadfastness of Christ.

The Gospel   Luke 20:27 (28-33) 34-38

Some Sadducees, those who say there is no resurrection, came to Jesus [and asked him a question, "Teacher, Moses wrote for us that if a man's brother dies, leaving a wife but no children, the man shall marry the widow and raise up children for his brother. Now there were seven brothers; the first married, and died childless; then the second and the third married her, and so in the same way all seven died childless. Finally the woman also died. In the resurrection, therefore, whose wife will the woman be? For the seven had married her."] Jesus said to them, "Those who belong to this age marry and are given in marriage; but those who are considered worthy of a place in that age and in the resurrection from the dead neither marry nor are given in marriage. Indeed they cannot die anymore, because they are like angels and are children of God, being children of the resurrection. And the fact that the dead are raised Moses himself showed, in the story about the bush, where he speaks of the Lord as the God of Abraham, the God of Isaac, and the God of Jacob. Now he is God not of the dead, but of the living; for to him all of them are alive."

Proper 28 *The Sunday closest to November 16*

The Collect

Blessed Lord, who caused all holy Scriptures to be written for our learning: Grant us so to hear them, read, mark, learn, and inwardly digest them, that we may embrace and ever hold fast the blessed hope of everlasting life, which you have given us in our Savior Jesus Christ; who lives and reigns with you and the Holy Spirit, one God, for ever and ever. *Amen.*

Blessed Lord, who hast caused all holy Scriptures to be written for our learning: Grant that we may in such wise hear them, read, mark, learn, and inwardly digest them; that, by patience and comfort of thy holy Word, we may embrace and ever hold fast the blessed hope of everlasting life, which thou hast given us in our Savior Jesus Christ; who liveth and reigneth with thee and the Holy Spirit, one God, for ever and ever. *Amen.*

Year A

The Lesson   Zephaniah 1:7, 12-18

Be silent before the Lord GOD! For the day of the LORD is at hand; the LORD has prepared a sacrifice, he has consecrated his guests. At that time, says the LORD, I will search Jerusalem with lamps, and I will punish the people who rest complacently on their dregs, those who say in their hearts, "The LORD will not do good, nor will he do harm." Their wealth shall be plundered, and their houses laid waste. Though they build houses, they shall not inhabit them; though they plant vineyards, they shall not drink wine from them. The great day of the LORD is near, near and hastening fast; the sound of the day of the LORD is bitter, the warrior cries aloud there. That day will be a day of wrath, a day of distress and anguish, a day of ruin and devastation, a day of darkness and gloom, a day of clouds and thick darkness, a day of trumpet blast and battle cry against the fortified cities and against the lofty battlements. I will bring such distress upon people that they shall walk like the blind; because they have sinned against the LORD, their blood shall be poured out like dust, and their flesh like dung. Neither their silver nor their gold will be able to save them on the day of the LORD's wrath; in the fire of his passion the whole earth shall be consumed; for a full, a terrible end he will make of all the inhabitants of the earth.

The Psalm 90 or 90:1-8, 12   *Domine, refugium*

1   [Lord, you have been our refuge *
       from one generation to another.

2   Before the mountains were brought forth,
       or the land and the earth were born, *
       from age to age you are God.

3   You turn us back to the dust and say, *
       "Go back, O child of earth."

4   For a thousand years in your sight are like yesterday when it is past *
       and like a watch in the night.

5   You sweep us away like a dream; *
       we fade away suddenly like the grass.

6   In the morning it is green and flourishes; *
       in the evening it is dried up and withered.

7   For we consume away in your displeasure; *
       we are afraid because of your wrathful indignation.

8   Our iniquities you have set before you, *
       and our secret sins in the light of your countenance.]

9   When you are angry, all our days are gone; *
       we bring our years to an end like a sigh.

10   The span of our life is seventy years,
       perhaps in strength even eighty; *
          yet the sum of them is but labor and sorrow,
          for they pass away quickly and we are gone.

11   Who regards the power of your wrath? *
       who rightly fears your indignation?

12 [So teach us to number our days *
    that we may apply our hearts to wisdom.]

13 Return, O LORD; how long will you tarry? *
    be gracious to your servants.

'14 Satisfy us by your loving-kindness in the morning; *
    so shall we rejoice and be glad all the days of our life.

15 Make us glad by the measure of the days that you afflicted us *
    and the years in which we suffered adversity.

16 Show your servants your works *
    and your splendor to their children.

17 May the graciousness of the LORD our God be upon us; *
    prosper the work of our hands;
    prosper our handiwork.

The Epistle   **1 Thessalonians 5:1-10**

Concerning the times and the seasons, brothers and sisters, you do not need to have anything written to you. For you yourselves know very well that the day of the Lord will come like a thief in the night. When they say, "There is peace and security," then sudden destruction will come upon them, as labor pains come upon a pregnant woman, and there will be no escape! But you, beloved, are not in darkness, for that day to surprise you like a thief; for you are all children of light and children of the day; we are not of the night or of darkness. So then let us not fall asleep as others do, but let us keep awake and be sober; for those who sleep, sleep at night and those who are drunk get drunk at night. But since we belong to the day, let us be sober, and put on the breastplate of faith and love, and for a helmet the hope of salvation. For God has destined us not for wrath but for obtaining salvation through our Lord Jesus Christ, who died for us, so that whether we are awake or asleep we may live with him.

The Gospel   **Matthew 25:14-15, 19-29**

Jesus said, "For it is as if a man, going on a journey, summoned his slaves and entrusted his property to them; to one he gave five talents, to another two, to another one, to each according to his ability. Then he went away. After a long time the master of those slaves came and settled accounts with them. Then the one who had received the five talents came forward, bringing five more talents, saying, 'Master, you handed over to me five talents; see, I have made five more talents.' His master said to him, 'Well done, good and trustworthy slave; you have been trustworthy in a few things, I will put you in charge of many things; enter into the joy of your master.' And the one with the two talents also came forward, saying, 'Master, you handed over to me two talents; see, I have made two more talents.' His master said to him, 'Well done, good and trustworthy slave; you have been trustworthy in a few things, I will put you in charge of many things; enter into the joy of your master.' Then the one who had received the one talent also came forward, saying, 'Master, I knew that you were a harsh man, reaping where you did not sow, and gathering where you did not scatter seed; so I was afraid, and I went and hid your talent in the ground. Here you have what is yours.' But his master replied, 'You wicked and lazy slave! You knew, did you, that I reap where I did not sow, and gather where I did not scatter? Then you ought to have invested my money with the bankers, and on my return I would have received what was my own with interest. So take the talent from him, and give it to the one with the ten talents. For to all those who have, more will be given, and they will have an abundance; but from those who have nothing, even what they have will be taken away.'"

Year B

The Lesson   Daniel 12:1-4a (5-13)

The LORD spoke to Daniel saying, "At that time Michael, the great prince, the protector of your people, shall arise. There shall be a time of anguish, such as has never occurred since nations first came into existence. But at that time your people shall be delivered, everyone who is found written in the book. Many of those who sleep in the dust of the earth shall awake, some to everlasting life, and some to shame and everlasting contempt. Those who are wise shall shine like the brightness of the sky, and those who lead many to righteousness, like the stars forever and ever. But you, Daniel, keep the words secret and the book sealed until the time of the end. [Then I, Daniel, looked, and two others appeared, one standing on this bank of the stream and one on the other. One of them said to the man clothed in linen, who was upstream, "How long shall it be until the end of these wonders?" The man clothed in linen, who was upstream, raised his right hand and his left hand toward heaven. And I heard him swear by the one who lives forever that it would be for a time, two times, and half a time, and that when the shattering of the power of the holy people comes to an end, all these things would be accomplished. I heard but could not understand; so I said, "My lord, what shall be the outcome of these things?" He said, "Go your way, Daniel, for the words are to remain secret and sealed until the time of the end. Many shall be purified, cleansed, and refined, but the wicked shall continue to act wickedly. None of the wicked shall understand, but those who are wise shall understand. From the time that the regular burnt offering is taken away and the abomination that desolates is set up, there shall be one thousand two hundred ninety days. Happy are those who persevere and attain the thousand three hundred thirty-five days. But you, go your way, and rest; you shall rise for your reward at the end of the days."]

The Psalm 16 or 16:5-11   *Conserva me, Domine*
1   Protect me, O God, for I take refuge in you; *
        I have said to the LORD, "You are my Lord,
        my good above all other."

2   All my delight is upon the godly that are in the land, *
        upon those who are noble among the people.

3   But those who run after other gods *
        shall have their troubles multiplied.

4   Their libations of blood I will not offer, *
        nor take the names of their gods upon my lips.

5   [O LORD, you are my portion and my cup; *
    it is you who uphold my lot.

6   My boundaries enclose a pleasant land; *
    indeed, I have a goodly heritage.

7   I will bless the LORD who gives me counsel; *
    my heart teaches me, night after night.

8   I have set the LORD always before me; *
    because he is at my right hand I shall not fall.

9   My heart, therefore, is glad, and my spirit rejoices; *
    my body also shall rest in hope.

10 For you will not abandon me to the grave, *
    nor let your holy one see the Pit.

11 You will show me the path of life; *
    in your presence there is fullness of joy,
    and in your right hand are pleasures for evermore.]

The Epistle

Hebrews 10:31-39

It is a fearful thing to fall into the hands of the living God. But recall those earlier days when, after you had been enlightened, you endured a hard struggle with sufferings, sometimes being publicly exposed to abuse and persecution, and sometimes being partners with those so treated. For you had compassion for those who were in prison, and you cheerfully accepted the plundering of your possessions, knowing that you yourselves possessed something better and more lasting. Do not, therefore, abandon that confidence of yours; it brings a great reward. For you need endurance, so that when you have done the will of God, you may receive what was promised. For yet "in a very little while, the one who is coming will come and will not delay; but my righteous one will live by faith. My soul takes no pleasure in anyone who shrinks back." But we are not among those who shrink back and so are lost, but among those who have faith and so are saved.

The Gospel

Mark 13:14-23

Jesus said, "But when you see the desolating sacrilege set up where it ought not to be (let the reader understand), then those in Judea must flee to the mountains; the one on the housetop must not go down or enter the house to take anything away; the one in the field must not turn back to get a coat. Woe to those who are pregnant and to those who are nursing infants in those days! Pray that it may not be in winter. For in those days there will be suffering, such as has not been from the beginning of the creation that God created until now, no, and never will be. And if the Lord had not cut short those days, no one would be saved; but for the sake of the elect, whom he chose, he has cut short those days. And if anyone says to you at that time, 'Look! Here is the Messiah!' or 'Look! There he is!' — do not believe it. False messiahs and false prophets will appear and produce signs and omens, to lead astray, if possible, the elect. But be alert; I have already told you everything."

Year C

The Lesson   **Malachi 3:13-4:2a, 5-6**

You have spoken harsh words against me, says the LORD. Yet you say, "How have we spoken against you?" You have said, "It is vain to serve God. What do we profit by keeping his command or by going about as mourners before the LORD of hosts? Now we count the arrogant happy; evildoers not only prosper, but when they put God to the test they escape." Then those who revered the LORD spoke with one another. The LORD took note and listened, and a book of remembrance was written before him of those who revered the LORD and thought on his name. They shall be mine, says the LORD of hosts, my special possessions on the day when I act, and I will spare them as parents spare their children who serve them. Then once more you shall see the difference between the righteous and the wicked, between one who serves God and one who does not serve him. See, the day is coming, burning like an oven, when all the arrogant and all evildoers will be stubble; the day that comes shall burn them up, says the LORD of hosts, so that it will leave them neither root nor branch. But for you who revere my name the sun of righteousness shall rise, with healing in its wings. Lo, I will send you the prophet Elijah before the great and terrible day of the LORD comes. He will turn the hearts of parents to their children and the hearts of children to their parents, so that I will not come and strike the land with a curse.

The Psalm 98 or 98:5-10   *Cantate Domino*

1   Sing to the LORD a new song, *
      for he has done marvelous things.

2   With his right hand and his holy arm *
      has he won for himself the victory.

3   The LORD has made known his victory; *
      his righteousness has he openly shown in the sight of the nations.

4   He remembers his mercy and faithfulness to the house of Israel, *
      and all the ends of the earth have seen the victory of our God.

5   [Shout with joy to the LORD, all you lands; *
      lift up your voice, rejoice, and sing.

6   Sing to the LORD with the harp, *
      with the harp and the voice of song.

7   With trumpets and the sound of the horn *
      shout with joy before the King, the LORD.

8   Let the sea make a noise and all that is in it, *
      the lands and those who dwell therein.

9   Let the rivers clap their hands, *
      and let the hills ring out with the joy before the LORD,
      when he comes to judge the earth.

10   In righteousness shall he judge the world *
        and the peoples with equity.]

The Epistle
2 Thessalonians 3:6-13

Now we command you, beloved, in the name of our lord Jesus Christ, to keep away from believers who are living in idleness and not according to the tradition that they received from us. For you yourselves know how you ought to imitate us; we were not idle when we were with you, and we did not eat anyone's bread without paying for it; but with toil and labor we worked night and day, so that we might not burden any of you. This was not because we do not have that right, but in order to give you an example to imitate. For even when we were with you, we gave you this command: Anyone unwilling to work should not eat. For we hear that some of you are living in idleness, mere busybodies, not doing any work. Now such persons we command and exhort in the Lord Jesus Christ to do their work quietly and to earn their own living. Brothers and sisters, do not be weary in doing what is right.

The Gospel
Luke 21:5-19

When some were speaking about the temple, how it was adorned with beautiful stones and gifts dedicated to God, Jesus said, "As for these things that you see, the days will come when not one stone will be left upon another; all will be thrown down." They asked him, "Teacher, when will this be, and what will be the sign that this is about to take place?" And he said, "Beware that you are not led astray; for many will come in my name and say, 'I am he!' and, 'The time is near!' Do not go after them. When you hear of wars and insurrections, do not be terrified; for these things must take place first, but the end will not follow immediately." Then he said to them, "Nation will rise against nation, and kingdom against kingdom; there will be great earthquakes, and in various places famines and plagues; and there will be dreadful portents and great signs from heaven. But before all this occurs, they will arrest you and persecute you; they will hand you over to synagogues and prisons, and you will be brought before kings and governors because of my name. This will give you an opportunity to testify. So make up your minds not to prepare your defense in advance; for I will give you words and a wisdom that none of your opponents will be able to withstand or contradict. You will be betrayed even by parents and brothers, by relatives and friends; and they will put some of you to death. You will be hated by all because of my name. But not a hair of your head will perish. By your endurance you will gain your souls."

Proper 29 *The Sunday closest to November 23*

The Collect

Almighty and everlasting God, whose will it is to restore all things in your well-beloved Son, the King of kings and Lord of lords: Mercifully grant that the peoples of the earth, divided and enslaved by sin, may be freed and brought together under his most gracious rule; who lives and reigns with you and the Holy Spirit, one God, now and for ever. *Amen.*

Almighty and everlasting God, whose will it is to restore all things in thy well-beloved Son, the King of kings and Lord of lords: Mercifully grant that the peoples of the

earth, divided and enslaved by sin, may be freed and brought together under his most gracious rule; who liveth and reigneth with thee and the Holy Spirit, one God, now and for ever. *Amen.*

Year A

The Lesson   **Ezekiel 34:11-17**

For thus says the Lord GOD: I myself will search for my sheep, and will seek them out. As shepherds seek out their flocks when they are among their scattered sheep, so I will seek out my sheep. I will rescue them from all the places to which they have been scattered on a day of clouds and thick darkness. I will bring them out from the peoples and gather them from the countries, and will bring them into their own land; and I will feed them on the mountains of Israel, by the watercourses, and in all the inhabited parts of the land. I will feed them with good pasture, and the mountain heights of Israel shall be their pasture; there they shall lie down in good grazing land, and they shall feed on rich pasture on the mountains of Israel. I myself will be the shepherd of my sheep, and I will make them lie down, says the Lord GOD. I will seek the lost, and I will bring back the strayed, and I will bind up the injured, and I will strengthen the weak, but the fat and the strong I will destroy. I will feed them with justice. As for you, my flock, thus says the Lord GOD: I shall judge between sheep and sheep, between rams and goats.

The Psalm 95:1-7   *Venite, exultemus*

1   Come, let us sing to the LORD; *
        let us shout for joy to the Rock of our salvation.

2   Let us come before his presence with thanksgiving *
        and raise a loud shout to him with psalms.

3   For the LORD is a great God, *
        and a great King above all gods.

4   In his hand are the caverns of the earth, *
        and the heights of the hills are his also.

5   The sea is his, for he made it, *
        and his hands have molded the dry land.

6   Come, let us bow down, and bend the knee, *
        and kneel before the LORD our Maker.

7   For he is our God,
    and we are the people of his pasture and the sheep of his hand. *
        Oh, that today you would hearken to his voice!

The Epistle   **1 Corinthians 15:20-28**

But in fact Christ has been raised from the dead, the first fruits of those who have died. For since death came through a human being, the resurrection of the dead has also come through a human being; for as all die in Adam, so all will be made alive in Christ. But each in his own order: Christ the first fruits, then at his coming those who belong to Christ. Then comes the end, when he hands over the kingdom to God the

Father, after he has destroyed every ruler and every authority and power. For he must reign until he has put all his enemies under his feet. The last enemy to be destroyed is death. For "God has put all things in subjection under his feet." But when it says, "All things are put in subjection," it is plain that this does not include the one who put all things in subjection under him. When all things are subjected to him, then the Son himself will also be subjected to the one who put all things in subjection under him, so that God may be all in all.

The Gospel   **Matthew 25:31-46**

Jesus said, "When the Son of Man comes in his glory, and all the angels with him, then he will sit on the throne of his glory. All the nations will be gathered before him, and he will separate people one from another as a shepherd separates the sheep from the goats, and he will put the sheep at his right hand and the goats at the left. Then the king will say to those at his right hand, 'Come, you that are blessed by my Father, inherit the kingdom prepared for you from the foundation of the world; for I was hungry and you gave me food, I was thirsty and you gave me something to drink, I was a stranger and you welcomed me, I was naked and you gave me clothing, I was sick and you took care of me, I was in prison and you visited me.' Then the righteous will answer him, 'Lord, when was it that we saw you hungry and gave you food, or thirsty and gave you something to drink? And when was it that we saw you a stranger and welcomed you, or naked and gave you clothing? And when was it that we saw you sick or in prison and visited you?' And the king will answer them, 'Truly I tell you, just as you did it to one of the least of these who are members of my family, you did it to me.' Then he will say to those at his left hand, 'You that are accursed, depart from me into the eternal fire prepared for the devil and his angels; for I was hungry and you gave me no food, I was thirsty and you gave me nothing to drink, I was a stranger and you did not welcome me, naked and you did not give me clothing, sick and in prison and you did not visit me.' Then they also will answer, 'Lord, when was it that we saw you hungry or thirsty or a stranger or naked or sick or in prison, and did not take care of you?' Then he will answer them, 'Truly I tell you, just as you did not do it to one of the least of these, you did not do it to me.' And these will go away into eternal punishment, but the righteous into eternal life."

Year B

The Lesson   **Daniel 7:9-14**

As I watched, thrones were set in place, and an Ancient One took his throne, his clothing was white as snow, and the hair of his head like pure wool; his throne was fiery flames, and its wheels were burning fire. A stream of fire issued and flowed out from his presence. A thousand thousands served him, and ten thousand times ten thousand stood attending him. The court sat in judgment, and the books were opened. I watched then because of the noise of the arrogant words that the horn was speaking. And as I watched, the beast was put to death, and its body destroyed and given over to be burned with fire. As for the rest of the beasts, their dominion was taken away, but their lives were prolonged for a season and a time. As I watched in the night visions, I saw one like a human being coming with the clouds of heaven. And he came to the Ancient One and was presented before him. To him was given dominion and glory and kingship, that all peoples, nations, and languages should serve him. His dominion is an everlasting dominion that shall not pass away, and his kingship is one that shall never be destroyed.

The Psalm 93   *Dominus regnavit*

1   The LORD is King;
     he has put on splendid apparel; *
         the LORD has put on his apparel
         and girded himself with strength.

2   He has made the whole world so sure *
         that it cannot be moved;

3   Ever since the world began, your throne has been established; *
         you are from everlasting.

4   The waters have lifted up, O LORD,
     the waters have lifted up their voice; *
         the waters have lifted up their pounding waves.

5   Mightier than the sound of many waters,
     mightier than the breakers of the sea, *
         mightier is the LORD who dwells on high.

6   Your testimonies are very sure, *
         and holiness adorns your house, O LORD,
         for ever and for evermore.

The Epistle   **Revelation 1:1-8**
The revelation of Jesus Christ, which God gave him to show his servants what must soon take place; he made it known by sending his angel to his servant John, who testified to the word of God and to the testimony of Jesus Christ, even to all that he saw. Blessed is the one who reads aloud the words of the prophecy, and blessed are those who hear and who keep what is written in it; for the time is near. John to the seven churches that are in Asia: Grace to you and peace from him who is and who was and who is to come, and from the seven spirits who are before his throne, and from Jesus Christ, the faithful witness, the firstborn of the dead, and the ruler of the kings of the earth. To him who loves us and freed us from our sins by his blood, and made us to be a kingdom, priests serving his God and Father, to him be glory and dominion forever and ever. Amen. Look! He is coming with the clouds; every eye will see him, even those who pierced him; and on his account all the tribes of the earth will wail. So it is to be. Amen. "I am the Alpha and the Omega," says the Lord God, who is and who was and who is to come, the Almighty.

The Gospel   **John 18:33-37**
Pilate entered the headquarters again, summoned Jesus, and asked him, "Are you the King of the Jews?" Jesus answered, "Do you ask this on your own, or did others tell you about me?" Pilate replied, "I am not a Jew, am I? Your own nation and the chief priests have handed you over to me. What have you done?" Jesus answered, "My kingdom is not from this world. If my kingdom were from this world, my followers

would be fighting to keep me from being handed over to the Jews. But as it is, my kingdom is not from here." Pilate asked him, "So you are a king?" Jesus answered, "You say that I am a king. For this I was born, and for this I came into the world, to testify to the truth. Everyone who belongs to the truth listens to my voice."

or Mark 11:1-11

When Jesus and those who followed were approaching Jerusalem, at Bethphage and Bethany, near the Mount of Olives, he sent two of his disciples and said to them, "Go into the village ahead of you, and immediately as you enter it, you will find tied there a colt that has never been ridden; untie it and bring it. If anyone says to you, 'Why are you doing this?' just say this, 'The Lord needs it and will send it back here immediately.'" They went away and found a colt tied near a door, outside in the street. As they were untying it, some of the bystanders said to them, "What are you doing, untying the colt?" They told them what Jesus had said; and they allowed them to take it. Then they brought the colt to Jesus and threw their cloaks on it; and he sat on it. Many people spread their cloaks on the road, and others spread leafy branches that they had cut in the fields. Then those who went ahead and those who followed were shouting, "Hosanna! Blessed is the one who comes in the name of the Lord! Blessed is the coming kingdom of our ancestor David! Hosanna in the highest heaven!" Then he entered Jerusalem and went into the temple; and when he had looked around at everything, as it was already late, he went out to Bethany with the twelve.

Year C

The Lesson   Jeremiah 23:1-6

Woe to the shepherds who destroy and scatter the sheep of my pasture! says the LORD. Therefore thus says the LORD, the God of Israel, concerning the shepherds who shepherd my people: It is you who have scattered my flock, and have driven them away, and you have not attended to them. So I will attend to you for your evil doings, says the LORD. Then I myself will gather the remnant of my flock out of all the lands where I have driven them, and I will bring them back to their fold, and they shall be fruitful and multiply. I will raise up shepherds over them who will shepherd them, and they shall not fear any longer, or be dismayed, nor shall any be missing, says the LORD. The days are surely coming, says the LORD, when I will raise up for David a righteous Branch, and he shall reign as king and deal wisely, and shall execute justice and righteousness in the land. In his days Judah will be saved and Israel will live in safety. And this is the name by which he will be called: "The LORD is our righteousness."

The Psalm 46   *Deus noster refugium*

1   God is our refuge and strength, *
       a very present help in trouble.

2   Therefore we will not fear, though the earth be moved, *
       and though the mountains be toppled into the depths of the sea;

3   Though its waters rage and foam, *
       and though the mountains tremble at its tumult.

4   The LORD of hosts is with us; *
         the God of Jacob is our stronghold.

5   There is river whose streams make glad the city of God, *
         the holy habitation of the Most High.

6   God is in the midst of her;
      she shall not be overthrown; *
         God shall help her at the break of day.

7   The nations make much ado, and the kingdoms are shaken; *
         God has spoken, and the earth shall melt away.

8   The LORD of hosts is with us; *
         the God of Jacob is our stronghold.

9   Come now and look upon the works of the LORD, *
         what awesome things he has done on earth.

10   It is he who makes war to cease in all the world; *
         he breaks the bow, and shatters the spear,
         and burns the shields with fire.

11   "Be still, then, and know that I am God; *
         I will be exalted among the nations;
         I will be exalted in the earth."

12   The LORD of hosts is with us; *
         the God of Jacob is our stronghold.

The Epistle   **Colossians 1:11-20**

May you be made strong with all the strength that comes from his glorious power, and may you be prepared to endure everything with patience, while joyfully giving thanks to the Father, who has enabled you to share in the inheritance of the saints in the light. He has rescued us from the power of darkness and transferred us into the kingdom of his beloved Son, in whom we have redemption, the forgiveness of sins. He is the image of the invisible God, the firstborn of all creation; for in him all things in heaven and on earth were created, things visible and invisible, whether thrones or dominions or rulers or powers — all things have been created through him and for him. He himself is before all things, and in him all things hold together. He is the head of the body, the church; he is the beginning, the firstborn from the dead, so that he might come to have first place in everything. For in him all the fullness of God was pleased to dwell, and through him God was pleased to reconcile to himself all things, whether on earth or in heaven, by making peace through the blood of his cross.

The Gospel   **Luke 23:35-43**

The people stood by, watching Jesus on the cross; but the leaders scoffed at him, saying, "He saved others; let him save himself if he is the Messiah of God, his chosen one!" The soldiers also mocked him, coming up and offering him sour wine, and saying, "If you are the King of the Jews, save yourself!" There was also an inscription over him, "This is the King of the Jews." One of the criminals who were hanged there kept deriding him and saying, "Are you not the Messiah? Save yourself and us!" But the other rebuked him, saying, "Do you not fear God, since you are under the same sentence of condemnation? And we indeed have been condemned justly, for we are getting what we deserve for our deeds, but this man has done nothing wrong." Then he said, "Jesus, remember me when you come into your kingdom." He replied, "Truly I tell you, today you will be with me in Paradise."

or Luke 19:29-38

When Jesus had come near Bethphage and Bethany, at the place called the Mount of Olives, he sent two of the disciples, saying, "Go into the village ahead of you, and as you enter it you will find tied there a colt that has never been ridden. Untie it and bring it here. If anyone asks you, 'Why are you untying it?' just say this, 'The Lord needs it.'" So those who were sent departed and found it as he had told them. As they were untying the colt, its owners asked them, "Why are you untying the colt?" They said, "The Lord needs it." Then they brought it to Jesus; and after throwing their cloaks on the colt, they set Jesus on it. As he rode along, people kept spreading their cloaks on the road. As he was now approaching the path down from the Mount of Olives, the whole multitude of the disciples began to praise God joyfully with a loud voice for all the deeds of power that they had seen, saying, "Blessed is the king who comes in the name of the Lord! Peace in heaven, and glory in the highest heaven!"

HOLY DAYS

St. Andrew — *November 30*

The Collect

Almighty God, who gave such grace to your apostle Andrew that he readily obeyed the call of your Son Jesus Christ, and brought his brother with him: Give us, who are called by your holy Word, grace to follow him without delay, and to bring those near to us into his gracious presence; who lives and reigns with you and the Holy Spirit, one God, now and for ever. *Amen.*

Almighty God, who didst give such grace to thine apostle Andrew that he readily obeyed the call of thy Son Jesus Christ, and brought his brother with him: Give unto us, who are called by thy Word, grace to follow him without delay, and to bring those near to us into his gracious presence; who liveth and reigneth with thee and the Holy Spirit, one God, now and for ever. *Amen.*

The Lesson

Deuteronomy 30:11-14

Moses said to the people of Israel, "Surely, this commandment that I am commanding you today is not too hard for you, nor is it too far away. It is not in heaven, that you should say, 'Who will go up to heaven for us, and get it for us so that we may hear it and observe it?' Neither is it beyond the sea, that you should say, "Who will cross to the other side of the sea for us, and get it for us so that we may hear it and observe it?" No, the word is very near to you; it is in your mouth and in your heart for you to observe."

The Psalm 19 or 19:1-6   *Caeli enarrant*

1   [The heavens declare the glory of God, *
       and the firmament shows his handiwork.

2   One day tells its tale to another, *
       and one night imparts knowledge to another.

3   Although they have no words or language, *
       and their voices are not heard,

4   Their sound has gone out into all lands, *
       and their message to the ends of the world.

5   In the deep has he set a pavilion for the sun; *
       it comes forth like a bridegroom out of his chamber;
       it rejoices like a champion to run its course.

6   It goes forth from the uttermost edge of the heavens
     and runs about to the end of it again; *
       nothing is hidden from its burning heat.]

7   The law of the LORD is perfect and revives the soul; *
       the testimony of the LORD is sure and gives wisdom to the innocent.

8   The statutes of the LORD are just and rejoice the heart; *
       the commandment of the LORD is clear and gives light to the eyes.

9　The fear of the Lord is clean and endures for ever; *
　　the judgments of the Lord are true and righteous altogether.

10　More to be desired are they than gold, more than much fine gold, *
　　sweeter far than honey, than honey in the comb.

11　By them also is your servant enlightened, *
　　and in keeping them there is great reward.

12　Who can tell how often he offends? *
　　cleanse me from my secret faults.

13　Above all, keep your servant from presumptuous sins;
　　let them not get dominion over me; *
　　　then shall I be whole and sound,
　　　and innocent of a great offense.

14　Let the words of my mouth and the meditation of my heart be acceptable in
　　your sight, *
　　　O Lord, my strength and my redeemer.

The Epistle　　　　　　　　　　　　　　　　　　　　　**Romans 10:8b-18**

"The word is near you, on your lips and in your heart" (that is, the word of faith that
we proclaim); because if you confess with your lips that Jesus is Lord and believe in
your heart that God raised him from the dead, you will be saved. For one believes
with the heart and so is justified, and one confesses with the mouth and so is saved.
The scripture says, "No one who believes in him will be put to shame." For there is
no distinction between Jew and Greek; the same Lord is Lord of all and is generous
to all who call on him. For, "Everyone who calls on the name of the Lord shall be
saved." But how are they to call on one in whom they have not believed? And how
are they to believe in one of whom they have never heard? And how are they to hear
without someone to proclaim him? And how are they to proclaim him unless they
are sent? As it is written, "How beautiful are the feet of those who bring good news!"
But not all have obeyed the good news; for Isaiah says, "Lord, who has believed our
message?" So faith comes from what is heard, and what is heard comes through the
word of Christ. But I ask, have they not heard? Indeed they have; for "Their voice
has gone out to all the earth, and their words to the ends of the world."

The Gospel　　　　　　　　　　　　　　　　　　　　　**Matthew 4:18-22**

As Jesus walked by the Sea of Galilee, he saw two brothers, Simon, who is called
Peter, and Andrew his brother, casting a net into the sea — for they were fishermen.
And he said to them, "Follow me, and I will make you fish for people." Immediately
they left their nets and followed him. As he went from there, he saw two other
brothers, James son of Zebedee and his brother John, in the boat with their father
Zebedee, mending their nets, and he called them. Immediately they left the boat and
their father, and followed him.

St. Thomas — *December 21*

The Collect

Everliving God, who strengthened your apostle Thomas with firm and certain faith in your Son's resurrection: Grant us so perfectly and without doubt to believe in Jesus Christ, our Lord and our God, that our faith may never be found wanting in your sight; through him who lives and reigns with you and the Holy Spirit, one God, now and for ever. *Amen.*

Everliving God, who didst strengthen thine apostle Thomas with sure and certain faith in thy Son's resurrection: Grant us so perfectly and without doubt to believe in Jesus Christ, our Lord and our God, that our faith may never be found wanting in thy sight; through him who liveth and reigneth with thee and the Holy Spirit, one God, now and for ever. *Amen.*

The Lesson

Habakkuk 2:1-4

I will stand at my watchpost, and station myself on the rampart; I will keep watch to see what he will say to me, and what he will answer concerning my complaint. Then the LORD answered me and said: Write the vision; make it plain on tablets, so that a runner may read it. For there is still a vision for the appointed time; it speaks of the end, and does not lie. If it seems to tarry, wait for it; it will surely come, it will not delay. Look at the proud! Their spirit is not right in them, but the righteous live by their faith.

The Psalm 126   *In convertendo*

1   When the LORD restored the fortunes of Zion, *
       then were we like those who dream.

2   Then was our mouth filled with laughter, *
       and our tongue with shouts of joy.

3   Then they said among the nations, *
       "The LORD has done great things for them."

4   The LORD has done great things for us, *
       and we are glad indeed.

5   Restore our fortunes, O LORD, *
       like the watercourses of the Negev.

6   Those who sowed with tears *
       will reap with songs of joy.

7   Those who go out weeping, carrying the seed, *
       will come again with joy, shouldering their sheaves.

The Epistle

Hebrews 10:35 - 11:1

Do not, therefore, abandon that confidence of yours; it brings a great reward. For you need endurance, so that when you have done the will of God, you may receive what was promised. For yet "in a very little while, the one who is coming will come and will not delay; but my righteous one will live by faith. My soul takes no pleasure in anyone who shrinks back." But we are not among those who shrink back and so are lost, but among those who have faith and so are saved. Now faith is the assurance of things hoped for, the conviction of things not seen.

The Gospel   John 20:24-29
Thomas (who was called the Twin), one of the twelve, was not with them when Jesus came. So the other disciples told him, "We have seen the Lord." But he said to them, "Unless I see the mark of the nails in his hands, and put my finger in the mark of the nails and my hand in his side, I will not believe." A week later his disciples were again in the house, and Thomas was with them. Although the doors were shut, Jesus came and stood among them and said, "Peace be with you." Then he said to Thomas, "Put your finger here and see my hands. Reach out your hand and put it in my side. Do not doubt but believe." Thomas answered him, "My Lord and my God!" Jesus said to him, "Have you believed because you have seen me? Blessed are those who have not seen and yet have come to believe."

St. Stephen — *December 26*

The Collect
We give thanks, O Lord of Glory, for the example of the first martyr Stephen, who looked up to heaven and prayed for his persecutors to your Son Jesus Christ, who stands at your right hand; where he lives and reigns with you and the Holy Spirit, one God, in glory everlasting. *Amen.*

We give thee thanks, O Lord of glory, for the example of the first martyr Stephen, who looked up to heaven and prayed for his persecutors to thy Son Jesus Christ, who standeth at thy right hand; where he liveth and reigneth with thee and the Holy Spirit, one God, in glory everlasting. *Amen.*

The Lesson   Jeremiah 26:1-9, 12-15
At the beginning of the reign of King Jehoiakim son of Josiah of Judah, this word came from the LORD: Thus says the LORD: Stand in the court of the LORD'S house, and speak to all the cities of Judah that come to worship in the house of the LORD; speak to them all the words that I command you; do not hold back a word. It may be that they will listen, all of them, and will turn from their evil way, that I may change my mind about the disaster that I intend to bring on them because of their evil doings. You shall say to them: Thus says the LORD: If you will not listen to me, to walk in my law that I have set before you, and to heed the words of my servants the prophets whom I send to you urgently — though you have not heeded — then I will make this house like Shiloh, and I will make this city a curse for all the nations of the earth. The priests and the prophets and all the people heard Jeremiah speaking these words in the house of the LORD. And when Jeremiah had finished speaking all that the LORD had commanded him to speak to all the people, then the priests and the prophets and all the people laid hold of him, saying, "You shall die! Why have you prophesied in the name of the LORD, saying, 'This house shall be like Shiloh, and this city shall be desolate, without inhabitant'?" And all the people gathered around Jeremiah in the house of the LORD. Then Jeremiah spoke to all the officials and all the people, saying, "It is the LORD who sent me to prophesy against this house and

this city all the words you have heard. Now therefore amend your ways and your doings, and obey the voice of the LORD your God, and the LORD will change his mind about the disaster that he has pronounced against you. But as for me, here I am in your hands. Do with me as seems good and right to you. Only know for certain that if you put me to death, you will be bring innocent blood upon yourselves and upon this city and its inhabitants, for in truth the LORD sent me to you to speak all these words in your ears."

The Psalm 31 or 31:1-5 *In te, Domine, speravi*

1   [In you, O LORD, have I taken refuge;
       let me never be put to shame; *
          deliver me in your righteousness.

2   Incline your ear to me; *
       make haste to deliver me.

3   Be my strong rock, a castle to keep me safe,
       for you are my crag and my stronghold; *
          for the sake of your Name, lead me and guide me.

4   Take me out of the net that they have secretly set for me, *
          for you are my tower of strength.

5   Into your hands I commend my spirit, *
       for you have redeemed me,
          O LORD, O God of truth.]

6   I hate those who cling to worthless idols, *
       and I put my trust in the LORD.

7   I will rejoice and be glad because of your mercy; *
       for you have seen my affliction;
       you know my distress.

8   You have not shut me up in the power of the enemy; *
       you have set my feet in an open place.

9   Have mercy on me, O LORD, for I am in trouble; *
       my eye is consumed with sorrow,
       and also my throat and my belly.

10   For my life is wasted with grief,
     and my years with sighing; *
       my strength fails me because of affliction,
       and my bones are consumed.

11   I have become a reproach to all my enemies and even to my neighbors,
     a dismay to those of my acquaintance; *
       when they see me in the street they avoid me.

12   I am forgotten like a dead man, out of mind; *
       I am as useless as a broken pot.

13   For I have heard the whispering of the crowd;
      fear is all around; *
            they put their heads together against me;
            they plot to take my life.

14   But as for me, I have trusted in you, O LORD. *
      I have said, "You are my God.

15   My times are in your hand; *
            rescue me from the hand of my enemies,
            and from those who persecute me.

16   Make your face to shine upon your servant, *
            and in your loving-kindness save me."

17   LORD, let me not be ashamed for having called upon you; *
            rather, let the wicked be put to shame;
            let them be silent in the grave.

18   Let the lying lips be silenced which speak against the righteous, *
            haughtily, disdainfully, and with contempt.

19   How great is your goodness, O LORD!
      which you have laid up for those who fear you; *
            which you have done in the sight of all
            for those who put their trust in you.

20   You hide them in the covert of your presence from those who slander them; *
            you keep them in your shelter from the strife of tongues.

21   Blessed be the LORD! *
            for he has shown me the wonders of his love in a besieged city.

22   Yet I said in my alarm,
      "I have been cut off from the sight of your eyes." *
            Nevertheless, you heard the sound of my entreaty
            when I cried out to you.

23   Love the LORD, all you who worship him; *
            the LORD protects the faithful,
            but repays to the full those who act haughtily.

24   Be strong and let your heart take courage, *
            all you who wait for the LORD.

The Epistle   Acts 6:8-7:2a, 51c-60

Stephen, full of grace and power, did great wonders and signs among the people.
Then some of those who belonged to the synagogue of the Freedmen (as it was
called), Cyrenians, Alexandrians, and others of those from Cilicia and Asia, stood up
and argued with Stephen. But they could not withstand the wisdom and the Spirit
with which he spoke. Then they secretly instigated some men to say, "We have heard
him speak blasphemous words against Moses and God." They stirred up the people

as well as the elders and the scribes; then they suddenly confronted him, siezed him, and brought him before the council. They set up false witnesses who said, "This man never stops saying things against this holy place and the law; for we have heard him say that this Jesus of Nazareth will destroy this place and will change the customs that Moses handed on to us." And all who sat in the council looked intently at him, and they saw that his face was like the face of an angel. Then the high priest asked him, "Are these things so?" And Stephen replied: "Brothers and fathers, listen to me. You are forever opposing the Holy Spirit, just as your ancestors used to do. Which of the prophets did your ancestors not persecute? They killed those who foretold the coming of the Righteous One, and now you have become his betrayers and murderers. You are the ones that received the law as ordained by angels, and yet you have not kept it." When they heard these things, they became enraged and ground their teeth at Stephen. But filled with the Holy Spirit, he gazed into heaven and saw the glory of God and Jesus standing at the right hand of God. "Look," he said, "I see the heavens opened and the Son of Man standing at the right hand of God!" But they covered their ears, and with a loud shout all rushed together against him. Then they dragged him out of the city and began to stone him; and the witnesses laid their coats at the feet of a young man named Saul. While they were stoning Stephen, he prayed, "Lord Jesus, receive my spirit." Then he knelt down and cried out in a loud voice, "Lord, do not hold this sin against them." When he had said this, he died.

The Gospel   **Matthew 23:34-39**
Jesus said, "Therefore I send you prophets, sages, and scribes, some of whom you will kill and crucify, and some you will flog in your synagogues and pursue from town to town, so that upon you may come all the righteous blood shed on earth, from the blood of righteous Abel to the blood of Zechariah son of Barachiah, whom you murdered between the sanctuary and the altar. Truly I tell you, all this will come upon this generation. "Jerusalem, Jerusalem, the city that kills the prophets and stones those who are sent to it! How often have I desired to gather your children together as a hen gathers her brood under her wings, and you were not willing! See, you house is left to you, desolate. For I tell you, you will not see me again until you say, 'Blessed is the one who comes in the name of the Lord.'"

St. John — *December 27*

The Collect
Shed upon your Church, O Lord, the brightness of your light, that we, being illumined by the teaching of your apostle and evangelist John, may so walk in the light of your truth, that at length we may attain to the fullness of eternal life; through Jesus Christ our Lord, who lives and reigns with you and the Holy Spirit, one God, for ever and ever. *Amen.*

Shed upon thy Church, we beseech thee, O Lord, the brightness of thy light; that we, being illumined by the teaching of thine apostle and evangelist John, may so walk in the light of thy truth, that we may at length attain to the fullness of life everlasting; through Jesus Christ our Lord, who liveth and reigneth with thee and the Holy Spirit, one God, for ever and ever. *Amen.*

The Lesson Exodus 33:18-23

Moses said, "Show me your glory, I pray." And he said, "I will make all my goodness pass before you, and will proclaim before you the name, 'The LORD'; and I will be gracious to whom I will be gracious, and will show mercy on whom I will show mercy. But," he said, "you cannot see my face; for no one shall see me and live." And the LORD continued, "See, there is a place by me where you shall stand on the rock; and while my glory passes by I will put you in a cleft of the rock, and I will cover you with my hand until I have passed by; then I will take away my hand, and you shall see my back; but my face shall not be seen."

The Psalm 92 or 92:1-4, 11-14   *Bonum est confiteri*

1   [It is a good thing to give thanks to the LORD, *
      and to sing praises to your Name, O Most High;

2   To tell of your loving-kindness early in the morning *
      and of your faithfulness in the night season;

3   On the psaltery, and on the lyre, *
      and to the melody of the harp.

4   For you have made me glad by your acts, O LORD; *
      and I shout for joy because of the works of your hands.]

5   LORD, how great are your works! *
      your thoughts are very deep.

6   The dullard does not know,
    nor does the fool understand, *
        that though the wicked grow like weeds,
        and all the workers of iniquity flourish,

7   They flourish only to be destroyed for ever; *
      but you, O LORD, are exalted for evermore.

8   For lo, your enemies, O LORD,
    lo, your enemies shall perish, *
        and all the workers of iniquity shall be scattered.

9   But my horn you have exalted like the horns of wild bulls; *
      I am anointed with fresh oil.

10   My eyes also gloat over my enemies, *
      and my ears rejoice to hear the doom of the wicked who rise up against me.

11   [The righteous shall flourish like a palm tree, *
      and shall spread abroad like a cedar of Lebanon.

12   Those who are planted in the house of the LORD *
        shall flourish in the courts of our God;

13   They shall still bear fruit in old age; *
        they shall be green and succulent;

¹⁴ That they may show how upright the L<small>ORD</small> is, *
　　my Rock, in whom there is no fault.]

The Epistle
1 John 1:1-9

We declare to you what was from the beginning, what we have heard, what we have seen with our eyes, what we have looked at and touched with our hands, concerning the word of life — this life was revealed, and we have seen it and testify to it, and declare to you the eternal life that was with the Father and was revealed to us — we declare to you what we have seen and heard so that you also may have fellowship with us; and truly our fellowship is with the Father and with his Son Jesus Christ. We are writing these things so that our joy may be complete. This is the message we have heard from him and proclaim to you, that God is light and in him there is no darkness at all. If we say that we have fellowship with him while we are walking in darkness, we lie and do not do what is true; but if we walk in the light as he himself is in the light, we have fellowship with one another, and the blood of Jesus his Son cleanses us from all sin. If we say that we have no sin, we deceive ourselves, and the truth is not in us. If we confess our sins, he who is faithful and just will forgive us our sins and cleanse us from all unrighteousness.

The Gospel
John 21:19b-24

Jesus said to Peter, "Follow me." Peter turned and saw the disciple whom Jesus loved following them; he was the one who had reclined next to Jesus at the supper and had said, "Lord, who is it that is going to betray you?" When Peter saw him, he said to Jesus, "Lord, what about him?" Jesus said to him, "If it is my will that he remain until I come, what is that to you ? Follow me!" So the rumor spread in the community that this disciple would not die. Yet Jesus did not say to him that he would not die, but, "If it is my will that he remain until I come, what is that to you?" This is the disciple who is testifying to these things and has written them, and we know that his testimony is true.

Holy Innocents — *December 28*

The Collect

We remember today, O God, the slaughter of the holy innocents of Bethlehem by King Herod. Receive, we pray, into the arms of your mercy all innocent victims; and by your great might frustrate the designs of evil tyrants and establish your rule of justice, love, and peace; through Jesus Christ our Lord, who lives and reigns with you, in the unity of the Holy Spirit, one God, for ever and ever. *Amen.*

We remember this day, O God, the slaughter of the holy innocents of Bethlehem by the order of King Herod. Receive, we beseech thee, into the arms of thy mercy all innocent victims; and by thy great might frustrate the designs of evil tyrants and establish thy rule of justice, love, and peace; through Jesus Christ our Lord, who liveth and reigneth with thee, in the unity of the Holy Spirit, one God, for ever and ever. *Amen.*

The Lesson
Jeremiah 31:15-17

Thus says the L<small>ORD</small>: A voice is heard in Ramah, lamentation and bitter weeping.

Rachel is weeping for her children; she refuses to be comforted for her children, because they are no more. Thus says the LORD: Keep your voice from weeping, and your eyes from tears; for there is a reward for your work, says the LORD: they shall come back from the land of the enemy; there is hope for your future, says the LORD: your children shall come back to their own country.

The Psalm 124   *Nisi quia Dominus*

1   If the LORD had not been on our side, *
      let Israel now say;

2   If the LORD had not been on our side, *
      when enemies rose up against us;

3   Then would they have swallowed us up alive *
      in their fierce anger toward us;

4   Then would the waters have overwhelmed us *
      and the torrent gone over us;

5   Then would the raging waters *
      have gone right over us.

6   Blessed be the LORD! *
      he has not given us over to be a prey for their teeth.

7   We have escaped like a bird from the snare of the fowler; *
      the snare is broken, and we have escaped.

8   Our help is in the Name of the LORD, *
      the maker of heaven and earth.

The Epistle   **Revelation 21:1-7**
Then I saw a new heaven and a new earth; for the first heaven and the first earth had passed away, and the sea was no more. And I saw the holy city, the new Jerusalem, coming down out of heaven from God, prepared as a bride adorned for her husband. And I heard a loud voice from the throne saying, "See, the home of God is among mortals. He will dwell with them as their God; they will be his peoples, and God himself will be with them; he will wipe every tear from their eyes. Death will be no more; mourning and crying and pain will be no more, for the first things have passed away." And the one who was seated on the throne said, "See, I am making all things new." Also he said, "Write this, for these words are trustworthy and true." Then he said to me, "It is done! I am the Alpha and the Omega, the beginning and the end. To the thirsty I will give water as a gift from the spring of the water of life. Those who conquer will inherit these things, and I will be their God and they will be my children.

The Gospel   **Matthew 2:13-18**
After the wisemen had left, an angel of the Lord appeared to Joseph in a dream and said, "Get up, take the child and his mother, and flee to Egypt, and remain there until I tell you; for Herod is about to search for the child, to destroy him." Then

Joseph got up, took the child and his mother by night, and went to Egypt, and remained there until the death of Herod. This was to fulfill what had been spoken by the Lord through the prophet, "Out of Egypt I have called my son." When Herod saw that he had been tricked by the wise men, he was infuriated, and he sent and killed all the children in and around Bethlehem who were two years old or under, according to the time that he had learned from the wise men. Then was fulfilled what had been spoken through the prophet Jeremiah: "A voice was heard in Ramah, wailing and loud lamentation, Rachel weeping for her children; she refused to be consoled, because they are no more."

Confession of St. Peter — *January 18*

The Collect
Almighty Father, who inspired Simon Peter, first among the apostles, to confess Jesus as Messiah and Son of the living God: Keep your Church steadfast upon the rock of this faith, so that in unity and peace we may proclaim the one truth and follow the one Lord, our Savior Jesus Christ; who lives and reigns with you and the Holy Spirit, one God, now and for ever. *Amen.*

Almighty Father, who didst inspire Simon Peter, first among the apostles, to confess Jesus as Messiah and Son of the living God: Keep thy Church steadfast upon the rock of this faith, that in unity and peace we may proclaim the one truth and follow the one Lord, our Savior Jesus Christ; who liveth and reigneth with thee and the Holy Spirit, one God, now and for ever. *Amen.*

The Lesson
Acts 4:8-13

Peter, filled with the Holy Spirit, said to them, "Rulers of the people and elders, if we are questioned today because of a good deed done to someone who was sick and are asked how this man has been healed, let it be known to all of you, and to all the people of Israel, that this man is standing before you in good health by the name of Jesus Christ of Nazareth, whom you crucified, whom God raised from the dead. This Jesus is 'the stone that was rejected by you, the builders; it has become the cornerstone.' There is salvation in no one else, for there is no other name under heaven given among mortals by which we must be saved." Now when they saw the boldness of Peter and John and realized that they were uneducated and ordinary men, they were amazed and recognized them as companions of Jesus.

The Psalm 23   *Dominus regit me*

1   The LORD is my shepherd; *
       I shall not be in want.

2   He makes me lie down in green pastures *
       and leads me beside still waters.

3   He revives my soul *
       and guides me along right pathways for his Name's sake.

4   Though I walk through the valley of the shadow of death,
       I shall fear no evil; *

for you are with me;
your rod and your staff, they comfort me.

5   You spread a table before me in the presence of those who trouble me; *
you have anointed my head with oil,
and my cup is running over.

6   Surely your goodness and mercy shall follow me all the days of my life, *
and I will dwell in the house of the LORD for ever.

The Epistle   1 Peter 5:1-4
As an elder myself and a witness of the sufferings of Christ, as well as one who shares
in the glory to be revealed, I exhort the elders among you to tend the flock of God
that is in your charge, exercising the oversight, not under compulsion but willingly, as
God would have you do it — not for sordid gain but eagerly. Do not lord it over
those in your charge, but be examples to the flock. And when the chief shepherd
appears, you will win the crown of glory that never fades away.

The Gospel   Matthew 16:13-19
When Jesus came into the district of Caesarea Philippi, he asked his disciples, "Who
do people say that the Son of Man is?" And they said, "Some say John the Baptist,
but others Elijah, and still others Jeremiah or one of the prophets." He said to them,
"But who do you say that I am?" Simon Peter answered, "You are the Messiah, the
Son of the living God." And Jesus answered him, "Blessed are you, Simon son of
Jonah! For flesh and blood has not revealed to this to you, but my Father in heaven.
And I tell you, you are Peter, and on this rock I will build my church, and the gates of
Hades will not prevail against it. I will give you the keys of the kingdom of heaven,
and whatever you bind on earth will be bound in heaven, and whatever you loose on
earth will be loosed in heaven."

Conversion of St. Paul — *January 25*

The Collect
**O God, by the preaching of your apostle Paul, you have caused the light of the Gospel
to shine throughout the world: Grant, we pray, that we, having his wonderful conversion
in remembrance, may show ourselves thankful to you by following his holy teaching;
through Jesus Christ our Lord, who lives and reigns with you, in the unity of the Holy
Spirit, one God, now and for ever.** *Amen.*

**O God, who, by the preaching of thine apostle Paul, has caused the light of the Gospel
to shine throughout the world: Grant, we beseech thee, that we, having his wonderful
conversion in remembrance, may show forth our thankfulness unto thee for the same
by following the holy doctrine which he taught; through Jesus Christ our Lord, who
liveth and reigneth with thee, in the unity of the Holy Spirit, one God, now and for
ever.** *Amen.*

The Lesson   Acts 26:9-21
Paul said to King Agrippa, "Indeed, I myself was convinced that I ought to do many
things against the name of Jesus of Nazareth. And that is what I did in Jerusalem;

with authority received from the chief priests, I not only locked up many of the saints in prison, but I also cast my vote against them when they were being condemned to death. By punishing them often in all the synagogues I tried to force them to blaspheme; and since I was so furiously enraged at them, I pursued them even to foreign cities. With this in mind, I was traveling to Damascus with the authority and commission of the chief priests, when at midday along the road, your Excellency, I saw a light from heaven, brighter than the sun, shining around me and my companions. When we had all fallen to the ground, I heard a voice saying to me in the Hebrew language, 'Saul, Saul, why are you persecuting me? It hurts you to kick against the goads.' I asked, 'Who are you, Lord?' The Lord answered, 'I am Jesus whom you are persecuting. But get up and stand on your feet; for I have appeared to you for this purpose, to appoint you to serve and testify to the things in which you have seen me and to those in which I will appear to you. I will rescue you from your people and from the Gentiles — to whom I am sending you to open their eyes so that they may turn from darkness to light and from the power of Satan to God, so that they may receive forgiveness of sins and a place among those who are sanctified by faith in me.' After that, King Agrippa, I was not disobedient to the heavenly vision, but declared first to those in Damascus, then in Jerusalem and throughout the countryside of Judea, and also to the Gentiles, that they should repent and turn to God and do deeds consistent with repentance. For this reason the Jews seized me in the temple and tried to kill me."

The Psalm 67   *Deus misereatur*

1   May God be merciful to us and bless us, *
        show us the light of his countenance and come to us.

2   Let your ways be known upon earth, *
        your saving health among all nations.

3   Let the peoples praise you, O God; *
        let all the peoples praise you.

4   Let the nations be glad and sing for joy, *
        for you judge the peoples with equity
        and guide all the nations upon earth.

5   Let the peoples praise you, O God; *
        let all the peoples praise you.

6   The earth has brought forth her increase; *
        may God, our own God, give us his blessing.

7   May God give us his blessing, *
        and may all the ends of the earth stand in awe of him.

The Epistle   **Galatians 1:11-24**

I want you to know, brother and sisters, that the gospel that was proclaimed by me is not of human origin; for I did not receive it from a human source, nor was I taught it, but I received it through a revelation of Jesus Christ. You have heard, no doubt, of my earlier life in Judaism. I was violently persecuting the church of God and was trying to destroy it. I advanced in Judaism beyond many among my people of the same age, for I was far more zealous for the traditions of my ancestors. But when God, who had set me apart before I was born and called me through his grace, was pleased to reveal his Son to me, so that I might proclaim him among the Gentiles, I did not confer with any human being, nor did I go up to Jerusalem to those who were already apostles before me, but I went away at once into Arabia, and afterwards I returned to Damascus. Then after three years I did go up to Jerusalem to visit Cephas and stayed with him fifteen days; but I did not see any other apostle except James the Lord's brother. In what I am writing to you, before God, I do not lie! Then I went into the regions of Syria and Cilicia, and I was still unknown by sight to the churches of Judea that are in Christ; they only heard it said, "The one who formerly was persecuting us is now proclaiming the faith he once tried to destroy." And they glorified God because of me.

The Gospel
Matthew 10:16-22

Jesus said to the twelve, "See, I am sending you out like sheep into the midst of wolves; so be wise as serpents and innocent as doves. Beware of them, for they will hand you over to councils and flog you in their synagogues; and you will be dragged before governors and kings because of me, as a testimony to them and the Gentiles. When they hand you over, do not worry about how you are to speak or what you are to say; for what you are to say will be given to you at that time; for it is not you who speak, but the Spirit of your Father speaking through you. Brother will betray brother to death, and a father his child, and children will rise against parents and have them put to death; and you will be hated by all because of my name. But the one who endures to the end will be saved.

The Presentation — *February 2*

The Collect
Almighty and everliving God, we humbly pray that, as your only-begotten Son was this day presented in the temple, so we may be presented to you with pure and clean hearts by Jesus Christ our Lord; who lives and reigns with you and the Holy Spirit, one God, now and for ever. *Amen.*

Almighty and everliving God, we humbly beseech thee that, as thy only-begotten Son was this day presented in the temple, so we may be presented unto thee with pure and clean hearts by the same thy Son Jesus Christ our Lord; who liveth and reigneth with thee and the Holy Spirit, one God, now and for ever. *Amen.*

The Lesson
Malachi 3:1-4

See, I am sending my messenger to prepare the way before me, and the Lord whom you seek will suddenly come to his temple. The messenger of the covenant in whom you delight — indeed, he is coming, says the LORD of hosts. But who can endure the day of his coming, and who can stand when he appears? For he is like a refiner's fire and like fullers' soap; he will sit as a refiner and purifier of silver, and he will purify the descendants of Levi and refine them like gold and silver, until they present offerings to the LORD in righteousness. Then the offering of Judah and Jerusalem will be pleasing to the LORD as in the days of old and as in former years.

The Psalm 84 or 84:1-6   *Quam dilecta!*

1   [How dear to me is your dwelling, O LORD of hosts! *
        My soul has a desire and longing for the courts of the LORD;
        my heart and my flesh rejoice in the living God.

2   The sparrow has found her a house
        and the swallow a nest where she may lay her young; *
        by the side of your altars, O LORD of hosts,
        my King and my God.

3   Happy are they who dwell in your house! *
        they will always be praising you.

4   Happy are the people whose strength is in you! *
        whose hearts are set on the pilgrims' way.

5   Those who go through the desolate valley will find it a place of springs, *
        for the early rains have covered it with pools of water.

6   They will climb from height to height, *
        and the God of gods will reveal himself in Zion.]

7   LORD God of hosts, hear my prayer; *
        hearken, O God of Jacob.

8   Behold our defender, O God; *
        and look upon the face of your Anointed.

9   For one day in your courts is better than a thousand in my own room, *
        and to stand at the threshold of the house of my God
        than to dwell in the tents of the wicked.

10   For the LORD God is both sun and shield; *
        he will give grace and glory;

11   No good thing will the LORD withhold *
        from those who walk with integrity.

12   O LORD of hosts, *
        happy are they who put their trust in you!

The Epistle   **Hebrews 2:14-18**

Since the children share flesh and blood, he himself likewise shared the same things, so that through death he might destroy the one who has the power of death, that is, the devil, and free those who all their lives were held in slavery by the fear of death. For it is clear that he did not come to help angels, but the descendants of Abraham. Therefore he had to become like his brothers and sisters in every respect, so that he might be a merciful and faithful high priest in the service of God, to make a sacrifice of atonement for the sins of the people. Because he himself was tested by what he suffered, he is able to help those who are being tested.

The Gospel Luke 2:22-40

When the time came for their purification according to the law of Moses, the parents of Jesus brought him up to Jerusalem to present him to the Lord (as it is written in the law of the Lord, "Every firstborn male shall be designated as holy to the Lord"), and they offered a sacrifice according to what is stated in the law of the Lord, "a pair of turtledoves or two young pigeons." Now there was a man in Jerusalem whose name was Simeon; this man was righteous and devout, looking forward to the consolation of Israel, and the Holy Spirit rested on him. It had been revealed to him by the Holy Spirit that he would not see death before he had seen the Lord's Messiah. Guided by the Spirit, Simeon came into the temple; and when the parents brought in the child Jesus, to do for him what was customary under the law, Simeon took him in his arms and praised God, saying, "Master, now you are dismissing your servant in peace, according to your word; for my eyes have seen your salvation, which you have prepared in the presence of all peoples, a light for revelation to the Gentiles and for glory to your people Israel." And the child's father and mother were amazed at what was being said about him. Then Simeon blessed them and said to his mother Mary, "This child is destined for the falling and the rising of many in Israel, and to be a sign that will be opposed so that the inner thoughts of many will be revealed — and a sword will pierce your own soul too." There was also a prophet, Anna the daughter of Phanuel, of the tribe of Asher. She was of a great age, having lived with her husband seven years after her marriage, then as a widow to the age of eighty-four. She never left the temple but worshiped there with fasting and prayer night and day. At that moment she came, and began to praise God and to speak about the child to all who were looking for the redemption of Jerusalem. When they had finished everything required by the law of the Lord, they returned to Galilee, to their own town of Nazareth. The child grew and became strong, filled with wisdom; and the favor of God was upon him.

St. Matthias — *February 24*

The Collect

Almighty God, who in the place of Judas chose your faithful servant Matthias to be numbered among the Twelve: Grant that your Church, being delivered from false apostles, may always be guided and governed by faithful and true pastors; through Jesus Christ our Lord, who lives and reigns with you, in the unity of the Holy Spirit, one God, now and for ever. *Amen.*

O Almighty God, who into the place of Judas didst choose thy faithful servant Matthias to be of the number of the Twelve: Grant that thy Church, being delivered from false apostles, may always be ordered and guided by faithful and true pastors; through Jesus Christ our Lord, who liveth and reigneth with thee, in the unity of the Holy Spirit, one God, now and for ever. *Amen.*

The Lesson Acts 1:15-26

In those days Peter stood up among the believers (together the crowd numbered about one hundred twenty persons) and said, "Friends, the scripture had to be fulfilled, which the Holy Spirit through David foretold concerning Judas, who became a guide for those who arrested Jesus — for he was numbered among us and was allotted his share in this ministry." (Now this man acquired a field with the reward of his wickedness; and falling headlong, he burst open in the middle and all his bowels gushed out. This became known to all the residents of Jerusalem, so that the field was called in their language Hakeldama, that is, Field of Blood.) "For it is written in the book of Psalms, 'Let his homestead become desolate, and let there be no one to live in it'; and 'Let another take his position of overseer.' So one of the men who have accompanied us during all the time that the Lord Jesus went in and out among us, beginning from the baptism of John until the day when he was taken up from us — one of these must become a witness with us to his resurrection." So they proposed two, Joseph called Barsabbas, who was also known as Justus, and Matthias. Then they prayed and said, "Lord, you know everyone's heart. Show us which one of these two you have chosen to take the place in this ministry and apostleship from which Judas turned aside to go to his own place." And they cast lots for them, and the lot fell on Matthias; and he was added to the eleven apostles.

The Psalm 15   *Domine, quis habitabit?*

1   LORD, who may dwell in your tabernacle? *
      who may abide upon your holy hill?

2   Whoever leads a blameless life and does what is right, *
      who speaks the truth from his heart.

3   There is no guile upon his tongue;
      he does no evil to his friend; *
         he does not heap contempt upon his neighbor.

4   In his sight the wicked is rejected, *
      but he honors those who fear the LORD.

5   He has sworn to do no wrong *
      and does not take back his word.

6   He does not give his money in hope of gain, *
      nor does he take a bribe against the innocent.

7   Whoever does these things *
      shall never be overthrown.

The Epistle   **Philippians 3:13b-21**

This one thing I do: forgetting what lies behind and straining forward to what lies ahead, I press on toward the goal for the prize of the heavenly call of God in Christ Jesus. Let those of us then who are mature be of the same mind; and if you think differently about anything, this too God will reveal to you. Only let us hold fast to what we have attained. Brothers and sisters, join in imitating me, and observe those who live according to the example you have in us. For many live as enemies of the cross of Christ; I have often told you of them, and now I tell you even with tears. Their end is destruction; their god is the belly; and their glory is in their shame; their minds are set on earthly things. But our citizenship is in heaven, and it is from there that we are expecting a Savior, the Lord Jesus Christ. He will transform the body of

St. Matthias — *February 24*   469

our humiliation that it may be conformed to the body of his glory, by the power that also enables him to make all things subject to himself.

The Gospel John 15:1, 6-16

Jesus said, "I am the true vine, and my Father is the vinegrower. Whoever does not abide in me is thrown away like a branch and withers; such branches are gathered, thrown into the fire, and burned. If you abide in me, and my words abide in you, ask for whatever you wish, and it will be done for you. My Father is glorified by this, that you bear much fruit and become my disciples. As the Father has loved me, so I have loved you; abide in my love. If you keep my commandments, you will abide in my love, just as I have kept my Father's commandments and abide in his love. I have said these things to you so that my joy may be in you, and that your joy may be complete. This is my commandment, that you love one another as I have loved you. No one has greater love than this, to lay down one's life for one's friends. You are my friends if you do what I command you. I do not call you servants any longer, because the servant does not know what the master is doing; but I have called you friends, because I have made known to you everything that I have heard from my Father. You did not choose me but I chose you. And I appointed you to go and bear fruit, fruit that will last, so that the Father will give you whatever you ask him in my name.

St. Joseph — *March 19*

The Collect
O God, who from the family of your servant David raised up Joseph to be the guardian of your incarnate Son and the spouse of his virgin mother: Give us grace to imitate his uprightness of life and his obedience to your commands; through Jesus Christ our Lord, who lives and reigns with you and the Holy Spirit, one God, for ever and ever. *Amen.*

O God, who from the family of thy servant David didst raise up Joseph to be the guardian of thy incarnate Son and the spouse of his virgin mother: Give us grace to imitate his uprightness of life and his obedience to thy commands; through the same thy Son Jesus Christ our Lord, who liveth and reigneth with thee, and of the Holy Spirit, one God, for ever and ever. *Amen.*

The Lesson 2 Samuel 7:4, 8-16

But that same night the word of the LORD came to Nathan: Now therefore thus you shall say to my servant David: Thus says the LORD of hosts: I took you from the pasture, from following the sheep to be prince over my people Israel; and I have been with you wherever you went, and have cut off all your enemies from before you; and I will make for you a great name, like the name of the great ones of the earth. And I will appoint a place for my people Israel and will plant them, so that they may live in their own place, and be disturbed no more; and evildoers shall afflict them no more, as formerly, from the time that I appointed judges over my people Israel; and I will give you rest from all your enemies. Moreover the LORD declares to you that the LORD will make you a house. When your days are fulfilled and you lie down with your ancestors, I will raise up your offspring after you, who shall come forth from your body, and I will establish his kingdom. He shall build a house for my name, and

I will establish the throne of his kingdom forever. I will be a father to him, and he shall be a son to me. When he commits iniquity, I will punish him with a rod such as mortals use, with blows inflicted by human beings. But I will not take my steadfast love from him, as I took it from Saul, whom I put away from before you. Your house and your kingdom shall be made sure forever before me; your throne shall be established forever.

The Psalm 89:1-29 or 89:1-4, 26-29   *Misericordias Domini*

1   [Your love, O LORD, for ever will I sing; *
        from age to age my mouth will proclaim your faithfulness.

2   For I am persuaded that your love is established for ever; *
        you have set your faithfulness firmly in the heavens.

3   "I have made a covenant with my chosen one; *
        I have sworn an oath to David my servant:

4   'I will establish your line for ever, *
        and preserve your throne for all generations.'"]

5   The heavens bear witness to your wonders, O LORD, *
        and to your faithfulness in the assembly of the holy ones;

6   For who in the skies can be compared to the LORD? *
        who is like the LORD among the gods?

7   God is much to be feared in the council of the holy ones, *
        great and terrible to all those round about him.

8   Who is like you, LORD God of hosts? *
        O mighty LORD, your faithfulness is all around you.

9   You rule the raging of the sea *
        and still the surging of its waves.

10   You have crushed Rahab of the deep with a deadly wound; *
        you have scattered your enemies with your mighty arm.

11   Yours are the heavens; the earth also is yours; *
        you laid the foundations of the world and all that is in it.

12   You have made the north and the south; *
        Tabor and Hermon rejoice in your Name.

13   You have a mighty arm; *
        strong is your hand and high is your right hand.

14   Righteousness and justice are the foundations of your throne; *
        love and truth go before your face.

15   Happy are the people who know the festal shout! *
        they walk, O LORD, in the light of your presence.

16   They rejoice daily in your Name; *
        they are jubilant in your righteousness.

17   For you are the glory of their strength, *
        and by your favor our might is exalted.

18   Truly, the LORD is our ruler; *
        the Holy One of Israel is our King.

19   You spoke once in a vision and said to your faithful people: *
        "I have set the crown upon a warrior
        and have exalted one chosen out of the people.

20   I have found David my servant; *
        with my holy oil have I anointed him.

21   My hand will hold him fast *
        and my arm will make him strong.

22   No enemy shall deceive him, *
        nor any wicked man bring him down.

23   I will crush his foes before him *
        and strike down those who hate him.

24   My faithfulness and love shall be with him, *
        and he shall be victorious through my Name.

25   I shall make his dominion extend *
        from the Great Sea to the River.

26   [He will say to me, 'You are my Father, *
        my God, and the rock of my salvation.'

27   I will make him my firstborn *
        and higher than the kings of the earth.

28   I will keep my love for him for ever, *
        and my covenant will stand firm for him.

29   I will establish his line for ever *
        and his throne as the days of heaven."]

The Epistle   **Romans 4:13-18**

The promise that he would inherit the world did not come to Abraham or to his descendants through the law but through the righteousness of faith. If it is the adherents of the law who are to be the heirs, faith is null and the promise is void. For the law brings wrath; but where there is no law, neither is there violation. For this reason it depends on faith, in order that the promise may rest on grace and be guaranteed to all his descendants, not only to the adherents of the law but also to those who share the faith of Abraham (for he is the father of all of us, as it is written, "I have made you the father of many nations") in the presence of the God in whom he believed, who gives life to the dead and calls into existence the things that do not exist. Hoping against hope, he believed that he would become "the father of many nations," according to what was said, "So numerous shall your descendants be."

The Gospel

Luke 2:41-52

Every year Jesus' parents went to Jerusalem for the festival of the Passover. And when he was twelve years old, they went up as usual for the festival. When the festival was ended and they started to return, the boy Jesus stayed behind in Jerusalem, but his parents did not know it. Assuming that he was in the group of travelers, they went a day's journey. Then they started to look for him among their relatives and friends. When they did not find him, they returned to Jerusalem to search for him. After three days they found him in the temple, sitting among the teachers, listening to them and asking them questions. And all who heard him were amazed at his understanding and his answers. When his parents saw him they were astonished; and his mother said to him, "Child, why have you treated us like this? Look, your father and I have been searching for you in great anxiety." He said to them, "Why were you searching for me? Did you not know that I must be in my Father's house?" But they did not understand what he said to them. Then he went down with them and came to Nazareth, and was obedient to them. His mother treasured all these things in her heart. And Jesus increased in wisdom and in years, and in divine and human favor.

The Annunciation — *March 25*

The Collect

Pour your grace into our hearts, O Lord, that we who have known the incarnation of your Son Jesus Christ, announced by an angel to the Virgin Mary, may by his cross and passion be brought to the glory of his resurrection; who lives and reigns with you, in the unity of the Holy Spirit, one God, now and for ever. *Amen.*

We beseech thee, O Lord, pour thy grace into our hearts, that we who have known the incarnation of thy Son Jesus Christ, announced by an angel to the Virgin Mary, may by his cross and passion be brought unto the glory of his resurrection; who liveth and reigneth with thee, in the unity of the Holy Spirit, one God, now and for ever. *Amen.*

The Lesson

Isaiah 7:10-14

The LORD spoke to Ahaz, saying, Ask a sign of the LORD your God; let it be deep as Sheol or high as heaven. But Ahaz said, I will not ask, and I will not put the LORD to the test. Then Isaiah said: "Hear then, O house of David! Is it too little for you to weary mortals, that you weary my God also? Therefore the Lord himself will give you a sign. Look, the young woman is with child and shall bear a son, and shall name him Immanuel.

The Psalm 40:1-11 or 40:5-10   *Expectans, expectavi*

1   I waited patiently upon the LORD; *
        he stooped to me and heard my cry.

2   He lifted me out of the desolate pit, out of the mire and clay; *
        he set my feet upon a high cliff and made my footing sure.

3   He put a new song in my mouth,
     a song of praise to our God; *
        many shall see, and stand in awe,
        and put their trust in the LORD.

4   Happy are they who trust in the LORD! *
        they do not resort to evil spirits or turn to false gods.

5   [Great things are they that you have done, O LORD my God!
     how great your wonders and your plans for us! *
        there is none who can be compared with you.

6   Oh, that I could make them known and tell them! *
        but they are more than I can count.

7   In sacrifice and offering you take no pleasure *
        (you have given me ears to hear you);

8   Burnt-offering and sin-offering you have not required, *
        and so I said, "Behold, I come.

9   In the roll of the book it is written concerning me: *
        'I love to do your will, O my God;
        your law is deep in my heart.'"

10   I proclaimed righteousness in the great congregation; *
        behold, I did not restrain my lips;
        and that, O LORD, you know.]

11   Your righteousness have I not hidden in my heart;
     I have spoken of your faithfulness and your deliverance; *
        I have not concealed your love and faithfulness from the great congregation.

or Canticle 3   **The Song of Mary**   *Magnificat*   *Luke 1:46-55*

My soul doth magnify the Lord, *
    and my spirit hath rejoiced in God my Savior.
For he hath regarded *
    the lowliness of his handmaiden.
For behold from henceforth *
    all generations shall call me blessed.
For he that is mighty hath magnified me, *
    and holy is his Name.
And his mercy is on them that fear him *
    throughout all generations.
He hath showed strength with his arm; *
    he hath scattered the proud in the imagination of their hearts.
He hath put down the mighty from their seat, *
    and hath exalted the humble and meek.
He hath filled the hungry with good things, *
    and the rich he hath sent empty away.

He remembering his mercy hath holpen his servant Israel, *
  as he promised to our forefathers,
    Abraham and his seed for ever.
Glory to the Father, and to the Son, and to the Holy Spirit: *
  as it was in the beginning, is now, and will be for ever. *Amen.*

or Canticle 15   The Song of Mary   *Magnificat*   *Luke 1:46-55*
My soul proclaims the greatness of the Lord,
my spirit rejoices in God my Savior; *
  for he has looked with favor on his lowly servant.
From this day all generations will call me blessed: *
  the Almighty has done great things for me,
    and holy is his Name.
He has mercy on those who fear him *
  in every generation.
He has shown the strength of his arm, *
  he has scattered the proud in their conceit.
He has cast down the mighty from their thrones, *
  and has lifted up the lowly.
He has filled the hungry with good things, *
  and the rich he has sent away empty.
He has come to the help of his servant Israel, *
  for he has remembered his promise of mercy,
The promise he made to our fathers, *
  to Abraham and his children for ever.
Glory to the Father, and to the Son, and to the Holy Spirit: *
  as it was in the beginning, is now, and will be for ever. *Amen.*

The Epistle   **Hebrews 10:5-10**
When Christ came into the world, he said, "Sacrifices and offerings you have not
desired, but a body you have prepared for me; in burnt offerings and sin offerings you
have taken no pleasure. Then I said, 'See, God, I have come to do your will, O God'
(in the scroll of the book it is written of me)." When he said above, "You have
neither desired nor taken pleasure in sacrifices and offerings and burnt offerings and
sin offerings" (these are offered according to the law), then he added, "See, I have
come to do your will." He abolishes the first in order to establish the second. And it
is by God's will that we have been sanctified through the offering of the body of Jesus
Christ once for all.

The Gospel   **Luke 1:26-38**
In the sixth month the angel Gabriel was sent by God to a town in Galilee called
Nazareth, to a virgin engaged to a man whose name was Joseph, of the house of
David. The virgin's name was Mary. And he came to her and said, "Greetings,
favored one! The Lord is with you." But she was much perplexed by his words and
pondered what sort of greeting this might be. The angel said to her, "Do not be
afraid, Mary, for you have found favor with God. And now, you will conceive in your
womb and bear a son, and you will name him Jesus. He will be great, and will be

called the Son of the Most High, and the Lord God will give to him the throne of his ancestor David. He will reign over the house of Jacob forever, and of his kingdom there will be no end." Mary said to the angel, "How can this be, since I am a virgin?" The angel said to her, "The Holy Spirit will come upon you, and the power of the Most High will overshadow you; therefore the child to be born will be holy; he will be called Son of God. And now, your relative Elizabeth in her old age has also conceived a son; and this is the sixth month for her who was said to be barren. For nothing will be impossible with God." Then Mary said, "Here am I, the servant of the Lord; let it be with me according to your word." Then the angel departed from her.

St. Mark *April 25*

The Collect
Almighty God, by the hand of Mark the evangelist you have given to your Church the Gospel of Jesus Christ the Son of God: We thank you for this witness, and pray that we may be firmly grounded in its truth; through Jesus Christ our Lord who lives and reigns with you and the Holy Spirit, one God, for ever and ever. *Amen.*

Almighty God, who by the hand of Mark the evangelist hast given to thy Church the Gospel of Jesus Christ the Son of God: We thank thee for this witness, and pray that we may be firmly grounded in its truth; through the same Jesus Christ our Lord, who liveth and reigneth with thee and the Holy Spirit, one God, for ever and ever. *Amen.*

The Lesson   Isaiah 52:7-10
How beautiful upon the mountains are the feet of the messenger who announces peace, who brings good news, who announces salvation, who says to Zion, "Your God reigns." Listen! Your sentinels lift up their voices, together they sing for joy; for in plain sight they see the return of the LORD to Zion. Break forth together into singing, you ruins of Jerusalem; for the LORD has comforted his people, he has redeemed Jerusalem. The LORD has bared his holy arm before the eyes of all the nations; and all the ends of the earth shall see the salvation of our God.

The Psalm 2 or 2:7-10   *Quare fremuerunt gentes?*
1   Why are the nations in an uproar? *
        Why do the peoples mutter empty threats?

2   Why do the kings of the earth rise up in revolt,
     and the princes plot together, *
        against the LORD and against his Anointed?

3   "Let us break their yoke," they say; *
        "let us cast off their bonds from us."

4   He whose throne is in heaven is laughing; *
        the Lord has them in derision.

5   Then he speaks to them in his wrath, *
        and his rage fills them with terror.

6   "I myself have set my king *
        upon my holy hill of Zion."

7   [Let me announce the decree of the LORD: *
        he said to me, "You are my Son;
        this day have I begotten you.

8   Ask of me, and I will give you the nations for your inheritance *
        and the ends of the earth for your possession.

9   You shall crush them with an iron rod *
        and shatter them like a piece of pottery."

10   And now, you kings, be wise; *
        be warned, you rulers of the earth.]

11   Submit to the LORD with fear, *
        and with trembling bow before him;

12   Lest he be angry and you perish; *
        for his wrath is quickly kindled.

13   Happy are they all *
        who take refuge in him!

The Epistle   Ephesians 4:7-8, 11-16

Each of us was given grace according to the measure of Christ's gift. Therefore it is said, "When he ascended on high he made captivity itself a captive; he gave gifts to his people." The gifts he gave were that some would be apostles, some prophets, some evangelists, some pastors and teachers, to equip the saints for the work of ministry, for building up the body of Christ, until all of us come to the unity of the faith and of the knowledge of the Son of God, to maturity, to the measure of the full stature of Christ. We must no longer be children, tossed to and fro and blown about by every wind of doctrine, by people's trickery, by their craftiness in deceitful scheming. But speaking the truth in love, we must grow up in every way into him who is the head, into Christ, from whom the whole body, joined and knit together by every ligament with which it is equipped, as each part is working properly, promotes the body's growth in building itself up in love.

The Gospel   Mark 1:1-15

The beginning of the good news of Jesus Christ, the Son of God. As it is written in the prophet Isaiah, "See, I am sending my messenger ahead of you, who will prepare your way; the voice of one crying out in the wilderness: 'Prepare the way of the Lord, make his paths straight,'" John the baptizer appeared in the wilderness, proclaiming a baptism of repentance for the forgiveness of sins. And people from the whole Judean countryside and all the people of Jerusalem were going out to him, and were baptized by him in the river Jordan, confessing their sins. Now John was clothed with camel's hair, with a leather belt around his waist, and he ate locusts and wild honey. He proclaimed, "The one who is more powerful than I is coming after me; I am not worthy to stoop down and untie the thong of his sandals. I have baptized you with water; but he will baptize you with the Holy Spirit." In those days Jesus came from Nazareth of Galilee and was baptized by John in the Jordan. And just as he was coming up out of the water, he saw the heavens torn apart and the Spirit descending like a dove on him. And a voice came from heaven, "You are my Son, the Beloved; with you I am well pleased." And the Spirit immediately drove him out into the wilderness. He was in the wilderness forty days, tempted by Satan; and he was with the wild beasts; and the angels waited on him. Now after John was arrested, Jesus came to Galilee, proclaiming the good news of God, and saying, "The time is fulfilled, and the kingdom of God has come near; repent, and believe in the good news."

or Mark 16:15-20

Jesus said to the apostles, "Go into all the world and proclaim the good news to the whole creation. The one who believes and is baptized will be saved; but the one who does not believe will be condemned. And these signs will accompany those who believe: by using my name they will cast out demons; they will speak in new tongues; they will pick up snakes in their hands, and if they drink any deadly thing, it will not hurt them; they will lay their hands on the sick, and they will recover." So then the Lord Jesus, after he had spoken to them, was taken up into heaven and sat down at the right hand of God. And they went out and proclaimed the good news everywhere, while the Lord worked with them and confirmed the message by the signs that accompanied it.

St. Philip & St. James — *May 1*

The Collect

Almighty God, who gave to your apostles Philip and James grace and strength to bear witness to the truth: Grant that we, being mindful of their victory of faith, may glorify in life and death the Name of our Lord Jesus Christ; who lives and reigns with you and the Holy Spirit, one God, now and for ever. *Amen.*

Almighty God, who didst give to thine apostles Philip and James grace and strength to bear witness to the truth: Grant that we, being mindful of their victory of faith, may glorify in life and death the Name of our Lord Jesus Christ; who liveth and reigneth with thee and the Holy Spirit, one God, now and for ever. *Amen.*

The Lesson   Isaiah 30:18-21

The LORD waits to be gracious to you; therefore he will rise up to show mercy to you. For the LORD is a God of justice; blessed are all those who wait for him. Truly, O people in Zion, inhabitants of Jerusalem, you shall weep no more. He will surely be gracious to you at the sound of your cry; when he hears it, he will answer you. Though the Lord may give you the bread of adversity and the water of affliction, yet your Teacher will not hide himself any more, but your eyes shall see your Teacher. And when you turn to the right or when you turn to the left, your ears shall hear a word behind you, saying, "This is the way; walk in it."

The Psalm 119:33-40   *Legem pone*

33 Teach me, O LORD, the way of your statutes, *
     and I shall keep it to the end.

34 Give me understanding, and I shall keep your law; *
     I shall keep it with all my heart.

35 Make me go in the path of your commandments, *
     for that is my desire.

36 Incline my heart to your decrees *
     and not to unjust gain.

37 Turn my eyes from watching what is worthless; *
     give me life in your ways.

38 Fulfill your promise to your servant, *
     which you make to those who fear you.

39 Turn away the reproach which I dread, *
     because your judgments are good.

40 Behold, I long for your commandments; *
     in your righteousness preserve my life.

The Epistle   2 Corinthians 4:1-6

Since it is by God's mercy that we are engaged in this ministry, we do not lose heart.
We have renounced the shameful things that one hides; we refuse to practice cunning
or falsify God's word; but by the open statement of the truth we commend ourselves
to the conscience of everyone in the sight of God. And even if our gospel is veiled, it
is veiled to those who are perishing. In their case the god of this world has blinded
the minds of the unbelievers, to keep them from seeing the light of the gospel of the
glory of Christ, who is the image of God. For we do not proclaim ourselves; we
proclaim Jesus Christ as Lord and ourselves as your slaves for Jesus' sake. For it is
the God who said, "Let light shine out of darkness," who has shone in our hearts to
give the light of the knowledge of the glory of God in the face of Jesus Christ.

The Gospel   John 14:6-14

Jesus said to Thomas, "I am the way, and the truth, and the life. No one comes to the
Father except through me. If you know me, you will know my Father also. From now
on you do know him and have seen him." Philip said to him, "Lord, show us the
Father, and we will be satisfied." Jesus said to him, "Have I been with you all this
time, Philip, and you still do not know me? Whoever has seen me has seen the
Father. How can you say, 'Show us the Father'? Do you not believe that I am in the
Father and the Father is in me? The words that I say to you I do not speak on my
own; but the Father who dwells in me does his works. Believe me that I am in the
Father and the Father is in me; but if you do not, then believe me because of the
works themselves. "Very truly, I tell you, the one who believes in me will also do the
works that I do and, in fact, will do greater works than these, because I am going to

the Father. I will do whatever you ask in my name, so that the Father may be glorified in the Son. If in my name you ask me for anything I will do it."

The Visitation — *May 31*

The Collect
Father in heaven, by your grace the virgin mother of your incarnate Son was blessed in bearing him, but still more blessed in keeping your word: Grant us who honor the exaltation of her lowliness to follow the example of her devotion to your will; through Jesus Christ our Lord, who lives and reigns with you and the Holy Spirit, one God, for ever and ever. *Amen.*

Father in heaven, by whose grace the virgin mother of thy incarnate Son was blessed in bearing him, but still more blessed in keeping thy word: Grant us who honor the exaltation of her lowliness to follow the example of her devotion to thy will; through the same Jesus Christ our Lord, who liveth and reigneth with thee and the Holy Spirit, one God, for ever and ever. *Amen.*

The Lesson
Zephaniah 3:14-18a

Sing aloud, O daughter Zion; shout, O Israel! Rejoice and exult with all your heart, O daughter Jerusalem! The LORD has taken away the judgments against you, he has turned away your enemies. The king of Israel, the LORD, is in your midst; you shall fear disaster no more. On that day it shall be said to Jerusalem: Do not fear, O Zion; do not let your hands grow weak. The LORD, your God, is in your midst, a warrior who gives victory; he will rejoice over you with gladness, he will renew you in his love; he will exult over you with loud singing as on a day of festival.

The Psalm 113   *Laudate, pueri*

1 Hallelujah!
   Give praise, you servants of the LORD; *
      praise the Name of the LORD.

2 Let the Name of the LORD be blessed, *
      from this time forth for evermore.

3 From the rising of the sun to its going down *
      let the Name of the LORD be praised.

4 The LORD is high above all nations, *
      and his glory above the heavens.

5 Who is like the LORD our God, who sits enthroned on high, *
      but stoops to behold the heavens and the earth?

6 He takes up the weak out of the dust *
      and lifts up the poor from the ashes.

7 He sets them with the princes, *
      with the princes of his people.

8 He makes the woman of a childless house *
      to be a joyful mother of children.

or Canticle 9   The First Son of Isaiah   *Ecce, Deus*   *Isaiah 12:2-6*

Surely, it is God who save me; *
    I will trust in him and not be afraid.
For the Lord is my stronghold and my sure defense, *
    and he will be my Savior.
Therefore you shall draw water with rejoicing *
    from the springs of salvation.
And on that day you shall say, *
    Give thanks to the Lord and call upon his Name;
Make his deeds known among the peoples; *
    see that they remember that his Name is exalted.
Sing the praises of the Lord, for he has done great things, *
    and this is known in all the world.
Cry aloud, inhabitants of Zion, ring out your joy, *
    for the great one in the midst of you is the Holy One of Israel.
Glory to the Father, and to the Son, and to the Holy Spirit: *
    as it was in the beginning, is now, and will be for ever. Amen.

The Epistle   **Colossians 3:12-17**

As God's chosen ones, holy and beloved, clothe yourselves with compassion, kindness, humility, meekness, and patience. Bear with one another and, if anyone has a complaint against another, forgive each other; just as the Lord has forgiven you, so you also must forgive. Above all, clothe yourselves with love, which binds everything together in perfect harmony. And let the peace of Christ rule in your hearts, to which indeed you were called in the one body. And be thankful. Let the word of Christ dwell in you richly; teach and admonish one another in all wisdom; and with gratitude in your hearts sing psalms, hymns, and spiritual songs to God. And whatever you do, in word or deed, do everything in the name of the Lord Jesus, giving thanks to God the Father through him.

The Gospel   **Luke 1:39-49**

Mary set out and went with haste to a Judean town in the hill country, where she entered the house of Zechariah and greeted Elizabeth. When Elizabeth heard Mary's greeting, the child leaped in her womb. And Elizabeth was filled with the Holy Spirit and exclaimed with a loud cry, "Blessed are you among women, and blessed is the fruit of your womb. And why has this happened to me, that the mother of my Lord comes to me? For as soon as I heard the sound of your greeting, the child in my womb leaped for joy. And blessed is she who believed that there would be a fulfillment of what was spoken to her by the Lord." And Mary said, "My soul magnifies the Lord, and my spirit rejoices in God my Savior, for he has looked with favor on the lowliness of his servant. Surely, from now on all generations will call me blessed; for the Mighty One has done great things for me, and holy is his name.

St. Barnabas — *June 11*

The Collect

Grant, O God, that we may follow the example of your faithful servant Barnabas, who, seeking not his own renown but the well-being of your Church, gave generously of his life and substance for the relief of the poor and the spread of the Gospel; through Jesus Christ our Lord, who lives and reigns with you and the Holy Spirit, one God, for ever and ever. *Amen.*

Grant, O God, that we may follow the example of thy faithful servant Barnabas, who, seeking not his own renown but the well-being of thy Church, gave generously of his life and substance for the relief of the poor and the spread of the Gospel; through Jesus Christ our Lord, who liveth and reigneth with thee and the Holy Spirit, one God, for ever and ever. *Amen.*

The Lesson   Isaiah 42:5-12

Thus says God, the LORD, who created the heavens and stretched them out, who spread out the earth and what comes from it, who gives breath to the people upon it and spirit to those who walk in it: I am the LORD, I have called you in righteousness, I have taken you by the hand and kept you; I have given you as a covenant to the people, a light to the nations, to open the eyes that are blind, to bring out the prisoners from the dungeon, from the prison those who sit in darkness. I am the LORD, that is my name; my glory I give to no other, nor my praise to idols. See, the former things have come to pass, and new things I now declare; before they spring forth, I tell you of them. Sing to the LORD a new song, his praise from the end of the earth! Let the sea roar and all that fills it, the coastlands and their inhabitants. Let the desert and its towns lift up their voice, the villages that Kedar inhabits; let the inhabitants of Sela sing for joy, let them shout from the tops of the mountains. Let them give glory to the LORD, and declare his praise in the coastlands.

The Psalm 112   *Beatus vir*

1   Hallelujah!
     Happy are they who fear the Lord *
         and have great delight in his commandments!

2   Their descendants will be mighty in the land; *
         the generation of the upright will be blessed.

3   Wealth and riches will be in their house, *
         and their righteousness will last for ever.

4   Light shines in the darkness for the upright; *
         the righteous are merciful and full of compassion.

5   It is good for them to be generous in lending *
         and to manage their affairs with justice.

6   For they will never be shaken; *
         the righteous will be kept in everlasting remembrance.

7　They will not be afraid of any evil rumors; *
　　　their heart is right;
　　　they put their trust in the Lord.

8　Their heart is established and will not shrink, *
　　　until they see their desire upon their enemies.

9　They have given freely to the poor, *
　　　and their righteousness stands fast for ever;
　　　they will hold up their head with honor.

10　The wicked will see it and be angry;
　　　they will gnash their teeth and pine away; *
　　　the desires of the wicked will perish.

The Epistle   Acts 11:19-30, 13:1-3

Those who were scattered because of the persecution that took place over Stephen
traveled as far as Phoenicia, Cyprus, and Antioch, and they spoke the word to no one
except Jews. But among them were some men of Cyprus and Cyrene who, on coming
to Antioch, spoke to the Hellenists also, proclaiming the Lord Jesus. The hand of the
Lord was with them, and a great number became believers and turned to the Lord.
News of this came to the ears of the church in Jerusalem, and they sent Barnabas to
Antioch. When he came and saw the grace of God, he rejoiced, and he exhorted them
all to remain faithful to the Lord with steadfast devotion; for he was a good man, full
of the Holy Spirit and of faith. And a great many people were brought to the Lord.
Then Barnabas went to Tarsus to look for Saul, and when he had found him, he
brought him to Antioch. So it was that for an entire year they met with the church
and taught a great many people, and it was in Antioch that the disciples were first
called "Christians." At that time prophets came down from Jerusalem to Antioch.
One of them named Agabus stood up and predicted by the Spirit that there would be
a severe famine over all the world; and this took place during the reign of Claudius.
The disciples determined that according to their ability, each would send relief to the
believers living in Judea; this they did, sending it to the elders by Barnabas and Saul.
Now in the church at Antioch there were prophets and teachers: Barnabas, Simeon
who was called Niger, Lucius of Cyrene, Manaen a member of the court of Herod the
ruler, and Saul. While they were worshiping the Lord and fasting, the Holy Spirit
said, "Set apart for me Barnabas and Saul for the work to which I have called them."
Then after fasting and praying they laid their hands on them and sent them off.

The Gospel   Matthew 10:7-16

Jesus said to the twelve, "As you go, proclaim the good news, 'The kingdom of
heaven has come near. Cure the sick, raise the dead, cleanse the lepers, cast out
demons. You received without payment; give without payment. Take no gold, or
silver, or copper in your belts, no bag for your journey, or two tunics, or sandals, or a
staff; for laborers deserve their food. Whatever town or village you enter, find out
who in it is worthy, and stay there until you leave. As you enter the house, greet it. If
the house is worthy, let your peace come upon it; but if it is not worthy, let your
peace return to you. If anyone will not welcome you or listen to your words, shake off

the dust from your feet as you leave that house or town. Truly I tell you, it will be more tolerable for the land of Sodom and Gomorrah on the day of judgment than for that town. "See, I am sending you out like sheep into the midst of wolves; so be wise as serpents and innocent as doves."

Nativity of St. John the Baptist — *June 24*

The Collect
Almighty God, by whose providence your servant John the Baptist was wonderfully born, and sent to prepare the way of your Son our Savior by preaching repentance: Make us so to follow his teaching and holy life, that we may truly repent according to his preaching; and, following his example, constantly speak the truth, boldly rebuke vice, and patiently suffer for the truth's sake; through Jesus Christ your Son our Lord, who lives and reigns with you and the Holy Spirit, one God, for ever and ever. *Amen.*

Almighty God, by whose providence thy servant John the Baptists was wonderfully born, and sent to prepare the way of thy Son our Savior by preaching repentance: Make us so to follow his doctrine and holy life, that we may truly repent according to his preaching; and after his example constantly speak the truth, boldly rebuke vice, and patiently suffer for the truth's sake; through the same thy Son Jesus Christ our Lord, who liveth and reigneth with thee and the Holy Spirit, one God, for ever and ever. *Amen.*

The Lesson   Isaiah 40:1-11
Comfort, O comfort my people, says your God. Speak tenderly to Jerusalem, and cry to her that she has served her term, that her penalty is paid, that she has received from the LORD'S hand double for all her sins. A voice cries out: "In the wilderness prepare the way of the LORD, make straight in the desert a highway for our God. Every valley shall be lifted up, and every mountain and hill be made low; the uneven ground shall become level, and the rough places a plain. Then the glory of the LORD shall be revealed, and all people shall see it together, for the mouth of the LORD has spoken." A voice says, "Cry out!" And I said, "What shall I cry?" All people are grass, their constancy is like the flower of the field. The grass withers, the flower fades, when the breath of the LORD blows upon it; surely the people are grass. The grass withers, the flower fades; but the word of our God will stand forever. Get you up to a high mountain, O Zion, herald of good tidings; lift up your voice with strength, O Jerusalem, herald of good tidings, lift it up, do not fear; say to the cities of Judah, "Here is your God!" See, the Lord GOD comes with might, and his arm rules for him; his reward is with him, and his recompense before him. He will feed his flock like a shepherd; he will gather the lambs in his arms, and carry them in his bosom, and gently lead the mother sheep.

The Psalm 85 or 85:7-13   *Benedixisti, Domine*
1   You have been gracious to your land, O LORD, *
           you have restored the good fortune of Jacob.

2   You have forgiven the iniquity of your people *
           and blotted out all their sins.

3   You have withdrawn all your fury *
        and turned yourself from your wrathful indignation.

4   Restore us then, O God our Savior; *
        let your anger depart from us.

5   Will you be displeased with us for ever? *
        will you prolong your anger from age to age?

6   Will you not give us life again, *
        that your people may rejoice in you?

7   [Show us your mercy, O LORD, *
        and grant us your salvation.

8   I will listen to what the LORD God is saying, *
        for he is speaking peace to his faithful people
        and to those who turn their hearts to him.

9   Truly, his salvation is very near to those who fear him, *
        that his glory may dwell in our land.

10   Mercy and truth have met together; *
        righteousness and peace have kissed each other.

11   Truth shall spring up from the earth, *
        and righteousness shall look down from heaven.

12   The LORD will indeed grant prosperity, *
        and our land will yield its increase.

13   Righteousness shall go before him, *
        and peace shall be a pathway for his feet.]

The Epistle   Acts 13:14b-26

On the sabbath day Paul and his companions went into the synagogue and sat down. After the reading of the law and the prophets, the officials of the synagogue sent them a message, saying, "Brothers, if you have any word of exhortation for the people, give it." So Paul stood up and with a gesture began to speak: "You Israelites, and others who fear God, listen. The God of this people Israel chose our ancestors and made the people great during their stay in the land of Egypt, and with uplifted arm he led them out of it. For about forty years he put up with them in the wilderness. After he had destroyed seven nations in the land of Canaan, he gave them their land as an inheritance for about four hundred fifty years. After that he gave them judges until the time of the prophet Samuel. Then they asked for a king; and God gave them Saul son of Kish, a man of the tribe of Benjamin, who reigned for forty years. When he had removed him, he made David their king. In his testimony about him he said, 'I have found David, son of Jesse, to be a man after my heart, who will carry out all my wishes.' Of this man's posterity God has brought to Israel a Savior, Jesus, as he promised; before his coming John had already proclaimed a baptism of repentance to all the people of Israel. And as John was finishing his work, he said, 'What do you suppose that I am? I am not he. No, but one is coming after me; I am not worthy to untie the thong of the sandals on his feet.' My brothers, you descendants of Abraham's family, and others who fear God, to us the message of this salvation has been sent."

The Gospel   Luke 1:57-80

The time came for Elizabeth to give birth, and she bore a son. Her neighbors and relatives heard that the Lord had shown his great mercy to her, and they rejoiced with her. On the eighth day they came to circumcise the child, and they were going to name him Zechariah after his father. But his mother said, "No; he is to be called John." They said to her, "None of your relatives has this name." Then they began motioning to his father to find out what name he wanted to give him. He asked for a writing tablet and wrote, "His name is John." And all of them were amazed. Immediately his mouth was opened and his tongue freed, and he began to speak, praising God. Fear came over all their neighbors, and all these things were talked about throughout the entire hill country of Judea. All who heard them pondered them and said, "What then will this child become?" For, indeed, the hand of the Lord was with him. Then his father Zechariah was filled with the Holy Spirit and spoke this prophecy: "Blessed be the Lord God of Israel, for he has looked favorably on his people and redeemed them. He has raised up a mighty savior for us in the house of his servant David, as he spoke through the mouth of his holy prophets from of old, that we would be saved from our enemies and from the hand of all who hate us. Thus he has shown the mercy promised to our ancestors, and has remembered his holy covenant, the oath that he swore to our ancestor Abraham, to grant us that we, being rescued from the hands of our enemies, might serve him without fear, in holiness and righteousness before him all our days. And you, child, will be called the prophet of the Most High; for you will go before the Lord to prepare his ways, to give knowledge of salvation to his people by the forgiveness of their sins. By the tender mercy of our God, the dawn from on high will break upon us, to give light to those who sit in darkness and in the shadow of death, to guide our feet into the way of peace." The child grew and became strong in spirit, and he was in the wilderness until the day he appeared publicly to Israel.

St. Peter & St. Paul — *June 29*

The Collect
Almighty God, whose blessed apostles Peter and Paul glorified you by the martyrdom: Grant that your Church, instructed by their teaching and example, and knit together in unity by your Spirit, may ever stand firm upon the one foundation, which is Jesus Christ our Lord; who lives and reigns with you, in the unity of the Holy Spirit, one God, now and for ever. *Amen.*

Almighty God, whose blessed apostles Peter and Paul glorified thee by their martyrdom: Grant that thy Church, instructed by their teaching and example, and knit together in unity by the Spirit, may ever stand firm upon the one foundation, which is Jesus Christ our Lord; who liveth and reigneth with thee, in the unity of the same Spirit, one God, for ever and ever. *Amen.*

The Lesson

For thus says the Lord GOD: I myself will search for my sheep, and will seek them out. As shepherds seek out their flocks when they are among their scattered sheep, so I will seek out my sheep. I will rescue them from all the places to which they have been scattered on a day of clouds and thick darkness. I will bring them out from the peoples and gather them from the countries, and will bring them into their own land; and I will feed them on the mountains of Israel, by the watercourses, and in all the inhabited parts of the land. I will feed them with good pasture, and the mountain heights of Israel shall be their pasture; there they shall lie down in good grazing land, and they shall feed on rich pasture on the mountains of Israel. I myself will be the shepherd of my sheep, and I will make them lie down, says the Lord GOD. I will seek the lost, and I will bring back the strayed, and I will bind up the injured, and I will strengthen the weak, but the fat and the strong I will destroy. I will feed them with justice.

The Psalm 87   *Fundamenta ejus*

1   On the holy mountain stands the city he has founded; *
         the LORD loves the gates of Zion
         more than all the dwellings of Jacob.

2   Glorious things are spoken of you, *
         O city of our God.

3   I count Egypt and Babylon among those who know me; *
         behold Philistia, Tyre, and Ethiopia:
         in Zion were they born.

4   Of Zion it shall be said, "Everyone was born in her, *
         and the Most High himself shall sustain her."

5   The LORD will record as he enrolls the peoples, *
         "These also were born there."

6   The singers and the dancers will say, *
         "All my fresh springs are in you."

The Epistle

In the presence of God and of Christ Jesus, who is to judge the living and the dead, and in view of his appearing and his kingdom, I solemnly urge you: proclaim the message; be persistent whether the time is favorable or unfavorable; convince, rebuke, and encourage, with the utmost patience in teaching. For the time is coming when people will not put up with sound doctrine, but having itching ears, they will accumulate for themselves teachers to suit their own desires, and will turn away from listening to the truth and wander away to myths. As for you, always be sober, endure suffering, do the work of an evangelist, carry out your ministry fully. As for me, I am already being poured out as a libation, and the time of my departure has come. I have fought the good fight, I have finished the race, I have kept the faith. From now on there is reserved for me the crown of righteousness, which the Lord, the righteous judge, will give me on that day, and not only to me but also to all who have longed for his appearing.

The Gospel

John 21:15-19

When they had finished breakfast, Jesus said to Simon Peter, "Simon son of John, do you love me more than these?" He said to him, "Yes, Lord; you know that I love you." Jesus said to him, "Feed my lambs." A second time he said to him, "Simon son of John, do you love me?" He said to him, "Yes, Lord; you know that I love you." Jesus said to him, "Tend my sheep." He said to him the third time, "Simon son of John, do you love me?" Peter felt hurt because he said to him the third time, "Do you love me?" And he said to him, "Lord, you know everything; you know that I love you." Jesus said to him, "Feed my sheep. Very truly, I tell you, when you were younger, you used to fasten you own belt and to go wherever you wished. But when you grow old, you will stretch out your hands, and someone else will fasten a belt around you and take you where you do not wish to go." (He said this to indicate the kind of death by which he would glorify God.) After this he said to him, "Follow me."

Independence Day *July 4*

The Collect

Lord God Almighty, in whose Name the founders of this country won liberty for themselves and for us, and lit the torch of freedom for nations then unborn: Grant that we and all the people of this land may have grace to maintain our liberties in righteousness and peace; through Jesus Christ our Lord, who lives and reigns with you and the Holy Spirit, one God, for ever and ever. *Amen.*

The Collect, "For the Nation," page 258 of the Book of Common Prayer, may be used instead.

Lord God Almighty, in whose Name the founders of this country won liberty for themselves and for us, and lit the torch of freedom for nations then unborn: Grant, we beseech thee, that we and all the people of this land may have grace to maintain these liberties in righteousness and peace; through Jesus Christ our Lord, who liveth and reigneth with thee and the Holy Spirit, one God, for ever and ever. *Amen.*

The Collect "For the Nation," page 207 of the Book of Common Prayer, may be used instead.

The Lesson

Deuteronomy 10:17-21

Moses said to Israel, "For the LORD your God is God of gods and Lord of lords, the great God, mighty and awesome, who is not partial and takes no bribe, who executes justice for the orphan and the widow, and who loves the strangers, providing them food and clothing. You shall also love the stranger, for you were strangers in the land of Egypt. You shall fear the LORD your God; him alone you shall worship; to him you shall hold fast, and by his name you shall swear. He is your praise; he is your God, who has done for you these great and awesome things that your own eyes have seen.

The Psalm 145 or 145:1-9   *Exaltabo te, Deus*

1   [I will exalt you, O God my King, *
        and bless your Name for ever and ever.

2   Every day will I bless you *
        and praise your Name for ever and ever.

3   Great is the LORD and greatly to be praised; *
        there is no end to his greatness.

4   One generation shall praise your works to another *
        and shall declare your power.

5   I will ponder the glorious splendor of your majesty *
        and all your marvelous works.

6   They shall speak of the might of your wondrous acts, *
        and I will tell of your greatness.

7   They shall publish the remembrance of your great goodness; *
        they shall sing of your righteous deeds.

8   The LORD is gracious and full of compassion, *
        slow to anger and of great kindness.

9   The LORD is loving to everyone *
        and his compassion is over all his works.]

10   All your works praise you, O LORD, *
        and your faithful servants bless you.

11   They make known the glory of your kingdom *
        and speak of your power;

12   That the peoples may know of your power *
        and the glorious splendor of your kingdom.

13   Your kingdom is an everlasting kingdom; *
        your dominion endures throughout all ages.

14   The LORD is faithful in all his words *
        and merciful in all his deeds.

15   The LORD upholds all those who fall; *
        he lifts up those who are bowed down.

16   The eyes of all wait upon you, O LORD, *
        and you give them their food in dues season.

17   You open wide your hand *
        and satisfy the needs of every living creature.

18   The LORD is righteous in all his ways *
        and loving in all his works.

19   The LORD is near to those who call upon him, *
      to all who call upon him faithfully.

20   He fulfills the desire of those who fear him; *
      he hears their cry and helps them.

21   The LORD preserves all those who love him, *
      but he destroys all the wicked.

22   My mouth shall speak the praise of the LORD; *
      let all flesh bless his holy Name for ever and ever.

The Epistle   **Hebrews 11:8-16**

By faith Abraham obeyed when he was called to set out for a place that he was to receive as an inheritance; and he set out, not knowing where he was going. By faith he stayed for a time in the land he had been promised, as in a foreign land, living in tents, as did Isaac and Jacob, who were heirs with him of the same promise. For he looked forward to the city that has foundations, whose architect and builder is God. By faith he received power of procreation, even though he was too old — and Sarah herself was barren — because he considered him faithful who had promised. Therefore from one person, and this one as good as dead, descendants were born, "as many as the stars of heaven and as the innumerable grains of sand by the seashore." All of these died in faith without having received the promises, but from a distance they saw and greeted them. They confessed that they were strangers and foreigners on the earth, for people who speak in this way make it clear that they are seeking a homeland. If they had been thinking of the land that they had left behind, they would have had opportunity to return. But as it is, they desire a better country, that is, a heavenly one. Therefore God is not ashamed to be called their God; indeed, he has prepared a city for them.

The Gospel   **Matthew 5:43-48**

Jesus said to the disciples, "You have heard that it was said, 'You shall love your neighbor and hate your enemy.' But I say to you, Love your enemies and pray for those who persecute you, so that you may be children of your Father in heaven; for he makes his sun rise on the evil and on the good, and sends rain on the righteous and on the unrighteous. For if you love those who love you, what reward do you have? Do not even the tax collectors do the same? And if you greet only your brothers and sisters, what more are you doing than others? Do not even the Gentiles do the same? Be perfect, therefore, as your heavenly Father is perfect.

The Psalm and Lessons "For the Nation," page 930 of the Book of Common Prayer, may be used instead.

St. Mary Magdalene — *July 22*

The Collect

Almighty God, whose blessed Son restored Mary Magdalene to health of body and mind, and called her to be a witness of his resurrection: Mercifully grant that by your

grace we may be healed from all your infirmities and know you in the power of his unending life; who with you and the Holy Spirit lives and reigns, one God, now and for ever. *Amen.*

Almighty God, whose blessed Son restored Mary Magdalene to health of body and mind, and called her to be a witness of his resurrection: Mercifully grant that by thy grace we may be healed of all our infirmities and know thee in the power of his endless life; who with thee and the Holy Spirit liveth and reigneth, one God, now and for ever. *Amen.*

The Lesson

Judith 9:1, 11-14

Then Judith prostrated herself, put ashes on her head, and uncovered the sackcloth she was wearing. At the very time when the evening incense was being offered in the house of God in Jerusalem, Judith cried out to the Lord with a loud voice, and said, "For your strength does not depend on numbers, nor your might on the powerful. But you are the God of the lowly, helper of the oppressed,upholder of the weak, protector of the forsaken, savior of those without hope. Please, please, God of my father, God of the heritage of Israel, Lord of heaven and earth, Creator of the waters, King of all your creation, hear my prayer! Make my deceitful words bring wound and bruise on those who have planned cruel things against your covenant, and against your sacred house, and against Mount Zion, and against the house your children possess. Let your whole nation and every tribe know and understand that you are God, the God of all power and might, and that there is no other who protects the people of Israel but you alone!"

The Psalm 42:1-7   *Quemadmodum*

1   As the deer longs for the water-brooks, *
     so longs my soul for you, O God.

2   My soul is athirst for God, athirst for the living God; *
     when shall I come to appear before the presence of God?

3   My tears have been my food day and night, *
     while all day long they say to me,
     "Where now is your God?"

4   I pour out my soul when I think on these things: *
     how I went with the multitude and led them into the house of God,

5   With the voice of praise and thanksgiving, *
     among those who keep holy-day.

6   Why are you so full of heaviness, O my soul? *
     and why are you so disquieted within me?

7   Put your trust in God; *
     for I will yet give thanks to him,
     who is the help of my countenance, and my God.

The Epistle   **2 Corinthians 5:14-18**

For the love of Christ urges us on, because we are convinced that one has died for all; therefore all have died. And he died for all, so that those who live might live no longer for themselves, but for him who died and was raised for them. From now on, therefore, we regard no one from a human point of view; even though we once knew Christ from a human point of view, we know him no longer in that way. So if anyone is in Christ, there is a new creation: everything old has passed away; see, everything has become new! All this is from God, who reconciled us to himself through Christ, and has given us the ministry of reconciliation.

The Gospel   **John 20:11-18**

Mary stood weeping outside the tomb. As she wept, she bent over to look into the tomb; and she saw two angels in white, sitting where the body of Jesus had been lying, one at the head and the other at the feet. They said to her, "Woman, why are you weeping?" She said to them, "They have taken away my Lord, and I do not know where they have laid him." When she had said this, she turned around and saw Jesus standing there, but she did not know that it was Jesus. Jesus said to her, "Woman, why are you weeping? Whom are you looking for?" Supposing him to be the gardener, she said to him, "Sir, if you have carried him away, tell me where you have laid him, and I will take him away." Jesus said to her, "Mary!" She turned and said to him in Hebrew, "Rabbouni!" (which means Teacher). Jesus said to her, "Do not hold on to me, because I have not yet ascended to the Father. But go to my brothers and say to them, 'I am ascending to my Father and your Father, to my God and your God.'" Mary Magdalene went and announced to the disciples, "I have seen the Lord"; and she told them that he had said these things to her.

St. James — *July 25*

The Collect

O gracious God, we remember before you today your servant and apostle James, first among the Twelve to suffer martyrdom for the Name of Jesus Christ; and we pray that you will pour out upon the leaders of your Church that spirit of self-denying service by which alone they may have true authority among your people; through Jesus Christ our Lord, who lives and reigns with you and the Holy Spirit, one God, now and for ever. *Amen.*

O gracious God, we remember before thee this day thy servant and apostle James, first among the Twelve to suffer martyrdom for the Name of Jesus Christ; and we pray that thou wilt pour out upon the leaders of thy Church that spirit of self-denying service by which alone they may have true authority among thy people; through the same Jesus Christ our Lord, who liveth and reigneth with thee and the Holy Spirit, one God, now and for ever. *Amen.*

The Lesson   **Jeremiah 45:1-5**

The word that the prophet Jeremiah spoke to Baruch son of Neriah, when he wrote these words in a scroll at the dictation of Jeremiah, in the fourth year of King Hehoiakim son of Josiah of Judah: Thus says the LORD, the God of Israel, to you, O Baruch: You said, "Woe is me! The LORD has added sorrow to my pain; I am weary with my groaning, and I find no rest." Thus you shall say to him, "Thus says the LORD: I am going to break down what I have built, and pluck up what I have planted — that is, the whole land. And you, do you seek great things for yourself? Do not seek them; for I am going to bring disaster upon all flesh, says the LORD; but I will give you your life as a prize of war in every place to which you may go."

The Psalm 7:1-10   *Domine, Deus meus*

1   O LORD my God, I take refuge in you; *
    save and deliver me from all who pursue me;

2   Lest like a lion they tear me in pieces *
    and snatch me away with none to deliver me.

3   O LORD my God, if I have done these things: *
    if there is any wickedness in my hands,

4   If I have repaid my friend with evil, *
    or plundered him who without cause is my enemy;

5   Then let my enemy pursue and overtake me, *
    trample my life into the ground,
    and lay my honor in the dust.

6   Stand up, O LORD, in your wrath; *
    rise up against the fury of my enemies.

7   Awake, O my God, decree justice; *
    let the assembly of the peoples gather round you.

8   Be seated on your lofty throne, O Most High; *
    O LORD, judge the nations.

9   Give judgment for me according to my righteousness, O LORD, *
    and according to my innocence, O Most High

10   Let the malice of the wicked come to an end,
    but establish the righteous; *
    for you test the mind and heart, O righteous God.

The Epistle   Acts 11:27-12:3

At that time prophets came down from Jerusalem to Antioch. One of them named Agabus stood up and predicted by the Spirit that there would be a severe famine over all the world; and this took place during the reign of Claudius. The disciples determined that according to their ability, each would send relief to the believers living in Judea; this they did, sending it to the elders by Barnabas and Saul. About that time King Herod laid violent hands upon some who belonged to the church. He had James, the brother of John, killed with the sword. After he saw that it pleased the Jews, he proceeded to arrest Peter also. (This was during the festival of Unleavened Bread.)

The Gospel
Matthew 20:20-28

The mother of the sons of Zebedee came to Jesus with her sons, and kneeling before him, she asked a favor of him. And he said to her, "What do you want?" She said to him, "Declare that these two sons of mine will sit, one at your right hand and one at your left, in your kingdom." But Jesus answered, "You do not know what you are asking. Are you able to drink the cup that I am about to drink?" They said to him, "We are able." He said to them, "You will indeed drink my cup, but to sit at my right hand and at my left, this is not mine to grant, but it is for those for whom it has been prepared by my Father." When the ten heard it, they were angry with the two brothers. But Jesus called them to him and said, "You know that the rulers of the Gentiles lord it over them, and their great ones are tyrants over them. It will not be so among you; but whoever wishes to be great among you must be your servant, and whoever wishes to be first among you must be your slave; just as the Son of Man came not to be served but to serve, and to give his life a ransom for many."

The Transfiguration *August 6*

The Collect
O God, who on the holy mount revealed to chosen witnesses your well-beloved Son, wonderfully transfigured, in raiment white and glistening: Mercifully grant that we, being delivered from the disquietude of this world, may by faith behold the King in his beauty; who with you, O Father, and you, O Holy Spirit, lives and reigns, one God, for ever and ever. *Amen.*

O God, who on the holy mount didst reveal to chosen witnesses thy well-beloved Son, wonderfully transfigured, in raiment white and glistening: Mercifully grant that we, being delivered from the disquietude of this world, may by faith behold the King in his beauty; who with thee, O Father, and thee, O Holy Ghost, liveth and reigneth, one God, world without end. *Amen.*

The Lesson
Exodus 34:29-35

Moses came down from Mount Sinai. As he came down from the mountain with the two tablets of the covenant in his hand, Moses did not know that the skin of his face shone because he had been talking with God. When Aaron and all the Israelites saw Moses, the skin of his face was shining, and they were afraid to come near him. But Moses called to them; and Aaron and all the leaders of the congregation returned to him, and Moses spoke with them. Afterward all the Israelites came near, and he gave them in commandment all that the LORD had spoken with him on Mount Sinai. When Moses had finished speaking with them, he put a veil on his face; but whenever Moses went in before the LORD to speak with him, he would take the veil off, until he came out; and when he came out, and told the Israelites what he had been commanded, the Israelites would see the face of Moses, that the skin of his face was shining; and Moses would put the veil on his face again, until he went in to speak with him.

The Psalm 99 or 99:5-9   *Dominus regnavit*
1 The LORD is King;
let the people tremble; *

he is enthroned upon the cherubim;
let the earth shake.

2   The LORD is great in Zion; *
    he is high above all peoples.

3   Let them confess his Name, which is great and awesome; *
    he is the Holy One.

4   "O mighty King, lover of justice,
    you have established equity; *
      you have executed justice and righteousness in Jacob."

5   [Proclaim the greatness of the LORD our God
    and fall down before his footstool; *
      he is the Holy One.

6   Moses and Aaron among his priests,
    and Samuel among those who call upon his Name, *
      they called upon the LORD, and he answered them.

7   He spoke to them out of the pillar of cloud; *
      they kept his testimonies and the decree that he gave them.

8   O LORD our God, you answered them indeed; *
    you were a God who forgave them,
    yet punished them for their evil deeds.

9   Proclaim the greatness of the LORD our God
    and worship him upon his holy hill; *
      for the LORD our God is the Holy One.]

The Epistle   2 Peter 1:13-21

I think it right, as long as I am in this body, to refresh your memory, since I know that my death will come soon, as indeed our Lord Jesus Christ has made clear to me. And I will make every effort so that after my departure you may be able at any time to recall these things. For we did not follow cleverly devised myths when we made known to you the power and coming of our Lord Jesus Christ, but we had been eyewitnesses of his majesty. For he received honor and glory from God the Father when that voice was conveyed to him by the Majestic Glory, saying, "This is my Son, my Beloved, with whom I am well pleased." We ourselves heard this voice come from heaven, while we were with him on the holy mountain. So we have the prophetic message more fully confirmed. You will do well to be attentive to this as to a lamp shining in a dark place, until the day dawns and the morning star rises in your hearts. First of all you must understand this, that no prophecy of scripture is a matter of one's own interpretation, because no prophecy ever came by human will, but men and women moved by the Holy Spirit spoke from God.

The Gospel   Luke 9:28-36

Now about eight days after Jesus had foretold his death and resurrection, Jesus took with him Peter and John and James, and went up on the mountain to pray. And while he was praying, the appearance of his face changed, and his clothes became dazzling white. Suddenly they saw two men, Moses and Elijah, talking to him. They appeared in glory and were speaking of his departure, which he was about to accomplish at Jerusalem. Now Peter and his companions were weighed down with sleep; but since they had stayed awake, they saw his glory and the two men who stood with him. Just as they were leaving him, Peter said to Jesus, "Master, it is good for us to be here; let us make three dwellings, one for you, one for Moses, and one for Elijah" — not knowing what he said. While he was saying this, a cloud came and overshadowed them; and they were terrified as they entered the cloud. Then from the cloud came a voice that said, "This is my Son, my Chosen; listen to him!" When the voice had spoken, Jesus was found alone. And they kept silent and in those days told no one any of the things they had seen.

St. Mary the Virgin — *August 15*

The Collect
O God, you have taken to yourself the blessed Virgin Mary, mother of your incarnate Son: Grant that we, who have been redeemed by his blood, may share with her the glory of your eternal kingdom; through Jesus Christ our Lord, who lives and reigns with you, in the unity of the Holy Spirit, one God, now and for ever. *Amen.*

O God, who hast taken to thyself the blessed Virgin Mary, mother of thy incarnate Son: Grant that we, who have been redeemed by his blood, may share with her the glory of thine eternal kingdom; through the same thy Son Jesus Christ our Lord, who liveth and reigneth with thee, in the unity of the Holy Spirit, one God, now and for ever. *Amen.*

The Lesson
Isaiah 61:10-11

I will greatly rejoice in the LORD, my whole being shall exult in my God; for he has clothed me with the garments of salvation, he has covered me with the robe of righteousness, as a bridegroom decks himself with a garland, and as a bride adorns herself with her jewels. For as the earth brings forth its shoots, and as a garden causes what is sown in it to spring up, so the Lord GOD will cause righteousness and praise to spring up before all the nations.

The Psalm 34 or 34:1-9
Benedicam Dominum

1 [I will bless the LORD at all times; *
   his praise shall ever be in my mouth.

2 I will glory in the LORD; *
   let the humble hear and rejoice.

3 Proclaim with me the greatness of the LORD; *
   let us exalt his Name together.

4 I sought the LORD, and he answered me *
   and delivered me out of all my terror.

5   Look upon him and be radiant, *
       and let not your faces be ashamed.

6   I called in my affliction and the LORD heard me *
       and saved me from all my troubles.

7   The angel of the LORD encompasses those who fear him, *
       and he will deliver them.

8   Taste and see that the LORD is good; *
       happy are they who trust in him!

9   Fear the LORD, you that are his saints, *
       for those who fear him lack nothing.]

10   The young lions lack and suffer hunger, *
       but those who seek the LORD lack nothing that is good.

11   Come, children, and listen to me; *
       I will teach you the fear of the LORD.

12   Who among you loves life *
       and desire long life to enjoy prosperity?

13   Keep your tongue from evil-speaking *
       and your lips from lying words.

14   Turn from evil and do good; *
       seek peace and pursue it.

15   The eyes of the LORD are upon the righteous, *
       and his ears are open to their cry.

16   The face of the LORD is against those who do evil, *
       to root out the remembrance of them from the earth.

17   The righteous cry, and the LORD hears them *
       and delivers them from all their troubles.

18   The LORD is near to the brokenhearted *
       and will save those whose spirits are crushed.

19   Many are the troubles of the righteous, *
       but the LORD will deliver him out of them all.

20   He will keep safe all his bones; *
       not one of them shall be broken.

21   Evil shall slay the wicked, *
       and those who hate the righteous will be punished.

22   The LORD ransoms the life of his servants, *
       and none will be punished who trust in him.

The Epistle   Galatians 4:4-7

When the fullness of time had come, God sent his Son, born of a woman, born under the law, in order to redeem those who were under the law, so that we might receive adoption as children. And because you are children, God has sent the Spirit of his Son into our hearts, crying, "Abba! Father!" So you are no longer a slave but a child, and if a child then also an heir, through God.

The Gospel   Luke 1:46-55

Mary said, "My soul magnifies the Lord, and my spirit rejoices in God my Savior, for he has looked with favor on the lowliness of his servant. Surely, from now on all generations will call me blessed; for the Mighty One has done great things for me, and holy is his name. His mercy is for those who fear him from generation to generation. He has shown strength with his arm; he has scattered the proud in the thoughts of their hearts. He has brought down the powerful from their thrones, and lifted up the lowly; he has filled the hungry with good things, and sent the rich away empty. He has helped his servant Israel, in remembrance of his mercy, according to the promise he made to our ancestors, to Abraham and to his descendants forever."

St. Bartholomew — *August 24*

The Collect

Almighty and everlasting God, who gave to your apostle Bartholomew grace truly to believe and to preach your Word: Grant that your Church may love what he believed and preach what he taught; through Jesus Christ our Lord, who lives and reigns with you and the Holy Spirit, one God, for ever and ever. *Amen.*

O Almighty and everlasting God, who didst give to thine apostle Bartholomew grace truly to believe and to preach thy Word: Grant, we beseech thee, unto thy Church to love what he believed and to preach what he taught; through Jesus Christ our Lord, who liveth and reigneth with thee and the Holy Spirit, one God, for ever and ever. *Amen.*

The Lesson   Deuteronomy 18:15-18

Moses said to the Israelites, "The LORD your God will raise up for you a prophet like me from among your own people; you shall heed such a prophet. This is what you requested of the LORD you God at Horeb on the day of the assembly when you said: 'If I hear the voice of the LORD my God any more, or ever again see this great fire, I will die.' Then the LORD replied to me: 'They are right in what they have said. I will raise up for them a prophet like you from among their own people; I will put my words in the mouth of the prophet, who shall speak to them everything that I command.'"

The Psalm 91 or 91:1-4   *Qui habitat*

1   [He who dwells in the shelter of the Most High, *
           abides under the shadow of the Almighty.

2 He shall say to the LORD,
"You are my refuge and my stronghold, *
my God in whom I put my trust."

3 He shall deliver you from the snare of the hunter *
and from the deadly pestilence.

4 He shall cover you with his pinions,
and you shall find refuge under his wings; *
his faithfulness shall be a shield and buckler.]

5 You shall not be afraid of any terror by night, *
nor of the arrow that flies by day;

6 Of the plague that stalks in the darkness, *
nor of the sickness that lays waste at mid-day.

7 A thousand shall fall at your side
and ten thousand at your right hand, *
but it shall not come near you.

8 Your eyes have only to behold *
to see the reward of the wicked.

9 Because you have made the LORD your refuge, *
and the Most High your habitation,

10 There shall no evil happen to you, *
neither shall any plague come near your dwelling.

11 For he shall give his angels charge over you, *
to keep you in all your ways.

12 They shall bear you in their hands, *
lest you dash your foot against a stone.

13 You shall tread upon the lion and adder; *
you shall trample the young lion and the serpent under your feet.

14 Because he is bound to me in love,
therefore will I deliver him; *
I will protect him, because he knows my Name.

15 He shall call upon me, and I will answer him; *
I am with him in trouble;
I will rescue him and bring him to honor.

16 With long life will I satisfy him, *
and show him my salvation.

The Epistle   **1 Corinthians 4:9-15**
I think that God has exhibited us apostles as last of all, as though sentenced to death, because we have become a spectacle to the world, to angels and mortals. We are fools

for the sake of Christ, but you are wise in Christ. We are weak, but you are strong.
You are held in honor, but we in disrepute. To the present hour we are hungry and
thirsty, we are poorly clothed and beaten and homeless, and we grow weary from the
work of our own hands. When reviled, we bless; when persecuted, we endure; when
slandered, we speak kindly. We have become like the rubbish of the world, the dregs
of all things, to this very day. I am not writing this to make you ashamed, but to
admonish you as my beloved children. For though you might have ten thousand
guardians in Christ, you do not have many fathers. Indeed, in Christ Jesus I became
your father through the gospel.

The Gospel Luke 22:24-30

A dispute also arose among the apostles as to which one of them was to be regarded
as the greatest. But Jesus said to them, "The kings of the Gentiles lord it over them;
and those in authority over them are called benefactors. But not so with you; rather
the greatest among you must become like the youngest, and the leader like one who
serves. For who is greater, the one who is at the table or the one who serves? Is it not
the one at the table? But I am among you as one who serves. You are those who have
stood by me in my trials; and I confer on you, just as my Father has conferred on me,
a kingdom, so that you may eat and drink at my table in my kingdom, and you will
sit on thrones judging the twelve tribes of Israel."

Holy Cross Day — *September 14*

The Collect

**Almighty God, whose Son our Savior Jesus Christ was lifted high upon the cross that
he might draw the whole world to himself: Mercifully grant that we, who glory in the
mystery of our redemption, may have grace to take up our cross and follow him; who
lives and reigns with you and the Holy Spirit, one God, in glory everlasting.** *Amen.*

**Almighty God, whose Son our Savior Jesus Christ was lifted high upon the cross that
he might draw the whole world unto himself: Mercifully grant that we, who glory in the
mystery of our redemption, may have grace to take up our cross and follow him; who
liveth and reigneth with thee and the Holy Spirit, one God, in glory everlasting.** *Amen.*

The Lesson Isaiah 45:21-25

Thus says the Lord, Declare and present your case; let them take counsel together!
Who told this long ago? Who declare it of old? Was it not I, the LORD? There is no
other god besides me, a righteous God and a Savior; there is no one besides me. Turn
to me and be saved, all the ends of the earth! For I am God, and there is no other. By
myself I have sworn, from my mouth has gone forth in righteousness a word that
shall not return: "To me every knee shall bow, every tongue shall swear." Only in the
LORD, it shall be said of me, are righteousness and strength; all who were incensed
against him shall come to him and be ashamed. In the LORD all the offspring of
Israel shall triumph and glory.

The Psalm 98 or 98:1-4   *Cantate Domino*

1   [Sing to the LORD a new song, *
       for he has done marvelous things.

2   With his right hand and his holy arm *
     has he won for himself the victory.

3   The LORD has made known his victory; *
     his righteousness has he openly shown in the sight of the nations.

4   He remembers his mercy and faithfulness to the house of Israel, *
     and all the ends of the earth have seen the victory of our God.]

5   Shout with joy to the LORD, all you lands; *
     lift up your voice, rejoice, and sing.

6   Sing to the LORD with the harp, *
     with the harp and the voice of song.

7   With trumpets and the sound of the horn *
     shout with joy before the King, the LORD.

8   Let the sea make a noise and all that is in it, *
     the lands and those who dwell therein.

9   Let the rivers clap their hands, *
     and let the hills ring out with the joy before the LORD,
     when he comes to judge the earth.

10 In righteousness shall he judge the world *
     and the peoples with equity.

The Epistle   **Philippians 2:5-11**

Let the same mind be in you that was in Christ Jesus, who, though he was in the form of God, did not regard equality with God as something to be exploited, but emptied himself, taking the form of a slave, being born in human likeness. And being found in human form, he humbled himself and became obedient to the point of death — even death on a cross. Therefore God also highly exalted him and gave him the name that is above every name, so that at the name of Jesus every knee should bend, in heaven and on earth and under the earth, and every tongue should confess that Jesus Christ is Lord, to the glory of God the Father.

or Galatians 6:14-18

May I never boast of anything except the cross of our Lord Jesus Christ, by which the world has been crucified to me, and I to the world. For neither circumcision nor uncircumcision is anything; but a new creation is everything! As for those who will follow this rule — peace be upon them, and mercy, and upon the Israel of God. From now on, let no one make trouble for me; for I carry the marks of Jesus branded on my body. May the grace of our Lord Jesus Christ be with your spirit, brothers and sisters. Amen.

The Gospel   **John 12:31-36a**

Jesus said, "Now is the judgment of this world; now the ruler of this world will be driven out. And I, when I am lifted up from the earth, will draw all people to myself." He said this to indicate the kind of death he was to die. The crowd answered him, "We have heard from the law that the Messiah remains forever. How can you say that the Son of Man must be lifted up? Who is this Son of Man?" Jesus said to them, "The light is with you for a little longer. Walk while you have the light, so that the darkness may not overtake you. If you walk in the darkness, you do not know where you are going. While you have the light, believe in the light, so that you may become children of light."

St. Matthew — *September 21*

The Collect
We thank you, heavenly Father, for the witness of your apostle and evangelist Matthew to the Gospel of your Son our Savior; and we pray that, after his example, we may with ready wills and hearts obey the calling of our Lord to follow him; through Jesus Christ our Lord, who lives and reigns with you and the Holy Spirit, one God, now and for ever. *Amen.*

We thank thee, heavenly Father, for the witness of thine apostle and evangelist Matthew to the Gospel of thy Son our Savior; and we pray that, after his example, we may with ready wills and hearts obey the calling of our Lord to follow him; through Jesus Christ our Lord, who liveth and reigneth with thee and the Holy Spirit, one God, now and for ever. *Amen.*

The Lesson
Proverbs 3:1-6

My child, do not forget my teaching, but let your heart keep my commandments; for length of days and years of life and abundant welfare they will give you. Do not let loyalty and faithfulness forsake you; bind them around your neck, write them on the tablet of your heart. So you will find favor and good repute in the sight of God and of people. Trust in the LORD with all your heart, and do not rely on your own insight. In all your ways acknowledge him, and he will make straight your paths.

The Psalm 119:33-40   *Legem pone*

33 Teach me, O LORD, the way of your statutes, *
      and I shall keep it to the end.

34 Give me understanding, and I shall keep your law; *
      I shall keep it with all my heart.

35 Make me go in the path of your commandments, *
      for that is my desire.

36 Incline my heart to your decrees *
      and not to unjust gain.

37 Turn my eyes from watching what is worthless; *
      give me life in your ways.

38 Fulfill your promise to your servant, *
      which you make to those who fear you.

39   Turn away the reproach which I dread, *
         because your judgments are good.

40   Behold, I long for your commandments; *
         in your righteousness preserve my life.

The Epistle   2 Timothy 3:14-17
As for you, continue in what you have learned and firmly believed, knowing from
whom you learned it, and how from childhood you have known the sacred writings
that are able to instruct you for salvation through faith in Christ Jesus. All scripture
is inspired by God and is useful for teaching, for reproof, for correction, and for
training in righteousness, so that everyone who belongs to God may be proficient,
equipped for every good work.

The Gospel   Matthew 9:9-13
As Jesus was walking along, he saw a man called Matthew sitting at the tax booth;
and he said to him, "Follow me." And he got up and followed him. And as he sat at
dinner in the house, many tax collectors and sinners came and were sitting with him
and his disciples. When the Pharisees saw this, they said to his disciples, "Why does
your teacher eat with tax collectors and sinners?" But when he heard this, he said,
"Those who are well have no need of a physician, but those who are sick. Go and
learn what this means, 'I desire mercy, not sacrifice.' For I have come to call not the
righteous but sinners."

St. Michael & All Angels — *September 29*

The Collect
**Everlasting God, you have ordained and constituted in a wonderful order the ministries
of angels and mortals: Mercifully grant that, as your holy angels always serve and
worship you in heaven, so by your appointment they may help and defend us here on
earth; through Jesus Christ our Lord, who lives and reigns with you and the Holy
Spirit, one God, for ever and ever.** *Amen.*

**O everlasting God, who hast ordained and constituted the ministries of angels and men
in a wonderful order: Mercifully grant that, as thy holy angels always serve and
worship thee in heaven, so by thy appointment they may help and defend us on earth;
through Jesus Christ our Lord, who liveth and reigneth with thee and the Holy Spirit,
one God, for ever and ever.** *Amen.*

The Lesson   Genesis 28:10-17
Jacob left Beer-sheba and went toward Haran. He came to a certain place and stayed
there for the night, because the sun had set. Taking one of the stones of the place, he
put it under his head and lay down in that place. And he dreamed that there was a
ladder set up on the earth, the top of it reaching to heaven; and the angels of God
were ascending and descending on it. And the Lord stood beside him and said, "I
am the Lord, the God of Abraham your father and the God of Isaac; the land on
which you lie I will give to you and to your offspring; and your offspring shall be like
the dust of the earth, and you shall spread abroad to the west and to the east and to

the north and to the south; and all the families of the earth shall be blessed in you and in your offspring. Know that I am with you and will keep you wherever you go, and will bring you back to this land; for I will not leave you until I have done what I have promised you." Then Jacob woke from his sleep and said, "Surely the LORD is in this place — and I did not know it!" And he was afraid, and said, "How awesome is this place! This is none other than the house of God, and this is the gate of heaven."

The Psalm 103 or 103:19-22   *Benedic, anima mea*

1   Bless the LORD, O my soul, *
        and all that is within me, bless his holy Name.

2   Bless the LORD, O my soul, *
        and forget not all his benefits.

3   He forgives all your sins *
        and heals all your infirmities;

4   He redeems your life from the grave *
        and crowns you with mercy and loving-kindness;

5   He satisfies you with good things, *
        and your youth is renewed like an eagle's.

6   The LORD executes righteousness *
        and judgment for all who are oppressed.

7   He made his ways known to Moses *
        and his works to the children of Israel.

8   The LORD is full of compassion and mercy, *
        slow to anger and of great kindness.

9   He will not always accuse us, *
        nor will he keep his anger for ever.

10   He has not dealt with us according to our sins, *
        nor rewarded us according to our wickedness.

11   For as the heavens are high above the earth, *
        so is his mercy great upon those who fear him.

12   As far as the east is from the west, *
        so far has he removed our sins from us.

13   As a father cares for his children, *
        so does the LORD care for those who fear him.

14   For he himself knows whereof we are made; *
        he remembers that we are but dust.

15   Our days are like the grass; *
        we flourish like a flower of the field;

16 When the wind goes over it, it is gone, *
    and its place shall know it no more.

17 But the merciful goodness of the LORD endures for ever on those who fear
    him, *
    and his righteousness on children's children;

18 On those who keep his covenant *
    and remember his commandments and do them.

19 [The LORD has set his throne in heaven, *
    and his kingship has dominion over all.

20 Bless the LORD, you angels of his,
    you mighty ones who do his bidding, *
    and hearken to the voice of his word.

21 Bless the LORD, all you his hosts, *
    you ministers of his who do his will.

22 Bless the LORD, all you works of his,
    in all places of his dominion; *
    bless the LORD, O my soul.]

The Epistle   **Revelation 12:7-12**
War broke out in heaven; Michael and his angels fought against the dragon. The
dragon and his angels fought back, but they were defeated, and there was no longer
any place for them in heaven. The great dragon was thrown down, that ancient
serpent, who is called the Devil and Satan, the deceiver of the whole world — he was
thrown down to the earth, and his angels were thrown down with him. Then I heard
a loud voice in heaven, proclaiming, "Now have come the salvation and the power
and the kingdom of our God and the authority of his Messiah, for the accuser of our
comrades has been thrown down, who accuses them day and night before our God.
But they have conquered him by the blood of the Lamb and by the word of their
testimony, for they did not cling to life even in the face of death. Rejoice then, you
heavens and those who dwell in them! But woe to the earth and the sea, for the devil
has come down to you with great wrath, because he knows that his time is short!"

The Gospel   **John 1:47-51**
When Jesus saw Nathanael coming toward him, he said of him, "Here is truly an
Israelite in whom there is no deceit!" Nathanael asked him, "Where did you get to
know me?" Jesus answered, "I saw you under the fig tree before Philip called you."
Nathanael replied, "Rabbi, you are the Son of God! You are the King of Israel!"
Jesus answered, "Do you believe because I told you that I saw you under the fig tree?
You will see greater things than these." And he said to him, "Very truly, I tell you,
you will see heaven opened and the angels of God ascending and descending upon
the Son of Man."

St. Luke — *October 18*

The Collect

Almighty God, who inspired your servant Luke the physician to set forth in the Gospel the love and healing power of your Son: Graciously continue in your Church this love and power to heal, to the praise and glory of your Name; through Jesus Christ our Lord, who lives and reigns with you, in the unity of the Holy Spirit, one God, now and for ever. *Amen.*

Almighty God, who didst inspire thy servant Luke the physician to set forth in the Gospel the love and healing power of thy Son: Graciously continue in thy Church the like love and power to heal, to the praise and glory of thy Name; through the same thy Son Jesus Christ our Lord, who liveth and reigneth with thee, in the unity of the Holy Spirit, one God, now and for ever. *Amen.*

The Lesson   Ecclesiasticus (Sirach) 38:1-4, 6-10, 12-14

Honor physicians for their services, for the Lord created them; for their gift of healing come from the Most High, and they are rewarded by the king. The skill of physicians makes them distinguished, and in the presence of the great they are admired. The Lord created medicines out of the earth, and the sensible will not despise them. And he gave skill to human beings that he might be glorified in his marvelous works. By them the physician heals and takes away pain; the pharmacist makes a mixture from them. God's works will never be finished; and from him health spreads over all the earth. My child, when you are ill, do not delay, but pray to the Lord, and he will heal you. Give up your faults and direct your hands rightly, and cleanse your heart from all sin. Then give the physician his place, for the Lord created him; do not let him leave you, for you need him. There may come a time when recovery lies in the hands of physicians, for they too pray to the Lord that he grant them success in diagnosis and in healing, for the sake of preserving life.

The Psalm 147 or 147:1-7   *Laudate Dominum*

1   [Hallelujah!
     How good it is to sing praises to our God! *
        how pleasant it is to honor him with praise!

2   The LORD rebuilds Jerusalem; *
        he gathers the exiles of Israel.

3   He heals the brokenhearted *
        and binds up their wounds.

4   He counts the number of the stars *
        and calls them all by their names.

5   Great is our LORD and mighty in power; *
        there is no limit to his wisdom.

6   The LORD lifts up the lowly, *
        but casts the wicked to the ground.

7   Sing to the LORD with thanksgiving; *
        make music to our God upon the harp.]

8   He covers the heavens with clouds *
        and prepares rain for the earth;

9   He makes grass to grow upon the mountains *
        and green plants to serve mankind.

10 He provides food for flocks and herds *
        and for the young ravens when they cry.

11 He is not impressed by the might of a horse; *
        he has no pleasure in the strength of a man;

12 But the LORD has pleasure in those who fear him, *
        in those who await his gracious favor.

13 Worship the LORD, O Jerusalem; *
        praise your God, O Zion;

14 For he has strengthened the bars of your gates; *
        he has blessed your children within you.

15 He has established peace on your borders; *
        he satisfies you with the finest wheat.

16 He sends out his command to the earth, *
        and his word runs very swiftly.

17 He gives snow like wool; *
        he scatters hoarfrost like ashes.

18 He scatters his hail like bread crumbs; *
        who can stand against his cold?

19 He sends forth his word and melts them; *
        he blows with his wind, and the waters flow.

20 He declares his word to Jacob, *
        his statutes and his judgments to Israel.

21 He has not done so to any other nation; *
        to them he has not revealed his judgments.
        Hallelujah!

The Epistle   2 Timothy 4:5-13

As for you, always be sober, endure suffering, do the work of an evangelist, carry out
your ministry fully. As for me, I am already being poured out as a libation, and the
time of my departure has come. I have fought the good fight, I have finished the race,
I have kept the faith. From now on there is reserved for me the crown of
righteousness, which the Lord, the righteous judge, will give me on that day, and not
only to me but also to all who have longed for his appearing. Do you best to come to

me soon, for Demas, in love with this present world, has deserted me and gone to Thessalonica; Crescens has gone to Galatia, Titus to Dalmatia. Only Luke is with me. Get Mark and bring him with you, for he is useful in my ministry. I have sent Tychicus to Ephesus. When you come, bring the cloak that I left with Carpus at Troas, also the books, and above all the parchments.

The Gospel Luke 4:14-21

Jesus, filled with the power of the Spirit, returned to Galilee, and a report about him spread through all the surrounding country. He began to teach in their synagogues and was praised by everyone. When he came to Nazareth, where he had been brought up, he went to they synagogue on the sabbath day, as was his custom. He stood up to read, and the scroll of the prophet Isaiah was given to him. He unrolled the scroll and found the place where it was written: "The Spirit of the Lord is upon me, because he has anointed me to bring good news to the poor. He has sent me to proclaim release to the captives and recovery of sight to the blind, to let the oppressed go free, to proclaim the year of the Lord's favor." And he rolled up the scroll, gave it back to the attendant, and sat down. The eyes of all in the synagogue were fixed on him. Then he began to say to them, "Today this scripture has been fulfilled in your hearing."

St. James of Jerusalem — *October 23*

The Collect

Grant, O God, that, following the example of your servant James the Just, brother of our Lord, your Church may give itself continually to prayer and to the reconciliation of all who are at variance and enmity; through Jesus Christ our Lord, who lives and reigns with you and the Holy Spirit, one God, now and for ever. *Amen.*

Grant, we beseech thee, O God, that after the example of thy servant James the Just, brother of our Lord, thy Church may give itself continually to prayer and to the reconciliation of all who are at variance and enmity; through the same our Lord Jesus Christ, who liveth and reigneth with thee and the Holy Spirit, one God, now and for ever. *Amen.*

The Lesson Acts 15:12-22a

The whole assembly kept silence, and listened to Barnabas and Paul as they told of all the signs and wonders that God had done through them among the Gentiles. After they finished speaking, James replied, "My brothers, listen to me. Simeon has related how God first looked favorably on the Gentiles, to take from among them a people for his name. This agrees with the words of the prophets, as it is written, 'After this I will return, and I will rebuild the dwelling of David, which has fallen; from its ruins I will rebuild it, and I will set it up, so that all other peoples may seek the Lord — even all the Gentiles over whom my name has been called. Thus says the Lord, who has been making these things known from long ago.' Therefore I have reached the decision that we should not trouble those Gentiles who are turning to God, but we should write to them to abstain only from things polluted by idols and from fornication and from whatever has been strangled and from blood. For in every city, for generations past, Moses has had those who proclaim him, for he has been read aloud every sabbath in the synagogues." Then the apostles and the elders, with the consent of the whole church, decided to choose men from among their members and to send them to Antioch with Paul and Barnabas.

The Psalm 1   *Beatus vir qui non abiit*

1   Happy are they who have not walked in the counsel of the wicked, *
     nor lingered in the way of sinners,
     nor sat in the seats of the scornful!

2   Their delight is in the law of the LORD, *
     and they meditate on his law day and night.

3   They are like trees planted by streams of water,
     bearing fruit in due season, with leaves that do not wither; *
     everything they do shall prosper.

4   It is not so with the wicked; *
     they are like chaff which the wind blows away.

5   Therefore the wicked shall not stand upright when judgment comes, *
     nor the sinner in the council of the righteous.

6   For the LORD knows the way of the righteous, *
     but the way of the wicked is doomed.

The Epistle   1 Corinthians 15:1-11

Now I would remind you, brothers and sisters, of the good news that I proclaimed to you, which you in turn received, in which also you stand, through which also you are being saved, if you hold firmly to the message that I proclaimed to you — unless you have come to believe in vain. For I handed on to you as of first importance what I in turn had received: that Christ died for our sins in accordance with the scriptures, and that he was buried, and that he was raised on the third day in accordance with the scriptures, and that he appeared to Cephas, then to the twelve. Then he appeared to more than five hundred brothers and sisters at one time, most of whom are still alive, though some have died. Then he appeared to James, then to all the apostles. Last of all, as to one untimely born, he appeared also to me. For I am the least of the apostles, unfit to be called an apostle, because I persecuted the church of God. But by the grace of God I am what I am, and his grace toward me has not been in vain. On the contrary, I worked harder than any of them — though it was not I, but the grace of God that is with me. Whether then it was I or they, so we proclaim and so you have come to believe.

The Gospel   Matthew 13:54-58

Jesus came to his hometown and began to teach the people in their synagogue, so that they were astounded and said, "Where did this man get this wisdom and these deeds of power? Is not this the carpenter's son? Is not his mother called Mary? And are not his brothers James and Joseph and Simon and Judas? And are not all his sisters with us? Where then did this man get all this?" And they took offense at him. But Jesus said to them, "Prophets are not without honor except in their own country and in their own house." And he did not do many deeds of power there, because of their unbelief.

St. Simon & St. Jude — *October 28*

The Collect
O God, we thank you for the glorious company of the apostles, and especially on this day for Simon and Jude; and we pray that, as they were faithful and zealous in their mission, so we may with ardent devotion make known the love and mercy of our Lord and Savior Jesus Christ; who lives and reigns with you and the Holy Spirit, one God, for ever and ever. *Amen.*

O God, we thank thee for the glorious company of the apostles, and especially on this day for Simon and Jude; and we pray that, as they were faithful and zealous in their mission, so we may with ardent devotion make known the love and mercy of our Lord and Savior Jesus Christ; who liveth and reigneth with thee and the Holy Spirit, one God, for ever and ever. *Amen.*

The Lesson   Deuteronomy 32:1-4
Moses spoke these words to the whole assembly of Israel; "Give ear, O heavens, and I will speak; let the earth hear the words of my mouth. May my teaching drop like the rain, my speech condense like the dew; like gentle rain on grass, like showers on new growth. For I will proclaim the name of the LORD; ascribe greatness to our God! The Rock, his work is perfect, and all his ways are just. A faithful God, without deceit, just and upright is he."

The Psalm 119:89-96   *In aeternum, Domine*
89   O LORD, your word is everlasting; *
    it stands firm in the heavens.

90   Your faithfulness remains from one generation to another; *
    you established the earth, and it abides.

91   By your decree these continue to this day, *
    for all things are your servants.

92   If my delight had not been in your law, *
    I should have perished in my affliction.

93   I will never forget your commandments, *
    because by them you give me life.

94   I am yours; oh, that you would save me! *
    for I study your commandments.

95   Though the wicked lie in wait for me to destroy me, *
    I will apply my mind to your decrees.

96   I see that all things come to an end, *
    but your commandment has no bounds.

The Epistle Ephesians 2:13-22

In Christ Jesus you who once were far off have been brought near by the blood of Christ. For he is our peace; in his flesh he has made both groups into one and has broken down the dividing wall, that is, the hostility between us. He has abolished the law with its commandments and ordinances, that he might create in himself one new humanity in place of the two, thus making peace, and might reconcile both groups to God in one body through the cross, thus putting to death that hostility through it. So he came and proclaimed peace to you who were far off and peace to those who were near; for through him both of us have access in one Spirit to the Father. So then you are no longer strangers and aliens, but you are citizens with the saints and also members of the household of God, built upon the foundation of the apostles and prophets, with Christ Jesus himself as the cornerstone. In him the whole structure is joined together and grows into a holy temple in the Lord; in whom you also are built together spiritually into a dwelling place for God.

The Gospel John 15:17-27

Jesus said to the disciples, "I am giving you these commands so that you may love one another. If the world hates you, be aware that it hated me before it hated you. If you belonged to the world, the world would love you as its own. Because you do not belong to the world, but I have chosen you out of the world — therefore the world hates you. Remember the word that I said to you, 'Servants are not greater than their master.' If they persecuted me, they will persecute you; if they kept my word, they will keep yours also. But they will do all these things to you on account of my name, because they do not know him who sent me. If I had not come and spoken to them, they would not have sin. Whoever hates me hates my Father also. If I had not done among them the works that no one else did, they would not have sin; but they have no excuse for their sin. But now they have seen and hated both me and my Father. It was to fulfill the word that is written in their law, 'They hated me without a cause.' When the Advocate comes, whom I will send to you from the Father, the Spirit of truth who comes from the Father, he will testify on my behalf. You also are to testify because you have been with me from the beginning."

All Saint's Day — *November 1*

The Collect

Almighty God, you have knit together your elect in one communion and fellowship in the mystical body of your Son Christ our Lord: Give us grace so to follow your blessed saints in all virtuous and godly living, that we may come to those ineffable joys that you have prepared for those who truly love you; through Jesus Christ our Lord, who with you and the Holy Spirit lives and reigns, one God, in glory everlasting. *Amen.*

O Almighty God, who hast knit together thine elect in one communion and fellowship in the mystical body of thy Son Christ our Lord: Grant us grace so to follow thy blessed saints in all virtuous and godly living, that we may come to those ineffable joys which thou hast prepared for those who unfeignedly love thee; through the same Jesus Christ our Lord, who with thee and the Holy Spirit liveth and reigneth, one God, in glory everlasting. *Amen.*

The Lesson   Ecclesiasticus (Sirach) 44:1-10, 13-14

Let us now sing the praises of famous men, our ancestors in their generations. The Lord apportioned to them great glory, his majesty from the beginning. There were those who ruled in their kingdoms, and made a name for themselves by their valor; those who gave counsel because they were intelligent; those who spoke in prophetic oracles; those who led the people by their counsels and by their knowledge of the people's lore; they were wise in their words of instruction; those who composed musical tunes, or put verses in writing; rich men endowed with resources, living peacefully in their homes — all these were honored in their generations, and were the pride of their times. Some of them have left behind a name, so that others declare their praise. But of others there is no memory; they have perished as though they had never existed; they have become as though they had never been born, they and their children after them. But these also were godly men, whose righteous deeds have not been forgotten; Their offspring will continue forever, and their glory will never be blotted out. Their bodies are buried in peace but their name lives on generation after generation.

or Ecclesiasticus (Sirach) 2:(1-6), 7-11

[My child, when you come to serve the Lord, prepare yourself for testing. Set your heart right and be steadfast, and do not be impetuous in time of calamity. Cling to him and do not depart, so that your last days may be prosperous. Accept whatever befalls you, and in times of humiliation be patient. For gold is tested in the fire, and those found acceptable, in the furnace of humiliation. Trust in him, and he will help you; make your ways straight, and hope in him.] You who fear the Lord, wait for his mercy; do not stray, or else you may fall. You who fear the Lord, trust in him, and your reward will not be lost. You who fear the Lord, hope for good things, for lasting joy and mercy. Consider the generations of old and see: has anyone trusted in the Lord and been disappointed? Or has anyone persevered in the fear of the Lord and been forsaken? Or has anyone called upon him and been neglected? For the Lord is compassionate and merciful; he forgives sins and saves in time of distress.

The Psalm 149   *Cantate Domino*

1   Hallelujah!
       Sing to the LORD a new song; *
          sing his praise in the congregation of the faithful.

2   Let Israel rejoice in his Maker; *
          let the children of Zion be joyful in their King.

3   Let them praise his Name in the dance; *
          let them sing praise to him with timbrel and harp.

4   For the LORD takes pleasure in his people *
          and adorns the poor with victory.

5   Let the faithful rejoice in triumph; *
          let them be joyful on their beds.

6   Let the praises of God be in their throat *
     and a two-edged sword in their hand;

7   To wreak vengeance on the nations *
     and punishment on the peoples;

8   To bind their kings in chains *
     and their nobles with links of iron;

9   To inflict on them the judgment decreed; *
     this is glory for all his faithful people.
     Hallelujah!

The Epistle   **Revelation 7:2-4, 9-17**

I saw another angel ascending from the rising of the sun, having the seal of the living God, and he called with a loud voice to the four angels who had been given power to damage earth and sea, saying, "Do not damage the earth or the sea or the trees, until we have marked the servants of our God with a seal on their foreheads." And I heard the number of those who were sealed, one hundred forty-four thousand, sealed out of every tribe of the people of Israel. After this I looked, and there was a great multitude that no one could count, from every nation, from all tribes and peoples and languages, standing before the throne and before the Lamb, robed in white, with palm branches in their hands. They cried out in a loud voice, saying, "Salvation belongs to our God who is seated on the throne, and to the Lamb!" And all the angels stood around the throne and around the elders and the four living creatures, and they fell on their faces before the throne and worshiped God, singing, "Amen! Blessing and glory and wisdom and thanksgiving and honor and power and might be to our God forever and ever! Amen." Then one of the elders addressed me, saying, "Who are these, robed in white, and where have they come from?" I said to him, "Sir, you are the one that knows." Then he said to me, "These are they who have come out of the great ordeal; they have washed their robes and made them white in the blood of the Lamb. For this reason they are before the throne of God, and worship him day and night within his temple, and the one who is seated on the throne will shelter them. They will hunger no more, and thirst no more; the sun will not strike them, nor any scorching heat; for the Lamb at the center of the throne will be their shepherd, and he will guide them to springs of the water of life, and God will wipe away every tear from their eyes."

or Ephesians 1:(11-14), 15-23

[In Christ we have also obtained an inheritance, having been destined according to the purpose of him who accomplished all things according to his counsel and will, so that we, who were the first to set our hope on Christ, might live for the praise of his glory. In him you also, when you had heard the word of truth, the gospel of your salvation, and had believed in him, were marked with the seal of the promised Holy Spirit; this is the pledge of our inheritance toward redemption as God's own people, to the praise of his glory.] I have heard of your faith in the Lord Jesus and your love toward all the saints, and for this reason I do not cease to give thanks for you as I remember you in my prayers. I pray that the God of our Lord Jesus Christ, the

Father of glory, may give you a spirit of wisdom and revelation as you come to know him, so that, with the eyes of your heart enlightened, you may know what is the hope to which he has called you, what are the riches of his glorious inheritance among the saints, and what is the immeasurable greatness of his power for us who believe, according to the working of his great power. God put this power to work in Christ when he raised him from the dead and seated him at his right hand in the heavenly places, far above all rule and authority and power and dominion, and above every name that is named, not only in this age but also in the age to come. And he has put all things under his feet and has made him the head over all things for the church, which is his body, the fullness of him who fills all in all.

The Gospel   **Matthew 5:1-12**

When Jesus saw the crowds, he went up the mountain; and after he sat down, his disciples came to him. Then he began to speak, and taught them, saying: "Blessed are the poor in spirit, for theirs is the kingdom of heaven. Blessed are those who mourn, for they will be comforted. Blessed are the meek, for they will inherit the earth. Blessed are those who hunger and thirst for righteousness, for they will be filled. Blessed are the merciful, for they will receive mercy. Blessed are the pure in heart, for they will see God. Blessed are the peacemakers, for they will be called children of God. Blessed are those who are persecuted for righteousness' sake, for theirs is the kingdom of heaven. Blesses are you when people revile you and persecute you and utter all kinds of evil against you falsely on my account. Rejoice and be glad, for your reward is great in heaven, for in the same way they persecuted the prophets who were before you.

or Luke 6:20-26 (27-36)

Jesus looked up at his disciples and said: "Blessed are you who are poor, for yours is the kingdom of God. Blessed are you who are hungry now, for you will be filled. Blessed are you who weep now, for you will laugh. Blessed are you when people hate you, and when they exclude you, revile you, and defame you on account of the Son of Man. Rejoice in that day and leap for joy, for surely your reward is great in heaven; for that is what their ancestors did to the prophets. But woe to you who are rich, for you have received your consolation. Woe to you who are full now, for you will be hungry. Woe to you who are laughing now, for you will mourn and weep. Woe to you when all speak well of you, for that is what their ancestors did to the false prophets. [But I say to you that listen, Love your enemies, do good to those who hate you, bless those who curse you, pray for those who abuse you. If anyone strikes you on the cheek, offer the other also; and from anyone who takes away your coat do not withhold even your shirt. Give to everyone who begs from you; and if anyone takes away your goods, do not ask for them again. Do to others as you would have them do to you. If you love those who love you, what credit is that to you? For even sinners love those who love them. If you do good to those who do good to you, what credit is that to you? For even sinners do the same. If you lend to those from whom you hope to receive, what credit is that to you? Even sinners lend to sinners, to receive as much again. But love your enemies, do good, and lend, expecting nothing in return. Your reward will be great, and you will be children of the Most High; for he is kind to the ungrateful and the wicked. Be merciful, just as your Father is merciful.]

Thanksgiving Day

The Collect

Almighty and gracious Father, we give you thanks for the fruits of the earth in their season and for the labors of those who harvest them. Make us, we pray, faithful stewards of your great bounty, for the provision of our necessities and the relief of all who are in need, to the glory of your Name; through Jesus Christ our Lord, who lives and reigns with you and the Holy Spirit, one God, now and for ever. *Amen.*

Almighty and gracious Father, we give thee thanks for the fruits of the earth in their season and for the labors of those who harvest them. Make us, we beseech thee, faithful stewards of thy great bounty, for the provision of our necessities and the relief of all who are in need, to the glory of thy Name; through Jesus Christ our Lord, who liveth and reigneth with thee and the Holy Spirit, one God, now and for ever. *Amen.*

The Lesson   Deuteronomy 8:1-3, 6-10, (17-20)

Moses said to Israel, "This entire commandment that I command you today you must diligently observe, so that you may live and increase, and go in and occupy the land that the LORD promised on oath to your ancestors. Remember the long way that the LORD your God has led you these forty years in the wilderness, in order to humble you, testing you to know what was in your heart, whether or not you would keep his commandments. He humbled you by letting you hunger, then by feeding you with manna, with which neither you nor your ancestors were acquainted, in order to make you understand that one does not live by bread alone, but by every word that comes from the mouth of the LORD. Therefore keep the commandments of the LORD your God, by walking in his ways and by fearing him. For the LORD your God is bringing you into a good land, a land with flowing streams, with springs and underground waters welling up in valleys and hills, a land of wheat and barley, of vines and fig trees and pomegranates, a land of olive trees and honey, a land where you may eat bread without scarcity, where you will lack nothing, a land whose stones are iron and from whose hills you may mine copper. You shall eat your fill and bless the LORD your God for the good land that he has given you. [Do not say to yourself, 'My power and the might of my own hand have gotten me this wealth.' But remember the LORD your God, for it is he who gives you power to get wealth, so that he may confirm his covenant that he swore to your ancestors, as he is doing today. If you do forget the LORD your God and follow other gods to serve and worship them, I solemnly warn you today that you shall surely perish. Like the nations that the LORD is destroying before you, so shall you perish, because you would not obey the voice of the LORD your God.]

The Psalm 65 or 65:9-14   *Te decet hymnus*

1   You are to be praised, O God, in Zion; *
     to you shall vows be performed in Jerusalem.

2   To you that hear prayer shall all flesh come, *
     because of their transgressions.

3 Our sins are stronger than we are, *
      but you will blot them out.

4 Happy are they whom you choose
   and draw to your courts to dwell there! *
      they will be satisfied by the beauty of your house,
      by the holiness of your temple.

5 Awesome things will you show us in your righteousness,
   O God of our salvation, *
      O Hope of all the ends of the earth
      and of the seas that are far away.

6 You make fast the mountains by your power; *
      they are girded about with might.

7 You still the roaring of the seas, *
      the roaring of their waves,
      and the clamor of the peoples.

8 Those who dwell at the ends of the earth will tremble at your marvelous signs; *
      you make the dawn and the dusk to sing for joy.

9 [You visit the earth and water it abundantly;
   you make it very plenteous; *
      the river of God is full of water.

10 You prepare the grain, *
      for so you provide for the earth.

11 You drench the furrows and smooth out the ridges; *
      with heavy rain you soften the ground and bless its increase.

12 You crown the year with your goodness, *
      and your paths overflow with plenty.

13 May the fields of the wilderness be rich for grazing, *
      and the hills be clothed with joy.

14 May the meadows cover themselves with flocks,
   and the valleys cloak themselves with grain; *
      let them shout for joy and sing.]

The Epistle   **James 1:17-18, 21-27**
Every generous act of giving, with every perfect gift, is from above, coming down
from the Father of lights, with whom there is no variation or shadow due to change.
In fulfillment of his own purpose he gave us birth by the word of truth, so that we
would become a kind of first fruits of his creatures. Therefore rid yourselves of all
sordidness and rank growth of wickedness, and welcome with meekness the
implanted word that has the power to save your souls. But be doers of the word, and
not merely hearers who deceive themselves. For if any are hearers of the word and
not doers, they are like those who look at themselves in a mirror; for they look at

hemselves and, on going away, immediately forget what they were like. But those who look into the perfect law, the law of liberty, and persevere, being not hearers who forget but doers who act — they will be blessed in their doing. If any think they are religious, and do not bridle their tongues but deceive their hearts, their religion is worthless. Religion that is pure and undefiled before God, the Father, is this: to care for orphans and widows in their distress, and to keep oneself unstained by the world.

The Gospel   **Matthew 6:25-33**

Jesus said, "Therefore I tell you, do not worry about your life, what you will eat or what you will drink, or about your body, what you will wear. Is not life more than food, and the body more than clothing? Look at the birds of the air; they neither sow nor reap nor gather into barns, and yet your heavenly Father feeds them. Are you not of more value than they? And can any of you by worrying add a single hour to your span of life? And why do you worry about clothing? Consider the lilies of the field, how they grow; they neither toil nor spin, yet I tell you, even Solomon in all his glory was not clothed like one of these. But if God so clothes the grass of the field, which is alive today and tomorrow is thrown into the oven, will he not much more clothe you — you of little faith? Therefore do not worry, saying, 'What will we eat?' or 'What will we drink?' or 'What will we wear?' For it is the Gentiles who strive for all these things; and indeed your heavenly Father knows that you need all these things. But strive first for the kingdom of God and his righteousness, and all these things will be given to you as well."